PEARSON

myHRlab™

Improve Your Grade

It's easy to prepare wisely with practice quizzes and tutorials.

PEARSON | **Human Resources Management in Canada**
Gary Dessler   Nina D. Cole | Canadian Eleventh Edition

Gradebook
Use the Grades section, to view grades for completed assignments/activities. Click to open different course content folders to view available grades for that content as applicable.

My Course > Chapter 6: Sensation and Perception > Study Plan - Chapter 6

Course Content

Back
- Our Sensational Senses
- Vision
- Hearing
- Other Senses
- Perceptual Powers: Origins and Influences
- Puzzles of Perception

Display: All items | Completed items | Assigned items

Filter by Content Type: No Filter Applied

Activity	Grade	Options
Chapter 6 Post-Test - Post-Test	70.3	
Chapter 6 Pre-Test - Pre-Test	22.2	

MyHRLab helps you focus your efforts where they are needed. Know your strengths and weaknesses before your first in-class exam.

Go to **www.pearsoned.ca/myhrlab** and follow the simple registration instructions on the Student Access Code Card provided with this text. Your unique access code is hidden there.

Save Time. Improve Results. www.pearsoned.ca/myhrlab

H0_006_MB

Personalized Learning

In MyHRLab you are treated as an individual with specific learning needs.

The study and assessment resources that come with your textbook allow you to review content and develop what you need to know, on your own time, and at your own pace.

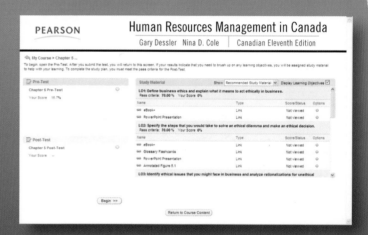

MyHRLab provides

- Quizzes with immeidate grades

- A personalized study plan that tells you where to study based on your results, and where you can find the key topics you need to review to improve

- A gradebook where you can find your grades to see your progress as the term unfolds

- An opportunity for your instructor to see the gradebook

- More than 200 video clips with closed-captioning and activities after you watch

Save Time. Improve Results. www.pearsoned.ca/myhrlab

Pearson eText

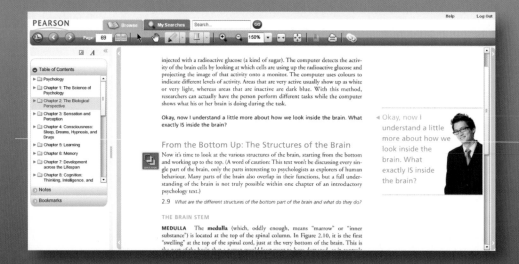

Pearson eText gives students access to the text whenever and wherever they have access to the internet. eText pages look exactly like the printed text, offering powerful new functionality for students and instructors.

Users can create notes, highlight text in different colours, create bookmarks, zoom, click hyperlinked words and phrases to view definitions, and choose single-page or two-page view.

Pearson eText allows for quick navigation using a table of contents and provides full-text search. The eText may also offer links to associated media files, enabling users to access videos, animations, or other activities as they read the text.

Save Time. Improve Results. www.pearsoned.ca/myhrlab

Human Resources Management in Canada

Gary Dessler | Canadian Eleventh Edition
Florida International University

Nina D. Cole
Ted Rogers School of Management, Ryerson University

Chapter 3 by Julie Bulmash
George Brown College

Pearson Canada
Toronto

Library and Archives Canada Cataloguing in Publication

Dessler, Gary, 1942–
  Human resources management in Canada/Gary Dessler, Nina D. Cole—Canadian 11th ed.

Includes bibliographical references and indexes.
ISBN 978-0-13-610750-7

1. Personnel management—Textbooks. 2. Personnel management—Canada—Textbooks. I. Cole, Nina D. (Nina Dawn).
II. Title.

HF5549.D49 2010   658.3   C2010-900143-5

ISBN: 978-0-13-610750-7

Vice-President, Editorial Director: Gary Bennett
Editor-in-Chief: Nicole Lukach
Acquisitions Editor: Karen Elliott
Executive Marketing Manager: Cas Shields
Developmental Editor: Catherine Belshaw
Production Editor: Kevin Leung
Production Coordinator: Patricia Ciardullo
Copy Editor: Patricia Jones
Proofreader: Strong Finish
Indexer: Belle Wong
Literary Permissions Research: Beth McAuley
Photo Research: Maria DeCambra
Compositor: MPS Limited, A Macmillan Company
Art Director: Julia Hall
Cover and Interior Designer: Miguel Acevedo
Cover Image: Getty Images

1 2 3 4 5   14 13 12 11

Printed and bound in the United States of America.

Dedication

To my mother
　　　　　　—*G.D.*

To Peggy Martin
　　　　　　—*N.C.*

BRIEF CONTENTS

CONTENTS

The eleventh edition of *Human Resources Management in Canada* shows students how human resources are the most important assets in organizations today. Human resources are a source of competitive advantage that is difficult to replicate. The strategic importance of human resources management (HRM) activities is emphasized throughout the book. Knowledge of HRM is important for supervisors and managers in every field and for employees at every level—not just those working in HR departments or aspiring to do so in the future. This book is designed to provide a complete, comprehensive review of HRM concepts and techniques in a highly readable and understandable form for a wide audience: students specializing in HRM and those in business programs, supervisory/managerial staff, and small-business owners.

As in previous editions, the Canadian eleventh edition provides extensive coverage of all HRM topics, such as job analysis, HR planning, recruitment, selection, orientation and training, career development, compensation and benefits, performance appraisal, health and safety, and labour relations. Practical applications are discussed in the Tips for the Front Line and Hints to Ensure Legal Compliance features. Research Insights are highlighted, and Ethical Dilemmas are presented for discussion.

NEW TO THE CANADIAN ELEVENTH EDITION

Revised Introductory Chapter. The first chapter has been revised to provide a comprehensive overview of the strategic importance of HR, the advances in measuring HRM's contribution to the bottom line, and HRM's critical role in strategy implementation.

Revised Chapter 3. Chapter 3 has been reorganized and completely updated.

Revised Chapter 11. Chapter 11 was substantially revised to incorporate more detailed coverage of the legal environment, including issues such as pay equity, employment equity, employment standards ("equal pay for equal work"), compensation policies, and privacy.

More coverage on the impact of globalization in HR. Further discussion on the impact of globalization in HR was added to programming: performance management (in addition to performance appraisal), the impact of immigration on the labour force, and employability skills.

Expanded and updated "The Labour Movement in Canada." This section was expanded to reflect the recent global economic downturn.

End-of-Chapter Cases and Exercises. More than 70 percent of the end-of-chapter cases and more than 50 percent of the end-of-chapter exercises are new or updated.

CBC Video Cases. All six accompanying video cases are new to this edition (see details under "Supplements" heading).

Boxed Features. The four boxed features—Strategic HR, Workforce Diversity, Global HRM, and Entrepreneurs and HR—have been updated and revised in all chapters.

Required Professional Capabilities (RPCs). Each chapter indicates where the specific required professional capabilities are discussed. These RPCs are set out by the Canadian Council of Human Resources Associations for students preparing to write the National Knowledge Exam.

KEY FEATURES OF THE CANADIAN ELEVENTH EDITION

Highlighted Themes

Workforce DIVERSITY

The Disconnect in Recruiting People with Disabilities

The good news is that employers want to hire people with disabilities, and qualified candidates are available. But putting employers and jobseekers together needs improved coordination to create more success stories. Employers have bottom-line reasons for building workforce diversity. Inclusiveness is a competitive advantage that lets an organization better connect with a diverse community and customer base. Inclusiveness provides access to a larger pool of strong job candidates in a time of skills shortages and enhances an organization's reputation as an employer of choice.

So why aren't more employers tapping into the wealth of human potential in people with disabilities? After all, as a group they make up some 13 percent of the working-age population. That is precisely what the Canadian Abilities Foundation set out to determine in its recently completed Neglected or Hidden study, the findings of which may surprise employers.

Likely the most revealing finding that illustrates the need for a new employment strategy for people with disabilities is the disconnect that exists among employers, people with disabilities, and the service providers who help these individuals enter the workforce.

With few exceptions, these stakeholders just don't seem to know how to communicate with one another, if they are fortunate enough to find one another in the first place. The commitment and passion of workers with disabilities and those assisting them is sound. Meanwhile, hundreds and hundreds of disability-related organizations across Canada provide some level of employment support to these clients. The Neglected or Hidden study suggests that the number of Canadian employers willing to hire people with disabilities should be more than adequate to meet the availability of disabled jobseekers.

The good news is that a small number of disability organizations have made significant inroads in their regions by using employer partnerships. One example is the Dartmouth Work Activity Society in Nova Scotia, which started its new approach with just a single employer "partner," who was highly satisfied with the services provided. EmployAbilities, a full-time service agency serving Edmonton and northern Alberta for more than 30 years, has also launched a partnership-building strategy. A unique feature of the agency's approach is its partnership with the local chamber of commerce through which it offers advice on disability issues to employers.

Source: Adapted from A. Prost, "Successful Recruiting from an Untapped Source," *Canadian HR Reporter* (January 16, 2006), pp. 11–12.

- **Workforce Diversity.** The Workforce Diversity boxes describe some of the issues and challenges involved in managing the diverse workforce found in Canadian organizations. The broad range of types of diversity addressed include generational/age, ethnic, gender, racial, and religious.

Strategic HR

Attracting the Younger Generation

The authors of the book Bridging the Generation Gap asked 500 Gen Ys this question: "What's important to you on the job?" The top three responses were quality of friendships, feeling they can make a contribution on the job, and a feeling of safety. These young workers want an organization where they can create friendships much as they did in school. In other words, the organization must have a social flair to catch their eye. Some examples include a company sports league and company social events like movie nights or meeting after work for a drink. But these quality relationships must go along with a feeling that what they do adds value to the organization.

The Gen Ys said that the top three ways to get their generation to join an organization are salary, casual work environment, and growth/development opportunities such as mentoring and training. Other benefits that organizations can offer to entice younger workers include state-of-the-art technology, opportunities to volunteer in the community (on company time), regular feedback, tuition reimbursement programs, strong reward and recognition programs, and a connection to the mission and vision of the organization.

The younger generation is going to take advantage of every ounce of technology to make their job search successful and easier. Organizations need to advertise jobs

on multiple online job boards, including local, national, and trade-related. Organizations should also create a job board on the company's website that should be regularly updated and provide an easy and responsive way for candidates to apply online. The posting should include an email address for the HR department or an application process. For the process to succeed, organizations must regularly check the responses and follow-up with candidates.

The actual copy of the ads is critical. Certain key words attract these individuals to an organization's ads when they do online searches. The younger generation likes short, snappy copy that gets right to the point of what they will be doing. But of equal or more importance, the ad needs to advertise the culture of the organization as it relates to the values of this generation. The ads should include statements such as "fast-paced environment," "individual contribution," "work-life balance," "do it your way," "opportunity to grow," "no rules," and "state-of-the-art technology." Organizations should only list these kinds of features in the ads if they truly offer them. Otherwise, the organization will see just how fast these workers will leave a company that doesn't fulfill its promises.

Source: Adapted from R. Throckmorton and L. Gravett, "Attracting the younger generation," *Canadian HR Reporter,* April 23, 2007.

- **Strategic HR.** These boxes provide examples that illustrate the ways in which organizations are using effective HRM policies and practices in order to achieve their strategic goals.

Entrepreneurs and HR

Alpha Safety Uses Personal Touch to Meet Labour Challenges

Alpha Safety Ltd. provides medics to the remote oil patches in northern British Columbia. It is a family-founded, family-run company. David Phibbs, manager and CEO, headed to Fort St. John with a Level III industrial first-aid certification, one of his sons, and a vehicle in 1997 and "the doors just opened up," he says.

Shifts for the medics can last as long as 65 days in fair to hardly tolerable camps. The HR planning challenges are obvious, but Alpha Safety was chosen as an industry leader in recruitment and retention by the Calgary-based Petroleum Human Resources Council of Canada.

Strong family values and building strong relationships with employees are at the heart of their success. One of their employees, medic Ted Thompson, says, "I liken it to a certain kindness. This company is really friendly. You're not just part of their policy and procedures. They have a real concern for the people who work for them."

The level of commitment extends far wider than an open-door policy at the office. Phibbs and his wife put

out welcome mats for workers in their own home, as accommodations for workers on their days off are few and far between during the height of the oil season. Phibbs once flew an employee to West Africa when his father died.

"We really try to get to know employees. We find out about their own relationships because if their wives or boyfriends don't support them being up here, it never works out," says Phibbs. Thus each medic is provided with 500 minutes of free cellphone service per month. The company's highly trained dispatchers are able to detect if any of their 70 field medics are becoming "bushed"—irrational and agitated as a result of losing a sense of reality—and get them back to base in Fort St. John.

Flexibility is also incredibly important at Alpha, especially considering the length of shifts. If a medic needs time off, has a family emergency, or just prefers to work a certain schedule, the company does its best to accommodate him or her.

Source: Excerpt adapted from L. Young, "Alpha Safety a leader with personal touch," *Canadian HR Reporter,* August 13, 2007.

- **Entrepreneurs and HR.** Suggestions, examples, and practical hints are provided to assist those in smaller businesses who have limited time and resources to implement effective HRM policies and procedures.

Global HRM

Recruiting European Candidates

An often overlooked option for managing the talent shortage is to recruit more candidates from Europe. Canada has strong ties to the European Union, and Europeans have a lot to offer the Canadian marketplace including global business perspectives.

"An important value-added Europeans can bring to the Canadian market is their ability to interact and negotiate within a multicultural environment and context. This aptitude strengthens Canadian companies' ability to function better in Canada's increasingly multicultural environment," says David Delfini, head of business development at Volareweb/Alitalia.

For Europeans, Canada offers an opportunity for advancement they might not get at home. In Italy, for example, it is almost impossible to move up the ranks if you haven't dedicated at least 20 years to the company. A 2007 study by Blusteps.com polled over 933 senior executives worldwide and revealed that traditional values about job tenure and loyalty remain well-ingrained with executives. The research also highlighted that 76 percent of European executives cited a lack of career advancement opportunities as the number one motivator to leave a company.

The borders have changed with the crisis of retiring baby boomers and impending talent shortages. Countries are opening their doors. The world is building broader intellectual capacity and perspectives and better preparation for the global market. Europeans can offer Canadian organizations needed experience and a global perspective in a tightening labour market.

One company pursuing this strategy is EBA Engineering Consultants of Edmonton. They have successfully recruited people in the UK to relocate to Western Canada by using a high-tech/high-touch promotional tool that communicates EBA's employment brand in a powerful way. A leather-bound album features stunning photographs of Western Canada, testimonials from EBA employees who had been previously recruited from overseas, and a USB key that links candidates to a comprehensive website. At the back of the album, a leather luggage tag is mounted as a call-to-action, inviting candidates to pack their bags and join the EBNA family in Canada.

Source: Adapted from A. Mirza, "Recruiting International Candidates," *HR Professional* (December 2008/January 2009), p. 27; and from K. Peters, "Public Image Ltd.," *HR Professional* (December 2007/January 2008), pp. 24–30. Reprinted with permission of HR Professional.

- **Global HRM.** In recognition of the increasing impact of globalization, topics highlighted in the Global HRM boxes include cultural issues in retirement plans, employment contracts in Europe, and the importance of personal relationships for business success in China.

Additional Features

Learning Outcomes. Specific learning goals are defined on each chapter-opening page.

Key Terms. Key terms appear in boldface within the text, are defined in the margins, and are listed at the end of each chapter.

Current Examples. Numerous real-world examples of HRM policies, procedures, and practices at a wide variety of organizations, ranging from small service providers to huge global corporations, can be found throughout the text.

Full-Colour Figures, Tables, and Photographs. Throughout each chapter, key concepts and applications are illustrated with strong, full-colour visual materials.

Weblinks. Helpful internet sites are provided throughout the text and are featured in the margins.

End-of-Chapter Summaries. At the end of each chapter, the summary reviews key points related to each of the learning outcomes.

End-of-Chapter Review and Discussion Questions. Each chapter contains a set of review and discussion questions.

Critical Thinking Questions. Each chapter contains end-of-chapter questions designed to provoke critical thinking and stimulate discussion.

Experiential Exercises. Each chapter includes a number of individual and group-based experiential exercises, which provide learners with the opportunity to apply the text material and develop some hands-on skills.

Running Cases. The running case at the end of each chapter illustrates the types of HRM challenges confronted by small-business owners and front-line supervisors. It is accompanied by critical thinking questions, which provide an opportunity to discuss and apply the text material.

Case Incidents. Case incidents can be found at the end of each chapter. These cases present current HRM issues in a real-life setting and are followed by questions designed to encourage discussion and promote the use of problem-solving skills.

CBC Videos. This book includes six CBC video cases relating to select chapter material, along with several critical thinking questions. All of the CBC videos can be found on MyHRLab at www.pearsoned.ca/myhrlab.

Supplements

Human Resources Management in Canada, Canadian Eleventh Edition, is accompanied by a complete supplements package:

Instructor Supplements

- **Instructor's Resource CD-ROM (0-13-704584-0).** This resource CD includes the following instructor supplements:

  - **Instructor's Manual with CBC Video Guide.** This comprehensive guide contains a detailed lecture outline of each chapter, descriptions of the discussion boxes, answers to review and critical thinking questions, answers to the case questions, hints regarding the experiential exercises, and helpful video case notes.

- **Computerized Testbank (Pearson TestGen).** This powerful computerized testing package contains more than 1500 multiple-choice, true/false, and short essay questions. This state-of-the-art software package allows instructors to view and edit the questions, generate tests, print tests in a variety of formats, administer tests on a local area network, and have the tests graded electronically.

- **PowerPoint® Lecture Slides.** This practical set of PowerPoint lecture slides outlines key concepts discussed in the text, and includes selected tables and figures from the text.

- **Clicker PowerPoint® Slides.** This set of Clicker-ready slides are suitable for use with any Personal Response System.

Most of these instructor supplements are also available for download from a password-protected section of Pearson Canada's online catalogue (vig.pearsoned.ca). Navigate to your book's catalogue page to view a list of the supplements that are available. See your local sales representative for details and access.

- **Pearson Canada/CBC Video Library.** Pearson Canada and the CBC have worked together to provide six new segments from the CBC series *The National*. Designed specifically to complement the text, this case collection is an excellent tool for bringing students in contact with the world outside the classroom. These programs have extremely high production quality and have been chosen to relate directly to chapter content.

- **MyHRLab.** Pearson Canada's online resource, MyHRLab, offers instructors and students all of their resources in one place, organized to accompany this text. With MyHRLab, you will be able to enliven your lectures with a variety of material. Your students will be able to "study smarter" with Pearson eText and a diagnostic test that creates a customized study plan to help them prepare for, and perform better on, exams. MyHRLab is available to instructors by going to www.pearsoned.ca/myhrlab and following the instructions on the page. Students get MyHRLab with an access code that is available with the purchase of a new text.

myHRlab

- **Pearson eText.** Pearson eText gives students access to the text whenever and wherever they have access to the internet. The eText pages look exactly like the printed text, offering powerful new functionality for students and instructors. Users can create notes, highlight text in different colours, create bookmarks, zoom, click hyperlinked words and phrases to view definitions, and view the text in either single-page or two-page format. Pearson eText allows for quick navigation to key parts of the eText, using a table of contents, and provides full-text search. The eText also offers links to associated media files, enabling users to access videos or other activities as they read the text.

- **MyTest.** MyTest from Pearson Canada is a powerful assessment generation program that helps instructors easily create and print quizzes, tests, and exams, as well as homework or practice handouts. Questions and tests can all be authored online, allowing instructors ultimate flexibility and the ability to efficiently manage assessments at any time, from anywhere.

MyTest for *Human Resources Management in Canada*, Canadian Eleventh Edition, includes more than 1500 multiple-choice, true/false, and short essay questions.

- **CourseSmart.** CourseSmart is a new way for instructors and students to access textbooks online anytime, from anywhere. With thousands of titles across hundreds of courses, CourseSmart helps instructors choose the best textbook for their class and give their students a new option for buying the assigned textbook as a lower-cost eTextbook. For more information visit www.coursesmart.com

- **Technology Specialists.** Pearson's technology specialists work with faculty and campus course designers to ensure that Pearson technology products, assessment tools, and online course materials are tailored to meet your specific needs. This highly qualified team is dedicated to helping schools take full advantage of a wide range of educational resources by assisting in the integration of a variety of instructional materials and media formats. Your local Pearson Canada sales representative can provide you with more details on this service program.

Student Supplements   **myHRlab**

- **MyHRLab.** Supplied with every new copy of this text, MyHRLab provides students with access to a wealth of resources, including:
  - diagnostic tests that assess students' understanding of the text
  - a custom study program that creates a personalized study plan using the eText and based on students' diagnostic test results
  - a media-enriched Pearson eText, loaded with animations, videos, and additional resources.

  Get started with the personal access code packaged with your new copy of the text. Personal access codes for MyHRLab can also be purchased separately at www.pearsoned.ca/myhrlab.

- **Pearson eText.** Pearson eText gives students access to the text whenever and wherever they have access to the internet. eText pages look exactly like the printed text, offering powerful new functionality for students and instructors. Users can create notes, highlight text in different colours, create bookmarks, zoom, click hyperlinked words and phrases to view definitions, and view in single-page or two-page view. Pearson eText allows for quick navigation to key parts of the eText, using a table of contents, and provides full-text search. The eText also offers links to associated media files, enabling users to access videos or other activities as they read the text.

Other Resources

- **Cawsey/Deszca/Templer, *Canadian Cases in Human Resources Management*, First Edition.** These 24 Canadian cases in human resources management are available through our Pearson Custom Business Resources database. Please ask your Pearson representative for details.

- **Sales/Owen/Lesperance, *Experiential Exercises in Human Resource Management*, First Edition.** Designed to accompany texts in the field of management, this resource meets the demand for more real-life, practical, and experiential material in management courses. In each book, the exercises follow an identical and innovative format to guide both instructors and students and to reinforce the goals of the series: increase students' awareness, apply theory, and build skills. (ISBN: 0-13-021805-7)

- **Pearson Practice Test for Human Resource Certification.** The Pearson Practice Test for Human Resource Certification is comprised of sample Knowledge Assessment and sample National Professional Practice Assessment questions and answers provided by the Canadian Council of Human Resources Associations (CCHRA). This supplement will assist those preparing for their Certified Human Resources Professional (CHRP) designation. (ISBN: 0-13-239843-5)

- **HRSim Selection and HR Simulation.** Two online simulations are available for students. Access code cards can be packaged with the text for an additional charge. Please see www.interpretive.com/hrsim.

- **Pearson Custom Publishing** (**www.prenhall.com/custombusiness**). Pearson Custom Publishing can provide you and your students with texts, cases, and articles to enhance your course. Choose material from Darden, Ivey, Harvard Business School Publishing, NACRA, and Thunderbird to create your own custom casebook. Contact your Pearson sales representative for more details.

- **New! Instructor's ASSET.** Pearson Canada is proud to introduce Instructor's ASSET, the Academic Support and Service for Educational Technologies. ASSET is the first integrated Canadian service program committed to meeting the customization, training, and support needs for your course. Ask your Pearson sales representative for details.

- **Your Pearson Sales Representative!** Your Pearson rep is always available to ensure you have everything you need to teach a winning course. Armed with experience, training, and product knowledge, your Pearson rep will support your assessment and adoption of any of the products, services, and technologies outlined here to ensure our offerings are tailored to suit your individual needs and the needs of your students. Whether it's getting instructions for TestGen software or specific content files for your new online course, your Pearson sales representative is here to help.

ACKNOWLEDGMENTS

The manuscript was reviewed at various stages of its development by a number of peers across Canada, and we want to thank those who shared their insights and constructive criticism. Among them are

- Stan Arnold, *Humber College*
- Lori Buchart, *Mount Royal University*
- Gary Gannon, *Durham College*
- Kathryn Taft, *Capilano University*
- Frank Vuo, *Lethbridge College*

At Pearson Canada, we are very grateful to Karen Elliott, acquisitions editor; Cas Shields, executive marketing manager; Catherine Belshaw, developmental editor; Kevin Leung, production editor; Patricia Jones, copyeditor; and all the other people behind the scenes who have helped make this edition possible.

A special note of thanks is extended to research assistant My-Binh Trung.

Gary Dessler
Florida International University

Nina D. Cole
Ryerson University

Dr. Nina Cole has over 30 years of experience in human resources management as a practitioner, consultant, researcher, and professor. She worked in business for 12 years as an HR management consultant and an HR manager with Federal Industries. Since 1990, she has worked as an academic, teaching and conducting research in human resources management and organizational behaviour. Dr. Cole is currently an Associate Professor at the Ted Rogers School of Management at Ryerson University in Toronto. She has been an active member of the Administrative Sciences Association of Canada, the Human Resources Professionals Association, and numerous other academic, industry, and community groups for many years.

THE STRATEGIC ROLE OF HUMAN RESOURCES MANAGEMENT

THE STRATEGIC ROLE OF HUMAN RESOURCES MANAGEMENT

human resources management (HRM) The management of people in organizations to drive successful organizational performance and achievement of the organization's strategic goals.

human capital The knowledge, education, training, skills, and expertise of an organization's workforce.

Research | INSIGHT

Human resources management (HRM) refers to the management of people in organizations. Human resources professionals are responsible for ensuring that the organization attracts, retains, and engages the diverse talent required to meet operational and performance commitments made to customers and shareholders. Their job is to ensure that the organization finds and hires the best individuals available, develops their talent, creates a productive work environment, and continually builds and monitors these human assets. They have the primary responsibility for managing the workforce that drives organizational performance and achievement of the organization's strategic goals.[1]

More specifically, HRM involves formulating and implementing HRM systems (such as recruitment, performance appraisal, and compensation) that are aligned with the organization's strategy in order to ensure that the workforce has the competencies and behaviours that are required to achieve the organization's strategic objectives. It is crucial that the HR strategy be aligned with the company's strategic plan (see **Figure 1.1**).

Just as important as the financial capital that is required for an organization to operate, the knowledge, education, training, skills, and expertise of a firm's workers represent the increasingly valuable **human capital**. More and more organizations are awakening to the importance of an organization's human capital as the next competitive advantage.[2] The contrasting results from companies that value human capital and those who do not are discussed in the Strategic HR box.

Research studies over the past 15 to 20 years have confirmed that effective HR practices are related to better organizational performance.[3] For example, outcome-based incentives for salespeople have a positive impact on sales, customer satisfaction, and profit;[4] three HR practices (profit sharing, results-oriented performance appraisal, and employment security) have strong relationships with important accounting measures of performance (return on assets and return on

FIGURE 1.1 | Linking Company-Wide and HR Strategies

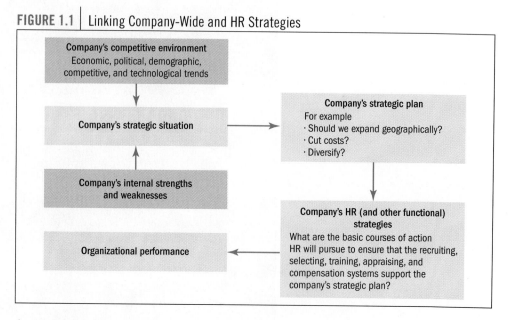

Source: © Gary Dessler, Ph.D., 2007.

Strategic HR

The Value of Human Resources: Four Seasons Hotels vs. Circuit City

For more than 40 years, Four Seasons Hotels and Resorts have built a reputation as the place to go for the friendliest and most customer-oriented hotel staff in the world. Their culture is built around employee empowerment and respect. Part of their strategic philosophy is "to create a culture and work ethic based on the Golden Rule, which would give employees a framework within which to pursue the creation of a superior international service culture." Debbie Brown, vice-president of human resources, North America, with Four Seasons, said it all comes down to the overall HR strategy. "Four Seasons hires motivated people, trains them to be the best that they can be, and offers them an environment in which to flourish," she said. "This strategy transcends boundaries because it is based on human nature."

Their retention strategies include mutual respect and recognition, visibility and accessibility of managers, informal and nonhierarchical interaction between all employees, competitive pay and benefits, and personal and professional growth. The results: Four Seasons has a 21 percent turnover rate in an industry where the average is 75.8 percent.

In contrast, Circuit City announced publicly in 2007 that it had decided to cut costs by getting rid of 3,400 of its "high paid" staff ($14 per hour) and replaced them with $9-per-hour workers. In the retail sector, customer service is everything, and customers obviously didn't like what they saw. Circuit City's holiday sales dropped 11.4 percent from the previous year, and their stock price plunged 80 percent.

Source: Adapted from J. Christofferson, "How Four Seasons Creates a 'Cycle of Success,'" *Workspan*, January 2007; and T. Humber, "Short-sighted move short circuits," *Canadian HR Reporter* (February 2007).

equity);[5] and high-performance HR practices (comprehensive employee recruitment and selection procedures, incentive compensation and performance management systems, and extensive employee involvement and training) have a positive relationship with turnover, productivity, and corporate financial performance (gross rate of return on capital).[6] A Watson Wyatt study of 51 large companies in North America and Europe showed that strong HRM was driving company performance. Those with the best HR practices provided a 64 percent total return to shareholders over a five-year period, more than three times the 21 percent return for companies with weaker HR practices.[7]

Human Resource Management Responsibilities

Human resource management responsibilities and activities fall into two categories. The first is the traditional *operational* (administrative) category, where HR professionals hire and maintain employees and then manage employee separations. This role requires HR staff to be administrative experts and employee champions. The second is the more recent *strategic* category, where HR is focused on ensuring that the organization is staffed with the most effective human capital to achieve its strategic goals. This role requires HR staff to be strategic partners and change agents.[8] **Table 1.1** illustrates the different focus of operational versus strategic HR activities.

Operational Responsibilities

Every line manager has responsibilities related to employees as they move through the stages of the human-capital life cycle: selection and assimilation into the organization, development of capabilities while working in the organization,

RPC

Advises on the status of dependent and independent contractors and determinants of employee status

Provides advice and counselling for employees

Monitors expenditures and timelines

TABLE 1.1 | Operational versus Strategic HR

Operational ⟵	⟶ Strategic
Skills	Concepts
Administrative tasks	Planning
Reactive	Proactive
Collecting metrics/measurements	Analyzing metrics/measurements
Working to achieve goals and objectives	Setting the goals and objectives
Following the laws, policies, and procedures	Interpreting, establishing, and revising the laws, policies, and procedures
Employee focus	Organizational focus
Explaining benefits to employees	Designing benefit plans that help the organization achieve its mission and goals
Setting up training sessions for employees	Assessing training needs for the entire organization
Recruiting and selecting employees	Workforce planning and building relationships with external resources
Administering the salary/wage plan	Creating a pay plan that maximizes employees' productivity, morale, and retention
Always doing things the same way	Recognizing that there may be better ways of doing things; recognizing how changes affect the entire organization—not just HR
Works within the organizational culture	Attempts to improve the organizational culture

Source: D.M. Cox & C.H. Cox, "At the Table: Transitioning to Strategic Business Partner," *Workspan*, November 2003, p. 22.

and transition out of the organization. HR professionals have traditionally served in a staff role as in-house consultants to line managers, offering advice on HR-related matters, formulating HR policies and procedures, and providing a wide range of HR services.

These services include analyzing jobs, planning future workforce requirements, selecting employees, orienting and training employees, managing compensation and reward plans, and communicating with employees (including counselling and disciplining). These responsibilities also include ensuring fair treatment, appraising performance, ensuring employee health and safety, managing labour relations and relationships with unions, handling complaints and grievances, and ensuring compliance with legislation affecting the workplace.

In recent years, there has been a trend to outsourcing much of the operational HR activities, so that HR staff in the organization can focus on strategic HRM. **Outsourcing** involves contracting with outside vendors to handle specified business functions on a permanent basis. Although using outside experts to provide employee counselling and payroll services has been common for many years, the outsourcing of other specific HR functions, including pension and benefits administration, recruitment, management development, and training, has become increasingly common.[9]

For example, Air Canada, CIBC, BMO Financial Group, Hewlett-Packard Canada, IBM Canada, Calgary Health, and Telus have all outsourced part or all of their administrative HR functions, allowing their remaining HR staff to be more strategically focused. Although most have been satisfied with their

outsourcing The practice of contracting with outside vendors to handle specified functions on a permanent basis.

outsourcing arrangement, some have not realized the full level of cost savings they initially anticipated. RBC Financial Group, for example, brought its recruitment function back in-house after experimenting with outsourcing.[10]

Strategic Responsibilities

strategy The company's plan for how it will balance its internal strengths and weaknesses with external opportunities and threats in order to maintain a competitive advantage.

More and more HR professionals are now devoting their time to helping their organization achieve its strategic objectives.[11] Traditionally, **strategy**—the company's plan for how it will balance its internal strengths and weaknesses with external opportunities and threats in order to maintain a competitive advantage—was formulated without HR input. But today, HR professionals are increasingly involved in both formulating and implementing organizational strategy.

For example, one of today's most critical strategic business challenges is an HR challenge—building the leadership pipeline. Almost half of the incumbents in senior positions in Canada achieve top performance ratings, but only 25 percent of second-level executives (the presumed feeder group for future senior executive roles) match that level of performance. For every two current senior executives, there is only one designated job-ready or nearly ready successor. Three out of every ten senior executive positions have no identified potential successors.[12] HR will play a critical role in managing this talent shortage.

CFT Training and Human Resources
www.cfthr.com
HR Dept
www.hrdept.co.uk

Role in Formulating Strategy Organizations are increasingly viewing the HR department as an equal partner in the strategic planning process. A survey of over 1100 corporate managers in Canada found that three-quarters of them strongly believe that the HR function contributes significantly to the overall success of their company and view having an HR professional on staff as strategic advantage.[13] HR professionals, together with line managers, play a role in what strategic planners call **environmental scanning**, which involves identifying and analyzing *external* opportunities and threats that may be crucial to the organization's success. These managers can also supply competitive intelligence that may be useful as the company formulates its strategic plans. Details regarding a successful incentive plan being used by a competitor, impending labour shortages, and information about pending legislative changes are examples. HR professionals can also add value to the strategy formulation process by supplying information regarding the company's *internal* strengths and weaknesses, particularly as they relate to the organization's workforce.

environmental scanning Identifying and analyzing external opportunities and threats that may be crucial to the organization's success.

Role in Executing Strategy Leading HR researcher Brian Becker says, "It isn't the content of the strategy that differentiates the winners and losers, it is the ability to execute."[14] Strategy execution is typically the area where HR makes the biggest strategic contribution. For example, HR professionals are heavily involved in the execution of downsizing and restructuring strategies through establishing training and retraining programs, arranging for outplacement services, instituting pay-for-performance plans, and helping to redesign jobs.

RPC

Provides support and expertise to managers and supervisors with respect to managing people

HR specialists are expected to be *change agents* who lead the organization and its employees through organizational change. Making the enterprise more responsive to product/service innovations and technological change is the objective of many management strategies. Flattening the pyramid, empowering employees, and organizing around teams are ways in which HRM can help an organization to respond quickly to its customers' needs and competitors' challenges.

Employees in fast-food establishments are taught how to provide courteous, efficient customer service.

The competitive strategy may involve differentiating the organization from its competitors by offering superior *customer service* through a highly committed, competent, and customer-oriented workforce. "Getting customer service right means getting HR right," says Lloyd Craig, president and CEO of Surrey Metro Savings Credit Union. His company has developed an extensive list of HR programs designed to help create and support happy, healthy, engaged employees.[15]

HR professionals and line managers play a pivotal role in *lowering labour costs*, the single largest operating expense in many organizations, particularly in the service sector. Doing so might involve introducing strategies to reduce turnover, absenteeism, and the rate of incidence of occupational illnesses and injuries. It could also mean adopting more effective recruitment, selection, and training programs. At one international tire manufacturing firm, for example, adopting a behaviour-based interview strategy as the basis for selection of entry-level engineers resulted in savings of $500 000 in three years. These savings were due to lower turnover, lower training costs, and improved capabilities of the engineering staff because of a better fit.[16]

Intense global competition and the need for more responsiveness to environmental changes put a premium on *employee engagement*, the emotional and intellectual involvement of employees in their work, such as intensity, focus, and involvement in his or her job and organization. Engaged employees drive desired organizational outcomes—they go beyond what is required; understand and share the values and goals of the organization; perceive that there are opportunities for growth, development, and advancement; enjoy collegial relationships with managers and co-workers; trust their leaders; and regard the success of the organization as their success.[17] There is a strong positive relationship between engagement and organizational performance (sales growth and total shareholder return), according to an analysis of a Hewitt Associates database of more than 4 million employees from almost 1500 companies.[18]

Although a recent Canadian study reported that 57 percent of the workforce is highly engaged, another 14 percent say they are not at all engaged. Employees reported their top reasons for disengagement as lack of recognition (59 percent), lack of opportunities for growth and advancement (46 percent), and ineffectiveness of managers and supervisors (43 percent).[19] Building employee engagement requires the joint efforts of HR professionals and line managers throughout the firm. Line managers need coaching to learn the skills it takes to build trusting and caring relationships with their employees. Other important strategic HR initiatives to build employee engagement include establishing recognition programs, instituting career-oriented performance-appraisal procedures, and providing management development programs.

Measuring the Value of HR: Metrics

metrics Statistics used to measure activities and results.

Today's HR professionals need to be able to measure the value and impact of their organization's human capital and HRM practices. The use of various **metrics**, or statistics to measure the activities and results of HR, is now quite common. Traditional operational measures focused on the amount of activity and the costs of the HR function (such as number of job candidates interviewed per month, cost per hire), but today's measures need to reflect the quality of people and the effectiveness of HRM initiatives that build workforce capability. These new measures provide critical information that can be linked to organizational outcomes like productivity, product or service quality, sales, market share, and profits. For example, the percentage of first-choice job candidates accepting first offer to hire indicates the strength of the organization's employment brand in the marketplace and directly affects the quality of the workforce.[20]

balanced scorecard A measurement system that translates an organization's strategy into a comprehensive set of performance measures.

Many organizations are using the **balanced scorecard** system that includes measures of the impact of HRM on organizational outcomes. The balanced scorecard approach translates an organization's strategy into a comprehensive set of performance measures. It includes financial measures that tell the results of actions already taken. It complements the financial measures with operational measures of organizational, business unit, or department success that will drive future performance. It balances long-term and short-term actions and balances measures of success relating to financial results, customers, internal business processes, and human capital management.[21] For example, one measure relating to HRM is the percentage of senior management positions with fully job-ready successors ready to move up.

ENVIRONMENTAL INFLUENCES ON HRM

There are numerous external and internal environmental influences that are driving the strategic focus of HRM. To be effective, all managers, including those with responsibility for HR, must monitor the environment on an ongoing basis, assess the impact of any changes, and be proactive in responding to such challenges.

External Environmental Influences

Five major external environmental influences on HRM will be discussed: economic conditions, labour market issues, government, technology, and globalization.

Economic Conditions

Economic conditions affect supply and demand for products and services, which, in turn, have a dramatic impact on the number and types of employees required as well as on an employer's ability to pay wages and provide benefits. When the economy is healthy, companies often hire more workers as demand for products and services increases. Consequently, unemployment rates fall, there is more competition for qualified employees, and training and retention strategies increase in importance. Conversely, during a downturn, some firms reduce pay and benefits in order to maintain workers' jobs. Other employers are forced to downsize by offering attractive early retirement and early leave programs or by laying off and terminating employees. Unemployment rates rise and employers are often overwhelmed with applicants when vacancies are advertised.

productivity The ratio of an organization's outputs (goods and services) to its inputs (people, capital, energy, and materials).

Productivity refers to the ratio of an organization's outputs (goods and services) to its inputs (people, capital, energy, and materials). Canada's relatively low productivity growth rate is of concern because of increasing global competition.

FIGURE 1.2 | Employment by Sector in Canada, 2008

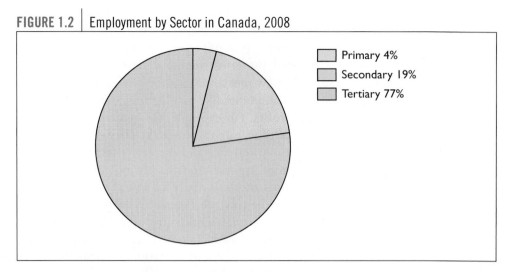

Primary 4%
Secondary 19%
Tertiary 77%

Source: Statistics Canada, CANSIM table 282-0008. Adapted from Statistics Canada website www40.statcan .ca/l01/cst01/labor10b-eng.htm (July 29, 2009).

To improve productivity, managers must find ways to produce more outputs with current input levels or to use fewer resources to produce current output levels. In most organizations today, productivity improvement is essential for long-term success.

Employment trends in Canada have been experiencing dramatic change. The **primary sector**, which includes agriculture, fishing and trapping, forestry, and mining, now represents only 4 percent of jobs. Employment in the **secondary sector** (manufacturing and construction) has decreased to 19 percent of jobs. The sector that has grown to represent 77 percent of jobs, dominating the Canadian economy, is the **tertiary or service sector**, which includes public administration, personal and business services, finance, trade, public utilities, and transportation/communications, as shown in **Figure 1.2**.

Since all jobs in the service sector involve the provision of service by employees to individual customers, effectively managing and motivating human resources is critical. Although there are some lesser-skilled jobs (in housekeeping and food services, for example), many service-sector jobs demand highly knowledgeable employees.

Workforce Issues

Increasing Workforce Diversity Canada's workforce is among the most diverse in the world. Diversity refers to the attributes that humans are likely to use to tell themselves "that person is different from me." These attributes include demographic factors (such as race, gender, age) as well as values and cultural norms.[22] Sexual orientation is one aspect of diversity that is becoming more recognized, as discussed in the Workforce Diversity box.

The proportion of visible and ethnic minorities entering the Canadian labour market is expected to continue growing at a faster pace than the rest of the population. Today, Canada admits more immigrants per capita than any other country. About two-thirds of visible minorities are immigrants, and approximately 20 percent of the Canadian population could be visible minorities by 2017. Ethnic diversity is also increasing. Currently, more than 200 different ethnic groups are represented among Canadian residents.[23]

primary sector Agriculture, fishing and trapping, forestry, and mining.

secondary sector Manufacturing and construction.

tertiary or service sector Public administration, personal and business services, finance, trade, public utilities, and transportation/communications.

Workforce DIVERSITY

Female Employee Complains about Transsexual Using Women's Washroom

Trans-sexualism is protected under human rights legislation under the category of gender. In some instances, it has been found to be protected as a disability—human rights tribunals have made such determinations based on evidence that trans-sexuals experience a complete disassociation between their gender identities and their physical conditions. Employers must balance the dignity of the trans-sexual employee with the rights of all other employees to feel comfortable in the workplace. A company's human rights training should include discussion of trans-gendered individuals, and such individuals should be consulted in the implementation of any changes to their routines.

In a British Columbia case, a female employee complained that there was a man using the women's washroom. The individual being referred to was a 12-year employee who was a biological male but had been living as a woman for more than two decades and had begun female hormone treatment over ten years ago. The employee was advised that there had been a complaint and that from now on she must knock to announce herself before entering the washroom. She refused to comply or to attend a follow-up meeting. Several days later, she was admitted to hospital with depression.

She filed a human rights complaint and the tribunal held that she had been discriminated against by the employer as she had been treated adversely compared to other employees. She was awarded $5000 as compensation for injury to dignity, feelings, and self-respect. She was also awarded an additional $1000 for lost wages.

Source: Fraser Milner Casgrain, LLP, "What Would You Do . . . if one of your female employees complained about 'a man using the women's washroom'?" Adapted from *Focus on Canadian Employment & Equality Rights*, published by and copyright CCH Canadian Limited, Toronto, Ontario.

As the employment rate for women has continued to converge toward that for men, organizations are accommodating working women and shared parenting responsibilities by offering on-site daycare, emergency childcare support, and flexible work arrangements. Women are now the primary breadwinners for 29 percent of dual-earner couples in Canada.[24]

The Aboriginal population is young and growing at a rate almost twice that of the rest of the Canadian population.[25] Young Aboriginal people represent an untapped source of employees who are still facing considerable difficulty in obtaining jobs and advancing in the workplace.

Canadians with disabilities continue to confront physical barriers to equality every day. Inaccessibility is still the rule, not the exception. Even though studies show that there are no performance differences in terms of productivity, attendance, and average tenure between employees who classify themselves as having a disability and those who do not, persons with disabilities continue, on average, to experience an unemployment rate that is 50 percent higher than that for the able-bodied population and an average income that is 17 percent lower.[26]

Another aspect of diversity is generational differences. There are four generations in the workplace, and nearly half of Canadians say they have experienced a clash with workers older or younger than themselves. On the other hand, about one-quarter of workers say they don't notice age differences and another one-quarter think this situation provides an excellent learning opportunity. Although the generations may not be all that different deep down, there are differences in their values and expectations due to the very different life-defining moments each group experienced as they came of age.[27]

Traditionalists/Silent Generation
Individuals born before 1946.

The senior group is the **Traditionalists** (also known as the **Silent Generation**), born before 1946. They grew up in era of hardship including world war and the Great Depression, and they tend to be quiet, loyal, and self-sacrificing. Although

Baby Boomers Individuals born between 1946 and 1964.

Sandwich Generation Individuals with responsibility for rearing young dependants as well as for assisting elderly relatives who are no longer capable of functioning totally independently.

Generation X Individuals born between 1965 and 1980.

Generation Y Individuals born since 1980.

many have retired, many others remain in the workforce.[28] For example, Walmart employs many seniors, even into their 90s, as greeters in their stores.[29]

The **Baby Boomers**, born between 1946 and 1964, are the largest group in the workforce. They grew up in a time of major optimism and change amidst the moon landing and the women's movement. They tend to be career-focused workaholics who experienced a lot of competition in the workplace and are driven to succeed. They are now aging and approaching retirement.[30]

The aging of the population has had another impact. Growing numbers of middle-aged employees are caught in the **Sandwich Generation**, with responsibilities for rearing young dependants as well as caring for elderly relatives who are no longer capable of functioning independently. Most employers provide flexibility in work hours for their "sandwiched" employees, and a few, such as RBC Financial Group, have provided eldercare benefits. The federal government offers a compassionate care benefit to provide job and income protection for up to six weeks to workers who need to take time off work to provide care to a gravely ill or dying family member.[31]

Generation X (individuals born between 1965 and 1980) is a much smaller group than the Boomers and were originally called the Baby Busters. This group grew up as divorce rates skyrocketed, and they were the first technology-literate generation. They tend to be independent and believe that security comes from transferability of skills rather than corporate loyalty. They can provide "out-of-the-box" thinking that can help companies deal with uncertainty. Flexible work-life arrangements and continuous skill development are valued by this generation.[32]

Generation Y (also known as Millennials and the Net Generation), born since 1980, are the children of the Baby Boomers, who have a reputation for being over-involved parents.[33] Members of this sizeable group are just now beginning to enter the workforce. Although they are techno-savvy, comfortable with diversity, and eager to make a contribution, they tend also to be impatient and action-oriented. They expect to change jobs frequently. New approaches to work and career management will be required to keep this group challenged.[34] For example, almost 90 percent of recent graduates in one survey said that they would deliberately seek out an employer with corporate social responsibility behaviour that reflects their own values. Unfortunately, businesses have been slow to catch on.[35] A summary of the attitudes/values/expectations and key characteristics of each generation is shown in **Table 1.2**.

Demographic Issues Two interrelated demographic issues are providing the workplace challenge currently considered most serious by both senior executives and HR professionals.[36] The average age of the workforce is increasing as the huge group of Baby Boomers is aging. Boomers are just beginning to retire and as a result, the ratio of children and seniors per hundred people in the working population is expected to increase rapidly, from 44 per hundred in 2005 to 61 per hundred in 2031.[37] There are significantly fewer workers in Generation X. This will create a labour shortage because a large, experienced group will be leaving the labour force and there will not be enough workers behind them to take over their jobs. The top concerns about these retiring workers are shown in **Table 1.3**. In time, as the large Generation Y group are fully absorbed into the labour force and gain experience, the shortage will dissipate, but at the moment, they are only beginning to join the workforce in entry-level positions.[38]

TABLE 1.2 | The Four Generations

	Traditionalists 1922–1945	Baby boomers 1946–1964	GenXers 1965–1980	GenYs 1981–2000
Attitudes, Values and Expectations	• Loyalty • Respect for authority • Dedication • Sacrifice • Conformity • Honour • Privacy • Stability • Economic conservatism	• Optimism • Involvement • Team-oriented • Personal growth and gratification • Youthfulness • Equality • Career-focused	• Independence • Self-reliance • Pragmatism • Skepticism • Informality • Balance	• Confidence • Diversity • Civic duty • Optimism • Immediate access to information and services
Key Characteristics	• Compliant • Stable • Detail-oriented • Hard-working • Dedicated • Fiscally frugal • Trustworthy • Risk-averse • Long-term focused	• Driven to succeed • Team player • Relationship-focused • Eager to add value • Politically savvy in the workplace • Competitive	• Techno-literate • Flexible and adaptable • Creative • Entrepreneurial • Multi-tasker • Results-driven • Individualistic	• Techno-savvy • Collective action • Expressive and tolerant of differences • Eager to accept challenges • Innovative and creative

Source: Adwoa K. Buahene and Giselle Kovary. Reprinted with permission from *HR Professional* (October/November 2007).

TABLE 1.3 | Top Concerns as Workers Retire, by Sector* (per cent)

Concern	Private sector (n = 61)	Public sector (n = 48)
Loss of experienced leaders	93.4	91.7
Loss of corporate knowledge	86.9	87.5
Shortage of technical or other specialized skills	65.6	72.9
Shortage of workers	55.7	54.2
Shortage of future leadership talent	49.2	56.3
Loss in continuity of relationships with customers	45.9	31.3
Difficulty fulfilling current business demands	27.9	27.1
Difficulty meeting growth targets	27.9	12.5
Loss in continuity of relationships with suppliers	24.6	14.6
Reduced ability to relate to an aging customer base	8.2	6.3

*Respondents were asked to select the impacts their organization will face as workers retire from a list of 10 options, plus an "other" category.

Source: K. Thorpe, *Harnessing the Power: Recruiting, Engaging, and Retaining Mature Workers*, Ottawa ON: The Conference Board of Canada, October 2008, p. 7. Reprinted by permission of The Conference Board of Canada, Ottawa.

TABLE 1.4 | Initiatives to Support or Retain Mature Workers (per cent)

Initiative	Currently in place	Plan to implement
Flexible work hours (n = 85)	76.5	12.9
Pension benefits (n = 80)	76.3	5.0
Leaves of absence (n = 79)	74.7	8.9
Retirement counselling (n = 79)	67.1	11.4
Financial planning for retirement (n = 82)	65.9	9.8
Training programs (n = 74)	62.2	8.1
Extended health-care benefits (n = 79)	60.8	5.1
Special assignments (n = 73)	60.3	9.6
Education support (n = 76)	56.6	2.6
Reduced work hours (n = 80)	53.8	17.5
Mentoring opportunities (n = 72)	51.4	20.8
Job sharing (n = 77)	50.6	14.3
Special recognition programs (n = 72)	43.1	11.1
Volunteer opportunities (n = 64)	37.5	10.9
Job modification/redesign (n = 71)	33.8	18.3
Community involvement initiatives (n = 74)	32.4	5.4
Sabbaticals (n = 69)	30.4	13.0
Programs to reduce cultural biases against mature workers (n = 63)	6.3	12.7

Source: K. Thorpe, *Harnessing the Power: Recruiting, Engaging, and Retaining Mature Workers*, Ottawa: The Conference Board of Canada, 2008, p. 19. Reprinted by permission of The Conference Board of Canada, Ottawa.

The bottom line is that employers will have to address the labour shortage by competing for the scarce Generation X talent and the incoming Generation Y workers. Traditional rewards and managerial practices will require adjustments to attract and retain these younger people.[39] At the same time, many companies are planning to ask older Baby Boomers to postpone retirement past the traditional age of 65 and remain in the workforce. This strategy will require a different set of initiatives, as shown in **Table 1.4**. A 2008 Canadian research study found that the most important HR practice to influence older workers to remain in the workforce was to show recognition and respect for their accomplishments, experience, knowledge, and expertise.[40]

Education Half of Canada's population has some post-secondary education (trades, college, university).[41] Given the higher expectations of the better-educated labour force, managers are expected to ensure that the talents and capabilities of employees are fully utilized and that opportunities are provided for career growth.

On the other hand, a startlingly high proportion (26 percent) have only marginal literacy skills, meaning the ability to understand and use printed and written documents in daily activities to achieve goals and to develop knowledge and potential. A frightening reality is that inadequate reading and writing skills have replaced lack of experience as the major reason for rejecting entry-level candidates.[42] About 15 percent of

An Ethical | Dilemma

The maintenance department supervisor has just come to you, the HR manager, voicing concern about the safety of two of her reporting employees whom she recently discovered are functionally illiterate. What are your responsibilities to these employees, if any?

working-age Canadians are *functionally illiterate*—unable to read, write, calculate, or solve problems at a level required for independent functioning or the performance of routine technical tasks.[43] Functional illiteracy is exacting a toll, not only on individual social and economic opportunities but also on organizations' accident rates and productivity levels.

Contingent/nonstandard workers
Workers who do not have regular full-time employment status.

NonStandard/Contingent Workers For the last thirty years or more, the labour market has undergone major structural changes with the growth of **contingent (or "nonstandard") workers,** meaning workers that do not fit the traditional definition of permanent, full-time employment with the same employer on an indeterminate basis. The forms of employment involving part-time, fixed-term, temporary, home and standby workers, those who have more than one job, and the self-employed have become so significant numerically that they now affect about one-third of the workforce. More women fall into this category than men.[44] Nonstandard work is often poorly paid, offers little or no job security, and is generally not covered by employment legislation. Some are calling for these laws to be updated so that contingent workers are provided the same legal protection as other workers.[45]

Technology

RPC

Contributes to improvements in the organization's structures and work processes

From Twitter to Facebook to videoconferencing setups that make it seem like everyone is in the same room, there is a wide range of technology available to organizations today. All of this technology can make working in and managing a dispersed workforce easier and can enable people to work anywhere and everywhere. The workplace of today includes "hotels, cafes and conference venues, as well as public areas of lounges and airports."[46] However, it has also brought new concerns as the line between work and family time has become blurred.[47]

Questions concerning data control, accuracy, the right to privacy, and ethics are at the core of a growing controversy brought about by the new information technologies. Sophisticated computerized control systems are used to monitor employee speed, accuracy, and efficiency in some firms. More firms are also monitoring employee email, voice mail, telephone conversations, and computer usage, and some now monitor employee behaviour using video surveillance.[48]

Government

Hints | **TO ENSURE LEGAL COMPLIANCE**

Various laws enacted by governments have had and will continue to have a dramatic impact on the employer–employee relationship in Canada. One of the factors that makes employment law in Canada so challenging is that there are 14 different jurisdictions involved. Each of the ten provinces and three territories has its own human rights, employment standards, labour relations, health and safety, and workers' compensation legislation. In addition, about 10 percent of the workforce (including employees of the federal government and Crown corporations, chartered banks, airlines, national railways, and the Canadian Armed Forces) is covered by federal employment legislation.

Although there is some commonality across jurisdictions, there is also considerable variation. Minimum wage, overtime pay requirements, vacation entitlement, and grounds protected under human rights legislation, for example, vary from one province/territory to another. Furthermore, some jurisdictions have pay equity and employment equity legislation while others do not. This means that companies with employees in more than one jurisdiction have different rules

Global HRM

Lin Congyin Prizes His Staff

Lin Congyin is the founder and chairperson of Jiumuwang Western-Style Fashional Clothes Co. Ltd. in Quan-zhou, the third-largest city in Fujian province in China. His company makes men's trousers and has led the segment's market share for seven consecutive years, beating out more than 110 000 garment enterprises in China. For Lin, the most valuable assets of his undertaking are not capital, products, or brand. "Staff is paramount," he said. In the clothing industry, which has a high employee turnover rate, Jiumuwang's rate always stands at no higher than 1.5 percent, the lowest among his competitors. "Without my staff, we wouldn't have such a renowned brand with a reputation of high quality."

No matter how busy he is, Lin always makes time to sign birthday cards for all his 8000 staff, almost every day. And he has incorporated a monthly birthday party into his routine. "Just imagine a big party for at least 500 people every month," he says with excitement.

Lin has insisted on providing free annual physical examinations for every staff member for ten years. More-over, he arranges the same package tour for all of his staff, including cleaners, every year. "It's my responsibility to take care of all the staff."

"It's quite simple to explain: as a boss, staff is earning your money or helping you to make money," he says. "If being concerned with staff helps you make fortune, then they should be respected," he says. "When I started Jiumuwang, I realized this principle."

Jiumuwang creates a career path tailored to every new staff member when they join the company. "We provide training to help promote staff's abilities. As a result we gain a talent pool," he says. Earlier this year, the All-China Federation of Industry and Commerce and Federation of Trade Unions awarded Lin the National Outstanding Entrepreneur award for staff caring. "If we respect staff and offer them training, their value will be priceless," said Lin.

Source: Adapted from Li Fangfang, "Lin Means Business," *China Business Week*, March 31–April 6, 2008, p. 12.

applying to different employees. There are, however, certain laws that apply to all employers and employees across Canada, such as Employment Insurance and the Canada/Quebec Pension Plan.

Globalization

globalization The emergence of a single global market for most products and services.

The term **globalization** refers to the emergence of a single global market for most products and services. This growing integration of the world economy into a single, huge marketplace is increasing the intensity of competition and leading most organizations to expand their operations around the world.[49] Firms in other parts of the world are also seeing human resources as a source of competitive advantage, as discussed in the Global HRM box.

RPC

Gathers, analyzes, and reports relevant business and industry information (including global trends) to influence the development of strategic business HR plans

There are increasing numbers of multinational corporations—firms that conduct a large part of business outside the country in which they are headquartered and that locate a significant percentage of their physical facilities and human resources in other countries. For example, Toyota has a large market share in the United States, Europe, and Africa, and is the market leader in Australia. Toyota has factories all over the world, manufacturing or assembling vehicles such as the Corolla for local markets. Notably, Toyota has manufacturing or assembly plants in the United States, Japan, Australia, Canada, Indonesia, Poland, South Africa, Turkey, the United Kingdom, France, and Brazil, and has recently added plants in Pakistan, India, Argentina, the Czech Republic, Mexico, Malaysia, Thailand, China, and Venezuela.[50]

Globalization means that HR professionals need to become familiar with employment legislation in other countries and to manage ethical dilemmas when labour standards are substantially lower than those in Canada. Companies

Employees are increasingly concerned with social responsibility on the part of their employer.

doing business in sub-Saharan Africa, for example, have to deal with a high death rate among employees with AIDS. Some are paying for antiretroviral drugs to keep their employees alive.[51]

Environmental Concerns

Environmental concerns have suddenly (some might say finally) emerged as an issue for people, particularly the younger generations.[52] Sustainability, climate change, global warming, pollution and carbon footprint, extinction of wildlife species, ecosystem fragility, and other related issues are increasingly important to people around the world. There is increasing evidence that interest in environmental issues is motivating the behaviour of employees, and that they are concerned about whether they work for environmentally responsible companies. Companies like Fairmont Hotels have made environmental stewardship a priority for almost 20 years. They have found that developing a reputation as an environmental leader and demonstrating corporate social responsibility have not only helped them to gain market share but have also been a strong employee retention tool.[53]

Internal Environmental Influences

How a firm deals with the following three internal environmental influences has a major impact on its ability to meet its objectives.

First, **organizational culture** consists of the core values, beliefs, and assumptions that are widely shared by members of an organization. Culture is often conveyed through an organization's mission statement, as well as through stories, myths, symbols, and ceremonies. It serves a variety of purposes:

- communicating what the organization "believes in" and "stands for"
- providing employees with a sense of direction and expected behaviour (norms)
- shaping employees' attitudes about themselves, the organization, and their roles
- creating a sense of identity, orderliness, and consistency
- fostering employee loyalty and commitment

organizational culture The core values, beliefs, and assumptions that are widely shared by members of an organization.

All managers with HR responsibilities play an important role in creating and maintaining the type of organizational culture desired. For example, they may organize recognition ceremonies for high-performing employees and be involved in decisions regarding symbols, such as a logo or the design of new company premises. Having a positive culture has a positive impact on employer branding, recruitment, retention, and productivity.

organizational climate The prevailing atmosphere that exists in an organization and its impact on employees.

Second, **organizational climate** refers to the prevailing atmosphere or "internal weather" that exists in an organization and its impact on employees.[54] It can be friendly or unfriendly, open or secretive, rigid or flexible, innovative or stagnant. The major factors influencing the climate are management's leadership style, HR policies and practices, and the amount and style of organizational communication. The type of climate that exists is generally reflected in the level of employee motivation, job satisfaction, performance, and productivity. HR professionals play a key role in helping managers throughout the firm to establish and maintain a positive organizational climate.

Third, *management practices* have changed considerably over the past decade, with many HRM implications. For example, the traditional bureaucratic structure with many levels of management is being replaced by flatter organizational forms using cross-functional teams and improved communication. Since managers have more people reporting to them in flat structures, they cannot supervise their employees as closely, and employee **empowerment** has greatly increased.

empowerment Providing workers with the skills and authority to make decisions that would traditionally be made by managers.

A BRIEF HISTORY OF HRM

HRM has changed dramatically over time and has assumed an increasingly strategic role. The demands on HR staff and expectations regarding their role have evolved as HRM has changed. HR practices have been shaped by society's prevailing beliefs and attitudes about workers and their rights, which have evolved in three stages.

Scientific Management: Concern for Production

scientific management The process of "scientifically" analyzing manufacturing processes, reducing production costs, and compensating employees based on their performance levels.

Frederick Taylor was the driving force behind **scientific management**, the process of "scientifically" analyzing manufacturing processes, reducing production costs, and compensating employees based on their performance.[55] As a result, management practices in the late 1800s and early 1900s emphasized task simplification and performance-based pay. Such incentives were expected to lead to higher wages for workers, increased profits for the organization, and workplace harmony. Taylor's views were not accepted by all management theorists. For example, Mary Parker Follett, a writer ahead of her time, advocated the use of self-management, cross-functional cooperation, empowerment, and managers as leaders, not dictators.[56]

The Human Relations Movement: Concern for People

human relations movement A management philosophy based on the belief that the attitudes and feelings of workers are important and deserve more attention.

The primary aim of the **human relations movement**, which emerged in the 1920s and 1930s but was not fully embraced until the 1940s, was to consider jobs from an employee's perspective. Managers who treated workers as machines were criticized. This management philosophy was based on the results of the

Hawthorne Studies, a series of experiments that examined factors influencing worker morale and productivity. The conclusions had a significant and far-reaching impact on management practices.

The researchers discovered that the effect of the social environment was equal to or greater than that of the physical environment. They learned that worker morale was greatly influenced by such factors as working conditions, the supervisor's leadership style, and management's philosophy regarding workers. Treating workers with dignity and respect was found to lead to higher job satisfaction and productivity levels, with economic incentives being of secondary importance. In the many firms embracing the human relations approach, working conditions improved substantially. Managers focused on establishing better channels of communication, allowing employees to exercise more self-direction, and treating employees with consideration. This movement came under severe criticism for overcompensating for the dehumanizing effects of scientific management by failing to recognize the importance of structure and work rules, for oversimplifying the concept of employee motivation, and for failing to recognize individual differences in beliefs, needs, and abilities.

The Human Resources Movement: Concern for People and Productivity

human resources movement A management philosophy focusing on concern for people and productivity.

HRM is currently based on the theoretical assumptions of the **human resources movement.** Arriving at this joint focus on people and productivity involved four evolutionary phases.[57]

Phase 1 In the early 1900s, HRM—or personnel administration, as it was then called—played a very minor or nonexistent role. During this era, personnel administrators assumed responsibility for hiring and firing (a duty formerly looked after by first-line supervisors), ran the payroll department, and administered benefits. Their job consisted largely of ensuring that procedures were followed.

Phase 2 As the *scientific management movement* gained momentum, operational efficiency increased but wage increases did not keep up, causing workers to distrust management. The resulting increase in unionization led to personnel departments serving as the primary contact for union representatives. Following the depression of the 1930s, various pieces of legislation were enacted, including a minimum wage act, an unemployment insurance program, and protection of workers' right to belong to unions. Legal compliance was subsequently added to the responsibilities of personnel managers. During the 1940s and 1950s, personnel managers were also involved in dealing with the impact of the *human relations movement.* Orientation, performance appraisal, and employee relations responsibilities were added to their portfolio.

Phase 3 The third major phase in personnel management was a direct result of government legislation passed during the 1960s, 1970s, and 1980s that affected employees' human rights, wages and benefits, working conditions, and health and safety, and established penalties for failure to meet them. The role of personnel departments expanded dramatically. They continued to provide expertise in such areas as compensation, recruitment, and training but in an expanded capacity. During the latter part of this era, the term "human resources management" emerged. This change represented a shift in emphasis—from maintenance and administration to corporate contribution, proactive management, and initiation of change.[58]

Phase 4 The fourth phase of HRM is strategic. Organizations must leverage human capital in order to compete in today's global business world. They require employees who are fully engaged in their jobs so that the goals and aims of both management and employees can be achieved. In today's organizations, employees are often a firm's best competitive advantage. The role of HR departments has evolved to that of strategic partner.

This transformation has occurred because economic forces, such as global competition, increasing sophisticated technology, and major demographic shifts are making human capital more important. Many traditional sources of competitive advantage, such as market share, proprietary technology, access to capital, and regulated markets, are becoming less powerful. What remains as a crucial differentiating factor is the organization, its employees, and how they work. Experts believe that the latent creative and innovative capacity among employees of most organizations has the power to eclipse other forms of competitive advantage. They predict that HR managers will be the means through which organizations can realize the untapped potential of their workforces.[59]

According to esteemed HR expert Ed Lawler, "The time is right for HR executives to take on an important new role in organizations. They need to become major players in the development and implementation of business strategy. This is a role that adds a great deal of value and one that HR executives can and should perform."[60]

HR's transformation has been underway for several years, but progress has been slow because of lack of senior management support and the fact that many non-HR managers still view HR as a cost centre. Also, many HR professionals need to acquire more broad-based business knowledge and skill sets in order to be considered and respected as equal business partners by other executives in the company.[61] In many organizations HR remains locked in a transactional mode, processing forms and requests, administering compensation and benefits, managing policies and programs, and overseeing hiring and training.[62]

GROWING PROFESSIONALISM IN HRM

Today, HR practitioners must be professionals in terms of both performance and qualifications.[63] Every profession has several characteristics: (1) a common body of knowledge; (2) benchmarked performance standards; (3) a representative professional association; (4) an external perception as a profession; (5) a code of ethics; (6) required training credentials for entry and career mobility; (7) an ongoing need for skill development; and (8) a need to ensure professional competence is maintained and put to socially responsible uses. Every province has an association of HR practitioners (Prince Edward Island is included in Nova Scotia's) that currently assumes dual roles: first, as a professional association serving the interests of its members, and second, as a regulatory body serving the public. These two roles sometimes conflict, such as when the disciplinary role of a regulator conflicts with the professional interests of a member.[64]

The Canadian Council of Human Resources Associations (CCHRA) is the 40 000-member national body through which all provincial HR associations are affiliated. The CCHRA is in turn a member of the World Federation of People Management Associations (WFPMA). The International Personnel Management Association (IPMA)–Canada is the national association for public-sector and quasi-public-sector HR professionals.

RPC

Stays current with professional knowledge

Fosters and promotes advancement of the profession

Other important associations for HR specialists include the Canadian Industrial Relations Association; WorldatWork for compensation and rewards issues; health and safety associations, such as the Industrial Accident Prevention Association, the Construction Safety Association, and Safe Communities Canada; and the Canadian Society for Training and Development for training and development professionals.

certification Recognition for having met certain professional standards.

Canadian Council of Human Resources Associations
www.cchra.ca
World Federation of People Management Associations
www.wfpma.com

The Certified Human Resources Professional (CHRP) designation is a nationally recognized **certification** for Canadian HR professionals (approximately 19 000 of them at present).[65] Managed by the CCHRA and administered through provincial HR associations, the CHRP is similar to other professional designations, such as Chartered Accountant (CA) and Professional Engineer (P.Eng.), as it recognizes members' qualifications and experience based on established levels of 187 required professional capabilities in seven functional dimensions: (1) professional practice; (2) organizational effectiveness; (3) staffing; (4) employee and labour relations; (5) total compensation; (6) organizational learning, training and development; and (7) occupational health, safety, and wellness. The national certification requirements are shown in **Figure 1.3**. Some provincial associations have also begun to sponsor a Senior HR Professional designation that recognizes HR professionals who have made a significant impact on the profession.[66]

Ethics

RPC

Understands and adheres to the Canadian Council of Human Resources Association's code of ethics and applicable provincial/territorial HR associations' codes

The professionalization of HRM has created the need for a uniform code of ethics, as agreement to abide by the code of ethics is one of the requirements of maintaining professional status. The CCHRA Code of Ethics is shown in **Figure 1.4**. Since what is ethical or unethical is generally open to debate (except in a few very clear-cut cases such as willful misrepresentation), most codes do not tell employees what they should do. Rather, they provide a guide to help employees discover the best course of action by themselves.[67] Increasingly, HR departments are being given a greater role in providing ethics training and monitoring to ensure compliance with the code of ethics. Some organizations have such a commitment to ethics that they have a full-time ethics officer. On the other hand, a 2008 survey of Ontario HR professionals found that 78.2 percent had been coerced into doing something morally or legally ambiguous at least once in their careers.[68]

An Ethical |Dilemma

Can or should an employee reveal information that was disclosed in confidence about a troubled co-worker, and if so, under what circumstances?

Human Resources Professionals Association of Ontario
www.hrpa.ca
Ethics Resource Center
www.ethics.org
Business for Social Responsibility
www.bsr.org
Canadian Business for Social Responsibility
www.cbsr.ca

social responsibility The implied, enforced, or felt obligation of managers, acting in their official capacities, to serve or protect the interests of groups other than themselves.

The most prevalent ethical issues confronting Canadian organizations today pertain to security of information, employee and client privacy, environmental issues, governance, and conflicts of interest.[69] The major reasons for the failure of ethics programs to achieve the desired results are lack of effective leadership and inadequate training. Positive outcomes associated with properly implemented ethics programs include increased confidence among stakeholders, such as clients, partners, and employees; greater client/customer and employee loyalty; decreased vulnerability to crime; reduced losses because of internal theft; and increased public trust.[70]

In recent years, the concept of **social responsibility** has frequently been discussed as an important manifestation of ethics. A company that exercises social responsibility attempts to balance its commitments, not only to its investors but also to its employees and customers, other businesses, and the community or

FIGURE 1.3 | National CHRP Certification Requirements

Please note that throughout the certification and recertification process, provincial variations may apply. Always contact the provincial HR association of which you are a member to ensure you have the most updated information that applies to you (www.cchra.ca/MemberAssociations).

A. Initial Certification

To fulfill the academic requirements for the CHRP designation, a candidate must:

1. Become a member of a provincial human resources professionals association; and

2. Pass

(1) The National Knowledge Exam® (assesses knowledge of major human resources functions), and

(2) National Professional Practice Assessment® (measures human resources "experience"); must be written within 5 years of passing the National Knowledge Exam®. (Please note that the NPPA is not mandatory in Quebec and Ontario.)

As of January 1, 2011, CHRP Candidates—those who have passed the National Knowledge Exam® (NKE) – will require a minimum of a bachelor's degree from an accredited college or university in order to register for the National Professional Practice Assessment® and qualify for the CHRP designation. In some provinces, the degree requirement varies, or additional requirements may be applicable. Please contact your provincial HR association for more details.

B. Sign the National Code of Ethics (or your provincial association's equivalent)

C. Recertification

Every three years, all CHRPs will be required to recertify based on a set of professional development criteria, including seminars, conferences, volunteer work, or continuing education. Provincial variations may apply.

Source: Adapted from Canadian Council of Human Resources Associations, *What Is the CHRP Designation?* www.cchra.ca (July 29, 2009). Reproduced with permission of the Canadian Council of Human Resources Associations.

communities in which it operates. Mountain Equipment Co-op (MEC) is an example of a company that considers socially responsible approaches to all aspects of their business—selecting and designing products, manufacturing MEC-brand products, transporting products and people, greening operations, engaging employees, equipping members, supporting the community, economic performance, and governing the co-operative. They examine every aspect of a product's life cycle from a social responsibility perspective, from the resources that go into making and shipping it, to the satisfaction of the employees and the members who take the products home.[71]

FIGURE 1.4 | CCHRA National Code of Ethics

1. Preamble

- As HR practitioners in the following categories—
  - Certified Human Resources Professionals,
  - CHRP Candidates, or
  - CHRP Exam Registrants,

  we commit to abide by all requirements of the Code of Ethics of the Canadian Council of Human Resources Associations (CCHRA), as listed in this document. (Where provincial codes are legislated, those will prevail.)

2. Competence

- Maintain competence in carrying out professional responsibilities and provide services in an honest and diligent manner.
- Ensure that activities engaged in are within the limits of one's knowledge, experience and skill.
- When providing services outside one's level of competence, or the profession, the necessary assistance must be sought so as not to compromise professional responsibility.

3. Legal Requirements

- Adhere to any statutory acts, regulation or by-laws which relate to the field of Human Resources Management, as well as all civil and criminal laws, regulations and statutes that apply in one's jurisdiction.
- Not knowingly or otherwise engage in or condone any activity or attempt to circumvent the clear intention of the law.

4. Dignity in the Workplace

- Support, promote and apply the principles of human rights, equity, dignity and respect in the workplace, within the profession and in society as a whole.

5. Balancing Interests

- Strive to balance organizational and employee needs and interests in the practice of the profession.

6. Confidentiality

- Hold in strict confidence all confidential information acquired in the course of the performance of one's duties, and not divulge confidential information unless required by law and/or where serious harm is imminent.

7. Conflict of Interest

- Either avoid or disclose a potential conflict of interest that might influence or might be perceived to influence personal actions or judgments.

8. Professional Growth and Support of Other Professionals

- Maintain personal and professional growth in Human Resources Management by engaging in activities that enhance the credibility and value of the profession.

9. Enforcement

- The Canadian Council of Human Resources Associations works collaboratively with its Member Associations to develop and enforce high standards of ethical practice among all its members.

Source: The CCHRA Code of Ethics. www.cchra.ca/Web/ethics/content.aspx?f=29756 (July 28, 2009). Reproduced with the permission of the Canadian Council of Human Resources Associations.

Chapter | SUMMARY

1. Human resources management (HRM) refers to the management of people in organizations. Strategic HRM involves linking HRM with strategic goals and objectives to improve business performance. In more and more firms, HR professionals are becoming strategic partners in strategy formulation and strategy execution.

2. Human resources activities are now being seen as falling into two categories. The first is the traditional operational (administrative) category, where HR hires and maintains employees and then manages employee separations. This role requires HR staff to be administrative experts and employee champions. The second is the more recent strategic category, where HR is focused on ensuring that the organization is staffed with the most effective human capital to achieve its strategic goals. This role requires HR staff to be strategic partners and change agents.

3. Internal environmental factors influencing HRM include organizational culture, which consists of the core values, beliefs, and assumptions that are widely shared by members of the organization; organizational climate, which is the prevailing atmosphere; and management practices, such as the shift from traditional bureaucratic structures to flatter organizations where employees are empowered to make more decisions. A number of external factors have an impact on HRM, including economic factors, labour market issues, technology, government, globalization, and environmental concerns.

4. The three stages in the evolution of management thinking about workers are (1) scientific management, which focused on production; (2) the human relations movement, in which the emphasis was on people; and (3) the human resources movement, in which it was recognized that organizational success is linked to both.

5. HR professionals are certified by provincial HR associations that together form the Canadian Council of Human Resources Associations (CCHRA). The CCHRA fulfils both an association role in representing its members and a regulatory role. It regulates the human resources profession in Canada and has a code of ethics for HR professionals. It has compiled a common body of knowledge based on a list of 187 required professional capabilities that provide the foundation for a certification process leading to the Certified Human Resources Professional designation.

Test yourself on the material for this chapter at
www.pearsoned.ca/myhrlab

Key | TERMS

Baby Boomers *(p. 10)*
balanced scorecard *(p. 7)*
certification *(p. 19)*
contingent (nonstandard) workers *(p. 13)*
empowerment *(p. 16)*
environmental scanning *(p. 5)*
Generation X *(p. 10)*
Generation Y *(p. 10)*
globalization *(p. 14)*
human capital *(p. 2)*
human relations movement *(p. 16)*
human resources management (HRM) *(p. 2)*
human resources movement *(p. 17)*

metrics *(p. 6)*
organizational climate *(p. 16)*
organizational culture *(p. 15)*
outsourcing *(p. 4)*
primary sector *(p. 8)*
productivity *(p. 7)*
Sandwich Generation *(p. 10)*
scientific management *(p. 16)*
secondary sector *(p. 8)*
social responsibility *(p. 19)*
strategy *(p. 5)*
tertiary or service sector *(p. 8)*
Traditionalists/Silent Generation *(p. 9)*

Review and Discussion | QUESTIONS

1. Describe the transformation that HRM is currently undergoing.

2. Describe the role of HR in strategy formulation and strategy implementation.

3. Describe how the external environment influences HR.

4. Differentiate between organizational culture and organizational climate.

5. Describe the multiple jurisdictions related to employment legislation affecting HRM in Canada.

6. Describe scientific management and explain its impact on organizations.

7. Explain why HRM is a profession.

Critical Thinking | QUESTIONS

1. Given the costs associated with human resources, which is often the largest budget item in an organization, if the executive team in your organization was not convinced that the senior HR executive should participate in the strategic planning process, what would you do to try to convince its members?

2. Explain how changing demographics and increasing workforce diversity have had an impact on the organization in which you are working or one in which you have worked.

3. A firm has requested your assistance in ensuring that its multigenerational workforce functions effectively as a team. What strategies and/or programs would you recommend? Why?

4. Identify a company that is known for being both ethical and socially responsible. What types of behaviour and activities typify this organization? How has this behaviour affected the achievement of its corporate strategy?

5. Refer to the Workforce Diversity box on page 9. Describe other challenges that organizations can face in implementing diversity initiatives.

Experiential | EXERCISES

1. Working alone or with a small group of classmates, interview an HR manager and prepare a short essay regarding his or her role in strategy formulation and implementation.

2. Prepare a summary of the employment legislation affecting all employers and employees who are not under federal jurisdiction in your province or territory. Explain the impact of each of these laws on HRM policies and practices.

3. Working with a small group of classmates, contact several firms in your community to find out whether or not they have a code of ethics. If so, learn as much as possible about the specific initiatives devised to support and communicate the code. If not, find out if the firm is planning to implement such a code. If so, how does the firm intend to proceed? If not, why not?

4. Using the sample Balanced Scorecard template provided by your professor, in pairs, develop a balanced scorecard measure for a hypothetical company in the retail urban clothing sector. This company has many stores in large and small cities in Ontario and Quebec. Be sure to take into consideration current economic conditions as you develop your measures.

Exchange your completed set of measures with another pair. Compare and contrast your measures. Is one set "better" than the other? Why or why not? Debrief as instructed.

Running | CASE

Running Case: LearnInMotion.com

Introduction

The main theme of this book is that HRM—activities like recruiting, selecting, training, and rewarding employees—is not just the job of a central HR group, but rather one in which every manager must engage. Perhaps nowhere is this more apparent than in the typical small service business, where the owner-manager usually has no HR staff to rely on. However, the success of such an enterprise often depends largely on the effectiveness with which workers are recruited, hired, trained, evaluated, and rewarded. To help illustrate and emphasize the front-line manager's HR role, throughout this book we will use a continuing ("running") case, based on an actual small business in Ottawa's high-tech region. Each segment will illustrate how the case's main players—owner-managers Jennifer Lau and Pierre LeBlanc—confront and solve HRM problems each day by applying the concepts and techniques presented in that particular chapter. Here's some background information you'll need to answer questions that arise in subsequent chapters.

LearnInMotion.com: A Profile

Jennifer and Pierre graduated from university as business majors in June 2008 and got the idea for LearnInMotion.com as a result of a project they worked on together their last semester in their entrepreneurship class. The professor had divided the students into two- or three-person teams and given them the assignment to "create a business plan for a high-tech company." The idea the two came up with was LearnInMotion.com. The basic idea of the website was to list a vast array of web-based, CD-ROM–based, or textbook–based continuing education-type business courses for working people who wanted to take a course from the comfort of their own homes. The idea was that users could come to the website to find and then take a course in one of several ways. Some courses could be completed interactively on the web via the site; others were in a form that was downloadable directly to the user's computer; others (which were either textbook or CD-ROM–based) could be ordered and delivered (in several major metropolitan areas) by independent contractor delivery people. Their business mission was "to provide work-related learning when, where, and how you need it."

Based on their research, they knew the market for work-related learning like this was booming. At the same time, professional development activities like these were increasingly internet-based. Tens of thousands of on- and offline training firms, universities, associations, and other content providers were trying to reach their target customers via the internet. Jennifer and Pierre understandably thought they were in the right place at the right time. Jennifer's father had some unused loft space in Kanata, Ontario, so with about $45 000 of accumulated savings, Jennifer and Pierre incorporated and were in business. They retained the services of an independent programmer and hired two people—a web designer to create the graphics for the site (which would then be programmed by the programmer), and a content manager whose job was to enter information onto the site as it came in from content providers. By the end of 2008, they also completed upgrading their business plan into a form they could show to prospective venture capitalists. They sent the first version to three Canadian venture capitalists. Then they waited.

And then they waited some more. They never heard back from the first three venture capitalists, so they sent their plan to five more. They still got no response. But Pierre and Jennifer pressed on. By day they called customers to get people to place ads on their site, to get content providers to list their available courses, and to get someone—anyone—to deliver textbook- and CD-ROM–based courses, as needed, across Canada. By May 2009, they had about 300 content providers offering courses and content through LearnInMotion.com. In the summer, they got their first serious nibble from a venture capital firm. They negotiated with this company through much of the summer, came to terms in the early fall, and closed the deal—getting just over $1 million in venture funding—in November 2009.

After a stunning total of $75 000 in legal fees (they had to pay both their firm's and the venture capital firm's lawyers to navigate the voluminous disclosure documents and agreements), they had just over $900 000 to spend. The funding, according to the business plan, was to go toward accomplishing five main goals: redesigning and expanding the website; hiring about seven more employees; moving to a larger office; designing and implementing a personal information manager (PIM)/calendar (users and content providers could use the calendar to interactively keep track of their personal and business schedules); and, last but not least, driving up sales. LearnInMotion was off and running.

QUESTIONS

1   What is human resources management and does it have a role to play in this organization? If so, specifically what responsibilities?

2   What environmental influences will affect the role that human resources management could play within this organization?

Case | INCIDENT

Jack Nelson's Problem

As a new member of the board of directors for a local bank, Jack Nelson was being introduced to all the employees in the home office. When he was introduced to Ruth Johnson, he was curious about her work and asked her what the machine she was using did. Johnson replied that she really did not know what the machine was called or what it did. She explained that she had only been working there for two months. She did, however, know precisely how to operate the machine. According to her supervisor, she was an excellent employee.

At one of the branch offices, the supervisor in charge spoke to Nelson confidentially, telling him that "something was wrong," but she didn't know what. For one thing, she explained, employee turnover was too high, and no sooner had one employee been put on the job than another one resigned. With customers to see and loans to be made, she continued, she had little time to work with the new employees as they came and went.

All branch supervisors hired their own employees without communication with the home office or other branches. When an opening developed, the supervisor tried to find a suitable employee to replace the worker who had quit.

After touring the 22 branches and finding similar problems in many of them, Nelson wondered what the home office should do or what action he should take. The banking firm was generally regarded as a well-run institution that had grown from 27 to 191 employees during the past eight years. The more he thought about the matter, the more puzzled Nelson became. He couldn't quite put his finger on the problem, and he didn't know whether to report his findings to the president.

QUESTIONS

1   What do you think is causing some of the problems in the bank's home office and branches?

2   Do you think setting up an HR unit in the main office would help?

3   What specific functions should an HR unit carry out? What HR functions would then be carried out by supervisors and other line managers? What role should the Internet play in the new HR organization?

Source: From Claude S. George, *Supervision in Action*, 4th ed., 1985. Adapted by permission of Prentice Hall, Inc., Upper Saddle River, NJ.

PEARSON

myHRlab™

For additional cases and exercise material, go to **www.pearsoned.ca/myhrlab**

CHAPTER 2

LEARNING OUTCOMES

AFTER STUDYING THIS CHAPTER, YOU SHOULD BE ABLE TO

EXPLAIN how employment-related issues are governed in Canada.

DISCUSS at least five prohibited grounds for discrimination under human rights legislation, and **describe** the requirements for reasonable accommodation.

DESCRIBE behaviour that could constitute harassment, and **describe** employers' responsibilities regarding harassment.

DESCRIBE the six steps involved in implementing an employment equity program.

DISCUSS key characteristics of successful diversity management initiatives.

THE CHANGING LEGAL EMPHASIS

From Compliance to Valuing Diversity

REQUIRED PROFESSIONAL CAPABILITIES (RPC)

- Identifies and masters legislation and jurisprudence relevant to HR functions

- Ensures that the organization's HR policies and practices align with human rights legislation

- Promotes a productive culture in the organization that values diversity, trust, and respect for individuals and their contributions

THE LEGAL FRAMEWORK FOR EMPLOYMENT LAW IN CANADA

Government of Canada
http://canada.gc.ca

In Canada, the primary responsibility for employment-related laws resides with the provinces and territories. Today, provincial/territorial employment laws govern approximately 90 percent of Canadian workers. The remaining 10 percent of the workforce—employed in the federal civil service, Crown corporations, and agencies, and businesses engaged in transportation, banking, and communications—is governed by federal employment legislation. Thus there are 14 jurisdictions—10 provinces, 3 territories, and Canada as a whole—for employment law.

There is a great deal of commonality to the legislation, both federal and provincial/territorial; however, there are also some differences. For example, vacations, statutory holidays, and minimum wage standards are provided by all jurisdictions, but specific entitlements vary from jurisdiction to jurisdiction. Therefore, a company with employees in different provinces/territories must monitor the legislation in each of those jurisdictions and remain current as legislation changes. Ensuring legality across multiple jurisdictions can be very complex, since it is possible for a policy, practice, or procedure to be legal in one jurisdiction yet illegal in others.

The legal framework for employment also includes constitutional law, particularly the Charter of Rights and Freedoms; acts of Parliament; common law, which is the accumulation of judicial precedents that do not derive from specific pieces of legislation; and contract law, which governs collective agreements and individual employment contracts. Such laws impose specific requirements and constraints on management policies, procedures, and practices. One common example of common law is court decisions regarding allegations of wrongful dismissal of an employee by an employer.

To avoid flooding the courts with complaints and the prosecutions of relatively minor infractions, the government in each jurisdiction creates special regulatory bodies to enforce compliance with the law and aid in its interpretation. Such bodies, which include human rights commissions and ministries of labour, develop legally binding rules called **regulations** and evaluate complaints.

regulations Legally binding rules established by the special regulatory bodies created to enforce compliance with the law and aid in its interpretation.

There are laws that specifically regulate some areas of HRM—occupational health and safety (occupational health and safety acts), union relations (labour relations acts), pensions (pension benefits acts), and compensation (pay equity acts, the Income Tax Act, and others). These will be discussed later in the chapters covering these topics. In this chapter, broader laws affecting the overall practice

It is illegal in every jurisdiction in Canada to discriminate on the basis of disability.

of HRM will be reviewed. These include employment standards legislation, human rights legislation, and employment equity legislation.

Many organizations have moved beyond legal compliance with human rights and employment equity requirements and have begun to initiate and promote workplace diversity initiatives because the value of having a diverse workforce has proven to make good business sense. The chapter will also provide an overview of diversity management initiatives.

EMPLOYMENT/LABOUR STANDARDS LEGISLATION

employment (labour) standards legislation Laws present in every Canadian jurisdiction that establish minimum employee entitlements and set a limit on the maximum number of hours of work permitted per day or week.

All employers and employees in Canada, including unionized employees, are covered by **employment (labour) standards legislation.** Enforcement is complaint-based and violators can be fined. These laws establish minimum employee entitlements pertaining to such issues as wages; paid holidays and vacations; leave for some mix of maternity, parenting, and adoption; bereavement leave; compassionate care leave; termination notice; and overtime pay. They also set the maximum number of hours of work permitted per day or week; overtime pay is required for any work in excess of the maximum. Recently, non-management employees at financial services firms, including CIBC, Scotiabank, and KPMG, have launched lawsuits claiming that they have been working overtime on a regular basis and not been paid for it.[1]

Canadian Association of Administrators of Labour Legislation
www.caall-acalo.org

Workplace Standards
www.workplace.ca/laws/
employ_standard_comp.html

Every jurisdiction in Canada has legislation incorporating the principle of *equal pay for equal work*. In most jurisdictions, this entitlement is found in the employment (labour) standards legislation; otherwise, it is in the human rights legislation. Equal pay for equal work specifies that an employer cannot pay male and female employees differently if they are performing the same or substantially similar work. Pay differences based on a valid merit or seniority system or employee productivity are permitted; it is only sex-based discrimination that is prohibited. This principle makes it illegal, for example, for the Canadian government to employ nurses (mostly women) as "program administrators" and doctors (mainly men) as "health professionals" to do the same job adjudicating Canada Pension Plan disability claims and pay the men twice as much.[2]

LEGISLATION PROTECTING HUMAN RIGHTS

Human rights legislation makes it illegal to discriminate, even unintentionally, against various groups. Reactive (complaint-driven) in nature, the focus of such legislation is on the types of acts in which employers should *not* engage. Included in this category are

1. *the Charter of Rights and Freedoms*, federal legislation that is the cornerstone of human rights, and
2. *human rights legislation*, which is present in every jurisdiction.

The Charter of Rights and Freedoms

Charter of Rights and Freedoms Federal law enacted in 1982 that guarantees fundamental freedoms to all Canadians.

The cornerstone of Canada's legislation pertaining to issues of human rights is the Constitution Act, which contains the **Charter of Rights and Freedoms.** The Charter applies to the actions of all levels of government (federal, provincial/territorial, and municipal) and agencies under their jurisdiction as they go about their work of creating laws. The Charter takes precedence over all other laws, which means that all legislation must meet Charter standards; thus, it is quite far-reaching in scope.

There are two notable exceptions to this generalization. The Charter allows laws to infringe on Charter rights if they can be demonstrably justified as reasonable limits in a "free and democratic society." Since "demonstrably justified" and "reasonable" are open to interpretation, many issues challenged under the Charter eventually end up before the Supreme Court, its ultimate interpreter. The second exception occurs when a legislative body invokes the "notwithstanding" provision, which allows the legislation to be exempted from challenge under the Charter.

The Charter provides the following fundamental rights and freedoms to every Canadian:

1. freedom of conscience and religion

2. freedom of thought, belief, opinion, and expression, including freedom of the press and other media of communication

3. freedom of peaceful assembly

4. freedom of association

In addition, the Charter provides Canadian multicultural heritage rights, First Peoples' rights, minority language education rights, equality rights, the right to live and work anywhere in Canada, the right to due process in criminal proceedings, and the right to democracy.[3]

equality rights Section 15 of the Charter of Rights and Freedoms, which guarantees the right to equal protection and equal benefit of the law without discrimination.

Section 15—**equality rights**—provides the basis for human rights legislation, as it guarantees the right to

equal protection and benefit of the law without discrimination, and, in particular, without discrimination based on race, national or ethnic origin, colour, religion, sex, age, or mental or physical disability.[4]

Section 15 provides the foundation for Canada's human rights legislation.

Human Rights Legislation

Every employer in Canada is affected by human rights legislation, which prohibits intentional and unintentional discrimination in its policies pertaining to all aspects, terms, and conditions of employment. Human rights legislation is extremely broad in scope, affecting almost all aspects of HRM. The ways in which employees should be treated on the job every day and the climate in which they work are also addressed by this legislation. An important feature of the human rights legislation is that it supersedes the terms of any employment contract or collective agreement.[5] For these reasons, supervisors and managers must be thoroughly familiar with the human rights legislation and their legal obligations and responsibilities specified therein.

Human rights legislation prohibits discrimination against all Canadians in a number of areas, including employment. To review individual provincial and territorial human rights laws would be confusing because of the many but generally minor differences among them, often only in terminology (e.g., some provinces use the term "creed," others "religion"). As indicated in Figure 2.1, most provincial/territorial laws are similar to the federal statute in terms of scope, interpretation, and application. All jurisdictions prohibit discrimination on the grounds of race, colour, religion/creed, sex, marital status, age, physical and mental disability, and sexual orientation. Some but not all jurisdictions

FIGURE 2.1 | Prohibited Grounds of Discrimination in Employment by Jurisdiction

Prohibited Grounds of Discrimination	Federal	Alta.	B.C.	Man.	N.B.	N.L.	N.S.	Ont.	P.E.I.	Que.	Sask.	N.W.T.	Y.T.	Nunavut
Race	◆	◆	◆	◆	◆	◆	◆	◆	◆	◆	◆	◆	◆	◆
Colour	◆	◆	◆	◆	◆	◆	◆	◆	◆	◆	◆	◆	◆	◆
Creed or religion	◆	◆	◆	◆	◆	◆	◆	◆	◆	◆	◆	◆	◆	◆
Sex	◆	◆	◆	◆	◆	◆	◆	◆	◆	◆	◆	◆	◆	◆
Marital status	◆	◆	◆	◆	◆	◆	◆	◆	◆	◆	◆	◆	◆	◆
Age	◆	◆ 18+	◆ 19–65	◆	◆	◆ 19–65	◆	◆ 18+	◆	◆	◆ 18–64	◆	◆	◆
Mental & physical disability	◆	◆	◆	◆	◆	◆	◆	◆	◆	◆	◆	◆	◆	◆
Sexual orientation	◆	◆	◆	◆	◆	◆	◆	◆	◆	◆	◆	◆	◆	◆
National or ethnic origin	◆			◆	◆		◆	◆	◆	◆	◆	◆	◆	◆
Family status	◆		◆				◆	◆	◆	◆	◆	◆	◆	◆
Ancestry or place of origin		◆	◆	◆	◆	◆	◆	◆	◆	◆		◆	◆	◆
Political belief			◆	◆	◆		◆		◆				◆	
Association				◆	◆		◆	◆	◆			◆		◆
Source of income		◆	◆				◆		◆	◆	◆			
Social condition or origin					◆	◆				◆			◆	
Language										◆	◆		◆	
Pardoned conviction	◆											◆	◆	◆
Record of criminal conviction										◆			◆	
Assignment, attachment, or seizure of pay						◆								

Note: The legislation providing human rights protection and equal pay for equal work in Nunavut is titled the Fair Practices Act.

Source: Canadian Human Rights Commission, Prohibited Grounds of Discrimination in Canada. www.chrc-ccdp.ca/pdf/ProhibitedGrounds_en.pdf. Reproduced with the permission of the Ministry of Public Works and Government Services, 2009.

prohibit discrimination on the basis of national or ethnic origin, family status, ancestry or place of origin, and various other grounds.

Discrimination Defined

discrimination As used in the context of human rights in employment, a distinction, exclusion, or preference, based on one of the prohibited grounds, that has the effect of nullifying or impairing the right of a person to full and equal recognition and exercise of his or her human rights and freedoms.

Central to human rights laws is the concept of **discrimination**. When someone is accused of discrimination, it generally means that he or she is perceived to be acting in an unfair or prejudiced manner. The law prohibits unfair discrimination—making choices on the basis of perceived but inaccurate differences, to the detriment of specific individuals and/or groups. Standards pertaining to unfair discrimination have changed over time. Both intentional and unintentional discrimination is prohibited.

Intentional Discrimination

Except in specific circumstances that will be described later, intentional discrimination is prohibited. An employer cannot discriminate *directly* by deliberately refusing to hire, train, or promote an individual, for example, on any of the prohibited grounds. It is important to realize that deliberate discrimination is not necessarily overt. In fact, overt (blatant) discrimination is relatively rare today. Subtle direct discrimination can be difficult to prove. For example, if a 60-year-old applicant is not selected for a job and is told that there was a better-qualified candidate, it is often difficult for the rejected job-seeker to determine if someone else truly did more closely match the firm's specifications or if the employer discriminated on the basis of age.

An employer is also prohibited from intentional discrimination in the form of *differential or unequal treatment.* No individuals or groups may be treated differently in any aspects or terms and conditions of employment based on any of the prohibited grounds. For example, it is illegal for an employer to request that only female applicants for a factory job demonstrate their lifting skills or to insist that any candidates with a physical disability undergo a pre-employment medical unless all applicants are being asked to do so.

It is also illegal for an employer to engage in intentional discrimination *indirectly*, through another party. This means that an employer may not ask someone else to discriminate on his or her behalf. For example, an employer cannot request that an employment agency refer only male candidates for consideration as management trainees or instruct supervisors that racial minorities are to be excluded from consideration for promotions.

Discrimination because of association is another possible type of intentional discrimination listed specifically as a prohibited ground in several Canadian jurisdictions. It involves the denial of rights because of friendship or other relationship with a protected group member. An example would be the refusal of a firm to promote a highly qualified male into senior management on the basis of the assumption that his wife, who was recently diagnosed with multiple sclerosis, will require too much of his time and attention and that her needs may restrict his willingness to travel on company business.

Unintentional Discrimination

unintentional/constructive/ systemic discrimination Discrimination that is embedded in policies and practices that appear neutral on the surface and are implemented impartially but have an adverse impact on specific groups of people for reasons that are not job related or required for the safe and efficient operation of the business.

Unintentional discrimination (also known as **constructive** or **systemic discrimination**) is the most difficult to detect and combat. Typically, it is embedded in policies and practices that, although appearing neutral on the surface and being implemented impartially, have an adverse impact on specific groups of people for reasons that are not job related or required for the safe and efficient operation of the business. Examples are shown in Figure 2.2.

Requirement for Reasonable Accommodation

reasonable accommodation The adjustment of employment policies and practices that an employer may be expected to make so that no individual is denied benefits, disadvantaged in employment, or prevented from carrying out the essential components of a job because of grounds prohibited in human rights legislation.

undue hardship The point to which employers are expected to accommodate under human rights legislative requirements.

An important feature of human rights legislation is the requirement for **reasonable accommodation.** Employers are required to adjust employment policies and practices so that no individual is prevented from doing his or her job on the basis of prohibited grounds for discrimination. Accommodation may involve scheduling adjustments to accommodate religious beliefs or workstation redesign to enable an individual with a physical disability to perform a particular task. Employers are expected to accommodate to the point of **undue hardship,** meaning that the financial cost of the accommodation (even with outside sources of funding) or health and safety risks to the individual concerned or other employees would make accommodation impossible.[6]

Failure to make every reasonable effort to accommodate employees is a violation of human rights legislation in all Canadian jurisdictions. The Supreme

FIGURE 2.2 | Examples of Systemic Discrimination

- Minimum height and weight requirements, which screen out dispropor-tionate numbers of women and people from Asia, who tend to be shorter in stature.
- Internal hiring policies or word-of-mouth hiring in workplaces that have not embraced diversity.
- Limited accessibility to company premises, which poses a barrier to persons with mobility limitations.
- Culturally biased or non-job-related employment tests, which discriminate against specific groups.
- Job evaluation systems that are not gender-neutral; that is, they under-value traditional female-dominated jobs.
- Promotions based exclusively on seniority or experience in firms that have a history of being white-male-dominated.
- Lack of a harassment policy or guidelines, or an organizational climate in which certain groups feel unwelcome and uncomfortable.

Source: Based on material provided by the Ontario Women's Directorate and the Canadian Human Rights Commission.

The Job Accommodation Network
http://janweb.icdi.wvu.edu

Court of Canada recently clarified the scope of the duty to accommodate by stating that is does not require an employer to completely alter the essence of the employment contract, whereby the employee has a duty to perform work in exchange for remuneration. If the characteristics of an illness are such that the employee remains unable to work for the foreseeable future, even though the employer has tried to accommodate the employee, the employer will have satis-fied the test of undue hardship.[7]

Accommodation of employees with "invisible" disabilities such as chronic fatigue syndrome, fibromyalgia, and mental illnesses is becoming more com-mon. An employee with bipolar disorder was terminated when he began to exhibit pre-manic symptoms after waiting for a response from management regarding his request for accommodation. A human rights tribunal found that the company had not investigated the nature of his condition or possible accom-modation and awarded the employee over $80 000 in damages.[8]

Permissible Discrimination

bona fide occupational require-ment (BFOR) A justifiable reason for discrimination based on busi-ness necessity (that is, required for the safe and efficient operation of the organization) or a requirement that can be clearly defended as intrinsically required by the tasks an employee is expected to perform.

Employers are permitted to discriminate if employment preferences are based on a **bona fide occupational requirement (BFOR)**, defined as a justifiable reason for discrimination based on business necessity, such as the requirement for the safe and efficient operation of the organization (e.g., a person who is blind cannot be employed as a truck driver or bus driver). In some cases, a BFOR exception to human rights protection is fairly obvious. For example, when casting in the the-atre, there may be specific roles that justify using age, sex, or national origin as a recruitment and selection criterion.

The issue of BFORs gets more complicated in situations in which the occupa-tional requirement is less obvious; the onus of proof is then placed on the employer. There are a number of instances in which BFORs have been established. For example, adherence to the tenets of the Roman Catholic Church has been deemed a BFOR when selecting faculty to teach in a Roman Catholic school.[9]

The Royal Canadian Mounted Police has a requirement that guards be of the same sex as prisoners being guarded, which was also ruled to be a BFOR.[10]

Human Rights Case Examples

In order to clarify how the human rights legislation is applied and the types of discrimination prohibited, a few examples follow.

Race and Colour

Racism and Racial Harassment: Your Rights and Responsibilities
www.ohrc.on.ca/en/issues/racism

Urban Alliance on Race Relations
www.tgmag.ca/magic/uarr.html

Sexual Orientation: Your Rights and Responsibilities
www.ohrc.on.ca/en/issues/sexual_orientation/index_html/view

Discrimination on the basis of race and colour is illegal in every Canadian jurisdiction. For example, the British Columbia Human Rights Tribunal found that two construction companies had discriminated against 38 Latin American workers brought in to work on a public transit project; the Latin Americans were treated differently than workers brought in from European countries in that the Latin Americans were paid lower wages and provided with inferior accommodation. The Tribunal awarded each worker $100 000.[11]

Sexual Orientation

Discrimination on the basis of sexual orientation is prohibited in all jurisdictions. As a result of lawsuits by same-sex couples, the Supreme Court ruled that all laws must define "common-law partners" to include both same-sex and opposite-sex couples.[12] In a recent federal case, a lesbian employee alleged that she was harassed by a co-worker. She made a complaint to her supervisors but felt the complaint was not investigated properly. She alleged that she was given a poor performance review because of her complaint and that her request for a transfer to another work site was denied. The Canadian Human Rights Commission ordered her employer to provide a letter of apology, financial compensation for pain and suffering, and a transfer to another work site. The Commission also ordered a meeting with the employer's harassment coordinator to talk about the complainant's experiences with the internal complaint process.[13]

An Ethical | Dilemma

Your company president tells you not to hire any gay or lesbian employees to work as part of his office staff because it would make him uncomfortable. What would you do?

Age

Many employers believe that it is justifiable to specify minimum or maximum ages for certain jobs. In actual fact, evidence is rarely available to support the position that age is an accurate indicator of a person's ability to perform a particular type of work.[14] For example, because of an economic downturn, an Ontario company was forced to lay off staff. The complainant, a foreman, had worked for the company for more than 32 years and was 57 at the time he was selected for termination along with another foreman who was aged 56. Both were offered a generous retirement package. The two foremen who remained were younger than the two released. The vice-president had prepared a note indicating that the two older workers who were terminated were told of the need to reduce people and that they "hoped to keep people with career potential." The Ontario Human Rights Tribunal found age discrimination on the basis of the good employment record of the complainant, the ages of those selected for layoff compared with those retained, and the vice-president's statement, which was found to be a "euphemism; its meaning concerns age."[15]

Religion

Discrimination on the basis of religion can take many forms in Canada's multicultural society. For example, it is a violation of human rights laws across Canada to deny time to pray or to prohibit the wearing of a *hijaab*. According to a recent survey in Toronto, discriminatory hiring practices and workplace racism toward Muslim women are quite common. Of the 32 women surveyed, 29 said that their employer had commented on their *hijaab*, and 13 said that they were told that they would have to stop wearing their *hijaab* if they wanted the job.[16]

Family Status

The Canadian Council on Rehabilitation and Work **www.workink.com**

Decisions regarding the specific meaning of discrimination based on family status (the status of being in a parent-and-child relationship) are evolving.[17] In a recent B.C. case, an employee whose shift was changed by the employer requested a return to her previous shift because the new shift time made it difficult for her to find a caregiver that could provide for her son's special needs. The employer refused and an arbitrator upheld the decision, saying that family status did not encompass the many circumstances that arise in regard to daycare needs. However, the Court of Appeal overturned the arbitrator and adopted a middle ground between a narrow definition of family status as being a parent and a broad definition encompassing all possible parental obligations.[18]

Harassment

harassment Unwelcome behaviour that demeans, humiliates, or embarrasses a person and that a reasonable person should have known would be unwelcome.

Some jurisdictions prohibit harassment on all prescribed grounds, while others only expressly ban sexual harassment. **Harassment** includes unwelcome behaviour that demeans, humiliates, or embarrasses a person and that a reasonable person should have known would be unwelcome. Examples of harassment are included in Figure 2.3. Minority women often experience harassment based on both sex and race.[19]

FIGURE 2.3 | Examples of Harassment

Some examples of harassment include:

- unwelcome remarks, slurs, jokes, taunts, or suggestions about a person's body, clothing, race, national or ethnic origin, colour, religion, age, sex, marital status, family status, physical or mental disability, sexual orientation, pardoned conviction, or other personal characteristics;
- unwelcome sexual remarks, invitations, or requests (including persistent, unwanted contact after the end of a relationship);
- display of sexually explicit, sexist, racist, or other offensive or derogatory material;
- written or verbal abuse or threats;
- practical jokes that embarrass or insult someone;
- leering (suggestive staring) or other offensive gestures;
- unwelcome physical contact, such as patting, touching, pinching, hitting;
- patronizing or condescending behaviour;
- humiliating an employee in front of co-workers;
- abuse of authority that undermines someone's performance or threatens his or her career;
- vandalism of personal property; and
- physical or sexual assault.

Source: Canadian Human Rights Commission, *Anti-Harassment Policies for the Workforce: An Employer's Guide.* www.chrc-ccdp.ca/pdf/AHPoliciesWorkplace_en.pdf. Reproduced by permission of the Ministry of Public Works and Government Services, 2009.

Global HRM

U.K. Court Awards $1.7 Million to Bullied Employee

A banking employee in the U.K. was the victim of bullying from four female coworkers over a period of four years. Some examples of her co-workers' behaviour included

- ignoring her or staring silently at her, often with arms crossed, in a way intended to intimidate and unnerve her;

- greeting others within the department in a very overt manner, highlighting that they were not speaking to her;

- talking over her or pretending they could not hear anything she said;

- bursting out laughing when she walked by;

- making crude and lewd comments that made her feel uncomfortable; and

- removing her name from circulation lists, hiding her mail, and removing papers from her desk.

Another male colleague also bullied her by being vulgar, inappropriate, and hostile, and trying to undermine her work and authority in the eyes of others.

As a result, she suffered two major episodes of depressive disorder requiring hospitalization and a suicide watch, followed by a period of four years in which she was not able to return to work and in which her capacity to enjoy life to the fullest had been seriously disrupted. The court concluded that she was subjected to a relentless campaign of mean and spiteful behaviour designed to cause her distress, amounting to a deliberate and concerted campaign of bullying.

The court held the employer vicariously liable for the conduct of the co-workers because the managers collectively closed their eyes to what was going on. They awarded damages of $1.7 million, including $1.3 million for future loss of earnings because she had lost her lifetime career.

Source: Adapted from H. Gray, "British court punishes employer that let bullying go unchecked," *Canadian HR Reporter* (October 9, 2006).

Sexual Harassment: Your Rights and Responsibilities
www.ohrc.on.ca/en/issues/ sexual_harassment

One type of intentional harassment that is receiving increasing attention is bullying, which involves repeated and deliberate incidents of negative behaviour that cumulatively undermine a person's self-image. This psychological form of harassment is much more prevalent and pervasive in workplaces than physical violence.[20] In 2004, a Quebec law prohibiting workplace psychological harassment came into effect with the intent of ending bullying in the workplace. In the first year, more than 2500 complaints were received, surpassing expectations to such a degree that the number of investigators was increased from 10 to 34.[21] Saskatchewan prohibits psychological harassment in its occupational health and safety legislation.[22]

This issue is a concern in other countries as well, as described in the Global HRM box.

Employer Responsibility The Supreme Court has made it clear that protecting employees from harassment is part of an employer's responsibility to provide a safe and healthy working environment. If harassment is occurring and employers are aware or ought to have been aware, they can be charged as well as the alleged harasser.[23] Employer responsibility includes employee harassment by clients or customers once it has been reported. In a recent Ontario case, Bell Mobility was ordered to pay an employee more than $500 000 after a supervisor assaulted her in the office, and she developed post-traumatic stress disorder. The company was found vicariously liable

Psychological harassment is often called bullying.

for the supervisor's aggressive behaviours and found to have breached its duty of care to provide a safe and harassment-free working environment.[24]

Sexual Harassment   The type of harassment that has attracted the most attention in the workplace is **sexual harassment**. Sexual harassment is offensive or humiliating behaviour that is related to a person's sex, as well as behaviour of a sexual nature that creates an intimidating, unwelcome, hostile, or offensive work environment or that could reasonably be thought to put sexual conditions on a person's job or employment opportunities.

Sexual harassment can be divided into two categories: sexual coercion and sexual annoyance.[25] **Sexual coercion** involves harassment of a sexual nature that results in some direct consequence to the worker's employment status or some gain in or loss of tangible job benefits. Typically, this involves a supervisor using control over employment, pay, performance appraisal results, or promotion to attempt to coerce an employee to grant sexual favours. If the worker agrees to the request, tangible job benefits follow; if the worker refuses, job benefits are denied or taken away.

Sexual annoyance is sexually related conduct that is hostile, intimidating, or offensive to the employee but has no direct link to tangible job benefits or loss thereof. Rather, a "poisoned work environment" is created for the employee, the tolerance of which effectively becomes a term or condition of employment. An Alberta court upheld the dismissal of a male employee who had used profane language, sexually infused talk and jokes, and displayed pornographic and graphically violent images. The employee claimed that he was a misunderstood jokester who had never worked with a female engineer before and blamed the company for not training him on appropriate conduct. However, the court found that the company had embarked on a campaign to recruit women into trades positions many years earlier and that all employees had been provided with diversity training. In addition, the company had also implemented and widely publicized an anti-harassment policy.[26]

Harassment Policies   To reduce liability, employers should establish sound harassment policies, communicate such policies to all employees, enforce the policies in a fair and consistent manner, and take an active role in maintaining a working environment that is free of harassment. Effective harassment policies should include[27]

1. an anti-harassment policy statement, stating the organization's commitment to a safe and respectful work environment and specifying that harassment is against the law;

2. information for victims (e.g., how to identify harassment; what isn't harassment);

3. employees' rights and responsibilities (e.g., respect others, speak up, report harassment);

4. employers' and managers' responsibilities (e.g., put a stop to harassment, be aware, listen to employees);

5. anti-harassment policy procedures (e.g., what to do if you are being harassed, what to do if you are accused of harassment, what to do if you are

---

sexual harassment Offensive or humiliating behaviour that is related to a person's sex, as well as behaviour of a sexual nature that creates an intimidating, unwelcome, hostile, or offensive work environment or that could reasonably be thought to put sexual conditions on a person's job or employment opportunities.

sexual coercion Harassment of a sexual nature that results in some direct consequence to the worker's employment status or some gain in or loss of tangible job benefits.

sexual annoyance Sexually related conduct that is hostile, intimidating, or offensive to the employee but has no direct link to tangible job benefits or loss thereof.

Hints | **TO ENSURE LEGAL COMPLIANCE**

Alberta Human Rights and Citizenship Commission
www.albertahumanrights.ab.ca

British Columbia Human Rights Tribunal
www.bchrt.bc.ca

Manitoba Human Rights Commission
www.gov.mb.ca/hrc

New Brunswick Human Rights Commission
www.gnb.ca/hrc-cdp/index-e.asp

Newfoundland and Labrador Human Rights Commission
www.justice.gov.nl.ca/hrc

Northwest Territories Human Rights Commission
www.nwthumanrights.ca

Nova Scotia Human Rights
Commission
www.gov.ns.ca/humanrights

Nunavut Human Rights Act
**www.gov.nu.ca/hr/site/doc/
Nunavut%20Human%20Rights%2
0Act.pdf**

Ontario Human Rights Commission
www.ohrc.on.ca

Prince Edward Island Human Rights
Commission
www.gov.pe.ca/humanrights/

Québec Commission des droits de la
personne et des droits de la
jeunesse
www.cdpdj.qc.ca

Saskatchewan Human Rights
Commission
www.shrc.gov.sk.ca

Yukon Human Rights Commission
www.yhrc.yk.ca

a third-party employee, investigation guidelines, remedies for the victim and corrective action for harassers, guidelines for handling unsubstantiated complaints and complaints made in bad faith, confidentiality);

6. penalties for retaliation against a complainant;
7. guidelines for appeals;
8. other options such as union grievance procedures and human rights complaints;
9. how the policy will be monitored and adjusted.

Enforcement

Enforcement of human rights acts is the responsibility of the human rights commission in each jurisdiction. It should be noted that all costs are borne by the commission, not by the complainant, which makes the process accessible to all employees, regardless of financial means. The commission itself can initiate a complaint if it has reasonable grounds to assume that a party is engaging in a discriminatory practice.

If discrimination is found, a number of remedies can be imposed. The most common is compensation for lost wages; other remedies include compensation for general damages, complainant expenses, and pain and humiliation. The violator is generally asked to restore the rights, opportunities, and privileges denied the victim, such as employment or promotion. A written letter of apology may also be required. If a pattern of discrimination is detected, the employer will be ordered to cease such practices and may be required to attend a training session or hold regular human rights workshops.

EMPLOYMENT EQUITY LEGISLATION

occupational segregation The existence of certain occupations that have traditionally been male dominated and others that have been female dominated.

glass ceiling An invisible barrier, caused by attitudinal or organizational bias, which limits the advancement opportunities of qualified designated group members.

The Charter of Rights and Freedoms legalizes employment equity initiatives, which go beyond human rights laws in that they are proactive programs developed by employers to remedy past discrimination and/or prevent future discrimination. Human rights laws focus on prohibiting various kinds of discrimination; however, over time it became obvious that there were certain groups for whom this complaint-based, reactive approach was insufficient. Investigation revealed that four identifiable groups—women, Aboriginal people, persons with disabilities, and visible minorities—had been subjected to pervasive patterns of differential treatment by employers, as evidenced by lower pay on average, occupational segregation, higher rates of unemployment, underemployment, and concentration in low-status jobs with little potential for career growth.

For example, historically, the majority of women worked in a very small number of jobs, such as nursing, teaching, sales, and secretarial/clerical work. This is known as **occupational segregation**. Advancement of women and other designated group members into senior management positions has been hindered by the existence of a **glass ceiling**, an "invisible" barrier caused by attitudinal or organizational bias, which limits the advancement opportunities of qualified individuals.

FIGURE 2.4 │ The Catalyst Pyramid—Canadian Women in Business, 2009

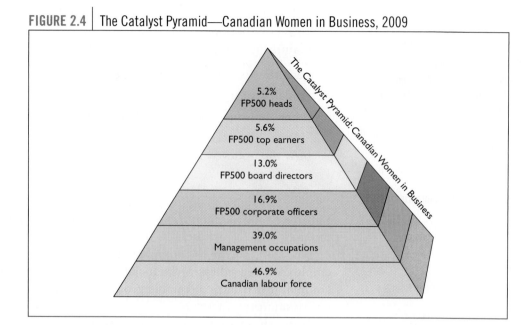

Sources: Catalyst, 2008 Catalyst Census of Women Corporate Officers and Top Earners of the FP500 (2009); Catalyst, 2007 Census of Women Board Directors of the FP500: Voices of the Boardroom (2008); Statistics Canada, Labour Force Survey (2008). Reproduced by permission of Catalyst, www.catalystwomen.org.

Catalyst
www.catalyst.org

Research │ INSIGHT

Annual studies involving Canada's *Financial Post* 500 (FP500) ranking—the 500 largest companies in Canada—conducted by Catalyst confirm that the glass ceiling is still intact (see Figure 2.4). In these firms, there is concrete evidence of underutilization of female employees. Although women made up almost one-half of the Canadian workforce in 2007, they were still under-represented on executive teams, composing 39 percent of management positions, 17 percent of corporate officers, and 13 percent of members on boards of directors. This situation creates a competitive opportunity for companies that utilize women to their full potential. Several studies have confirmed that as the number of female board members increases, so does financial performance.[28]

The Plight of the Four Designated Groups

1. Women

Women accounted for 47 percent of the employed workforce in 2006. Two-thirds of all employed women were working in teaching, nursing and related health occupations, clerical or other administrative positions, and sales and service occupations. There has been virtually no change in the proportion of women employed in these traditionally female-dominated occupations over the past decade. Women continue to be under-represented in engineering, natural sciences, and mathematics, a trend unlikely to change in the near future since women are still under-represented in university programs in these fields.[29]

Workforce DIVERSITY

Intellectually Disabled Workers Take Pride in High-Quality, Cost-Effective Services

Versatech Industries Inc. of Winnipeg is a non-profit organization that assembles and packages consumer goods and provides recycling and document destruction services. Its many customers include the Province of Manitoba, the Government of Canada, Boeing, and its oldest and largest client, Coghlan's—The Outdoor Accessory People. Started in 1962 by a group of parents of children with intellectual disabilities in order to help them develop job skills, their first customer needed someone to assemble and package camp stove toasters.

From those humble beginnings, the company now has three locations in Winnipeg and continues to assemble and package Coghlan's small accessories for camping, picnicking, fishing, and hiking. It employs close to 300 people, of which 43 are full-time employees trained to help people with special needs and 260 are intellectually disabled. Eighty percent of the revenue the workers generate is paid back to them in wages, dividends, and bonuses. When skeptics imply that customers are hiring cheap labour, they are quickly corrected. The cost is based on the amount of time it would take a fully functioning person to do the job. However much time that takes, that's the rate of pay customers are charged for the service provided to them.

Using Versatech to assemble and package Coghlan's products is, nevertheless, cost-effective compared to automated factories. And while its competitors tend to have their products manufactured, packaged, and assembled in Asia, working with Versatech allows Coghlan's to keep the work local. Versatech automates some applications, but most work is done by hand, which allows for better quality control. "And this workforce is very good," says Justin Vandenberg, Coghlan's director of marketing. "They take a lot of pride in their work."

Versatech CEO Richard Doyle says that whenever visitors tour Versatech, "they say they've never seen a happier place." For himself, he says, "This is the most amazing place. They make you feel like a million bucks. We're here because we want to make their lives better, but you should see what they do for our lives." As for the workforce of people with intellectual disabilities, Doyle says, "We have a pool of very talented people. They work with power tools, machines, sort lines, and some have taken a food-handling course and gotten their certificates. Some might have difficulty reading, but that's not needed for putting hinges together." And they might have a longer learning curve, which is why each employee starts out with a job coach for three months, or however long it takes to become a fully functional employee.

In light of the increasing labour gap that has Canadian employers in all sectors scrambling to recruit, Doyle wonders what's stopping other companies from tapping into this workforce. Employment agencies for the disabled, he says, often have trouble finding jobs for people. "It's the employers that have to give their heads a shake," he says. "These people can contribute."

Source: Adapted from M. Morra, "Take a chance on me: Companies that hire disabled workers receive back tenfold results," *Workplace* (November/December 2008), pp. 22–24. Reprinted with permission of the author.

2. Aboriginals

Most Aboriginal employees in the workforce are concentrated in low-skill, low-paid jobs such as trades helpers. The unemployment rate for Aboriginal people is significantly higher than the rate among non-Aboriginals, and their income is significantly lower.[30]

3. People with Disabilities

About 45 percent of people with disabilities are in the labour force, compared with almost 80 percent of the non-disabled population. Although 63 percent of people with a mild disability are in the workforce, only 28 percent of those with a severe to very severe disability are working. The median employment income of workers with disabilities is 83 percent of that of other Canadian workers.[31] The Workforce Diversity box provides an example of the capabilities of disabled workers.

KSAs Knowledge, skills, and abilities.

underemployment Being employed in a job that does not fully utilize one's knowledge, skills, and abilities (KSAs).

4. Visible Minorities

Many immigrants are highly educated visible minorities. They are typically unable to obtain employment that takes full advantage of their knowledge, skills, and abilities (**KSAs**), and thus face **underemployment**. An example is provided in the Entrepreneurs and HR box. The unemployment rate for newly arrived skilled immigrants, who are more likely than the Canadian-born population to have a university education, was more than double that of the Canadian–born population.[32] A recent study on diversity in the Greater Toronto Area highlighted the continuing disadvantaged status of visible minorities. The study looked at 3257 leaders in the GTA in all sectors and found that just 13 percent were visible minorities (who make up half of the population).[33] There are only four visible minority city councillors.[34]

Mel Garbe, a Métis law student, gained experience through the Alberta Law Society's Aboriginal Law Summer Student Employment program.

Legislation to Address Employment Barriers

After realizing that simple prohibition of discrimination would not correct these patterns, a number of jurisdictions passed employment equity legislation aimed at identifying and eliminating systemic barriers to employment opportunities that adversely affect these four groups. Employment equity legislation is focused on bringing the four traditionally disadvantaged groups identified above into the mainstream of Canada's labour force. The use of the term "employment equity" distinguishes Canada's approach from the "affirmative action" used in the

Entrepreneurs and HR

Diversity Works for Steam Whistle Brewing

One day Sybil Taylor, director of marketing at Steam Whistle Brewing, noticed a resumé on her desk. Someone named Stefan Atton, who had immigrated to Canada only two months before, was applying for a delivery job. "But when I read his credentials," says Taylor, "I thought, Oh my God. What is this guy doing?"

The applicant had worked in Sri Lanka and in India as a brand and market manager for multinational companies Procter & Gamble, Reckitt & Coleman Inc., and Lion—the largest brewery in Sri Lanka, where he oversaw export sales of Carlsberg and Guinness in the United States, Germany, United Kingdom, and France. Yet since arriving in Canada, Atton had sent out 700 resumés for jobs in his field, which yielded nothing, except for one job he narrowly missed out on because he lacked Canadian work experience. To get at least some experience, he had worked for his first two months here as a telemarketer.

Then a friend suggested he approach companies in a different way—by applying for an entry-level position. He tried Steam Whistle, having heard that company was involved in several community marketing initiatives. The

small brewery didn't have an HR department, so Atton strategically sent his resumé to Steam Whistle's director of marketing. What he didn't know was that Taylor was preparing to step down to a less-demanding position within the company to spend more time with her young family.

He'll never forget the email. "Sybil wrote to me and said, 'Why don't you interview for my job?'" says Atton. "I nearly fell out of my chair." Since hiring Stefan Atton at Steam Whistle five years ago, the company has never looked back. The small brewery has since hired a colleague of his from Sri Lanka, who is now Steam Whistle's chief financial officer.

As employers start hiring new Canadians, they need to move beyond inclusiveness, such as honouring different religious customs, and move toward a culture that really enhances and trains the skill development across the whole spectrum of their people. Then they can really engage individuals and get the best performance from them.

Source: Adapted from M. Morra, "Diversity: Smart hiring brews success," *Workplace News* (November/December 2007) pp. 26–28. Reprinted with permission of the author.

United States. Affirmative action has come to be associated with quotas, a divisive political issue.[35]

Employment equity legislation is intended to remove employment barriers and promote equality for the members of the four designated groups. For example, employers under federal jurisdiction must prepare an annual plan with specific goals to achieve better representation of the designated group members at all levels of the organization and timetables for goal implementation. Employers must also submit an annual report on the company's progress in meeting its goals, indicating the representation of designated group members by occupational groups and salary ranges, and information on those hired, promoted, and terminated.

Employment Equity Programs

Mandatory employment equity programs are virtually non-existent in provincial and territorial jurisdictions. Some provinces have employment equity policies that encourage employment equity plans in provincial departments and ministries. Quebec has a contract compliance program where employers in receipt of more than $100 000 in provincial funding must implement an employment equity plan.[36] In the federal jurisdiction, the Federal Contractors Program requires firms bidding on federal contracts of $200 000 or more to implement an employment equity plan.

employment equity program A detailed plan designed to identify and correct existing discrimination, redress past discrimination, and achieve a balanced representation of designated group members in the organization.

An **employment equity program** is designed to achieve a balanced representation of designated group members in the organization. It is a major management exercise because existing employees must become comfortable working with others from diverse backgrounds, cultures, religions, and so on, and this represents a major change in the work environment. A deliberately structured process is involved, which can be tailored to suit the unique needs of the firm. The employment equity process includes six main steps, each of which will now be described.

Step 1: Senior-Management Commitment and Support

Senior management's total commitment to employment equity is essential to a program's success. A *written policy*, endorsed by senior management and distributed to every employee, is an essential first step. The employment equity policy for Ryerson University is shown in Figure 2.5. An organization should *appoint a senior official* (preferably reporting to the CEO) to whom overall responsibility and authority for program design and implementation is assigned.

Step 2: Data Collection and Analysis

The development of an internal workforce profile is necessary in order to compare internal representation with external workforce availability data, set reasonable goals, and measure progress. To obtain data pertaining to the distribution of designated group members, a self-identification process is often used. Under federal employment equity legislation, employers may collect such data, as long as employees voluntarily agree to be identified or identify themselves as designated group members and the data are only used for employment equity planning and reporting purposes.

utilization analysis The comparison of the internal workforce representation with external workforce availability.

Comparison data from Statistics Canada and other sources must also be collected on the number of designated group members available in the labour markets from which the organization recruits. The comparison of the internal workforce representation with external workforce availability is called a **utilization analysis.** This type of comparison is necessary in order to determine

FIGURE 2.5 | Ryerson University Employment Equity Policy

Ryerson University—Employment Equity

Principles

Ryerson University is committed to principles of equity and diversity in the workplace. Employment equity is a principle at the core of Ryerson's overall mandate as a community leader and as an institution of higher learning. The University is committed to promoting employment equity within the University community, and to ensuring there is equal opportunity and equitable representation in employment for all current and potential faculty and staff.

Employment equity involves hiring the best-qualified candidate while ensuring a fair and equitable hiring process for all persons. The University shall hire and make employment and promotion decisions on the basis of qualifications and merit. Within this context, the University shall make proactive efforts to increase the participation from the four groups designated for employment equity, namely women, visible minorities, persons with disabilities, and aboriginal persons.

Objectives

The following objectives apply to the *Employment Equity* policy:

1. Achieve and maintain a representative workforce for all employees by actively seeking to attract individuals of diverse background while affirmatively addressing the historic under-representation of aboriginal peoples, people with disabilities, visible minorities, and women.
2. Develop and implement an employment equity plan (including goals and timetables) to achieve and maintain representational hiring among faculty and staff.
3. Identify and remove discriminatory barriers (systemic or otherwise), implement special programs, and work with the Ryerson community to foster an environment that promotes the principles of employment equity in the workplace.
4. Work collaboratively with academic and administrative leaders, unions, and employee groups to develop an effective communication strategy that will educate, inform, and raise the level of awareness within the community towards employment equity and diversity-related issues.
5. Manage an effective outreach program that will facilitate the wide promotion of employment opportunities in order to enhance the diversity of the candidate pool and ultimately enhance the representation of designated groups among faculty and staff.
6. Ensure continued compliance with the requirements of all relevant legislation (including the Ontario Human Rights Code and the Federal Contractors Program) as well as internal policies and collective agreements that govern the various groups of faculty and staff.

Policy

Ryerson University is committed to actively seeking and attracting qualified individuals of diverse background while affirmatively addressing the historic under-representation of aboriginal peoples, people with disabilities, visible minorities, and women.

The University is committed to actively promoting employment equity within the Ryerson community and to promoting a climate that is favourable to the successful integration of members of designated groups.

The University shall ensure that there are no discriminatory barriers in the selection, development and training, promotion, and retention and termination of employees. The University will make reasonable accommodations to enable employees to compete on an equitable basis.

Scope

This policy applies to all employees of Ryerson University, including faculty (career or tenure stream), academic and administrative support staff, supervisors, managers, academic administrators and senior administrators and the executive.

Source: From *Ryerson University Employment Equity Policy-Procedure.* www.ryerson.ca/about/vpadministration/assets/pdf/EmploymentEquity.pdf

employment systems review A thorough examination of corporate policies and procedures, collective agreements, and informal practices to determine their impact on designated group members so that existing intentional or systemic barriers can be eliminated.

the degree of underutilization and concentration of designated group members in specific occupations or at particular organizational levels.

Step 3: Employment Systems Review

It is also essential that the organization undertake a comprehensive **employment systems review** to determine the impact of policies and procedures manuals, collective agreements, and informal practices on designated group members so that existing intentional or systemic barriers can be eliminated. Typically, employment systems that require review include job classifications and descriptions, recruitment and selection processes, performance appraisal systems, training and development programs, transfer and promotion procedures, compensation policies and practices, and discipline and termination procedures.

Step 4: Plan Development

Once the workforce profile and systems reviews have been completed, the employment equity plan can be prepared. *Goals and timetables* are the core of an employment equity program. Goals, ranging from short to long term in duration, should be flexible and tied to reasonable timetables. *Goals are not quotas.*[37] They are estimates of the results that experts in the firm have established based on knowledge of the workplace and its employees, the availability of individuals with the KSAs required by the firm in the external labour force, and the special measures that are planned. Quantitative goals should be set, specifying the number or percentage of qualified designated group members to be hired, trained, or promoted into each occupational group within a specified period of time. Qualitative goals, referred to as special measures, should also be included.

Three types of special measures are (1) **positive measures** designed to accelerate the entry, development, and promotion of designated group members, such as targeted recruitment; (2) **accommodation measures** to assist designated group members in carrying out their essential job duties, such as upgrading facilities for an employee with disabilities; and (3) **supportive measures** that enable all employees to achieve a better work/life balance, such as flexible work schedules in northern Canada to allow Aboriginal employees to take part in traditional fishing and hunting activities.

Giving preference to designated group members to the extent that non-members believe they are being discriminated against can result in accusations of **reverse discrimination.** It is possible to avoid the entire issue of reverse discrimination if the approach taken to employment equity is goals. When goals are seen as targets, the end result is that a *better-qualified* candidate who is not a designated group member is never denied an employment-related opportunity. However, when there are two *equally qualified candidates,* based on non-discriminatory job specifications and selection criteria, preference will be given to the designated group member. The term "equally qualified" needs to be explained, since it does not necessarily imply identical educational qualifications or years of work experience but rather the possession of the qualifications required to perform the job. Thus, if a job requires two years of previous related experience, the candidate with four years of related experience is no more qualified than the individual with two.

positive measures Initiatives designed to accelerate the entry, development, and promotion of designated group members, aimed at overcoming the residual effects of past discrimination.

accommodation measures Strategies to assist designated group members.

supportive measures Strategies that enable all employees to achieve better balance between work and other responsibilities.

reverse discrimination Giving preference to designated group members to the extent that non-members believe they are being discriminated against.

An Ethical | Dilemma

Your executive team has just selected a white male for a senior management position in your company instead of a similarly qualified visible minority candidate. How would you handle this situation?

Step 5: Implementation

Implementation is the process that transforms goals, timetables, and special measures into reality. Implementation strategies will be different in every firm because of each organization's unique culture and climate.

Step 6: Monitoring, Evaluating, and Revising

An effective employment equity program requires a control system so that progress and success, or lack thereof, can be evaluated.

TABLE 2.1 | Impact of Employment Equity in Federally Regulated Organizations

Private Sector

Designated Group	Representation 1987	Representation 2007	Availability 2007
Women	40.1	42.7	47.3
Visible minorities	4.9	15.9	12.6
Aboriginal	.6	1.9	2.6
People with disabilities	1.6	2.7	5.8

Public Sector

Designated Group	Representation 1987	Representation 2007	Availability 2007
Women	42.0	54.4	52.2
Visible minorities	2.7	9.2	10.4
Aboriginal	1.8	4.4	2.5
People with disabilities	2.6	5.9	3.6

Source: Adapted from *Employment Equity Act: Annual Report 2008.* Ottawa ON: Human Resources and Skills Development Canada, 2009.

Impact of Employment Equity

According to the Canadian Human Rights Commission 2008 Annual Report, employment equity has gradually been making a difference, as shown in Table 2.1.

DIVERSITY MANAGEMENT

diversity management Activities designed to integrate all members of an organization's multicultural workforce and use their diversity to enhance the firm's effectiveness.

Diversity Best Practices
www.diversitybestpractices.com

Diversity Central
www.diversitycentral.com

Although many people perceive "diversity management" to be another term for "employment equity," the two are very distinct. Managing diversity is a strategic approach to talent management, which goes far beyond legal compliance or even implementing an employment equity plan voluntarily (see the example in the Strategic HRM box). **Diversity management** is broader and more inclusive in scope and involves a set of activities designed to integrate all members of an organization's multicultural workforce and use their diversity to enhance the firm's effectiveness. Professional services firm Deloitte appointed Jane Allen as chief diversity officer in 2008. Her mandate is to ensure that the firm's diversity strategy is linked to its business strategy. The main focus of the diversity strategy is to attract and retain the best talent.[38]

Although there are ethical and social responsibility issues involved in embracing diversity, there are other more pragmatic reasons for doing so. Employees with different ethnic backgrounds often possess foreign language skills, have knowledge of different cultures and business practices, and may even have established trade links in other nations, which can lead to competitive advantages. Visible minorities can also help to increase an organization's competitiveness and

Strategic HR

Xerox Research Centre Reaps Economic Advantage of Diversity

Over its 33-year history, the Xerox Research Centre of Canada in Mississauga, Ontario, has prided itself on its diverse workforce, according to Hadi Mahabadi, vice-president and manager. The centre has more than 130 employees from more than 35 countries. In the process of trying to come up with new ideas for Xerox, research centre employees do a lot of brainstorming. When the people involved in brainstorming come from different cultures, the ideas are more creative. "You get a much richer pool of ideas to select from, which helps innovation," said Mahabadi.

This richness of ideas has paid off. Last year, the centre reached a milestone in research: It received its 1000th patent. As a testament to the role of diversity in innovation, three of the centre's top performers, who have more than 100 patents each, are skilled immigrants.

Over the past few years, that high number of patents has led to an average of five to six ideas each year going to market. "Having a lot of patents is a good thing, but taking it to market and commercializing it is much more important," said Mahabadi.

To make the most of skilled immigrants, the centre provides courses on language, public speaking, and writing. The centre also pairs a new skilled immigrant with a buddy—either someone from the same field or someone from a similar background who shares the new hire's language. "Our aim is that the person gets used to the system, learns the language fast, and becomes familiar with the situation as fast as possible and not delay in their progress," said Mahabadi.

Source: Adapted from S. Klie, "Diverse workforce helps research centre reach milestone," *Canadian HR Reporter* (December 17, 2007), pp. 13, 15.

As chief diversity officer at professional services firm Deloitte in Toronto, Jane Allen holds decision makers accountable to acting in a manner that encourages a culture of diversity.

international savvy in the global business arena. Specifically, cultural diversity can help fine-tune product design, marketing, and ultimately customer satisfaction.

Although embracing employee diversity offers opportunities to enhance organizational effectiveness, transforming an organizational culture presents a set of challenges that must be handled properly. Diversity initiatives should be undertaken slowly, since they involve a complex change process. Resistance to change may have to be overcome, along with stereotyped beliefs or prejudices and employee resentment.

Creating an Inclusive Environment

Organizations that have been successful in managing diversity have worked hard to create an inclusive environment in a variety of ways.

Top Management Commitment

As with any major change initiative, unless there is commitment from the top, it is unlikely that other managers will become champions of diversity. For example, 30 Ontario deputy ministers partnered with 87 Queen's Park employees in a year-long diversity mentorship program rather unique in the public sector. Even Secretary of the Cabinet Shelly Jamieson—Ontario's most senior public servant—took part.[39]

Integration of Diversity Initiatives and Talent Management

Diversity and inclusion initiatives work best when they are integrated into recruiting, training and development, and succession planning processes. For example, executive search firms that work with Royal Bank of Canada (RBC) are required to include a diverse slate of candidates for key positions, and they also have a commitment to having at least one candidate who is representative of that diverse mix for mid-level positions.[40] Air Canada regularly reviews its physical requirements for jobs such as ramp agents and pilots to see if accommodations can be made for workers with disabilities.[41]

Diversity Training Programs

Diversity training programs are designed to reduce stereotypes by providing awareness of diversity issues and educating employees about specific types of differences. They can also identify appropriate ways to handle differences through inclusive behaviours. For example, TransCanada, a gas transmission and power generation company based in Calgary, worked with the Aboriginal Human Resources Council to develop a new management training program called Mastering Aboriginal Inclusion. The training is designed to help managers develop expertise in the recruitment, retention, and advancement of Aboriginals. TransCanada also provides training for all employees so they can be more knowledgeable about Aboriginal cultures, beliefs, and ways of thinking.[42]

Support Groups

Support groups have been established in some firms to provide a means for employees with similar backgrounds to share their experiences. For example, KPMG has established member networks for women, international employees, and parents of children with special needs.[43] IBM encourages employees to form interest clubs, such as the Black Network Group and Aboriginal Peoples Network.[44] Groups for lesbian, gay, bisexual, and transgender (LGBT) employees are offered by KPMG, Scotiabank, TD Bank Financial Group, Hewlett-Packard Canada, and Edmonton-based software firm Intuit.[45]

Critical Relationship Networks

It is important to think critically about where informal networking takes place and how this may exclude certain groups. Providing employees with access to senior-level executives and employees from other departments and backgrounds is crucial to developing career-enhancing networks. Ernst & Young has a long-standing mentorship program where partners coach visible minority managers, and the Assiniboine Credit Union in Winnipeg offers an Aboriginal integration program which includes mentoring for the participants.[46]

Open Dialogue

Firms that want to ensure that employees from different backgrounds don't feel the need to suppress their true identities in order to fit in encourage open dialogue to address sensitive issues: LGBT employees often find that they cannot realize their potential when hiding their sexual orientation; female minorities often have difficulty communicating their achievements without feeling uncomfortable about self-promoting; Asian employees are typically very uncomfortable speaking directly about a problem issue, and so on. For example, KPMG operates a "micro-inequities" program designed to promote diversity through awareness of body language, spoken language, and differing cultural norms.[47]

Management Responsibility and Accountability

Diversity management initiatives will not receive high priority unless supervisors and managers are held accountable and results are part of their formal assessment. Quarterly reports on the progress regarding diversity goals are provided to the RBC Diversity Leadership Council, chaired by the CEO.[48] At FedEx Canada, managers are held accountable for the count of personnel from each of the four designated groups in their departments. A new performance appraisal system for managers considers it a core competency "to ensure the workplace is a diverse workplace."[49]

Conclusion

The Canadian labour force offers a large pool of diverse talent that is underrepresented and underutilized. Harnessing and maximizing this talent offers substantial benefits to organizations in terms of productivity, profitability, and competitive advantage. If Canadian organizations want to reap the benefits of a diverse workforce, they must make diversity an essential element of their operations, creating strong links between diversity and corporate strategies.

A Conference Board of Canada study found that Canadian organizations appear to be shifting their approach from a compliance-driven focus on employment equity to a business-driven focus on workplace diversity. Many indicate a high level of commitment to diversity and clearly identify key business reasons for investing in diversity and inclusiveness. If this commitment can be translated into strategies and practices that are successful in building and maintaining a high-performing and diverse workforce, then Canadian organizations will be in an excellent position to create a competitive advantage.[50]

Chapter | SUMMARY

1. The responsibility for employment-related law resides with the provinces and territories; however, employees of the federal civil service; Crown corporations and agencies; and businesses engaged in transportation, banking, and communications are federally regulated. There are 14 jurisdictions for employment law—10 provinces, 3 territories, and the federal jurisdiction. Ninety percent of Canadians are covered by provincial/territorial employment legislation and 10 percent are covered by federal employment legislation.

2. All jurisdictions prohibit discrimination on the grounds of race, colour, sexual orientation, religion/creed, physical and mental disability, sex,

age, and marital status. Employers are required to make reasonable accommodation for employees by adjusting employment policies and practices so that no one is disadvantaged in employment on any of the prohibited grounds to the point of undue hardship.

3. Harassment includes a wide range of behaviours that a reasonable person *ought to know* are unwelcome. Employers and managers have a responsibility to provide a safe and healthy working environment. If harassment is occurring and they are aware or ought to have been aware, they can be charged along with the alleged harasser. To reduce liability, employers should establish harassment policies, communicate these to employees, enforce the policies, and play an active role in maintaining a work environment free of harassment.

4. The six steps involved in implementing an employment equity program are (1) senior management commitment and support; (2) data collection and analysis; (3) an employment systems review; (4) plan development; (5) plan implementation; and (6) a follow-up process encompassing monitoring, evaluation, and revision.

5. Organizations that have been successful in managing diversity have worked hard to create an inclusive environment in a variety of ways: top management commitment, integration of diversity initiatives and talent management, diversity training programs, support groups, critical relationship networks/mentoring programs, open dialogue, and management responsibility and accountability.

Key | TERMS

accommodation measures   *(p. 43)*
bona fide occupational requirement (BFOR)
   (p. 32)
Charter of Rights and Freedoms   *(p. 28)*
common law   *(p. 27)*
contract law   *(p. 27)*
discrimination   *(p. 30)*
diversity management   *(p. 44)*
employment (labour) standards legislation   *(p. 28)*
employment equity program   *(p. 41)*
employment systems review   *(p. 42)*
equality rights   *(p. 29)*
glass ceiling   *(p. 37)*
harassment   *(p. 34)*
KSAs   *(p. 40)*

occupational segregation   *(p. 37)*
positive measures   *(p. 43)*
reasonable accommodation   *(p. 31)*
regulations   *(p. 27)*
reverse discrimination   *(p. 43)*
sexual annoyance   *(p. 36)*
sexual coercion   *(p. 36)*
sexual harassment   *(p. 36)*
supportive measures   *(p. 43)*
underemployment   *(p. 40)*
undue hardship   *(p. 31)*
unintentional/constructive/systemic
   discrimination   *(p. 31)*
utilization analysis   *(p. 42)*

Review and Discussion | QUESTIONS

1. Describe the impact of the Charter of Rights and Freedoms on HRM.

2. Differentiate among the following types of discrimination and provide one example of each: direct, differential treatment, indirect, because of association, and systemic.

3. Provide five examples of prohibited grounds for discrimination in employment in Canadian jurisdictions.

4. Define "sexual harassment" and describe five types of behaviour that could constitute such harassment.

5. Define the concepts of occupational segregation, underutilization, underemployment, and the glass ceiling.

6. Explain how "diversity management" differs from "employment equity and explain three reasons (other than ethics and social responsibility) for embracing workforce diversity.

7. Identify the steps in implementing an employment equity program and the importance of each step.

Critical Thinking | QUESTIONS

1. The owner of your company has just informed you, the HR manager, that there are certain moving company jobs, namely the movers, for which he feels minimum strength requirements are BFORs. How would you handle this situation?

2. An employee who has been off for two months with a stress-related ailment has just contacted you, indicating that she would like to return to work next week but won't be able to work full-time for another month or so. How would you handle this?

3. Discuss how organizations such as Versatech (see Workforce Diversity box on page 000) can increase their market share. What arguments can be made to persuade other companies to work with Versatech and other similar organizations?

4. Do you think that the approach taken by Steam Whistle Brewery's Stefan Atton (see Entrepreneurs and HR box on page 40) is commonly used by newcomers to Canada to obtain jobs in their field? Why or why not? What can Canadian businesses do to better attract, assess, and hire newcomers?

5. Explain the difference between goals and quotas and discuss the ways in which employers can avoid the issue of reverse discrimination.

6. If your head office in Toronto sent you a diversity poster focusing on LGBT (lesbian, gay, bisexual, and transgendered) employees and many of your employees are Mormons, what would you do?

Experiential | EXERCISES

1. Go to your provincial or territorial employment (labour) standards website and determine the following:
   - minimum legal age to work in this jurisdiction
   - minimum hourly wages
   - maximum number of hours worked in a week before overtime must be paid

   How does this information apply to you, your friends and family? Did you notice anything else that caught your interest that you were previously unaware of?

2. Prepare a report outlining legally acceptable questions that may be asked at a selection interview with a young female engineer applying for the job of engineering project manager at an oil field in rural northern Alberta, with an otherwise all-male group. (Refer to Appendix 7.1 on page 206.)

3. Working with a small group of classmates, search the Web for a company in your community that has an employment equity or diversity management program. Contact the company's HR manager and request more information on the program. Prepare a brief report summarizing its key features.

Running | CASE

Running Case: LearnInMotion.com

Legal Issues

One of the problems that Jennifer and Pierre faced at LearnInMotion.com concerned the inadequacies of the firm's current human resources management practices and procedures. The previous year had been a swirl of activity—creating and testing the business model, launching the site, writing and rewriting the business plan, and finally getting venture funding. And it would be accurate to say that in all that time, they put absolutely no time into employee manuals, HR policies, or other HR-related matters. Even the 25-page business plan was of no help in this regard. The plan provided considerable detail regarding budgetary projections, competition, market growth, and business strategy. However, it was silent when it came to HR except for containing short bios of the current employees and projections of the types of positions that would have to be staffed in the first two years.

Almost from the beginning, it was apparent to both Jennifer and Pierre that they were (as Pierre put it) "out of our depth" when it came to the letter and spirit of equal employment opportunity laws. Having both been through business school, they were familiar with the general requirements, such as not asking applicants about their ages. However, those general guidelines weren't always easy to translate into practice during the actual applicant interviews. Two incidents particularly concerned them. One of the applicants for a sales position was in his 50s, which made him about twice as old as any other applicant. Although Pierre didn't mean to be discriminatory, he found himself asking this candidate such questions as "Do you think you'll be able to get up to speed selling an internet product?" and "You know, we'll be working very long hours here; are you up to that?"— questions that he did not ask of other, younger candidates. There was also a problem with a candidate for the content manager position. The candidate was a single mother with two children, and Pierre asked her quite pointed questions, such as "What are your children's ages and what daycare arrangements do you have?" and "This job involves quite a bit of overtime and weekend work. Are you sure your kids won't get in the way of that?" Jennifer thought questions like these were probably okay, but she wasn't sure.

There was also a disturbing incident in the office. There were already two content management employees, Maya and Dan, whose job it was to actually place the course and other educational content on the website. Dan, along with Alex the web surfer, occasionally used vulgarity, for instance, when referring to the problems the firm was having getting the computer supplier to come to the office and repair a chronic problem with the firm's server. Pierre's attitude was that "boys will be boys." However, Jennifer and Maya cringed several times when "the boys" were having one of these exchanges and felt strongly that this behaviour had to stop. However, Jennifer was not sure language like this constituted harassment under the law, although she did feel that at a minimum it was uncivil. The two owners decided it was time to institute and implement some HR policies that would ensure their company and its employees adhered to the letter and the spirit of the various employment laws. Now they want you, their management consultant, to help them actually do it.

QUESTIONS

1   Is the Employment Standards Act applicable to this employer as they are situated in Ontario? As LearnInMotion's management consultant, what areas of the Act do you feel Jennifer and Pierre need to be aware of in regards to their current employee relations issues? Specifically what areas would you recommend they start updating in their human resource policy manual?

2   Should Pierre and Jennifer put a "respectful workplace policy" in place? If so, please develop a draft of this type of policy utilizing the web resources listed in Chapter 2.

Case | INCIDENT

A New HR Professional's First Workplace Dilemma

Laura, a recent graduate from a human resources diploma program from a local community college, has just landed her first role as a human resources coordinator at a small bottling company. Upper management has made it clear that they want Laura to make her first priority the updating of the current human resources manual. During her second week on the job, Laura was strolling down the hallway toward the break room to get herself a cup of coffee when she passed the director of marketing's office. As she passed she noticed an inappropriate picture of a woman was visible on his computer. Shocked at what she had just seen, Laura continued down the hall, not sure what to do next. Upon returning to her office, Laura decided the best way to start revising the manual was to introduce a policy on appropriate computer use. She felt this would address the problem as she didn't want to start her new job on a negative

note by reporting the director of marketing to the CEO without a clear policy in place.

QUESTIONS

1   Do you agree with how Laura handled this situation? If so why? If not, what would you have done differently?

2   Is it important for this company to have such a policy in place? If so, how can the employment (labour) standards act in your province/territory help in drafting a policy on appropriate computer use?

For additional cases and exercise material, go to
www.pearsoned.ca/myhrlab

CHAPTER 3

LEARNING OUTCOMES

AFTER STUDYING THIS CHAPTER, YOU SHOULD BE ABLE TO

EXPLAIN the strategic importance of technology in HRM.

DESCRIBE the impact that HR technology has on the role of the HR professional and the seven core competencies that have emerged.

DEFINE HRIS and describe its main components.

EXPLAIN the key functions of an HRIS and its key stakeholders.

DISCUSS what is meant by e-HR and the benefits of web-enabled service applications.

DESCRIBE the three-step process involved in selecting and implementing an HRIS.

EXPLAIN how HR technology has evolved.

IDENTIFY the key trends in HR technology.

HUMAN RESOURCES MANAGEMENT AND TECHNOLOGY
by Julie Bulmash

REQUIRED PROFESSIONAL CAPABILITIES (RPC)

- Provides the organization with timely and accurate information
- Ensures compliance with legislated and contractual requirements for information management
- Contributes to the development of specifications for the acquisition and/or development of HR information management systems and for their implementation
- Evaluates alternatives for meeting current and future information management needs
- Contributes to the development of information management systems
- Ensures the availability of information needed to support the management decision-making process
- Ensures HR administrative requirements conform to organizational policies as well as best practices, balancing confidentiality and operational requirements
- Applies principles of project management to HR activities
- Evaluates progress on deliverables
- Assesses requests for HR information in light of corporate policy, freedom of information legislation, evidentiary privileges, and contractual or other releases

HUMAN RESOURCES MANAGEMENT AND TECHNOLOGY

When new employees are hired, they are required to complete forms in order to provide information such as first and last name, address, emergency contacts, banking information, beneficiary information for pension and benefits, marital status, and Social Insurance Number. This is data, and HR has always been the custodian of this data. How the data is used, the type of data collected, how the data is updated, where the data is stored, and the type of system used to collect the data has changed over time, but the need to collect the information relating to hiring, promoting, and firing employees has not changed. However, the systems that HR uses to capture this data and the importance that HR now places on technology have fundamentally changed. According to a recent report from Towers Perrin, global organizations are increasing their investments in HR technology. Surprisingly, even in today's uncertain economic times, a third of organizations are increasing their investments in HR technology systems while half have maintained their budgets.[1]

Technology permeates business life today.

This chapter will begin by explaining the strategic importance of technology in HRM.

Changes to the role of HR professionals due to their increasing use of technology and the new key competencies that HR professionals must exhibit in order to deliver superior service to employees will be discussed. Then the role of human resources information systems in managing the human capital of an organization will be reviewed, including web-based electronic HR. Finally, trends in HR and technology will be discussed.

THE STRATEGIC IMPORTANCE OF TECHNOLOGY IN HRM

HR technology Any technology that is used to attract, hire, retain and maintain talent, support workforce administration, and optimize workforce management.

HR technology can be defined as any technology that is used to attract, hire, retain and maintain talent, support workforce administration, and optimize workforce management.[2] This technology can be resident in different types of human resource information systems (HRIS), can be used by various stakeholders, such as managers, employees, and HR professionals, and can be accessed in different ways, such as via the company intranet.

There is no doubt that technology has made it easier and faster to gather, collate, and deliver information, and to communicate with employees. More importantly, it has the potential to reduce the administrative burden on the HR department members so they are able to focus on more meaningful HR activities, such as providing line managers with the appropriate decision-making tools that will enable managers to make more effective HR-related decisions.[3] Research has indicated that companies who use technology effectively to manage their HR functions will be more effective than those that do not.[4] Perhaps not surprisingly, Google is using technology in an innovative way to help manage employee retention, as discussed in the Strategic HR box.

Over the next decade, there will be significant pressures on the HR department to manage costs and deliver effective and efficient services. Being responsive and providing service 24/7, 365 days a year across an organization's global networks is the new norm.[5]

Strategic HR

Google Tackles Retention Issues with "Predictive Attrition"

Google has worked hard to keep employees happy. But it is facing some retention challenges, as several senior people reportedly have departed in the past year. In response, Google has intensified its efforts in the area of "predictive attrition" to "find situations that may increase the likelihood of some Googlers leaving the company so that managers and HR staff can work on avoiding those very situations," said Wendy Rozeluk of global communications and public affairs at Google Canada in Toronto.

Google is not providing specific details about its analysis, but the algorithm looks at data from employees who have left the company, studying factors such as where people work, team size, and compensation. The tool analyzes less obvious factors that may contribute to the decision to leave the company but identifies groups versus specific people at risk of leaving. For example, are tenured, high-performing engineers in North America more likely to stay or leave than junior ones in Europe?

"As anyone who has observed Google over the years knows, we're serious about keeping our employees happy," said Rozeluk. "What we were looking for was general trends that might indicate an increased likelihood that someone might leave."

Source: Adapted from S. Dobson, "Google searches for way to keep staff," *Canadian HR Reporter,* July 13, 2009.

A strong strategic relationship between HR and technology will enable HR to achieve three key objectives:

1. *strategic alignment* with the business objectives,
2. *business intelligence*—providing users with relevant data, and
3. *effectiveness and efficiency*—changing how HR work is performed by reducing lead times, costs, and service levels.[6]

The expectations are high for HR. Achievement of these objectives will require HR professionals to be very effective at leveraging technology in order to reduce the time spent on administrative and legal compliance work so that it can focus on delivering strategic services.[7] Demonstrating that HR is adding value to the bottom line continues to be a major challenge for HR. A recent Mercer survey suggested that over 60 percent of chief financial officers continue to view HR as a cost centre that focuses primarily on executing administrative and compliance functions and that only 15 percent of them reported that HR was focused on strategic activities.[8]

THE IMPACT OF TECHNOLOGY ON THE ROLE OF HR

The impact of technology has fundamentally changed the HR role. It has enabled HR to decrease its involvement in transactional (administrative) activities and to increase its focus on how to improve its delivery of strategic services. As a result, seven core competencies have emerged that are critical to the development of the HR professional, as shown in **Figure 3.1**. Wayne Brockbank and David Ulrich from the University of Michigan Business School identified five key competencies for HR;[9] a recent study by Mercer highlighted two additional competencies.[10] These competencies are mastery of HR technology, strategic contribution, personal credibility, HR service delivery, business knowledge, data management, and financial management.

The traditional HR role has changed in three major ways as a result of the technologically enabled environment: (1) deceased transactional activities, (2) increased client/customer focus, and (3) increased delivery of strategic services.

FIGURE 3.1 | Emerging Role of the HR Professional: Seven Key Competencies

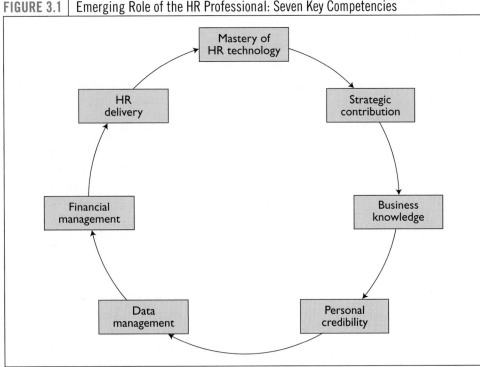

Source: Julie Bulmash, 2009.

Decreased Transactional Activities

Technology enables the reduction of the administrative burden, resulting in lowering basic transaction costs. Proactive HR professionals leverage technology to improve the design and delivery of basic HR services. In order to do so, HR professionals develop business knowledge with respect to the key drivers of organizational productivity and become cognizant of costs associated with enhancing efficiencies and effectiveness of the workforce. Reducing administrative and compliance activities through automation is considered necessary if HR is going to liberate itself from these day-to-day activities. Selecting the appropriate technology and ensuring that it is deployed appropriately are very important activities to ensure the organization can meet its goals. A recent survey published by the Society of Human Resource Management indicated that technical skills such as software and internet literacy, as well as database skills, are considered most important for the HR specialist to develop.[11]

Increased Client/Customer Focus

In organizations, HR deals with many internal customers, including managers, employees, and all the other departments in the organization. These customers expect HR to understand and respond to their requests quickly, reduce bureaucracy, and provide information that is meaningful, useful, and accurate. In today's economic climate, there is a significant need for HR professionals to understand the financial side of organizations, in particular how to help the organization control its people costs.

Managers expect HR to understand their key business issues and to provide relevant and meaningful information to help them make better decisions. For

RPC

Provides the organization with timely and accurate HR information

example, managers are responsible for creating and maintaining their staffing budgets. Information about the number of employees who quit or were terminated or the numbers of maternity and other planned leaves is important to help the manager plan more effectively.

Today's employees expect responsiveness, flexibility, and access to information 24/7. To be effective, HR must understand how technology can best meet the needs of their customers. When these stakeholders become more comfortable with the fact that HR is listening and cares about their needs, they will gain respect for HR and trust HR. This trust will lead them to sharing their concerns to a greater degree and trusting HR with their data requirements.

A significant partner of HR is the information technology (IT) department. The next section will focus on how HR can work to develop a good working relationship with this very critical group.

Gartner Inc.
www.gartner.com
Forrester Research
www.forrester.com
International Data Corporation
www.idc.com
Technology Publications
www.bitpipe.com
Software & Information Industry Associations
www.siia.com
International Association for Human Resource Information Management
www.ihrim.org
Society for Human Resource Management
www.SHRM.org

HR and the IT Department: Developing Good Working Relationships

If HR is going to gain credibility with the IT department and work effectively, it must demonstrate its knowledge of and respect for the IT discipline. Specifically, it is important for HR to exhibit knowledge of different types of HR systems, technology delivery methods, best practices of other organizations, and the types of technology enhancements that set these organizations apart. For example, when AT&T long distance services decided to implement an HR/payroll system, HR met with several different vendors to explore the functionalities of the different HR/payroll systems and worked with a team of IT professionals to help them make an informed decision.

In order for HR to build this technological knowledge, they can seek out learning opportunities such as trade shows, meetings with software vendors, formal courses in IT, and reading material about technological trends and issues. Not only will HR practitioners be able to speak the language of IT, but they will also gain a greater understanding of the IT discipline and the challenges facing IT professionals.[12]

Increased Strategic Activities

HR guru Ed Lawler has suggested that HR consider itself to be a business and that a business must consider the types of products it should offer to ensure sustainability.[13] Those products and services must relate to implementing the organization's strategy, so that HR will be "strategically proactive versus reactive."[14] HR must understand and respond to changing strategic requirements and effectively use technology to reduce the time and effort spent on maintenance and compliance work in HR so that more effort can be shifted to strategic business needs. Currently, the area of most importance to businesses has been identified as talent management. Managing human capital effectively to positively impact the bottom line is a major focus for executives today.[15]

RPC

Ensures the availability of information needed to support the management decision-making process

HUMAN RESOURCES INFORMATION SYSTEMS (HRIS)

There are over 140 human resources information systems being offered by over a hundred vendors in the United States and Canada.[16] The costs of implementing such a system range from $1000 to $12 million.[17] Licensing fees cost anywhere from three to eight times the cost of the software license for implementation costs.[18]

Not all companies have the latest and greatest technology, nor do all companies need the most advanced technology. However, all companies do have HR-related information needs. The information needs of a small company with 40 employees may only require the use of a simple Microsoft Word or Microsoft Excel file to keep basic employee data. A company with 3000 employees manages a greater volume of data, which can be daunting without a more sophisticated tool to store and retrieve data.

Also referred to as human resources management systems (HRMS) in the literature,[19] **human resources information systems (HRIS)** can be defined as integrated systems used to gather, store, and analyze information regarding an organization's human resources.[20] These systems consist of software applications that work in conjunction with an electronic database.[21] HRIS enable HR professionals to collaborate with the organization to ensure efficiency and effectiveness of the workforce, become more customer focused, and align their activities to the business plan, thus contributing to the bottom line. Using HRIS technology can help HR automate and simplify tasks, reduce administration and record keeping, and provide management with data and resources.

All these systems have different functionalities (or capabilities) and some are much more complex than others, but they all provide a repository for information/data to be stored and maintained. HRIS possess varying degrees of reporting capability. However, the system must transform basic data into information that is meaningful to managers. This is the challenge facing HR departments today and will ultimately determine whether HR is able to deliver strategic HR services. Much of the data now available to HR comes from a **data warehouse**— a specialized type of database that is optimized for reporting and analysis and is the raw material for managers' decision support.[22]

human resources information system (HRIS) Integrated system used to gather, store, and analyze information regarding an organization's human resources.

data warehouse A specialized type of database that is optimized for reporting and analysis and is the raw material for managers' decision support.

The Relationship between HRM and HRIS

HRIS is the composite of databases, computer applications, hardware, and software necessary to collect, record, store, manage, deliver, manipulate, and present data regarding human resources.[23] It is primarily a transaction processor, editor, and record keeper, maintaining employee, organizational, and HR-related data.[24] Its primary function is to provide information to its clients, such as employees, managers, payroll staff, and HR professionals.

It is important to note that the term "systems" refers not just to the technical hardware and software. From an HR perspective, "systems" is about the people, policies, procedures, and data required to manage the HR function. In reality, computer technology is not the key to being successful at managing HR information; what it does do well is provide a very useful tool for "operationalizing" the information, making it easier to obtain and disseminate information and ensuring that the information is specific to the organization's HR policies and practices.[25]

An HRIS must allow for the assimilation and integration of HR policies and procedures in addition to operating the computer hardware and software applications.[26] For example, a simple business rule—promotional raises are not to exceed 8 percent of salary—can easily be programmed into the system.

FIGURE 3.2 | HRIS Subsystems

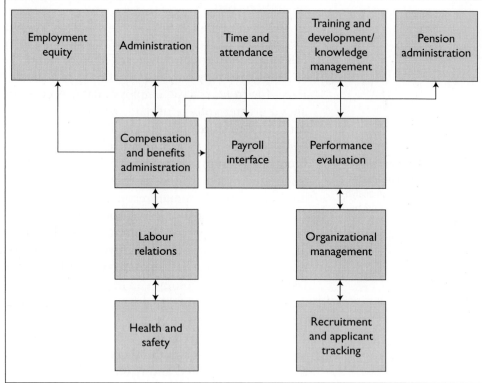

Source: Julie Bulmash, 2006.

The Major Components of an HRIS

There are several different generic subsystems that comprise an HRIS:[27] administration; recruitment; compensation, and benefit administration; payroll; time and attendance; employment equity; performance evaluation; and health and safety, as shown in **Figure 3.2**.

HR Administration

A basic component of an HRIS is its administrative function. The typical information in an HRIS system includes employee name, address, phone number and email address; birth date; hire date; sex; salary; emergency contact information; department code; location; employment status, such as full-time, part-time, or contract; the start date of each position held; position titles; and benefit information.

Recruitment and Applicant Tracking

One of the first lessons a HR professional learns is not to hire anyone unless the company approves the hiring budget. In organizations that effectively manage their costs, approval for filling a position is a formalized process. This module contains information on the position name and number, the department in which the position resides, whether the position has been approved, and whether the position is going to be a full-time or part-time position. Depending on the sophistication of the HRIS, online forms may be available, and it may be possible to track applicants and scan their résumés for key words identifying skills and experience.

Time and Attendance

Typically, vacation entitlement is based on service. For example, Ontario legislation states that employees are entitled to two weeks after completing one year of service. However, some organizations may choose to be more generous and they may offer three weeks of vacation. To calculate this information the HR specialist would need the hire date, any leaves of absences paid or unpaid, termination date if applicable, and any other events that interrupted service. This information can be found in an HRIS. In addition, the company's policy (such as a "use it or lose it" policy) might be programmed into the system. If there are any special rules, this information is programmed into the system; for example, employees often continue to accumulate vacation on some type of leaves.

Other data that can be found with respect to time and attendance includes information on absenteeism (the number of days an employee was absent); leaves of absence; whether these leaves were sabbatical or personal; parental leaves; and the dates the employee started and ended the leave. Policy details would be programmed; for example, some companies have a policy that states that, if an employee is absent for more than a certain number of days, his or her pay is decreased by a certain amount. **Figure 3.3** shows a related screen from a popular HRIS from PeopleSoft, whose subsystem is called the Enterprise Time and Labour system.

Training and Development/Knowledge Management

This HRIS subsystem includes information about an employee's skills and competencies, training courses and development activities undertaken, and the costs of such activities. It may also contain career planning information in terms of which positions might be most appropriate for particular employees, based on their skills and competencies.

Pension Administration

For organizations that sponsor retirement plans for their employees, information necessary to produce annual pension statements will be recorded. This data includes date of plan entry, normal retirement date, employee elections regarding contributions, and the company contribution each year.

FIGURE 3.3 | PeopleSoft Enterprise Time and Labour Screen

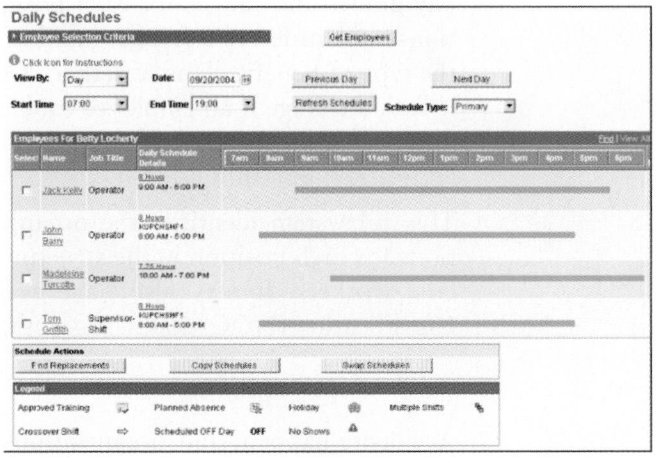

Source: Reproduced with permission of Oracle.

FIGURE 3.4 | PeopleSoft Enterprise ePerformance Screen

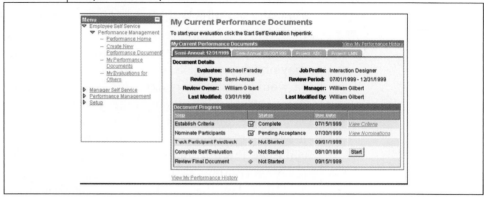

Source: Reproduced with permission of Oracle.

Employment Equity Information

Federally regulated organizations are responsible for annual reporting of their employment equity information to the government. This information, including the types of industry the organization competes in and the geographic region that the organization operates in, can be recorded in the HRIS and easily retrieved to create reports required under the legislation.

Performance Evaluation

New managers need information regarding the performance history of the employees reporting to them and thus must be able to look back at their past ratings. An HRIS can store information regarding ratings, the date these ratings were received, the type of appraisals that were used, and comments about the appraisal, as well as performance objectives and goals that arose out of the performance evaluation process. **Figure 3.4** shows a screen with performance evaluation information from PeopleSoft's Enterprise ePerformance subsystem.

Compensation and Benefits Administration

The HRIS includes information regarding the company's compensation and benefits plans and their policies relating to these plans. For example, information can include the pay increase associated with a promotion, data regarding pay grades and ranges for each position, the bonus structure, and which positions are entitled to a bonus. In addition, information can be entered regarding the type of benefit plans, whether there is a cost sharing arrangement, and how it would change if an employee took an unpaid leave.

Organization Management

This subsystem identifies the organizational structure and stores job descriptions for each position in the structure. It can also link the positions/jobs to specific workers. It may also have a field to enter the National Occupational Classification (NOC) codes.

Health and Safety

Accidents happen, and organizations are responsible for reporting these accidents to Workers' Compensation authorities. Information as to the number of accidents, types of accidents, health and safety complaints and resolutions, workers compensation claims, and workers' compensation forms can also be kept in the system.

Labour Relations

Information such as union membership, seniority lists, grievances, and resolutions can be found in this subsystem.

Payroll Interface

Most HRIS today have a subsystem with information on salary, wages, and benefits to make it easier to interface with the payroll system in accounting. The more sophisticated systems have an ability to interface with external payroll providers such as ADP and Ceridian.

Key Functions of an HRIS

An HRIS is made up of a number of subsystems and data can be stored, maintained, and generated from the system. Through a number of business software applications, this data is then transformed into information. This information is utilized by different stakeholders, can become essential for business operations, and can aid in decision making.[28] These stakeholders include employees, managers, and HR/payroll professionals.

The key functions of an HRIS are shown in **Figure 3.5**, along with the way in which stakeholders use the information generated.[29] The data in the HRIS system can be used to create and maintain employee records, ensure legal compliance, enable managers to forecast and plan their staffing requirements, enable managers and HR to manage knowledge and talent through career and succession planning, ensure the organization is aligned more effectively with their

FIGURE 3.5 | Key Functions of an HRIS

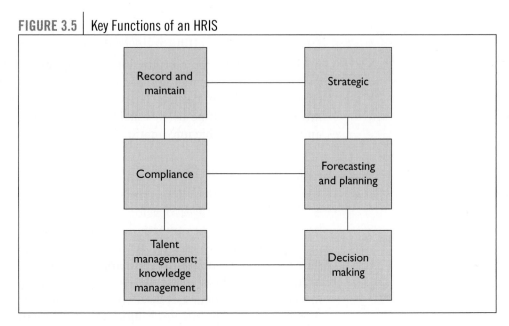

Source: Julie Bulmash, 2006.

strategic plan, and assist managers with decision making by providing the relevant data required to make effective and informed decisions.

Create and Maintain Employee Records

A record is established for every employee once they are hired into an organization. This record is maintained throughout his or her period of employment and includes all the details regarding the individual's employment history with the organization, such as personal data (for example, address and telephone number), and job data (for example, job title[s], salary increases, and performance appraisals). In most organizations, the HRIS administrator is responsible for creating and maintaining these records. Accuracy and timeliness are critical. For example, when an employee is promoted, salary increase information needs to be entered into the system immediately. Over time, managers, the employee, and HR professionals will require access to the employee's record. Typically, employees want to check this data for accuracy, or they may want to use the information to help them advance in the organization, whereas managers and HR would use this information to help them make decisions.

Legal Compliance

Information entered into the HRIS ensures that organizations can comply with government regulations by providing data in an accurate and timely manner. Ensuring data integrity and accuracy is very important and a key responsibility of the HR professional. For example, organizations that are subject to employment equity legislation are required to file an annual report. These reports can be generated with ease if this information has been recorded and maintained appropriately. Some HRIS software interfaces directly with the Employment Equity Computerized Reporting System (EECRS) software provided by the government.[30] In this case, the information from the HRIS can be downloaded directly into the required reporting system. Payroll is another example of a function with a multitude of compliance responsibilities, such as the generation of an employee's T4 information.

Forecasting and Planning HR Requirements

Information from the recruitment, training, and development, and administrative subsystems, such as number of open positions, types of positions, current employee skills and competencies, job rates (salaries), retirement eligibility, and attrition rates, can be used to help managers develop long-range staffing plans and provide valuable information to human resources professionals.

Talent Management/Knowledge Management

The data that is entered into the system, such as skills, competencies, jobs held, training, and employee development interests, can be used to help managers provide development opportunities for their employees. It will ensure that the appropriate employees are offered positions that will enhance their skills, provide the appropriate training for employees so they can advance in the organization, and highlight an employee's interests and development paths. This information will help HR staff to provide more targeted advice and counsel to managers and help HR work more effectively with employees and managers to create a development plan that meets organizational and employee needs.

Strategic Alignment

Information from the system can help organizations align more effectively with their strategic plan. For example, if the organization's plan was to enter into a new market and it required a certain number and type of employees, the data from the system can provide the manager with a barometer as to whether they are moving towards the goal and leverage the information on the skills employees possess to help the organization effectively obtain the goal.

Enhancing Decision Making: Decision Support Systems

The ability to be able to extract data from the HRIS and use this data not just for information purposes but to improve the quality of decisions made by managers and HR professionals has become important in the effective management of human capital.[31] It is not only a matter of interpreting the data but also using the data within a meaningful context to help managers and HR professionals make effective business decisions.

It is not uncommon for managers to request reports from the HRIS. For example, a manager might be responsible for his or her own salary budget and, when it comes time for annual increases, managers are typically asked to recommend appropriate salary increases for their employees based on their budgets. In order to make a quality decision, the manager might need to confirm each employee's current salary, look at the history of salary increases, review compensation policies, and review the employees' performance history. To make the most informed decision, the manager needs information that is relevant, useful, timely, and accurate.

Human resources might request a report on the number of hires within each department. They may want to look at a particular division to assess how many new hires there were within a given time frame and whether they were full time, contract, or part time. Using this information would be an example of utilizing the system to help the HR professional make a decision as to what resources a particular business unit may need in the future.

Some common reports that managers request from the HRIS are basic information reports, including information such as name, address, and phone number; compensation reports such as salary histories; performance evaluations; leaves of absence (length of time, paid or unpaid); number of jobs held and position titles; number of vacation days taken and number outstanding; and types of training taken and skills acquired.

In addition to these reports, managers utilize the system to perform HR calculations. The Saratoga Institute has identified a list of the most common calculations requested by managers: health care cost per employee, pay and benefits as a percentage of operating expenses, cost per hire, return on training, voluntary turnover rate, turnover cost, time to fill jobs, return on human capital invested, and human value added.[32]

metrics (workforce analytics)
Statistical measures of the impact of HRM practices on the performance of an organization's human capital.

Metrics, also known as *workforce analytics*, are statistical measures of the impact of HRM practices on the performance of an organization's human capital. An example of a metric is the cost of the HR department per employee, calculated as the total cost of the HR department for a given period of time divided by the total number of employees employed during that time. Metrics can help managers to identify opportunities to take action to improve performance and control costs. There are many possible metrics to use, and they are chosen by identifying key HR issues, gathering data from HR and other areas, setting applicable standards for rigor, and ensuring relevance.[33] Leading edge organizations

FIGURE 3.6 | HRIS Users

	Employee*	Manager	HR
Record and maintain	✓	✓	✓
Compliance			✓
Forecasting and Planning		✓	✓
Talent management: knowledge management	✓	✓	✓
Strategic		✓	✓
Decision making	✓	✓	✓

*Employee is only able to record and maintain data in the HRIS system if it is web-enabled
Source: Julie Bulmash, 2009.

have adopted metrics/workforce analytics and are using sophisticated HRIS capabilities to generate relevant and high-quality data. An example in the area of health and safety is obtaining HRIS data on the number of accidents and injuries and also on the causes of these injuries. Knowing the causes will enable HR to develop the applicable policies and practices to reduce the number of health and safety problems.[34]

Effective HR departments utilize precision data analysis to aid managers in effective decision making. This ability to contribute to decisions has enabled HR to demonstrate that the effective management of human capital can have a significant and measurable impact on a company's bottom line.[35] **Figure 3.6** summarizes the main user groups for the HRIS and the key information provided to each group.

SELECTING AND IMPLEMENTING AN HRIS

So far, some generic subsystems of an HRIS, major functions of an HRIS, and the stakeholders who use these systems have been described. Companies vary in terms of their information needs, their existing technology and their commitment to technology. They are also different in terms of their ability to afford technology and the value they place on HR information and people resources available to devote to a technology upgrade.[36] A company may only need a very simple system that captures time card and payroll information or they may need a very sophisticated system that can calculate significant workforce analytics.

Organizations can choose from many different systems in all sorts of sizes and with varying degrees of functionality and sophistication. The choice of technology revolves around two basic questions: (1) What is the desired amount of customization? and (2) What type of system is required/preferred? Organizations can decide whether they want to purchase a standard system and adapt to its processes, or alternatively to purchase a system and customize the software to fit the organization's existing processes. Some of the criteria that may affect this decision are the cost of the system, the number of employees, the degree of efficiency, and the company's existing hardware and software. Irrespective of the type of system selected, the key reasons for purchase are generally cost savings, faster processing of information, and access to relevant information that will help the organization to achieve its goals.[37]

RPC

Contributes to development of specifications for the acquisition and/or development of HR information management systems and for their implementation.

Contributes to development of information management systems

Types of HRIS Systems

An effective HRIS system matches its technical capabilities with the needs of the organization. These needs typically increase with the size of the organization.[38] Smaller firms might use very generic software applications such as Microsoft Excel and Access. These firms might only require payroll and benefits administration, time and attendance reporting, and an employee scheduling function.

Mid-sized firms typically require compliance tracking and reporting, health claims administration, payroll, and compensation and benefits administration. Managers may require information on performance appraisal, time and attendance, succession planning, skills testing, and employee scheduling. Employees may use the system to aid in career development. Mid-sized firms require greater data integration and the systems will have better backup and recovery capability. They will also allow for many users. In mid-sized systems, all HRIS functions typically flow through the single system and therefore data redundancies can be identified and eliminated. Some popular HRIS vendors for small to mid-sized organizations are Spectrum Human Resource Systems Corp., Genesys software systems, Best Software Inc., Ultimate Software (UltiPro workforce management), People Track Inc., and Organization Plus.[39]

Large organizations typically require greater functionality than the mid-sized firms. In addition to those functions mentioned above, these firms will require employee screening, résumé processing and tracking, and additional compliance and reporting requirements such as employment equity. They may also require self-service options, which are web-based applications that enable managers and employees to access and manage information directly without having to go through HR or the manager.

enterprise-wide or enterprise resource planning (ERP) system A system that supports enterprise-wide or cross-functional requirements rather than a single department within the organization.

The type of HRIS systems they might require can be part of a larger **enterprise-wide system/enterprise resource planning (ERP) system** that supports enterprise-wide or cross-functional requirements rather than a single department within the organization.[40] These systems originated from software that integrated information from the organization's functional areas (finance, marketing, operations and so on) into one universal database so that financial information could be linked to marketing information and so on. An enterprise-wide system typically includes several HR modules, such as a payroll module and a training and development module. These systems vary with respect to cost, functionality, and robustness, so depending on the organization's requirements, some systems will be more appropriate than others. Some popular ERP systems are SAP, PeopleSoft, and Oracle ERP systems.[41]

The largest ERP systems provider is SAP, a German company that was founded as "*Systemanalyse und Programmentwicklung*" in 1972 by five former IBM employees in Germany. This acronym was changed to *Systeme, Anwendungen und Produkte in der Datenverarbeitung*, which means "Systems, Applications and Products in Data Processing" and in 2005 the name was officially changed to SAP AG. SAP products are used by over 12 million people in more than 120 countries and its market has typically been Fortune 500 companies. Recently they have targeted small- to medium-sized organizations with some of their new products. SAP is made up of individual, integrated software modules that perform various organizational system tasks such as finance/accounting, controlling, project systems, funds management, materials management, and sales distribution. One of its major modules is Human Resource Management Systems (HRMS). These systems are robust, and SAP offers a full range of functionality, HR products, and web-based offerings.[42]

FIGURE 3.7 | Three-Step HRIS Implementation Process

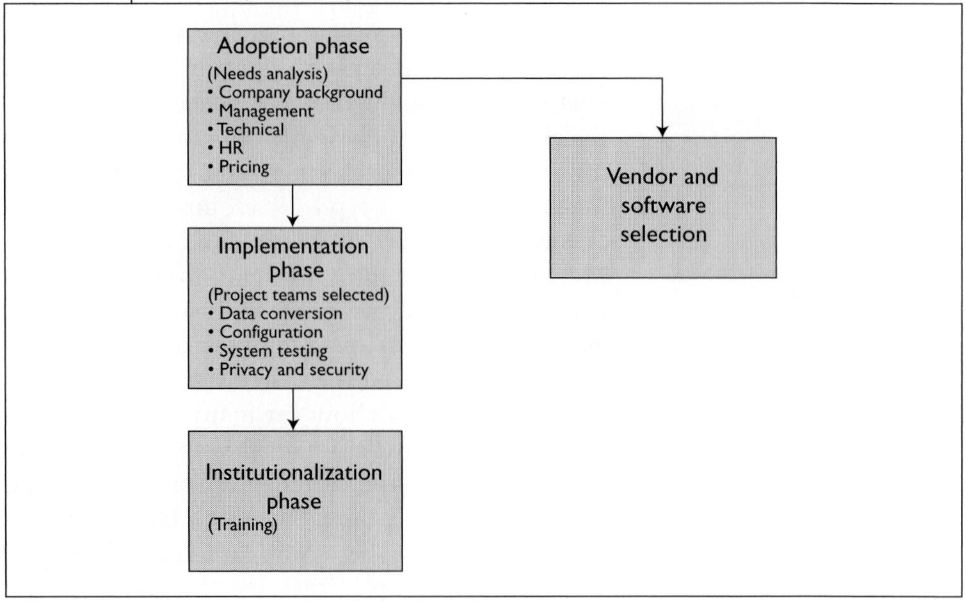

Adoption phase
(Needs analysis)
• Company background
• Management
• Technical
• HR
• Pricing

Implementation phase
(Project teams selected)
• Data conversion
• Configuration
• System testing
• Privacy and security

Institutionalization phase
(Training)

Vendor and software selection

Source: Julie Bulmash, 2009.

RPC

Evaluates alternatives for meeting current and future information management needs

stand-alone system A self-contained system that does not rely on other systems to operate.

PeopleSoft is a company that provides HRIS, manufacturing, financial, enterprise performance management, student administration, and customer relationship management (CRM) systems to large corporations and governments. It was founded in 1987 by David Duffield and Ken Morris. Its software is well known for its ability to be easily customized, so that it can fit the specific business needs of each client. In 2005, PeopleSoft was acquired by Oracle.[43] One company that uses PeopleSoft is the Canadian Imperial Bank of Commerce (CIBC). Their employees are provided with online access to HR services and information. The system enables employees to add dependants to health insurance, change payroll deductions, enroll in benefits programs, calculate pension benefits, and do retirement planning.[44]

HR technology can also be provided by a **stand-alone system**, meaning a self-contained system that does not rely on other systems to operate. These systems are not enterprise-wide but do perform specific HR related functions. Examples include Halogen Software Inc.[45] and Sage Abra Inc.

Typically organizations follow a three-step process to choose an HRIS, as shown in **Figure 3.7**. The three steps are (1) adoption phase, (2) implementation phase, and (3) integration (institutionalization) phase.[46]

Phase 1: Adoption—Determining the Need

In this phase, organizations typically engage in a needs analysis to determine what type of system they will purchase. A needs analysis helps the organization decide on what the system should be capable of doing and what the technical specifications will be. It helps the organization develop an information policy about how the information should be managed with respect to storage and access. A needs analysis also will provide the organization with a framework with which to evaluate vendors of software. There are several main areas to be considered: company background, management considerations, technical considerations, HR considerations, and cost considerations.[47]

Company Background

The industry, the size of company and the projected growth are important elements to consider. For example, if the company is very small and has only four people and the HR forecast is to add an additional five people in the next two years, then the type of system that is needed could be something as simple as an Excel spreadsheet. Typically, organizations require HR software after they reach 100 employees.

Management Considerations

Normally, management would have some preconceived views regarding what they want the system to do and the type of software that might be required. They may want a complex system with enterprise-wide capabilities or a stand-alone system.

Technical Considerations

Elements such as hardware, operating systems, networking, databases, and telecommunications all need to be considered. It is very important to understand the kind of technology the company currently has because, in some cases, integrating new software into existing systems can be costly.

HR Considerations

The HR department must consider its needs. What type of daily requests and which employee transactions would make the most sense to automate? What types of forms, reports, or listings are maintained? For example, every time management wants to notify the entire organization about some key event, has it been necessary to pull together a list manually? If so, this activity could be automated. The most critical area to be assessed is the decision support activities of HR. As discussed earlier, providing reports to help managers make better decisions is an important activity where HR can add value. The needs assessment would identify the types of data required to produce reports, where this data can be found, and how reliable the data is. HR would look at the manual reports currently being maintained and decide how these can be automated.

Cost Considerations

RPC

Applies principles of project management to HR activities

request for proposal (RFP)
Document requesting that vendors provide a proposal detailing how the implementation of their particular HRIS will meet the organization's needs.

Organizations may want to have the best possible system but might not be able to afford all the "bells and whistles." Factored into the price that an organization can afford are considerations such as additional hardware purchases required, the number of additional staff needed during the implementation phase, training costs, and ongoing support costs.

Once the needs analysis is complete, companies send out a **request for proposal (RFP)** to a number of vendors, requesting details of how the implementation of their particular HRIS will meet the organization's needs. Then demonstrations of the various systems are scheduled and the system that most closely aligns with the organization's needs is selected.

At this point, the adoption phase is complete, and the organization will move into the implementation phase.

Phase 2: Implementation

In this phase the company selects a project team which typically includes outside consultants who have knowledge and expertise on the technical side and expertise in change management to help the organization with the implementation. In addition to the outside consultants, there is usually a senior project manager who leads the team, subject matter experts from HR and payroll, and management from the various functional areas across the organization. These managers will be using the system, so it is important for them to ensure that the system is implemented effectively and that their requirements are clearly understood.

The activities involved in this phase focus on getting the system "up and running" within a controlled environment so that the system can be tested to ensure that it is functioning in the way the organization requires. The existing data is "converted" into the new system, meaning that the old system data is transformed to make it compatible with the new system. The software is tested and the users are expected to provide feedback before the system goes live. "Going live" means disengaging any previous HRIS and providing users access to the new system only. In this phase, security profiles are established for the users.

Privacy and Security

There are major privacy concerns when setting up an HRIS due to the sensitive personal nature of much of the data stored there, such as medical claims. Careful decisions must be made regarding who will have access to the computer hardware, software, and databases, and who will be able to modify the databases.[48] Establishing security profiles is a very important activity when implementing an HRIS. The staff members who will be working with the HRIS must be identified and security profiles established. These profiles specify which staff members have access to each screen, which data elements (fields) each staff person can have access to, and which staff persons can enter or change data. Security profiles typically are attached to positions in the organization rather than to individuals.

For example, the profile for an HR administrator who enters employee information into the system and who is the point of contact for all changes that employees make to their "tombstone data" would include viewing, entering, and changing data. A line manager's profile typically includes viewing information relating to their employee but not confidential data that is irrelevant to the work situation and would not include changing employee records.

A final, critical piece of HRIS security is making sure the system users clearly understand and adhere to the company confidentiality policy and code of ethics. All users need to understand that they must not share passwords, post them in view of others, or compromise them in any way.

Phase 3: Integration

The final step in implementing an HRIS system is to train the users on the system. The organization's goal is for the stakeholders to use the system and reap the benefits from the system identified through the needs analysis. However, many difficulties can arise with the implementation of a new system and, as with any change, people need to become comfortable. People often have difficulties in transitioning to an HRIS, so the organization can experience inertia.[49]

Employees need to be trained but even after training they may not feel fully competent and might not use the system. With any new system, stakeholders can underestimate its complexity.

ELECTRONIC HR

electronic HR (e-HR) A form of technology that enables HR professionals to integrate an organization's HR strategies, processes, and human capital to improve overall HR service delivery.

Electronic HR (e-HR) enables HR professionals to integrate an organization's HR strategies, processes, and human capital to improve overall HR service delivery.[50] By the mid-1990s, organizations were beginning to embrace ways in which to incorporate electronic and computer functions into their HR strategies.[51] Companies continue to look for better ways to manage costs, provide better service, and effectively manage their human capital. e-HR has become integral to helping organizations achieve these goals.

One of the most successful innovations is the migration of HRIS applications onto an intranet.[52] An **intranet** is a network that is interconnected within one organization, using web technologies for the sharing of information internally.[53] The internet has enabled organizations to harness web-based technology and use web-based applications to enhance HR services. A **web-based application** can be accessed from any computer connected to the internet by using a password-protected login page. More than 90 percent of companies are currently using the web for HR purposes.[54]

intranet A network that is interconnected within one organization, using web technologies for the sharing of information internally.

web-based application An application that can be accessed from any computer connected to the Internet.

HR portal A single Internet access point for customized and personalized HR services.

The most significant development in HR technology that enables direct employee access to HR applications is the web-based **HR portal** which provides users with a single internet access point for customized and personalized HR services.[55]

e-HR and Web-Based Self-Service Trends

The two most popular web-based applications enable HR self-service and therefore save time and reduce paperwork for HR staff.[56] These applications have allowed companies to shift responsibility for viewing and updating records onto employees and managers and have fundamentally changed the manner in which employees acquire information and interact with their HR departments.

Employee Self-Service (ESS)

employee self-service (ESS) Enables employees to access and manage their personal information directly.

interactive voice response (IVR) A telephone technology in which a touch-tone telephone is used to interact with a database to acquire information from or enter data into the database.

Employee self-service (ESS) systems enable employees to access and manage their personal information directly on a 24/7 basis without having to go through their HR departments or their managers. Employees often access ESS systems via the internet, sometimes using a portal on the company's intranet site. An **interactive voice response (IVR)** system is a telephone technology often used to access ESS, in which a touch-tone telephone is used to interact with a database to acquire information from or enter data into the database.[57] For example, employees can call in to report their attendance by entering in a specific code.

Some common ESS options allow employees to update personal information such as address, phone number, emergency contact name and number; revise banking information; enroll in benefit programs; research benefit options; view payroll information such as salary deductions; record vacation time and sick days; record travel expenses; access HR policies; participate in training delivered via the web; and access company communications and newsletters issued by the

FIGURE 3.8 | PeopleSoft Enterprise eProfile Screen

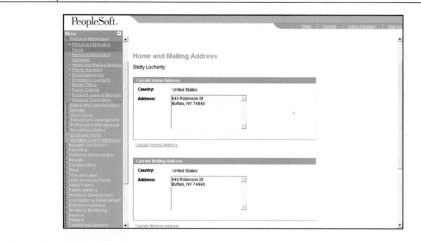

Source: Reproduced with permission of Oracle.

HR department. For example, an employee who recently split with his or her spouse can log on through the company's intranet site, click on the HR portal, and make all the required changes to emergency contact name, beneficiary information, and other benefit details that list the former spouse's name, all in the privacy of the employee's own home. **Figure 3.8** provides a sample PeopleSoft Enterprise eProfile screen.

ESS systems have fundamentally changed the way employees relate to their HR departments. Employees are able to access information that is relevant only to them and they no longer need to speak with an HR representative directly for fairly routine data updates. These systems have also helped HR departments to manage their operational costs effectively. From the perspective of the HR professional, the responsibility for basic administrative and transactional activities has been shifted onto the employee. This shift in responsibility enables HR professionals to have more time to focus on strategic issues.

ESS systems can be very effective. A recent study found that HR generalist workloads were reduced by an average of 15 percent.[58] Two organizations that have benefited from upgrading their technology and adding ESS are the Toronto Police Services and Time Warner.

For the Toronto Police Services, one of the most time-consuming and onerous activities was the scheduling and the payment of both overtime and court time for officers. In 2002, the Police Services spent over $500 million of their operating budget on salaries, of which $32 million went to paying overtime and court time costs to 7000 officers. With the implementation of an ESS system, officers were able to revise their schedules online using the ESS system, which in turn reduced administrative costs.[59]

Time Warner's challenge was to find a way to unify its 80 000 employees in geographically diverse regions and give them access to their HR services. They created an employee portal, called "Employee Connection." The portal gives employees varying levels of access to benefits enrollment, compensation planning, merit reviews, stock option information, payroll information, administrative HR forms, expense reimbursement forms, and travel planning information.[60]

RPC

Stays current with professional knowledge

Management Self-Service (MSS)

management self-service (MSS)
Enables managers to access a range of information about themselves and about employees who report to them and to process HR-related paperwork that pertains to their staff.

Management self-service (MSS) systems allow managers to access a range of information about themselves and about the employees who report to them. MSS systems also give managers the opportunity to process HR related paperwork that pertains to their staff. Managers can view résumés that are on file, view merit reviews, submit position requisitions, view employee salaries, and keep track of employee performance and training histories. Typically, this type of system offers a broader range of services than is available to non-managerial staff. In addition to providing HR-related information, MSS systems often provide managers with additional tools to help them with tasks such as budget reviews, report writing, and authorization of expense reimbursements.

The major benefit of MSS is that it provides managers with ready access to information that is useful both to themselves and to their employees without having to go through a third party. In this way, MSS systems reduce overall company workloads. In fact, research has indicated that when used properly, MSS systems reduce the workload of HR generalists by more than 21 percent because they are not spending the same amount of time on planning annual compensation increases, viewing employee histories, initiating requests for positions, or posting jobs.[61]

Managers are receptive to MSS systems because they contribute to data integrity and accuracy. The number of edits to the data decreases as managers can validate the data right away. In addition, the time needed to process the data improves as the manager can view the information in real time, authorize the activity, and communicate directly with the employee.[62] Imagistics International Inc., formally Pitney Bowes Office Systems, recently implemented an MSS system. Since the system has been in place, they have reported a significant reduction in administrative costs, process steps, and number of entry errors, and an overall streamlining of their HR reporting process.[63]

MSS can be a very valuable tool, but this technology is currently not as popular as ESS and has been slower to gain acceptance. **Figure 3.9** summarizes web-based service applications and their benefits.

FIGURE 3.9 | Web-Based Self-Service Applications and Benefits

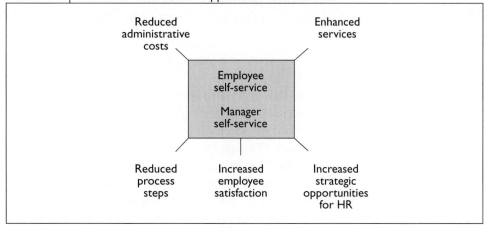

Source: Julie Bulmash, 2006.

e-HR and Talent Management Systems

As mentioned earlier, human capital management has become a key priority in organizations. The importance of acquiring and managing talent has increased and is expected to continue to increase over the next decade. Even in the current uncertain economic times, organizations are dedicating significant resources to this important activity, and the allocation of a sizable portion of HR budget dollars on new talent management technologies is expected.[64]

Talent management systems offer HR an integrated approach to managing its talent. They enable proactive workforce planning, applicant screening, and candidate assessment. They can help HR access employee performance and competency information, run performance management processes, and assign high performers into succession plans. They can also provide increased access to managers so that they can be more effective at compensation planning and budgeting and offer employees increased access to online career planning tools.

e-HR Vendors

There are numerous vendors in the marketplace offering products to help HR automate its functions. Some are stand-alone applications while others are enterprise-wide solutions. Some software vendors who offer high quality web-based hiring tools such as applicant tracking and e-recruiting tools are Brass Ring, Deploy, Icarian, Taleo (formally RecruitSoft), and Web Hire.[65] Halogen Software's eAppraisal product is a web-based system for employee performance appraisal. Forms can be created and completed electronically, including 360-degree feedback.[66] ExecuTRACK Software Group has developed software solutions for human capital. Their software can create succession-planning matrices and candidate placement scenarios, as well as many other tasks.[67] OrgPlus software has a sophisticated tool for graphically depicting organizational charts and transforming this information into decision-making tools.[68] The Entrepreneurs and HR box provides an example of two Canadian entrepreneurs who offer innovative HRIS software.

However, it is important to note that these systems are enablers only. Understanding how to use the technology effectively to manage talent is critical for HR. Web-based systems have the potential to revolutionize how HR delivers service, but research has indicated that HR is still struggling with how to effectively optimize these new technologies and web-based tools.[69]

Cautions Regarding e-HR

Recent surveys of ESS and MSS system users indicate that although 80 percent of respondents agreed that web-based self-service systems can lower HR operation costs, only 40 percent believe that their company is actually achieving this result. Two-thirds of those surveyed agree that web-based self-service systems can effectively support the transformation of the HR department into a more strategic partner by redirecting some of their responsibilities onto employees, but only 37 percent actually felt there was a change.[70]

Why does this discrepancy exist? Could it be that employees and managers view this new technology as the "work of HR" and therefore are resistant to

Entrepreneurs and HR

Cronus Technologies

Cary and Shaun Schuler were awarded the Young Entrepreneur Award by the Business Development Bank of Canada (BDC). Cary, Shaun, and older brother Rodney founded Cronus Technologies Inc., an IT company located in the heart of Saskatoon's high-tech businesses area. Cronus specializes in custom software development and project management and has won the prestigious HR Technology Excellence Award for its products. Currently they export to the United States but are developing partnerships in Western Europe.

"The Schulers epitomize a new generation of young Canadian entrepreneurs who, in creating jobs for themselves and members of their communities, are giving a great deal back to the regions that host their businesses," says BDC President and CEO Michel Vennat. "I salute their drive and determination."

Cronus continues to grow as a leading developer of innovative software. It is also a good corporate citizen.

The founders of Cronus Technologies Inc.—Rodney, Cary, and Shaun Schuler.

The Schulers believe in giving back to the community and have sponsored and made donations to various organizations such as the Arthritis Society, the Hope Cancer Centre, the United Way, and the Dragon Boat Races.

Source: Business Development Bank of Canada. www.bdc.ca/en/about/mediaroom/news_releases/2003/2003102011.htm?iNoC=1 (June 29, 2006).

using it? Perhaps the technology is not as user-friendly as it should be? The usefulness of this technology will depend on whether the content is considered beneficial and relevant, on how easy the system is to navigate, and on its cultural fit with the organization. Realizing the potential of any new technology means that processes associated with the technology must be changed. People need to use the system in the right way. Only then will they reap the expected benefits.[71]

Another interesting issue to consider is how HR has responded to this new technology. As was mentioned earlier, with these technological developments, the traditional transactional HR activities are no longer required and, as a result, HR may feel disenfranchised. A recent survey found that implementation of HR technology does not necessarily mean a reduction in the number of HR staff—in fact, the number of staff either increased or remained the same.[72] e-HR is about redistributing administrative HR work in order to provide HR professionals with more time to focus on the strategic activities that add value to the bottom line. The expectations are high for HR in terms of what it is expected to deliver to sustain innovation.[73]

A BRIEF HISTORY OF THE EVOLUTION OF HR TECHNOLOGY

The HR function has evolved significantly in terms of technology. Four main stages of development can be identified: (1) paper-based systems, (2) early personal computer (PC) technology, (3) electronic databases, and (4) web-based technology.[74]

Stage 1: Paper-Based Systems

Initially HR systems were paper-based. These systems operated independently and did not integrate with any other business-related functions. Features were added as needed. Data was typically stored on mainframe computers. The reporting was very rudimentary. HR data was only available to and used by HR staff. It was common for managers during this period to send employees to HR to get all their "personnel" questions answered.

Stage 2: Early Personal Computer (PC) Technology

In the next stage, HR continued to be the only department with access to the data. The fundamental difference was where the data was stored. HR departments began to store data in personal computers (PCs) and on local area network systems. These HR databases were simple, yet able to produce reports that listed basic employee information. Advances in database technology included payroll systems.

Stage 3: Electronic Database Systems

relational database One piece of data stored in several different data files so that information from the separate files can be linked and used together.

In the next phase, relational database technology emerged. A **relational database** stores one piece of data in several different data files in order that the information from the separate files can be linked and used together. This technology provided organizations with the ability to develop more complex reports that integrated several databases.[75] For example, a report could be generated from two different databases—one that included basic information such as name and address, and another containing salary and benefit information—as long as each database included employee number to link the data.

With the advent of electronic databases, HR systems began to become integrated with other business-related systems, and HR began using information systems to speed up transactional activities. Also at this time, the use of the internet was increasing, and managers began to realize just how powerful a tool it was and the benefits that could be derived from an HR technology perspective.

Leading HR organizations began to purchase ERP systems (that included HR modules) that leveraged relational database technology. For example, if a company decided to give all of its employees a salary increase, this information could be recorded on the employee file in the HR system and the financial module could be notified of this increase so that it would automatically debit cash and credit salary expense in the company's general ledger. It was at this point that HR entered fully into the digital world of electronic HR and the term "e-HR" began to appear.

Stage 4: Web-Based Technology

At the present time, most companies use HR technology, and the benefits of automation are widely known. The focus has shifted to automating as many transactions as possible to achieve effectiveness and efficiency. Call centres and IVR systems are becoming widely used by organizations. As was discussed earlier, web-based applications are becoming increasingly popular methods to deliver information. These applications allow users to access the applications from any computer connected to the internet via a secure, password-protected login page.

An Ethical | Dilemma

A senior manager (a very good friend of your parents) asks if you (the HR administrator) could tell him what his upcoming bonus will be; he has serious financial problems and may have to take out a loan today if his bonus is not high enough. What would you do?

For the most part, HR continues to be the owner of the information: The shift has been in terms of how HR utilizes the system capabilities. It is minimizing HR time spent on administration by providing tools to managers to take over some of this work. This frees up time for HR staff to focus on making more strategic contributions to organizational effectiveness.

TRENDS IN HR AND TECHNOLOGY

HR technology strategy A plan that is aimed at increasing the effectiveness of HR programs, processes, and service delivery by shortening cycle times, increasing customer service levels, reducing costs, and adding new service capabilities.

The technology of the future will be about speedy access to accurate real-time information. The ability to access this information via multiple delivery systems will give organizations a strategic edge. HR will continue to move towards providing managers and employees with information so they can manage their own HR issues using web-based systems.[76] Future technology will transform information into knowledge that can be used by the organization as a decision-making tool, and it will require HR and IT to work together to leverage this technology.[77] A recent study by the Hackett Group, a business process advisory firm, found that high-performing organizations spend 25 percent less on HR compared to their peers because they use technology effectively to improve effectiveness and efficiency.[78] Companies will need to develop a comprehensive HR technology strategy for the acquisition and use of technology to ensure future success in this area. An **HR technology strategy** is a plan that is aimed at "increasing the effectiveness of the HR programs, processes, and service delivery by shortening cycle times, increasing customer service levels, reducing costs, and adding new service capabilities." It is a document that will guide future technology investments.[79]

Watson Wyatt consultants have identified several major technology trends that will influence HR management in the future.[80]

1. *The increased use of portals and intranets and a greater focus on the use of virtual tools.* A recent survey of over 182 companies by Watson Wyatt found that one in five expect to change their HR service delivery systems. The most commonly planned changes are implementing a health care portal that provides employees with health improvement information (73 percent) and offering total compensation information to employees via the web (65 percent).[81] Training and education will be required to ease the transition for employees to learn to access their own information as opposed to going to HR.[82]

2. *Greater access to technology.* This will require HR to ensure that the appropriate security measures are in place and to be highly diligent in terms of access protocols.

3. *Continued optimization of current systems.* This will mean that HR must continue to be "technologically educated."

4. *Enhanced focus on workforce analytics.* This will require HR to continue its evolution with respect to providing managers with valuable information for decision-making.

5. *Increased focus on reducing costs.* This will require HR to optimize the functionality of HR technology.

6. *Increased use of standards for data exchange and processes (XML).* Companies who operate globally will need to find ways to streamline wide variations in HR processes. Developing a standard global architecture for HR data will be important, as will ensuring that the vendor they work with is capable of complying with this global standard.

7. *Contingency planning.* This will require HR to ensure that plans are in place to deal with disasters, helping organizations get employees back to work, and providing them with the appropriate emotional support.

8. *Heightened awareness of HR data privacy.* Government legislation will continue to increase and require organizations to comply.[83] Currently, Canada has two federal privacy acts, the Privacy Information Act and the Personal Information Protection and Electronic Documents Act (PIPEDA). This will require HR to stay current with respect to legislation and to use their information systems to ensure compliance.

outsourcing Subcontracting of work that is not considered part of a company's core business.

9. *Continued use of outsourcing of non-core HR related work.* The main strategies behind **outsourcing** are cost reduction and the ability to focus on core business objectives. The growth in HR outsourcing has been in areas relating to basic HR transactions and those services that focus on managing the employee life cycle, such as recruiting. Studies have shown that 96 percent of large companies currently outsource some portion of their HR related activities.[84] The outsourcing of Unilever's administrative HR functions is highlighted in the Global HRM box.

Today's HR professionals must be technically savvy and be able to "speak the language of business." They must understand the business environment and the major drivers relating to workforce productivity as determined by management. The use of HR metrics will be increasingly important for HR to assess whether they are providing services that provide value to the organization.

HR departments today are faced with significant challenges if they are going to contribute to organizational effectiveness. How HR utilizes technology to evaluate its own effectiveness and leverages emerging technologies to

Global HRM

Outsourcing HR Functions

Accenture, a global management consulting, technology, and outsourcing company, has recently entered into an agreement with Unilever Corporation. Unilever is a multinational marketing organization with familiar products such as Dove soap, Becel margarine, and Lipton soup, that employs 206 000 people in 100 countries worldwide. To optimize its HR services to its employees, Unilever has decided to outsource its administrative HR functions to Accenture. The agreement will cover three geographic regions—Europe, the Americas, and Asia—and provide services to approximately 200 000 employees in more than 20 languages. Accenture will manage critical HR software applications.

Some of the services it will provide are recruitment, payroll administration, total rewards administration, performance management workforce reporting, and core HR administration.

This arrangement will change the way Unilever manages and delivers its HR services across the company. Once these functions are outsourced, the remaining HR activities will be redesigned to focus more on the customer and establish a targeted service delivery model.

Source: J. Finlaw, "Accenture to Help Unilever Transform Human Resources Operations in 100 Countries with a Seven-Year Outsourcing Agreement," Press Release, June 6, 2006. Used with permission of Accenture.

drive productivity and the management of human capital will make the difference between an HR department that just plays a support role and one that is truly a business partner.

Chapter | SUMMARY

1. Technology has the potential to reduce the administrative burden on the HR department so they are able to focus on more meaningful HR activities, such as providing line managers with the appropriate decision-making tools that will enable managers to make more effective HR-related decisions. Companies who use technology appropriately to manage their HR functions will be more effective than those that do not. Enhancing the relationship between HR and technology will enable HR to achieve three key objectives: (1) strategic alignment with the business objectives, (2) business intelligence—providing users with relevant data, and (3) effectiveness and efficiency—changing how the work is performed by reducing lead times, costs, and service levels.

2. The role of the HR professional has changed fundamentally as a result of technology. It has enabled HR to decrease its involvement in transactional (administrative) activities and to increase its focus on how to increase its delivery of strategic services. The core competencies that have developed are mastery of HR technology, strategic contribution, business knowledge, personal credibility, data management, HR delivery, and financial management.

3. An HRIS is a group of integrated systems used to gather, store, and analyze information regarding an organization's human resources. Its main components are administration, recruitment, compensation and benefit administration, payroll, time and attendance, employment equity, performance evaluation, and health and safety.

4. The key functions of an HRIS are to create and maintain employee records; ensure legal compliance; enable managers to forecast and plan their staffing requirements; enable managers and HR to manage knowledge and talent through career and succession planning; ensure the organization is aligned more effectively with their strategic plan; and assist managers with decision making by providing the relevant data required to make

effective and informed decisions. The key stakeholders include employees, managers, and HR/payroll professionals.

5. Electronic HR (e-HR) refers to a form of technology that enables HR professionals to integrate an organization's HR strategies, processes, and human capital to improve overall HR service delivery. Examples include the migration of HRIS applications onto an intranet, the use of web-based HR portals that provide users with a single internet access point for customized and personalized HR services, and the use of web-based applications such as employee self-service (ESS) and management self-service (MSS) to enhance HR services.

6. The three steps in the process of selecting and implementing an HRIS are: (1) the adoption phase whereby organizations carry out a needs analysis to determine requirements, (2) the implementation phase where project teams are created, the software is tested, and privacy and security concerns are addressed, and (3) the institutionalization phase where training and change management activities are highlighted.

7. HR technology has evolved from paper and pencil systems to PCs, then to relational databases, and finally to web-based technology and integration with enterprise-wide systems.

8. Current technology trends that will impact HR are the use of HR portals, outsourcing, the focus on talent management, the need to develop an HR technology strategy, and a continued focus on measuring the value that HR brings to the organization.

PEARSON
myHRlab™

Test yourself on material for this chapter at
www.pearsoned.ca/myhrlab

Key | TERMS

data warehouse   *(p. 57)*
electronic HR (e-HR)   *(p. 69)*
employee self-service (ESS)   *(p. 69)*
enterprise-wide system/enterprise resource
    planning (ERP) system   *(p. 65)*
HR technology   *(p. 53)*
HR technology strategy   *(p. 75)*
human resources information system
    (HRIS)   *(p. 57)*
HR portal   *(p. 69)*

interactive voice response (IVR)   *(p. 69)*
intranet   *(p. 69)*
management self-service (MSS)   *(p. 71)*
metrics (workforce analytics)   *(p. 63)*
outsourcing   *(p. 76)*
relational database   *(p. 74)*
request for proposal (RFP)   *(p. 67)*
stand-alone system   *(p. 66)*
web-based application   *(p. 69)*

Review and Discussion | QUESTIONS

1. Enhancing the strategic relationship between HR and technology will necessitate the achievement of three key objectives. What are these objectives?

2. Discuss the seven key competencies of an HR professional in an IT-enabled world.

3. Describe two web-based service delivery applications that are popular today.

4. Describe several technological trends that HR must be aware of in order to offer value-added technology solutions.

5. Explain what an HR technology strategy plan is and why it is important.

6. What are the eight generic subsystem components that reside in an HRIS?

7. Discuss the six key functions of an HRIS system.

8. Describe the three steps involved in selecting and implementing an HRIS system.

9. Explain the four stages in the evolution of HR technology.

Critical Thinking | QUESTIONS

1. In order for HR to demonstrate that it is a strategic partner with the business, it must be aware of its customer requirements. In terms of technology, what actions and initiatives would HR have to take to demonstrate this awareness?

2. The role of HR has fundamentally changed as a result of technology. How will HR deliver service in the future? What delivery mechanisms will work best?

3. Do you think that it is important for all types of organizations to have an HRIS? Why or why not?

4. Compare and contrast the costs and benefits of being a member of an HRIS implementation team.

5. Do you think that maintaining the security of an HRIS system is a major concern for HR technology professionals? What security issues are most important today?

6. How does HR technology help organizations deliver transactional HR activities in a more efficient way?

7. In today's economic climate, organizations are concerned with talent management. How can HR technology be used to ease these concerns?

Experiential | EXERCISES

1. Explore two vendors who offer technology related solutions for talent management such as Taleo (www.taleo.com) and Halogen software (www.halogensoftware.com). Consider how these programs can contribute to organizational effectiveness. How will they help managers manage more effectively? How will they aid HR in delivering strategic services?

2. Go to www.workopolis.com and/or www.monster.ca. Find a job posting for an HRIS manager and HRIS analyst/administrator. How are the jobs different? What types of activities does each role carry out?

3. Investigate what workers are saying about how the web has helped them work more effectively.

Go to http://webworkerdaily.com. What types of issues are being discussed there? Are there some trends?

4. To accommodate a diverse workforce, HR must consider various types of delivery methods to communicate HR information. Explore the difference between video and audio podcasts, Interactive Voice Response (IVR) and a company intranet. Describe these methods of delivery and how they can be used to deliver HR information. (Some interesting HR related podcasts—such as the Harvard Business Review Idea Cast—can be found at www.apple.com by accessing the iTunes store.)

Running | CASE

Does LearnInMotion Need an HRIS?

Jennifer was getting frustrated. With only a few employees, the company kept a paper-based file for each employee with personal information, benefits forms, and so on. She and Pierre had decided to outsource payroll, but she still had to spend several hours every two weeks gathering payroll information, such as regular hours, overtime hours, vacation time and sick time that had been taken, and so on, to send to the payroll company. The benefits information and calculations were supposed to be carried out by the payroll company, but there had been several instances where mistakes had been made.

Jennifer and Pierre discussed the issue and decided that as a high-tech company, they should investigate the possibility of computerizing their employee files and information. Even with a very small number of employees, they both thought it might be easier for them to use some sort of HRIS. They have asked you, their management consultants, to provide answers to the following questions.

QUESTIONS

1 What data should be stored for each employee? How would the company use these data?

2 Conduct an HRIS needs analysis for the company. What would the results be?

3 Would you recommend an HRIS to Jennifer and Pierre? If so, what kind of system?

Case | INCIDENT

Integration and Transfer of HR Functions Using HRIS

Jack Newman had recently been appointed regional director of Boomerang Water Corporation, a major service utility in Australia. Jack's previous appointment was with a large manufacturing company in the United States, where he had made a reputation for himself as a visionary specializing in customer service and performance management. Jack was the youngest person and only non-Australian ever to be appointed as a director of Boomerang Water Corporation. This particular region of the utility employed approximately 2000 workers engaged in the customer service and maintenance provision side of the business. These employees operated in groups of about 30 workers. One supervisor managed each work group. These groups were located in five departments across the region, with each department specializing in a particular customer service or maintenance function. The region serviced about 500 000 customers.

A central division controlled the human resource management functions for the region. This division was located in the region's main town. Elaine MacVain headed the HR division. Elaine had been with the utility for nearly 25 years and over these years had developed a reputation for running a strong, controlled division that provided the customer service and maintenance department with a diversity of HR services. Elaine considered that the main focus of the division was to process day-to-day HR transactions and maintain employee records. Elaine managed a staff of 10 HR professionals who processed employee data that included workers' pay, leave entitlements and requests, and shift work entitlements. The HR department was responsible for recruitment and selection, the performance management system, occupational health and safety records, and career planning. Ron Locat, a member of Elaine's division, had developed a stand-alone HRIS to maintain the HR department's records. Ron had little formal IT training but had undergone in-house training in the use of Microsoft Access and had used Access to create the division's database system. Elaine and the other members of the HR division did not have a high level of IT literacy, but they could operate the

Access system that Ron had developed. Elaine was indebted to Ron for the work he had put into the database system and felt indebted to him for the support that he gave to the HR staff.

A major focus of the utility was training the customer service and maintenance employees. The utility had a promotion system based on the employee's level of technical skills. Employees were promoted to high levels of competency and pay scales on completion of skills training. Peter Noall, who had been with the utility for about four years, headed the training division, which had three staff in addition to Peter. One staff member was an ex-technical college teacher, and two had been technical supervisors in the organization. Due to the small size of the training division, Peter was forced to outsource much of the organization's training needs. A major responsibility of Peter's was work safety, and he was very proud of the organization's safety record. Peter had contracted the purchase of an expensive, dedicated, training database system to support the organization's training function. The system provided the training division with a powerful tool with which to profile the total skills base of the organization, identify present and future training needs, track employees' competency levels, and evaluate training outcomes in relation to productivity gains. The training division was proud of its use of high-level technology to support strategic training initiatives.

On commencing his appointment, Jack Newman decided his immediate focus was on improving the organization's customer service. He engaged the Fast Track–Immediate Success consultancy group to run a number of focus groups and conduct a strategic analysis related to the delivery of customer service. Eddie Wanton from Fast Track organized focus groups within the HR division and the training division, and ran three focus groups of 20 randomly selected supervisors. Eddie's report to Jack Newman included the following concerns and recommendations aimed to improve customer service.

REPORT FROM FAST TRACK

Concern 1: At present, customer complaints are directed to work group supervisors.

Recommendation: Introduce a new division dedicated to customer service quality.

Concern 2: Customer service is not supported by an integration of customer feedback, work group practices, training, and HR strategies.

Recommendation: Link the new customer service quality division to HR, training, and work group supervision.

Concern 3: At present, the HR division has sole responsibility for performance management, not the training division or work group supervisors.

Recommendation: Link performance management responsibilities to work group supervisors via training plans and HR recruitment strategies.

Concern 4: Communications among the HR division, training division, and work group supervisors are low-level and infrequent.

Recommendation: Introduce an organization structure that seamlessly integrates and promotes strategic communication between HR, training, and work group supervision.

Concern 5: The HR division and the training division have created tightly controlled centres of knowledge that do not directly inform work group supervisors.

Recommendation: Introduce the transfer of targeted HR and training responsibilities directly to work group supervisors.

EDDIE WANTON'S RECOMMENDED STRATEGY

Introduce a database information system that will seamlessly integrate HR functions, training functions, and customer service functions. Use the information system to develop strategic links between these functions. Use the new information system to break down information channel barriers between the HR and training divisions. Use the system to devolve appropriate HR and training operations to work group supervisors. Create a new customer service quality division and use the new IT system to integrate it with the other divisions and work group supervisors. In short, change the organization's communication and information architecture to promote the integration of cross-divisional information sharing, decision making, and control.

JACK NEWMAN'S RESPONSE

Jack Newman's response to Fast Track's recommendations was to target changes to the organization's structure and design necessary to promote the improvement of customer service. Jack immediately decided to act as champion of the cause and constituted a taskforce with the responsibility of implementing Fast Tack's recommendations. Jack appointed to the change taskforce Elaine, Peter, Bobby Bea (a work group supervisor who was a union official and had been with the utility for nearly 30 years), and two consultants from IT Now, a company marketing an integrated HRIS. Jack decided to act as chairperson of the taskforce. The objectives of the taskforce were to assist the consultants in identifying the organization's needs, and to inform the consultants as to the type of configuration necessary for the off-the-shelf HRIS to meet those needs. Jack expected the consultants to have the new system up and running within six months.

At the very first meeting of the taskforce it was apparent that, while Peter shared Jack's vision for change, Elaine was very concerned about the implication of these proposed changes for her division. Jack told Elaine that the HR staff would have to significantly upgrade their IT skills, or the organization might have to offer HR division staff redeployment or redundancy packages. Peter quickly pointed out that greater integration between HR and training should place all occupational health and safety responsibilities within the training division. Peter also emphasized that the need to train employees in the new system would entail increasing the number of training division staff. Bobby Bea was concerned that any transfer of HR transactions, such as employees' leave applications or performance management responsibilities, onto work group supervisors would cut down on their time to oversee service or maintenance operations. Bobby also pointed out that any changes to supervisors' job descriptions would need to be approved by the union and would involve pay raises. The consultant drew the taskforce's attention to the fact that if the organization required the new system to be functional within six months, they would most likely be forced to implement the off-the-shelf version with little specific tailoring to meet organizational needs. Both Elaine and Peter were concerned as to whom would head the new customer service quality division and the implications of the creation of this new division for their divisional budgets.

QUESTIONS

1   How can the assignment of a champion facilitate the introduction of the new HRIS? Is Jack Newman the best person to act as champion?

2   Why have the HR and training divisions built quite different database systems? What are the difficulties involved in integrating the functions of these divisions?

3   What are the advantages of integrating the functions of the HR division, training division, and those of the work group supervisors?

4   What are the advantages and disadvantages of the Boomerang Water Corporation buying an off-the-shelf integrated HR database system?

5   In what ways may the transfer of some HR functions to work group supervisors improve the efficiency of the HR division? In what ways may work group supervisors be advantaged or disadvantaged by the transfer of HR functions?

Source: G. Dessler, J. Griffiths, and B. Lloyd-Walker, *Human Resources Management*, 2nd ed. Frenchs Forest, New South Wales: Pearson Education Australia, 2004, pp. 97–99. Reprinted with permission of the publisher.

For additional cases and exercise material, go to
www.pearsoned.ca/myhrlab

 To view the CBC Videos, read a summary, and answer discussion questions, go to MyHRLab at
www.pearsoned.ca/myhrlab

CHAPTER 4

LEARNING OUTCOMES

AFTER STUDYING THIS CHAPTER, YOU SHOULD BE ABLE TO

DEFINE job design and **EXPLAIN** the difference between a job and a position.

DESCRIBE the job specialization, behavioural, and ergonomic considerations involved in job design.

EXPLAIN the six steps in job analysis.

DESCRIBE four basic narrative methods and three quantitative methods of collecting job analysis information.

EXPLAIN the difference between a job description and a job specification.

EXPLAIN the three reasons why competency-based job analysis has become more common.

DESIGNING AND ANALYZING JOBS

REQUIRED PROFESSIONAL CAPABILITIES (RPC)

- Provides the information necessary for the organization to effectively manage its people practices

- Identifies the data required to support HR planning

ORGANIZING WORK FOR STRATEGIC SUCCESS

An organization consists of one or more employees who perform various tasks. The relationships between people and tasks must be structured so that the organization achieves its strategic goals in an efficient and effective manner through a motivated and engaged workforce. There are many ways to distribute work between employees, and careful consideration of how this is done can provide a strategic advantage over competitors.

organizational structure The formal relationships among jobs in an organization.

organization chart A "snapshot" of the firm, depicting the organization's structure in chart form at a particular point in time.

Organizational structure refers to the formal relationships among jobs in an organization. An **organization chart** is often used to depict the structure. As illustrated in Figure 4.1, the chart indicates the types of departments established and the title of each manager's job. By means of connecting lines, it clarifies the chain of command and shows who is accountable to whom. An organization chart presents a "snapshot" of the firm at a particular point in time, but it does not provide details about actual communication patterns, degree of supervision, amount of power and authority, or specific duties and responsibilities.

Example of Online Organization Chart
www.IntranetOrgChart.com

Online Organization Charts
www.nakisa.com

Designing an organization involves choosing a structure that is appropriate, given the company's strategic goals. Figure 4.2 depicts three common types of organizational structure: bureaucratic, flat, and matrix. In flatter organizations, managers have increased spans of control (number of employees reporting to them) and thus less time to manage each one. Therefore employees' jobs involve

FIGURE 4.1 | A Sample Organization Chart

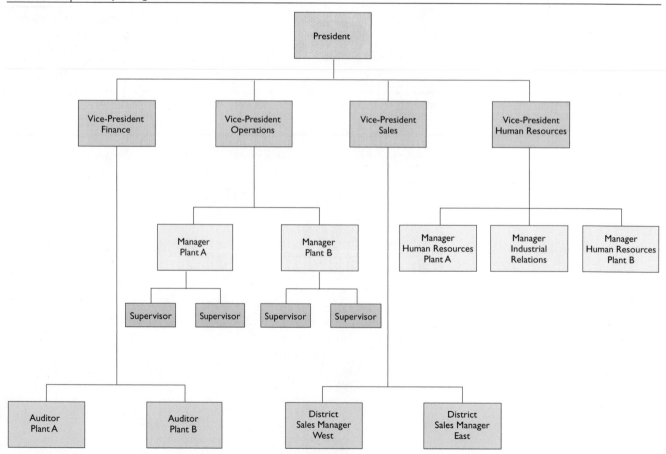

FIGURE 4.2 | Bureaucratic, Flat, and Matrix Organizational Structures

Structure   **Characteristics**

BUREAUCRATIC

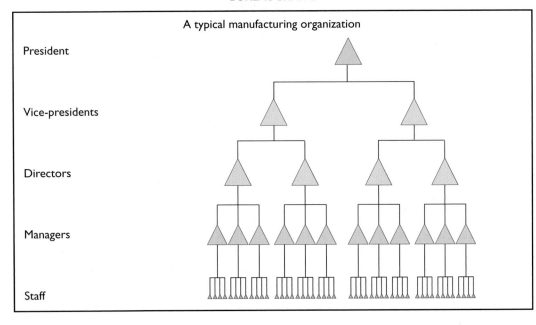

- Top-down management approach
- Many levels, and hierarchical communication channels and career paths
- Highly specialized jobs with narrowly defined job descriptions
- Focus on independent performance

FLAT

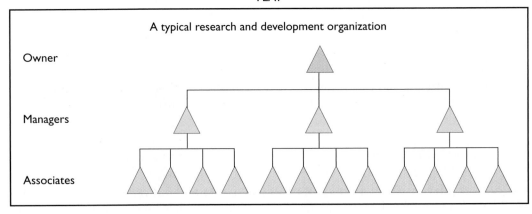

- Decentralized management approach
- Few levels and multi-directional communication
- Broadly defined jobs, with general job descriptions
- Emphasis on teams and on product development

MATRIX

A consumer products company

	Product A	Product B	Product C
Marketing	△	△	△
Finance	△	△	△
Sales	△	△	△
Production	△	△	△

- Each job has two components: functional and product
- Finance personnel for product B are responsible to both the finance executive and the product B executive

Strategic HR

IKEA Canada doesn't just want to fill jobs; it wants to partner with people. It recruits unique individuals who share the corporate values of togetherness, cost-consciousness, respect, and simplicity. IKEA listens and supports each employee to identify his or her needs, ambitions, and capabilities. Employees are expected not to ask others what they should be doing but to ask themselves and then get on with it. It is important for IKEA employees to have a strong desire to learn and the motivation to continually do things better, because the IKEA way of working is less structured than that of many other organizations.

IKEA Canada employee Ingeborg, a sales co-worker who is 71 years young, says, "Everyone asks me why I am still working. I tell them I love my job. There is always a great atmosphere in the store; I really enjoy the company of my managers and co-workers. We work together very well."

Source: Adapted from IKEA Canada. www.ikea.com/ms/en_CA/jobsjoin_us/ikea_values/index.html and www.ikea.com/ms/en_CA/jobs/true_stories/ingeborg/index.html (April 6, 2009).

more responsibility. In organizations using self-managed work teams, employees' jobs change daily, so management intentionally avoids having employees view their jobs as a specific, narrow set of responsibilities. The focus is on defining the job at hand in terms of the overall best interests of the organization, as is the case at IKEA, described in the Strategic HR box.

JOB DESIGN

job design The process of systematically organizing work into tasks that are required to perform a specific job.

job A group of related activities and duties, held by a single employee or a number of incumbents.

position The collection of tasks and responsibilities performed by one person.

In most organizations, work is divided into manageable units and ultimately into jobs that can be performed by employees. **Job design** is the process of systematically organizing work into tasks that are required to perform a specific job. An organization's strategy and structure influence the ways in which jobs are designed. In bureaucratic organizations, for example, because a hierarchical division of labour exists, jobs are generally highly specialized. In addition, effective job design also takes into consideration human and technological factors.

A **job** consists of a group of related activities and duties. Ideally, the duties of a job should be clear and distinct from those of other jobs, and they should involve natural units of work that are similar and related. This approach helps to minimize conflict and enhance employee performance. A job may be held by a single employee or may have a number of incumbents. The collection of tasks and responsibilities performed by one person is known as a **position**. To clarify, in a department with 1 supervisor, 1 clerk, 40 assemblers, and 3 tow-motor operators, there are 45 positions and 4 jobs.

Job Specialization (Industrial Engineering)

The term "job" as it is known today is largely an outgrowth of the efficiency demands of the industrial revolution. As the substitution of machine power for people power became more widespread, experts wrote glowingly about the positive correlation between (1) job specialization and (2) productivity and efficiency.[1] The popularity of specialized, short-cycle jobs soared—at least among management experts and managers.

work simplification An approach to job design that involves assigning most of the administrative aspects of work (such as planning and organizing) to supervisors and managers, while giving lower-level employees narrowly defined tasks to perform according to methods established and specified by management.

Work simplification evolved from scientific management theory. It is based on the premise that work can be broken down into clearly defined, highly specialized, repetitive tasks to maximize efficiency. This approach to job design involves assigning most of the administrative aspects of work (such as planning and organizing) to supervisors and managers while giving lower-level employees narrowly defined tasks to perform according to methods established and specified by management.

Work simplification can increase operating efficiency in a stable environment and may be very appropriate in settings employing individuals with intellectual disabilities or those lacking education and training (as in some operations in the developing world); it is not effective, however, in a changing environment in which customers/clients demand custom-designed products and/or high-quality services, or one in which employees want challenging work. Moreover, among educated employees, simplified jobs often lead to lower satisfaction, higher rates of absenteeism and turnover, and sometimes to a demand for premium pay to compensate for the repetitive nature of the work.

industrial engineering A field of study concerned with analyzing work methods; making work cycles more efficient by modifying, combining, rearranging, or eliminating tasks; and establishing time standards.

Another important contribution of scientific management was the study of work. **Industrial engineering**, which evolved with this movement, is concerned with analyzing work methods and establishing time standards to improve efficiency. Industrial engineers systematically identify, analyze, and time the elements of each job's work cycle and determine which, if any, elements can be modified, combined, rearranged, or eliminated to reduce the time needed to complete the cycle.

Too much emphasis on the concerns of industrial engineering—improving efficiency and simplifying work methods—may result in human considerations being neglected or downplayed. For example, an assembly line, with its simplified and repetitive tasks, embodies the principles of industrial engineering but may lead to repetitive strain injuries, high turnover, and low satisfaction because of the lack of psychological fulfillment. Thus, to be effective, job design must also satisfy human psychological and physiological needs.

Behavioural Aspects of Job Design

By the mid-1900s, reacting to what they viewed as the "dehumanizing" aspects of highly repetitive and specialized jobs, various management theorists proposed ways of broadening the activities in which employees engaged. **Job enlargement,** also known as **horizontal loading,** involves assigning workers additional tasks at the same level of responsibility to increase the number of tasks they have to perform. Thus, if the work was assembling chairs, the worker who previously only bolted the seat to the legs might take on the additional tasks of assembling the legs and attaching the back as well. Job enlargement reduces monotony and fatigue by expanding the job cycle and drawing on a wider range of employee skills.

job enlargement (horizontal loading) A technique to relieve monotony and boredom that involves assigning workers additional tasks at the same level of responsibility to increase the number of tasks they have to perform.

job rotation Another technique to relieve monotony and employee boredom that involves systematically moving employees from one job to another.

Another technique to relieve monotony and employee boredom is **job rotation**. This involves systematically moving employees from one job to another. Although the jobs themselves don't change, workers experience more task variety, motivation, and productivity. The company gains by having more versatile, multi-skilled employees who can cover for one another efficiently.

job enrichment (vertical loading) Any effort that makes an employee's job more rewarding or satisfying by adding more meaningful tasks and duties.

It has also been suggested that the best way to motivate workers is to build opportunities for challenge and achievement into jobs through **job enrichment,** also known as **vertical loading.**[2] This is defined as any effort that makes an

Workforce DIVERSITY

Accommodating and Utilizing the Aging Workforce

Arthritis is a complex of diseases often associated with advancing age. At Ontario Power Generation (OPG), ergonomics specialists adjust work to the physical capacity of individual employees who develop arthritis. Don Russell, who has been with OPG for 34 years, was diagnosed with rheumatoid arthritis in 1991 but has continued to work as an authorized nuclear operator for the past 17 years. "In 1991, I was in bad shape. I could barely move and my whole body hurt. I had problems walking, getting up and down stairs, and sitting for any length of time," he says. "I was lucky that I had an employer that allowed me to continue to work."

OPG was open to a proposal to work at home, setting up a computer long before telecommuting was common. Once he was back at work, Russell was given a motorized cart to get around the large plant. His manager recognized that shift work was taking a toll on Russell and made adjustments to his work schedule.

Elfie Bennett is another OPG employee who suffers from arthritis, which eventually required surgery

on both knees. "Once I was back, the nursing team did an assessment and came up with a plan for reduced work for the first couple of months, phasing in to full-time work," says Bennett. "The ergonomics team set up a desk that allowed me to be pain free. I find that I have to stay on top of the pain because once it starts hurting it seems to spread everywhere." Bennett is a specialist in nuclear operations and her current role is section manager in outages at OPG. Since her surgery, OPG has adjusted her work to focus more on strategic planning and less on immediate execution. This allows Bennett to do more work at her desk.

Better work site and job design were critical in retaining these two employees. OPG looked for opportunities to modify their work using new technology and ergonomic adjustments. Changes to the workplace such as push-button door openers and lever faucets will help not only the person with arthritis but also other workers and members of the public.

Source: Adapted from S. Singh, "Easing the pain of arthritis at work," *Canadian HR Reporter* (November 3, 2008).

---

employee's job more rewarding or satisfying by adding more meaningful tasks and duties. Job enrichment involves increasing autonomy and responsibility by allowing employees to assume a greater role in the decision-making process.

Enriching jobs can be accomplished through such activities as

Tips FOR THE FRONT LINE

- increasing the level of difficulty and responsibility of the job;
- assigning workers more authority and control over outcomes;
- providing feedback about individual or unit job performance directly to employees;
- adding new tasks requiring training, thereby providing an opportunity for growth; and
- assigning individuals entire tasks or responsibility for performing a whole job rather than only parts of it, such as conducting an entire background check rather than just checking educational credentials.

Job enrichment is not always the best approach. It is more successful in some jobs and settings than in others; for example, not all employees want additional responsibility and challenge. Some people prefer routine jobs and may resist job redesign efforts. In addition, job redesign efforts almost always fail when employees lack the physical or mental skills, abilities, or education needed to perform the job.

Team-Based Job Designs

A logical outgrowth of job enrichment and the job characteristics model has been the increasing use of **team-based job designs**, which focus on giving a **team**,

team-based job designs Job designs that focus on giving a team, rather than an individual, a whole and meaningful piece of work to do and empowering team members to decide among themselves how to accomplish the work.

team A small group of people, with complementary skills, who work toward common goals for which they hold joint responsibility and accountability.

rather than an individual, a whole and meaningful piece of work to do. Team members are empowered to decide among themselves how to accomplish the work.[3] Often they are cross-trained and then rotated through different tasks. Team-based designs are best suited to flat and matrix organization structures. Increasingly, organizations are using "virtual teams"—people working together effectively and efficiently across boundaries of time and space and using software to make team meetings more productive.[4]

Ergonomic Aspects of Job Design

ergonomics An interdisciplinary approach that seeks to integrate and accommodate the physical needs of workers into the design of jobs. It aims to adapt the entire job system—the work, environment, machines, equipment, and processes—to match human characteristics.

By the late 20th century, it became apparent that in addition to considering psychological needs, effective job design also required taking physiological needs and health and safety issues into account. **Ergonomics** seeks to integrate and accommodate the physical needs of workers into the design of jobs. It aims to adapt the entire job system—the work, environment, machines, equipment, and processes—to match human characteristics. Doing so results in eliminating or minimizing product defects, damage to equipment, and worker injuries or illnesses caused by poor work design.

In addition to designing jobs and equipment with the aim of minimizing negative physiological effects for all workers, ergonomics can aid in meeting the unique requirements of individuals with special needs, such as older workers and people with disabilities, as discussed in the Workforce Diversity box.

It is important to note that the ergonomic considerations involved in the design of jobs, workstations, and office space are important to all employees, not just to those with special needs. The Institute for Research in Construction (part of Canada's National Research Council) conducted a field study of the effects of the physical conditions on occupant satisfaction. The results showed that predictable, positive relationships exist among satisfaction with the physical environment, overall environment satisfaction, and job satisfaction. Thus, people who are more satisfied with the physical setup of their workstations have higher job satisfaction.[5]

Research | INSIGHT

At a Nissan factory in Tokyo, Japan, workers meet at a productivity session, surrounded by unfinished car frames hanging along the assembly line. Work teams like this are part of the trend toward a multi-skilled, cross-functional, self-directed team organization that allows workers greater autonomy in meeting goals. In plants like these, broadly described jobs that emphasize employees' required competencies are replacing narrowly defined jobs.

Increasing Job Flexibility

In the 21st century, the traditional meaning of a "job" as a set of well-defined and clearly delineated responsibilities has changed. Companies are grappling with challenges such as rapid product and technological change, global competition, deregulation, political instability, demographic changes, and a shift to a service economy. This has increased the need for firms to be responsive, flexible, and much more competitive. In turn, the organizational methods managers use to accomplish this have helped weaken the meaning of "job" as a well-defined and clearly delineated set of responsibilities. Requiring that employees limit themselves to narrow jobs runs counter to the need to have them willingly switch from task to task as jobs and team assignments change.

All these changes have led work to become more cognitively complex, more team-based and collaborative, more dependent on social skills, more dependent on technological competence, more time pressured, more mobile, and less dependent on geography.[6]

This situation has led some organizations to focus on personal competencies and skills in job analysis, hiring, and compensation management, rather than on specific duties and tasks.

THE NATURE OF JOB ANALYSIS

Once jobs have been designed or redesigned, an employer's performance-related expectations need to be defined and communicated. This is best accomplished through job analysis, a process by which information about jobs is systematically gathered and organized. **Job analysis** is the procedure firms use to determine the tasks, duties, and responsibilities of each job and the human attributes (in terms of knowledge, skills, and abilities) required to perform it. Once this information has been gathered, it is used for developing job descriptions (what the job entails) and job specifications (what the human requirements are).

job analysis The procedure for determining the tasks, duties, and responsibilities of each job, and the human attributes (in terms of knowledge, skills, and abilities) required to perform it.

Uses of Job Analysis Information

Job analysis is sometimes called the cornerstone of HRM. As illustrated in Figure 4.3, the information gathered, evaluated, and summarized through job analysis is the basis for a number of interrelated HRM activities.

Human Resources Planning

Knowing the actual requirements of jobs is essential for planning future staffing needs. When this information is combined with knowledge about the skills and qualifications of current employees, it is possible to determine which jobs can be filled internally and which will require external recruitment.

RPC

Provides the information necessary for the organization to effectively manage its people practices

Identifies the data required to support HR planning

Recruitment and Selection

The job description and job specification information should be used to decide what sort of person to recruit and hire. Identifying bona fide occupational

FIGURE 4.3 | Uses of Job Analysis Information

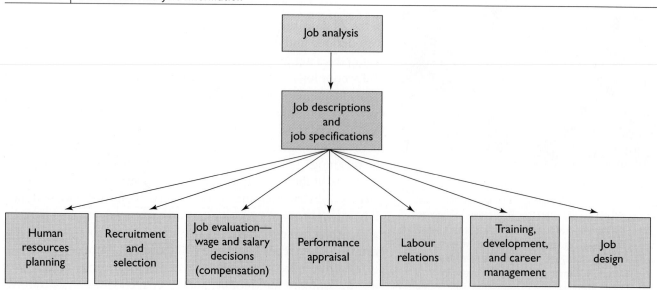

requirements and ensuring that all activities related to recruitment and selection (such as advertising, screening, and testing) are based on these requirements is necessary for legal compliance in all Canadian jurisdictions.

Compensation

Job analysis information is also essential for determining the relative value of and appropriate compensation for each job. Job evaluation should be based on the required skills, physical and mental demands, responsibilities, and working conditions—all assessed through job analysis. The relative value of jobs is one of the key factors used to determine appropriate compensation and justify pay differences if challenged under human rights or pay equity legislation. Information about the actual job duties is also necessary to determine whether a job qualifies for overtime-pay and maximum-hours purposes, as specified in employment standards legislation.

Performance Appraisal

To be legally defensible, the criteria used to assess employee performance must be directly related to the duties and responsibilities identified through job analysis. For many jobs involving routine tasks, especially those of a quantifiable nature, performance standards are determined through job analysis. For more complex jobs, performance standards are often jointly established by employees and their supervisors. To be realistic and achievable, such standards should be based on actual job requirements as identified through job analysis.

Labour Relations

In unionized environments, the job descriptions developed from the job analysis information are generally subject to union approval before being finalized. Such union-approved job descriptions then become the basis for classifying jobs and bargaining over wages, performance criteria, and working conditions. Once approved, significant changes to job descriptions may have to be negotiated.

Training, Development, and Career Management

By comparing the knowledge, skills, and abilities (KSAs) that employees bring to the job with those that are identified by job analysis, managers can determine gaps that require training programs. Having accurate information about jobs also means that employees can prepare for future advancement by identifying gaps between their current KSAs and those specified for the jobs to which they aspire.

Job Design

Job analysis is useful for ensuring that all of the duties having to be done have actually been assigned and for identifying areas of overlap. Also, having an accurate description of each job sometimes leads to the identification of unnecessary requirements, areas of conflict or dissatisfaction, and/or health and safety concerns that can be eliminated through job redesign. Such redesign may increase morale and productivity and ensure compliance with human rights and occupational health and safety regulations.

Steps in Job Analysis

The six steps involved in analyzing jobs are outlined here.

Step 1

Identify the use to which the information will be put, since this will determine the types of data that should be collected and the techniques used. Some data-collection techniques—such as interviewing the employee and asking what the job entails and what his or her responsibilities are—are good for writing job descriptions and selecting employees for the job. Other job analysis techniques provide numerical ratings for each job, which can be used to compare jobs for compensation purposes.

Step 2

process chart A diagram showing the flow of inputs to and outputs from the job under study.

Review relevant background information, such as organization charts, process charts, and existing job descriptions.[7] A **process chart** (like the one in Figure 4.4) shows the flow of inputs to and outputs from the job under study. (In Figure 4.4, the inventory control clerk is expected to receive inventory from suppliers, take requests for inventory from the two plant managers, provide requested inventory to these managers, and give information to the plant accountant on the status of in-stock inventories.)

Step 3

Select the representative positions and jobs to be analyzed. This selection is necessary when there are many incumbents in a single job and when a number of similar jobs are to be analyzed because it would be too time-consuming to analyze every position and job.

Step 4

Next, analyze the jobs by collecting data on job activities, required employee behaviours, working conditions, and human traits and abilities needed to perform

---

FIGURE 4.4 | Process Chart for Analyzing a Job's Workflow

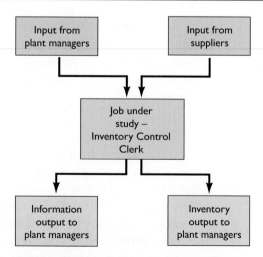

Source: Henderson, Richard I., ed., *Compensation Management in a Knowledge-based World*, 10th ed., Upper Saddle River, NJ: Pearson Education, Inc., 2006, p. 114. Reprinted by permission of the publisher.

the job, and using one or more of the job analysis techniques explained later in this chapter.

An Ethical | Dilemma

If a supervisor reviews the job analysis information provided by an employee and says that the job duties and responsibilities have been inflated, but the employee says that the supervisor does not really know what the job entails, how can a decision be made about what information is accurate?

It is helpful to spend several minutes prior to collecting job analysis information explaining the process that you will be following.

Step 5

Review the information with job incumbents. The job analysis information should be verified with any workers performing the job and with the immediate supervisor. This corroboration will help to confirm that the information is factually correct and complete, and it can also help gain the employees' acceptance of the job analysis data.

Step 6

Develop a job description and job specification, which are the two concrete products of the job analysis.

METHODS OF COLLECTING JOB ANALYSIS INFORMATION

Various qualitative and quantitative techniques are used to collect information about the duties, responsibilities, and requirements of the job; the most important ones will be discussed in this section. In practice, when the information is being used for multiple purposes, ranging from developing recruitment criteria to compensation decisions, several techniques may be used in combination.

Collecting job analysis data usually involves a joint effort by an HR specialist, the incumbent, and the jobholder's supervisor. The HR specialist (an HR manager, job analyst, or consultant) might observe and analyze the work being done and then develop a job description and specification. The supervisor and incumbent generally also get involved, perhaps by filling out questionnaires. The supervisor and incumbent typically review and verify the job analyst's conclusions regarding the job's duties, responsibilities, and requirements.

Qualitative Job Analysis Techniques

The Interview

The interview is probably the most widely used method for determining the duties and responsibilities of a job. Three types of interviews are used to collect job analysis data: *individual interviews* with each employee; *group interviews* with employees who have the same job; and *supervisory interviews* with one or more supervisors who are thoroughly knowledgeable about the job being analyzed. The group interview is used when a large number of employees are performing similar or identical work, and it can be a quick and inexpensive way of learning about the job. As a rule, the immediate supervisor attends the group session; if not, the supervisor should be interviewed separately to get that person's perspective on the duties and responsibilities of the job.

The most fruitful interviews follow a structured or checklist format. A job analysis questionnaire, like the one presented in Figure 4.5, may be used to

FIGURE 4.5 | Job Analysis Questionnaire

Job title: _____   Job grade: _____
Department: _____   Location: _____
Prepared by: _____   Date: _____

1. Purpose of job
   • What is the purpose of the job? Why does the job exist?
   _____
   _____
   _____

2. Major responsibilities and essential functions (list in order of importance)

• What are the responsibilities?	• Why is the activity performed?
• How are they done?	• What is the measure of success?
• Percentage of time?	• What direction of others is involved?

   _____
   _____
   _____
   _____

3. Knowledge
   • What techniques and/or practices are necessary? Why?
   _____
   _____

   • List specific education requirement(s).
   _____
   _____

   • List experience requirement(s) and number of years required in each.
   _____
   _____

   • List required licences or certificates.
   _____
   _____

4. Problem solving and decision making
   • List how the jobholder solves problems (i.e., planning, scheduling, creativity techniques, complexity of procedures, degree of independent thinking, and resourcefulness or ingenuity required). List examples of required development of new methods. What are the consequences if problems are not solved?
   _____
   _____
   _____
   _____
   _____
   _____

5. Resource responsibility
   • List annual pay of personnel who report to jobholder: _____
   • List annual operating budget (include pay): _____

continued

- List any other financial resources (i.e., annual project value/cost, shop order value, total sales, total unit payroll, gross sales booked, purchasing/contracts volume, transportation costs, facilities budget, assets, investment income, program development costs, and gross sales billed):

_____

_____

- What is the jobholder's role in planning, organizing, acquiring, or monitoring these resources?

_____

_____

- What is the jobholder's impact in planning, organizing, acquiring, or monitoring these resources?

_____

_____

6. Skills of persuasion
- Describe the communication skills required in the job (e.g., explaining, convincing, and selling).
- Are contacts inside or outside?
- What are the levels of contacts?
- What type of oral or written communications are involved?
- Who is communicated with and why?

_____

_____

_____

_____

_____

_____

7. Working conditions
Read the list of working conditions below and put a check mark if they impact on your job.

Condition	Amount of Exposure		
	Occasional	Regular	Frequent
Dust, dirt, fumes	_____	_____	_____
Heat, cold	_____	_____	_____
Noise	_____	_____	_____
Vibration	_____	_____	_____
Inclement weather	_____	_____	_____
Lighting	_____	_____	_____

Describe any health or safety hazards related to the job.

_____

_____

_____

Source: Carswell's Compensation Guide, ed. D.E. Tyson, CHRP, Tab 3 Job Analysis and Evaluation, Chapter 9, "Job Analysis and Job Descriptions," by T.J. Hackett and E.G. Vogeley, adapted by S. Weeks, P. Drouillard and D.E. Tyson, pages 9–21 and 9–23. Reprinted by permission of Carswell, a division of Thomson Reuters Canada Limited.

interview job incumbents or may be filled out by them. It includes a series of detailed questions regarding such matters as the general purpose of the job; responsibilities and duties; the education, experience, and skills required; physical and mental demands; and working conditions.

Tips | FOR THE FRONT LINE

Interview Guidelines When conducting a job analysis interview, supervisors and job analysts should keep several things in mind:

1. The job analyst and supervisor should work together to identify the employees who know the job best as well as those who might be expected to be the most objective in describing their duties and responsibilities.

2. Rapport should be established quickly with the interviewee by using the individual's name, speaking in easily understood language, briefly reviewing the purpose of the interview (job analysis, not performance appraisal), and explaining how the person came to be chosen.

3. A structured guide or checklist that lists questions and provides spaces for answers should be used. Using a form ensures that crucial questions are identified ahead of time, that complete and accurate information is gathered, and that all interviewers (if there is more than one) glean the same types of data, thereby helping to ensure comparability of results. However, leeway should also be permitted by including some open-ended questions, such as "Was there anything that we didn't cover with our questions?"

4. When duties are not performed in a regular manner—for instance, when the incumbent doesn't perform the same tasks or jobs over and over again many times a day—the incumbent should be asked to list his or her duties *in order of importance* and *frequency of occurrence*. This will ensure that crucial activities that occur infrequently—like a nurse's occasional emergency room duties—aren't overlooked.

5. The data should be reviewed and verified by both the interviewee and his or her immediate supervisor.

Questionnaires

Having employees fill out questionnaires to describe their job-related duties and responsibilities is another good method of obtaining job analysis information. The major decision involved is determining how structured the questionnaire should be and what questions to include. Some questionnaires involve structured checklists. Each employee is presented with a long list of specific duties or tasks (such as "change and splice wire") and is asked to indicate whether or not he or she performs each and, if so, how much time is normally spent on it. At the other extreme, the questionnaire can be open-ended and simply ask the employee to describe the major duties of his or her job. In practice, a typical job analysis questionnaire often falls between the two extremes.

Observation

Direct observation is especially useful when jobs consist mainly of observable physical activities. Jobs like those of janitor, assembly-line worker, and accounting clerk are examples. Conversely, observation is usually not appropriate when the job entails a lot of immeasurable mental activity (e.g., lawyer, design engineer). Nor is it useful if the employee engages in important activities that might occur only occasionally, such as compiling year-end reports. Direct observation and interviewing are often used together.

Participant Diary/Log

diary/log Daily listings made by employees of every activity in which they engage, along with the time each activity takes.

Another technique involves asking employees to keep a **diary/log** or list of what they do during the day. Each employee records every activity in which he or she is involved (along with the time spent) in a log. This can produce a very complete picture of the job, especially when supplemented with subsequent interviews with the employee and his or her supervisor. The employee might, of course, try to exaggerate some activities and underplay others. However, the detailed, chronological nature of the log tends to minimize this problem.

Advantages and Disadvantages of Qualitative Methods

Interviews, questionnaires, observation, and participant diaries/logs are all qualitative in nature. They are the most popular methods for gathering job analysis data, and they provide realistic information about what job incumbents actually do and the qualifications and skills required. Associated with each are certain advantages and disadvantages, as summarized in Table 4.1. By combining two or more qualitative techniques, some of the disadvantages can be overcome.

TABLE 4.1 | A Summary of Conventional Data Collection Methods for Job Analysis and the Advantages/Disadvantages of Each

Method	Variations	Brief Description	Advantages	Disadvantages
Observation	Structured	• Watch people go about their work; record frequency of behaviours or nature of performance on forms prepared in advance	• Third-party observer has more credibility than job incumbents, who may have reasons for distorting information • Focuses more on reality than on perceptions	• Observation can influence behaviour of job incumbents • Meaningless for jobs requiring mental effort (in that case, use information processing method) • Not useful for jobs with a long job cycle
	Unstructured	• Watch people go about their work; describe behaviours/tasks performed		
	Combination	• Part of the form is prepared in advance and is structured; part is unstructured		
Questionnaire	Structured	• Ask job incumbents/supervisors about work performed using fixed responses	• Relatively inexpensive • Structured questionnaires lend themselves easily to computer analyses • Good method when employees are widely scattered or when data must be collected from a large number of employees	• Developing and testing a questionnaire can be time-consuming and costly • Depends on communication skills of respondents • Does not allow for probing • Tends to focus on perceptions of the job
	Unstructured	• Ask job incumbents/supervisors to write essays to describe work performed		
	Combination	• Part of the questionnaire is structured; part is unstructured		

continued

TABLE 4.1 | *continued*

Method	Variations	Brief Description	Advantages	Disadvantages
Diary/Log	Structured	• Ask people to record their activities over several days or weeks in a booklet with time increments provided	• Highly detailed information can be collected over the entire job cycle • Quite appropriate for jobs with a long job cycle	• Requires the job incumbent's participation and cooperation • Tends to focus on perceptions of the job
	Unstructured	• Ask people to indicate in a booklet over how long a period they worked on a task or activity		
	Combination	• Part of the diary is structured; part is unstructured		
Individual Interview	Structured	• Read questions and/or fixed response choices to job incumbent and supervisor; must be face to face	• Provides an opportunity to explain the need for and functions of job analysis • Relatively quick and simple way to collect data • More flexible than surveys • Allows for probing to extract information and provides the interviewee with an opportunity to express views and/or vent frustrations that might otherwise go unnoticed • Activities and behaviours may be reported that would be missed during observation	• Depends heavily on rapport between interviewer and respondent • May suffer from validity/ reliability problems • Information may be distorted due to outright falsification or honest misunderstanding
	Unstructured	• Ask questions and/or provide general response choices to job incumbent and supervisor; must be face to face		
	Combination	• Part of the interview is structured; part is unstructured		
Group Interview	Structured	• Same as structured individual interviews except that more than one job incumbent/ supervisor is interviewed	• Groups tend to do better than individuals with open-ended problem solving • Reliability/validity are likely to be higher than with individuals because group members cross check each other	• Cost more because more people are taken away from their jobs to participate • Like individual interviews, tends to focus on perceptions of the job
	Unstructured	• Same as unstructured individual interviews except that more than one job incumbent/supervisor is interviewed		
	Combination	• Same as combination individual interview except more than one job incumbent/supervisor is interviewed		

Source: Adapted from William J. Rothwell and H.C. Kazanas, *Planning and Managing Human Resources: Strategic Planning for Personnel Management*, 2nd ed. Amherst, MA: Human Resources Development Press, 2003, pp. 66–68. Reprinted by permission of the publisher.

Quantitative Job Analysis Techniques

Although most employers use interviews, questionnaires, observations, and/ or diaries/logs for collecting job analysis data, there are many times when these narrative approaches are not appropriate. For example, when the aim is to assign a quantitative value to each job so that jobs can be compared for pay purposes, a more quantitative job analysis approach may be better. The Position Analysis Questionnaire and Functional Job Analysis are two popular quantitative methods.

Position Analysis Questionnaire

The **Position Analysis Questionnaire (PAQ)** is a very structured job analysis questionnaire, a portion of which is shown in Figure 4.6.[8] The PAQ itself is filled in by a job analyst, who should already be acquainted with the particular job to be analyzed. The PAQ contains 194 items, each of which represents a basic element that may or may not play an important role in the job. The job analyst decides whether each item plays a role in the job and, if so, to what extent. If, for example, "written materials" received a rating of four, this would indicate that such materials as books, reports, and office notes play a considerable role in this job.

The advantage of the PAQ is that it provides a quantitative score or profile of the job in terms of how that job rates on six basic dimensions: (1) information input, (2) mental processes, (3) work output (physical activities and tools), (4) relationships with others, (5) job context (the physical and social environment), and (6) other job characteristics (such as pace and structure). Because it allows for the assignment of a quantitative score to each job based on these six dimensions, the PAQ's real strength is in classifying jobs. Results can be used to compare jobs with one another; this information can then be used to determine appropriate pay levels.[9]

Functional Job Analysis

Functional Job Analysis (FJA) rates the job on responsibilities for data, people, and things from simple to complex. For example, working with "things" literally means the physical interaction with tangibles such as desktop equipment (pencils, paper clips, telephone), groceries, luggage, or a bus. Physical involvement with tangibles such as a telephone may not seem very important in tasks primarily concerned with data (such as data analysis) or people (such as nursing), but its importance is quickly apparent for a worker with a disability. This technique also identifies performance standards and training requirements. Thus, FJA allows the analyst to answer the question: "To do this task and meet these standards, what training does the worker require?"[10]

The National Occupational Classification

The **National Occupational Classification (NOC)**, the product of systematic, field-based research by Human Resources and Skills Development Canada (HRSDC), is an excellent source of standardized job information. It was updated and revised in 2006 and contains comprehensive descriptions of approximately 30 000 occupations and the requirements for each. To illustrate the types of information included, the NOC listing for specialists in human resources is shown in Figure 4.7.

The NOC and its counselling component, the *Career Handbook* (2nd ed.), both focus on occupations rather than jobs. An **occupation** is defined as a collection of jobs that share some or all of a set of main duties. The list of examples of job titles within each of the 520 Unit Groups in the NOC provides a frame of reference for the boundaries of that occupational group. The jobs within each group are characterized by similar skills.

FIGURE 4.6 | Position Analysis Questionnaire (Excerpt)

A1. Visual Sources of Job Information

Using the response scale at the left, rate each of the following items on the basis of the extent to which it is used by the worker as a source of information in performing the job.

1. **Written materials**
   E.g., books, reports, office notes, articles, job instructions, or signs
2. **Quantitative materials**
   Materials that deal with quantities or amounts, e.g., graphs, accounts, specifications, or tables of numbers
3. **Pictorial materials**
   Pictures or picturelike materials used as sources of information, e.g., drawings, blueprints, diagrams, maps, tracings, photographic films, x-ray films, or TV pictures
4. **Patterns or related devices**
   E.g., templates, stencils, or patterns used as sources of information when observed during use (Do not include materials described in item 3.)
5. **Visual displays**
   E.g., dials, gauges, signal lights, radarscopes, speedometers, or clocks
6. **Measuring devices**
   E.g., rules, calipers, tire pressure gauges, scales, thickness gauges, pipettes, thermometers, or protractors used to obtain visual information about physical measurements (Do not include devices described in item 5.)
7. **Mechanical devices**
   E.g., tools, equipment, or machinery that are sources of information when observed during use or operation
8. **Materials in process**
   E.g., parts, materials, or objects which are sources of information when being modified, worked on, or otherwise processed, such as bread dough being mixed, a workpiece being turned in a lathe, fabric being cut, or a shoe being resoled
9. **Materials not in process**
   E.g., parts, materials, or objects not in the process of being changed or modified, which are sources of information when being inspected, handled, packaged, distributed, or selected, such as items or materials in inventory, storage, or distribution channels, or items being inspected
10. **Features of nature**
    E.g., landscapes, fields, geological samples, vegetation, cloud formations, and other natural features that are observed or inspected to provide information
11. **Constructed features of environment**
    E.g., structures, buildings, dams, highways, bridges, docks, railroads, and other "constructed" or altered aspects of the indoor or outdoor environment which are observed or inspected to provide job information (Do not consider equipment, machines, etc., that individuals use in their work, as covered by item 7.)
12. **Behaviour**
    Observing the actions of people or animals, e.g., in teaching, supervising, or sports officiating, where the behaviour is a source of job information
13. **Events or circumstances**
    Events the worker observed and may participate in, such as flow of traffic, movement of materials, or airport control tower operations
14. **Art or décor**
    Artistic or decorative objects or arrangements used as *sources* of job information, e.g., paintings, sculpture, jewellery, window displays, or interior design

Note: The 194 PAQ elements are grouped into six dimensions. This figure exhibits 14 of the "information input" questions or elements. Other PAQ pages contain questions regarding mental processes, work output, relationships with others, job context, and other job characteristics.

Source: E.J. McCormick, P.R. Jeanneret, and R.D. Mecham, *Position Analysis Questionnaire.* West Lafayette, IN: Purdue Research Foundation, 1989. Copyright © 1989 by Purdue Research Foundation. Reprinted with permission.

FIGURE 4.7 | *NOC* Job Description for Specialists in Human Resources

Specialists in Human Resources develop, implement, and evaluate human resources and labour relations policies, programs, and procedures and advise managers and employees on personnel matters. Specialists in Human Resources are employed throughout the private and public sectors, or may be self-employed.

Examples of titles classified in this unit group

Business Agent, Labour Organization
Classification Officer—human resources
Classification Specialist
Compensation Research Analyst
Conciliator
Consultant, Human Resources
Employee Relations Officer
Employment Equity Officer
Human Resources Research Officer
Job Analyst
Labour Relations Officer
Mediator
Union Representative
Wage Analyst

Main duties

Specialists in Human Resources perform some or all of the following duties:

- Plan, develop, implement, and evaluate personnel and labour relations policies, programs, and procedures to address an organization's human resource requirements
- Advise managers and employees on the interpretation of personnel policies, compensation and benefit programs, and collective agreements
- Negotiate collective agreements on behalf of employers or workers, mediate labour disputes and grievances and provide advice on employee and labour relations
- Research and prepare occupational classifications, job descriptions, salary scales, and competency appraisal measures and systems
- Plan and administer staffing, total compensation, training and career development, employee assistance, employment equity and affirmative action programs
- Manage programs and maintain human resources information and related records systems
- Hire and oversee training of staff
- Coordinate employee performance and appraisal programs
- Research employee benefit and health and safety practices and recommend changes or modifications to existing policies

Employment requirements

- A university degree or college diploma in a field related to personnel management, such as business administration, industrial relations, commerce, or psychology
  or
  Completion of a professional development program in personnel administration is required.
- Some experience in a clerical or administrative position related to personnel administration is required.

Additional information

- Progression to management positions is possible with experience.

Classified elsewhere

- *Human Resources Managers* (0112)
- *Personnel and Recruitment Officers* (1223)
- *Personnel Clerks* (1442)
- *Professional Occupations in Business Services to Management* (1122)
- Training officers and instructors (in 4131 *College and Other Vocational Instructors*)

Source: Adapted from Human Resources and Skills Development Canada, *National Occupational Classification*, 2001. Reproduced with the permission of Her Majesty The Queen in Right of Canada 2009. www5.hrsdc.gc.ca/NOC/English/NOC/2006/ProfileQuickSearch.aspx?val65=1121 (March 29, 2009).

Occupational Information Network
http://online.onetcenter.org

Job Analysis.Network
www.job-analysis.net

To provide a complete representation of work in the Canadian economy, the NOC classifies occupations into Major Groups based on two key dimensions—skill level and skill type. The Major Groups, which are identified by two-digit numbers, are then broken down further into Minor Groups, with a third digit added, and Unit Groups, at which level a fourth digit is added. Within these three levels of classification, a Unit Group provides the actual profile of an occupation.[11] For example,

Major Group 31—Professional Occupations in Health

Minor Group 311—Physicians, Dentists, and Veterinarians

Unit Group 3113—Dentists

Internet-Based Job Analysis

Most of these job analysis methods suffer from one or more problems. Face-to-face interviews and observations can be slow and time-consuming. The information (usually collected orally or in writing) is difficult to update quickly. Collecting the information from internationally dispersed employees is even more challenging.[12] Internet-based job analysis is an obvious solution, and the use of web-based job analysis surveys have become increasingly common.

Using Multiple Sources of Job Analysis Information

Job analysis information can be obtained from individual workers, groups, supervisors, or observers. Interviews, observations, or questionnaires can be used. Some firms use a single approach, but one study suggests that using just one source is not wise because each approach has drawbacks. For example, in a group interview, some group members may feel pressure to go along with the group's consensus, or an employee may be careless about how or she completes a questionnaire. Thus collecting job analysis data from only one source may lead to inaccurate conclusions, so when possible, job analysis data should be collected from several sources.

An Ethical | Dilemma

If a job analyst is on the other side of the world from an employee who completed a web-based job analysis questionnaire, should another method of job analysis also be used to confirm the accuracy of the information?

WRITING JOB DESCRIPTIONS AND JOB SPECIFICATIONS

Job Descriptions

job description A list of the duties, responsibilities, reporting relationships, and working conditions of a job—one product of a job analysis.

A **job description** is a written statement of *what* the jobholder actually does, *how* he or she does it, and *under what conditions* the job is performed. The description in Figure 4.8—in this case for a vice-president, human resources, Asia-Pacific region—provides an example. As can be seen, the description is quite comprehensive and includes such essential elements as job identification, summary, and duties and responsibilities, as well as the human qualifications for the job.

FIGURE 4.8 | Sample Job Description

Sample Job Description

Position:	Vice-President, Human Resources, Asia-Pacific
Location:	Hong Kong
Division:	Asia-Pacific
Department:	Human Resources
Reports to:	President Asia-Pacific (administrative), Vice-President, Human Resources—Corporate (functional)
Date:	2 April 2009

Job Summary

Under the administrative direction of the President, Asia-Pacific, and the functional guidance of the Vice-President, Human Resources—Corporate, develop, recommend and implement approved HRM strategies, policies and practices that will facilitate the achievement of the company's stated business and HRM objectives.

Duties and Responsibilities

- Develop and recommend HRM strategies, policies and practices that promote employee commitment, competence, motivation and performance, and that facilitate the achievement of the Asia-Pacific region's business objectives.
- Provide policy guidance to senior management regarding the acquisition, development, reward, maintenance and existence of the division's human resources so as to promote the status of the company as an ethical and preferred employer of choice.
- Identify, analyze and interpret for Asia-Pacific regional senior management and corporate HR management those influences and changes in the division's internal and external environment and their impact on HRM and divisional business objectives, strategies, policies and practices.

Relationships

Internally, relate with senior line and functional managers within the Asia-Pacific region and corporate headquarters in New York. Externally, successfully relate with senior academic, business, government and trade union personnel. Directly supervise the following positions: Manager, Compensation and Benefits, Asia-Pacific and Manager, Training and Development, Asia-Pacific. Functionally supervise the HR managers in 13 geographic locations within the Asia-Pacific region.

Problem Solving

Diverse cultures and varying stages of economic development within the Asia-Pacific region create a unique and tough business environment. The incumbent will often face complex HR and business problems demanding solutions that need to be creative and, at the same time, sensitive to local and company requirements.

Authority

This position has the authority to:

- approve expenditures on budgeted capital items up to a total value of $100 000 in any one financial year
- hire and fire subordinate personnel in accord with company policies and procedures
- approve expense accounts for subordinate personnel in accord with company policies and procedures

continued

- authorize all non-capital item expenditures within approved budgetary limit
- exercise line authority over all direct reporting positions

Accountability

Employees: 3000. Sales: $4 billion. Direct budget responsibility: $2.7 million. Assets controlled: $780 000. Locations: Australia, China, Hong Kong, India, Indonesia, Japan, South Korea, Malaysia, New Zealand, the Philippines, Singapore, Taiwan, Thailand.

Special Circumstances

Successful performance requires the incumbent to work long hours, to travel extensively (50–60 percent of the time), to quickly adapt to different cultures and business conditions, to successfully handle high-stress situations and to constantly work under pressure in a complex and very competitive business environment.

Performance Indicators

Performance indicators will include both quantitative and qualitative measures as agreed by the President, Asia-Pacific Division, and Vice-President, Human Resources—Corporate and the incumbent. Indicators may be market based (e.g., share price improvement), business based (e.g., division profitability, budget control, days lost through industrial unrest, positive changes in employee commitment, job satisfaction and motivation) and individual based (e.g., performance as a leader and manager as assessed by superiors, peers and subordinates). Performance expectations and performance indicators generally will be defined on an annual basis. A formal performance appraisal will be conducted at least once a year.

Source: Adapted from R.J. Stone, *Human Resource Management*, 4th ed. Milton, Queensland: John Wiley & Sons, 2002, pp. 131–132. Reprinted with permission of the author.

No standard format is used in writing job descriptions, but most include the following types of information: job identification, job summary, relationships, duties and responsibilities, authority of incumbent, performance standards, and working conditions. As mentioned previously, job specifications (human qualifications) may also be included, as is the case in Figure 4.8.

Job Identification

As in Figure 4.8, the job identification section generally contains several categories of information. The *position title* specifies the title of the job, such as vice-president, marketing manager, recruiter, or inventory control clerk. The *department* and *location* are also indicated, along with the title of the immediate supervisor—in this case under the heading *reports to*.

Job Summary

The *job summary* should describe the general nature of the job, listing only its major functions or activities. Thus (as in Figure 4.8), the vice-president, human resources, Asia-Pacific region, will "develop, recommend and implement approved HRM strategies, policies and practices that will facilitate the achievement of the company's stated business and HRM objectives." For the job of materials manager, the summary might state that he or she will "purchase economically, regulate deliveries of, store, and distribute all material necessary on the production line," while that for a mailroom supervisor might indicate that he or she will "receive, sort, and deliver all incoming mail properly, and he or she will handle all outgoing mail, including the accurate and timely posting of such mail."[13]

Relationships

The *relationships* section indicates the jobholder's relationships with others inside and outside the organization, as shown in Figure 4.8. Others directly and indirectly supervised are included, along with peers, superiors, and outsiders relevant to the job.

Duties and Responsibilities

This section presents a detailed list of the job's major duties and responsibilities. As in Figure 4.8, each of the job's major duties should be listed separately and described in a few sentences. In the figure, for instance, the duties of the vice-president, human resources, Asia-Pacific region, include developing and recommending HRM strategies, policies, and practices; providing policy guidance; and identifying, analyzing, and interpreting internal and external environmental changes. Typical duties of other jobs might include maintaining balanced and controlled inventories, making accurate postings to accounts payable, maintaining favourable purchase price variances, and repairing production line tools and equipment.

Most experts state unequivocally that "one item frequently found that should *never* be included in a job description is a 'cop-out clause' like 'other duties, as assigned.'" This phrase leaves open the nature of the job and the people needed to staff it, and it can be subject to abuse.[14]

An Ethical | Dilemma

In view of the fact that job descriptions are not required by law and that some organizations have found them no longer relevant, would abolishing job descriptions raise any moral or legal concerns?

Authority

This section of a job description should define the limits of the jobholder's authority, including his or her decision-making authority, direct supervision of other employees, and budgetary limitations. For example, the vice-president, human resources, Asia-Pacific region (in Figure 4.8), has the authority to approve all budgeted non-capital expenditures and budgeted capital expenditures up to $100 000; approve expense accounts for subordinates; hire and fire subordinates; and exercise line authority over direct reporting positions.

Performance Standards/Indicators

Some job descriptions also contain a performance standards/indicators section, which indicates the standards the employee is expected to achieve in each of the job description's main duties and responsibilities.

Setting standards is never easy. Most managers soon learn, however, that just telling employees to "do their best" doesn't provide enough guidance to ensure top performance. One straightforward way of setting standards is to finish the statement: "I will be completely satisfied with your work when . . ." This sentence, if completed for each duty listed in the job description, should result in a usable set of performance standards.[15] Some examples would include the following:

Duty: Accurately Posting Accounts Payable

- All invoices received are posted within the same working day.

- All invoices are routed to the proper department managers for approval no later than the day following receipt.
- No more than three posting errors per month occur on average.
- The posting ledger is balanced by the end of the third working day of each month.

Duty: *Meeting Daily Production Schedule*

- Work group produces no fewer than 426 units per working day.
- No more than 2 percent of units are rejected at the next workstation, on average.
- Work is completed with no more than 5 percent overtime per week, on average.

Working Conditions and Physical Environment

The job description should also list the general working conditions involved in the job. This section generally includes information about noise level, temperature, lighting, degree of privacy, frequency of interruptions, hours of work, amount of travel, and hazards to which the incumbent may be exposed.

Special guidelines for entrepreneurial and small businesses are provided in the Entrepreneurs and HR box.

Entrepreneurs and HR

A Practical Approach to Job Analysis and Job Descriptions

Without their own job analysts or even their own HR managers, many small-business owners need a more streamlined approach to job analysis. A resource that includes all of the possible positions that they might encounter, with a detailed listing of the duties normally assigned to these positions, exists in the National Occupational Classification (NOC) mentioned earlier. The practical approach to job analysis for small-business owners presented next is built around this invaluable reference tool.

Step 1: Develop an Organization Chart.

Drawing up the organization chart of the present structure comes first. Then, depending on how far in advance planning is being done, a chart can be produced that shows how the organization should look in the immediate future (say, in two months), as well as two or three other charts showing how the organization is likely to evolve over the next two or three years.

Step 2: Use a Job Analysis Questionnaire.

Next, a job analysis questionnaire can be used to determine what each job entails. A shorter version of one of the more comprehensive job analysis questionnaires such as that in Figure 4.5 may be useful for collecting job analysis data. An example of a job summary for a customer service clerk follows:

> Answers inquiries and gives directions to customers, authorizes cashing of customers' cheques, records and returns lost credit cards, sorts and reviews new credit applications, and works at the customer service desk.

Step 3: Obtain a Copy of the National Occupational Classification (NOC) and Related Publications for Reference.

Next, standardized examples of the job descriptions needed should be obtained from the NOC website at www.hrsdc.gc.ca/eng/workplaceskills/noc/index.shtml. A related publication entitled Job Descriptions: An Employers' Handbook is also available for downloading from the NOC website at www.hrsdc.gc.ca/eng/workplaceskills/noc/employers/emplr_handbooks.shtml.

Step 4: Choose Appropriate Job Titles and Job Descriptions and Copy Them for Reference.

For each department, the NOC job titles and job descriptions that are believed to be appropriate should be chosen. The NOC definition will provide a firm foundation for the job description being created. It will provide

continued

a standardized list and constant reminder of the specific duties that should be included.

Step 5: Complete the Job Description.
An appropriate job description for the job under consideration can then be written. The job analysis information, together with the information from the NOC, can be used to create a complete listing of the tasks and duties of each of the jobs. The working conditions section can be completed once all of the tasks and duties have been specified.

Job Descriptions and Human Rights Legislation

Human rights legislation requires employers to ensure that there is no discrimination on any of the prohibited grounds in any aspect of terms and conditions of employment. To ensure that job descriptions comply with this legislation, a few key points should be kept in mind:

- Job descriptions are not legally required but are highly advisable.
- Essential job duties should be clearly identified in the job description. Indicating the percentage of time spent on each duty and/or listing duties in order of importance are strategies used to differentiate between essential and nonessential tasks and responsibilities.
- When assessing suitability for employment, training program enrollment, and transfers or promotions, and when appraising performance, the only criteria examined should be knowledge, skills, and abilities (KSAs) required for the essential duties of the job.
- When an employee cannot perform one or more of the essential duties because of reasons related to a prohibited ground, such as a physical disability or religion, reasonable accommodation to the point of undue hardship is required.

Job Specifications

job specification A list of the "human requirements," that is, the requisite knowledge, skills, and abilities, needed to perform the job—another product of a job analysis.

Writing the **job specification** involves examining the duties and responsibilities and answering the question "What human traits and experience are required to do this job?" Much of this information can be obtained from the job analysis questionnaire. The job specification clarifies what kind of person to recruit and for which qualities that person should be tested. It is sometimes included with the job description.

Complying with human rights legislation means keeping a few pointers in mind:

Hints TO ENSURE LEGAL COMPLIANCE

- All listed qualifications are bona fide occupational requirements (BFORs), based on the current job duties and responsibilities.
- Unjustifiably high educational and/or lengthy experience requirements can lead to systemic discrimination.
- The qualifications of the current incumbent should not be confused with the minimum requirements, since he or she might be underqualified or overqualified.
- For entry-level jobs, identifying the actual physical and mental demands is critical. For example, if the job requires detailed manipulation on a circuit-board assembly line, finger dexterity is extremely important and is something for which candidates should be tested. A **physical demands analysis**—which identifies the senses used and the type, frequency, and amount of physical effort involved in the job—is often used to supplement the job specification. A sample form is included as Figure 4.9. Having such

physical demands analysis Identification of the senses used and the type, frequency, and amount of physical effort involved in a job.

FIGURE 4.9 | Physical Demands Analysis

Division:	Job Title:
Job Code:	Level:
Date:	Date of Last Revision:

Physical Requirements
Review the chart below. Indicate which of the following are essential to perform the functions of this job, with or without accommodation. Check one box in each section.

Section I					Section 2		Section 3			Section 4		
Incumbent Uses:	NA	Right	Left	Both	Repetitive motion		The job requires the use of the first category up to 2 hours per day	The job requires the use of the first category up to 4 hours per day	The job requires the use of the first category up to 8 hours per day	Frequent breaks: Normal breaks plus those caused by performing jobs outside of the area.	Limited breaks: Two short breaks and one lunch break.
					Y	N					
Hands: (requires manual manipulation)											
Feet: (functions requiring foot pedals and the like)											

Lifting capacity: Indicate, by checking the appropriate box, the amount of lifting necessary for this job, with or without accommodation.

	NA	Occasionally (As Needed)	Often (Up to 4 Hours Per Day)	Frequently (Up to 8 Hours Per Day)
5 kg				
5–10 kg				
10–25 kg				
25–50 kg				
50+ kg				

Mobility: Indicate which category the job functions fall under by placing a check next to those that apply.
☐ Sits constantly (6 hours or more with two breaks and one lunch break)
☐ Sits intermittently (6 hours or more with frequent change, due to breaks and getting up to perform jobs outside of the area)
☐ Stands intermittently (6 hours or more with frequent changes, due to breaks and getting up to perform jobs outside of the area)
☐ Bending constantly (4 hours or more with two breaks and one lunch break)
☐ Bending intermittently (4 hours or more with frequent changes, due to breaks and getting up to perform jobs outside of the area)
☐ Walks constantly (6 hours or more with two breaks and one lunch break)
☐ Walks intermittently (6 hours or more with frequent changes, due to breaks and getting up to perform jobs outside of the area)

continued

Visual acuity: Indicate the minimum acceptable level, with or without accommodation, necessary for the job
☐ Excellent visual acuity
☐ Good visual acuity
☐ Not relevant to the job

Auditory acuity: Indicate the minimum acceptable level, with or without accommodation, necessary for the job.
☐ Excellent auditory acuity
☐ Good auditory acuity
☐ Not relevant to the job

Source: M. Rock and D.R. Berger, eds., *The Compensation Handbook: A State-of-the-Art Guide to Compensation Strategy and Design*, 4th ed. Columbus, OH: McGraw-Hill, 2000, pp. 69–70 © 2000 The McGraw-Hill Companies, Inc.

detailed information is particularly beneficial when determining accommodation requirements. The mental and emotional demands of a job are typically missing from job analysis information. They should be specified so that the mental and emotional competencies of job applicants can be assessed and any need for accommodation can be identified.

Identifying the human requirements for a job can be accomplished through a judgmental approach (based on educated guesses of job incumbents, supervisors, and HR managers) or statistical analysis (based on the relationship between some human trait of skill and some criterion of job effectiveness). Basing job specifications on statistical analysis is more legally defensible. For example, the Personality-Related Position Requirements Form (PPRF) is a survey instrument designed to assist managers in identifying potential personality-related traits that may be important in a job. Identifying personality dimensions is difficult when using most job analysis techniques, because they tend to be much better suited to unearthing human aptitudes and skills—like manual dexterity. The PPRF uses questionnaire items to assess the relevance of such basic personality dimensions as agreeableness, conscientiousness, and emotional stability to the job under study. The relevance of these personality traits can then be assessed through statistical analysis.[16]

An Ethical | Dilemma

Are personality traits really part of the KSAs and bona fide occupational requirements/essential duties of a job?

Completing the Job Specification Form

Once the required human characteristics have been determined, whether using statistical analysis or a judgmental approach, a job specification form should be completed. To illustrate the types of information and amount of detail that should be provided in a well-written job specification, a sample has been included as Figure 4.10.

COMPETENCY-BASED JOB ANALYSIS

Not coincidentally, many employers and job analysis experts say traditional job analysis procedures can't go on playing a central role in HR management.[17] Their basic concern is this: In high-performance work environments in which employers need workers to seamlessly move from job to job and exercise

FIGURE 4.10 | Job Specification

Job Title: Lifeguard   **Location:** Lethbridge Community Pool
Job Code: LG1   **Supervisor:** Head Lifeguard
Department: Recreation   **Division:** Parks and Recreation
Date: May 1, 2007

Job Summary
The incumbent is required to safeguard the health of pool users by patrolling the pool, rescuing swimmers in difficulty, treating injuries, advising pool users of safety rules, and enforcing safety rules.

Skill
Formal Qualifications: Royal Life Saving Society Bronze Medallion or equivalent
Experience: No prior experience required but would be an asset.
Communication Skills: Good oral communication skills are required. Proficiency in one or more foreign languages would be an asset. The incumbent must be able to communicate courteously and effectively. Strong interpersonal skills are required. All interaction with the public must be handled with tact and diplomacy.

Effort
Physical Effort: The incumbent is required to stand during the majority of working hours. In the event of an emergency where a swimmer is in distress, the incumbent must initiate rescue procedures immediately, which may involve strenuous physical exertion.
Mental Effort: Continuous mental attention to pool users. Must remain vigilant despite many simultaneous demands on his or her attention.
Emotional Effort: Enforcement of safety rules and water rescue can be stressful. Must maintain a professional demeanour when dealing with serious injuries or death.

Working Conditions
Job is performed in humid indoor environment, temperature-controlled. No privacy. Shift work to cover pool hours from 7 A.M. to 11 P.M., seven days a week. Some overtime and split shifts may be required.

Approval Signatures
Incumbent: _____
Supervisor: _____ Date: _____

---

competencies Demonstrable characteristics of a person that enable performance of the job.

self-control, job descriptions based on lists of job-specific duties may actually inhibit (or fail to encourage) the flexible behaviour companies need. Employers are therefore shifting toward newer approaches for describing jobs, such as competency-based analysis.

Competency-based job analysis basically means writing job descriptions based on competencies rather than job duties. It emphasizes what the employee must be capable of doing, rather than a list of the duties he or she must perform. **Competencies** are demonstrable characteristics of a person that enable performance. Job competencies are always observable and measurable behaviours comprising part of a job. The job's required competencies can be identified by simply completing this sentence: "In order to perform this job competently, the employee should be able to . . ."

competency-based job analysis Describing a job in terms of the measurable, observable behavioural competencies an employee must exhibit to do a job well.

Competency-based job analysis means describing the job in terms of the measurable, observable behavioural competencies (knowledge, skills, and/or behaviours) that an employee doing that job must exhibit to do the job well. This contrasts with the traditional way of describing the job in terms of job duties and responsibilities. Traditional job analysis focuses on "what" is accomplished—

on duties and responsibilities. Competency-based analysis focuses more on "how" the worker meets the job's objectives or actually accomplishes the work. Traditional job analysis is thus job focused. Competency-based analysis is worker focused—specifically, what must he or she be competent to do?

Three Reasons to Use Competency Analysis

There are three reasons to describe jobs in terms of competencies rather than duties. *First,* as mentioned earlier, traditional job descriptions (with their lists of specific duties) may actually backfire if a *high-performance work system* is your goal. The whole thrust of these systems is to encourage employees to work in a self-motivated way, by organizing the work around teams, by encouraging team members to rotate freely among jobs (each with its own skill set), by pushing more responsibility for things like day-to-day supervision down to the workers, and by organizing work around projects or processes in which jobs may blend or overlap. Employees here must be enthusiastic about learning and moving among jobs. Giving someone a job description with a list of specific duties may simply breed a "that's-not-my-job" attitude by pigeonholing workers too narrowly.

Second, describing the job in terms of the skills, knowledge, and competencies the worker needs is *more strategic.* For example, a company with a strategic emphasis on miniaturization and precision manufacturing should encourage some employees to develop their expertise in these two strategically crucial areas.

Third, measurable skills, knowledge, and competencies support the employer's *performance management process.* Training, appraisals, and rewards should be based on fostering and rewarding the skills and competencies required to achieve work goals. Describing the job in terms of skills and competencies facilitates understanding of those required competencies.

Examples of Competencies

In practice, managers often write paragraph-length competencies for jobs and organize these into two or three clusters. For example, the job's required competencies might include *general or core competencies* (such as reading, writing, and mathematical reasoning), *leadership competencies* (such as leadership, strategic thinking, and teaching others), and *technical/task/functional competencies* (which focus on the specific technical competencies required for specific types of jobs and/or occupations).

So, some technical competencies for the job of systems engineer might include the following:

- Design complex software applications, establish protocols, and create prototypes.
- Establish the necessary platform requirements to efficiently and completely coordinate data transfer.
- Prepare comprehensive and complete documentation including specifications, flow diagrams, process patrols, and budgets.[18]

Similarly, for a corporate treasurer, technical competencies might include the following:

- Formulate trade recommendations by studying several computer models for currency trends and using various quantitative techniques to determine the financial impact of certain financial trades.

- Recommend specific trades and when to make them.
- Present recommendations and persuade others to follow the recommended course of action.[19] (Note: Exhibiting this competency presumes the treasurer has certain knowledge and skills that one could measure.)

Comparing Traditional versus Competency-Based Job Analysis

In practice, in almost any job description today some of the job's listed duties and responsibilities are competency-based, while most are not. For example, consider the typical duties you might find in a marketing manager's job description. Which of the duties would complete this phrase: "In order to perform this job competently, the employee should be able to: . . . ?"

Some familiar duties and responsibilities would not easily fit these requirements. For example, "works with writers and artists and oversees copywriting, design, layout, and production of promotional materials" is not particularly measurable. How can the extent to which the employee "works with writers and artists" or "oversees copywriting, design, and layout" be measured? Put another way, in devising a training program for this job's incumbent, how would one determine whether the person had been adequately trained to work with writers and artists? In fact, what sort of training would that duty and responsibility even imply? It's not clear at all.

On the other hand, some of the job's typical duties and responsibilities are more easily expressed as competencies. For example, the phrase, "to perform this job competently, the employee should be able to . . ." could easily be completed with "conduct marketing surveys on current and new-product concepts; prepare marketing activity reports; and develop and execute marketing plans and programs."

Writing Competency-Based Job Descriptions

Defining the job's competencies and writing them up involves a process that is similar in most respects to traditional job analysis. In other words, the manager will interview job incumbents and their supervisors, ask open-ended questions regarding job responsibilities and activities, and perhaps identify critical incidents that pinpoint success on the job. These job descriptions can be particularly useful in organizations that use competency-based pay, as discussed in Chapter 11.

Chapter | SUMMARY

1. In any organization, work has to be divided into manageable units and ultimately into jobs that can be performed by employees. The process of organizing work into tasks that are required to perform a specific job is known as job design. The term "job" means a group of tasks and duties, and several employees may have the same job. The collection of tasks and responsibilities performed by one person is known as a "position."

2. Industrial engineering is concerned with analyzing work methods; making work cycles more efficient by modifying, combining, rearranging, or eliminating tasks; and establishing time standards. Behavioural scientists focus on identifying various job dimensions that would simultaneously improve the efficiency of organizations and job satisfaction of employees. Effective job design must also take physiological needs and health

and safety issues into account by using ergonomics to integrate and accommodate the physical needs of workers into the design of jobs.

3. Job analysis involves six steps: (1) determine the use to which the information will be put, (2) collect background information, (3) select the representative positions and jobs to be analyzed, (4) collect data, (5) review the information collected with the incumbents and their supervisors, and (6) develop the job descriptions and job specifications.

4. Four qualitative techniques are used to gather job analysis data: interviews, questionnaires, direct observation, and participant diaries/logs. Quantitative job analysis techniques include the Position Analysis Questionnaire (PAQ), Functional Job Analysis (FJA), and the National Occupational Classification (NOC).

5. A job description is a written statement of what the jobholder actually does, how he or she does it, and under what conditions the job is performed. The job specification involves examining the duties and responsibilities and answering this question: "What human traits and experience are required to do this job?"

6. Competency-based job analysis, focusing on how the job is done (the behaviours required) more than on task requirements, has become more common for three reasons. First, traditional job descriptions may not be appropriate in organizations with flexible jobs. Second, describing the job in terms of the skills, knowledge, and competencies the worker needs is more strategic. Third, competency-based job analysis supports the employer's performance management process.

PEARSON
myHRlab

Test yourself on material for this chapter at
www.pearsoned.ca/myhrlab

Key | TERMS

competencies   *(p. 110)*
competency-based job analysis   *(p. 110)*
diary/log   *(p. 97)*
ergonomics   *(p. 89)*
Functional Job Analysis (FJA)   *(p. 99)*
industrial engineering   *(p. 87)*
job   *(p. 86)*
job analysis   *(p. 90)*
job description   *(p. 102)*
job design   *(p. 86)*
job enlargement (horizontal loading)   *(p. 87)*
job enrichment (vertical loading)   *(p. 87)*
job rotation   *(p. 87)*

job specification   *(p. 107)*
National Occupational Classification (NOC)   *(p. 99)*
occupation   *(p. 99)*
organization chart   *(p. 84)*
organizational structure   *(p. 84)*
physical demands analysis   *(p. 107)*
position   *(p. 86)*
Position Analysis Questionnaire (PAQ)   *(p. 99)*
process chart   *(p. 92)*
team   *(p. 88)*
team-based job design   *(p. 88)*
work simplification   *(p. 87)*

Review and Discussion | QUESTIONS

1. Explain the two main elements of the job specialization approach to job design. In what situations is this approach to job design appropriate?

2. Differentiate among job enlargement, job rotation, and job enrichment, and provide an example of each.

3. What is involved in the ergonomic approach to job design? Why is it becoming increasingly important?

4. Several qualitative and quantitative methods for collecting job analysis data are available—interviews, the Position

Analysis Questionnaire, and so on. Compare and contrast these methods, explaining what each is useful for and listing the pros and cons of each.

5. Although not legally required, having job descriptions is highly advisable. Why? How can firms ensure that their job specifications are legally defensible?

6. What are competencies? Why are companies starting to use competency-based job analysis? How is this approach different from the traditional approach?

Critical Thinking | QUESTIONS

1. Why isn't it always desirable or appropriate to use job enrichment when designing jobs? How would you determine how enriched an individual employee's job should be?

2. Assume that you are the job analyst at a bicycle manufacturing company in British Columbia and have been assigned responsibility for preparing job descriptions (including specifications) for all the supervisory and managerial positions. One of the production managers has just indicated that he will not complete the job analysis questionnaire you have developed.
   (a) How would you handle this situation?
   (b) What arguments would you use to attempt to persuade him to change his mind?
   (c) If your persuasion efforts failed, how would you go about obtaining the job analysis information you need to develop the job description for his position?

3. Because the top job in a firm (such as president, executive director, or CEO) is by nature more strategic and broader in scope than any other job, is competency-based job analysis more appropriate? Is there less need for a job description for the president? Why or why not?

4. If you were designing a job for a new marketing and sales representative for a small entrepreneurial company that is experiencing rapid growth, what approach would you take? Explain why you would take this approach. How would you go about determining job specifications?

5. Identify all of the reasons why getting the job analysis and resulting job description and specifications correct is important to both an organization and its employees. What would the impact be if incorrect information were included?

Experiential | EXERCISES

1. Use organization chart software to draw an organization chart that accurately depicts the structure of the organization in which you are currently employed or one with which you are thoroughly familiar. Once you have completed this task, form a group with several of your classmates. Taking turns, have each member show his or her organization chart to the group; briefly describe the structure depicted, explain whether or not the structure seems to be appropriate to him or her, and identify several advantages and disadvantages he or she experienced working within this structure.

2. Working individually or in groups and using the HRSDC website, find the National Occupational Classification (NOC) job descriptions for both a university professor and a college professor. Compare the two descriptions, noting similarities and differences. Using the NOC descriptions and your own observations of people in this role, create a competency profile for each job. How similar are they? Why do you think this is so? Compare and discuss your results with other individual students or groups.

3. Working individually, prepare a job description (including job specifications) for a position that you know well, using the job analysis questionnaire in this chapter. Once you have done so, exchange job descriptions with someone else in the class. Critique your colleague's job description

and provide specific suggestions regarding any additions/deletions/revisions that you would recommend to ensure that the job description accurately reflects the job and is legally defensible.

4. Working in groups of three or four, identify the jobs that have been or are held by students in your group. Select one job to analyze. Use the job analysis questionnaire shown in Figure 4.5 to conduct a job analysis interview and document a job description and specifications. Compare and critique your work with the work done by another group.

Running | CASE

Running Case: Learn in Motion.com

Who Do We Have to Hire?

As the excitement surrounding the move into their new offices wound down, the two principal owners of LearnInMotion.com, Pierre and Jennifer, turned to the task of hiring new employees. In their business plan they'd specified several basic goals for the venture capital funds they'd just received, and hiring a team topped the list. They knew their other goals—boosting sales and expanding the website, for instance—would be unreachable without the right team.

They were just about to place their ads when Pierre asked a question that brought them to a stop: "What kind of people do we want to hire?" It seemed they hadn't really considered this. They knew the answer in general terms, of course. For example, they knew they needed at least two salespeople, a programmer, a web designer, and several content management people to transform the incoming material into content they could post on their site. But it was obvious that job titles alone really didn't provide enough guidance. For example, if they couldn't specify the exact duties of these positions, how could they decide whether they needed experienced employees? How could they decide exactly what sorts of experiences and skills they had to look for in their candidates if they didn't know exactly what these candidates would have to do? They wouldn't even know what questions to ask.

And that wasn't all. For example, there were obviously other tasks to do, and these weren't necessarily included in the sorts of things that salespeople, programmers, web designers, or content management people typically do. Who was going to answer the phones? (Jennifer and Pierre had originally assumed they'd put in one of those fancy automated call directory and voicemail systems—until they found out it would cost close to $10 000.) As a practical matter, they knew they had to have someone answering the phones and directing callers to the proper extensions. Who was going to keep track of the monthly expenses and compile them for the accountants, who'd then produce monthly reports for the venture capitalist? Would the salespeople generate their own leads? Or would LearnInMotion.com have to hire web surfers to search and find the names of people for the sales staff to call or email? What would happen when the company had to purchase supplies, such as fax paper or printer ink? Would the owners have to do this themselves or should they have someone in house do it for them? The list, it seemed, went on and on.

It was obvious, in other words, that the owners had to get their managerial act together and draw up the sorts of documents they'd read about as business majors—job descriptions, job specifications, and so forth. The trouble was, it had all seemed a lot easier when they read the textbook. Now they want you, their management consultant, to help them actually do it. Here's what they want you to do for them.

QUESTIONS

1 To assist Pierre and Jennifer in developing much needed job descriptions, follow the steps outlined in the job analysis process and design a job description for the positions of web designers, salespeople, and receptionist.

2 As part of the job analysis process you will follow in question 1, evaluate the methods of collecting job analysis information and discuss which ones you would recommend (including why) to Pierre and Jennifer as part of developing the job descriptions.

3 As their management consultant would you recommend they only use quantitative or qualitative methods, or both, and why?

Case | INCIDENT

What Is a Human Resources Consultant to Do?

Anthony LePage is the owner of a local recruitment agency that has an established presence in the Northern Ontario market. He is looking to expand its service offerings to include consulting services to small businesses. A recent marketing blitz advertising this new service offering has led to a new partnership with a large local manufacturing business.

After the meeting with the owner of the manufacturing business, the mandate is clear that the owner is seeking the agency's assistance in creating and writing job descriptions for all of the positions within his company. Some of these positions include administrative assistants, sales, engineering, and skilled trades, along with many others. There are more than 100 descriptions to write. The owner would like to see a sample job description within one week before he signs the contract to complete the remainder of the job descriptions.

Anthony LePage has just hired you on as the human resources consultant in charge of producing this job description sample for his new client and has asked you to answer the following questions.

QUESTIONS

1   Outline what the crucial differences are between a job description and a job specification.

2   The owner of the business has heard that only qualitative methods produce the best job descriptions. Would you attempt to persuade him otherwise?

3   Develop a sample job description for the position of administrative assistant for the owner and explain why you included the various sections that you did.

4   The owner has heard from some of his colleagues about the use of competencies. He wants to know what they are and if these should be incorporated into the job descriptions he requires.

For additional cases and exercise material, go to
www.pearsoned.ca/myhrlab

CHAPTER 5

HUMAN RESOURCES PLANNING

LEARNING OUTCOMES

AFTER STUDYING THIS CHAPTER, YOU SHOULD BE ABLE TO

DEFINE human resources planning (HRP) and **DISCUSS** its strategic importance.

DESCRIBE four quantitative and two qualitative techniques used to forecast human resources demand.

DISCUSS briefly the four strategies used to forecast internal human resources supply and four types of market conditions assessed when forecasting external human resources supply.

DESCRIBE the ways in which a surplus of human resources can be handled.

EXPLAIN how organizations deal with a shortage of human resources.

REQUIRED PROFESSIONAL CAPABILITIES (RPC)

- Maintains an inventory of HR talent for the use of the organization
- Identifies the organization's staffing needs
- Researches, analyzes, and reports on potential people issues affecting the organization

THE STRATEGIC IMPORTANCE OF HUMAN RESOURCES PLANNING

human resources planning (HRP)
The process of forecasting future human resources requirements to ensure that the organization will have the required number of employees with the necessary skills to meet its strategic objectives.

Human resources planning (HRP) is the process of forecasting future human resources requirements to ensure that the organization will have the required number of employees with the necessary skills to meet its strategic objectives. HRP is a proactive process, which both anticipates and influences an organization's future by systematically forecasting the demand for and supply of employees under changing conditions and by developing plans and activities to satisfy these needs. Effective HRP helps an organization to achieve its strategic goals and objectives, achieve economies in hiring new workers, make major labour market demands more successfully, anticipate and avoid shortages and surpluses of human resources, and control and/or reduce labour costs.

HRP has recently become a key strategic priority not just for HR departments but for strategic business planners as well. The existing labour shortage in Canada is forecast to increase to one million workers over the next 15 years, as shown in **Figure 5.1**. HRP will be critical aspect of strategic planning and absolutely essential for successful strategy implementation.[1]

As illustrated in **Figure 5.2**, key steps in the HRP process include forecasting demand for labour, analyzing the labour supply, and planning and implementing HR programs to balance supply and demand. As illustrated in **Figure 5.3**, there are many alternative techniques to manage labour surpluses and labour shortages.

Lack of or inadequate human resources planning within an organization can result in significant costs when unstaffed positions create costly inefficiencies and when severance pay is required for large numbers of employees being laid

FIGURE 5.1 | Labour Shortage Hitting Canada Hard

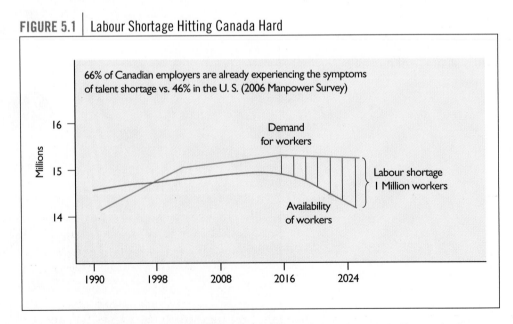

Source: Performance and Potential 2000–2001: Seeking "Made in Canada" Solutions (Ottawa: Conference Board of Canada 2000), 51. Reprinted by permission of The Conference Board of Canada, Ottawa.

FIGURE 5.2 | Human Resources Planning Model

Step 1: Forecast Demand for Labour

Considerations
- Organizational strategic plans
- Organizational tactical plans
- Economic conditions
- Market and competitive trends
- Government and legislative issues
- Social concerns
- Technological changes
- Demographic trends

Techniques Utilized
- Trend analysis
- Ratio analysis
- Scatter plot
- Regression analysis
- Nominal group technique
- Delphi technique
- Managerial judgment
- Staffing tables

Step 2: Analyze Supply

Internal Analysis
- Markov analysis
- Skills inventories
- Management inventories
- Replacement charts and development tracking
- Replacement summaries
- Succession planning

External Analysis
- General economic conditions
- Labour market conditions (national and local)
- Occupational market conditions

Step 3: Implement Human Resources Programs to Balance Supply and Demand

Labour Shortage
- Overtime
- Hire temporary employees
- Subcontract work
- Recruitment
- Transfer
- Promotion

Labour Surplus
- Hiring freeze
- Attrition
- Buyouts and early retirement programs
- Job sharing
- Part-time work
- Work sharing
- Reduced workweek
- Alternative jobs within the organization
- Layoffs (reverse seniority or juniority)
- Supplemental unemployment benefits (SUBs)
- Termination
- Severance pay
- Outplacement assistance

off. It can also create situations in which one department is laying off employees while another is hiring individuals with similar skills, which can reduce morale and productivity and cause turnover. Perhaps most importantly, ineffective HRP can lead to the inability to accomplish short-term operational plans and/or long-range strategic plans.

Unfortunately, a 2006 Conference Board of Canada study found that Canadian employers are doing little to tackle the impending labour shortage from a strategic perspective.[2] Two years later, in 2008, a survey by the Human

FIGURE 5.3 | Balancing Supply and Demand Considerations

Conditions and Possible Solutions

A. When labour demand exceeds labour supply
- Scheduling overtime hours
- Hiring temporary workers
- Subcontracting
- External recruitment
- Internal promotions and transfers
- *Performance management, training and retraining, and career development play a critical role.*

B. When labour supply exceeds labour demand
- Hiring freeze: reassigning current workers to job openings
- Attrition: standard employee resignation, retirement, or death
- Incentives to leave the organization: buyouts or early retirement programs
- Job sharing
- Reducing positions to part-time
- Work sharing and reduced workweek
- Finding employees alternative jobs within the organization
- Employee layoffs
- Termination of employment
- *Evaluating the effectiveness of layoffs and downsizing is critical, as is managing "survivor sickness."*

C. When labour demand equals labour supply
- Vacancies are filled internally through transfers or promotions, or externally by hiring new employees
- *Performance management, training, and career development are critical in achieving balance.*

In their HR planning, employers closely monitor trends, such as the availability of entry-level labour.

Resources Professionals Association found that, although a quarter of companies expect retirement levels to hit 20 percent or higher over the next five years, only 14 percent of the companies said they were fully prepared.[3]

The Relationship between HRP and Strategic Planning

Strategic plans are created and carried out by people. Thus, determining how many people will be available is a critical element of the strategic planning process. For example, plans to enter new businesses, build new plants, or reduce the level of activities all influence the number and types of positions to be filled. At the same time, decisions regarding how positions will be filled must be integrated with other aspects of the firm's HR plans, for instance, those pertaining to training current and new employees, appraising performance, and terminating, transferring, or promoting staff members, as shown in **Figure 5.4.**

Although production, financial, and marketing plans have long been recognized as important cornerstones in the strategic

FIGURE 5.4 | Linkage of Strategic Planning and HR Planning

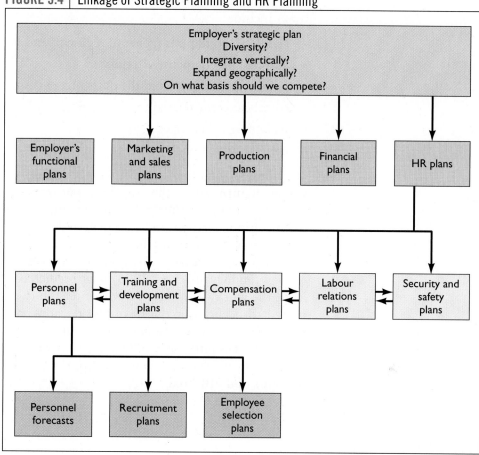

planning process, more and more firms are realizing that HR plans are another essential component. It is becoming clear that HRP and strategic planning become effective when a reciprocal and interdependent relationship exists between them.[4]

Failure to integrate HRP and strategic planning can have very serious consequences. For example, despite the fact that the Canadian Nurses Association (CNA) warned governments in 1998 that an aging workforce and an inability to attract and retain nurses could leave the system short 113 000 nurses by 2011, it is clear that a long-term nationwide HR plan for nurses is overdue.[5] Provinces are still trying to cope by poaching nurses from each other without any overall coordinated plan.[6]

The shortage is having a direct impact on nurses' physical and mental health. They are reporting higher rates of absenteeism, emotional exhaustion, and higher injury claim rates than workers in other professions. And because of the inaction to date, the next time Canada faces a communicable disease outbreak, the health system may not be able to cope.[7]

The Importance of Environmental Scanning

Environmental scanning is a critical component of HRP and strategic planning processes; the most successful organizations are prepared for changes before they occur. The external environmental factors most frequently monitored include

- economic conditions (general, regional, and local)
- market and competitive trends
- new or revised laws and the decisions of courts and quasi-judicial bodies
- social concerns related to health care, childcare, and educational priorities
- technological changes
- demographic trends

Economic conditions affect supply and demand for products and services, which in turn affect the number and types of employees required. In the severe recession of the 1990s, for example, both private- and public-sector organizations restructured or downsized. Today, the most significant environmental factor relates to the dramatic demographic changes in labour force composition. Starting in 2011, labour force growth will be entirely dependent on new immigrants.[8] By 2026, it is predicted that for every 13 people who leave the workforce, only 10 will enter. Thus, a severe labour shortage is expected to occur over the next two decades as the baby boomers retire and there are not enough Generation X and Generation Y employees to replace them all.[9] Despite this challenging environment, one family business in the ultra-competitive oil patch is rising to the challenge, as described in the Entrepreneurs and HR box.

Entrepreneurs and HR

Alpha Safety Uses Personal Touch to Meet Labour Challenges

Alpha Safety Ltd. provides medics to the remote oil patches in northern British Columbia. It is a family-founded, family-run company. David Phibbs, manager and CEO, headed to Fort St. John with a Level III industrial first-aid certification, one of his sons, and a vehicle in 1997 and "the doors just opened up," he says.

Shifts for the medics can last as long as 65 days in fair to hardly tolerable camps. The HR planning challenges are obvious, but Alpha Safety was chosen as an industry leader in recruitment and retention by the Calgary-based Petroleum Human Resources Council of Canada.

Strong family values and building strong relationships with employees are at the heart of their success. One of their employees, medic Ted Thompson, says, "I liken it to a certain kindness. This company is really friendly. You're not just part of their policy and procedures. They have a real concern for the people who work for them."

The level of commitment extends far wider than an open-door policy at the office. Phibbs and his wife put out welcome mats for workers in their own home, as accommodations for workers on their days off are few and far between during the height of the oil season. Phibbs once flew an employee to West Africa when his father died.

"We really try to get to know employees. We find out about their own relationships because if their wives or boyfriends don't support them being up here, it never works out," says Phibbs. Thus each medic is provided with 500 minutes of free cellphone service per month. The company's highly trained dispatchers are able to detect if any of their 70 field medics are becoming "bushed"—irrational and agitated as a result of losing a sense of reality—and get them back to base in Fort St. John.

Flexibility is also incredibly important at Alpha, especially considering the length of shifts. If a medic needs time off, has a family emergency, or just prefers to work a certain schedule, the company does its best to accommodate him or her.

Source: Excerpt adapted from L. Young, "Alpha Safety a leader with personal touch," *Canadian HR Reporter,* August 13, 2007.

Steps in HRP

Once the human resources implications of the organization's strategic plans have been analyzed, three subsequent processes are involved in HRP:

1. forecasting future human resources needs (demand)
2. forecasting the availability of internal and external candidates (supply)
3. planning and implementing HR programs to balance supply and demand

STEP 1: FORECASTING FUTURE HUMAN RESOURCES NEEDS (DEMAND)

RPC

Identifies the organization's staffing needs

A key component of HRP is forecasting the number and type of people needed to meet organizational objectives. Managers should consider several factors when forecasting such requirements. From a practical point of view, the demand for the organization's product or service is paramount. Thus, in a manufacturing firm, sales are projected first. Then, the volume of production required to meet these sales requirements is determined. Finally, the staff needed to maintain this volume of output is estimated. In addition to this "basic requirement" for staff, several other factors should be considered, including

1. *projected turnover* as a result of resignations or terminations
2. *quality and nature of employees* in relation to what management sees as the changing needs of the organization
3. *decisions to upgrade* the quality of products or services *or enter into new markets,* which might change the required employee skill mix
4. *planned technological and administrative changes aimed at increasing productivity and reducing employee headcount,* such as the installation of new equipment or introduction of a financial incentive plan
5. the *financial resources* available to each department: For example, a budget increase may enable managers to pay higher wages and/or hire more people; conversely, a budget crunch might result in wage freezes and/or layoffs

In large organizations, needs forecasting is primarily quantitative in nature and is the responsibility of highly trained specialists. *Quantitative techniques* for determining human resources requirements include trend analysis, ratio analysis, scatter plot analysis, regression analysis, and computerized forecasting. *Qualitative approaches* to forecasting range from sophisticated analytical models to informal expert opinions about future needs, such as a manager deciding that the cost of overtime in his or her department is beginning to outweigh that involved in hiring an additional staff member and then making plans to amend his or her staff complement during the next budget year.

Quantitative Approaches

Trend Analysis

trend analysis The study of a firm's past employment levels over a period of years to predict future needs.

Trend analysis involves studying the firm's employment levels over the last five years or so to predict future needs. For example, the number of employees in the firm at the end of each of the last five years—or perhaps the number in each subgroup (such as sales, production, and administration)—might be computed. The purpose is to identify employment trends that might continue into the future.

Trend analysis is valuable as an initial estimate only, since employment levels rarely depend solely on the passage of time. Other factors (like changes in sales volume and productivity) will also affect future staffing needs.

Ratio Analysis

ratio analysis A forecasting technique for determining future staff needs by using ratios between some causal factor (such as sales volume) and the number of employees needed.

Another approach, **ratio analysis**, involves making forecasts based on the ratio between some causal factor (such as sales volume) and the number of employees required (e.g., number of salespeople). For example, suppose a salesperson traditionally generates $500 000 in sales and that plans call for increasing the firm's sales by $3 million next year. Then, if the sales revenue–salespeople ratio remains the same, six new salespeople would be required (each of whom produces an extra $500 000 in sales).

Ratio analysis can also be used to help forecast other employee requirements. For example, a salesperson–secretary ratio could be computed to determine how many new secretaries will be needed to support the extra sales staff.

Like trend analysis, ratio analysis assumes that productivity remains about the same—for instance, that each salesperson can't be motivated to produce much more than $500 000 in sales. If sales productivity were to increase or decrease, then the ratio of sales to salespeople would change. A forecast based on historical ratios would then no longer be accurate.

The Scatter Plot

scatter plot A graphical method used to help identify the relationship between two variables.

A **scatter plot** is another option. Scatter plots can be used to determine whether two factors—a measure of business activity and staffing levels—are related. If they are, then when the measure of business activity is forecast, HR requirements can also be estimated.

An example to illustrate follows. Legislative changes to the health-care system require that two 500-bed Canadian hospitals be amalgamated. Both previously had responsibility for acute, chronic, and long-term care. The government's plan is for Hospital A to specialize in acute care while Hospital B assumes responsibility for chronic and long-term care. In general, providing acute care requires staffing with registered nurses (RNs), while chronic and long-term care facilities can be staffed primarily with registered practical nurses (RPNs).

By the end of the calendar year, 200 beds at Hospital A must be converted from chronic and long-term care beds to facilities for acute patients. At the same time, Hospital A's 200 chronic and long-term patients must be transferred to Hospital B. In a joint meeting, the directors of nursing and HR decide that a good starting point in the planning process would be to calculate the relationship between hospital size (in terms of number of acute beds) and the number of RNs required. After placing telephone calls to their counterparts at eight hospitals in larger centres across the country, they obtain the following information:

Size of Hospital (Number of Acute Beds)	Number of Registered Nurses
200	240
300	260
400	470
500	500
600	620
700	660
800	820
900	860

FIGURE 5.5 | Determining the Relationship between Hospital Size and Number of Nurses

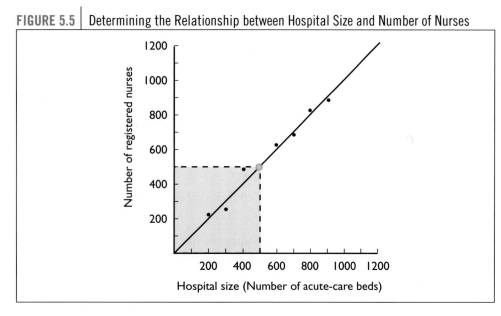

Note: After fitting the line, the number of employees needed, given the projected volume, can be extrapolated (projected).

To determine how many RNs would be needed, they use the data obtained to draw the scatter plot shown in **Figure 5.5**, in which hospital size is shown on the horizontal axis and number of RNs is shown on the vertical axis. If the two factors are related, then the points will tend to fall along a straight line, as they do in this case. Carefully drawing a line that minimizes the distances between the line and each of the plotted points (the line of best fit) permits an estimate of the number of nurses required for hospitals of various sizes. Thus, since Hospital A will now have 500 acute-care beds, the estimated number of RNs needed is 500.

Regression Analysis

regression analysis A statistical technique involving the use of a mathematical formula to project future demands based on an established relationship between an organization's employment level (dependent variable) and some measurable factor of output (independent variable).

Regression analysis is a more sophisticated statistical technique to determine the line of best fit. It involves the use of a mathematical formula to project future demands based on an established relationship between an organization's employment level (dependent variable) and some measurable factor of output (independent variable), such as revenue, sales, or production level. When there are several dependent and/or independent variables, multiple regression analysis is used.

Qualitative Approaches

In contrast to quantitative approaches, which utilize statistical formulas, qualitative techniques rely solely on expert judgments. Two approaches used to gather such opinions in order to forecast human resources demand (or supply) are the nominal group and Delphi techniques.

Nominal Group Technique

nominal group technique A decision-making technique that involves a group of experts meeting face to face. Steps include independent idea generation, clarification and open discussion, and private assessment.

The **nominal group technique** involves a group of experts (such as first-line supervisors and managers) meeting face to face. Although one of its uses is human resources demand forecasting, this technique is used to deal with issues and problems ranging from identifying training needs to determining safety program incentives. The steps involved are as follows:[10]

1. Each member of the group independently writes down his or her ideas on the problem or issue (in this case, the causes of demand).

2. Going around the table, each member then presents one idea. This process continues until all ideas have been presented and recorded, typically on a flipchart or chalkboard. No discussion is permitted during this step.

3. Clarification is then sought, as necessary, followed by group discussion and evaluation.

4. Finally, each member is asked to rank the ideas. This is done independently and in silence.

The advantages of this technique include involvement of key decision makers, a future focus, and the fact that the group discussion involved in the third step can facilitate the exchange of ideas and greater acceptance of results. Drawbacks include subjectivity and the potential for group pressure to lead to less accurate assessment than could be obtained through other means.

The Delphi Technique

Delphi technique A judgmental forecasting method used to arrive at a group decision, typically involving outside experts as well as organizational employees. Ideas are exchanged without face-to-face interaction and feedback is provided and used to fine-tune independent judgments until a consensus is reached.

Although short-term forecasting is generally handled by managers, the **Delphi technique** is useful for long-range forecasting and other strategic planning issues. It typically involves outside experts as well as company employees, based on the premise that outsiders may be able to assess changes in economic, demographic, governmental, technological, and social conditions and their potential impact more objectively. The Delphi technique involves the following steps:[11]

1. The problem is identified (in this case, the causes of demand) and each group member is requested to submit a potential solution by completing a carefully designed questionnaire. Direct face-to-face contact is not permitted.

2. After each member independently and anonymously completes the initial questionnaire, the results are compiled at a centralized location.

3. Each group member is then given a copy of the results.

4. If there are differences in opinion, each individual uses the feedback from other experts to fine-tune his or her independent assessment.

5. The third and fourth steps are repeated as often as necessary until a consensus is reached.

As with the nominal group technique, the advantages include involvement of key decision makers and a future focus; however, the Delphi technique permits the group to critically evaluate a wider range of views. Drawbacks include the fact that judgments may not efficiently use objective data, the time and costs involved, and the potential difficulty in integrating diverse opinions.

Managerial Judgment

Although managerial judgment is central to qualitative forecasting, it also plays a key role when quantitative techniques are used. It's rare that any historical trend, ratio, or relationship will continue unchanged into the future. Judgment is thus needed to modify the forecast based on anticipated changes.

FIGURE 5.6 | A Sample Staffing Table

Job Title (As on Job Description)	Department	Anticipated Openings												
		Total	Jan.	Feb.	Mar.	Apr.	May	June	July	Aug.	Sept.	Oct.	Nov.	Dec.
General Manager	Administration	1					1							
Director of Finance	Administration	1												1
Human Resources Officer	Administration	2	1					1						
Collection Clerk	Administration	1		1										
Groundskeeper	Maintenance	4						1	1					2
Service and Maintenance Technician	Maintenance	5	1			2					2			
Water Utility Engineer	Operations	3									2			1
Apprentice Lineperson	Operations	10	6						4					
Water Meter Technician	Operations	1												1
Engineering Technician	Operations	3			2							1		
Field Technician	Operations	8						8						
Senior Programmer/ Analyst	Systems	2				1				1				
Programmer/Operator	Systems	4		2						1			1	
Systems Operator	Systems	5					2						3	
Customer Service Representative	Sales	8	4					3				1		

Springbrook Utilities Commission Staffing Table
Date compiled:_____

Summarizing Human Resources Requirements

The end result of the forecasting process is an estimate of short-term and long-range HR requirements. Long-range plans are general statements of potential staffing needs and may not include specific numbers.

Short-term plans—although still approximations—are more specific and are often depicted in a **staffing table**. As illustrated in **Figure 5.6,** a staffing table is a pictorial representation of all jobs within the organization, along with the number of current incumbents and future employment requirements (monthly or yearly) for each.

staffing table A pictorial representation of all jobs within the organization, along with the number of current incumbents and future employment requirements (monthly or yearly) for each.

STEP 2: FORECASTING THE AVAILABILITY OF INTERNAL AND EXTERNAL CANDIDATES (SUPPLY)

Short-term and long-range HR demand forecasts only provide half of the staffing equation by answering the question "How many employees will we need?" The next major concern is how projected openings will be filled. There are two sources of supply:

1. *internal*—present employees who can be transferred or promoted to meet anticipated needs

RPC

Researches, analyzes, and reports on potential people issues affecting the organization

2. *external*—people in the labour market not currently working for the organization, including those who are employed elsewhere and those who are unemployed

Forecasting the Supply of Internal Candidates

Before estimating how many external candidates will need to be recruited and hired, management must determine how many candidates for projected openings will likely come from within the firm. This is the purpose of forecasting the supply of internal candidates.

Markov Analysis

Markov analysis A method of forecasting internal labour supply that involves tracking the pattern of employee movements through various jobs and developing a transitional probability matrix.

Estimating internal supply involves much more than simply calculating the number of employees. Some firms use the **Markov analysis** technique to track the pattern of employee movements through various jobs and develop a transitional probability matrix for forecasting internal supply by specific categories, such as position and gender. As illustrated in **Figure** 5.7, such an analysis shows the actual number (and percentage) of employees who remain in each job from one year to the next, as well as the proportions promoted, demoted, transferred, and leaving the organization. These proportions (probabilities) are used to forecast human resources supply.

In addition to such quantitative data, the skills and capabilities of current employees must be assessed and skills inventories prepared. From this information, replacement charts and/or summaries and succession plans can be developed.

FIGURE 5.7 | Hypothetical Markov Analysis for a Manufacturing Operation

2007 \ 2008	Plant Manager	Foreperson	Team Leader	Production Worker	Exit
Plant Manager (n = 5)	80% / 4				20% / 1
Foreperson (n = 35)	8% / 3	82% / 28			10% / 4
Team Leader (n = 110)		11% / 12	70% / 77	7% / 8	12% / 13
Production Worker (n = 861)			6% / 52	72% / 620	22% / 189
Projected Supply	7	40	129	628	

Percentages represent transitions (previous year's actuals).
Actual numbers of employees are shown as whole numbers in each block
(projections for 2008 based on current staffing).

Skills Inventories and Management Inventories

Skills inventories contain comprehensive information about the capabilities of current employees. Data gathered for each employee include name, age, date of employment, current position, present duties and responsibilities, educational background, previous work history, skills, abilities, and interests. Information about current performance and readiness for promotion is generally included as well. Data pertaining to managerial staff are compiled in **management inventories**. Records summarizing the background, qualifications, interests, and skills of management employees, as well as information about managerial responsibilities and management training, are used to identify internal candidates eligible for promotion opportunities.

To be useful, skills and management inventories must be updated regularly. Failure to do so can lead to present employees being overlooked for job openings. Updating every two years is generally adequate if employees are encouraged to report significant qualifications changes (such as new skills learned and/or courses completed) to the HR department as they occur.

Replacement Charts and Replacement Summaries

Replacement charts are typically used to keep track of potential internal candidates for the firm's most important positions. As can be seen in **Figure 5.8**, such charts typically indicate the age of potential internal candidates (which cannot be used as a criterion in making selection or promotion decisions but which is necessary to project retirement dates), the current performance level of the employee, and his or her promotion potential. The latter is based on the employee's future career aspirations and a supervisory assessment of readiness for promotion.

To provide a more objective estimate of future potential, this information may be supplemented by results of psychological tests, interviews with HR specialists, and other selection techniques.

Although replacement charts provide an excellent quick reference tool, they contain very little information. For that reason, many firms prefer to use **replacement summaries**. Such summaries list likely replacements for each position and their relative strengths and weaknesses, as well as information about current position, performance, promotability, age, and experience. These additional data can be extremely helpful to decision makers, although caution must be taken to ensure that no discrimination occurs on the basis of age, sex, and so on.

Succession Planning

Forecasting the availability of inside candidates is particularly important in succession planning. In a nutshell, **succession planning** refers to the plans a company makes to fill its most important executive positions. In the days when companies were hierarchical and employees tended to remain with the firm for years, executive succession was often straightforward: Staff climbed the ladder one rung at a time, and it wasn't unusual for someone to start on the shop floor and end up in the president's office. Although that kind of ascent is still possible, employee turnover and flatter structures mean that the lines of succession are no longer as direct. For example, potential successors for top positions might be routed through the top jobs at several key divisions, as well as overseas, and sent through a university graduate-level, advanced management program.

Succession planning is extremely important today. The result of the limited attention paid to succession planning in the public sector over the last several

FIGURE 5.8 | Management Replacement Chart

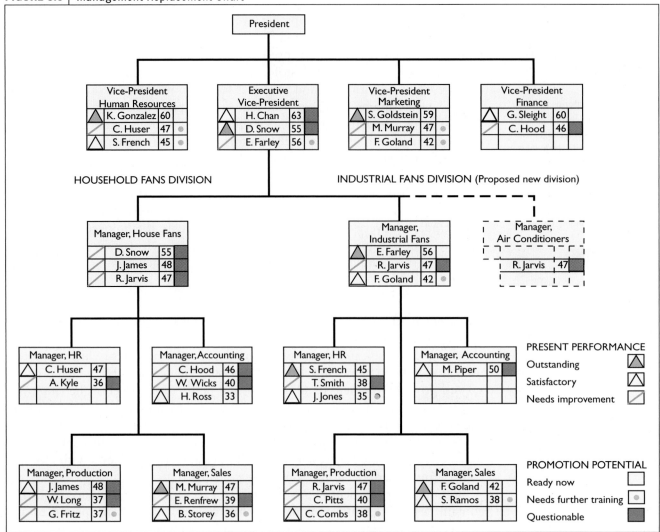

decades is that now, for every two senior executives, there is only one job-ready successor. For example, a 2007 Statistics Canada study showed that the rate at which federal public servants are retiring has tripled since 2000.[12]

Because succession planning requires balancing the organization's top-management needs with the potential and career aspirations of available candidates, it includes these activities:

Tips | **FOR THE FRONT LINE**

- analysis of the demand for managers and professionals in the company
- audit of existing executives and projection of likely future supply
- planning of individual career paths based on objective estimates of future needs, performance appraisal data, and assessments of potential
- career counselling and performance-related training and development to prepare individuals for future roles
- accelerated promotions, with development targeted at future business needs
- planned strategic recruitment, aimed at obtaining people with the potential to meet future needs, as well as at filling current openings[13]

It should be noted that replacement charts, replacement summaries, and succession plans are considered highly confidential in most organizations.

Forecasting the Supply of External (Outside) Candidates

Some jobs cannot be filled with internal candidates, such as entry-level jobs and jobs for which no current employees are qualified. In these situations, the firm looks for external candidates. Employer growth is primarily responsible for the number of entry-level openings. Although there are some higher-level jobs that require such unique talents and skills that they are impossible to fill internally and some jobs are vacated unexpectedly, a key factor in determining the number of positions that must be filled externally is the effectiveness of the organization's training and development and career-planning initiatives. If employees are not encouraged to expand their capabilities, they may not be ready to fill vacancies as they arise, and external sources must be tapped.

To project the supply of outside candidates, employers assess general economic conditions, national labour market conditions, local labour market conditions, and occupational market conditions.

General Economic Conditions

The first step is to forecast general economic conditions and the expected unemployment rate. The national unemployment rate provides an estimate of how difficult it is likely to be to recruit new employees in the immediate future. In general terms, the lower the rate of unemployment, the smaller the labour supply and the more difficult it will be to recruit employees. It is important to note, though, that even when unemployment rates are high, some positions will still be difficult to fill, because unemployment rates vary by occupation and geographic location.

National Labour Market Conditions

Statistics Canada
www.statcan.gc.ca

Demographic trends have a significant impact on national labour market conditions. Fortunately, a wealth of labour market information is available from Statistics Canada and other government and private sources. A crucial reality is that just as the baby boom cohort approaches retirement, relatively fewer young workers will be entering the labour pool.[14] Thus, the supply of labour in Canada will be dramatically lowered over the next two decades.

Highly educated immigrants are the predominant drivers of growth in the Canadian labour pool.[15] Because of Canada's aging population and declining birth rate, it is expected that by 2011 almost all labour force growth will be made up by immigrant workers. Federal, provincial, and major municipality governments are all adjusting legislation to make it easier to import foreign workers and, together with industry groups, are addressing recognition of foreign credentials.[16] CareerBridge, a private-sector not-for-profit organization, helps foreign-trained professionals start their careers in Canada.[17] According to Gord Nixon, president and CEO of RBC Financial Group, it is clear that more talented immigrants will be part of Canada's response to the

Strategic HR

Pumping Up People Supply

Building an aortic pericardial heart valve is no easy task. The intricate medical device, measuring mere millimetres, requires highly specialized skills in its production and engineering. Therefore, there is a very small talent pool available to Burnaby, B.C.–based Sorin Group Canada. They hire engineers who focus on custom-engineered machinery and equipment, quality assurance experts who ensure that regulations are followed, and production technicians who hand-sew and hand-suture the heart valves.

According to Judith Thompson, senior manager of HR at Sorin Group, "Canada isn't well-known for its biomedical engineers so even when we hire now, to ask for medical device experience, we wouldn't get it. So we hire an engineer or scientist and train on the rest of it." The company has come to realize the benefits, and necessity, of new immigrants as a major source of talent. "Our culture is very diverse. About 90 percent of our staff speak English as a second language, from production people to vice-presidents, so we don't look for Canadian-born, Canadian-educated, Canadian experience because in these economic times that would set us back," she says. "I would

never have filled 60 positions last year with those criteria."

Training is extensive as it takes three or four months before workers, wearing gowns and gloves in a super-clean environment, can make a product that is usable, And even then they can only make a certain number of valves or components per week—it takes another six months to ramp up to regular production, says Thompson.

Sorin supports its employees with in-house English-language training, through a partnership with Immigration Services, and provides subsidies to foreign-trained engineers who want to pursue an engineering degree in British Columbia.

"We just can't speak enough about the program and the return on investment we've gotten," says Thompson. "We're getting better feedback on problems on the floor because the employees are more comfortable speaking to the researchers and scientists and surgeons who come in on tours. The confidence level of the group has gone up and they are very devoted to the company and the product they make."

Source: Adapted from S. Dobson, "Pumping up people supply at Sorin Group Canada to build heart valves," *Canadian HR Reporter,* February 23, 2009.

coming labour shortage, and employers will have to stop overlooking immigrants in their HR plans, start hiring immigrants to work at the level at which they were trained, and work harder at integrating immigrant workers into the workforce.[18] An example of a company that has come to realize the benefits of new immigrants as a major source of talent is provided in the Strategic HR box.

Local Labour Market Conditions

Toronto Region Immigrant
Employment Council
www.hireimmigrants.ca
Career Bridge
www.careerbridge.ca
Human Resources and Social
Development Canada
www.hrsdc.gc.ca

Local labour markets are affected by many conditions, including community growth rates and attitudes. Communities that do not support existing businesses may experience declining population as residents move away to find jobs, which then makes it difficult to attract new business, because potential employers fear future local HR supply shortages. The end result is that there are fewer and fewer jobs and more and more people leaving the local labour market—a vicious downward spiral. Conversely, one reason growing cities are attractive to employers is the promise of large future labour markets. Chambers of commerce and provincial/local development and planning agencies can be excellent sources of local labour market information.

Physiotherapy is a skills-shortage occupation; the demand for physiotherapists exceeds the supply.

Occupational Market Conditions

In addition to looking at the overall labour market, organizations also generally want to forecast the availability of potential candidates in specific occupations (engineers, drill press operators, accountants, and so on) for which they will be recruiting. The ongoing shortage of nurses was discussed earlier in the chapter. Alberta is already facing a severe labour shortage of workers in the oil and gas sector.[19] The mining industry, the construction industry, the electricity industry, the manufacturing industry, as well as the non-profit sector are all facing labour shortages.[20] A shortage of information technology workers is projected to cost the Canadian economy $10 billion per year until it is resolved.[21] Shortages of civil service workers, accountants, lawyers, engineers, meteorologists, funeral directors (to bury the baby boomers), and hospitality industry workers are also expected.[22] There is even a shortage of foreign exotic dancers![23]

STEP 3: PLANNING AND IMPLEMENTING HR PROGRAMS TO BALANCE SUPPLY AND DEMAND

Once the supply and demand of human resources have been estimated, program planning and implementation commence. To successfully fill positions internally, organizations must manage performance and careers. Performance is managed through effectively designing jobs and quality of working life initiatives; establishing performance standards and goals; coaching, measuring, and evaluating; and implementing a suitable reward structure (compensation and benefits).

To manage careers effectively, policies and systems must be established for recruitment, selection and placement (including transfer, promotion, retirement, and termination), and training and development. Policies and systems are also required for job analysis, individual employee assessment, replacement and succession planning, and career tracking, as well as career planning and development.

Specific strategies must be formulated to balance supply and demand considerations. As was illustrated in Figure 5.3, there are three possible scenarios:

1. labour supply exceeds demand (surplus)
2. labour demand exceeds supply (shortage)
3. expected demand matches supply

Labour Surplus

hiring freeze A common initial response to an employee surplus. Openings are filled by reassigning current employees, and no outsiders are hired.

attrition The normal separation of employees from an organization because of resignation, retirement, or death.

A labour surplus exists when the internal supply of employees exceeds the organization's demand. Most employers respond initially by instituting a **hiring freeze**, which means that openings are filled by reassigning current employees, and no outsiders are hired. The surplus is slowly reduced through **attrition**, which is the normal separation of employees because of resignation, retirement, or death. When employees leave, the ensuing vacancies are not filled, and the staffing level decreases gradually without any involuntary terminations. In addition to the time it takes, a major drawback of this approach is that the firm has no control over who stays and who leaves.

early retirement buyout programs Strategies used to accelerate attrition that involve offering attractive buyout packages or the opportunity to retire on full pension with an attractive benefits package.

job sharing A strategy that involves dividing the duties of a single position between two or more employees.

work sharing Employees work three or four days a week and receive EI benefits on their non-workday(s).

reduced workweek Employees work fewer hours and receive less pay.

layoff The temporary withdrawal of employment to workers for economic or business reasons.

supplemental unemployment benefits (SUBs) A top-up of EI benefits to bring income levels closer to what an employee would receive if on the job.

termination Permanent separation from the organization for any reason.

severance package A lump-sum payment, continuation of benefits for a specified period of time, and other benefits that are provided to employees who are being terminated.

Some organizations attempt to accelerate attrition by offering incentives to employees to leave, such as **early retirement buyout programs**. Staffing levels are reduced and internal job openings created by offering attractive buyout packages or the opportunity to retire on full pension with an attractive benefits package, at a relatively early age (often 50 or 55). To be successful, buyouts must be handled very carefully. Selection criteria should be established to ensure that key people who cannot be easily replaced do not leave the firm. A drawback of buyouts and early retirement packages is that they often require a great deal of money up-front. Care must also be taken to ensure that early retirement is voluntary, since forced early retirement is a contravention of human rights legislation.

Another strategy used to deal with an employee surplus involves reducing the total number of hours worked. **Job sharing** involves dividing the duties of a single position between two or more employees. Reducing full-time positions to *part-time work* is sometimes more effective, especially if there are peak demand periods. Creating a job-share position and/or offering part-time employment can be win–win strategies, since layoffs can be avoided. Although the employees involved work fewer hours and thus have less pay, they are still employed, and they may enjoy having more free time at their disposal. The organization benefits by retaining good employees.

Twenty-five years ago, the federal government introduced a **work-sharing** scheme, a layoff-avoidance strategy that involves employees working three or four days a week and receiving Employment Insurance (EI) benefits on their non-workday(s). The program was temporarily extended to provide 52 weeks of benefits from February 1, 2009, to April 3, 2010, during the recent economic slowdown.[24] Similar to work sharing, but without a formal arrangement with government regarding EI benefits, is a **reduced workweek**. Employees simply work fewer hours and receive less pay. The organization retains a skilled workforce, lessens the financial and emotional impact of a full layoff, and reduces production costs. The only potential drawback is that it is sometimes difficult to predict in advance, with any degree of accuracy, how many hours of work should be scheduled each week.

Another strategy used to manage an employee surplus is a **layoff**, the temporary withdrawal of employment to workers for economic or business reasons. Layoffs may be short in duration, as when plants close for brief periods to adjust inventory levels or to retool for a new product line, but can last months or even years if caused by a major change in the business cycle. Layoffs are not easy for either managers or workers, but they are sometimes necessary if attrition will take too long to reduce the number of employees to the required level.

To ease the financial burden of layoffs, some organizations offer **supplemental unemployment benefits (SUBs)**, which are a top-up of EI benefits to bring income levels of temporarily laid-off workers closer to their regular pay on the job. SUB programs are generally negotiated through collective bargaining. Benefits are payable until the pool of funds set aside has been exhausted.

When employees are no longer required, the employment relationship may be severed. **Termination** is a broad term that encompasses permanent separation from the organization for any reason. In situations in which employment is terminated involuntarily, employees with acceptable or better performance ratings are often offered severance pay and outplacement assistance.

A **severance package** is typically provided when employees are being terminated through no fault of their own in order to avoid wrongful dismissal lawsuits. Severance pay is legally required in certain situations, such as mass layoffs.

In addition to pay, severance packages often include the continuation of benefits for a specified period. In determining the appropriate package, employers should take salary, years of service, the employee's age, and his or her likelihood of obtaining another job into consideration.[25] Executives may be protected by a *golden parachute clause* in their contract of employment, a guarantee by the employer to pay specified compensation and benefits in the case of termination because of downsizing or restructuring. To soften the blow of termination, *outplacement assistance,* generally offered by an outside agency, can assist affected employees in finding employment elsewhere.

Although restructuring initiatives ranging from layoffs to mergers and acquisitions were prevalent in the 1990s, the consequences were not as positive as anticipated. In a study of 6418 workforce reductions in Fortune 500 firms over 18 years (1982 to 2000), researchers found no consistent evidence that downsizing led to improved financial performance.[26]

As those firms discovered, a high cost associated with downsizing is **survivor sickness**, a range of emotions that can include feelings of betrayal or violation, guilt, and detachment. The remaining employees, anxious about the next round of terminations, often suffer stress symptoms including depression, increased errors, and reduced performance.

Labour Shortage

A labour shortage exists when the internal supply of human resources cannot meet the organization's needs. Scheduling overtime hours is often the initial response. Employers may also subcontract work on a temporary or permanent basis. Another short-term solution is to hire temporary employees.

As vacancies are created within the firm, opportunities are generally provided for employee transfers and promotions, which necessitate performance management, training (and retraining), and career development. Of course, internal movement does not eliminate a shortage, which means that recruitment will be required. It is hoped, though, that resultant vacancies will be for entry-level jobs, which can be filled more easily externally.

A **transfer** involves a lateral movement from one job to another that is relatively equal in pay, responsibility, and/or organizational level. Transfers can lead to more effective utilization of human resources, broaden an employee's skills and perspectives, and help make him or her a better candidate for future promotions. Transfers also offer additional technical and interpersonal challenges and increased variety of work, which may enhance job satisfaction and motivation.

A **promotion** involves the movement of an employee from one job to another that is higher in pay, responsibility, and/or organizational level. Such a move may be based on merit, seniority, or a combination of both. Merit-based promotions are awarded in recognition of a person's outstanding performance in his or her present job or as an assessment of his or her future potential.

Looming Labour Shortage in Canada

Today, Canada is entering a long-term labour shortage. Over the next 20 years, the vast majority of baby boomers will transition from working life to retirement, creating a critical undersupply of labour.[27] As a result, many employers are seeking strategies to increase the workforce participation of older Canadians, setting aside the stereotypes and prejudices that older workers are less productive, resistant to change, and hard to get along with. Instead, employers are seizing the opportunity to retain a wealth of knowledge and maturity. Although many older workers leave the workforce because of health problems, those who remain are in very good or excellent physical and mental condition.[28]

Another strategy involves increasing the number of Aboriginal employees (Nunavut is setting up a trade school in Rankin Inlet) and visible minority employees, increasing the number of female employees in male-dominated workplaces (Yukon College is encouraging women to train in the trades), and accessing the largely untapped pool of talent available from people with disabilities.[29] Provincial governments have been expanding apprenticeship programs (Ontario and British Columbia have already done so) and wooing workers with lifestyle (Saskatchewan's affordable housing, slower pace, and shorter commutes that leave more time for family activities).[30]

One increasingly common approach to manage the coming labour shortage is through the use of flexible work arrangements. These have been commonly used in the past to attract and retain workers seeking work/life balance, which is a key factor in employment decisions for Generations X and Y. Today, many older workers are expected to respond to flexible options that will bridge work and retirement.[31]

Flexible Work Arrangements

Employees of all ages are increasingly demanding flexible work arrangements.[32] Younger workers want time to have a "life" outside work and time to balance work with their family responsibilities. A recent study of 1439 young associate lawyers at major Canadian law firms found that 62 percent of the females and almost half of the males plan to change jobs within five years (costing law firms $315 000 each to replace them) to find an environment that is more supportive of their family and personal commitments and that provides them with more control over their work schedules.[33]

Older workers want less stress and more time for recreational and leisure activities. Work is the number one cause of stress in the lives of Canadians.[34] In between is the Sandwich Generation with both childcare and eldercare responsibilities, which comprises about 25 percent of the workforce.[35]

Employers must be aware of the value of flexible schedules for attracting and retaining talent, as labour becomes increasingly scarce.[36] This is true in most places around the world, as described in the Global HRM box.

Although flexible work arrangements have traditionally been associated with improving work/life balance, they are increasingly seen as part of a business strategy, because they can assist organizations in meeting customer needs when and where they need to be met.[37] For example, one British Columbia firm used flexible work arrangements to enhance customer service by offering employees the option to start work at 6 A.M. Pacific Time in order to deal with customers at 9 A.M. Eastern Time.

Scotiabank is one Canadian employer that offers flexible work arrangements as part of its philosophy regarding its 70 percent female workforce.[38] At IBM Canada, flexible work arrangements help keep employees committed to the workplace.[39] Efforts to assist workers in adapting to ongoing societal and demographic changes can also help organizations to achieve a competitive advantage through increased productivity and lower costs.[40]

Global HRM

Flexible Work Arrangements for Work/Life Balance Popular Around the World

Managing talent is the most critical HR challenge worldwide in every region and industry for the foreseeable future, according to a survey of 4741 executives in 83 countries conducted by the Boston Consulting Group, the World Federation of Personnel Management Associations, and the Canadian Council of Human Resources Associations. Companies around the world are expecting to boost global sourcing of talented employees.

Managing work/life balance was also rated as a top HR challenge in most countries, with the exception of the Pacific Region. It was a top-three challenge in Argentina, Chile, Brazil, Canada, India, Italy, Singapore, and South Africa. As skilled labour becomes harder to

obtain, as employees' loyalty to a single company decreases, and as traditional means of delivering on recruiting and staffing—such as newspaper advertisements and web pages—lose effectiveness, HR departments should renovate their current recruiting and staffing processes. In particular, they should pay close attention to HR branding and marketing activities. HR will also need to work closely with line managers on this topic, paying special attention to internal staffing. The time it takes to fill a new position is often a key performance indicator that is analyzed by corporate leaders.

Source: Creating People Advantage: How to Address HR Challenges Worldwide Through 2015. Boston MA: Boston Consulting Group, World Federation of Personnel Management Associations and the Canadian Council of Human Resources Associations, 2008.

flextime A plan whereby employees build their workday around a core of midday hours.

There are many different flexible work options. Some of the most commonly used ones will be described here. **Flextime** is a plan whereby employees' flexible workdays are built around a core of midday hours, such as 11 A.M. to 2 P.M. Workers determine their own flexible starting and stopping hours. For example, they may opt to work from 7 A.M. to 3 P.M. or from 11 A.M. to 7 P.M. In practice, most employers who use flextime give employees only limited freedom regarding the hours that they work. Typical schedules dictate the earliest starting time, latest starting time, and core periods. Employers often prefer a schedule that is fairly close to the traditional 9 A.M. to 5 P.M. workday. For example, starting times may be between 7 A.M. and 10 A.M., and the core time from 10 A.M. to 3 P.M. The effect of flextime for many employees is to have about an hour or two of leeway before 9 A.M. or after 5 P.M.

Telecommuting (or *teleworking*) is a common flexible work arrangement. Here, employees work at home, using their computers, iPhones, and email to transmit completed work to the office. For employees, telecommuting reduces travel time, permits the employee to work whenever he or she is most productive, and provides flexibility for dealing with family responsibilities. Organizations using this virtual work approach report stunning improvements in cost savings, productivity, and employee morale.[41] Many managers are not comfortable supervising telecommuters, fearing a loss of control. Successful telecommuting requires that mutual trust be established between an employee and his or her supervisor.[42] Successful telecommuters are highly motivated and have the self-discipline to work independently.[43] Best Buy calculated a 35 percent increase in productivity for its employees who were teleworking.[44]

An Ethical Dilemma

Is it ethical for an employer to deny employees the right to flexible work arrangements just because managers are concerned about the additional communication required and about losing control over their employees?

As mentioned earlier in the chapter, *job sharing* is a strategy that allows two or more employees to share a single full-time job. For example, two people may share a 40-hour-per-week job, with one working mornings and the other working afternoons, or one person working Monday through Wednesday noon, and the other from Wednesday noon through Friday. A *reduced workweek*

compressed workweek An arrangement that most commonly allows employees to work four ten-hour days instead of the more usual five eight-hour days.

is another option for employees who want to reduce their overall work hours. Cara Flight Kitchen recently negotiated a reduced workweek of three or four days for employees aged 50 or over.[45]

The most common **compressed workweek** arrangement involves employees working four ten-hour days instead of the more usual five eight-hour days. Compressed workweek plans have been fairly successful as they have several advantages. Productivity seems to increase since there are fewer startups and shutdowns. Workers are also more willing to work some evenings and weekends as part of these plans. The compressed workweek is generally effective in terms of reducing paid overtime, reducing absenteeism, and improving efficiency. Furthermore, workers also gain: There is a 20 percent reduction in commuter trips and an additional day off per week. Additional savings (e.g., in childcare expenses) may also result. However, there has not been a lot of experience with shortened workweeks, and it is possible that the improvements are short-lived. Fatigue is a potential drawback of the four-day workweek. (Note that fatigue was a main reason for adopting eight-hour workdays in the first place.)

flexyear A work arrangement under which employees can choose (at six-month intervals) the number of hours that they want to work each month over the next year.

Other employers, especially in Europe, are switching to a plan that they call **flexyear**. Under this plan, employees can choose (at six-month intervals) the number of hours that they want to work each month over the next year. A full-timer, for instance, might be able to work up to 173 hours a month. In a typical flexyear arrangement, an employee who wants to average 110 hours a month might work 150 hours in January (when the children are at school and the company needs extra help to cope with January sales). In February, the employee may work only 70 hours because he or she wants to go skiing. This arrangement may be particularly attractive to older employees or those who have already retired but are willing to work for part of the year.

Labour Supply Matches Labour Demand

When the expected supply matches the demand, organizations replace employees who leave the firm with individuals transferred or promoted from inside or hired from outside. As in shortage situations, performance management, training, and career development play crucial roles.

Chapter | SUMMARY

1. Human resources planning (HRP) is the process of reviewing HR requirements to ensure that the organization has the required number of employees with the necessary skills to meet its strategic goals. Forecasting future labour demand and supply is a critical element of the strategic planning process. HRP and strategic planning become effective when a reciprocal and interdependent relationship exists between them.

2. Four quantitative techniques for forecasting future HR demand are trend analysis, ratio analysis, scatter plots, and regression analysis.

Two qualitative techniques used to forecast demand are the nominal group technique and the Delphi technique.

3. Four strategies used to forecast internal HR supply are Markov analysis, skills and management inventories, replacement charts and summaries, and succession planning. Forecasting external HR supply requires an assessment of general economic conditions, national labour market conditions, local labour market conditions, and occupational labour market conditions.

Chapter 5   Human Resources Planning   139

4. Strategies to manage a labour surplus include a hiring freeze; downsizing through attrition; early retirement buyout programs; reduced hours through job sharing, part-time work, work sharing, or reduced workweeks; and termination of employment.

5. Strategies to manage a human resources shortage include hiring temporary employees, subcontracting work, employee transfers and promotions, and flexible work arrangements to increase work/life balance.

Test yourself on material for this chapter at
www.pearsoned.ca/myhrlab

Key | TERMS

attrition   *(p. 133)*
compressed workweek   *(p. 138)*
Delphi technique   *(p. 126)*
early retirement buyout programs   *(p. 134)*
flextime   *(p. 137)*
flexyear   *(p. 138)*
hiring freeze   *(p. 133)*
human resources planning (HRP)   *(p. 118)*
job sharing   *(p. 134)*
layoff   *(p. 134)*
management inventories   *(p. 129)*
Markov analysis   *(p. 128)*
nominal group technique   *(p. 125)*
promotion   *(p. 135)*
ratio analysis   *(p. 124)*
reduced workweek   *(p. 134)*

regression analysis   *(p. 125)*
replacement charts   *(p. 129)*
replacement summaries   *(p. 129)*
scatter plot   *(p. 124)*
severance package   *(p. 134)*
skills inventories   *(p. 129)*
staffing table   *(p. 127)*
succession planning   *(p. 129)*
supplemental unemployment benefits (SUBs)   *(p. 134)*
survivor sickness   *(p. 135)*
termination   *(p. 134)*
transfer   *(p. 135)*
trend analysis   *(p. 123)*
work sharing   *(p. 134)*

Review and Discussion | QUESTIONS

1. Describe the costs associated with a lack of or inadequate HRP.

2. After analyzing the human resources implications of the organization's strategic plans, what are the three subsequent processes involved in HRP?

3. Discuss the pros and cons of five of the approaches to dealing with a labour surplus from both the organization and employee perspectives.

4. Differentiate between replacement charts and replacement summaries, and explain why replacement summaries are generally preferred.

5. Discuss various methods of easing the burden of a layoff or termination.

6. Differentiate between the seniority and merit-based approaches to promotion and describe the advantages and disadvantages associated with each.

7. Describe several flexible work arrangements that can help employers retain employees.

Critical Thinking | QUESTIONS

1. A number of quantitative and qualitative techniques for forecasting human resources demand were discussed in this chapter. Working in groups, identify which strategies would be most appropriate for (a) small versus large companies, (b) industries undergoing rapid change, and

(c) businesses/industries in which there are seasonal variations in HR requirements.

2. Suppose that it has just been projected that, because of a number of technological innovations, your firm will need 20 percent fewer clerical employees within the next five years. What actions would you take to try to retain your high-performing clerical staff members?

3. Suppose that you are the HR manager at a firm at which a hiring freeze has just been declared. The plan is to downsize through attrition. What steps would you take to ensure that you reap the advantages of this strategy while minimizing the disadvantages?

4. Work/life balance is important for both older workers and the younger generations in the workforce. What are some of the operational issues that need to be managed in implementing widespread flexible work arrangements?

5. Assume that you are a hospital administrator and must plan to replace retiring nurses who make up 25 percent of your staff. Using the information provided in the text about the projected shortfall starting in 2011, describe some options you might want to consider to ensure that you have enough nurses.

6. Using the Entrepreneurs and HR box on page 000 as an example of a good response to a challenging staffing environment, brainstorm a list of actions the following types of industries/businesses could take to attract and retain employees:
   - international structural engineering firm
   - midwives cooperative in Nunavut
   - large bank expanding into developing countries
   - cleaning service company specializing in medical facilities such as small hospitals and clinics

Experiential | EXERCISES

1. Develop a realistic, hypothetical staffing table for a department or organization with which you are familiar.

2. Contact the HR manager at a firm in your area and find out whether the firm uses any of the following: (a) skills/management inventories, (b) replacement charts or summaries, and (c) a succession plan. Prepare a brief summary of the information gathered. Once you have completed these tasks, form a group with several of your classmates. Share your findings with the group members. Were there similarities across firms? Did company size seem to make a difference in terms of strategies used for forecasting the supply of internal candidates? Can you identify any other factors that seem to play a role in the choice of forecasting techniques used?

3. This assignment requires working within teams of five or six. Half of each team is to assume the role of management at a firm that is about to undergo major downsizing. The other half of each team is to assume the roles of employees—some of whom will be affected and others of whom will remain. Each management team is paired with an employee team and must prepare and roleplay a realistic meeting of the two parties. Managers should work toward minimizing the negative impact on those who will be affected, as well as on those who will remain. Individuals in employee roles are asked to envision what their thoughts and feelings would be (if they have never actually been in this situation, that is) and to portray them as realistically as possible.

4. Form teams of three or four people. Your professor will assign you your position on the following statement: "All employees in an organization should be aware of their personal standing with respect to replacement charts and succession planning." Formulate your arguments to support your assigned position and then debate the statement with another team as instructed.

5. With a partner, research "survivor sickness" and what specific companies have done to successfully mitigate this response and regain full employee commitment. Prepare a brief (two to three minutes maximum) oral presentation to share what you have learned.

Running | CASE

Running Case: LearnInMotion.com

To Plan or Not to Plan?

One aspect of HRM that Jennifer and Pierre studied at university was HR planning. Their professor emphasized its importance, especially for large organizations. Although LearnInMotion.com was certainly small at this point, with only a few employees, they were planning to expand, and it seemed that detailed HRP should be an essential part of their plans. There is no succession plan—after all, they have just started the business! But they both knew that the market for technology workers, in general, was competitive. Jennifer and Pierre have asked for some assistance with the following questions.

QUESTIONS

1 What is Human Resources Planning and how will it help LearnInMotion's strategic plans?

2 Describe the steps in the Human Resources Planning process and discuss the important elements within each that will benefit LearnInMotion.

Case | INCIDENT

How to Expand Successfully While Utilizing HRP Fundamentals

A successful franchise owner of a prestigious sporting goods chain is looking to expand into the province of Alberta. Typically each store needs the following positions staffed for optimum profitability and success: a store manager, an assistant manager, 5 department managers, and 20 customer service representatives.

The owner wants each store to be fully operational within six months. Currently, all stores are on schedule to be built by this deadline. The owner needs your assistance to decide where to locate the new stores and to implement necessary human resource planning initiatives to source the talent to staff the positions within the new stores. Please help the owner by answering the following questions.

QUESTIONS

1 Discuss the importance of environmental scanning and how it will benefit this franchise owner in choosing where to locate the stores in Alberta.

2 What qualitative and quantitative approaches should be used to source talent for each store?

For additional cases and exercise material, go to
www.pearsoned.ca/myhrlab

CHAPTER 6

RECRUITMENT

LEARNING OUTCOMES

AFTER STUDYING THIS CHAPTER, YOU SHOULD BE ABLE TO

DEFINE recruitment, and discuss the increasing use of employer branding.

EXPLAIN the recruitment process.

ANALYZE the role of job posting, human resources records, and skills inventories in recruiting from within.

IDENTIFY at least 10 methods used for external recruitment.

EXPLAIN two strategies used to recruit non-permanent staff.

DISCUSS strategies for recruiting a more diverse workforce.

EXPLAIN the importance of application forms.

REQUIRED PROFESSIONAL CAPABILITIES (RPC)

- Develops, implements and monitors processes for attracting qualified candidates
- Evaluates recruiting effectiveness
- Identifies the potential sources of internal and external qualified candidates.
- Evaluates the relevance of alternatives to recruitment (developing, outsourcing, contingent workers, agencies etc.)

THE STRATEGIC IMPORTANCE OF RECRUITMENT

recruitment The process of searching out and attracting qualified job applicants, which begins with the identification of a position that requires staffing and is completed when résumés and/or completed application forms are received from an adequate number of applicants.

Human talent is beginning to be referred to as the world's most sought-after commodity.[1] The quality of an organization's human resources begins with a strategic perspective in the management of recruitment. **Recruitment** is the process of searching out and attracting qualified job applicants. It begins with the identification of a position that requires staffing and is completed when résumés and/or completed application forms are received from an adequate number of applicants. A Watson Wyatt study found that organizations with superior recruiting practices financially outperform those with less effective programs and that successful recruiting is a strong indicator of higher shareholder value.[2]

recruiter A specialist in recruitment, whose job it is to find and attract capable candidates.

Authority for recruitment is generally delegated to HR staff members, except in small businesses, where line managers usually recruit their own staff. In large organizations where recruiting is done on a continual basis, the HR team typically includes specialists, known as **recruiters**, whose job it is to find and attract qualified applicants. Recruiters are becoming increasingly critical to achieving an organization's strategic objectives as competition for the employees necessary for strategy implementation increases due to the growing talent shortage.

Recruiters Café
www.recruiterscafe.com
Great Place to Work
Institute Canada
www.greatplacetowork.ca

Organizations are increasingly seeking the high profile given to an "employer of choice," such as those included in lists such as Mediacorp's "Top 100 Employers," the Hewitt Associates "50 Best Employers" and the Financial Post's "Ten Best Companies to Work For." Employers such as Scotiabank, Purolator Courier, Tim Hortons and many others are also applying the marketing concept of branding to strengthen their recruitment activities.[3]

Employer Branding

Gabriel Bouchard, founder of the Monster Canada online job board says, "In an increasingly tight job market, employers must remain permanently visible to potential employees, establishing and maintaining relationships with potential candidates before they even begin pursuing a new job. This is particularly crucial when it comes to hard-to-fill or mission-critical positions."[4] Proactive employers are trying to obtain a competitive advantage in recruitment by establishing themselves as employers of choice through employer branding. The purpose of an employer brand is to attract people to apply to work at the organization, and to earn the loyalty of current employees.

employer branding The image or impression of an organization as an employer based on the benefits of being employed by the organization.

Employer branding is the image or impression of an organization as an employer based on the perceived benefits of being employed by the organization. It is the experience of an employee when working for a company, based on feelings, emotions, senses, realities, and benefits (functional benefits such as personal development; economic benefits such as monetary rewards; and psychological benefits such as feelings of purpose, belonging, and recognition). It is essentially a promise made to employees and their perception of how well that promise is delivered.[5]

Employer branding is particularly important during the recruitment process, not just for applicants who are eventually hired but also for those not hired who are out in the marketplace communicating their experience as an applicant to other job-seekers.[6] Inconsiderate recruiting practices can be brand suicide for companies. Branding includes the experiences a candidate goes through while interacting with a company throughout the recruitment process, including:[7]

- what candidates experience when they go to the company's website,
- whether HR sends an acknowledgement letter or email thanking each candidate who sends in a résumé,
- how candidates are greeted by the receptionist when they make initial contact by phone or in person, and
- whether the HR person who interviews candidates is a good spokesperson who can articulate the organization's values and culture.

Employer branding involves three steps.[8] Step 1 is to define the target audience, where to find them, and what they want from an employer. The target group may be one of the four generations in today's workforce, the underemployed, or the four employment equity groups. McDonald's may target potential Generation Y employees who are seeking career development. At Southland Transportation, a school bus service provider in Alberta, the target audience is retired police officers, recent retirees, and parents with young children.[9]

Step 2 is to develop the employee value proposition—the specific reasons why the organization is a unique place to work and a more attractive employer for the target audience compared to other organizations. The use of concrete facts, programs, policies, survey results, and information will clearly portray the organization as an employer of choice. It is also very important to ensure that current managers are prepared to deliver the value proposition by guiding and mentoring employees.[10] Loblaws and Fairmont Hotels offer potential employees the opportunity to participate in "green" environmental initiatives.[11] At PCL Construction of Alberta, 80 percent of employees own stock in the company.[12]

Step 3 is to communicate the brand by incorporating the value proposition into all recruitment efforts. The communication should reinforce and remind current and potential employees of promises in the employee value proposition and of the organization's ability to deliver it through their managers. An integrated marketing approach to internal and external communication should use various channels such as television, radio, print, websites, and so on.[13]

McDonald's has young people as its target market; the company used focus groups to find that their interests are themselves and making money; it offers flexible hours, uniform choices, scholarships, and discount cards to support its value proposition slogan "we take care of our employees"; and it communicated this proposition through television ads and a recruiting website. Following the introduction of this branding initiative, McDonald's saw a surge in the number of young people who recognized McDonald's as a great place to work.[14] With the right branding strategy, job seekers line up to apply for jobs. A successful brand results in job seekers saying "I'd like to work there."[15]

McDonald's Recruiting
www.worksforme.ca

THE RECRUITMENT PROCESS

As illustrated in **Figure 6.1**, the recruitment process has a number of steps:

RPC

Develops, implements and monitors processes for attracting qualified candidates

1. Job openings are identified through HR planning (based on the organization's strategic plan) or manager request. HR plans play a vital role in the identification process, because they indicate present and future openings and specify which should be filled internally and which externally. Openings do

FIGURE 6.1 | An Overview of the Recruitment Process

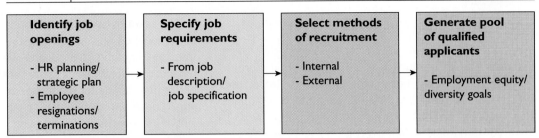

Identify job openings	Specify job requirements	Select methods of recruitment	Generate pool of qualified applicants
- HR planning/ strategic plan - Employee resignations/ terminations	- From job description/ job specification	- Internal - External	- Employment equity/ diversity goals

arise unexpectedly, however, in which case managers request that a new employee be hired.

2. The job requirements are determined. This step involves reviewing the job description and the job specification and updating them, if necessary. Manager comments may also prove helpful in identifying requirements.

3. Appropriate recruiting source(s) and method(s) are chosen. The major decision here is whether to start with internal or external recruiting. There is no single, best recruiting technique, and the most appropriate for any given position depends on a number of factors, which will be discussed in the next section.

4. A pool of qualified recruits is generated. The requirements of employment equity legislation (if any) and the organization's diversity goals should be reflected in the applicant pool.

A recruiter must be aware of constraints affecting the recruitment process in order to be successful in his or her job. Constraints arise from organizational policies, such as promote-from-within policies, which means that a recruiter cannot start recruiting externally for a specified period, even if he or she is aware that there are no suitable internal candidates. Constraints also arise from compensation policies, since they influence the attractiveness of the job to potential applicants. If there is an employment equity plan, it will specify goals for increasing recruitment from the designated groups. Monetary and nonmonetary inducements offered by competitors impose a constraint, since recruiters must try to meet the prevailing standards or use alternative inducements.

Perhaps the biggest constraint on recruiting activity at this time is the current labour shortage, which makes recruiting more difficult. One survey by Hewitt Associates found that recruitment practices will have to undergo "enormous change" over the next several years.[16] Some initiatives are already underway to attract foreign recruits, as explained in the **Global HRM** box.

RECRUITING WITHIN THE ORGANIZATION

Although recruiting often brings job boards and employment agencies to mind, current employees are generally the largest source of recruits. Filling open positions with inside candidates has several advantages. Firstly, employees see that competence is rewarded, thus enhancing their commitment, morale, and performance. Having already been with the firm for some time, insiders may be more committed to the company's goals and less likely to leave, and managers are provided with a longer-term perspective when making business decisions. It is generally safer to promote from within, because the firm is likely to have a more accurate assessment of the person's skills and performance level than would otherwise be the case. Finally, inside candidates require less orientation than outsiders do.

Global HRM

Recruiting European Candidates

An often overlooked option for managing the talent shortage is to recruit more candidates from Europe. Canada has strong ties to the European Union, and Europeans have a lot to offer the Canadian marketplace including global business perspectives.

"An important value-added Europeans can bring to the Canadian market is their ability to interact and negotiate within a multicultural environment and context. This aptitude strengthens Canadian companies' ability to function better in Canada's increasingly multicultural environment," says David Delfini, head of business development at Volareweb/Alitalia.

For Europeans, Canada offers an opportunity for advancement they might not get at home. In Italy, for example, it is almost impossible to move up the ranks if you haven't dedicated at least 20 years to the company. A 2007 study by Blusteps.com polled over 933 senior executives worldwide and revealed that traditional values about job tenure and loyalty remain well-ingrained with executives. The research also highlighted that 76 percent of European executives cited a lack of career advancement opportunities as the number one motivator to leave a company.

The borders have changed with the crisis of retiring baby boomers and impending talent shortages. Countries are opening their doors. The world is building broader intellectual capacity and perspectives and better preparation for the global market. Europeans can offer Canadian organizations needed experience and a global perspective in a tightening labour market.

One company pursuing this strategy is EBA Engineering Consultants of Edmonton. They have successfully recruited people in the UK to relocate to Western Canada by using a high-tech/high-touch promotional tool that communicates EBA's employment brand in a powerful way. A leather-bound album features stunning photographs of Western Canada, testimonials from EBA employees who had been previously recruited from overseas, and a USB key that links candidates to a comprehensive website. At the back of the album, a leather luggage tag is mounted as a call-to-action, inviting candidates to pack their bags and join the EBNA family in Canada.

Source: Adapted from A. Mirza, "Recruiting International Candidates," *HR Professional* (December 2008/January 2009), p. 27; and from K. Peters, "Public Image Ltd.," *HR Professional* (December 2007/January 2008), pp. 24–30. Reprinted with permission of *HR Professional*.

Recruiting from within also has a number of drawbacks, however. Employees who apply for jobs and don't get them may become discontented (informing unsuccessful applicants as to why they were rejected and what remedial action they might take to be more successful in the future is thus essential.)[17] Managers may be required to post all job openings and interview all inside candidates, even when they already know whom they want to hire, thus wasting considerable time and creating false hope on the part of those employees not genuinely being considered. Employees may be less satisfied with and accepting of a boss appointed from within their own ranks than they would a newcomer; it is sometimes difficult for a newly chosen leader to adjust to no longer being "one of the gang."[18] There is also a possibility of "inbreeding." When an entire management team has been brought up through the ranks, they may have a tendency to make decisions "by the book" and to maintain the status quo, when a new and innovative direction is needed.

Recruiting from within can be accomplished by using job posting, human resources records, and skills inventories.

Job Posting

job posting The process of notifying current employees about vacant positions.

Job posting is a process of notifying current employees about vacant positions. Most companies now use computerized job-posting systems, where information about job vacancies can be found on the company's intranet. This involves a notice outlining the job title, duties (as listed in the job description), qualifications (taken from the job specification), hours of work, pay range, posting date, and closing date, as shown in **Figure 6.2**. Not all

FIGURE 6.2 | Sample Job Posting

Director, Office of Sustainability
Facilities and Operations—F&O Sustainability Office
Competition No.—**A10398404**
Closing Date—**May 20, 2009**

Come join one of Canada's Top 30 Greenest Employers. The Offices of the Vice President (Facilities & Operations) and the Vice President (Academic) invite applications for the position of Director, Office of Sustainability.

The role of the new Office of Sustainability is to inspire campus-wide initiatives around sustainability within the context of the University's adopted *Sustainability Commitment and Guiding Principles*. Initiatives will focus on global and local challenges including energy, climate, water, health, ecology, and social transformation—all related to the integrity of living systems. The Office will nurture open and frank conversations on campus in a welcoming and safe environment that can advance our understanding of responsible global citizenship. Stakeholders will look to the Office to establish the University of Alberta as a model of sustainability and a centre for sustainability education globally. See http://www.sustainability.ualberta.ca/ to learn more about the 30-year history in the area of sustainable operations in Facilities and Operations, and the many research and learning activities at the University. See http://www.canadastop100.com/environmental/ to learn why we are one of Canada's Greenest Employers.

Reporting to the Associate Vice-President, Facilities and Operations, the Director will act as a catalyst, working with support from the Academic Coordinator, to facilitate the mission of the Office by providing a clearinghouse for courses, events, research projects, funding sources, and collaborations. The Director will seek funding opportunities and leverage programs and opportunities from operations within Facilities and Operations. The Director will also create capacity within the Office of Sustainability to deliver the mandate of the broader institution, with the support of the Office of the Technical Director of Sustainability and numerous support positions.

The responsibilities of the Director of the Office of Sustainability include:
- Positioning the University of Alberta as a recognized national and international leader in the field of sustainability and higher education at the provincial, regional, national and international levels
- Providing strategic leadership to place the office on strong financial and operating principles
- Supporting "Discovery Learning" through collaborative problem-solving exercises on campus and by enabling service learning and student projects around the question of sustainability
- Identifying and working through the Academic Coordinator to facilitate the development of applied learning and research opportunities for staff, faculty, alumni, students, and the broader community—sensitive to individual disciplinary and cultural differences that exist on and off campus

The successful candidate will have:
- A Bachelor or graduate degree in environmental studies, or a related degree in management or science, with a broad environmental, biological, or ecological focus
- Seven years of progressive management experience that includes implementing environmental or sustainability programs
- Leadership experience in environmental initiatives, resource management and teaching/presenting information and advancing knowledge
- Experience with the development of business plans, business cases and fund development
- Strong communication skills including the writing of reports and public speaking on topics of local and global importance ranging from metrics and triple bottom line returns

This full-time regular continuing Administrative Professional Officer (APO) position offers a comprehensive benefits package and annual salary range of $64,011 to $101,349.

Please submit a cover letter, resume and the names of three references to the attention of the Human Resources Manager (Facilities & Operations). Consideration of applications will begin May 20, 2009; however, the competition will remain open until filled.

We thank all applicants; however, only those selected for an interview will be contacted.

How to Apply
Apply Online
Note: Online applications are accepted until midnight Mountain Standard Time of the closing date.
Online
http://www.careers.ualberta.ca/apply.aspx?id=A10398404
Email
recruit@ualberta.ca
The University of Alberta hires on the basis of merit. We are committed to the principle of equity in employment. We welcome diversity and encourage applications from all qualified women and men, including persons with disabilities, members of visible minorities, and Aboriginal persons.

Source: Reprinted by permission of Recruitment Services, Human Resources, University of Alberta.

FIGURE 6.3 | Advantages and Disadvantages of Job Posting

Advantages

- Provides every qualified employee with a chance for a transfer or promotion.
- Reduces the likelihood of special deals and favouritism.
- Demonstrates the organization's commitment to career growth and development.
- Communicates to employees the organization's policies and guidelines regarding promotions and transfers.
- Provides equal opportunity to all qualified employees.

Disadvantages

- Unsuccessful job candidates may become demotivated, demoralized, discontented, and unhappy if feedback is not communicated in a timely and sensitive manner.
- Tensions may rise if it appears that a qualified internal candidate was passed over for an equally qualified or less qualified external candidate.
- The decision about which candidate to select may be more difficult if there are two or more equally qualified candidates.

firms use intranets. Some post jobs on bulletin boards or in employee publications. As illustrated in **Figure 6.3**, there are advantages and disadvantages to using job postings to facilitate the transfer and promotion of qualified internal candidates.

An Ethical | Dilemma

Suppose a manager has already made up his or her mind about who will be selected for an internal position. But an internal job posting and subsequent interviews have shown another equally qualified candidate. Who should be offered the position?

Human Resources Records

Human resources records are often consulted to ensure that qualified individuals are notified, in person, of vacant positions. An examination of employee files, including résumés and application forms, may uncover employees who are working in jobs below their education or skill levels, people who already have the requisite KSAs, or persons with the potential to move into the vacant position if given some additional training.

Skills Inventories

Skills inventories are an even better reference tool. Although such inventories may be used instead of job postings, they are more often used as a supplement. Whether computerized or manual, referring to such inventories ensures that qualified internal candidates are identified and considered for transfer or promotion when opportunities arise.

Limitations of Recruiting from Within

It is rarely possible to fill all non-entry-level jobs with current employees. Middle- and upper-level jobs may be vacated unexpectedly, with no internal replacements yet qualified or ready for transfer or promotion; or the jobs may require such specialized training and experience that there are no potential internal replacements. Even in firms with a policy of promoting from within, potential external candidates are increasingly being considered in order to meet strategic objectives. Hiring someone from outside may be preferable in order to acquire the latest knowledge and expertise or gain new ideas and revitalize the department or organization.[19]

RECRUITING OUTSIDE THE ORGANIZATION

RPC

Identifies the potential sources of internal and external qualified candidates

Unless there is a workforce reduction, even in firms with a promote-from-within policy, a replacement from outside must eventually be found to fill the job left vacant once all eligible employees have been given the opportunity for transfer and/or promotion. In addition, most entry-level positions must be filled by external candidates. The advantages of external recruitment include:

- the generation of a larger pool of qualified candidates, which may have a positive impact on the quality of the selection decision
- the availability of a more diverse applicant pool, which can assist in meeting employment equity goals and timetables
- the acquisition of skills or knowledge not currently available within the organization and/or new ideas and creative problem-solving techniques
- the elimination of rivalry and competition caused by employees jockeying for transfers and promotions, which can hinder interpersonal and interdepartmental cooperation
- the potential cost savings resulting from hiring individuals who already have the skills, rather than providing extensive training.

Planning External Recruitment

When choosing external recruitment method(s), in addition to the constraints mentioned earlier several factors should be considered. The type of job to be filled has a major impact on the recruitment method selected. For example, most firms normally rely on professional search firms for recruiting executive-level employees. In contrast, internet advertising is commonly used for recruiting other salaried employees.

yield ratio The percentage of applicants that proceed to the next stage of the selection process.

Yield ratios help to indicate which recruitment methods are the most effective at producing qualified job candidates. A **yield ratio** is the percentage of applicants that proceed to the next stage of the selection process. A recruiting yield pyramid, such as that shown in **Figure 6.4**, can be devised for each method by calculating the yield ratio for each step in the selection process.

FIGURE 6.4 | Recruiting Yield Pyramid

The firm in this example typically hires 50 entry-level accountants each year. The firm has calculated that using this method leads to a ratio of offers made to actual new hires of two to one (about half of the candidates to whom offers are made accept). The firm also knows that the ratio of candidates interviewed to offers made is three to two, while the ratio of candidates invited for interviews to candidates actually interviewed is generally four to three. Finally, the firm knows that the ratio between leads generated and candidates selected for interviews is six to one. In other words, of six leads generated through college/university recruiting efforts, one applicant is invited to attend an interview. Given these ratios, the firm knows that, using this particular recruitment method, 1200 leads must be generated in order to hire 50 new accountants.

RPC

Evaluates effectiveness of recruitment process

The average number of days from when the company initiates a recruitment method to when the successful candidate begins to work is called time-lapse data. Assume that the accounting company in the above example found the following scenario: Six days elapsed between submission of application forms and résumés to invitation for an interview; five days then passed from invitation to actual interview; five days from interview to job offer; six days from job offer to acceptance; and 23 days from acceptance of job offer to commencement of work. These data indicate that, using on-campus recruiting, the firm must initiate recruitment efforts at least 45 days before the anticipated job opening date. Calculating time-lapse data for each recruitment method means that the amount of lead time available can be taken into account when deciding which strategy or strategies would be most appropriate.

External Recruitment Methods

Many methods of recruiting from the external labour market are in use, but online recruiting has quickly become the most popular for many jobs. Several of the most common external recruitment methods will now be reviewed.

Online Recruiting

The majority of companies now use online recruitment, and a majority of Canadian workers use the internet to research prospective employers, review job postings, complete online applications, and post their résumés. The internet provides recruiters with a large audience for job postings and a vast talent pool. Online recruiting can involve accessing one or more internet job boards, using a corporate website, or using social networking sites.

Recruiting Online
www.Jobster.com
Nicejob.ca
www.nicejob.ca
Canadajobs.com
www.canadajobs.com
Canjobs.com
www.canjobs.com
Monster Board Canada
www.monster.ca
Workopolis.com
www.workopolis.com
HotJobs.com
www.hotjobs.com
CareerBuilder
www.careerbuilder.ca

Internet Job Boards Online job boards are fast, easy, and convenient and allow recruiters to search for candidates for positions in two ways. First, for a fee, companies can post a job opening online and customize it by using corporate logos and adding details about the company benefits and culture. Job seekers can search through the job postings, often by job type, region, or other criterion, and apply for the position online through the job board. The popularity of internet job boards among job seekers is high because of the number of job postings available on one site.

Second, job seekers can post their résumés on job boards, and firms can search the database. Canada has hundreds of job boards, ranging from the two largest, Workopolis.com and Monster.ca, to many smaller job boards serving specific fields from tourism to medicine.[20] Job board meta-crawlers such as actualjobs.com enable job seekers to search multiple job boards with one query.

The advantages of job boards include candidate assistance with self-assessment and résumé writing and pre-screening assistance for recruiters. One problem with internet job boards is their vulnerability to privacy breaches. Fake job postings can lead to identity theft from submitted résumés, and résumés are sometimes copied onto competing job boards or other sites.[21] As a result, job boards are now providing tips for job seekers on maintaining privacy and confidentiality.[22]

Corporate Websites   With the overabundance of applicants now found on most online job boards, employers are now using their own corporate websites to recruit. Career pages provide a single platform for recruitment that promotes the employer brand, educates the applicant about the company, captures data about the applicant, and provides an important link to job boards where a company's positions may be advertised.[23] Virtual workplace tours using video can be provided to attract top talent aligned with the employer brand.[24] Corporate websites help the company create a pool of candidates who have already expressed interest in the organization.[25]

Using pre-screening strategies is essential, however. The volume of résumés definitely does not diminish when the firm accepts them online. At Hewlett Packard, for example, more than 1 million online applications are received each year.[26] One way of coping with this volume is to generate automatic replies acknowledging receipt of applications.[27] Applicant tracking software is available to help recruiters track individual candidates through the recruitment and selection processes and to enable candidates to keep their profiles up to date.

Active job seekers are not the only potential future employees who visit corporate websites. Customers, investors, and competitors also visit them.[28] Many of those visiting career websites are "happily employed" individuals (known as "passive" job seekers) who are likely to arrive at the career site after browsing the company's main pages for other reasons, such as research into products or services. Therefore, it is important that a firm have a prominently positioned link on the homepage leading directly to the careers section to make it easy for passive job seekers to pursue job opportunities within the company.[29]

Tips | FOR THE FRONT LINE

Best practices for career websites include the following:

- Include candid information about company culture, career paths, and business prospects
- Include third-party sources of information on your company, such as articles, rankings, and awards
- Design separate sections for different types of job seekers, such as students and part-timers
- Have a direct link from the homepage to the career page
- Have a job search tool that allows applicants to search open job positions by location and job category
- Have a standardized application or résumé builder to allow for easy applicant screening
- Use "e-mail to a friend" options for visitor referrals.[30]

An Ethical | Dilemma

Is it ethical to use personal information on social networking sites to assess job candidates?

Social Networking Sites

Many organizations are turning to social networking sites such as Facebook to find young, tech-savvy recruits. Some create virtual recruitment booths and others create a company profile where they can post jobs and publicize their employer brand. Other users seeking jobs can become "friends" of potential employers and upload their profiles, which contain more information than résumés. Ernst & Young is one firm that has used this approach—it has even established its own company social networking site for employees and alumni.[31]

The advantage of using social networking for recruitment purposes is the opportunity to connect with millions of other users at little or no cost. One disadvantage is the possibility of unhappy employees or customers posting negative comments on the site.[32]

Print Advertising

Despite the advent of online recruiting, traditional advertising in newspapers and other print media is still a very common method of recruiting.[33] For advertising to bring the desired results, two issues must be addressed: the media to be used and the construction of the ad.[34] The selection of the best medium— whether it is the local newspaper, a national newspaper, a technical journal, or even a billboard—depends on the types of positions for which the organization is recruiting. Reaching individuals who are already employed and not actively seeking alternative employment requires a different medium than is appropriate to attract those who are unemployed.

To achieve optimum results from an advertisement, the following four-point guide, called AIDA, should be kept in mind as the ad is being constructed:

1. The ad should attract attention. The ads that stand out have borders, a company logo or picture, and effective use of empty white space. To attract attention, key positions should be advertised in display ads, rather than classified ads.
2. The ad should develop interest in the job. Interest can be created by the nature of the job itself, by pointing out the range of duties and/or the amount of challenge or responsibility involved. Sometimes other aspects of the job, such as its location or working conditions, are useful in attracting interest. To ensure that the individuals attracted are qualified, the job specifications should always be included.
3. The ad should create a desire for the job. This may be done by capitalizing on the interesting aspects of the job itself and by pointing out any unique benefits or opportunities associated with it, such as the opportunity for career development or travel. Desire may also be created by stressing the employer's commitment to employment equity. The target audience should be kept in mind as the ad is being created.
4. The ad should instigate action. To prompt action, ads often include a closing date and a statement such as "Call today," "Send your résumé today," "Check out our website for more information," or "Go to the site of our next job fair."

When properly constructed, advertisements can be an effective instrument for recruiting, as well as for communicating the organization's corporate image

FIGURE 6.5 | Recruitment Advertisement Illustrating AIDA Principles

We offer stimulating jobs in an exciting work environment.

Anapharm is an international organization specialized in clinical research on innovative and generic drugs. The company offers advanced services for marketing new drugs around the world.

Become one of our close to 800 employees who have chosen to:

- Join dynamic work teams with multidisciplinary expertises
- Increase your professional experience
- Become involved in continuous improvement projects/innovative research projects

- Evolve in a work environment that offers personal and professional challenges as well as **very competitive salaries and benefits**
- Participate in recognized training activities
- Work with state-of-the-art equipment.

Anapharm is opening a new clinic in Toronto...

- Training coordinator (screening coordinator)
- Clinical technical support coordinator (operational supervisor)
- Clinical project coordinator (study coordinator)
- Clinical ambulatory coordinator (scrennig coordinator)

- Medication coordinator
- Registered pratical nurses (RPN)
- Maintenance Technician
- Registered nurse

Other position available...

Be part of our team!

We offer employment opportunities in Québec, Montréal, Trois-Rivières and Toronto.
For more details, visit our Web site.
www.anapharm.com/career
We subscribe to the principle of equality in employment.

anapharm

Source: Reprinted with permission of Anapharm.

RecruitAd
www.recruitad.com

want ad A recruitment ad describing the job and its specifications, the compensation package, and the hiring employer. The address to which applications and/or résumés should be submitted is also provided.

blind ad A recruitment ad in which the identity and address of the employer are omitted.

to the general public. A newspaper ad incorporating the AIDA principles is shown in **Figure 6.5**.

There are two general types of newspaper advertisements: want ads and blind ads. **Want ads** describe the job and its specifications, the compensation package, and the hiring employer. Although the content pertaining to the job, specifications, and compensation is identical in **blind ads**, such ads omit the identity and address of the hiring employer. Although many job seekers do not like responding to blind ads because there is always the danger of unknowingly sending a résumé to the firm at which they are currently employed, such ads do result in the opening remaining confidential (which may be necessary if the position is still staffed).

Many factors make advertising a useful recruiting method. Employers can use advertisements to reach and attract potential job applicants from a diverse labour market in as wide or narrow a geographical area as desired. To meet employment equity goals and timetables, ads can be placed in publications read by designated group members, such as a minority-language newspaper or the newsletter of a non-profit agency assisting individuals who have a particular mental or physical disability.

Private Employment Agencies

Private employment agencies are often called on to provide assistance to employers seeking clerical staff, functional specialists, and technical employees. The "staffing" business has grown into a $6 billion industry that places hundreds of thousands of job seekers each year.[35] Generally, it is the employer who pays the agency fee. It is not uncommon for employers to be charged a fee equal to 15 to 30 percent of the first year's salary of the individual hired through agency referral. This percentage may vary depending on the volume of business provided by the client and the type of employee sought.

These agencies take an employer's request for recruits and then solicit job seekers, relying primarily on internet job boards, advertising, and walk-ins/write-ins. Employment agencies serve two basic functions: (1) expanding the applicant pool and (2) performing preliminary interviewing and screening. Specific situations in which an employment agency might be used for recruiting include the following:

- The organization does not have an HR department or does not have anyone with the requisite time and/or expertise.
- The firm has experienced difficulty in generating a pool of qualified candidates for the position or a similar type of position in the past.
- A particular opening must be filled quickly.
- There is a desire to recruit a greater number of designated group members than the firm has been able to attract on its own.
- The recruitment effort is aimed at reaching individuals who are currently employed and might therefore feel more comfortable answering ads placed by and dealing with an employment agency.

Tips | FOR THE FRONT LINE

It should be noted, however, that the amount of service provided varies widely, as does the level of professionalism and the calibre of staff. Although most agencies carefully screen applicants, some simply provide a stream of applicants and let the client's HR department staff do the screening. Agency staff is usually paid on a commission basis, and their desire to earn a commission may occasionally compromise their professionalism (for example, encouraging job seekers to accept jobs for which they are neither qualified nor suited).

Executive Search Firms

Employers retain executive search firms to fill critical positions in a firm, usually middle- to senior-level professional and managerial employees. Such firms often specialize in a particular type of talent, such as executives, sales, scientific, or middle-management employees. They typically know and understand the marketplace, have many contacts, and are especially adept at contacting qualified candidates who are employed and not actively looking to change jobs (which is why they have been given the nickname "headhunters"). Generally, one-third of the fee is payable as a retainer at the outset. Compared with the value of the time savings realized by the client firm's executive team, however, such a fee often turns out to be insignificant.

Association of Canadian Search, Employment, and Staffing Services (ACSESS)
www.acsess.org

Using this recruitment method has some potential pitfalls.[36] Executive search firms cannot do an effective job if they are given inaccurate or incomplete information about the job and/or the firm. It is therefore essential for employers to explain in detail the type of candidate required—and why. A few headhunters are more salespeople than professionals, and they are more interested in persuading the employer to hire a candidate than in finding one who really meets the job specifications. Some firms have also been known to present an unpromising candidate to a client simply to make their one or two other prospects look that much better. The Association of Canadian Search, Employment, and Staffing Services (ACSESS) sponsors the Certified Personnel Consultant (CPC) designation, which signifies that recruiters have met specific educational and

testing requirements and confirms an individual's commitment to the best industry practices.[37]

Walk-Ins and Write-Ins

Individuals who go to organizations in person to apply for jobs without referral
or invitation are called walk-ins. People who submit unsolicited résumés to
organizations are known as write-ins. Walk-ins and write-ins are an inexpensive
recruitment method. Their résumés are generally screened by the HR department and if an applicant is considered suitable, his or her résumé is retained on
file for three to six months or passed on to the relevant department manager if
there is an immediate or upcoming opening for which the applicant is qualified.
Some organizations, such as RBC Financial Group, are using computer databases to store the information found on the résumés and application forms of
walk-in and write-in candidates. Whether the original document is paper-based
or submitted online, it can be scanned and stored on databases for fast, easy
access using a few key words.[38]

Employee Referrals

Some organizations encourage applications from friends and relatives of current
employees by mounting an employee referral campaign. Openings are announced in the company's intranet or newsletter, along with a request for referrals. Cash awards or prizes may be offered for referrals that culminate in a new
hire. Because no advertising or agency fees are involved, paying bonuses still
represents a low recruiting cost.

nepotism A preference for hiring
relatives of current employees.

The disadvantages associated with employee referrals include the potential
for inbreeding and **nepotism** to cause morale problems and dissatisfaction
among employees whose referrals are not hired. Perhaps the biggest drawback,
however, is that this method may result in systemic discrimination.

Former Employees

In these times of talent shortage and diminishing employee loyalty, some organizations are making efforts to keep in touch with former employees who may
be interested in rejoining the organization in future. Organizations such as
Microsoft, Ernst & Young, and Procter & Gamble are establishing alumni
networks that offer benefits such as health care, job boards, and alumni parties.
About 25 percent of hires at the manager level and above at Microsoft are
returning employees, known as "boomerangs."[39]

Educational Institutions

Recruiting at educational institutions is extremely effective when candidates require formal training but need relatively little full-time work experience. High
schools can provide recruits for clerical and some blue-collar jobs. For example,
EnCana, an oil and gas company headquartered in Calgary, is facing an ongoing
shortage of skilled workers. It has started a program called "Oil and Gas
Production Field Operator Career Pathway," which offers high school students
an opportunity to earn credits while learning about field production work.
Beginning in grade 10, students in participating high schools can sign up for a
distance-learning course supplied by Calgary-based Southern Alberta Institute
of Technology (SAIT). Students who progress through the course in all three

Many companies take recruitment campaigns into high schools to sell careers to a younger generation. This type of recruitment helps a variety of industries meet future recruitment demands. Here, students learn how to work on a car.

years will graduate with a production field operation certificate from SAIT. Students will have a chance of getting one of at least six paid internship positions with EnCana that last through eight weeks in the summer following each year.[40]

Most high schools, colleges, and universities have counselling centres that provide job-search assistance to students through such activities as skills assessment testing and workshops on résumé preparation and interview strategies. Sometimes they arrange for on-site job fairs, at which employers set up displays outlining the types of job opportunities available. The Halifax Career Fair, a partnership among Nova Scotia's universities and colleges, is the foremost recruiting event in Atlantic Canada. Every year, the event attracts about 100 companies from across the country and 1200 students.[41]

Co-operative (co-op) education and field placement programs have become increasingly popular in Canada. These programs require students to spend a specified time working in organizations as an integral part of their academic program, thereby gaining some hands-on skills in an actual work setting. Co-op programs are offered in some high schools, as well as in colleges and universities.

Summer internship programs hire college and/or university students to complete summer projects between their second-last and final year of study. Their performance is assessed, and those who are judged to be superior are offered permanent positions following graduation. Other firms offer internship opportunities to graduates, thereby enabling them to acquire hands-on skills to supplement their education. As with student internships, outstanding performers are often offered full-time employment at the end of the program. It is now possible for firms to recruit graduate interns online through Career Edge, an organization committed to helping university, college, and high-school graduates gain essential career-related experience through internships. Career Edge uses the internet as its sole means of bringing companies and youth together. More

Career Edge
www.careeredge.org
Job Postings (Student Job Magazine)
www.jobpostings.ca
Halifax Career Fairs
www.halifaxcareerfairs.com

than 8000 young Canadians have started their careers through the program in more than 1000 organizations. Within a few months of completing their internship, nearly 80 percent of interns have found permanent employment with competitive salaries, and nearly 60 percent of the interns are hired by host organizations on a full-time basis.[42]

Internship, co-op, and field placement programs can produce a win–win result. The employer is provided with an inexpensive opportunity to assess potential employees while benefiting from the current knowledge and enthusiasm of bright, talented individuals. Because co-op students and interns have been exposed to the organization, they are less likely to leave shortly after permanent hire than recruits with no previous exposure to the firm.[43] Recognizing these benefits has made such programs a major recruitment method in many organizations.

Human Resources and Skills Development Canada (HRSDC)

Job Bank
www.jobbank.gc.ca
Training and Careers
www.jobsetc.gc.ca

Through various programs, including those for youth, Aboriginals, and persons with disabilities, HRSDC helps unemployed individuals to find suitable jobs and helps employers to locate qualified candidates to meet their needs—at no cost to either party. The Job Bank is the largest web-based network of job postings available to Canadian employers free of charge, and it provides access to 700 000 new jobs each year, to more than 40 000 jobs at any given time, and up to 2 000 new jobs posted every day. HRSDC also operates Job Match, a web-based recruitment tool that can match employers' skill requirements with individuals' skill sets. Job seekers receive a list of employers with a matching job vacancy and employers receive a list of qualified candidates.[44]

Professional and Trade Associations

CA Source
www.casource.com
Hire Authority
www.hrpa.org

Professional and trade associations can be extremely helpful when recruiters are seeking individuals with specialized skills in such fields as IT, engineering, HR, and accounting, particularly if experience is a job requirement. Many such associations conduct ongoing placement activities on behalf of their members, and most regularly send their members newsletters or magazines in which organizations can place job advertisements. Such advertising may attract individuals who hadn't previously thought about changing jobs, as well as those actively seeking employment. For example, the Human Resources Professionals Association (HRPA) in Ontario has an employment service called the Hire Authority. For a nominal fee, employers can post HR-related employment opportunities on the HRPA website, where they can be viewed by HRPA members. Additionally, employers can pay for access to an online database of member résumés and can search, sort, and pre-screen qualified candidates for vacant positions.[45]

Labour Organizations

Some firms, particularly in the construction industry, obtain recruits through union hiring halls. The union maintains a roster of members (typically skilled trades people, such as carpenters, pipe fitters, welders, plumbers, and electricians), whom it sends out on assignment as requests from employers are received. Once the union members have completed their contracted work at one firm, they notify the union of their availability for another assignment.

Military Personnel

The Canadian Force Liaison Council (CFLC)
www.cflc.forces.gc.ca
Civiside.com
www.civiside.com

Military reservists are also potential recruits. The Canadian Forces Liaison Council (CFLC) is responsible for promoting the hiring of reservists by civilian employers. The CFLC also encourages civilian employers to give reservists time off for military training. Reserve force training develops skills and attributes sought after in the civilian workforce, such as leadership, planning, coordination, and teamwork.[46] Many organizations—such as Home Depot Canada and Énergie New Brunswick Power—have recognized the value of such leave and have joined the 4700 organizations in Canada that have signed a Statement of Support for the Reserve Forces with the CFLC.[47] The CFLC's Reserve Employment Assistance Program (REAP) allows employers to place job postings for skilled personnel at more than 300 military units across the country at no charge.[48]

Open Houses and Job Fairs

Another popular recruitment method involves holding an open house. Common in retail firms looking to staff a new store from the ground up, open houses have also been the choice of corporations trying to draw out scarce talent in an ultra-tight job market. A similar recruitment method involves holding a job fair on site. At such events, recruiters share information about the organization and job opportunities with those attending in an informal, relaxed setting. Some organizations are now holding job fairs online (known as virtual job fairs) in order to connect with a wider geographical audience. Top prospects are invited to visit the firm or to return at a later date for a more in-depth assessment.

Recruiting Non-Permanent Staff

In recent years, many companies have increased their use of contingent workers in order to attain labour flexibility and to acquire employees with special skills on an as-needed basis. In these firms, recruiters are spending more time seeking temporary (term, seasonal, casual) and contract workers and less time recruiting permanent staff.[49] Three sources of non-permanent staff are temporary help agencies, contract workers, and employee leasing.

Temporary Help Agencies

RPC

Evaluates the relevance of alternatives to recruitment (developing, outsourcing, contingent workers, agencies, etc.)

Temporary help agencies, such as Kelly Services and Office Overload, exist in major cities in Canada. They specialize in providing temporary workers to cover for employees who are ill, on vacation, or on a leave of absence. Firms also use temporary employees to handle seasonal work, peak workloads, and special projects for which no current employees have the time and/or expertise. Temporary workers are agency employees and are reassigned to another employer when their services are no longer required.

Temps provide employers with three major benefits:

1. They cost much less than permanent employees, as they generally receive less compensation than permanent staff. There are also savings related to the hiring and training costs associated with permanent employees. In fact, training has become the central investment in the business strategy of many temporary employment agencies. For example, Accountemps invests in the skills

The numbers of temporary and freelance workers are increasing all over the world. Alemi Takada is a noted Japanese freelance animator who manages her workload and does projects for companies all over the world through an Internet agency that represents about 15,000 freelancers in media and publishing.

and training of employees after they have worked for a specified amount of time. This training includes online tutoring in software they may use on the job and tuition reimbursement for skills training.[50]

2. If a temp performs unsatisfactorily, a substitute can be requested immediately. Generally, a suitable replacement is sent to the firm within one business day.

3. Individuals working as temps who are seeking full-time employment are often highly motivated, knowing that many firms choose full-time employees from the ranks of their top-performing temps.

Contract Workers

contract workers Employees who develop work relationships directly with the employer for a specific type of work or period of time.

Contract workers are employees who develop work relationships directly with the employer for a specific type of work or period of time.[51] For example, Parc Aviation is a major supplier of contract workers to the airline industry. Airline organizations benefit from the services of contract engineers by having them cover seasonal or unplanned peaks in business, carry out special tasks or projects, and reduce the necessity for airlines to downsize permanent staff during cyclical downturns.[52]

Many professionals with specialized skills become contract workers, including project managers, accountants, and lawyers. Some have consciously made a decision to work for themselves; others have been unable to obtain full-time employment in their field of expertise or have found themselves out of a full-time job because of cutbacks. Thus, some want to remain self-employed; others work a contract while hoping to obtain a full-time position eventually. Some firms hire former employees (such as retirees) on a contract basis.

An Ethical | Dilemma

Is it ethical to keep extending the contracts of contract workers rather than hiring them as permanent employees in order to avoid the cost of employee benefits?

RECRUITING A MORE DIVERSE WORKFORCE

Recruiting a diverse workforce is not just socially responsible—it's a necessity. As noted previously, the composition of Canada's workforce is changing dramatically. Trends of particular significance include the increasing necessity of hiring older employees, a decrease in the availability of young workers, and an increase in the number of women, visible minorities, Aboriginal people, and persons with disabilities in the workforce.

Attracting Older Workers

Prime50
www.prime50.com

Many employers, recognizing the fact that the workforce is aging, are encouraging retirement-age employees to stay with the company or are actively recruiting employees who are at or beyond retirement age. For example, 20 percent of Home Depot Canada's workforce is over age 50.[53] Hiring and retaining older employees has significant benefits. These workers typically have high job satisfaction, a strong sense of loyalty and organizational commitment, a strong work ethic, good people skills, and willingness to work in a variety of roles, including part time.[54]

To make a company attractive to older workers, it is important to deal with stereotypical attitudes toward older workers through education, ensure that HR policies do not discourage recruitment of older workers, develop flexible work arrangements, and redesign jobs to accommodate decreased dexterity and strength. Canadian employers have been encouraged to take action to retain and recruit older workers, as they represent a large, underutilized, skilled labour pool, but so far little effort has been made to attract these people.[55] A 2008 Conference Board of Canada study found that the most common recruitment strategy for older workers was rehiring former employees and retirees. Less than 20 percent were using recruitment campaigns directed specifically to mature workers.[56]

Attracting Younger Employees

Many firms are recognizing the benefits of a multigenerational workforce and not only are trying to attract older workers but also are taking steps to address the pending shortage of younger employees. Although older employees have comparatively wider experience and wisdom, the young bring energy, enthusiasm, and physical strength to their positions.

Successful organizations balance these different kinds of experience. McDonald's Restaurants of Canada Ltd. (one of the largest employers of youth in the country and an active recruiter of seniors) feels that it is critical for organizations in the service industry to have employees who mirror their customer base. Its experience is that each member of the multi-age teams brings a particular strength, which leads to synergy, respect, and team-building.[57]

Younger members of the workforce are part of the Generation X and Generation Y cohorts. To appeal to Generation Xers, it is important to stress that they will be able to work independently and that work/life balance is supported. Potential employees from Generation Y will want to know that they will be working with experts from across the organization and that they will have a variety of experiences, as described in the **Strategic HR** box. They will be attracted by

Strategic HR

Attracting the Younger Generation

The authors of the book Bridging the Generation Gap asked 500 Gen Ys this question: "What's important to you on the job?" The top three responses were quality of friendships, feeling they can make a contribution on the job, and a feeling of safety. These young workers want an organization where they can create friendships much as they did in school. In other words, the organization must have a social flair to catch their eye. Some examples include a company sports league and company social events like movie nights or meeting after work for a drink. But these quality relationships must go along with a feeling that what they do adds value to the organization.

The Gen Ys said that the top three ways to get their generation to join an organization are salary, casual work environment, and growth/development opportunities such as mentoring and training. Other benefits that organizations can offer to entice younger workers include state-of-the-art technology, opportunities to volunteer in the community (on company time), regular feedback, tuition reimbursement programs, strong reward and recognition programs, and a connection to the mission and vision of the organization.

The younger generation is going to take advantage of every ounce of technology to make their job search successful and easier. Organizations need to advertise jobs on multiple online job boards, including local, national, and trade-related. Organizations should also create a job board on the company's website that should be regularly updated and provide an easy and responsive way for candidates to apply online. The posting should include an email address for the HR department or an application process. For the process to succeed, organizations must regularly check the applications and follow-up with candidates.

The actual copy of the ads is critical. Certain key words attract these individuals to an organization's ads when they do online searches. The younger generation likes short, snappy copy that gets right to the point of what they will be doing. But of equal or more importance, the ad needs to advertise the culture of the organization as it relates to the values of this generation. The ads should include statements such as "fast-paced environment," "individual contribution," "work-life balance," "do it your way," "opportunity to grow," "no rules," and "state-of-the-art technology." Organizations should only list these kinds of features in the ads if they truly offer them. Otherwise, the organization will see just how fast these workers will leave a company that doesn't fulfill its promises.

Source: Adapted from R. Throckmorton and L. Gravett, "Attracting the younger generation," *Canadian HR Reporter*, April 23, 2007.

organizations that value social responsibility, diversity, and creativity.[58] Accounting firm Meyers Norris Penny built an award-winning student recruiting campaign around the question "What do you want?" that resulted in continuously improving quality of the students hired.[59]

Recruiting Designated Group Members

Aboriginal Human Resource Development Council of Canada
www.ahrdcc.com
Canadian Council for Rehabilitation and Work
www.ccrw.org
WORK*ink*
www.workink.com
Toronto Region Immigrant Employment Council
www.hireimmigrants.ca

Most of the recruitment methods discussed previously can be used to attract members of designated groups, provided that the employer's commitment to equity and diversity is made clear to all involved in the recruitment process—whether it is employees asked for referrals or private employment agencies. This can also be stressed in all recruitment advertising. Alternative publications targeted at designated group members should be considered for advertising, and linkages can be formed with organizations and agencies specializing in assisting designated group members. Specific examples follow:

The Aboriginal Human Resource Development Council of Canada, headquartered in Saskatoon, Saskatchewan, sponsors the Aboriginal Inclusion

After struggling to restart his career in Canada, Sibaway Issah found the assistance he needed with Career Edge, a non-profit agency that links qualified immigrants with possible employers.

Network (iN), which offers a job board, résumé database, and other tools to hire, retain, and promote Aboriginal talent. The iN is linked to 350 Aboriginal employment centres across Canada.[60]

WORKink is Canada's most powerful online career development and employment portal for Canadians with disabilities. The WORKink site offers a full complement of employment and recruitment resources and services for job seekers with disabilities and for employers looking to create an inclusive workplace. WORKink is sponsored by the Canadian Council on Rehabilitation and Work. Employers can post job openings free of charge, browse résumés of people with disabilities, or access information on how to adapt the work environment to accommodate people with disabilities in their region.[61]

The Society for Canadian Women in Science and Technology (SCWIST) is a non-profit, volunteer organization aimed at improving attitudes and stereotypes about and assisting women in scientific, technological, and engineering careers. Employers can access valuable information about resources, such as websites, employment agencies, and publications, to attract professional women for employment opportunities in industries where they generally have a low representation.[62]

The Ontario Ministry of Community and Social Services sponsors a program called Paths to Equal Opportunity intended to provide links to information on removing and preventing barriers so that people with disabilities can work, learn, and play to their fullest potential. In conjunction with the Canadian Abilities Foundation, the program publishes a resource booklet called Abilities @ Work, which provides specific information to employers who want to find out about recruiting, interviewing, hiring, and working with people with disabilities. It also provides information to employees and jobseekers with disabilities who want information on looking for work, on accommodation in the workplace, and on maintaining employment.

Another useful tool is the guidebook Tapping the Talents of People with Disabilities: A Guidebook for Employers, which is available through the Conference Board of Canada. More information on hiring people with disabilities is provided in the **Workforce Diversity** box.

Workforce DIVERSITY

The Disconnect in Recruiting People with Disabilities

The good news is that employers want to hire people with disabilities, and qualified candidates are available. But putting employers and jobseekers together needs improved coordination to create more success stories. Employers have bottom-line reasons for building workforce diversity. Inclusiveness is a competitive advantage that lets an organization better connect with a diverse community and customer base. Inclusiveness provides access to a larger pool of strong job candidates in a time of skills shortages and enhances an organization's reputation as an employer of choice.

So why aren't more employers tapping into the wealth of human potential in people with disabilities? After all, as a group they make up some 13 percent of the working-age population. That is precisely what the Canadian Abilities Foundation set out to determine in its recently completed Neglected or Hidden study, the findings of which may surprise employers.

Likely the most revealing finding that illustrates the need for a new employment strategy for people with disabilities is the disconnect that exists among employers, people with disabilities, and the service providers who help these individuals enter the workforce.

With few exceptions, these stakeholders just don't seem to know how to communicate with one another, if they are fortunate enough to find one another in the first place. The commitment and passion of workers with disabilities and those assisting them is sound. Meanwhile, hundreds and hundreds of disability-related organizations across Canada provide some level of employment support to these clients. The Neglected or Hidden study suggests that the number of Canadian employers willing to hire people with disabilities should be more than adequate to meet the availability of disabled jobseekers.

The good news is that a small number of disability organizations have made significant inroads in their regions by using employer partnerships. One example is the Dartmouth Work Activity Society in Nova Scotia, which started its new approach with just a single employer "partner," who was highly satisfied with the services provided. EmployAbilities, a full-time service agency serving Edmonton and northern Alberta for more than 30 years, has also launched a partnership-building strategy. A unique feature of the agency's approach is its partnership with the local chamber of commerce through which it offers advice on disability issues to employers.

Source: Adapted from A. Prost, "Successful Recruiting from an Untapped Source," *Canadian HR Reporter* (January 16, 2006), pp. 11–12.

DEVELOPING AND USING APPLICATION FORMS

For most employers, completion of an application form is the last step in the recruitment process. An application form provides an efficient means of collecting verifiable historical data from each candidate in a standardized format; it usually includes information about education, prior work history, and other job-related skills.

A completed application form can provide the recruiter with information on the applicant's education and experience, a brief overview of the applicant's career progress and growth, and information that can be used to predict whether or not the candidate will succeed on the job. Even when detailed résumés have been submitted, most firms also request that a standardized company application form be completed. There are many reasons for this practice:

- Candidate comparison is facilitated because information is collected in a uniform manner.
- The information that the company requires is specifically requested, rather than just what the candidate wants to reveal

- Candidates are typically asked to complete an application form while on the company premises, and thus it is a sample of the candidate's own work (obtaining assistance with résumés is common, given that many job boards offer online résumé building options).
- Application forms typically ask the candidate to provide written authorization for reference checking.
- Candidates are asked to acknowledge that the information provided is true and accurate, which protects the company from applicants who falsify their credentials.
- Many application forms today have an optional section regarding designated group member status. An example is provided in **Figure 6.6**. The data collected are used for employment equity tracking purposes.

Human Rights Legislation and Application Forms

Application forms cannot ask questions that would directly or indirectly classify candidates on the basis of any of the prohibited grounds under human rights legislation; potential employers cannot ask for a photograph, information about illnesses, disabilities, or workers' compensation claims, or information that could lead to direct, intentional discrimination, such as age, gender, sexual orientation, marital status, maiden name, date of birth, place of origin, number of dependants, and so on.

If an application form has any illegal questions, an unsuccessful candidate may challenge the legality of the entire recruitment and selection processes. In such case, the burden of proof is on the employer. Thus, taking human rights legislation requirements into consideration when designing application forms is imperative. The Guide to Screening and Selection in Employment in the Appendix to Chapter 7 provides helpful hints. Specific guidelines regarding questions that can and cannot be asked on application forms are available through the human rights commissions in each jurisdiction. **Figure 6.7**, a sample application form developed by the Ontario Human Rights Commission, illustrates the types of information that can legally be requested.

Using Application Forms to Predict Job Performance

Some firms use application forms to predict which candidates will be successful and which will not, in much the same way that employers use tests for screening.

weighted application blank (WAB)
A job application form on which applicant responses have been weighted based on their statistical relationship to measures of job success.

One approach involves designing a **weighted application blank (WAB)**. Statistical studies are conducted to find the relationship between responses on the application form (such as "dollar sales achieved" or "received cash bonus for good job") and measures of success on the job.[63] A scoring system is subsequently developed by weighting the different possible responses to those particular items. By scoring an applicant's response to each of those questions and then totalling the scores obtained, a composite score can be calculated for each applicant. Although studies have shown that WABs can be highly valid predictors and although they can be developed fairly easily, such forms are used by relatively few organizations.

FIGURE 6.6 | Self-Identification for Employment Equity Purposes

Employee Self-Identification Form

(Confidential when completed)

- This form is designed to collect information on the composition of the Public Service workforce to comply with legislation on employment equity and to facilitate the planning and implementation of employment equity activities. Your response is **voluntary** and you may identify in more than one designated group.

- The information you provide will be used in compiling statistics on employment equity in the federal Public Service. With your consent (see Box E), it may also be used by the employment equity coordinator of your department for human resource management purposes. This includes referral for training and developmental assignments and, in the case of persons with disabilities, facilitating appropriate accommodation in the workplace.

- Employment equity information will be retained in the Employment Equity Data Bank (EEDB) of the Treasury Board Secretariat and its confidentiality is protected under the *Privacy Act*. You have the right to review and correct information about yourself and can be assured that it will not be used for unauthorized purposes.

Step 1:   Complete boxes A to E. In boxes B, C and D, refer to the definitions provided.

Step 2:   Sign and date the form and return it to your department's EE coordinator.

Thank you for your cooperation.

TBS/PPB 300-02432
TBS/SCT 330-78 (Rev. 1999–02)

A.

Family Name	Given Name and Initial

Department or Agency/Branch

( )	
Telephone # (office)	Personal Record Identifier (PRI)

○ Female   ○ Male

B. A person with a disability . . . (i) . . . has a long-term or recurring physical, mental, sensory, psychiatric, or learning impairment and

1. considers himself/herself to be disadvantaged in employment by reason of that impairement, or,

2. believes that an employer or potential employer is likely to consider him/her to be disadvantaged in employment by reason of that impairment,
   and includes persons whose functional limitations owing to their impairment have been accommodated in their current job or workplace.

ARE YOU A PERSON WITH A DISABILITY?

○ No

○ Yes, check all that apply

11 ○ **Co-ordination or dexterity** *(difficulty using hands or arms, for example, grasping or handling a stapler or using a keyboard)*

12 ○ **Mobility** *(difficulty moving around, for example, from one office to another or up and down stairs)*

16 ○ **Blind or visual impairment** *(unable to see or difficulty seeing)*

19 ○ **Deaf or hard of hearing** *(unable to hear or difficulty hearing)*

13 ○ **Speech impairment** *(unable to speak or difficulty speaking and being understood)*

23 ○ **Other disability** *(including learning disabilities, developmental disabilities and all other types of disabilities)*

(Please specify) _____

C. An Aboriginal person . . .

. . . is a North American Indian or a member of a First Nation or who is Métis, or Inuit. North American Indians or members of a First Nation include status, treaty or registered Indians, as well as non-status and non-registered Indians.

ARE YOU AN ABORIGINAL PERSON

○ No

○ Yes, check the appropriate circle

03 ○ North American Indian/First Nation

02 ○ Métis

01 ○ Inuit

D. A person in a visible minority . . .

. . . in Canada is someone (other than an Aboriginal person as defined in C above) who is non-white in colour/race, regardless of place of birth.

ARE YOU IN A VISIBLE GROUP

○ No

○ Yes, check the circle which best describes your visible minority group or origin

41 ○ Black

45 ○ Chinese

51 ○ Filipino

47 ○ Japanese

48 ○ Korean

56 ○ South Asian/East Indian *(including Indian from India; Bangladeshi; Pakistani; East Indian from Guyana; Trinidad; East Africa; etc.)*

58 ○ Southeast Asian *(including Burmese; Cambodian; Laotian; Thai; Vietnamese; etc.)*

57 ○ Non-White West Asian, North African and Arab *(including Egyptian; Libyan; Lebanese; Iranian; etc.)*

42 ○ Non-White Latin American *(including indigenous persons from Central and South America, etc.)*

44 ○ Persons of Mixed Origin *(with one parent in one of the visible minority groups listed above)*

59 ○ Other Visible Minority Group

(Please specify) _____

E. 99○ The information in this form may be used for human resources management

_____   _____
Signature   Date (DD/MM/YY)

Source: Employee Self-Identification Form, www.tbs-sct.gc.ca/gui/iden2-eng.asp, Treasury Board of Canada Secretariat, 2009. Reproduced with the permission of the Minister of Public Works and Government Services Canada, 2000.

biographical information blank (BIB) A detailed job application form requesting biographical data found to be predictive of success on the job, pertaining to background, experiences, and preferences. As with a WAB, responses are scored.

Another type of application form that can be used to predict performance is a **biographical information blank (BIB)**, also known as a biodata form.[64] Essentially, it is a more detailed version of an application form, focusing on biographical data found to be predictive of job success. Questions relating to age, gender, race or other grounds prohibited under human rights legislation cannot be used. Candidates respond to a series of questions about their background, experiences, and preferences, including willingness to travel and leisure activities, as shown in **Figure 6.8**. Because biographical questions rarely have right or wrong

FIGURE 6.7 | Sample Application Form

Appendix "D"—Sample Application for Employment

Position being applied for _____   Date available to begin work _____

- -

PERSONAL DATA

Last name _____   Given name(s) _____

Address _____   Street _____   Apt. No. _____

Home Telephone Number _____

City _____   Province _____   Postal Code _____

Business Telephone Number _____

Are you legally eligible to work in Canada?   Yes ☐   No ☐

Are you 18 years or more?   Yes ☐   No ☐

Are you willing to relocate in Ontario?   Yes ☐   No ☐

Preferred Location _____

To determine your qualification for employment, please provide below and on the reverse, information about your academic and other achievements including volunteer work, as well as employment history. Attach any additional information on a separate sheet.

- -

EDUCATION

SECONDARY SCHOOL ☐

BUSINESS OR TRADE SCHOOL ☐

Highest grade or level completed _____   Name of program _____

Length of program _____

Licence, certificate or diploma awarded?   Yes ☐   No ☐

Type: _____

- -

COMMUNITY COLLEGE ☐   UNIVERSITY ☐

Name of program _____   Length of Program _____

Diploma/Degree awarded?

Yes ☐   No ☐   Honours ☐

Major Subject _____

Other courses, workshops, seminars,
Licences, Certificates, Degrees_____

- -

WORK-RELATED SKILLS

Describe any of your work-related skills, experience or training that relates to the position being applied for.

_____

_____

- -

EMPLOYMENT

Name of present/last employer _____   Job title _____

Period of employment (includes time spent away from work due to disability or maternity/parental leave but it is not necessary to refer to this)

From _____   To _____

Type of Business _____

Reason for leaving (do not refer to issues related to maternity/parental leave, Workers' Compensation claims, handicap/disability, or human rights complaints)_____

- -

Functions/Responsibilities _____

_____

Name of previous employer _____   Job title _____

Period of employment (includes time spent away from work due to disability or maternity/ parental leave but it is not necessary to refer to this)

From _____   To _____

Type of Business _____

Reason for leaving (do not refer to issues related to maternity/parental leave, Workers' Compensation claims, handicap/disability, or human rights complaints)_____ _____

Functions/Responsibilities _____

- -

Name of previous employer _____   Job title _____

Period of employment (includes time spent away from work due to disability or maternity/ parental leave but it is not necessary to refer to this)

From _____   To _____

Type of Business _____

Reason for leaving (do not refer to issues related to maternity/parental leave, Workers' Compensation claims, handicap/disability, or human rights complaints)_____

Functions/Responsibilities _____

- -

For employment references we may approach:

Your present/last employer?   Yes ☐   No ☐

Your former employer(s)?   Yes ☐   No ☐

List references if different from above on a separate sheet. _____

- -

PERSONAL INTEREST AND ACTIVITIES (civic, athletic, etc.) _____ _____ _____ _____

I hereby declare that the foregoing information is true and complete to my knowledge. I understand that a false statement may disqualify me from employment, or cause my dismissal.

Have you attached an additional sheet? Yes ☐   No ☐

Signature _____   Date _____

Source: Sample Application for Employment, from *Human Rights at Work* (Toronto: Ontario Human Rights Commission, 2005). © Queen's Printer for Ontario, 2005. Reproduced with permission.

FIGURE 6.8 | Example of a Biographical Information Blank

Personal Information

Name _____   _____
               Last   First

Mailing Address _____
                        Street, City, Province, Postal Code

How long have you lived at your current address? _____

Do you consider your net worth to be low _____   moderate _____   or high _____?

Have you ever been turned down for a loan?   Yes _____   No _____

How many credit cards do you have? _____

Education and Training

Highest level of education completed:

High School _____   Vocational _____   College _____   University _____   Postgraduate _____

What educational degrees do you have? Diploma/Certificate _____   B.A. _____   B.Sc. _____ B.Comm. _____   M.B.A. _____   Master's _____   Other (Identify) _____

What subjects did you major in? _____

What was your grade-point average in college or university?   A _____   B _____   C _____   D _____

Did you graduate with honours?   Yes _____   No _____

continued

Did you receive any awards for academic excellence?   Yes _____   No _____

Did you receive any scholarships?   Yes _____   No _____

List the extracurricular activities you participated in during school:

_____

Information about You

Did you find school stimulating _____   boring _____?

Did you hold a job while attending school?   Yes _____   No _____

How did you pay for your post-high-school training? (Check as many as appropriate)

Parents paid _____   Loans _____   Scholarships _____   Paid own way _____

Have you ever held a job where you earned commissions on sales?   Yes _____   No _____

If "Yes," were your commissions low _____   moderate _____   high _____?

Five years from now, what do you expect your salary to be? _____

Do you enjoy meeting new people?   Yes _____   No _____

How many social phone calls do you receive a week? _____

Do people count on you to "cheer up" others?   Yes _____   No _____

How many parties do you go to in a year? _____

Do you enjoy talking to people?   Yes _____   No _____

Rate your conversational skills:

Excellent _____   Very Good _____   Good _____   Fair _____   Poor _____

How often do you introduce yourself to other people you don't know?

Always _____   Sometimes _____   Never _____

Do you enjoy social gatherings?   Yes _____   No _____

Do you go to social gatherings out of a sense of duty?   Yes _____   No _____

How many times a year do you go out to dinner with friends? _____

Do you enjoy talking to people you don't know?   Yes _____   No _____

What are your hobbies?

_____

What sports, recreational, or physical activities do you engage in?

_____

How confident are you in your ability to succeed?

Very Confident _____   Confident _____   Somewhat Confident _____

Source: From *Recruitment and Selection in Canada*, Third Canadian Edition, by Catano/Cronshaw, 2005. Reprinted with permission of Nelson, a division of Thomson Learning.

answers, BIBs are difficult to fake. The development of a BIB requires that the items that are valid predictors of job success be identified and that weights be established for different responses to these items. By totalling the scores for each item, it is possible to obtain a composite score for each applicant.

Chapter | SUMMARY

1. Recruitment is the process of searching out and attracting qualified job applicants. It begins with the identification of a position that requires staffing and is completed when résumés and/or completed application forms are received. In order to manage the increasing talent shortage, proactive employers are trying to obtain a competitive advantage in recruitment by establishing themselves as employers of choice through employer branding.

2. The recruitment process has four steps. First, job openings are identified through HR planning or manager request. Second, the job description and

job specification are then reviewed to determine the job requirements. Third, appropriate recruiting source(s) and method(s) are chosen. Fourth, using these strategies, a pool of qualified candidates is generated.

3. Job posting is the process of notifying existing employees about vacant positions. Human resources records may indicate appropriate applicants for vacant positions. Skills inventories may provide even better information.

4. External recruitment methods include online recruiting, print advertising, private employment agencies, executive search firms, walk-ins/write-ins, employee referrals, educational institutions, HRSDC, professional and trade associations, labour organizations, military personnel, and open houses/job fairs.

5. Two strategies for obtaining nonpermanent staff include using temporary help agencies and hiring contract workers.

6. Recruiting a diverse workforce is a necessity, given the shrinking labour force. In particular, recruiters are trying to attract older workers, younger workers, women, visible minorities, Aboriginal people, and people with disabilities.

7. Application forms are important because they provide information on the applicant's education and experience, a brief overview of the applicant's career progress, and information that can be used to predict whether an applicant will succeed on the job.

PEARSON
myHRlab™

Test yourself on material for this chapter at
www.pearsoned.ca/myhrlab

Key | TERMS

biographical information blank (BIB) *(p. 166)*
blind ad *(p. 153)*
contract workers *(p. 159)*
employer branding *(p. 143)*
job posting *(p. 148)*
nepotism *(p. 155)*

recruiter *(p. 143)*
recruitment *(p. 143)*
want ad *(p. 153)*
weighted application blank
  (WAB) *(p. 164)*
yield ratio *(p. 149)*

Review and Discussion | QUESTIONS

1. Discuss the advantages and disadvantages of recruiting within the organization. Identify and describe the three tools that are used in this process.

2. List the advantages of external recruitment.

3. Explain the difference between an internet job board and a corporate career website.

4. Describe the AIDA guidelines for print advertising.

5. Under what circumstances should a private employment agency be used?

6. Describe the advantages of using application forms as part of the recruitment process.

Critical Thinking | QUESTIONS

1. What potential problems may result if the employer branding value proposition presented during the recruitment process is not reinforced once the new recruit is working for the organization? What could organizations do to avoid this situation?

2. What potential problems could be created by offering referral bonuses to existing employees?

3. Compare and contrast the advantages and disadvantages of traditional and virtual career fairs.

4. As the labour supply gets tighter and tighter, would you be in favour of loosening requirements for foreign-trained professionals to become qualified in Canada?

5. What are some of the specific reservations that a 30-year-old candidate might have about applying for a job that requires managing a workforce that is on average ten years older than he or she is?

6. Assume you are the HR manager in a highly homogenous company that now wants to better reflect the diversity of the target client group in its employee population. What must you consider as you think about implementing your new recruitment strategy?

Experiential | EXERCISES

1. Examine classified and display ads appearing in the "help wanted" section of a recent newspaper. Choose three ads and, using the AIDA guidelines presented in this chapter, analyze the effectiveness of each one.

2. Go to your university's or college's career centre and gather information on all the services they provide. How many companies come to recruit students through the centre each year? What services does the centre provide to employers seeking to hire graduating students? Employers seeking to hire summer students? Employers seeking to hire students for internships?

3. Considering the current economic situation and using the following list of jobs, identify all of the sources that could be used to recruit qualified applicants:

- Registered Nurses to work in the critical care unit of a new regional hospital

- carpenters to work on a new home building project

- Chief Financial Officer for an international engineering firm with a head office located in Vancouver

- retail sales associates to work in an urban clothing chain

- customer service representatives to work in a bank branch

- bilingual (English plus one other language) administrative assistants for Canadian financial services company operating internationally

Running | CASE

Running Case: LearnInMotion.com

Getting Better Applicants

If Jennifer and Pierre were asked what the main problem was in running their business, their answer would be quick and short: hiring good people. They were simply astonished at how hard it was to attract and hire good candidates. After much debate, they decided to post openings for seven positions: two salespeople, one web designer, two content management people, one office manager, and one web surfer.

Their first approach was to design and place a large display ad in two local newspapers. The display ad listed all the positions available. Jennifer and Pierre assumed that by placing a large ad with the name of the company prominently displayed and a bold border around the ad, it would draw attention and therefore generate applicants. For two consecutive weekends, the ad cost the fledgling company close to $1000, but it produced only a handful of applicants. After speaking with them by phone, Jennifer and Pierre rejected three outright, two said they weren't interested, and two scheduled interviews but never showed up.

The owners therefore decided to change their approach. They used different recruiting methods for each position. In the paper, they placed ads for the salespeople under "Sales" and for the office manager under "Administrative."

They advertised for a web designer by placing an ad on Monster.ca. And for the content managers and web surfer, they placed neatly typed help wanted ads in the career placement offices of a technical college and a community college about ten minutes away from their office. They also used this job posting approach to find independent contractors they could use to deliver courses physically to users' homes or offices.

The results were disappointing. Over a typical weekend, literally dozens of want ads for experienced salespeople appear, as well as almost as many for office managers. The ad for salespeople generated three calls, one of whom Jennifer and Pierre felt might be a viable candidate, although the person wanted a much higher salary than they had planned to pay. One possible candidate emerged for the office manager position.

They decided to change the positioning of the sales ad (since the job involved entirely inside phone sales) in the newspaper from "Salespersons Wanted" to "Phone Sales," which is a separate category. Many of the calls they got (not all of them, but many) were from salespeople who were used to working in what some people called "boiler-room" operations. In other words, they sit at the phone all day making

cold calls from lists provided by their employers, selling anything from burglar alarms to investments, all under very high-pressure conditions. They weren't interested in LearnInMotion, nor was LearnInMotion interested in them.

They fared a little better with the web designer ad, which produced four possible applicants. They got no phone calls from the local college job postings; when they called to ask the placement offices why, they were told that their posted salary of $8 per hour was "much too low." They went back and replaced the job postings with $10 hourly rates.

"I just don't understand it," Jennifer finally said. Especially for the sales job, Jennifer and Pierre felt that they were offering perfectly acceptable compensation packages, so the lack of applicants surprised them. "Maybe a lot of people just don't want to work for dot-coms anymore," said Pierre, thinking out loud. "When the bottom fell out of the dot-com market, a lot of good people were hurt by working for a series of two or three failed dot-coms. Maybe they've just had enough of the wired world."

QUESTIONS

1 Describe how the recruitment process (including all of the steps) outlined in Figure 6.1 will be of assistance to Jennifer and Pierre to solve their problems.

2 Draft a new job posting for each of the seven positions discussed in the case. Then discuss how you put the job posting(s) together and why, using Figures 6.2 and 6.3 as examples.

Case | INCIDENT

Solving a Potential Recruitment Dilemma

Rachel Lucas is the Human Resources manager of a prestigious accounting firm. Rachel recently attended a local human resources professionals' association meeting where recruitment was the topic up for discussion. At this meeting all aspects of the recruitment process, including recruitment methods and how to increase diversity through the use of application forms, were to be discussed. Rachel couldn't wait to apply what she learned at this meeting to her job.

While listening to the scheduled speaker for the evening, Rachel started to think about the current recruitment initiatives she was dealing with at work. The firm was entering its traditional busy season where many clients would need tax returns completed. This time every year she needed to source and hire quality, qualified candidates to fill 50 tax preparer positions. The partners were relying heavily on her this year to get higher quality candidates this year due to the complex returns that would have to be completed and to have them in place within three weeks.

As the speaker was finishing his presentation, Rachel wondered what recruitment process and techniques she should use. What would be the best decisions for the firm?

QUESTIONS

1   Should Rachel utilize internal or external recruitment techniques to staff these 50 positions?

2   Rachel is hoping to recruit qualified candidates from a variety of diverse demographics. Will she have to use different recruitment techniques to do this? If so, what ones are the most effective to attract these candidates (i.e. older workers, designated group members, etc.)?

3   Rachel plans on hiring recruiters to assist her in staffing these 50 positions. Knowing the company will require the recruiters to adhere to the concept of employer branding, describe what steps Rachel should take to orientate the new recruiters to the branding process.

Test yourself on material for this chapter at
www.pearsoned.ca/myhrlab

CHAPTER 7

LEARNING OUTCOMES

AFTER STUDYING THIS CHAPTER, YOU SHOULD BE ABLE TO

DEFINE selection, and **DISCUSS** its strategic importance.

DEFINE reliability and validity, and **EXPLAIN** their importance in selection techniques.

DESCRIBE at least four types of testing used in selection, and **ANALYZE** the conflicting legal concerns related to alcohol and drug testing.

DESCRIBE the major types of selection interviews by degree of structure, type of content, and manner of administration.

EXPLAIN the importance of reference checking, **DESCRIBE** strategies to make such checking effective, and **ANALYZE** the legal issues involved.

SELECTION

REQUIRED PROFESSIONAL CAPABILITIES (RPC)

- Analyzes position and competency requirements to establish selection criteria
- Establishes screening and assessment procedures
- Determines the appropriate selection tools and develops new tools as required
- Administers a variety of selection tools, including tests, interviews, reference checks, etc.

- Evaluates the effectiveness of selection processes, tools, and outcomes
- Establishes appointment procedures for candidates selected through the recruitment process, ensuring that conditions of employment are documented and consistent with established policies
- Supports managers in the negotiation of terms and conditions of employment

THE STRATEGIC IMPORTANCE OF EMPLOYEE SELECTION

selection The process of choosing among individuals who have been recruited to fill existing or projected job openings.

Selection is the process of choosing among individuals who have been recruited to fill existing or projected job openings. Whether considering current employees for a transfer or promotion or outside candidates for a first-time position with the firm, information about the applicants must be collected and evaluated. Selection begins when a pool of applicants has submitted their résumés or completed application forms as a result of the recruiting process.

The selection process has important strategic significance. More and more managers have realized that the quality of the company's human resources is often the single most important factor in determining whether the firm is going to survive and be successful in reaching the objectives specified in its strategic plan. Those individuals selected will be implementing strategic decisions and, in some cases, creating strategic plans. Thus, the successful candidates must fit with the strategic direction of the organization. For example, if the organization is planning to expand internationally, language skills and international experience will become important selection criteria.

When a poor selection decision is made and the individual selected for the job is not capable of acceptable performance in the job, strategic objectives will not be met. In addition, when an unsuccessful employee must be terminated, the recruitment and selection process must begin all over again, and the successor must be properly oriented and trained. The "hidden" costs are frequently even higher, including internal disorganization and disruption and customer alienation. For example, the City of Waterloo was forced to fire its new chief administrative officer after three weeks on the job when it was found that he had provided inaccurate and misleading information to city council in a previous job.[1]

There are also legal implications associated with ineffective selection. *Human rights* legislation in every Canadian jurisdiction prohibits discrimination in all aspects, terms, and conditions of employment on such grounds as race, religion or creed, colour, marital status, gender, age, and disability. Firms must ensure that all their selection procedures are free of both intentional and systemic discrimination (see Appendix 7.1, which provides the Canadian Human Rights Commission's *Guide to Screening and Selection in Employment*). Organizations required by law to implement an employment equity plan must ensure that all their employment systems, including selection, are bias-free and do not have an adverse impact on members of the four designated groups—women, visible minorities, Aboriginals, and persons with disabilities.

Another legal implication is employer liability for *negligent or wrongful hiring*. Courts are increasingly finding employers liable when employees with unsuitable backgrounds are hired and subsequently engage in criminal activities falling within the scope of their employment. British Columbia has a law that requires schools, hospitals, and employers of childcare workers to conduct criminal record checks for all new employees.[2]

Suggested guidelines for avoiding negative legal consequences, such as human rights complaints, liability for negligent hiring, and wrongful dismissal suits, include the following:

1. ensuring that all selection criteria and strategies are based on the job description and the job specification

An Ethical | Dilemma

As the company recruiter, how would you handle a request from the CEO that you hire her son for a summer job, knowing that, given current hiring constraints, the sons and daughters of other employees will not be able to obtain such positions?

Hints | TO ENSURE LEGAL COMPLIANCE

2. adequately assessing the applicant's ability to meet performance standards or expectations

3. carefully scrutinizing all information supplied on application forms and résumés

4. obtaining written authorization for reference checking from prospective employees, and checking references very carefully

5. saving all records and information obtained about the applicant during each stage of the selection process

6. rejecting applicants who make false statements on their application forms or résumés

Supply Challenges

selection ratio The ratio of the number of applicants hired to the total number of applicants.

Although it is desirable to have a large, qualified pool of recruits from which to select applicants, this is not always possible. The emerging labour supply shortage situation in Canada will result in increasingly small selection ratios. A **selection ratio** is the ratio of the number of applicants hired to the total number of applicants available, as follows:

$$\frac{\text{Number of Applicants Hired}}{\text{Total Number of Applicants}} = \text{Selection Ratio}$$

A small selection ratio, such as 1:2, means that there are a limited number of applicants from which to select, and it may also mean low-quality recruits. If this is the case, it is generally better to start the recruitment process over again, even if it means a hiring delay, rather than taking the risk of hiring an employee who will be a marginal performer at best.

The Selection Process

multiple-hurdle strategy An approach to selection involving a series of successive steps or hurdles. Only candidates clearing the hurdle are permitted to move on to the next step.

Most firms use a sequential selection system involving a series of successive steps—a **multiple-hurdle strategy**. Only candidates clearing a "hurdle" (selection techniques including prescreening, testing, interviewing, and background/reference checking) are permitted to move on to the next step. Clearing the hurdle requires meeting or exceeding the minimum requirements established for that hurdle. Thus, only candidates who have cleared all of the previous hurdles remain in contention for the position at the time that the hiring decision is being made.

To assess each applicant's potential for success on the job, organizations typically rely on a number of sources of information. The number of steps in the selection process and their sequence vary with the organization. An abbreviated selection process for entrepreneurs and small business owners is provided in the Entrepreneurs and HR box. The types of selection instruments and screening devices used are also not standardized across organizations. Even within a firm, the number and sequence of steps often vary with the type and level of the job, as well as the source and method of recruitment. **Figure 7.1** illustrates the steps commonly involved.

At each step in the selection process, carefully chosen selection criteria must be used to determine which applicants will move on to the next step. It is through job analysis that the duties, responsibilities, and human requirements

RPC

Analyzes position and competency requirements to establish selection criteria

Entrepreneurs and HR

Employment Testing and Interviewing

For the small business, one or two hiring mistakes could be disastrous, so a formal testing program is advisable. Some tests are so easy to use that they are particularly good for smaller firms. Several examples follow.

- One is the Wonderlic Personnel Test, which measures general mental ability. It takes less than 15 minutes to administer the four-page booklet. The tester reads the instructions and then keeps time as the candidate works through the 50 problems on the two inside sheets. The tester scores the test by adding up the number of correct answers. Comparing the candidate's score with the minimum scores recommended for various occupations shows whether the candidate achieved the minimally acceptable score for the type of job in question.

- The Predictive Index is another example. It measures work-related personality traits, drives, and behaviours—in particular, dominance, extroversion, patience, and blame avoidance—on a two-sided sheet. A template makes scoring simple. The Predictive Index program includes 15 standard personality patterns. For example, there is the "social interest" pattern for a person who is generally unselfish, congenial, persuasive, patient, and unassuming. This person would be good with people and a good personnel interviewer, for instance.

- Computerized testing programs are especially useful for small employers. For example, many employers rely on informal typing tests when hiring office help. A better approach is to use a program like the Minnesota Clerical Assessment Battery published by Assessment Systems Corporation. It runs on a PC and includes a typing test, proofreading test, filing test, business vocabulary test, business math test, and clerical knowledge test.

Interviewing

A practical, streamlined employment interview process would proceed as follows:

- Preparing for the Interview. Even a busy entrepreneur or small business manager can quickly specify the kind of person who would be best for the job. One way to do so is to focus on four basic required factors—knowledge and experience, motivation, intellectual capacity, and personality—and to ask the following questions:

  - Knowledge and experience: What must the candidate know to perform the job? What experience is absolutely necessary to perform the job?

  - Motivation: What should the person like doing to enjoy this job? Is there anything the person should not dislike? Are there any essential goals or aspirations the person should have? Are there any unusual energy demands on the job?

  - Intellectual capacity: Are there any specific intellectual aptitudes required (mathematical, mechanical, and so on)? How complex are the problems the person must solve? What must a person be able to demonstrate he or she can do intellectually? How should the person solve problems (cautiously, deductively, and so on)?

  - Personality factor: What are the critical personality qualities needed for success on the job (ability to withstand boredom, decisiveness, stability, and so on)? How must the job incumbent handle stress, pressure, and criticism? What kind of interpersonal behaviour is required in the job up the line, at peer level, down the line, and outside the firm with customers?

- Specific Factors to Probe in the Interview. A combination of situational questions and open-ended questions like those in **Figure 7.6** should be asked in order to probe the candidate's suitability for the job. For example:

  - Intellectual factor: Here, such things as complexity of tasks the person has performed, grades in school, test results (including scholastic aptitude tests and so on), and how the person organizes his or her thoughts and communicates are assessed.

  - Motivation factor: The person's likes and dislikes (for each thing done, what he or she liked or disliked about it), aspirations (including the validity of each goal in terms of the person's reasoning about why he or she chose it), and energy level should be probed, perhaps by asking what he or she does on, say, a "typical Tuesday."

  - Personality factor: Questions probing for self-defeating behaviours (aggressiveness, compulsive fidgeting, and so on) and exploring the

continued

person's past interpersonal relationships should be asked. Additional questions about the person's past interactions (working in a group at school, working with fraternity brothers or sorority sisters, leading the work team on the last job, and so on) should also be asked. A judgment about the person's behaviour in the interview itself can also be made—is the candidate personable? Shy? Outgoing?

- Knowledge and experience factor: Situational questions such as "How would you organize such a sales effort?" or "How would you design that kind of web site?" can probe for information on this factor.

- Conducting the Interview. Devise and use a plan to guide the interview. According to interviewing expert John Drake, significant areas to cover include the candidate's
  - college experiences
  - work experiences—summer, part-time
  - work experience—full-time
  - goals and ambitions
  - reactions to the job you are interviewing for
  - self-assessments (by the candidate of his or her strengths and weaknesses)
  - military experiences
  - present outside activities.

- Follow the Plan. Begin with an open-ended question for each topic, such as, "Could you tell me about what you did when you were in high school?" Keep in mind that information must be elicited regarding four main traits—intelligence, motivation, personality, and knowledge and experience. The information in each of these four areas can then be accumulated as the person answers. Follow-up questions on particular areas such as "Could you elaborate on that, please?" can then be used.

- Match the Candidate to the Job. After following the interview plan and probing for the four factors, conclusions can be drawn about the person's intellectual capacity, knowledge and experience, motivation, and personality, and the candidate's general strengths and limitations can be summarized using an interview evaluation form (for instance, see **Figure 7.7**). The conclusions can then be compared to both the job description and the list of behavioural requirements developed when preparing for the interview. This should provide a rational basis for matching the candidate to the job based on an analysis of the traits and aptitudes the job actually requires.

Source: Based on John Drake, *Interviewing for Managers: A Complete Guide to Employment Interviewing.* New York: AMCOM, 1982. Reprinted with permission.

FIGURE 7.1 | Typical Steps in the Selection Process

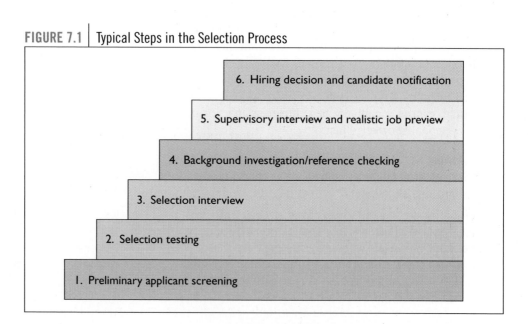

6. Hiring decision and candidate notification

5. Supervisory interview and realistic job preview

4. Background investigation/reference checking

3. Selection interview

2. Selection testing

1. Preliminary applicant screening

for each job are identified. By basing selection criteria on these requirements, firms can create a legally defensible hiring system.[3] Individuals hired after thorough screening against these carefully developed selection criteria (based directly on the job description and job specification) learn their jobs readily, are productive, and generally adjust to their jobs with a minimum of difficulty.

STEP 1: PRELIMINARY APPLICANT SCREENING

RPC

Establishes screening and assessment procedures

Initial applicant screening is generally performed by members of the HR department. Application forms and résumés are reviewed, and those candidates not meeting the essential selection criteria are eliminated first. Then, the remaining applications are examined and those candidates who most closely match the remaining job specifications are identified and given further consideration.

The use of technology is becoming increasingly popular to help HR professionals improve the initial screening process. An increasing number of firms, such as Blockbuster and Home Depot, are using technological applications to help screen large numbers of candidates and generate short-lists of individuals who will move on to the next step in the selection process.

STEP 2: SELECTION TESTING

Selection testing is a common screening device used by approximately two-thirds of Canadian organizations to assess specific job-related skills, as well as general intelligence, personality characteristics, mental abilities, interests, and preferences.[4] Testing techniques provide efficient, standardized procedures for screening large numbers of applicants. Several thousand psychological and personality tests are on the market.[5]

The Importance of Reliability and Validity

Tests and other selection techniques are only useful if they provide reliable and valid measures.[6] All reputable tests will provide information to users about the reliability and validity of the test.

Reliability

reliability The degree to which interviews, tests, and other selection procedures yield comparable data over time; in other words, the degree of dependability, consistency, or stability of the measures used.

The degree to which interviews, tests, and other selection procedures yield comparable data over time is known as **reliability**. Reliability is the degree of dependability, consistency, or stability of the measures used. For example, a test that results in widely variable scores (such as 60 percent, 82 percent, and 71 percent) when it is administered on different occasions to the same individual is unreliable. Reliability also refers to the extent to which two or more methods yield the same results or are consistent. For example, applicants with high scores on personality tests for impulsivity, or lack of self-control, are correlated with the likelihood of failing background checks due to criminal behaviour.[7] Reliability also means the extent to which there is agreement between two or more raters (inter-rater reliability).

When dealing with tests, another measure of reliability that is taken into account is internal consistency. For example, suppose a vocational interest test has ten items, all of which were supposed to measure, in one way or another, the person's interest in working outdoors. To assess internal reliability, the degree to which responses to those ten items vary together would be statistically analyzed. (That is one reason that tests often include questions that appear rather repetitive.) Reliability can be diminished when questions are answered randomly, when the test setting is noisy or uncomfortable, and when the applicant is tired or unwell.

Validity

validity The accuracy with which a predictor measures what it is intended to measure.

Validity, in the context of selection, is an indicator of the extent to which data from a selection technique, such as a test or interview, are related to or predictive of subsequent performance on the job. For example, high impulsivity is correlated with low productivity.[8] Separate validation studies of selection techniques should be conducted for different subgroups, such as visible minorities and women, in order to assess **differential validity.** In some cases, the technique may be a valid predictor of job success for one group (such as white males) but not for other applicants, thereby leading to systemic discrimination.

differential validity Confirmation that the selection tool accurately predicts the performance of all possible employee subgroups, including white males, women, visible minorities, persons with disabilities, and Aboriginal people.

Three types of validity are particularly relevant to selection: criterion-related, content, and construct validity.

Criterion-Related Validity The extent to which a selection tool predicts or significantly correlates with important elements of work behaviour is known as **criterion-related validity.** Demonstrating criterion-related validity requires proving that those who exhibit strong sales ability on a test or in an interview, for example, also have high sales on the job, and that those individuals who do poorly on the test or in the interview have poor sales results.

criterion-related validity The extent to which a selection tool predicts or significantly correlates with important elements of work behaviour.

Content Validity When a selection instrument, such as a test, adequately samples the knowledge and skills needed to perform the job, **content validity** is assumed to exist. The closer the content of the selection instrument is to actual samples of work or work behaviour, the greater the content validity. For example, asking a candidate for a secretarial position to demonstrate word processing skills, as required on the job, has high content validity.

content validity The extent to which a selection instrument, such as a test, adequately samples the knowledge and skills needed to perform the job.

Construct Validity The extent to which a selection tool measures a theoretical construct or trait deemed necessary to perform the job successfully is known as **construct validity.** Intelligence, verbal skills, analytical ability, and leadership skills are all examples of constructs. Measuring construct validity requires demonstrating that the psychological trait or attribute is related to satisfactory job performance, as well as showing that the test or other selection tool used accurately measures the psychological trait or attribute. As an example of poor construct validity, an accounting firm was selecting applicants for auditor positions based on a test for high extroversion, when the job in fact required working alone with data. A test to select applicants with high introversion would have had higher construct validity and would have helped to avoid the high turnover rate the firm was experiencing.[9]

construct validity The extent to which a selection tool measures a theoretical construct or trait deemed necessary to perform the job successfully.

RPC

Evaluates the effectiveness of selection processes, tools, and outcomes

Professional standards for psychologists require that tests be used as supplements to other techniques, such as interviews and background checks; that tests be validated in the organization where they will be used; that a certified psychologist be used to choose, validate, administer, and interpret tests; and that private, quiet, well-lit, and well-ventilated settings be provided to all applicants taking the test.[10]

Tests of Cognitive Abilities

Ensuring validity of selection tools when assessing candidates with disabilities may require accommodation of the disability. Some guidelines are provided in the Workforce Diversity box on page 183. Included in the category of test of cognitive abilities are tests of general reasoning ability (intelligence), tests of emotional intelligence, and tests of specific thinking skills, like memory and inductive reasoning.

Intelligence Tests

intelligence (IQ) tests Tests that measure general intellectual abilities, such as verbal comprehension, inductive reasoning, memory, numerical ability, speed of perception, spatial visualization, and word fluency.

Intelligence (IQ) tests are tests of general intellectual abilities. They measure not a single "intelligence" trait, but rather a number of abilities, including memory, vocabulary, verbal fluency, and numerical ability. An IQ score is actually a *derived* score, reflecting the extent to which the person is above or below the "average" adult's intelligence score. Intelligence is often measured with individually administered tests, such as the Stanford-Binet Test or the Wechsler Test. Other IQ tests, such as the Wonderlic, can be administered to groups of people.

Emotional Intelligence Tests

emotional intelligence (EI) tests Tests that measure ability to monitor one's own emotions and the emotions of others and to use that knowledge to guide thoughts and actions.

Emotional intelligence (EI) tests measure ability to monitor one's own emotions and the emotions of others and to use that knowledge to guide thoughts and actions. Someone with a high emotional quotient (EQ) is self-aware, can control his or her impulses, is self-motivated, and demonstrates empathy and social awareness. Many people believe that EQ, which can be modified through conscious effort and practice, is actually a more important determinant of success than a high IQ. Self-assessment EI tests include the Emotional Quotient Inventory (EQi), the EQ Map, the Mayer Salovey Caruso Emotional Intelligence Test (MSCEIT), and the Emotional Intelligence Questionnaire (EIQ). The Emotional Competence Inventory (ECI) is a 360-degree assessment in which several individuals evaluate one person to get a more complete picture of the individual's emotional competencies.[11]

Emotional Quotient Inventory
www.eiconsortium.org

Specific Cognitive Abilities

aptitude tests Tests that measure an individual's aptitude or potential to perform a job, provided he or she is given proper training.

There are also measures of specific thinking skills, such as inductive and deductive reasoning, verbal comprehension, memory, and numerical ability. Tests in this category are often called **aptitude tests**, since they purport to measure the applicant's aptitude for the job in question, that is, the applicant's potential to perform the job once given proper training. An example is the test of mechanical comprehension illustrated in **Figure 7.2**. It tests the applicant's understanding of basic mechanical principles. It may therefore reflect a person's aptitude for jobs—like that of machinist or engineer—that require mechanical comprehension. Multidimensional aptitude tests commonly used in applicant selection include the General Aptitude Test Battery (GATB).

Tests of Motor and Physical Abilities

There are many *motor abilities* that a firm might want to measure. These include finger dexterity, manual dexterity, speed of arm movement, and reaction time. The Crawford Small Parts Dexterity Test, as illustrated in **Figure 7.3**, is an example. It measures the speed and accuracy of simple judgment, as well as the speed of finger, hand, and arm movements. Other tests include the Stromberg Dexterity Test, the Minnesota Rate of Manipulation Test, and the Purdue Peg Board.

FIGURE 7.2 | Two Problems from the Test of Mechanical Comprehension

Look at Sample X on this page. It shows two men carrying a weighted object on a plank, and it asks, "Which man carries more weight?" Because the object is closer to man "B" than to man "A," man "B" is shouldering more weight; so blacken the circle under "B" on your answer sheet. Now look at Sample Y and answer it yourself. Fill in the circle under the correct answer on your answer sheet.

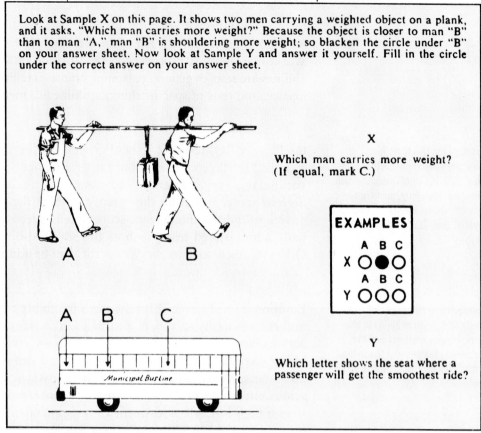

X

Which man carries more weight?
(If equal, mark C.)

EXAMPLES

Y

Which letter shows the seat where a passenger will get the smoothest ride?

Note: 1969 is latest copyright on this test, which is still most commonly used for this purpose.

Source: Reproduced by permission. Copyright 1967, 1969 by The Psychological Corporation, New York, NY. All rights reserved.

FIGURE 7.3 | Crawford Small Parts Dexterity Test

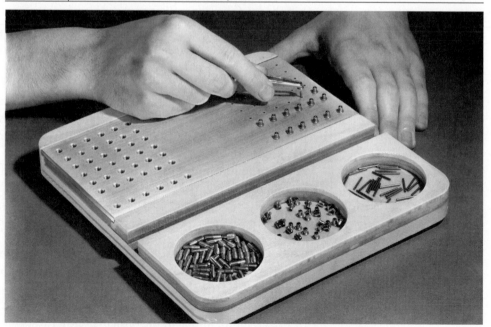

Source: The Psychological Corporation.

Tests of physical abilities may also be required.[12] For example, some firms are now using Functional Abilities Evaluations (FAE) to assist with placement decisions. An FAE, which measures a whole series of physical abilities—ranging from lifting, to pulling and pushing, sitting, squatting, climbing, and carrying—is particularly useful for positions with a multitude of physical demands, such as firefighter and police officer.[13] Ensuring that physical abilities tests do not violate human rights legislation requires basing such tests on job duties identified

Workforce DIVERSITY

Principles for Assessment Accommodations

There are four principles by which those responsible for assessment should be guided in determining accommodations when assessing persons with disabilities:

Principle 1: Provide all applicants with an equal opportunity to fully demonstrate their qualifications.

A disability may hinder a person from fully demonstrating his or her qualifications using a particular assessment instrument. Therefore, adjustments need to be made to the administration procedures or to the assessment instrument itself so that the person is in a position to fully demonstrate his or her qualifications.

Principle 2: Determine assessment accommodations on a case-by-case basis.

Three key elements must be considered when determining appropriate accommodations:

- The nature and the extent of the individual's functional limitation
- The type of assessment instrument being used
- The nature and level of the qualification being assessed

Principle 3: Do not alter the nature or level of the qualification being assessed.

For example, although providing additional time to complete a test could be appropriate when the qualification "knowledge of the organization's mandate and its business" is assessed, providing additional time could be inappropriate for a test assessing the qualification "verify information rapidly and accurately." In the latter case, the obtained result may not be representative of the applicant's true ability to do the task rapidly, considering the additional time given.

Principle 4: Base assessment accommodations on complete information.

To make appropriate decisions when determining assessment accommodations, there is a need to rely on complete information on the three elements mentioned earlier justifying the case-by-case approach:

1. The nature and the extent of the individual's functional limitations: For example, the appropriate accommodation for one person who is partially sighted may require a large print format of a test; while for another person who is also partially sighted, the appropriate accommodation may require special lighting. These differences arise because the nature and extent of the functional limitations vary from one individual to another.

2. Type of assessment instrument: For example, someone who has functional limitations that affect his or her manual writing speed may need some additional time to write an essay-style exam, while the same person may not need additional time for a multiple choice exam that does not require written responses beyond filling in circles on a response sheet.

3. Nature of the qualification being assessed: For example, allowing the use of a calculator for a test assessing "ability to perform financial calculation" could be appropriate. However, allowing the use of a calculator when the "ability to do mental calculation" is assessed would be inappropriate. In the latter case, the provision of the calculator would invalidate the result, as it would then not be representative of the applicant's ability to do the task mentally.

Source: Adapted from *Guide for Assessing Persons with Disabilities* (pp. 10–12). Policy Development Directorate, Public Service Commission of Canada, July 2007.

through job analysis and a physical demands analysis, ensuring that the tests duplicate the actual physical requirements of the job, developing and imposing such tests honestly and in good faith, ensuring that those administering the tests are properly trained and administer the tests in a consistent manner, and ensuring that testing standards are objectively related to job performance.[14]

Measuring Personality and Interests

A person's mental and physical abilities are seldom sufficient to explain his or her job performance. Other factors such as the person's motivation and interpersonal skills are important too. Personality and interest inventories are sometimes used as predictors of such intangibles.

personality tests Instruments used to measure basic aspects of personality, such as introversion, stability, motivation, neurotic tendency, self-confidence, self-sufficiency, and sociability.

Personality tests can measure basic aspects of an applicant's personality, such as introversion, stability, and motivation. The use of such tests for selection assumes that it is possible to find a relationship between a measurable personality trait (such as conscientiousness) and success on the job.[15] Many of these tests are *projective*. In the Thematic Apperception Test, an ambiguous stimulus (like an inkblot or clouded picture) is presented to the test taker, and he or she is asked to interpret or react to it. Because the pictures are ambiguous, the person's interpretation must come from within—he or she supposedly *projects* into the picture his or her own emotional attitudes about life. Thus, a security-oriented person might describe the woman in **Figure 7.4** as "my mother worrying about what I will do if I lose my job."

Myers-Briggs Type Indicator
www.psychometrics.com

The Myers-Briggs instrument, which has been in use for more than 50 years, is believed to be the most widely used personality inventory in the world. More than two million assessments are administered annually in the United States alone.[16] Another example of a common personality test is the Minnesota Multiphasic Personality Inventory (MMPI), which taps traits like hypochondria and paranoia.

Research | **INSIGHT**

Research studies confirm that personality tests can help companies to hire more effective workers. For example, industrial psychologists often talk in terms

FIGURE 7.4 | Sample Picture from Thematic Apperception Test

How do you interpret this picture?

of the "Big Five" personality dimensions as they apply to employment testing: *extroversion, emotional stability, agreeableness, conscientiousness,* and *openness to experience.*[17] These dimensions can be measured using the NEO Five-Factor Inventory (NEO-FFI) and similar tests. One study focused on the extent to which these dimensions predicted performance (in terms of job and training proficiency, for example) for professionals, police officers, managers, sales workers, and skilled/semi-skilled workers. Conscientiousness showed a consistent relationship with all performance criteria for every occupation. Extroversion was a valid predictor of performance for managers and sales employees—the two occupations involving the most social interaction. Both openness to experience and extroversion predicted training proficiency for all occupations.[18] Another study involving a sample of 89 university employees concluded that absenteeism was inversely related to extroversion and conscientiousness.[19]

Interest inventories compare a candidate's interests with those of people in various occupations. Thus, a person taking the Strong-Campbell Inventory would receive a report comparing his or her interests with those of people already in occupations such as accountant, engineer, manager, or medical technologist. Interest inventories have many uses. One is career planning, since people generally do better in jobs involving activities in which they have an interest. Another is selection. If the firm can select people whose interests are roughly the same as those of high-performing incumbents in the jobs for which it is hiring, the new employees are more likely to be successful.[20]

Achievement Tests

An **achievement test** is basically a measure of what a person has learned. Most of the tests taken in school are achievement tests. They measure knowledge and/or proficiency in such areas as economics, marketing, or HRM. Achievement tests are also widely used in selection. For example, the Purdue Test for Machinists and Machine Operators tests the job knowledge of experienced machinists with such questions as "What is meant by 'tolerance'?" Other tests are available for electricians, welders, carpenters, and so forth. In addition to job knowledge, achievement tests measure the applicant's abilities; a keyboarding test is one example.

Work Sampling

Work samples focus on measuring job performance directly and thus are among the best predictors of job performance. In developing a work-sampling test, experts first list all the possible tasks that jobholders would be required to perform. Then, by listing the frequency of performance and relative importance of each task, key tasks are identified. Each applicant then performs the key tasks, and his or her work is monitored by the test administrator, who records the approach taken. Finally, the work-sampling test is validated by determining the relationship between the applicants' scores on the work samples and their actual performance on the job. Then, once it is shown that the work sample is a valid predictor of job success, the employer can begin using it for selection.[21]

Research Psychologists Press Inc.
www.rpp.on.ca

interest inventories Tests that compare a candidate's interests with those of people in various occupations.

achievement tests Tests used to measure knowledge and/or proficiency acquired through education, training, or experience.

Management Assessment Centres

management assessment centre A strategy used to assess candidates' management potential that uses a combination of realistic exercises, management games, objective testing, presentations, and interviews.

In a two- to three-day **management assessment centre**, the management potential of 10 or 12 candidates is assessed by expert appraisers who observe them performing realistic management tasks. The centre may be a plain conference room, but it is often a special room with a one-way mirror to facilitate unobtrusive observations. Examples of the types of activities and exercises involved include the following:

1. *An in-basket exercise.* Each candidate is faced with an accumulation of reports, memos, messages from incoming phone calls, letters, and other materials collected in the in-basket of the simulated job that he or she is to take over and is required to take appropriate action. For example, he or she must write letters, return phone calls, and prepare meeting agendas. The trained evaluators then review the results.

2. *A leaderless group discussion.* A leaderless group is given a discussion question and told to arrive at a group decision. The raters evaluate each candidate's interpersonal skills, acceptance by the group, leadership ability, and individual influence.

3. *Management games.* Participants engage in realistic problem solving, usually as members of two or more simulated companies that are competing in the marketplace. Decisions might have to be made about such issues as how to advertise and manufacture and how much inventory to keep in stock.

4. *Individual presentations.* During oral presentations on an assigned topic, each participant's communication skills and persuasiveness are evaluated.

5. *Objective tests.* Candidates may be asked to complete paper-and-pencil or computer-based personality, aptitude, interest, and/or achievement tests.

6. *An interview.* Most centres also require an interview between at least one of the expert assessors and each participant to evaluate interests, background, past performance, and motivation.

International Congress on Assessment Center Methods
www.assessmentcenters.org

Situational Testing

situational tests Tests in which candidates are presented with hypothetical situations representative of the job for which they are applying and are evaluated on their responses.

In **situational tests**, candidates are presented with hypothetical situations representative of the job for which they are applying (often on video) and are evaluated on their responses.[22] Several of the assessment centre exercises described previously are examples. In a typical test, a number of realistic scenarios are presented and each is followed by a multiple-choice question with several possible courses of action, from which candidates are asked to select the "best" response, in their opinion.[23] The level of each candidate's skills is then evaluated, and an assessment report can be easily generated, making the simulation easier and less expensive to administer than other screening tools. Simulations also provide a realistic job preview by exposing candidates to the types of activities that they will encounter on the job.

A research study of situational testing on 160 civil service employees demonstrated the validity of the situational test in predicting overall job performance as well as three performance dimensions: core technical proficiency, job dedication, and interpersonal facilitation. The situational test provided valid predictive

Research INSIGHT

A management game or simulation is a typical component in a management assessment centre.

Interactive employment tests administered on the computer are becoming popular as screening devices at many firms.

micro-assessment A series of verbal, paper-based, or computer-based questions and exercises that a candidate is required to complete, covering the range of activities required on the job for which he or she is applying.

information over and above cognitive ability tests, personality tests, and job experience.[24]

Micro-assessments

An entirely performance-based testing strategy that focuses on individual performance is a **micro-assessment**. In a micro-assessment, each applicant completes a series of verbal, paper-based, or computer-based questions and exercises that cover the range of activities required on the job for which he or she is apply ing. In addition to technical exercises, participants are required to solve a set of work-related problems that demonstrate their ability to perform well within the confines of a certain department or corporate culture. Exercises are simple to develop because they are taken directly from the job.

Physical Examination and Substance Abuse Testing

The use of medical examinations in selection has decreased, in part because of the loss of physically demanding manufacturing and natural resource jobs. Before 1980, 25 percent of new hires underwent a medical exam, but by 2001, only 11 percent were required to do so.[25] Three main reasons that firms may include a medical examination as a step in the selection process are (1) to determine that the applicant *qualifies for the physical requirements* of the position and, if not, to document any *accommodation requirements*; (2) to establish a *record and baseline* of the applicant's health for the purpose of future insurance or compensation claims; and (3) to *reduce absenteeism and accidents* by identifying any health issues or concerns that need to be addressed, including communicable diseases of which the applicant may have been unaware. Medical exams are only permitted after a written offer of employment has been extended (except in the case of bona fide occupational requirements, as for food handlers).

The purpose of pre-employment substance abuse testing is to avoid hiring employees who would pose unnecessary risks to themselves or others and/or perform below expectations. However, in Canada, employers are not permitted to screen candidates for substance abuse. Alcohol and drug addiction is considered to be a disability under human rights codes, and an employee cannot be discriminated against during the selection process based on a disability.[26]

STEP 3: THE SELECTION INTERVIEW

selection interview A procedure designed to predict future job performance on the basis of applicants' oral responses to oral inquiries.

The interview is used by virtually all organizations for selecting job applicants. The **selection interview**, which involves a process of two-way communication between the interviewee(s) and the interviewer(s), can be defined as "a procedure designed to predict future job performance on the basis of applicants' oral responses to oral inquiries."[27]

Interviews are considered to be one of the most important aspects of the selection process and generally have a major impact on both applicants and interviewers. Interviews significantly influence applicants' views about the job and organization, enable employers to fill in any gaps in the information provided on application forms and résumés, and supplement the results of any tests administered. They may also reveal entirely new types of information.

A major reason for the popularity of selection interviews is that they meet a number of the objectives of both interviewer and interviewee. Interviewer objectives include assessing applicants' qualifications and observing relevant aspects of applicants' behaviour, such as verbal communication skills, degree of self-confidence, and interpersonal skills; providing candidates with information about the job and expected duties and responsibilities; promoting the organization and highlighting its attractiveness; and determining how well the applicants would fit into the organization. Typical objectives of job applicants include presenting a positive image of themselves; selling their skills and marketing their positive attributes to the interviewer(s); and gathering information about the job and the organization so that they can make an informed decision about the job, career opportunities in the firm, and the work environment.[28]

Types of Interviews

Selection interviews can be classified according to the degree of structure, their content, and the way in which the interview is administered.

The Structure of the Interview

unstructured interview An unstructured, conversational-style interview. The interviewer pursues points of interest as they come up in response to questions.

structured interview An interview following a set sequence of questions.

First, interviews can be classified according to the degree to which they are structured. In an **unstructured interview**, questions are asked as they come to mind. Interviewees for the same job thus may or may not be asked the same or similar questions, and the interview's unstructured nature allows the interviewer to ask questions based on the candidate's last statements and to pursue points of interest as they develop. Unstructured interviews have low reliability and validity.[29]

The interview can also be structured. In the classical **structured interview**, the questions and acceptable responses are specified in advance and the responses are rated for appropriateness of content.[30] In practice, however, most structured interviews do not involve specifying and rating responses in advance. Instead, each candidate is asked a series of predetermined, job-related questions, based on the job description and specification. Such interviews are generally high in validity and reliability. However, a totally structured interview does not provide the flexibility to pursue points of interest as they develop, which may result in an interview that seems quite mechanical to all concerned.

mixed (semi-structured) interview An interview format that combines the structured and unstructured techniques.

Between these two extremes is the **mixed (semi-structured) interview**, which involves a combination of preset, structured questions based on the job description and specification, and a series of preset candidate-specific, job-related questions based on information provided on the application form and/or résumé. The questions asked of all candidates facilitate candidate comparison, while the job-related, candidate-specific questions make the interview more conversational. A realistic approach that yields comparable answers and in-depth insights, the mixed interview format is extremely popular.

Research | INSIGHT

A study of 92 real employment interviews found that the interviewers using high levels of structure in the interview process evaluated applicants less favourably than those who used semi-structured or unstructured interviews, and those applicants who were evaluated using a semi-structured interview were rated slightly higher than those evaluated by unstructured interviews. Additionally, the study found that significant differences occur in the way that female and male interviewers evaluate their applicants. Although male interviewers' ratings were unaffected by the interview structure, female interviewers' ratings were substantially higher in unstructured and semi-structured interviews than in highly structured interviews.[31]

The Content of the Interview

Interviews can also be classified according to the content of their questions. A **situational interview** is one in which the questions focus on the individual's ability to project what his or her *future* behaviour would be in a given situation.[32] The underlying premise is that intentions predict behaviour. For example, a candidate for a supervisory position might be asked how he or she would respond to an employee coming to work late three days in a row. The interview can be both *structured* and *situational*, with predetermined questions requiring the candidate to project what his or her behaviour would be. In a structured situational interview, the applicant could be evaluated, say, on whether he or she would try to determine if the employee was experiencing some difficulty in getting to work on time or would simply issue a verbal or written warning to the employee.

The **behavioural interview**, also known as a **behaviour description interview (BDI)**, involves describing various situations and asking interviewees how they behaved *in the past* in such situations.[33] The underlying assumption is that the best predictor of future performance is past performance in similar circumstances.

Administering the Interview

Interviews can also be classified based on how they are administered:

- one-on-one or by a panel of interviewers;
- sequentially or all at once; and
- face-to-face or using videoconferencing (30 percent of interviews and growing).

The majority of interviews are sequential, face-to-face, and one-on-one. In a *sequential interview* the applicant is interviewed by several persons in sequence before a selection decision is made. In an *unstructured sequential interview* each interviewer may look at the applicant from his or her own point of view, ask different questions, and form an independent opinion of the candidate. Conversely, in a *structured sequential* (or serialized) interview, each interviewer rates the candidate on a standard evaluation form, and the ratings are compared before the hiring decision is made.[34]

A **panel interview** involves the candidate being interviewed simultaneously by a group (or panel) of interviewers, including an HR representative, the hiring manager, and potential co-workers, superiors, and/or reporting employees. The key advantages associated with this technique are the increased likelihood that the information provided will be heard and recorded accurately; varied questions pertaining to each interviewer's area of expertise; minimized time and travel/accommodation expenses as each interviewee only attends one interview; reduced likelihood of human rights/employment equity violations since an HR representative is present; and less likelihood of interviewer error, because of advanced planning and preparation.

A more stressful variant of the panel interview is the *mass interview*, which involves a panel simultaneously interviewing several candidates. The panel poses a problem to be solved and then sits back and watches which candidate takes the lead in formulating an answer.

situational interview A series of job-related questions that focus on how the candidate would behave in a given situation.

behavioural or behaviour description interview (BDI) A series of job-related questions that focus on relevant past job-related behaviours.

panel interview An interview in which a group of interviewers questions the applicant.

A panel interview is an efficient and cost-effective way of permitting a number of qualified persons to assess a candidate's KSAs.

Interviewing and the Law

As a selection procedure, interviews must comply with human rights legislation. Doing so requires keeping the following guidelines in mind:

1. Interviewers cannot ask questions that would violate human rights legislation, either directly or indirectly. Questions cannot be asked about candidates' marital status, childcare arrangements, ethnic background, or workers' compensation history, for example.

2. All interviewees must be treated in the same manner. An interviewer cannot ask only female factory position applicants to demonstrate their lifting abilities, for example, or question female sales applicants about their willingness to travel but not ask male candidates. However, accommodation must be provided to applicants with disabilities.

3. Cutting short an interview based on preconceived notions about the gender or race of the "ideal" candidate should also be avoided, because this is another example of illegal differential treatment.

4. A helpful phrase to keep in mind when designing interview questions is "This job requires. . . ." Interviewers who focus on the job description and job specification can gather all the information required to assess applicants without infringing on the candidates' legal rights.

Common Interviewing Mistakes

Several common interviewing errors that can undermine the usefulness of interviews are discussed in the following pages.

Poor Planning

Many selection interviews are simply not carefully planned and may be conducted without having prepared written questions in advance. Lack of planning often leads to a relatively unstructured interview, in which whatever comes up is discussed. The end result may be little or no cross-candidate job-related information. The less structured the interview is, the less reliable and valid the evaluation of each candidate will be.[35]

Snap Judgments

One of the most consistent literature findings is that interviewers tend to jump to conclusions—make snap judgments—during the first few minutes of the interview or even before the interview begins, based on the candidates' test scores or résumé data. Thus, it is important for a candidate to start off on the right foot with the interviewer.

Negative Emphasis

Many interviewers seem to have a consistent negative bias. They are generally more influenced by unfavourable than favourable information about the candidate. Also, their impressions are much more likely to change from favourable to unfavourable than vice versa.

Halo Effect

halo effect A positive initial impression that distorts an interviewer's rating of a candidate because subsequent information is judged with a positive bias.

It is also possible for a positive initial impression to distort an interviewer's rating of a candidate, because subsequent information is judged with a positive bias. This is known as the **halo effect**. An applicant who has a pleasant smile and firm handshake, for example, may be judged positively before the interview even begins. Having gained that positive initial impression, the interviewer may not seek contradictory information when listening to the candidate's answers to the questions posed.

Poor Knowledge of the Job

Interviewers who do not know precisely what the job entails and what sort of candidate is best suited for it usually make their decisions based on incorrect stereotypes about what a good applicant is. Interviewers who have a clear understanding of what the job entails conduct more effective interviews.

Contrast (Candidate-Order) Error

contrast or candidate-order error An error of judgment on the part of the interviewer because of interviewing one or more very good or very bad candidates just before the interview in question.

Contrast or candidate-order error means that the order in which applicants are seen can affect how they are rated. In one study, managers were asked to evaluate a candidate who was "just average" after first evaluating several "unfavourable" candidates. The average candidate was evaluated more favourably than he or she might otherwise have been because, in contrast to the unfavourable candidates, the average one looked better than he or she actually was.

Influence of Nonverbal Behaviour

Interviewers are also influenced by the applicant's nonverbal behaviour, and the more eye contact, head moving, smiling, and other similar nonverbal behaviours, the higher the ratings. These nonverbal behaviours often account for more than 80 percent of the applicant's rating. This finding is of particular concern since nonverbal behaviour is tied to ethnicity and cultural background. An applicant's attractiveness and gender also play a role. Research has shown that those rated as being more physically attractive are also rated as more suitable for employment, well ahead of those rated average looking and those regarded as physically unattractive. Although this bias is considered to be unconscious, it may have serious implications for aging employees.[36]

Telegraphing

Some interviewers are so anxious to fill a job that they help the applicants to respond correctly to their questions by telegraphing the expected answer. An obvious example might be a question like: "This job calls for handling a lot of stress. You can do that, can you not?" The telegraphing is not always so obvious. For example, favourable first impressions of candidates tend to be linked to use of a more positive interview style. This can translate into sending subtle cues regarding the preferred response, such as a smile or nod.[37]

Too Much/Too Little Talking

If the applicant is permitted to dominate the interview, the interviewer may not have a chance to ask his or her prepared questions and often learns very little about the candidate's job-related skills. At the other extreme, some interviewers talk so much that the interviewee is not given enough time to answer questions. One expert suggests using the 30/70 rule: During a selection interview, encourage the candidate to speak 70 percent of the time, and restrict the interviewer speaking to just 30 percent of the time.[38]

Similar-to-Me Bias

Interviewers tend to provide more favourable ratings to candidates who possess demographic, personality, and attitudinal characteristics similar to their own.[39]

Designing an Effective Interview

Problems like those just described can be avoided by designing and conducting an effective interview. Combining several of the interview formats previously discussed enables interviewers to capitalize on the advantages of each.[40] To allow for probing and to prevent the interview from becoming too mechanical in nature, a semi-structured format is recommended. Given their higher validity in predicting job performance, the focus should be on situational and behavioural questions.

Designing an effective interview involves composing a series of job-related questions to be asked of all applicants for a particular job, as well as a few job-related candidate-specific questions. Doing so involves the following five steps, the first two of which should occur before recruitment.[41]

The first step is to decide who will be involved in the selection process and to *develop selection criteria*. Specifying selection criteria involves clarifying and weighting the information in the job description and job specification and holding discussions among the interview-team members, especially those most familiar with the job and co-workers.

The second step is to *specify musts* and *wants* and weight the *wants*. Once agreed on, the selection criteria should be divided into the two categories: musts and wants.[41] **Must criteria** are those that are absolutely essential for the job, include a measurable standard of acceptability, or are absolute. There are often only two musts: a specific level of education (or equivalent combination of education and work experience) and a minimum amount of prior, related work experience. The **want criteria** include skills and abilities that cannot be screened on paper (such as verbal skills) or are not readily measurable (such as leadership ability, teamwork skills, and enthusiasm), as well as qualifications that are desirable but not critical.

The third step is to determine assessment strategies and to *develop an evaluation form*. Once the must and want criteria have been identified, appropriate strategies for learning about each should be specified. For some qualifications, especially those that are critically important, the team may decide to use several assessment strategies. For example, leadership skills might be assessed through behavioural questions, situational questions, a written test, and an assessment centre. Once all want criteria have been agreed on and weighted, they become the basis for candidate comparison and evaluation, as illustrated in **Figure 7.5**.

The fourth step is to *develop interview questions* to be asked of all candidates. Questions should be developed for each KSA to be assessed during the interview. *Job-knowledge questions* and *worker-requirements questions* to gauge the applicants' motivation and willingness to perform under prevailing working conditions, such as shift work or travel, should also be included.

The fifth and final step is to *develop candidate-specific questions*. A few open-ended, job-related questions that are candidate-specific should be planned, based on each candidate's résumé and application form. Some examples are shown in **Figure 7.6**.

Conducting an Effective Interview

Although the following discussion focuses on a semi-structured panel interview, the steps described apply to all selection interviews.[43]

Planning the Interview

Before the first interview, agreement should be reached on the procedure that will be followed. Sometimes all members of the team ask a question in turn; in other situations, only one member of the team asks questions and the others serve as observers. Sitting around a large table in a conference room is much more appropriate and far less stressful than having all panel members seated across from the candidate behind a table or desk, which forms both a physical and a psychological barrier. As noted earlier, special planning is required when assessing candidates with disabilities.

Establishing Rapport

The main reason for an interview is to find out as much as possible about the candidate's fit with the job specifications, something that is difficult to do if the individual is tense and nervous. The candidate should be greeted in a friendly manner and put at ease.

Asking Questions

The questions written in advance should then be asked in order. Interviewers should listen carefully, encourage the candidate to

The rapport established with a job applicant not only puts the person at ease but also reflects the company's attitude toward its public.

FIGURE 7.5 | Worksheet—Comparison of Candidates for an Administrative Assistant Position

Criteria			Alternatives				
			A Smith	**B** Brown		**C** Yuill		
Must			Info	Go/No	Info	Go/No	Info	Go/No
Education — Office Admin. diploma or equivalent experience (3 years' clerical/secretarial experience)			Office admin. diploma	Go	Office admin. diploma	Go	No diploma, 1 year related experience	No Go
Experience — At least 2 years' secretarial/clerical experience			3 years' experience	Go	2 years' experience	Go		Go
Wants	Wt.	Info		Wt. Sc.	Sc.	Info	Wt. Sc.	Sc.	Info
Keyboarding/word processing	10	Word processing test		90	9	Word processing test	100	10	
Good oral communication	9	Interview assessment		81	9	Interview assessment	81	9	
Good spelling/grammar	9	Test results		72	8	Test results	81	9	
Organizational ability	9	Interview questions/simulation/reference checking		72	8	Interview questions/simulation/reference checking	81	9	
Initiative	8	Interview questions/simulation/reference checking		56	7	Interview questions/simulation/reference checking	64	8	
High ethical standards	7	Interview questions/simulation/reference checking		49	7	Interview questions/simulation/reference checking	49	7	
Shorthand skills (or speed writing)	4	Interview question and test results		16	4	Interview question and test results	0	0	
Designated group member, other than white female	2	Application form		4	2	Application form	0	0	
				440			**456**		TOP CANDIDATE

FIGURE 7.6 | Suggested Supplementary Questions for Interviewing Applicants

1. How did you choose this line of work?
2. What did you enjoy most about your last job?
3. What did you like least about your last job?
4. What has been your greatest frustration or disappointment on your present job? Why?
5. What are some of the pluses and minuses of your last job?
6. What were the circumstances surrounding your leaving your last job?
7. Did you give notice?
8. Why should we be hiring you?
9. What do you expect from this employer?
10. What are three things you will not do in your next job?
11. What would your last supervisor say your three weaknesses are?
12. What are your major strengths?
13. How can your supervisor best help you obtain your goals?
14. How did your supervisor rate your job performance?
15. In what ways would you change your last supervisor?
16. What are your career goals during the next 1–3 years? 5–10 years?
17. How will working for this company help you reach those goals?
18. What did you do the last time you received instructions with which you disagreed?
19. What are some of the things about which you and your supervisor disagreed? What did you do?
20. Which do you prefer, working alone or working with groups?
21. What motivated you to do better at your last job?
22. Do you consider your progress on that job representative of your ability? Why?
23. Do you have any questions about the duties of the job for which you have applied?
24. Can you perform the essential functions of the job for which you have applied?

Source: Reprinted from www.HR.BLR.com with permission of the publisher Business and Legal Reports, Inc. 141 Mill Rock Road East, Old Saybrook, CT © 2004.

express his or her thoughts and ideas fully, and record the candidate's answers briefly but thoroughly. Taking notes increases the validity of the interview process, since doing so (1) reduces the likelihood of forgetting job-relevant information and subsequently reconstructing forgotten information in accordance with biases and stereotypes; (2) reduces the likelihood of making a snap judgment and helps to prevent the halo effect, negative emphasis, and candidate-order errors; and (3) helps to ensure that all candidates are assessed on the same criteria.[44]

Closing the Interview

Toward the end of the interview, time should be allocated to answer any questions that the candidate may have and, if appropriate, to advocate for the firm and position.

Evaluating the Candidate

Immediately following each interview, the applicant's interview performance should be rated by each panel member independently, based on a review of his or her notes or an observation form like the one shown in **Figure 7.7**. Since interviews are only one step in the process and since a final decision cannot be reached until all assessments (including reference checking) have been completed, these evaluations should not be shared at this time.

FIGURE 7.7 | Interview Evaluation Form

Name of candidate:

Date interviewed:

Position:

Completed by:

Date:

Instructions: Circle one number for each criterion, then add them together for a total.

KNOWLEDGE OF SPECIFIC JOB AND JOB-RELATED TOPICS

0. No knowledge evident.
1. Less than we would prefer.
2. Meets requirements for hiring.
3. Exceeds our expectations of average candidates.
4. Thoroughly versed in job and very strong in associated areas.

EXPERIENCE

0. None for this job; no related experience either.
1. Would prefer more for this job. Adequate for job applied for.
2. More than sufficient for job.
3. Totally experienced in job.
4. Strong experience in all related areas.

COMMUNICATION

0. Could not communicate. Will be severely impaired in most jobs.
1. Some difficulties. Will detract from job performance.
2. Sufficient for adequate job performance.
3. More than sufficient for job.
4. Outstanding ability to communicate.

INTEREST IN POSITION AND ORGANIZATION

0. Showed no interest.
1. Some lack of interest.
2. Appeared genuinely interested.
3. Very interested. Seems to prefer type of work applied for.
4. Totally absorbed with job content. Conveys feeling only this job will do.

OVERALL MOTIVATION TO SUCCEED

0. None exhibited.
1. Showed little interest in advancement.
2. Average interest in advancement.
3. Highly motivated. Strong desire to advance.
4. Extremely motivated. Very strong desire to succeed and advance.

POISE AND CONFIDENCE

0. Extremely distracted and confused. Displayed uneven temper.
1. Sufficient display of confusion or loss of temper to interfere with job performance.
2. Sufficient poise and confidence to perform job.
3. No loss of poise during interview. Confidence in ability to handle pressure.
4. Displayed impressive poise under stress. Appears unusually confident and secure.

COMPREHENSION

0. Did not understand many points and concepts.
1. Missed some ideas or concepts.
2. Understood most new ideas and skills discussed.
3. Grasped all new points and concepts quickly.
4. Extremely sharp. Understood subtle points and underlying motives.

_____ **TOTAL POINTS**

ADDITIONAL REMARKS:

Source: Reprinted from www.HR.BLR.com with permission of the publisher Business and Legal Reports, Inc. 141 Mill Rock Road East, Old Saybrook, CT © 2004.

STEP 4: BACKGROUND INVESTIGATION/REFERENCE CHECKING

Background investigation and reference checking are used to verify the accuracy of the information provided by candidates on their application forms and résumés. In an ideal world, every applicant's story would be completely accurate, but in real life, this is often not the case, as illustrated in **Figure 7.8.** At least one-third of applicants lie—overstating qualifications or achievements, attempting to hide negative information, or being deliberately evasive or untruthful.[45]

Unfortunately, some employers do not check references, which can have grave consequences. Recent cases in Canada have included a nurse who practised in a Toronto hospital for almost two years without a registered nurse qualification, a manufacturing plant payroll officer who embezzled almost $2 million, and a teacher arrested for possessing child pornography.[46] Background checks are thus necessary to avoid negligent hiring lawsuits when others are placed in situations of unnecessary and avoidable risk.[47] Other problems can also be addressed through background checks. Loblaws recently took action to reduce its $1 billion disappearing goods problem by making criminal record checks mandatory for all prospective employees. So far, 7.5 percent of prospective hires have been eliminated because of criminal records.[48]

Surveys indicate that at least 90 percent of Canadian organizations conduct background checks.[49] Many firms use reference-checking services or hire a consultant to perform this task. Obtaining such assistance may be a small price to pay to avoid the time and legal costs associated with the consequences.

Whether requesting reference information in writing or asking for such information over the telephone, questions should be written down in advance. **Figure 7.9** is an example of a form used for written reference checking. If enough time is taken and the proper questions are asked, such checking is an inexpensive and straightforward way of verifying factual information about the applicant. This may include current and previous job titles, salary, dates of employment, and reasons for leaving, as well as information about the applicant's fit with the job and organizational culture.

King-Reed Associates
www.king-reed.com
Back Check
www.backcheck.ca
Investigative Research Group
www.irg-investigation.com

FIGURE 7.8 | Top Seven Résumé Lies

- Dates of employment
- Job title (inflated rank)
- Salary level
- Criminal records
- Education (bogus degrees diploma mills)
- Professional license (MD, RN etc.)
- "Ghost" company (self-owned business)

Source: AccuScreen Inc., www.accuscreen.com/TOP7. (May 24, 2009). Used with permission.

FIGURE 7.9 | Form Requesting Written Reference Information

We are in the process of considering James Ridley Parrish (SIN Number: 123-456-789) for a sales position in our firm. In considering him/her, it would be helpful if we could review your appraisal of his/her previous work with you. For your information, we have enclosed a statement signed by him/her authorizing us to contact you for information on his/her previous work experience with you. We would certainly appreciate it if you would provide us with your candid opinions of his/her employment. If you have any questions or comments you would care to make, please feel free to contact us at the number listed in the attached cover letter. At any rate, thank you for your consideration of our requests for the information requested below. As you answer the questions, please keep in mind that they should be answered in terms of your knowledge of his/her previous work with you.

1. When was he/she employed with your firm? From _____ to _____
2. Was he/she under your direct supervision? ☐ Yes ☐ No
3. If not, what was your working relationships with him/her? _____
4. How long have you had an opportunity to observe his/her job performance? _____
5. What was his/her last job title with your firm? _____
6. Did he/she supervise any employees? ☐ Yes ☐ No If so, how many?
7. Why did he/she leave your company? _____

Below is a series of questions that deal with how he/she might perform at the job for which we are considering him/her. Read the question and then use the rating scale to indicate how you think he/she would perform based on your previous knowledge of his/her work.

8. For him/her to perform best, how closely should he/she be supervised?
   ☐ Needs no supervision
   ☐ Needs infrequent supervision
   ☐ Needs close, frequent supervision
9. How well does he/she react to working with details?
   ☐ Gets easily frustrated
   ☐ Can handle work that involves some details but works better without them
   ☐ Details in a job pose no problems at all
10. How well do you think he/she can handle complaints from customers?
    ☐ Would generally refuse to help resolve a customer complaint
    ☐ Would help resolve a complaint only if a customer insisted
    ☐ Would feel the customer is right and do everything possible to resolve a complaint
11. In what type of sales job do you think he/she would be best?
    ☐ Handling sales of walk-in customers
    ☐ Traveling to customer locations out-of-town to make sales
12. With respect to his/her work habits, check all of the characteristics below that describe his/her work situation:
    ☐ Works best on a regular schedule
    ☐ Works best under pressure
    ☐ Works best only when in the mood
    ☐ Works best when there is a regular series of steps to follow for solving a problem
13. Do you know of anything that would indicate if he/she would be unfit or dangerous (for example, in working with customers or co-workers or in driving an automobile) in a position with our organization? ☐ Yes ☐ No
    If "yes" please explain. _____
14. If you have any additional comments, please make them on the back of this form.

Your Name: _____

Your Title: _____

Address: _____
              City   Province   Postal Code

Company: _____

Telephone: _____

Thank you for your time and help. The information you provided will be very useful as we review all application materials.

Note: This form is completed by the reference giver.

Source: From *Human Resource Selection*, 5th ed., by Gatewood/Field. © 2001. Reprinted with permission of South-Western, a division of Thomson Learning: www.thomsonrights.com. Fax 800-730-2215.

Information to Be Verified

A basic background check includes a criminal record check, independent verification of educational qualifications, verification of at least five years' employment, together with checks of three performance-related references from past supervisors. For financially sensitive positions, a credit check may also be included.

Obtaining Written Permission

Written permission is not only required for credit checking. As a legal protection for all concerned, applicants should be asked to indicate, in writing, their willingness for the firm to check with current and/or former employers and other references. There is generally a section on the application form for this purpose. Many employers will not give out any reference information until they have received a copy of such written authorization. Because background checks may provide information on age or other prohibited grounds for discrimination, some employers do not conduct background checks until a conditional offer of employment has been extended.[50]

However, other employers do not hesitate to seek out information in the public domain at any time, without permission. A recent survey found that almost one-quarter of employers are using social networking sites such as Facebook to gather information on job applicants. A third of those employers find enough negative information (such as the items listed in **Figure 7.10**) to eliminate a candidate from further consideration, and one-quarter of them find favourable content that supports the candidate's application.[51]

Making Reference Checks More Effective

Several things can be done to make reference checks more effective. One is to use a structured form to ensure that important questions are not overlooked.

FIGURE 7.10 | Online Postings by Job Candidates that Concern Hiring Managers

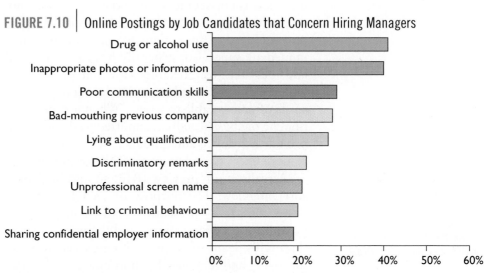

Source: careerbuilder.ca/Article/CB-417-Interviewing-Is-Your-Future-Boss-Researching-You-Online/?sc_extcmp=cbca_9417&cblang=CAEnglish&pf=true&SiteId=cbca_9417&ArticleID=417&cbRecursionCnt=1&cbsid=02a1e103f09840968597bacd20a26d98-296480762-VG-4 (May 24, 2009); shown in *Canadian HR Reporter* October 6, 2008, p. 4.

An Ethical | Dilemma

As the HR manager, how would you balance your ethical responsibilities to those providing reference information and to the job applicant in a situation in which a candidate is being eliminated from a competition based on negative reference information from a number of sources?

Another suggestion is to use the references offered by the applicant as a source for other references who may know of the applicant's performance. Thus, each of the applicant's references might be asked, "Could you please give me the name of another person who might be familiar with the applicant's performance?" In that way, information may be obtained from references that are more objective because they weren't referred directly by the applicant. Making reference checks productive also requires persistence.

Providing References

In providing reference information, the concept of *qualified privilege* is important. Generally speaking, if comments are made in confidence for a public purpose, without malice, and are honestly believed, the defence of qualified privilege exists. Thus, if honest, fair, and candid references are given by an individual who is asked to provide confidential information about the performance of a job applicant, then the doctrine of qualified privilege generally protects the reference giver, even if negative information is imparted about the candidate.[52] An overly positive reference, however, describing an employee dismissed for theft as "trustworthy" can be considered *negligent misrepresentation* if the former employee steals from a new employer.[53] Due to concerns about the possibility of civil litigation, some Canadian companies have adopted a "no reference" policy regarding previous employees or are only willing to confirm the position held and dates of employment—especially in the case of discharged employees.[54]

STEP 5: SUPERVISORY INTERVIEW AND REALISTIC JOB PREVIEW

The two or three top candidates typically return for an interview with the immediate supervisor, who usually makes the final selection decision. The supervisory interview is important because the supervisor knows the technical aspects of the job, is most qualified to assess the applicants' job knowledge and skills, and is best equipped to answer any job-specific questions from the candidate. Also, the immediate supervisor generally has to work closely with the selected individual and must feel comfortable with that person. The selected individual must fit with the current members of the hiring department, something that the supervisor is often best able to assess. When a supervisor makes a hiring recommendation, he or she is usually committed to the new employee's success and will try to provide assistance and guidance. If the new hire is not successful, the supervisor is more likely to accept some of the responsibility.

realistic job preview (RJP) A strategy used to provide applicants with realistic information—both positive and negative—about the job demands, the organization's expectations, and the work environment.

A **realistic job preview (RJP)** should be provided at the time of the supervisory interview. The purpose of an RJP is to create appropriate expectations about the job by presenting realistic information about the job demands, the organization's expectations, and the work environment.[55] Studies have reported that RJPs lead to improved employee job satisfaction, reduced voluntary turnover, and enhanced communication.[56] Although some candidates may choose not to accept employment with the firm after an RJP, those individuals probably would not have remained with the firm long had they accepted the job offer.[57]

STEP 6: HIRING DECISION AND CANDIDATE NOTIFICATION

statistical strategy A more objective technique used to determine to whom the job should be offered; involves identifying the most valid predictors and weighting them through statistical methods, such as multiple regression.

To make the hiring decision, information from the multiple selection techniques used must be combined, and the applicant who is the best fit with the selection criteria must be identified. HR department staff members generally play a major role in compiling all the data. It is the immediate supervisor who is usually responsible for making the final hiring decision, however. Firms generally make a subjective evaluation of all the information gleaned about each candidate and arrive at an overall judgment. The validity and reliability of these judgments can be improved by using tests that are objectively scored and by devising a candidate-rating sheet based on the weighted want criteria.

Another approach involves combining all the pieces of information according to a formula and giving the job to the candidate with the highest score. Research studies have indicated that this approach, called a **statistical strategy**, is generally more reliable and valid than is a subjective evaluation.[58]

Regardless of collection methodology, all information used in making the selection decision should be kept in a file, including interview notes, test results, reference-checking information, and so on. In the event of a human rights challenge, negligent hiring charge, or union grievance about the selection decision, such data are critical.

Once the selection decision has been made, a job offer is extended to the successful candidate. Often, the initial offer is made by telephone, but it should be followed up with a written employment offer that clearly specifies important terms and conditions of employment, such as starting date, starting salary, probation period, and so on.

Candidates should be given a reasonable length of time in which to think about the offer and not be pressured into making an immediate decision. If there are two candidates who are both excellent and the first-choice candidate declines the offer, the runner-up can then be offered the job.

An Ethical | Dilemma

As the HR manager, how much feedback should you provide to those individuals not selected for a position?

Chapter | SUMMARY

1. Selection is the process of choosing among individuals who have been recruited to fill existing or projected job openings. The purpose of selection is to find the "best" candidate. Because the quality of the company's human resources is often a competitive advantage in achieving the company's strategic objectives, selection of those employees has considerable strategic importance. Those individuals selected will be implementing strategic decisions and, in some cases, creating strategic plans. Thus, the successful candidates must fit with the strategic direction of the organization.

2. Reliability (the degree to which selection techniques are dependable, consistent, and stable) and validity (which relates to accuracy) of selection tests and interviews are critically important for effective selection of the best candidate and to satisfy legal requirements.

3. The different types of tests used for selection include intelligence tests, emotional intelligence tests, aptitude tests, tests of motor and physical abilities, personality tests, interest inventories, achievement tests, the work-sampling technique, management assessment centres, situational testing, micro-assessments, and medical examinations. Pre-employment substance abuse testing is not permitted under human rights legislation.

4. Selection interviewing can be unstructured, structured, or semi-structured. The content varies between situational interviews (focus on future behaviour) and behavioural interviews (focus on past behaviour). Interviews can be administered on a one-on-one basis, sequentially, or by using a panel.

5. Reference checking is a very important source of information about job candidates. Failure to check references can lead to negligent or wrongful hiring lawsuits. When providing references, the legal concept of qualified privilege means that if honest, fair, and candid references are given, the reference-giver is protected from litigation, even if negative information is imparted about the candidate. Providing overly positive references can lead to charges of negligent misrepresentation by subsequent employers. Fear of civil litigation has led some Canadian companies to adopt a policy of "no references" or to only confirm a former employee's position and dates of employment.

PEARSON
myHRlab

Test yourself on the material for this chapter at
www.pearsoned.ca/myhrlab

Key | TERMS

achievement tests   *(p. 184)*
aptitude tests   *(p. 181)*
behavioural or behaviour description
    interview (BDI)   *(p. 188)*
construct validity   *(p. 180)*
content validity   *(p. 180)*
contrast or candidate-order error   *(p. 191)*
criterion-related validity   *(p. 180)*
differential validity   *(p. 180)*
emotional intelligence (EI) tests   *(p. 181)*
halo effect   *(p. 191)*
intelligence (IQ) tests   *(p. 181)*
interest inventories   *(p. 184)*
management assessment centre   *(p. 185)*
micro-assessment   *(p. 186)*
mixed (semi-structured) interview   *(p. 187)*

multiple-hurdle strategy   *(p. 176)*
must criteria   *(p. 193)*
panel interview   *(p. 188)*
personality tests   *(p. 183)*
realistic job preview (RJP)   *(p. 200)*
reliability   *(p. 179)*
selection   *(p. 175)*
selection interview   *(p. 186)*
selection ratio   *(p. 176)*
situational interview   *(p. 188)*
situational tests   *(p. 185)*
statistical strategy   *(p. 201)*
structured interview   *(p. 187)*
unstructured interview   *(p. 187)*
validity   *(p. 180)*
want criteria   *(p. 193)*

Review and Discussion | QUESTIONS

1. Explain the differences among criterion-related validity, content validity, and construct validity.

2. Describe five different types of testing that may be used in the selection process and give an example of each.

3. Describe any four activities involved in a management assessment centre.

4. Name and describe the pros and cons of the three different types of interview structures.

5. Explain the difference between situational and behavioural interviews. Give examples of situational and behavioural interview questions.

6. Briefly discuss any five common interviewing mistakes and explain how such errors can be avoided.

7. Why is the supervisory interview so important in the selection process?

Critical Thinking | QUESTIONS

1. If you were asked to design an effective selection process for retail sales representatives working on a 100 percent commission basis, which of the steps described in this chapter would you include and why? Justify the omission of any steps and explain why the quality of the selection decision will not be compromised by their elimination.

2. Assume that you have just been hired as the employment manager in a small manufacturing firm that has never done any selection testing. Write a memorandum to the CEO describing the types of tests that you would recommend the firm consider using in the future, some of the legal and ethical concerns pertaining to such testing and how such concerns can be overcome, and the benefits to the firm of using the recommended testing.

3. Describe strategies that you could use to (a) establish rapport with an extremely nervous candidate, (b) get an interviewee who is rambling "back on track," (c) clarify a statement made by an applicant during an interview, and (d) obtain detailed reference information from an individual who seems reluctant to say much.

4. Alberta oil and gas companies are using pre-employment substance abuse testing even though it is prohibited. Their argument is that, because they have multibillion-dollar projects underway with a lot of potential for accidents, environmental damage, and so on, they want to be sure that they are not hiring employees who have substance abuse problems. They know that their young, transient, and relatively wealthy oil sands workforce commonly abuses drugs and alcohol. How could this situation be resolved in the spirit of the law on accommodating disabilities?

Experiential | EXERCISES

1. Design a semi-structured interview questionnaire for a position with which you are extremely familiar, basing the candidate-specific questions on your own résumé. Ensure that behavioural, situational, job-knowledge, and worker-requirements questions are included. Once you have done so, select a partner. Role-play two selection interviews—one based on your questionnaire and the other based on your partner's questionnaire. The individual who wrote the questions is to play the role of interviewee, with his or her partner serving as the interviewer. Do not forget to build rapport, ask the questions in order, take effective notes, and bring the interview to a close. Once you have completed the two role-plays, critically evaluate each interview questionnaire.

2. Create an offer of employment for a successful customer service representative at a call centre, outlining the terms and conditions of employment. Keep in mind that a copy of the letter should be signed and returned by the new hire and that a signed letter of offer becomes an employment contract.

3. Using the NOC job description and the competency job analysis you created earlier in the course, for either a university or college professor, develop two situational and two behavioural interview questions along with an outline of a "good" answer for each that you expect from the interviewees. Share and critique both questions and answers. Discuss how taking the time to complete this activity can help in candidate selection.

Running | CASE

Running Case: LearnInMotion.com

The Better Interview

Like virtually all the other HR-related activities at LearnInMotion.com, the company has no organized approach to interviewing job candidates. Three people, Jennifer, Pierre, and Greg (from the board of directors), interview each candidate, and the three then get together for a discussion. Unfortunately, they usually reach strikingly different conclusions. For example, Greg thought a particular candidate was "stellar" and would not only be able to sell but also eventually assume various administrative responsibilities to take the load off Jennifer and Pierre. Pierre thought this particular candidate was hopeless: "I've been selling for eight years and have hired many salespeople, and there's no way this person's going to be a closer," he said. Jennifer, noting that a friend of her mother had recommended this particular candidate, was willing to take a wait-and-see attitude: "Let's hire her and see how she does," she said. Pierre replied that this was no way to hire a salesperson, and, in any case, hiring another administrator was pretty far down their priority list. "I wish Greg would stick to the problem at hand, namely hiring a 100-percent salesperson."

Jennifer was sure that inadequate formal interviewing practices, procedures, and training accounted for at least some of the problems they were having in hiring and keeping good salespeople. They did hire one salesperson whom they thought was going to be terrific, based on the praise provided by her references

and on what they understood her previous sales experience had been; she stayed for a month and a half, sold hardly anything, cost the company almost $10 000 of its precious cash, and then left for another job.

The problem wasn't just with the salespeople. For one thing, they hired a programmer largely based on his assertion that he was expert in various web-related programming, including HTML, XML, and Java script. They followed up with one of his references, who was neutral regarding the candidate's programming abilities. But, being desperate, Jennifer and Pierre hired him anyway—only to have him leave three weeks later, more or less by mutual consent.

"This is a total disaster," said Jennifer, and Pierre could only agree. It was obvious that in some respects their interviews were worse than not interviewing at all: For example, if they didn't have interviews, perhaps they would have used more caution in following up with the candidates' references. In any case, they now want you, their management consultant, to tell them what to do.

QUESTIONS

1   How would you restructure LearnInMotion's selection process?

2   Should Pierre and Jennifer utilize the multiple hurdle strategy? Why or why not?

3   What are some of the legal implications of a new selection process Jennifer and Pierre need to be aware of?

Case | INCIDENT

The Case of What Should Have Been Known

Sunrise Academy, a privately run technical college, has been operating now for four successful years. Executive Director Ron Phillips is responsible for overseeing the college. He has just been reviewing the latest enrolment figures and is pleasantly surprised again by the projected number for the upcoming new

school year. This will mean that a new professor will be needed in the Business Administration program. At that moment, Ron picks up the phone and calls the Director of Human Resources to start the process for drafting a job posting to advertise the position both internally and externally.

A week goes by and HR calls Ron to indicate that they have many applications available to be reviewed for potential interviews. Ron reviews the applicants and a short-list is developed and called for interviews. After a round of four "okay but not spectacular" interviews, Ron was beginning to think they would never find a good candidate. However, the last interviewee, Rita Miller, turned out to be the successful choice and was subsequently offered the position. HR checked two references prior offering Rita the position in writing. HR also asked Rita to bring an original copy of her Masters of Business Administration degree once it was received, as this degree was a requirement in the professor posting.

Rita brought a copy of her degree to HR within a week of being offered the position. HR's policy is also to call the issuing institution to verify degrees. Things became busy in the department so it was nearly two months later when someone finally checked Rita's degree. The results indicated Rita's degree was forged. HR called Ron with the news, and

Ron has asked you to come in to help him decide what to do next.

QUESTIONS

1   Are there any legal implications to be aware of as a result of this selection decision?

2   What should have been done differently in the selection process?

3   How should the background checking process be improved at Sunrise Academy?

For additional cases and exercise material, go to
www.pearsoned.ca/myhrlab

 To view the CBC Videos, read a summary, and answer discussion questions, go to MyHRLab at
www.pearsoned.ca/myhrlab

Subject	Avoid Asking	Preferred	Comment
Name	about name change: whether it was changed by court order, marriage, or other reason maiden name		ask after selection if needed to check on previously held jobs or educational credentials
Address	for addresses outside Canada	ask place and duration of current or recent address	
Age	for birth certificates, baptismal records, or about age in general	ask applicants whether they are eligible to work under Canadian laws regarding age restrictions	if precise age required for benefits plans or other legitimate purposes, it can be determined after selection
Sex	males or females to fill in different applications about pregnancy, child bearing plans, or child care arrangements	ask applicant if the attendance requirements can be met	during the interview or after selection, the applicant, for purposes of courtesy, may be asked which of Dr., Mr., Mrs., Miss, Ms. is preferred
Marital Status	whether the applicant is single, married, divorced, engaged, separated, widowed, or living common-law whether an applicant's spouse may be transferred about spouse's employment	if transfer or travel is part of the job, the applicant can be asked if he or she can meet these requirements ask whether there are any circumstances that might prevent completion of a minimum service commitment	information on dependants can be determined after selection if necessary
Family Status	number of children or dependants about child care arrangements	if the applicant would be able to work the required hours and, where applicable, overtime	contacts for emergencies and/or details on dependants can be determined after selection
National or Ethnic Origin	about birthplace, nationality of ancestors, spouse, or other relatives whether born in Canada for proof of citizenship	since those who are entitled to work in Canada must be citizens, permanent residents, or holders of valid work permits, applicants can be asked if they are legally entitled to work in Canada	documentation of eligibility to work (papers, visas, etc.) can be requested after selection
Military Service	about military service in other countries	inquire about Canadian military service where employment preference is given to veterans by law	
Language	mother tongue where language skills obtained	ask whether applicant understands, reads, writes, or speaks languages required for the job	testing or scoring applicants for language proficiency is not permitted unless job related
Race or Colour	about race or colour, including colour of eyes, skin, or hair		

continued

Subject	Avoid Asking	Preferred	Comment
Photographs	for photo to be attached to applications or sent to interviewer before interview	photos for security passes or company files can be taken after selection	
Religion	whether applicant will work a specific religious holiday about religious affiliation, church membership, frequency of church attendance for references from clergy or religious leader	explain the required work shift, asking whether such a schedule poses problems for the applicant	reasonable accommodation of an employee's religious beliefs is the employer's duty
Height and Weight			no inquiry unless there is evidence they are genuine occupational requirements
Disability	for list of all disabilities, limitations, or health problems whether applicant drinks or uses drugs whether applicant has ever received psychiatric care or been hospitalized for emotional problems whether applicant has received workers' compensation		the employer should: – disclose any information on medically-related requirements or standards early in the application process – then ask whether the applicant has any condition that could affect his or her ability to do the job, preferably during a pre-employment medical examination a disability is only relevant to job ability if it: – threatens the safety or property of others – prevents the applicant from safe and adequate job performance even when reasonable efforts are made to accommodate the disability
Medical Information	whether currently under a physician's care name of family doctor whether receiving counselling or therapy		medical exams should be conducted after selection and only if an employee's condition is related to job duties offers of employment can be made conditional on successful completion of a medical exam
Pardoned Conviction	whether applicant has ever been convicted whether applicant has ever been arrested whether applicant has a criminal record	if bonding is a job requirement, ask whether the applicant is eligible	inquiries about criminal record or convictions are discouraged unless related to job duties

continued

Subject	Avoid Asking	Preferred	Comment
Sexual Orientation	about the applicant's sexual orientation		contacts for emergencies and/or details on dependants can be determined after selection
References			the same restrictions that apply to questions asked of applicants apply when asking for employment references

Souce: A Guide to Screening and Selection in Employment, Canadian Human Rights Commission. www. chrc-ccdp.ca/publications/screening_employment-en.asp. Reprinted with permission of the Minister of Public Works and Government Services Canada, 2009.

CHAPTER 8

LEARNING OUTCOMES

AFTER STUDYING THIS CHAPTER, YOU SHOULD BE ABLE TO

EXPLAIN how to develop an orientation program.

DESCRIBE the five-step training process.

DISCUSS two techniques used for assessing training needs.

EXPLAIN at least five traditional training techniques.

DESCRIBE the three types of e-learning.

DESCRIBE how to evaluate the training effort.

EXPLAIN several common types of training for special purposes.

ORIENTATION AND TRAINING

REQUIRED PROFESSIONAL CAPABILITIES (RPC)

- Develops orientation policies and procedures for new employees

- Ensures compliance with legislated training obligations

- Conducts training needs assessments

- Recommends the most appropriate way to meet identified learning needs

- Facilitates post-training support activities to ensure transfer of learning to the workplace

- Identifies and accesses external sources of training funding available to employees

- Recommends the selection of external training providers

- Participates in course design and selection and delivery of learning materials

- Ensures arrangements are made for training schedules, facilities, trainers, participants, and equipment and course material

ORIENTING EMPLOYEES

Once employees have been recruited and selected, the next step is orienting them to their new company and their new job. A strategic approach to recruitment and retention of employees includes a well-integrated orientation program, both before and after hiring.[1] New employees need a clear understanding of company policies, of expectations regarding their performance, and of operating procedures. In the long term, a comprehensive orientation (also called onboarding) program can lead to reductions in turnover, increased morale, fewer instances of corrective discipline, and fewer employee grievances. It can also reduce the number of workplace injuries, particularly for young workers.[2] The bottom-line implications of successful orientation can be dramatic, as described in the **Strategic HR** box.

Purpose of Orientation Programs

employee orientation (onboarding)
A procedure for providing new employees with basic background information about the firm and the job.

Employee orientation (onboarding) provides new employees with basic background information about the employer and specific information that they need to perform their jobs satisfactorily. At the Law Society of Upper Canada, any time a new employee walks through the door, the organization acts quickly to help the person get started on the right foot. The Law Society views orientation as an investment in the retention of talent. The essence of the orientation

Strategic HR

Onboarding: The First Step in Motivation and Retention

Professor Jerry Newman is one of the authors of a best-selling book on compensation. He worked undercover as a crew member in seven fast-food restaurants during a 14-month period in order to research total rewards. One of his findings was that the onboarding (also known as employee orientation) process played a very significant role in long-term perceptions of management's leadership abilities and the quality of non-monetary rewards.

In the best restaurant he worked for, he walked in and asked a counter worker for an application. She handed it to him, suggested that he fill out the application in the lobby, and in one simple gesture, created a positive first impression by asking "Would you like a soda?" Although it may seem trivial, it was one of the few times anyone went to any lengths, however minor, to satisfy the needs of a future employee.

The first days and weeks of employment are crucial in the turnover reduction process as reality begins to converge or diverge with an employee's needs and aspirations. Making good first impressions goes a long way toward shaping a future view of non-monetary rewards.

In recent years, the fast food industry has made concerted efforts to reduce turnover. Many chains have cut turnover in half during the past five years. Why? Because when they start to analyze costs, the results of successful onboarding are dramatic.

Assume a typical store does $1 million in sales and profits are 10 percent ($100 000). A typical turnover, according to most brands, costs between $1500 and $2000. If turnover is 150 percent and the typical store has 40 employees, then 60 employees turn over during the course of the year. Taking the midpoint of the replacement cost, 60 employees at $1750 each equals $105 000. With profits at $100 000, the turnover costs eat up a store's profitability. This is why fast food has made reducing turnover a high priority. And the cost of turnover in, say, high-tech industries is much higher than $1500 or $2000. It quickly becomes apparent that reducing turnover, partially accomplished through a positive and successful onboarding experience, can have very positive payoffs.

program is to introduce people to the culture, give them a common bond, teach the importance of teamwork in the workplace, and provide the tools and information to be successful at the Law Society.[3]

socialization The ongoing process of instilling in all employees the prevailing attitudes, standards, values, and patterns of behaviour that are expected by the organization.

Orientation is actually one component of the employer's new-employee socialization process. **Socialization** is the ongoing process of instilling in all employees the prevailing attitudes, standards, values, and patterns of behaviour that are expected by the organization.[4] During the time required for socialization to occur, a new employee is less than fully productive. A strong onboarding program can speed up the socialization process and result in the new employee achieving full productivity as quickly as possible.

Orientation helps the employee to perform better by providing necessary information about company rules and practices. It helps to clarify the organization's expectations of an employee regarding his or her job, thus helping to reduce the new employee's first-day jitters and **reality shock**—the discrepancy between what the new employee expected from his or her new job and its realities.

reality shock The state that results from the discrepancy between what the new employee expects from his or her new job and the realities of it.

An important part of any effective orientation program is sitting down and deciding on work-related goals with the new employee. These goals provide the basis for early feedback and establish a foundation for ongoing performance management.[5] Orientation is the first step in helping the new employee to manage the learning curve; it helps new employees to become productive more quickly than they might otherwise.

Some organizations commence orientation activity before the first day of employment. At Ernst & Young, the firm keeps in touch with people who have been hired but have not yet started work by sending them internal newsletters, inviting them to drop by for chats, and hosting dinners for them.[6] Others use orientation as an ongoing "new-hire development process" and extend it in stages throughout the first year of employment, in order to improve retention levels and reduce the overall costs of recruitment.[7]

Online onboarding systems that can be provided to new employees as soon as they accept the job offer are increasingly being used to engage employees more quickly and accelerate employee performance.[8] Online onboarding provides strategic benefits starting with building the brand as an employer of choice. This approach engages new hires in a personalized way and accelerates their time-to-productivity by completing benefits decisions, payroll forms, new-hire data, introduction of policies and procedures, and preliminary socialization using videos and graphics before the first day on the job, leading to a productive day one.[9]

Content of Orientation Programs

RPC

Develops orientation policies and procedures for new employees

Orientation programs range from brief, informal introductions to lengthy, formal programs. In the latter, the new employee is usually given (over an extended time) the following:

- a handbook that covers matters like company history and current mission; working hours and attendance expectations; vacations and holidays; payroll, employee benefits, and pensions; and work regulations and policies such as personal use of company technology
- a tour of the company facilities and introductions to the employee's supervisor and co-workers

- an explanation of job procedures, duties, and responsibilities
- a summary of training to be received (when and why)
- an explanation of performance appraisal criteria, including the estimated time to achieve full productivity.

As illustrated in **Figure 8.1**, other information typically includes HR policies, strategic objectives, company organization and operations, and safety measures and regulations. At Ernst & Young, after a review of best practices, both internally and externally, the orientation program was redesigned to include the following:[10]

- a presentation providing an overview of the firm
- an administrative checklist of tasks to be conducted before a new employee's start date and during the first three months of employment
- a binder explaining the firm's vision, values, strategies, and structures
- information technology training
- a form for employee feedback
- an intranet site with information about the firm.

Note that some courts have found employee handbook contents to represent a contract with the employee. Therefore, disclaimers should be included that make it clear that statements of company policies, benefits, and regulations do not constitute the terms and conditions of an employment contract, either express or implied. Firms should think twice before including such statements in the handbook as "No employee will be terminated without just cause," or statements that imply or state that employees have tenure; they could be viewed as legal and binding commitments.

Responsibility for Orientation

The first day of the orientation usually starts with the HR specialist, who explains such matters as working hours and vacation. The employee is then introduced to his or her new supervisor, who continues the orientation by explaining the exact nature of the job, introducing the person to his or her new colleagues, and familiarizing the new employee with the workplace. Sometimes, another employee at a peer level will be assigned as a "buddy" or mentor for the newly hired employee for the first few weeks or months of employment.[11] It is a good idea for the HR department to follow up with each new employee about three months after the initial orientation to address any remaining questions.

Special Orientation Situations

Diverse Workforce

In an organization that has not had a diverse workforce in the past, orienting new employees from different backgrounds poses a special challenge. The values of the organization may be new to them if these values were not part of their past experience. New employees should be advised to expect a variety of reactions from current employees to someone from a different background and be given some tips on how to

In an orientation, the supervisor explains the exact nature of the job, introduces new colleagues, and familiarizes new employees with the workplace.

FIGURE 8.1 | Orientation Checklist

Orientation Checklist for New Employees
Instructions to Departmental HR Administrator:

a. Supply a copy of this Employee Orientation Checklist to each new employee for his/her information.

b. Complete or coordinate the completion of each of the tasks indicated on this Checklist.

c. When all activities have been completed, sign in the space indicated below and forward a copy to the Department of Human Resources.

EMPLOYMENT DOCUMENTATION

- Employee has met with a Benefits Officer in Human Resources to sign all necessary payroll and benefit plan documentation

INTRODUCTION AND WELCOME

- Employee has received a copy of this Orientation Checklist
- All necessary equipment required by the employee, including computer, telephone and other facilities are available
- Employee has been provided with an e-mail account
- Employee has been introduced to his/her immediate supervisor
- Employee has been introduced to co-workers and others with whom she/he will regularly interact in her/his job
- Employee has been assigned a "mentor/buddy"
- Business cards have been supplied, if required

OVERVIEW OF DEPARTMENT AND POSITION

The following have been reviewed with the employee:

- The Department's organizational structure
- The role of the Department within the university
- The current objectives and priorities of the Department
- A written job description, the latest Job Fact Sheet for the position, or some other written statement of job responsibilities
- Specific performance standards and expectations
- The probationary period and probationary review process.

WORK SITE FAMILIARIZATION

Employee has been shown how to locate or access the following:

- The Department's local area network
- Computer assistance—HELP Desk
- Unit or departmental files, reports and other records
- Lunch and rest room facilities
- Office supplies and office equipment

DEPARTMENTAL POLICIES AND PROCEDURES

The Department's policies and procedures have been reviewed with the employee, including those pertaining to the following:

- Hours of operation and overtime requirements, if any
- Phone greetings
- Dress code
- Personal use of university equipment

WORKPLACE SAFETY

The university's safety policies and procedures in relation to the following have been reviewed with the employee:

- Reporting of accidents and incidents
- Duty to report unsafe conditions
- Right to refuse unsafe work
- Building evacuation and fire alarm
- Location of emergency exits; fire extinguishers; the nearest first aid station; and the closest qualified first aid attendant.

All activities noted above have been reviewed with the employee.

HR Administrator: **Date:**

Employee's Name:

Employee: **Date:**

Position Title:

Source: Memorial University, www.mun.ca/finance/forms/OrientationChecklist_New_Employees.doc (May 29, 2009). Used with permission of Memorial University of Newfoundland.

deal with these reactions. In particular, they need to know which reactions are prohibited under human rights legislation and how to report these, should they occur.

Mergers and Acquisitions

Employees hired into a newly merged company need to receive information about the details of the merger or acquisition as part of the information on company history. They also need to be made aware of any ongoing, as-yet-unresolved difficulties regarding day-to-day operational issues related to their work. A further orientation issue arises with respect to the existing employees at the time of the merger or acquisition: A new company culture will evolve in the merged organization, and everyone will experience a resocialization process. This presents an opportunity for the merged organization to emphasize the new organizational values and beliefs, in order to reinforce corporate culture and further the new organization's business objectives.[12]

Union versus Non-Union Employees

New employees in unionized positions need to be provided with a copy of the collective agreement and be told which information relates specifically to their particular job. They also need to be introduced to their union steward, have payroll deduction of union dues explained, and be informed of the names of union executive members. New employees, both unionized and non-unionized, need to be made aware of which jobs are unionized and which ones are not.

Multi-Location Organizations

New employees in a multi-location company need to be made aware of where the other locations are and what business functions are performed in each location. The Ontario Ministry of Education and Training is one such organization, and it uses a web-based, online orientation to deliver corporate-level information.[13] All employees have equal access regardless of their location, and the same message is delivered to each one. Updates can be made instantaneously, and employees can view the information at their own pace.

IBM has been piloting two virtual onboarding programs for interns in China and India. In the Chinese pilot, U.S.–based HR staff and Chinese interns create individual avatars to build relationships, learn about their functions, and hold meetings within Second Life (an online artificial 3-D world). In India, IBM is using another virtual tool called Plane Shift to allow virtual teams to simulate project work.[14]

Problems with Orientation Programs

A number of potential problems can arise with orientation programs. Often, *too much information* is provided in a short time (usually one day) and the new employee is overwhelmed. New employees commonly find themselves inundated with forms to fill out for payroll, benefits, pensions, and so on. Another problem is that *little or no orientation* is provided, which means that new employees must personally seek answers to each question that arises and work without a good understanding of what is expected of them. This is a common problem for part-time and contract workers. Finally, the orientation information provided by the HR department can be *too broad* to be meaningful to a new employee, especially on the first day, whereas the orientation information provided by the immediate supervisor may be *too detailed* to realistically expect the new employee to remember it all.

Evaluation of Orientation Programs

Orientation programs should be evaluated to assess whether they are providing timely, useful information to new employees in a cost-effective manner. Three approaches to evaluating orientation programs are as follows:

1. *Employee reaction.* Interview or survey new employees for their opinion on the usefulness of the orientation program.
2. *Socialization effects.* Review new employees at regular intervals to assess progress toward understanding and acceptance of the beliefs, values, and norms of the organization.
3. *Cost/benefit analysis.* Compare (1) orientation costs, such as printing handbooks and time spent orienting new employees by HR staff and immediate supervisors, with (2) benefits of orientation, including reduction in errors, rate of productivity, efficiency levels, and so on.

Executive Integration

Typically, executives do not participate in formal orientation activities, and there is little planning regarding how they will be integrated into their new position and

An Ethical | Dilemma

Is it ethical to withhold information from an incoming executive about critical problems that he or she will face?

company. The common assumption is that the new executive is a professional and will know what to do, but full executive integration can take up to 18 months.[15] To make things even more difficult, executives are often brought in as change agents, in which case they can expect to face considerable resistance. Thus, a lack of attention to executive integration can result in serious problems with assimilation and work effectiveness. It is common to perceive executive integration as an orientation issue, but integration at senior levels in the organization requires an ongoing process that can continue for months as the new executive learns about the unspoken dynamics of the organization that are not covered in orientation programs, such as how decisions are really made and who holds what type of power.[16]

Executive integration is of critical importance to a productive relationship between a new executive and his or her organization, and it is important to review previous successes and failures at executive integration on an ongoing basis. Key aspects of the integration process include the following:

- identifying position specifications (particularly the ability to deal with and overcome jealousy)
- providing realistic information to job candidates and providing support regarding reality shock
- assessing each candidate's previous record at making organizational transitions
- announcing the hiring with enthusiasm
- stressing the importance of listening as well as demonstrating competency, and promoting more time spent talking with the boss

- assisting new executives who are balancing their work to change cultural norms while they themselves are part of the culture itself.[17]

THE TRAINING PROCESS

training The process of teaching employees the basic skills/competencies that they need to perform their jobs.

Canadian Society for Training and Development (CSTD)
www.cstd.ca

Training employees involves a learning process in which workers are provided with the information and skills that they need to successfully perform their jobs. Training might thus mean showing a production worker how to operate a new machine, a new salesperson how to sell the firm's product, or a new supervisor how to interview and appraise employees. Whereas *training* focuses on skills and competencies needed to perform employees' current jobs, *development* is training of a long-term nature. Its aim is to prepare current employees for future jobs within the organization.

It is important to ensure that business and training goals are aligned and that training is part of an organization's strategic plan.[18] A training professional in today's business world has to understand the organization's business, speak its language, and demonstrate the business value of training investment.[19] Purolator, one of Canada's largest courier services, has 13 000 employees, and Stephen Gould, senior vice-president of HR, says it's critical to the success of the business that the company's trainers understand the business strategy.[20]

In today's service-based economy, highly knowledgeable workers can be the company's most important assets. Thus, it is important to treat training as a strategic investment in human capital.[21] For example, Vancouver's Sierra Systems, an information technology consulting company, offers ongoing in-house training and more than 2000 online courses for its employees. Their Senior HR manager explains, "Training and development is critical to our business. We're a professional services firm and our people are how we deliver our business."[22] Unfortunately, training is more likely to occur at certain ages and income levels, as discussed in the **Workforce Diversity** box.

A recent federal government report concluded that

> To remain competitive and keep up with the accelerating pace of technological change, Canada must continuously renew and upgrade the skills of its workforce. We can no longer assume that the skills acquired in youth will carry workers through their active lives. Rather, the working life of most adults must be a period of continuous learning.[23]

Already, a skills crisis has arisen in the manufacturing sector, where lack of qualified personnel is a major problem. Skills in greatest need of improvement are problem solving, communications, and teamwork.[24] Training is therefore moving to centre stage as a necessity for improving employers' competitiveness. The federal government has called for businesses to increase spending on training, and business has asked the government to expand programs for professional immigrants to get Canadian qualifications in their fields. In response, the Canadian Council on Learning was created by the federal government to promote best practices in workplace learning. The Quebec government has legislated that all firms with a payroll of more than $250 000 must spend 1 percent of payroll on employee training (or else pay tax in the same amount).[25]

Another benefit of increased training is the fact that training can strengthen employee commitment. It implies faith in the future of the company and of the individual. Few things can better illustrate a firm's commitment to its employees than continuing developmental opportunities to improve themselves, and such

Workforce DIVERSITY

Variations in Amount of Job-Related Training

A Statistics Canada survey revealed interesting facts about differences in the amount of job-related training received by Canadians based on a number of demographic variables. Workers aged 25 to 34 spent triple the time in job-related training than those in the 55 to 64 age group did. In the 55 to 64 age group, women were more likely than men to engage in job-related training. Giving more training to younger workers makes sense, in that older employees have had longer to accumulate not only general work skills but also job-specific skills. In addition, many older employees may be winding down before retirement.

Job-related training was accessed more by employees who were already well-educated. The amount of job-related training increased with household income, particularly for younger people Employees aged 25 to 34 in professional or managerial occupations were more likely to take training than those in clerical, sales, or service occupations.

The most common type of training for all groups was in business, management, and public administration.

The primary motive for taking job-related training was to improve job performance, particularly for older workers. Different objectives highlighted different career stages. The second most common motivation for older workers was to avoid losing their jobs, while for younger workers it was to help them find or change jobs. The third most common motivation for taking job-related training was to increase income, but this was much more important for younger workers compared to older ones.

In conclusion, training opportunities are not equally distributed. Those who are younger and more highly educated, for example, tend to participate in job-related training at a higher rate. However, those who are educationally disadvantaged likely stand to gain more when they are given the opportunity for training. Indeed, although the least educated are less likely to participate in training, they are the most likely to benefit.

Source: C. Underhill, "Training Through the Ages," *Perspectives*, October 2006, pp. 17–27. Statistics Canada Catalogue no. 75-001-XIE.

commitment is usually reciprocated.[26] This loyalty is one reason that a high-commitment firm like the Bank of Montreal provides seven days of training per year for all employees, at a cost of $1800 per employee—more than double the national average.[27] Today's young employees view learning and growth as the pathway to a successful and secure future and are attracted to organizations that have a commitment to keeping and growing their talent.[28]

Training and Learning

Training is essentially a learning process. To train employees, therefore, it is useful to know something about how people learn. For example, people have three main learning styles: *auditory*, learning through talking and listening; *visual*, learning through pictures and print; and *kinesthetic*, tactile learning through a whole-body experience. Training effectiveness can be enhanced by identifying learning styles and personalizing the training accordingly.[29]

Research INSIGHT

First, it is easier for trainees to understand and remember material that is meaningful. At the start of training, provide the trainees with an overall picture of the material to be presented. When presenting material, use as many visual aids as possible and a variety of familiar examples. Organize the material so that it is presented in a logical manner and in meaningful units. Try to use terms and concepts that are already familiar to trainees.

Second, make sure that it is easy to transfer new skills and behaviours from the training site to the job site. Maximize the similarity between the training situation and the work situation, and provide adequate training practice. Give trainees the chance to use their new skills immediately on their return to work. Train managers first and employees second in order to send a message about the importance of the training, and control contingencies by planning rewards for trainees who successfully complete and integrate the new training.[30]

Third, motivate the trainee. Motivation affects training outcomes independently of any increase in cognitive ability. Training motivation is affected by individual characteristics, such as conscientiousness, and by the training climate.[31] Therefore, it is important to try to provide as much realistic practice as possible. Trainees learn best at their own pace and when correct responses are immediately reinforced, perhaps with a quick "Well done." For many younger employees, the use of technology can motivate learning. Simulations, games, virtual worlds, and online networking are revolutionizing how people learn and how learning experiences are designed and delivered. Learners who are immersed in deep experiential learning in highly visual and interactive environments become intellectually engaged in the experience.[32]

Fourth, effectively prepare the trainee. Research evidence shows that the trainee's pre-training preparation is a crucial step in the training process. It is important to create a perceived need for training in the minds of participants.[33] Also, provide preparatory information that will help to set the trainees' expectations about the events and consequences of actions that are likely to occur in the training environment (and, eventually, on the job). For example, trainees learning to become first-line supervisors might face stressful conditions, high workload, and difficult employees. Studies suggest that the negative impact of such events can be reduced by letting trainees know ahead of time what might occur.[34]

Legal Aspects of Training

Hints | **TO ENSURE LEGAL COMPLIANCE**

RPC

Ensures compliance with legislated training obligations

Under human rights and employment equity legislation, several aspects of employee training programs must be assessed with an eye toward the program's impact on designated group members.[35] For example, if relatively few women or visible minorities are selected for the training program, there may be a requirement to show that the admissions procedures are valid—that they predict performance on the job for which the person is being trained. It could turn out that the reading level of the training manuals is too advanced for many trainees for whom English is not their first language, which results in their doing poorly in the program, quite aside from their aptitude for the jobs for which they are being trained. The training program might then be found to be unfairly discriminatory. On the other hand, employees who refuse a lawful and reasonable order to attend a training program may be considered to have abandoned their position.[36]

Negligent training is another potential problem. *Negligent training* occurs when an employer fails to train adequately, and an employee subsequently harms a third party. Also, employees who are dismissed for poor performance or disciplined for safety infractions may claim that the employer was negligent in that the employee's training was inadequate.

The Five-Step Training Process

A typical training program consists of five steps, as summarized in **Figure 8.2**. The purpose of the *needs analysis* step is to identify the specific job performance skills needed, to analyze the skills and needs of the prospective trainees, and to

FIGURE 8.2 | The Five Steps in the Training and Development Process

1. NEEDS ANALYSIS

- Identify specific job performance skills needed to improve performance and productivity.
- Analyze the audience to ensure that the program will be suited to their specific levels of education, experience, and skills, as well as their attitudes and personal motivations.
- Use research to develop specific measurable knowledge and performance objectives.

2. INSTRUCTIONAL DESIGN

- Gather instructional objectives, methods, media, description of and sequence of content, examples, exercises, and activities. Organize them into a curriculum that supports adult learning theory and provides a blueprint for program development.
- Make sure all materials (such as video scripts, leaders' guides, and participants' workbooks) complement each other, are written clearly, and blend into unified training geared directly to the stated learning objectives.
- Carefully and professionally handle all program elements—whether reproduced on paper, film, or tape—to guarantee quality and effectiveness.

3. VALIDATION

- Introduce and validate the training before a representative audience. Base final revisions on pilot results to ensure program effectiveness.

4. IMPLEMENTATION

- When applicable, boost success with a train-the-trainer workshop that focuses on presentation-knowledge and skills in addition to training content.

5. EVALUATION AND FOLLOW-UP

- Assess program success according to
  REACTION—Document the learners' immediate reactions to the training.
  LEARNING—Use feedback devices or pre- and post-tests to measure what learners have actually learned.
  BEHAVIOUR—Note supervisors' reactions to learners' performance following completion of the training. This is one way to measure the degree to which learners apply new skills and knowledge to their jobs.
  RESULTS—Determine the level of improvement in job performance and assess needed maintenance.

Source: This article was originally published in IOMA's monthly newsletter HRFocus® and is republished here with the express written permission of IOMA. © 2009. Further use of, electronic distribution, or reproduction of this material requires the permission of IOMA. www.ioma.com

develop specific, measurable knowledge and performance objectives. (Managers must make sure that the performance deficiency is amenable to training rather than caused by, say, poor morale because of low salaries.) In the second step, *instructional design*, the actual content of the training program is compiled and produced, including workbooks, exercises, and activities. The third step is *validation*, in which the bugs are worked out of the training program by presenting it to a small representative audience. Fourth, the training program is *implemented*,

Training and Development
www.ipmaac.org

using techniques like those discussed in this chapter and the next (such as on-the-job training and programmed learning). Fifth, there should be an *evaluation* and follow-up step in which the program's successes or failures are assessed.

STEP 1: TRAINING NEEDS ANALYSIS

RPC

Conducts training needs assessments

The first step in training is to determine what training is required, if any. The main task in assessing the training needs of new employees is to determine what the job entails and break it down into subtasks, each of which is then taught to the new employee. Assessing the training needs of current employees can be more complex, because it involves the added task of deciding whether or not training is the solution. For example, performance may be down not because of lack of training but because the standards are not clear or because the person is not motivated.

Task analysis and performance analysis are the two main techniques for identifying training needs. **Task analysis**—an analysis of the job's requirements—is especially appropriate for determining the training needs of employees who are *new* to their jobs. **Performance analysis** appraises the performance of *current* employees to determine whether training could reduce performance problems (such as excess scrap or low output). Other techniques used to identify training needs include supervisors' reports, HR records, management requests, observations, tests of job knowledge, and questionnaire surveys.[37]

task analysis A detailed study of a job to identify the skills and competencies it requires so that an appropriate training program can be instituted.

performance analysis Verifying that there is a performance deficiency and determining whether that deficiency should be rectified through training or through some other means (such as transferring the employee).

Whichever technique is used—task analysis, performance analysis, or some other—employee input is essential. It is often true that no one knows as much about the job as the people actually doing it, so soliciting employee input is usually wise.[38]

Task Analysis: Assessing the Training Needs of New Employees

Task analysis—identifying the broad competencies and specific skills required to perform job-related tasks—is used for determining the training needs of employees who are new to their jobs. Particularly with entry-level workers, it is common to hire inexperienced people and train them.[39] Thus, the aim is to develop the skills and knowledge required for effective performance—like soldering (in the case of an assembly worker) or interviewing (in the case of a supervisor).

The job description and job specification are helpful here. These list the specific duties and skills required on the job and become the basic reference point in determining the training required to perform the job.

Task Analysis Record Form

Some employers supplement the current job description and specification with a task analysis record form. This consolidates information regarding the job's required tasks and skills in a form that is especially helpful for determining training requirements. As illustrated in **Table 8.1**, a task analysis record form contains six types of information:

1. *Column 1, Task List.* Here, the job's main tasks and subtasks are listed.
2. *Column 2, When and How Often Performed.* Here, the frequency with which the task and subtasks are performed is indicated.

TABLE 8.1 | Task Analysis Record Form

Task List	When and How Often Performed	Quantity and Quality of Performance	Conditions Under Which Performed	Competencies and Specific Knowledge Required	Where Best Learned
1. Operate paper cutter	4 times per day		Noisy press room: distractions		
1.1 Start motor					
1.2 Set cutting distance		± tolerance of 0.007 in.		Read gauge	On the job
1.3 Place paper on cutting table		Must be completely even to prevent uneven cut		Lift paper correctly	On the job
1.4 Push paper up to cutter				Must be even	On the job
1.5 Grasp safety release with left hand	100% of time, for safety			Essential for safety	On the job but practise first with no distractions
1.6 Grasp cutter release with right hand				Must keep both hands on releases	On the job but practise first with no distractions
1.7 Simultaneously pull safety release with left hand and cutter release with right hand					
1.8 Wait for cutter to retract	100% of time, for safety			Must keep both hands on releases	On the job but practise first with no distractions
1.9 Retract paper				Wait till cutter retracts	On the job but practise first with no distractions
1.10 Shut off	100% of time, for safety				On the job but practise first with no distractions
2. Operate printing press					
2.1 Start motor					
.					
.					
.					

Note: Task analysis record form showing some of the tasks and subtasks performed by a right-handed printing press operator.

3. *Column 3, Quantity and Quality of Performance.* Here, the standards of performance for each task and subtask are described in measurable terms, like "tolerance of 0.007 in.," or "within two days of receiving the order," for instance.

4. *Column 4, Conditions Under Which Performed.* This column indicates the conditions under which the tasks and subtasks are to be performed.

5. *Column 5, Competencies and Specific Knowledge Required.* This is the heart of the task analysis form. Here, the competencies and specific skills or knowledge required for each task and subtask are listed, specifying exactly what knowledge or skills must be taught. Thus, for the subtask "Set cutting distance," the trainee must be taught how to read the gauge.

6. *Column 6, Where Best Learned.* The decision as to whether the task is learned best on or off the job is based on several considerations. Safety is one: For example, prospective jet pilots must learn something about the plane off the job in a simulator before actually getting behind the controls.

Once the essential skills involved in doing the job are determined, new employees' proficiency in these skills can be assessed and training needs identified for each individual.

Performance Analysis: Determining the Training Needs of Current Employees

Performance analysis means verifying whether there is a significant performance deficiency and, if so, determining whether that deficiency should be rectified through training or some other means (such as transferring the employee). The first step is to appraise the employee's performance because, to improve it, the firm must first compare the person's current performance with what it should be. Examples of specific performance deficiencies follow:

"Salespeople are expected to make ten new contacts per week, but John averages only six."

"Other plants our size average no more than two serious accidents per month; we are averaging five."

Distinguishing between *can't do* and *won't do* problems is at the heart of performance analysis. First, the firm must determine whether it is a *can't do* problem and, if so, its specific causes. For example, the employees do not know what to do or what the standards are; there are obstacles in the system (such as a lack of tools or supplies); job aids are needed; poor selection has resulted in hiring people who do not have the skills to do the job; or training is inadequate. Conversely, it might be a *won't do* problem. In this case, employees *could* do a good job if they wanted to. If so, the reward system might have to be changed, perhaps by implementing an incentive program.

Training Objectives

Once training needs have been identified, training objectives can be established. Concrete, measurable training objectives should be set after training needs have been analyzed. Objectives specify what the trainee should be able to accomplish after successfully completing the training program. They thus provide a focus for the efforts of both the trainee and the trainer and provide a benchmark for evaluating the success of the training program. A training program can then be developed and implemented, with the intent to achieve these objectives. These objectives must be accomplished within the organization's training budget.

STEP 2: INSTRUCTIONAL DESIGN

After the employees' training needs have been determined and training objectives have been set, the training program can be designed. Descriptions of the most popular traditional training techniques and more recent e-learning techniques follow.

Traditional Training Techniques

On-the-Job Training

On-the-job training (OJT) involves having a person learn a job by actually performing it. Virtually every employee—from mailroom clerk to company president—gets some on-the-job training when he or she joins a firm. In many companies, OJT is the only type of training available. It usually involves assigning new employees to experienced workers or supervisors who then do the actual training.[40]

OJT has several advantages: It is relatively inexpensive, trainees learn while producing, and there is no need for expensive off-job facilities, like classrooms or manuals. The method also facilitates learning, since trainees learn by actually doing the job and get quick feedback about the quality of their performance.

Apprenticeship Training

More employers are going "back to the future" by implementing apprenticeship-training programs, an approach that began in the Middle Ages. Apprenticeship training basically involves having the learner/apprentice study under the tutelage of a master craftsperson.

Apprentices become skilled workers through a combination of classroom instruction and on-the-job training. Apprenticeships are widely used to train individuals for many occupations, including those of electrician and plumber. In Canada, close to 170 established trades have recognized apprenticeship programs.[41]

On-the-job training is structured and concrete. Here, a supervisor teaches an employee to use a drum-forming machine.

Apprenticeship training is critical today as more than half of skilled trades workers are expecting to retire by 2020. Federal, provincial, and territorial governments are increasing their funding of apprenticeship training programs in order to meet this growing need for more tradespeople.[42]

Informal Learning

About two-thirds of industrial training is not "formal" at all but rather results from day-to-day unplanned interactions between the new worker and his or her colleagues. Informal learning may be defined as "any learning that occurs in which the learning process is not determined or designed by the organization."[43]

Job Instruction Training

job instruction training (JIT) The listing of each job's basic tasks, along with key points, in order to provide step-by-step training for employees.

Many jobs consist of a logical sequence of steps and are best taught step by step. This step-by-step process is called **job instruction training** (**JIT**). To begin, all necessary steps in the job are listed, each in its proper sequence. Alongside each step, a corresponding "key point" (if any) should be noted. The steps show *what* is to be done, while the key points show *how* it is to be done, and *why*. Here is an example of a job instruction training sheet for teaching a right-handed trainee how to operate a large, motorized paper cutter:

Steps	Key Points
1. Start motor	None
2. Set cutting distance	Carefully read scale, to prevent wrong-sized cut
3. Place paper on cutting table	Make sure paper is even, to prevent uneven cut
4. Push paper up to cutter	Make sure paper is tight, to prevent uneven cut
5. Grasp safety release with left hand	Do not release left hand, to prevent hand from being caught in cutter
6. Grasp cutter release with right hand	Do not release right hand, to prevent hand from being caught in cutter
7. Simultaneously pull cutter and safety releases	Keep both hands on corresponding releases, to avoid hands being on cutting table
8. Wait for cutter to retract	Keep both hands on releases, to avoid having hands on cutting table
9. Retract paper	Make sure cutter is retracted; keep both hands away from releases
10. Shut off motor	None

In today's service economy, job instruction training for step-by-step manual work is being superseded by behaviour modelling for service workers. Behaviour modelling is discussed in the next chapter.

Classroom Training

Classroom training continues to be the primary method of providing corporate training in Canada, and lectures are a widely used method of classroom training delivery. Lecturing has several advantages. It is a quick and simple way of providing knowledge to large groups of trainees, as when the sales force must be taught the special features of a new product.

Classroom learning has evolved to maintain its relevance in the technological age. For Generation Y employees familiar with Web 2.0 features such as wikis, blogs, and podcasts, learning opportunities must reflect their new abilities and needs. Blended learning, using a combination of instructor-led training and online e-learning, has been found to provide better learning results and higher learner engagement and enthusiasm than expected. In blended learning, the in-class training becomes tightly integrated with the online experience, and the relevance to the learner is vastly improved. Thus the classroom has evolved to include interactions with remote colleagues, instructors, e-learning in many forms, coaching, assessment and feedback.[44]

Audiovisual Techniques

Audiovisual techniques (videotapes and CDs) can be very effective and are widely used. Audiovisuals are more expensive than conventional lectures but offer some advantages. Trainers should consider using them in the following situations:

1. *When there is a need to illustrate how a certain sequence should be followed over time*, such as when teaching wire soldering or telephone repair. The stop-action, instant-replay, or fast- or slow-motion capabilities of audiovisuals can be useful.

2. When there is a need to expose trainees to events not easily demonstrable in live lectures, such as a visual tour of a factory or open-heart surgery.

3. *When the training is going to be used organization-wide* and it is too costly to move the trainers from place to place.

There are three options when it comes to audiovisual material: buying an existing product, making one, or using a production company. Dozens of businesses issue catalogues that list audiovisual programs on topics ranging from applicant interviewing to zoo management.

Videoconferencing, in which an instructor is televised live to multiple locations, is now a common method for training employees. It has been defined as "a means of joining two or more distant groups using a combination of audio and visual equipment."[45] Videoconferencing allows people in one location to communicate live with people in another city or country or with groups in several places at once. It is particularly important to prepare a training guide ahead of time, as most or all of the learners will not be in the same location as the trainer. It is also important for the trainer to arrive early and test all equipment that will be used.

videoconferencing Connecting two or more distant groups by using audiovisual equipment.

Programmed Learning

Whether the programmed instruction device is a textbook or a computer, **programmed learning** consists of three functions:

1. presenting questions, facts, or problems to the learner

2. allowing the person to respond

3. providing feedback on the accuracy of his or her answers.

The main advantage of programmed learning is that it reduces training time by about one-third.[46] In terms of the principles of learning listed earlier, programmed instruction can also facilitate learning because it lets trainees learn at their own pace, provides immediate feedback, and (from the learner's point of view) reduces the risk of error. However, trainees do not learn much more from programmed learning than they would from a traditional textbook. Therefore,

programmed learning A systematic method for teaching job skills that involves presenting questions or facts, allowing the person to respond, and giving the learner immediate feedback on the accuracy of his or her answers.

Vestibule training simulates flight conditions at NASA headquarters.

vestibule or simulated training Training employees on special off-the-job equipment, as in airplane pilot training, whereby training costs and hazards can be reduced.

e-learning Delivery and administration of learning opportunities and support via computer, networked, and web-based technology, to enhance employee performance and development.

the cost of developing the manuals and/or software for programmed instruction has to be weighed against the accelerated but not improved learning that should occur.

Vestibule or Simulated Training

Vestibule or simulated training is a technique by which trainees learn on the actual or simulated equipment that they will use on the job, but they are trained off the job. Therefore, it aims to obtain the advantages of on-the-job training without actually putting the trainee on the job. Vestibule training is virtually a necessity when it is too costly or dangerous to train employees on the job. Putting new assembly-line workers right to work could slow production, for instance, and when safety is a concern—as with pilots—vestibule training may be the only practical alternative.

Vestibule training may just place a trainee in a separate room with the equipment that he or she will actually be using on the job; however, it often involves the use of equipment simulators. In pilot training, for instance, the main advantages of flight simulators are safety, learning efficiency, and cost savings (on maintenance costs, pilot cost, fuel cost, and the cost of not having the aircraft in regular service).[47]

E-Learning

Electronic training techniques have been developed that allow training professionals to provide learning in a more flexible, personalized, and cost-effective manner. **E-learning** is the delivery and administration of learning opportunities and support via computer, networked, and web-based technology, to enhance employee performance and development. Canadian employers are using e-learning to become more productive and innovative and to make self-directed, lifelong learners of their employees.[48]

Effective e-learning requires good instructional design. It is critical to motivate learners by describing the benefits they will gain from the training, providing content designed to the learner's specific needs, and offering interactivity, such as application of the material to common problems in the context of the learner's workplace and intrinsic feedback.[49]

The Canadian Society for Training and Development has found that e-learning is generally as effective as other forms of learning, at a reduced cost. The primary users of e-learning in Canada are professional and technical employees; clerical, service, and support employees; and managers. Interestingly, learners are more satisfied when web-based learning involves high levels of human interaction.[50] Mobile technologies are growing in influence in training and development. Short videos, instant messages, podcasts and email are examples of smart phone features that can be used for training.[51]

There are three major types of e-learning: computer-based training, online training, and electronic performance support systems (EPSS).

Computer-Based Training

In computer-based training (CBT), the trainee uses a computer-based system to interactively increase his or her knowledge or skills. Computer-based training almost always involves presenting trainees with integrated computerized simulations and using multimedia (including video, audio, text, and graphics) to help the trainee to learn how to do the job.[52] Cisco Systems developed a binary math game intended to improve the effectiveness of network engineers, and made it available for free on its website and for use on mobile devices. This simple game solved a key training problem and also turned out to be an effective corporate marketing tool.[53]

A new generation of simulations has been developed to simulate role-play situations designed to teach behavioural skills and emotional intelligence. Body language, facial expressions, and subtle nuances are programmed in. These new simulations offer authentic and relevant scenarios involving pressure situations that tap users' emotions and force them to act.[54] At L'Oréal Canada, new product managers participate in a training program that combines e-learning and a virtual simulation where they apply their new skills. Teams of trainees compete as virtual companies in the marketplace and continue to learn when they see their results compared to the others.[55]

A higher percentage of Canadian firms use CBT compared with American firms, primarily because of Canada's geography. CBT is often more cost-effective than traditional training methods, which require instructors and/or trainees to travel long distances to training sites.[56] Alberta Pacific Forest Industries (AL-Pac) had such good results from using CBT as a staple of its training program that it launched a new component to enable employees to learn the skills of another trade. Employees benefit from having training that is accessible 24 hours a day, which addresses shift work and different learning styles. This training program also helps to keep non-union staff members satisfied, as the multi-skilling resulting from CBT enables many employees to rotate jobs.[57]

CBT programs can be very beneficial. Advantages include instructional consistency (computers, unlike human trainers, do not have good days and bad days), mastery of learning (if the trainee does not learn it, he or she generally cannot move on to the next step in the CBT), flexibility for the trainee, and increased trainee motivation (resulting from the responsive feedback of the CBT program).

Online Training

Web-based training is now commonly used by Canadian organizations. It is generally estimated that online training costs about 50 percent less than traditional classroom-based training. Also, online learning is ideal for adults, who learn what they want, when they want, and where they want. Online training is often the best solution for highly specialized business professionals, who have little time available for ongoing education. Students (the workers of tomorrow) thrive in online learning environments. They do not find it to be an isolated or lonely experience, and they find that they have more time to reflect on the learning material, which leads to livelier interaction.[58] Further, online training is ideal for global organizations that want consistent training for all employees worldwide. Alcan Inc. is using this approach to standardize its training programs for 72 000 employees in 55 countries.[59]

However, critics point out that content management, sound educational strategy, learner support, and system administration should receive more attention, as they are often the critical determining factors in successful training outcomes. In the last few years, "learner content management systems" have been developed to deliver personalized content in small "chunks" or "nuggets" of learning. These systems complement "learning management systems" that are

RPC

Recommends the selection of external training providers

focused on the logistics of managing learning. Together, they form a powerful combination for an e-learning platform. This development is considered to be part of the "second wave" of e-learning, involving greater standardization and the emergence of norms. Another problem is that the freedom of online learning means that unless learners are highly motivated, they may not complete the training. It is estimated that learners don't complete 50 to 90 percent of online courses. In general, it is important to seek "blended learning," including both personal interaction and online training tools.[60]

Electronic Performance Support Systems (EPSS)

electronic performance support systems (EPSS) Computer-based job aids, or sets of computerized tools and displays that automate training, documentation, and phone support.

Electronic performance support systems (EPSS) are computer-based job aids, or sets of computerized tools and displays that automate training, documentation, and phone support. EPSS provides support that is faster, cheaper, and more effective than traditional paper-based job aids, such as manuals. When a customer calls a Dell Computer service representative about a problem with a new computer, the representative is probably asking questions prompted by an EPSS, which takes the service representative and the customer through an analytical sequence, step by step. Without the EPSS, Dell would have to train its service representatives to memorize an unrealistically large number of solutions. Learners say that EPSS provides significant value in maximizing the impact of training. If a skill is taught but the trainees don't need to use it until several weeks or months later, the learning material is always available through the EPSS.[61]

STEPS 3 AND 4: VALIDATION AND IMPLEMENTATION

RPC

Ensures arrangements are made for training schedules, facilities, trainers, participants, equipment, and course materials

Validation of the training program that has been designed is an often-overlooked step in the training process. In order to ensure that the program will accomplish its objectives, it is necessary to conduct a pilot study, or "run through," with a representative group of trainees. The results of the pilot study are used to assess the effectiveness of the training.

Revisions to the program can be made to address any problems encountered by the pilot group of trainees in using the training material and experiences provided to them. Testing at the end of the pilot study can measure whether or not the program is producing the desired improvement in skill level. If the results fall below the level of the training objectives, then more work must be undertaken to strengthen the instructional design.

Once the program has been validated, it is ready to be implemented by professional trainers. In some cases, a train-the-trainer workshop may be required to familiarize trainers with unfamiliar content or with unique and innovative new methods for presenting the training content.

STEP 5: EVALUATION OF TRAINING

transfer of training Application of the skills acquired during the training program into the work environment, and the maintenance of these skills over time.

It is important to assess the return on investment in human capital made through training by determining whether the training actually achieved the objectives. **Transfer of training** is the application of the skills acquired during the training program into the work environment and the maintenance of these skills over time. A number of actions can be taken before, during, and after a training program to enhance transfer of training.[62]

Before training, potential trainees can be assessed on their level of ability, aptitude, and motivation regarding the skill to be taught, and those with higher levels can be selected for the training program. Trainees can be involved in designing the training, and management should provide active support at this stage.

During the training, it is important to provide frequent feedback, opportunities for practice, and positive reinforcement. After the training program, trainees can use goal-setting and relapse-prevention techniques to increase the likelihood of applying what they have learned. Management can enhance transfer of training by providing opportunities to apply new skills and by continuing to provide positive reinforcement of the new skills while being tolerant of errors.

After trainees complete their training (or at planned intervals during the training), the program should be evaluated to see how well its objectives have been met and the extent to which transfer of training has occurred. Thus, if assemblers should be able to solder a junction in 30 seconds, or a photocopier technician repair a machine in 30 minutes, then the program's effectiveness should be measured based on whether these objectives are attained. For example, are trainees learning as *much* as they can? Are they learning as *fast* as they can? Is there a *better method* for training them? These are some of the questions that are answered by properly evaluating training efforts.

Overall, there is little doubt that training and development can be effective. Formal studies of training programs substantiate the potential positive impact of such programs. Profitable companies spend the most on training, and those rated as being among the 100 best companies to work for in Canada spend the most per employee on training.[63]

There are two basic issues to address when evaluating a training program. The first is the design of the evaluation study and, in particular, whether controlled experimentation will be used. The second is the training effect to be measured.

Controlled experimentation is the best method to use in evaluating a training program. A controlled experiment uses both a training group and a control group (that receives no training). Data (for example, on quantity of production or quality of soldered junctions) should be obtained both before and after the training effort in the training group, and before and after a corresponding work period in the control group. In this way, it is possible to determine the extent to which any change in performance in the training group resulted from the training itself, rather than from some organization-wide change like a raise in pay, which would likely have affected employees in both groups equally.

Training Effects to Measure

Four basic categories of training outcomes can be measured:[64]

1. *Reaction.* First, evaluate trainees' reactions to the program. Did they like the program? Did they think it worthwhile? One expert suggests at least using an evaluation form like the one shown in **Figure 8.3** to evaluate reaction to the training program.[65]

2. *Learning.* Second, test the trainees to determine whether they learned the principles, skills, and facts that they were supposed to learn.

3. *Behaviour.* Next, ask whether the trainees' behaviour on the job changed because of the training program. For example, are employees in the store's

---

RPC

Facilitates post training support activities to ensure transfer of learning to the workplace

---

controlled experimentation Formal methods for testing the effectiveness of a training program, preferably with a control group and with tests before and after training.

FIGURE 8.3 | Sample Training Evaluation Form

PROGRAM NAME: _____   DATE: _____

YOUR NAME (Optional): _____   FACILITATOR(S): _____

OVERALL PROGRAM RATING	Poor		Fair		Good		Excellent
	1	2	3	4	5	6	7

What did you like <u>best</u> about the program?	What did you like <u>least</u> about the program?	What would you like to have spent <u>more</u> time on?

Please complete this form to help us assess how well this program met your needs and our objectives. Your feedback is important to us and will be used in our continuous efforts to improve the quality and usefulness of this program. Circle the number that best expresses your reaction to each item.

	Strongly Disagree		Disagree		Agree		Strongly Agree
1. The program was well-organized:	1	2	3	4	5	6	7
2. The sequence of material presented was logical:	1	2	3	4	5	6	7
3. The content of the program was understandable:	1	2	3	4	5	6	7
4. The program activities were effective in helping me learn the concepts and skills presented:	1	2	3	4	5	6	7
5. The objectives of the program were clear:	1	2	3	4	5	6	7
6. The program met its stated objectives:	1	2	3	4	5	6	7
7. The facilitator(s) grasped the material and activities they presented:	1	2	3	4	5	6	7
8. The knowledge and skills learned in this program will help me do my job better:	1	2	3	4	5	6	7

9. The length of the program   was appropriate   should be shorter   should be longer

Thank you for your participation and feedback!

Source: *CCH Ultimate HR Manual* (Training and Development par. 15187), 2005, p. 19116.

complaint department more courteous toward disgruntled customers than they were previously? These measures determine the degree of transfer of training.

4. *Results*. Last, but probably most important, ask questions such as these: "Did the number of customer complaints about employees drop? Did the rejection rate improve? Was turnover reduced? Are production quotas now being met?" and so on. Improvements in these "metrics"—specific measures of workplace results—are especially important. The training program may

succeed in terms of the reactions from trainees, increased learning, and even changes in behaviour, but if the results are not achieved, then in the final analysis the training has not achieved its goals. If so, the problem may be related to inappropriate use of a training program. For example, training is ineffective when environmental factors are the cause of poor performance.

Although the four basic categories are understandable and widely used, there are several things to keep in mind when using them to measure training effects. First, there are usually only modest correlations among the four types of training criteria (i.e., scoring "high" on learning does not necessarily mean that behaviour or results will also score "high," and the converse is true as well). Similarly, studies show that "reaction" measures (e.g., "How well did you like the program?") may provide some insight into how they liked the program but probably will not provide much insight into what they learned or how they will behave once they are back on the job.

TRAINING FOR SPECIAL PURPOSES

Training increasingly does more than just prepare employees to perform their jobs effectively. Training for special purposes—increasing literacy and adjusting to diversity, for instance—is required too. The following is a sampling of such special-purpose training programs.

Literacy and Essential Skills Training

National Adult Literacy Database
www.nald.ca

Functional illiteracy is a serious problem for many employers. As the Canadian economy shifts from goods to services, there is a corresponding need for workers who are more skilled, more literate, and better able to perform at least basic arithmetic. Not only does enhanced literacy give employees a better chance for success in their careers, but it also improves bottom-line performance of the employer—through time savings, lower costs, and improved quality of work.[66]

In 2008, the Canadian Council on Learning reported that almost half of Canadian adults are below the internationally accepted literacy standard for coping in a modern society.[67] Research by University of Ottawa economists for Statistics Canada has shown that investments in essential skills training to improve literacy and numeracy pay off. For every increase of 1 percent in national literacy scores relative to the international average, a country will realize a 2.5 percent gain in productivity and a 1.5 percent increase in per capita GDP over the long term.[68]

RPC

Identifies and accesses external sources of training funding available to employees

Employers are responding to this issue in two main ways. Organizations such as diamond mining company BHP Billiton, steel giant Dofasco, the Construction Sector Council, and the Canadian Trucking Human Resources Council have implemented a training strategy with the objective of raising the essential skills of their workforce. Essential skills of workers can be measured with the Test of Workplace Essential Skills (TOWES), developed by Bow Valley College in Calgary. In 2005, the federal government made funding available for training professionals to develop Enhanced Language Training (ELT) to provide job-specific English instruction to help immigrants gain employment in their area of expertise.[69]

Diversity Training

With increasingly diverse workforces and customers, there is a strong business case for implementing diversity-training programs. Diversity training enhances cross-cultural sensitivity among supervisors and nonsupervisors, with the aim of creating more harmonious working relationships among a firm's employees. It also enhances the abilities of salespeople to provide effective customer service.[70]

Two broad approaches to diversity training are cross-cultural communication training and cultural sensitivity training. *Cross-cultural communication training* focuses on workplace cultural etiquette and interpersonal skills. *Cultural sensitivity training* focuses on sensitizing employees to the views of different cultural groups toward work so that employees from diverse backgrounds can work together more effectively. All employees should be involved in managing diversity, and diversity initiatives should be planned and supported as any other business opportunity would be.[71]

Handidactis, a nonprofit organization in Montreal, provides sensitivity training to help people interact with those who have a disability, including those with a vision or hearing impairment, and individuals who have a physical or mental disability. The first step is to ask the person with the disability if he or she needs anything special to do the job. This practice is often overlooked as people jump in to help someone with a disability, which in effect takes away that person's independence. Furthermore, the person may not need help. The training also involves discovering what it is like to have a disability, through simulated blindness and speech impediments.[72]

Customer-Service Training

More and more retailers are finding it necessary to compete based on the quality of their service, and many are therefore implementing customer-service training programs. The basic aim is to train all employees to (1) have excellent product knowledge and (2) treat the company's customers in a courteous and hospitable manner. The saying "The customer is always right" is emphasized by countless service companies today. However, putting the customer first requires employee customer-service training.

The Canadian retail industry has struggled in the past with poorly trained workers who were not equipped to provide quality customer service. Retailers now understand that they need to make a serious investment in their employees.[73] The Retail Council of Canada offers a national customer service certification program for retail sales associates and retail first-level managers, based on national occupational standards and essential skills profiles for each group. Certification requires the completion of a workbook, a multiple-choice exam, an in-store evaluation-of-performance interview, and experience (600 hours for sales associates, one year for first-level managers). The certification program for sales associates includes the topics of professionalism, customer service and sales, inventory, store appearance, security and safety, and communication. Topics for first-level managers include professionalism, communication, leadership, human resources, operations, marketing, sales, customer service, administration, and planning.[74]

Diversity Training Links
www.diversityatwork.com
www.diversitytraining.com

Training for Teamwork

An increasing number of firms today use work teams to improve their effectiveness. However, many firms find that teamwork does not just happen and that employees must be trained to be good team members.

Some firms use outdoor training—such as Outward Bound programs—to build teamwork. Outdoor training usually involves taking a group of employees out into rugged terrain, where, by overcoming physical obstacles, they learn team spirit, co-operation, and the need to trust and rely on each other.[75] An example of one activity is the "trust fall." Here, an employee has to slowly lean back and fall backward from a height of, say, three metres into the waiting arms of five or ten team members. The idea is to build trust in one's colleagues.

An Ethical | Dilemma

Is it ethical to require employees to participate in weekend and evening training programs if they do not want to because it is going to take time that they would otherwise be spending on personal and family responsibilities?

Not all employees are eager to participate in such activities. Such firms as Outward Bound have prospective participants fill out extensive medical evaluations to make sure that participants can safely engage in risky outdoor activities. Others feel that the outdoor activities are too contrived to be applicable back at work. However, they do illustrate the lengths to which employers will go to build teamwork.

Training for First-Time Supervisors/Managers

As baby boomers head into retirement, young employees are rising to positions of authority quickly and in large numbers. They are assuming supervisory and managerial roles at a much younger age than their counterparts were only 10 to 15 years ago, with some university graduates being hired into management training programs right after graduation. Along with the steep learning curve that all first-time supervisors/managers face, the latest group faces the challenges of managing employees from previous generations still present in the workforce.

New supervisors/managers are often chosen for their technical ability, and their interpersonal and communication skills get overlooked. But it is precisely these skills that will determine success as a manager, which requires networking and the ability to get work done through other people. New managers also need to learn to define their personal management style, how to give and receive feedback, how to motivate others, and how to manage conflict.[76]

The transition demands crucial training because first-time supervisors/managers need to learn a new set of skills. Formal training is required, and higher-level managers need to coach, mentor, and provide performance feedback to new young supervisors.[77] This type of training can be provided by external organizations such as the Canadian Management Centre.

Canadian Management Centre
www.cmctraining.org

Training for Global Business

Firms competing in the global marketplace often implement special global training programs. The reasons for doing so include avoiding lost business because of cultural insensitivity, improving job satisfaction and retention of overseas staff, and enabling a newly assigned employee to communicate with colleagues abroad.[78]

Research | INSIGHT

Recent research by Healthy Companies International has found that success in the global marketplace is predicted by developing leaders at all levels of business and by placing a high value on multicultural experience and competencies. The research identified four global literacies, or critical competencies, required to succeed in the global economy:

- personal literacy—understanding and valuing oneself
- social literacy—engaging and challenging other people
- business literacy—focusing and mobilizing the business
- cultural literacy—understanding and leveraging cultural differences.[79]

Chapter | SUMMARY

1. A strategic approach to recruitment and retention of employees includes a well-integrated orientation (onboarding) program both before and after hiring. New employees need a clear understanding of company policies, of expectations regarding their performance, and of operating procedures. Orientation is part of the socialization process that instills in new employees the prevailing attitudes, standards, values, and patterns of behaviour that are expected by the organization. Onboarding helps to reduce reality shock—the discrepancy between what the new employee expected from his or her new job and its realities.

2. The basic training process consists of five steps: needs analysis, instructional design, validation, implementation, and evaluation.

3. Two techniques for assessing training needs are (1) task analysis to determine the training needs of employees who are new to their jobs, and (2) performance analysis to appraise the performance of current employees to determine whether training could reduce performance problems.

4. Traditional training techniques include on-the-job-training, apprenticeship training, informal learning, job instruction training, classroom training, audiovisual techniques, programmed learning, and vestibule or simulated training.

5. Three types of e-learning are computer-based training, online training, and electronic performance support systems.

6. In evaluating the effectiveness of a training program, four categories of outcomes can be measured: reaction, learning, behaviour, and results.

7. Today's organizations often provide training for special purposes, including literacy training, diversity training, customer-service training, training for teamwork, training for first-time supervisors/managers, and training for global business.

PEARSON
myHRlab

Test yourself on material for this chapter at
www.pearsoned.ca/myhrlab

Key | TERMS

controlled experimentation   *(p. 229)*
electronic performance support
   systems (EPSS)   *(p. 228)*
e-learning   *(p. 226)*
employee orientation (onboarding)   *(p. 210)*
job instruction training (JIT)   *(p. 224)*
performance analysis   *(p. 220)*
programmed learning   *(p. 225)*

reality shock   *(p. 211)*
socialization   *(p. 211)*
task analysis   *(p. 220)*
training   *(p. 216)*
transfer of training   *(p. 228)*
vestibule or simulated training   *(p. 226)*
videoconferencing   *(p. 225)*

Review and Discussion | QUESTIONS

1. Prepare an orientation program checklist for your current or most recent job.
2. Identify and describe three special orientation situations that may be encountered.
3. Choose a task with which you are familiar—such as mowing the lawn or using a chat room—and develop a job instruction training sheet for it.
4. Ali Khan is an undergraduate business student majoring in accounting. He has just failed the first accounting course, Accounting 101, and is understandably upset. Explain how you would use performance analysis to identify what, if any, are Ali's training needs.
5. Describe how you would go about determining the best way to train a group of newly hired managers on how to conduct selection interviews.
6. Think about the jobs that you have had in the past. For which of these jobs could an electronic performance support system be used? Prepare an outline for such a system.

Critical Thinking | QUESTIONS

1. "A well-thought-out onboarding program is especially important for employees (like many recent graduates) who have had little or no work experience." Explain why you agree or disagree with this statement.
2. What do you think are some of the main drawbacks of relying on informal on-the-job training for teaching new employees their jobs?
3. This chapter points out that one reason for implementing special global training programs is to avoid business loss because of cultural insensitivity. What sort of cultural insensitivity do you think is meant, and how might that translate into lost business? What sort of training programs would you recommend to avoid such cultural insensitivity?
4. Most training programs are not formally evaluated beyond a reaction measure. Why do you think employers do not measure the impact of training on learning, behaviour, and results more often?
5. Assume that your company president wants to develop a more customer-focused organization. For the past ten years, the company has focused on cost containment while growing the business. Write a memo to your company president that supports the investment in customer service training as part of the strategic plan.

Experiential | EXERCISES

1. Obtain a copy of an employee handbook from your employer or from some other organization. Review it and make recommendations for improvement.
2. Working individually or in groups, follow the steps in Figure 8.2 and prepare a training program for a job that you currently hold or have had in the past.
3. In small groups of four to six students, complete the following exercise:

JetBlue Airlines has asked you to quickly develop the outline of a training program for its new reservation clerks. Airline reservation clerks obviously need numerous skills to perform their jobs. (You may want to start by listing the job's main duties, using the information provided below.) Produce the requested training outline, making sure to be very specific about what you want to teach the new clerks and what methods and aids you suggest using to train them.

Duties of Airline Reservation Clerks: Customers contact airline reservation clerks to obtain flight schedules, prices, and itineraries. The reservation clerks look up the requested information on the airline's flight schedule systems, which are updated continuously. The reservation clerk must deal courteously and expeditiously with the customer and be able to quickly find alternative flight arrangements in order to provide the customer with the itinerary that fits his or her needs. Alternative flights and prices must be found quickly so that the customer is not kept waiting and so that the reservations operations group maintains its efficiency standards. It is often necessary to look under various routings, since there may be a dozen or more alternative routes between the customer's starting point and destination.

4. Working in groups of four to six students, complete the following exercise:

Determine who in your group knows how to make paper objects such as cranes, boxes, balloons, ninja darts, fortunes, boats, etc. Select one person who is willing to be a Subject Matter Expert (SME) to assist your group in developing an on-the-job training program to make one product.

Using the expertise of your SME, develop, document (refer to the sample job instruction template earlier in the chapter), and validate a training plan to make the chosen product. Modify the documented plan as required after your pilot. Ensure that everyone in your group has a copy of the plan and can reliably make the product to standards. Once this is accomplished, each group member will pair up with a member of another group that made a different product. Each person in the resulting dyads will train his or her partner on how to make the products using the training plan and sample he or she created.

Debrief the exercise as instructed.

Running | CASE

Running Case: LearnInMotion.com

The New Training Program

"I just don't understand it," said Pierre. "No one here seems to follow instructions, and no matter how many times I've told them how to do things, they seem to do them their own way." At present, LearnInMotion.com has no formal onboarding or training policies or procedures. Jennifer believes this is one reason that employees generally ignore the standards that she and Pierre would like employees to adopt.

Several examples illustrate this problem. One job of the web designer (her name is Maureen) is to take customer copy for banner ads and adapt it for placement on LearnInMotion.com. She has been told several times not to tinker in any way with a customer's logo: Most companies put considerable thought and resources into logo design, and as Pierre has said, "Whether or not Maureen thinks the logo is perfect, it's the customer's logo, and she's to leave it as it is." Yet just a week ago, they almost lost a big customer when Maureen, to "clarify" the customer's logo, modified its design before posting it on LearnInMotion.com.

That's just the tip of the iceberg. As far as Jennifer and Pierre are concerned, it is the sales effort that is completely out of control. For one thing, even after several months on the job, it still seems as if the sales people don't know what they're talking about. For example, LearnInMotion has several co-brand arrangements with websites like Yahoo! This setup allows users on other sites to easily click through to LearnInMotion.com if they are interested in ordering educational courses or CDs. Jennifer has noticed that, during conversations with customers, the two salespeople have no idea of which sites co-brand with LearnInMotion, or how to get to the LearnInMotion site from the partner website. The salespeople also need to know a lot more about the products themselves. For example, one salesperson was trying to sell someone who produces programs on managing call centres on the idea of listing its products under LearnInMotion's "communications" community. In fact, the "communications" community is for courses on topics like interpersonal communications and how to be a better listener; it has nothing to do with managing the sorts of call centres that, for instance, airlines use for handling customer inquiries. As another example, the web surfer is supposed to get a specific email address with a specific person's name for the salespeople to use; instead he often just comes back with an "information" email address from a website. The list goes on and on.

Jennifer feels the company has had other problems because of the lack of adequate employee training and orientation. For example, a question came up recently when employees found they weren't paid for the Canada Day holiday. They assumed they would be paid, but they were not. Similarly, when a salesperson left after barely a month on the job, there was considerable debate about whether the person should receive severance pay and accumulated vacation pay. Other matters to cover during an orientation, says Jennifer, include company policy regarding lateness and absences; health and hospitalization benefits (there are none, other than workers' compensation); and matters like maintaining a safe and healthy workplace, personal appearance and cleanliness, personal telephone calls and email, substance abuse, and eating on the job.

Jennifer believes that implementing orientation and training programs would help ensure that employees know how to do their jobs. She and Pierre further believe that it is only when employees understand the right way to do their jobs that there is any hope those jobs will in fact be carried out in the way the owners want them to be. Now they want you, their management consultant, to help them.

QUESTIONS

1 How would you change LearnInMotion's orientation program? Should this company rename this process to an onboarding program instead?

2 Should Pierre and Jennifer be involved to emphasize the importance of this process to their staff?

3 Should management of each department assist in the development and subsequent enforcement of the new onboarding program? Why or why not?

Case | INCIDENT

A Case of Too Little Training Too Late!

It's late Friday afternoon in Thunder Bay, Ontario, and Jeff Hartley, a returning summer student, is looking forward to the end of the workday so that he can join his team from the paint department at the baseball game tonight. At the same time, in the office area adjacent to the plant, Julie Adler is working on the finishing touches to a new training program she will be requiring all new employees to take prior to being hired at Simplas Inc. Julie just completed hiring back all of the summer students who were on staff last year and is anxious to have them attend this required training/onboarding program scheduled for Monday morning.

The company has never had a formal onboarding program before, including no WHMIS training regarding chemicals and their affects in the workplace. Julie has been noticing some unsafe behaviours lately and wants to take this opportunity to put appropriate training in place. Another part of Julie's plan for this training is to emphasize the supervisor's role in each department with regard to promoting safe behaviours, especially in the area of proper handling of chemicals in the workplace.

An hour later Julie has put the finishing touches on her new orientation/training program, has confirmed the trainer scheduled to certify everyone in WHMIS on Monday, and has received top management support for her program when she hears screams coming from the paint department. Running down the stairs to the paint department, she sees Jeff Hartley unconscious on the floor. The sound of the arrival of the ambulance erupts into the air. After Jeff is taken to the hospital, Julie is desperate to investigate what happened. She turns to his supervisor and demands to know all the details. Apparently in his hurry to be done for the day, Jeff did not wear his face mask while he was painting a final part and must have passed out from the paint fumes collecting in the area. Julie sighs and just realizes now how much more training will be needed at this employer. Onboarding is just a start. Please assist Julie by answering the following questions.

QUESTIONS

1   What legal aspects regarding the obvious lack of training in this case will Julie, as HR Manager, and the company have to deal with?

2   How can the five-step training process assist in this scenario?

3   Should Julie put together specific training for all summer students?

For additional cases and exercise material, go to
www.pearsoned.ca/myhrlab

CHAPTER 9

CAREER DEVELOPMENT

LEARNING OUTCOMES

AFTER STUDYING THIS CHAPTER, YOU SHOULD BE ABLE TO

EXPLAIN the strategic importance of career planning and development in the context of today's talent shortage.

ANALYZE the factors that affect career choices.

EXPLAIN the responsibilities of the organization in the career development process.

RECOMMEND how to manage transfers and promotions more effectively.

EXPLAIN what management development is and why it is important.

DESCRIBE on-the-job and off-the-job management-development techniques.

REQUIRED PROFESSIONAL CAPABILITIES (RPC)

- Assesses and recommends internal and external suppliers of development programs
- Applies general principles of adult learning to ensure appropriate development methods and techniques
- Uses a variety of methods to deliver development programs
- Helps supervisors/managers to identify career options for employees that align with business needs
- Provides assessment tools for career development
- Ensures performance management information is an integral component of employee development

- Assists employees in identifying career paths, establishing learning plans and activities required for achieving personal and organizational success
- Facilitates the implementation of developmental work assignments
- Monitors, documents, and reports on career development activities
- Monitors and reports on the impact of development activities on organizational performance
- Implements deployment procedures ensuring that necessary compensation and benefits changes and education plans are addressed

CAREER PLANNING AND DEVELOPMENT

career planning and development
The deliberate process through which a person becomes aware of personal career-related attributes and the lifelong series of activities that contribute to his or her career fulfillment.

Career Planning Exercises
www.careerstorm.com
Career Networking
www.careerkey.com

Career planning has become a critical strategic issue for CEOs and boards of directors, as well as HR executives.[1] The talent shortage has created a sense of urgency regarding the development of careers for the next generation of managers and executives needed to take responsibility for strategic leadership. Increasing competition for talent is expected to create a serious challenge for retaining high-potential employees. Proactive organizations have already started to take action to manage the need for more managerial talent. For example, Labatt Breweries' global management trainee program is helping to ensure a supply of future leaders, as described in the Strategic HR box.

At the same time, there is an increasing need for employees who are interested in global careers; in virtual work as a key aspect of their careers; in careers that involve continuously changing technology; and many other variations on traditional career paths. HRM activities play an important role in **career planning and development.** Career-related programs help HR professionals to maintain employee commitment—an employee's identification with and agreement to pursue the company's or the unit's strategic goals. Most employees appreciate and respond well to having their skills and potential enhanced, and to knowing that they will be more marketable. Developmental activities, such as providing the educational and training resources required to help employees identify and develop their promotion and career potential, are extremely important to younger employees today. Career-oriented firms also stress career-oriented appraisals that link the employee's past performance, career preferences, and developmental needs in a formal career plan.

Career planning can play a significant role in retaining employees in the organization and reducing turnover of valued workers. The key factors in employee retention today are an organizational culture that values and nurtures talented employees, fair processes in "people" decisions, and managers who understand what motivates employees.[2] Employers and employees also recognize the need for lifelong learning. Retention can be strengthened by providing extensive, continuing training—from basic remedial skills to advanced decision-making techniques—throughout employees' careers.

Before proceeding, it would be useful to clarify some of the terms that will be used throughout this chapter.[3] A *career* is a series of work-related positions, paid or unpaid, that help a person to grow in job skills, success, and fulfillment. *Career development* is the lifelong series of activities (such as workshops) that contribute to a person's career exploration, establishment, success, and fulfillment. *Career planning* is the deliberate process through which someone becomes aware of personal skills, interests, knowledge, motivations, and other characteristics; acquires information about opportunities and choices; identifies career-related goals; and establishes action plans to attain specific goals.

Roles in Career Development

The individual, the manager, and the employer all have roles in the individual's career development. Ultimately, however, it is the *individual* who must accept responsibility for his or her own career. This requires an entrepreneurial, goal-oriented approach that uses four key skills: self-motivation, independent learning, effective time and money management, and self-promotion.[4] Younger

Strategic HR

Brewing Up Management Trainee Programs

For the past two months, Luca Lorenzoni has gone to work every day in a lab coat and goggles—not exactly where the University of Waterloo business major expected to find himself after graduating. "If you'd told me that I'd be in the quality control lab analyzing chemicals in beer, I would have laughed at you," he says. "But that's the opportunity we're given here."

Lorenzoni is in the midst of Labatt Breweries of Canada's global management trainee program, a cross-sectional program aimed at building leaders who understand the beer business from start to finish. Having learned about brewing, Lorenzoni is now going on the road with sales reps to learn how to sell beer. Later he'll move to head office, where he'll train in the HR, information technology, and the legal and corporate affairs side of the business. Then he'll be assigned to a five-month project before moving into his first management role with the company. In all, Lorenzoni will spend ten months in the program, where he'll learn every aspect of the business and travel across the country—all while receiving a full salary.

The program has helped Labatt entice the best and the brightest as future leaders, says Amy Secord, manager of people development. Last year, 3000 students and recent graduates (within two years of graduating) applied for the program. Only 15, including Lorenzoni, were chosen. The selection process involves five rigorous rounds of interviews, including a business simulation that resembles the game of Risk, says Secord. Applicants are divided into teams and assigned a continent where they manage a beer company. "We go through different rounds to represent different years. We throw in factors such as another entry into the market, or perhaps they had a bad year with weather," she says. "It's not so much to see what their results are but how they interact as a team and who steps up as a natural leader."

Lorenzoni jokes that he still has nightmares about the intense selection process but says that's what attracted him to the program in the first place. It also gives him the time and experience to decide whether Labatt is the right fit for him and vice versa. "Any time you spend that much time and dedicate that many resources to actually finding candidates, you know that the company has got a lot behind the program," he says. "You get to see, round through round, who's staying on and to see if you really fit with them."

Before applying for the program, Lorenzoni did consulting work in Toronto with little vision for the future. The management training program has opened up more opportunities than he could have imagined, he says. "You see a path. It's something that at every step you have to earn, but, at the same time, there is a lot of opportunity here," he says.

"The program is already paying off for Labatt," says Secord. Several trainees from the first intake have shot straight up the corporate ranks, landing roles just below the director level—roles that have traditionally taken 10 to 15 years to achieve. "These are people two to three years out of school," she says. "[The program] is imperative. We have to make sure we have the right people in the right places."

Some components of the program have been modified along the way and, more significantly, Labatt has condensed the interview process to have candidates in the door by November instead of December. "We've had to speed up the recruitment process quite a bit," says Secord. "Even in this tough market, more and more companies are trying to get the best talent. Last year, in Luca's year, we actually lost a lot of candidates because we were only offering to them at the beginning of December."

Labatt is also trying to reach a broader audience through a Facebook group and trainees' blogs. Secord declines to say how much the program costs per trainee but will say it's one of the company's more expensive—and valued—programs. "If we don't take the time to make sure that we have the right people, who are trained the right way, we're in a lot of trouble further down the line. We need them now."

Source: Adapted from D. Harder, "Brewing up Management Trainee Programs," *Canadian HR Reporter*, December 15, 2008.

workers today are increasingly expecting to develop these skills by pursuing a career path that involves moving through multiple organizations.[5]

Networking is the foundation of active career management and is essential for accessing the most valuable career resource—people. Networking is an organized process whereby the individual arranges and conducts a series of face-to-face meetings with his or her colleagues and contacts, plus individuals they

FIGURE 9.1 | Personal Networking Chart

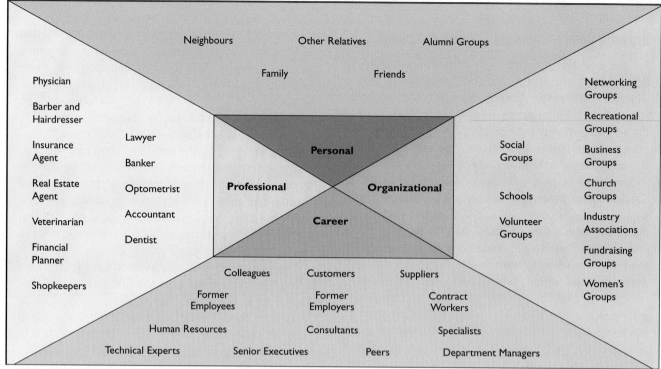

recommend. Networking does not involve asking for a job, and it is not a one-sided encounter where only one individual benefits, but rather a mutual sharing process. Its objectives are to let people know about background and career goals, and to exchange information, advice, and referrals.[6] A personal networking chart is shown in **Figure 9.1.**

Within the organization, the individual's *manager* plays a role, too. The manager should provide timely and objective performance feedback, offer developmental assignments and support, and participate in career-development discussions. The manager acts as a coach, an appraiser, an advisor, and a referral agent, for instance, listening to and clarifying the individual's career plans, giving feedback, generating career options, and linking the employee to organizational resources and career options.

Finally, the *employer* plays a career-development role. For example, an organization wanting to retain good employees should provide career-oriented training and development opportunities, offer career information and career programs, and give employees a variety of career options. Most employees will ultimately assess their employers on the extent to which the organization allowed them to excel and to become the people they believed they had the potential to become. That will help to determine their overall job satisfaction and their commitment to their employers.[7]

Factors That Affect Career Choices

The first step in planning a career is to learn as much as possible about the person's interests, aptitudes, and skills.

Identify Career Stage

Each person's career goes through stages, and the current stage will influence the employee's knowledge of and preference for various occupations. The typical stages of this **career cycle** follow.[8]

career cycle The stages through which a person's career evolves.

Growth Stage The **growth stage** lasts roughly from birth to age 14 and is a period during which the person develops a self-concept by identifying with and interacting with other people, such as family, friends, and teachers. Early in this period, role-playing is important, and children experiment with different ways of acting; this helps them to form impressions of how other people react to different behaviours and contributes to their developing a unique self-concept or identity. Toward the end of this stage, the adolescent (who by this time has developed preliminary ideas about what his or her interests and abilities are) begins to think realistically about occupational alternatives.

growth stage The period from birth to around age 14 during which the person develops a self-concept by identifying with and interacting with other people, such as family, friends, and teachers.

Exploration Stage The **exploration stage** is the period (roughly from age 15 to 24) during which a person seriously explores various occupational alternatives. The person attempts to match these alternatives with what he or she has learned about them and about his or her own interests and abilities from school, leisure activities, and work. Tentative broad occupational choices are usually made during the beginning of this period. Toward the end of this period, a potentially appropriate choice is made and the person tries out an entry-level job.

Probably the most important task that the person has in this and the preceding stage is to develop a realistic understanding of his or her abilities and talents. Similarly, the person must make sound educational decisions based on reliable sources of information about occupational alternatives.

exploration stage The period from around age 15 to 24 during which a person seriously explores various occupational alternatives, attempting to match these alternatives with his or her interests and abilities.

Establishment Stage The **establishment stage** spans the period from roughly age 24 to 44 and is the heart of most people's work lives. During this period, a suitable occupation is typically found and the person engages in activities that help him or her to earn a permanent place in the chosen field. Often, and particularly in the professions, the person locks into a chosen occupation early. In most cases, however, this is a period during which the person is continually testing his or her capabilities and ambitions against those of the initial occupational choice. Some people, however, do not settle into one occupation and continue to change jobs throughout their life.

establishment stage The period, roughly from age 24 to 44, that is the heart of most people's work lives.

Maintenance Stage Between the ages of 45 and 65, many people simply slide from the establishment stage into the **maintenance stage**. During this latter period, most efforts are now typically directed at maintaining the place that the person has created in the world of work. As mentioned above, some people continue to change jobs during this stage as well.

maintenance stage The period from about age 45 to 65 during which the person secures his or her place in the world of work.

Decline Stage As retirement age approaches, there may be a slowing-down period known as the **decline stage**. However, it is becoming more common for older workers, despite some decline in physical capabilities, to continue to work until normal retirement age and some even embark on new careers after "retirement."

decline stage The period during which many people are faced with the prospect of having to accept reduced levels of power and responsibility.

Identify Occupational Orientation

Career-counselling expert John Holland says that a person's personality (including values, motives, and needs) determines his or her **occupational orientation**, which is another important factor in career choices. For example, a person with

occupational orientation The theory, developed by John Holland, that there are six basic personal orientations that determine the sorts of careers to which people are drawn.

a strong social orientation might be attracted to careers that entail interpersonal rather than intellectual or physical activities and to such occupations as social work.

Based on research with his Vocational Preference Test (VPT), John Holland found six basic personality types or orientations:[9]

1. *Realistic orientation.* These people are attracted to occupations that involve physical activities requiring skill, strength, and coordination. Examples include forestry, farming, and agriculture.

2. *Investigative orientation.* Investigative people are attracted to careers that involve cognitive activities (thinking, organizing, and understanding) rather than affective activities (feeling, acting, or interpersonal and emotional tasks). Examples include biologists, chemists, and university professors.

3. *Social orientation.* These people are attracted to careers that involve interpersonal rather than intellectual or physical activities. Examples include clinical psychology, foreign service, and social work.

4. *Conventional orientation.* A conventional orientation favours careers that involve structured, rule-regulated activities, as well as careers in which it is expected that the employee subordinate his or her personal needs to those of the organization. Examples include accountants and bankers.

5. *Enterprising orientation.* Verbal activities aimed at influencing others are attractive to enterprising personalities. Examples include managers, lawyers, and public relations executives.

6. *Artistic orientation.* People here are attracted to careers that involve self-expression, artistic creation, expression of emotions, and individualistic activities. Examples include artists, advertising executives, and musicians.

Most people have more than one orientation (they might be social, realistic, and investigative, for example), and Holland believes that the more similar or compatible these orientations are, the less internal conflict or indecision a person will face in making a career choice.

Identify Skills and Aptitudes

Successful performance depends not just on motivation but also on ability. Someone may have a conventional orientation, but whether he or she has the skills to be an accountant, banker, or credit manager will largely determine the specific occupation ultimately chosen. Therefore, each individual's skills must be identified, based on his or her education and experience. In organizations using competency- or skill-based pay, a formal system for evaluating skills will already be in place.

For career-planning purposes, a person's aptitudes are usually measured with a test battery, such as the general aptitude test battery (GATB). This instrument measures various aptitudes, including intelligence and mathematical ability. Considerable work has been done to relate aptitudes, such as those measured by the GATB, to specific occupations.

Identify a Career Anchor

career anchor A concern or value that you will not give up if a choice has to be made.

Edgar Schein says that career planning is a continuing process of self-discovery. As a person learns more about him- or herself, a dominant **career anchor** may become apparent. Career anchors, as their name implies, are concerns or values that a person will not give up if a choice has to be made. Schein identified eight career anchors:[10]

1. *Technical/functional as a career anchor.* People who have a strong technical/ functional career anchor tend to avoid decisions that would drive them toward general management. Instead, they make decisions that will enable them to remain and grow in their chosen technical or functional fields.

2. *Managerial competence as a career anchor.* Other people show a strong motivation to become managers, and their career experience convinces them that they have the skills and values required to rise to general-management positions. A management position of high responsibility is their ultimate goal.

3. *Creativity as a career anchor.* People who become successful entrepreneurs have a need to build or create something that is entirely their own product— a product or process that bears their name, a company of their own, or a personal fortune that reflects their accomplishments.

4. *Autonomy and independence as career anchors.* Some people seem driven to be on their own, free of the dependence that can arise when a person works in a large organization where promotions, transfers, and salary decisions make them subordinate to others.

5. *Security as a career anchor.* Some people are mostly concerned with long-run career stability and job security. A stable future with one organization that offers a good retirement program and benefits and/or maintaining similar geographic surroundings may be important.

6. *Service/dedication as a career anchor.* More and more people feel a need to do something meaningful in a larger context. Information technology has made global problems, such as the environment, overpopulation, and poverty, highly visible.

7. *Pure challenge as a career anchor.* A small group of people define their career in terms of overcoming impossible odds, solving unsolved problems, and winning out over competitors.

8. *Lifestyle as a career anchor.* A growing number of people, particularly dual career couples, define their careers as part of a larger lifestyle integrating two careers and two sets of personal and family concerns.

Responsibilities of the Organization

Along with the employee, the manager, employer, and HR staff all have career-management responsibilities. Some guidelines follow.

Provide Realistic Job Previews

Tips | **FOR THE FRONT LINE**

Providing recruits with realistic previews of what to expect should they be selected to work in the organization—previews that describe both the attractions and the possible pitfalls—can be an effective way of minimizing reality shock and improving employees' long-term performance.

Avoid Reality Shock

Perhaps at no other stage in the person's career is it more important for the employer to be career development-oriented than at the initial entry stage, when the person is recruited, hired, and given a first assignment and a boss. This is (or should be) a period of *reality testing* during which his or her initial hopes and goals first confront the realities of organizational life and of the person's talents and needs.

For many first-time workers, this turns out to be a disastrous period, one in which their often naïve expectations confront unexpected workplace realities, such as being relegated to an unimportant low-risk job where they "cannot cause any trouble while being tried out," interdepartmental conflict and politicking, or a boss who is neither rewarded for nor trained in the unique mentoring tasks needed to properly supervise new employees.[11]

Provide Challenging Initial Jobs

Most experts agree that one of the most important things is to provide new employees with challenging first jobs. In most organizations, however, providing such jobs seems more the exception than the rule. This imbalance, as one expert has pointed out, is an example of "glaring mismanagement" when one considers the effort and money invested in recruiting, hiring, and training new employees.[12]

Be Demanding

There is often a "Pygmalion effect" in the relationship between a new employee and his or her boss.[13] In other words, the more the supervisor expects and the more confident and supportive he or she is, the better new employees will perform.

Provide Periodic Developmental Job Rotation

The best way in which new employees can test themselves and crystallize their career anchors is to try out a variety of challenging jobs. By rotating to jobs in various specializations—from financial analysis to production to HR, for example—the employee gets an opportunity to assess his or her aptitudes and preferences. At the same time, the organization gets a manager with a broader, multifunctional view of the organization.[14]

Provide Career-Oriented Performance Appraisals

Supervisors must understand that valid performance appraisal information is, in the long run, more important than protecting the short-term interests of their staff.[15] Therefore, a supervisor needs concrete information regarding the employee's potential career path—information, in other words, about the nature of the future work for which he or she is appraising the employee or which the employee desires.[16]

Provide Career-Planning Workshops

Employers should also take steps to increase their employees' involvement and expertise in planning and developing their own careers. One option here is to organize periodic

Giving an employee responsibility for a major presentation to an important client is one way to front-load entry-level jobs with challenge and to foster employee commitment.

career-planning workshops. A **career-planning workshop** has been defined as "a planned learning event in which participants are expected to be actively involved, completing career-planning exercises and inventories, and participating in career-skills practice sessions."[17]

Such workshops usually contain a *self-assessment* activity in which individual employees actively analyze their own career interests, skills, and career anchors. There is then an *environmental assessment* phase in which relevant information about the company and its career options and staffing needs is presented. Finally, a career-planning workshop typically concludes with *goal setting and action planning* in which the individual sets career goals and creates a career plan.

A career-planning workbook may be distributed to employees either as part of a workshop or as an independent career-planning aid. This is "a printed guide that directs its users through a series of assessment exercises, models, discussions, guidelines, and other information to support career planning."[18] The workbook may also contain practical career-related information, such as how to prepare a résumé. Finally, career-planning workbooks usually contain guides for creating a career-development action plan. A career-planning workbook underlines the employee's responsibility to initiate the career-development process, whereas career workshops may reinforce the perception that the employer will do so.[19]

Provide Opportunities for Mentoring

Mentoring has traditionally been defined as "the use of an experienced individual (the mentor) to teach and train someone [the protégé] with less knowledge in a given area." Through individualized attention, "the mentor transfers needed information, feedback, and encouragement to the protégé," and in that way, the opportunities for the protégé to optimize his or her career success are improved. Effective mentoring builds trust both ways in the mentor–protégé relationship. Mentoring provides benefits to both mentors, who demonstrate enhanced attitudes and job performance, and protégés, who become more self-confident and productive and experience greater career satisfaction and faster career growth.[20]

Organizational mentoring may be formal or informal. Informally, of course, middle- and senior-level managers will often voluntarily take up-and-coming employees under their wings, not only to train them but also to give career advice and to help them steer around political pitfalls. However, many employers also establish formal mentoring programs. Here employers actively encourage mentoring relationships to take place and may pair protégés with potential mentors.[21] Training may be provided to facilitate the mentoring process and, in particular, to aid both mentor and protégé in understanding their respective responsibilities in the mentoring relationship.

A recent study by Peer Resources, a nonprofit centre for mentoring in Victoria, B.C., found that mentoring is not being used to its full potential in Canadian workplaces. This is surprising, given the emphasis on learning organizations and knowledge workers in today's businesses. Mentoring is one of the best and cheapest ways to transfer knowledge. Mentoring also keeps skilled employees motivated, loyal, and committed to the organization. Ultimately, an effective mentoring program supports corporate strategy by retaining future leaders.[22]

career-planning workshop A planned learning event in which participants are expected to be actively involved in career-planning exercises and career-skills practice sessions.

RPC
Assists employees in identifying career paths, establishing learning plans and activities required for achieving personal and organizational success

mentoring An experienced individual (the mentor) teaching and training another person (the protégé) who has less knowledge in an area.

RPC
Helps supervisors/managers to identify career options for employees that align with business needs

Mentors—Peer Resources
www.mentors.ca

Through reverse mentoring, a younger employee can provide an older one with guidance in using modern technology.

A new development in mentoring is *reverse mentoring* programs where younger employees provide guidance to senior executives on how to use the web for messaging, buying products and services, finding new business opportunities, and so forth. Procter & Gamble, General Electric, and the Wharton Business School are all using reverse mentoring. The relationship that develops often provides benefits to the young mentor when the web-challenged older manager reciprocates in the form of career advice and guidance. Younger employees can also contribute toward understanding the ever-changing consumer marketplace.[23]

Become a Learning Organization

learning organization An organization skilled at creating, acquiring, and transferring knowledge and at modifying its behaviour to reflect new knowledge and insights.

Learning is a survival technique for both individuals and organizations. Today, employees at all levels know that they must engage in lifelong learning in order to remain employable and have a satisfying career. A **learning organization** "is an organization skilled at creating, acquiring, and transferring knowledge and at modifying its behaviour to reflect new knowledge and insights."[24] The HR department is often the driving force behind ensuring that the training and development opportunities necessary to create a learning organization are in place, particularly in transferring knowledge, learning from experience, experimentation through searching for and testing new knowledge, learning from others, and systematic problem solving.

MANAGING TRANSFERS AND PROMOTIONS

Transfers and promotions are significant career-related decisions that managers make on an ongoing basis. These decisions have important career development implications for the transferred and/or promoted employee and substantial benefits for the organization in terms of creating a pool of potential future managers with broad experience throughout the firm.

Managing Transfers

Employees may seek transfers into jobs that offer greater possibility for career advancement or opportunities for personal enrichment or into those that are more interesting or more convenient—better hours, location of work, and so on.[25]

Employers may transfer a worker in order to fill a vacant position or, more generally, to find a better fit for the employee within the firm. Transfers are thus increasingly used as a way to give employees opportunities for diversity of job assignment and, therefore, personal and career growth. Many organizations are recognizing that future leaders will need international experience to effectively manage their organizations in the increasingly globalized world of business, and they are providing international assignments as a career development experience.

RPC

Implements deployment procedures ensuring that necessary compensation and benefit changes and education plans are addressed

Policies of routinely transferring employees from locale to locale, either to give their employees more exposure to a wide range of jobs or to fill open positions with trained employees, have fallen into disfavour, partly because of the cost of relocating employees and partly because of the assumption that frequent transfers have a bad effect on an employee's family life. Companies are facing a record number of rejections of their relocation offers. About two-thirds of all transfer refusals are due to family or spousal concerns. Providing reassurances that relocation costs will be covered is often no longer enough to persuade employees to upset their lifestyles, their spouses' careers, and their children's activities. To overcome this problem, companies are offering spousal support in the form of career transition programs in order to encourage employees to accept transfers.[26]

Making Promotion Decisions

Employers must decide on the criteria on which to promote employees, and the way that these decisions are made will affect the employees' motivation, performance, and commitment.

Decision 1: Is Seniority or Competence the Rule?

From the point of view of motivation, promotion based on competence is best. However, union agreements often contain a clause that emphasizes seniority in promotions, meaning that only *substantial differences in abilities* can be taken into account.[27]

Decision 2: How Is Competence Measured?

Hints | **TO ENSURE LEGAL COMPLIANCE**

If promotion is to be based on competence, how will competence be defined and measured? Defining and measuring *past* performance are relatively straigh forward matters, but promotion also requires predicting the person's *potential*; thus, there must be a valid procedure for predicting a candidate's future performance. Tests and assessment centres can be used to evaluate employees and identify those with executive potential.[28]

Decision 3: Is the Process Formal or Informal?

Many employers still depend on an informal system where the availability and requirements of open positions are kept secret. Key managers make promotion decisions among employees whom they know personally and who have impressed them.[29] The problem is that when employees are not made aware of the jobs that are available, the criteria for promotion, and how promotion decisions are made, the link between performance and promotion is severed, thereby diminishing the effectiveness of promotion as a reward. For this reason, many employers establish formal, published promotion policies and procedures that describe the criteria by which promotions are awarded. Skills inventories, replacement charts, and replacement summaries (like those discussed in Chapter 5) can be used to compile detailed information about the qualifications of hundreds or thousands of employees. The net effect of such actions is twofold: (1) an employer ensures that all qualified employees are considered for openings, and (2) promotion becomes more closely linked with performance in the minds of employees.

Decision 4: Vertical, Horizontal, or Other Career Path?

Finally, employers are increasingly facing the question of how to "promote" employees in an era of flattened organizations that have eliminated many of the higher-management positions to which employees might normally aspire.[30]

An Ethical | Dilemma

Is it ethical for employers to keep promotion policies and procedures secret in an era of flattened organizations, where so many employees who aspire to higher positions will not get them but might achieve them elsewhere?

Some firms have created two parallel career paths: one for managers and another for "individual contributors," such as engineers, who can move up to nonsupervisory but still more-senior positions, such as "senior engineer," with most of the perks and financial rewards attached to management-track positions at that level.[31] Another option is to provide career-development opportunities by moving the person horizontally, such as a production employee being moved horizontally to HR in order to give him or her an opportunity to develop new skills.

MANAGEMENT DEVELOPMENT

management development Any attempt to improve current or future management performance by imparting knowledge, changing attitudes, or increasing skills.

Management development is any attempt to improve managerial performance by imparting knowledge, changing attitudes, or increasing skills. Management development is particularly important as baby boomers enter retirement and the next generation of managers assumes senior management responsibilities. It can also help to attract top talent or achieve employer-of-choice status. The ultimate aim of management-development programs is to achieve business strategy. For this reason, the management-development process consists of (1) assessing the company's human resources needs to achieve its strategic objectives, (2) creating a talent pool, and then (3) developing the managers themselves.[32]

Another critical issue in management development is training local managers in other parts of the world to take over from the original expatriate managers first sent out to initiate operations. Many organizations are focusing on management development in the Asia-Pacific region, as outlined in the Global HRM box.

Global HRM

Leadership Development in the Asia-Pacific Region

The Asia-Pacific region represents the major source of growth within the local market and internationally for many corporations over the next ten years. It is forecast that by 2015 the region will account for 45 percent of world GDP, compared to 20 percent for the United States and 17 percent for Western Europe. Inherent within such rapid growth projections are both opportunities and challenges that organizations will need to surmount.

The growth opportunities are often in locations where there is currently a limited supply of leadership capability, so it has been necessary for organizations to import excellence from their home base rather than to source locally. While this solution is effective over the short term, only the development of local leadership competence, in terms of quantity and quality, over the long term will ensure the achievement of future growth targets.

The Asia-Pacific region embodies wide socio-economic and cultural diversity and has examples of both the most and least developed countries in the world. The primary focus of leadership development for most organizations is on people who are native to Asia-Pacific and who, over the long term, will keep their home base there. This is because the localization of leadership has been found to have a positive impact on performance and because the cost of expatriate assignments is high.

In Asia-Pacific, the current limitations of local leadership supply are serious, creating severe competition for talent. As well, the planned reduction in the number of expatriates has taken longer than expected due to job fulfillment and interest in career development (on the part of expatriates), and due to the efficiency and familiarity of working within established networks and behaviours and preservation of common cultural characteristics and behaviours (on the part of organizations).

A Conference Board survey of 55 companies in the region found that these companies have a genuine interest in changing the balance between expatriate and local leadership, and they are looking to attract, inspire, and retain their best local and regional talent by offering challenging career opportunities and improved leadership development programs and by recruiting the best new talent from all available sources. Almost 80 percent are trying to accelerate talent development in the Asia-Pacific region. More than half have developed competency models that take a consistent global view of what composes global leadership effectiveness. A clear majority of 83 percent say that global skills and competencies are transferable across geographies and cultures; however, they also said that other competencies need to be developed and learned, or re-learned, for different locations.

Although these companies found that experiential activities such as challenging assignments were the most effective in developing leaders, they were actually using formal training and learning activities more often. Therefore, organizations may get a better return on investment if they rebalanced their resources and processes more toward experiential development opportunities/responsibilities than formal learning interventions.

Source: Excerpt from A. Bell, *Leadership in Asia-Pacific: Identifying and Developing Leaders for Growth*, Research Report #R-1387-06-RR. New York: The Conference Board, 2006. Reprinted with permission.

Succession Planning

succession planning A process through which senior-level and critical strategic job openings are planned for and eventually filled.

Most organizations take special measures to plan ahead to develop replacements for senior executives because of their key strategic role. This process is called **succession planning.** Succession planning provides "a significant competitive advantage to companies that take it seriously—and serious risks to those that do not."[33] Although succession planning has traditionally been focused only on management jobs, many organizations today include other strategic positions as well. When an organization loses a top salesperson or a talented engineer, the loss will not make headlines, but the impact on the bottom line could still be significant. A vacant position can mean that important decisions are delayed or made by other employees with less knowledge and expertise.[34]

Successful succession planning begins with CEO leadership and involvement in the following steps:[35]

1. establishing a strategic direction for the organization and jobs that are critical to achieving that strategic direction

2. identifying core skills and competencies needed in jobs that are critical to achieve the strategy

3. identifying people inside the organization who have, or can acquire, those skills and providing them with developmental opportunities (being prepared to recruit externally as well)

Succession planning for senior managers needs to be overseen by the CEO, as it can easily become an emotional issue for ambitious managers and can evoke political behaviour that can only be dealt with at the highest level.[36] HR staff ensure that all the required information for effective succession planning (such as skills inventories) is available, help to ensure objectivity in the process, and provide the development activities required for employees identified in the succession plan.[37]

Once potential successors have been identified, a *replacement chart* is often prepared. As shown in **Figure 9.2**, this chart summarizes potential candidates for each job in the succession management plan, and their development needs.[38] It is very important to ensure that these plans are implemented and carefully managed. A recent survey showed that only half of North American companies with succession plans did not actively manage them.[39]

Employees should be encouraged to be proactive and accept responsibility for their own career, including seeking out opportunities for leadership training. Employees who feel empowered and motivated to be the initiators of their own management-development process may already be demonstrating leadership

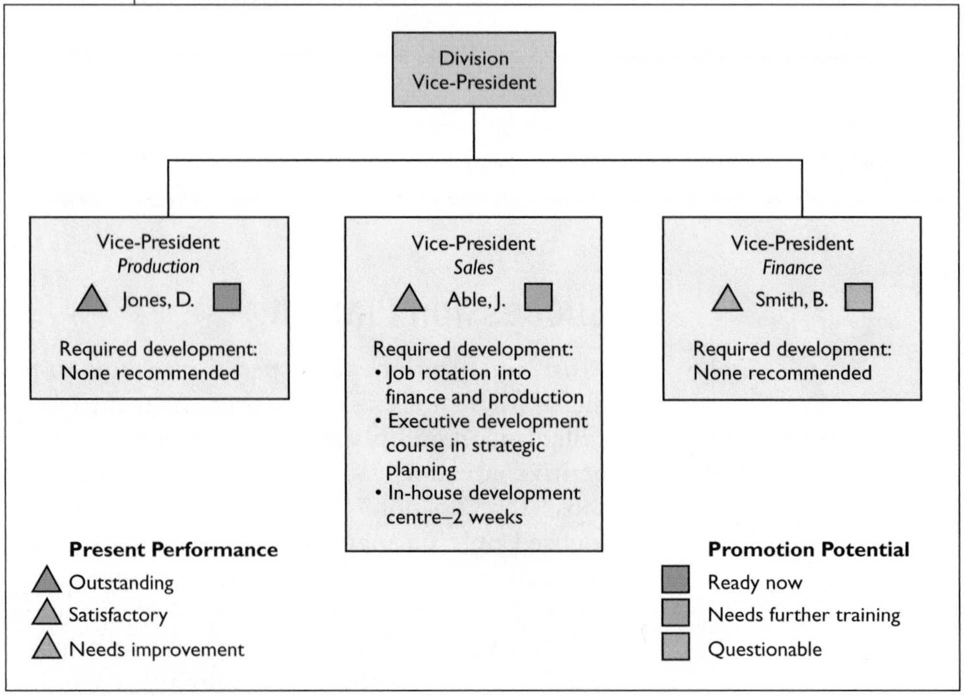

FIGURE 9.2 | Replacement Chart Showing Development Needs of Future Divisional Vice-President

potential. Empowering employees in the organization to be part of a mutual succession-planning process increases the potential for its success.[40] However, it may be necessary to pay special attention to career development for older workers, as discussed in the Workforce Diversity box.

On-the-Job Management-Development Techniques

On-the-job training is one of the most popular development methods. Important techniques here include developmental job rotation, the coaching/understudy approach, and action learning.

Developmental Job Rotation

developmental job rotation
A management-training technique that involves moving a trainee from department to department to broaden his or her experience and identify strong and weak points.

Developmental job rotation involves moving management trainees from department to department to broaden their understanding of all parts of the

Workforce DIVERSITY

Career Development for Older Workers

If an employer doesn't pay attention to the career development of staff as they approach age 60, it won't have the benefit of their productivity during their second middle age. The "second middle age" is a term coined by Helen Harkness in the book *Don't Stop the Career Clock*. It refers to the 20-year period when an individual is between ages 60 and 80. It ought to be viewed as a time of potential and valuable contribution rather than as "the retirement years" or, worse, "old age."

Here are practical career development strategies that will help keep employees fully engaged during their second middle age:

Adopt a new attitude. Discard the stereotypes. Older workers are not necessarily closed-minded, reluctant to embrace change, risk averse, and focused on the past. Their views are grounded in years of hard-earned experience and many of them are open-minded, flexible, forward-thinking, and willing to take calculated risks.

Provide career counselling. People want to do work that interests them, takes advantage of their knowledge, honours their values, and uses their key skills. These factors change for the individual over time, and often a person's career path takes him or her away from work that is truly enjoyed. Returning to an earlier role could be rejuvenating in second middle age or it might be feasible to launch into a completely new endeavour as an alternative to retirement. To help employees stay on a productive career track, it is crucial to provide good career counselling.

Invest in training and development. Recent research debunks the myth of the inevitable decline of mental ability with age. Although slower processing and some memory loss are typical of aging, these are not necessarily signs of diminishing capacity in primary mental functions, such as verbal meaning, spatial orientation, inductive reasoning, numerical ability, or word fluency. These important mental competencies, which can remain intact well into someone's 90s in the absence of illness, make second middle-agers worthy candidates for training and development. It is easy to compensate for a slower mental pace and occasional memory lapse when intellectual capability is respected.

Honour the need for work/life balance. After decades of commuting, working long hours, and taking short holidays, many people look forward to retirement as a welcome break from the unrelenting routine. The prospect of sleeping in seven days a week, taking an extended trip, or spending the winter in Florida can have a lot of appeal. Creative work arrangements could offer some of these perks to second middle-agers.

Second middle-agers could be organizational gold. Research has shown that they have lower rates of absenteeism, fewer accidents, higher levels of job satisfaction, and a stronger work ethic. Why wouldn't employers encourage them to develop their careers and remain productive in the workforce as long as possible?

Source: Adapted from M. Watters, "Career Development for Employees Heading into Their 'Second Middle Age,'" *Canadian HR Reporter*, February 13, 2006, p. 13.

business.[41] The trainee—often a recent college or university graduate—may work for several months in each department; this not only helps to broaden his or her experience but also helps the trainee discover which jobs he or she prefers. TD Bank Financial Group provides MBA graduates with four customized six-month rotations within fast-paced and exciting areas throughout the organization.[42]

In addition to providing a well-rounded training experience for each person, job rotation helps to prevent stagnation through the constant introduction of new points of view in each department. It also tests the trainee and helps to identify the person's strong and weak points.[43] Job rotation is more appropriate for developing general line managers than functional staff experts.

Coaching/Understudy Approach

In the *coaching/understudy approach*, the trainee works directly with the person that he or she is to replace; the latter is, in turn, responsible for the trainee's coaching. Normally, the trainee relieves the executive of certain responsibilities and learns the job by doing it.[44] This helps to ensure that the employer will have trained managers to assume key positions.

To be effective, the executive has to be a good coach and mentor. His or her motivation to train the replacement will depend on the quality of the relationship between them.

Action Learning

action learning A training technique by which management trainees are allowed to work full-time, analyzing and solving problems in other departments.

Action learning releases managers from their regular duties in order that they can work full-time on projects, analyzing and solving problems in departments other than their own. The trainees meet periodically with a project group of four or five people, with whom their findings and progress are discussed and debated. TD Bank Financial Group and Telus use this method.[45]

The idea of developing managers in this way has pros and cons. It gives trainees real experience with actual problems, and to that extent, it can develop skills like problem analysis and planning. Furthermore, working with the others in the group, the trainees can and do find solutions to major problems. The main drawback is that, in releasing trainees to work on outside projects, the employer loses the full-time services of a competent manager.

Off-the-Job Management-Development Techniques

There are many techniques that are used to develop managers off the job, perhaps in a conference room at headquarters or off the premises entirely at a university or special seminar. These techniques are addressed next.

The Case Study Method

case study method A development method in which a trainee is presented with a written description of an organizational problem to diagnose and solve.

The **case study method** presents a trainee with a written description of an organizational problem. The person then analyzes the case in private, diagnoses the problem, and presents his or her findings and solutions in a discussion with other trainees.[46] The case method approach is aimed at giving trainees realistic experience in identifying and analyzing complex problems in an environment in which their progress can be subtly guided by a trained discussion leader. Through the class discussion of the case, trainees learn that there are usually

Trainees participating in a case-study discussion

many ways to approach and solve complex organizational problems. Trainees also learn that their own needs and values often influence their solutions.

Several things can be done to increase the effectiveness of the case approach. If possible, the cases should be actual scenarios from the trainees' own firms; this will help to ensure that trainees understand the background of the case, as well as make it easier for trainees to transfer what they learn to their own jobs and situations. Instructors have to guard against dominating the case analysis and make sure that they remain no more than a catalyst or coach. Finally, they must carefully prepare the case discussion and let the participants discuss the case in small groups before class.[47]

Management Games

management game A computerized development technique in which teams of managers compete with one another by making decisions regarding realistic but simulated companies.

Development Dimensions International
www.ddiworld.com

In a computerized **management game**, trainees are divided into five- or six-person companies, each of which has to compete with the others in a simulated marketplace. Each company sets a goal (e.g., "maximize sales") and is told that it can make several decisions, such as (1) how much to spend on advertising, (2) how much to produce, (3) how much inventory to maintain, and (4) how many of which product to produce. As in the real world, each company usually cannot see what decisions the other firms have made, although these decisions do affect their own sales. For example, if a competitor decides to increase its advertising expenditures, it may end up increasing its sales at the expense of the other firms.[48] A board game called Making Sense of Business: A Simulation designed by Development Dimensions International provides participants with the opportunity to carry out strategic decision making and learn about the hard decisions and trade-offs that business leaders deal with every day.[49]

Management games can be good development tools. People learn best by getting involved in the activity itself, and the games can be useful for gaining such involvement. They help trainees to develop their problem-solving skills and leadership skills, as well as foster cooperation and teamwork.

Outside Seminars

Niagara Institute
www.niagarainstitute.com

Many organizations offer special seminars and conferences aimed at providing skill-building training for managers. For example, the Niagara Institute in

Adventure learning participants enhance their leadership skills, team skills, and risk-taking behaviour.

Niagara-on-the-Lake, Ontario, offers programs that develop skills essential for strong leadership; and the Institute of Professional Management offers a professional accreditation program leading to the Canadian Management Professional (CMP) designation.[50] Outdoor experiential expeditions, or adventure learning experiences, are sometimes used to enhance leadership skills, team skills, and risk-taking behaviour.[51]

College/University-Related Programs

Colleges and universities provide three types of management-development activities. First, many schools provide *executive-development programs* in leadership, marketing, HRM, operations management, and so on. The programs use cases and lectures to provide senior-level managers with the latest management skills, as well as practice in analyzing complex organizational problems. Most of these programs take the executives away from their jobs, putting them in university-run learning environments for their entire stay.

Second, many colleges and universities also offer *individualized courses* in areas like business, management, and health-care administration. Managers can take these to fill gaps in their backgrounds. Thus, a prospective division manager with a gap in experience with accounting controls might sign up for a two-course sequence in managerial accounting.

Finally, many schools also offer *degree programs*, such as the MBA or Executive MBA. The latter is a Master of Business Administration degree program geared especially to middle managers and above, who generally take their courses on weekends and proceed through the program with the same group of colleagues.

The employer usually plays a role in university-related programs.[52] First, many employers offer *tuition refunds* as an incentive for employees to develop job-related skills. Thus, engineers may be encouraged to enroll in technical courses aimed at keeping them abreast of changes in their field. Supervisors may be encouraged to enroll in programs to develop them for higher-level management jobs. Employers are also increasingly granting technical and professional employees extended *sabbaticals*—periods of time off—to attend a college or university to pursue a higher degree or to upgrade skills.

Role-Playing

The aim of **role-playing** is to create a realistic situation and then have the trainees assume the parts (or roles) of specific people in that situation.[53] Roles that can be used in an employee discipline role-playing exercise are presented in **Figure 9.3.** When combined with the general instructions for the role-playing exercise, roles like these for all of the participants can trigger a spirited discussion among the role-players, particularly when they all throw themselves into the roles. The idea of the exercise is to solve the problem at hand and thereby develop trainees' skills in areas like leadership and delegation.

The role-players can also give up their inhibitions and experiment with new ways of acting. For example, a supervisor could experiment with both a considerate and an autocratic leadership style, whereas in the real world the person might not have this harmless avenue for experimentation. Role-playing also trains a person to be aware of and sensitive to the feelings of others.[54]

RPC

Assesses and recommends internal and external suppliers of development programs

role-playing A training technique in which trainees act the parts of people in a realistic management situation.

Queen's Executive Development Centre
www.execdev.com

FIGURE 9.3 | Typical Roles in an Employee Discipline Role-Playing Exercise

Manager: Dale has failed to adapt to the new requirements for production planning. His/her plans are often incomplete or inadequate. Dale's attitude is defensive and he/she is often nasty to co-workers when they are working on their plans. Dale doesn't seem to understand the importance of the new planning procedure. You have given him/her two verbal warnings in the past. You need to get Dale to understand why production planning is so important in this business. You have just asked Dale to come into your office.

Employee: For 25 years in this job, you have never had any complaints about your work. However, in your performance appraisal last month your manager said that you needed to complete your production planning more quickly. Your manager is also very concerned about the accuracy of your production planning and has warned you a couple of times to be more careful. He/she has just asked you to come into his/her office, and you think it may be about your production planning work.

An Ethical | Dilemma

Is it ethical to require employees to participate in role-playing exercises when they are uncomfortable in this situation?

behaviour modelling A training technique in which trainees are first shown good management techniques, then asked to play roles in a simulated situation, and finally given feedback regarding their performance.

Tips | FOR THE FRONT LINE

Role-playing has some drawbacks. An exercise can take an hour or more to complete, only to be deemed a waste of time by participants if the instructor does not prepare a wrap-up explanation of what the participants were to learn. Some trainees also feel that role-playing is childish, while others who may be uncomfortable with acting are reluctant to participate at all. Knowing the audience and preparing a wrap-up are thus advisable.

Behaviour Modelling

Behaviour modelling involves (1) showing trainees the right (or "model") way of doing something, (2) letting each person practise the right way to do it, and then (3) providing feedback regarding each trainee's performance.[55] It has been used to train first-line supervisors to better handle common supervisor–employee interactions; this includes giving recognition, disciplining, introducing changes, and improving poor performance. It has also been used to train middle managers to better handle interpersonal situations, such as performance problems and undesirable work habits. Finally, it has been used to train employees and their supervisors to take and give criticism, give and ask for help, and establish mutual trust and respect.

The basic behaviour-modelling procedure can be outlined as follows:

1. *Modelling.* First, trainees watch films or videotapes that show model persons behaving effectively in a problem situation. In other words, trainees are shown the right way to behave in a simulated but realistic situation. The film or video might thus show a supervisor effectively disciplining an employee, if teaching how to discipline is the aim of the training program.

2. *Role-playing.* Next, the trainees are given roles to play in a simulated situation; here they practise and rehearse the effective behaviours demonstrated by the models.

3. *Social reinforcement.* The trainer provides reinforcement in the form of praise and constructive feedback based on how the trainee performs in the role-playing situation.

4. *Transfer of training.* Finally, trainees are encouraged to apply their new skills when they are back on their jobs.

In-House Development Centres

in-house development centre
A company-based method for exposing prospective managers to realistic exercises to develop improved management skills.

BMO Financial Group
www.bmo.com

Some employers have **in-house development centres,** also called "corporate universities." These centres usually combine classroom learning (lectures and seminars, for instance) with other techniques, like assessment centres, in-basket exercises, and role-playing, to help develop employees and other managers. The number of corporate universities in North America has grown exponentially over the last several years because of their effectiveness in recruiting and retaining the brightest minds and in developing employee loyalty.[56] In Canada, BMO Financial Group, Canada Post, the City of Richmond, and many others all find that corporate universities can create a competitive advantage.[57]

EXECUTIVE DEVELOPMENT

RPC

Monitors and reports on the impact of development activities on organizational performance

Canada is facing a shortage of leadership talent. At the same time, leadership values are evolving. The traditional command-and-control leadership style is losing its effectiveness, and there is a growing need for leaders who can listen to others and tolerate mistakes made in good faith as part of a learning process. Organizations can gain competitive advantage by addressing this leadership gap.[58]

Bob Hedley, vice-president of Leadership at Maple Leaf Foods, says, "Where I lose sleep right now is we still don't have enough bench strength. One of the challenges is to acquire enough talent within the company and grow them fast enough so that we are ready to grow ourselves."[59] Maple Leaf Foods believes that employees' success guarantees the success of the company. They call it the "Leadership Edge"—thousands of high-performing people, thriving in a high-performance culture. Employees are provided with ongoing feedback about their performance through a state-of-the-art performance assessment and development process. Employees receive recognition for both their accomplishments and their potential. This feedback is followed up with well-targeted developmental activities to ensure continued growth and development.[60]

At the executive level, 70 percent of learning comes from job experiences, 20 percent comes from other individuals such as mentors and coaches, and 10 percent comes from formal training.[61] Many companies are trying to enhance learning from others by providing one-on-one executive coaching by independent coaches as part of the executive development process. In some cases, company managers are being provided with training in coaching skills, indicating the growing interest in developing coaching competencies throughout the management ranks.[62] For example, SaskEnergy created a long-term coaching program for 200 managers from all levels to help them develop successful leadership behaviours and provide skills they could apply to their teams. Coaching goals were tied to the organizational strategy and to succession planning, and senior management actively supported the program. The success of the program is helping to build leaders and position SaskEnergy for future success.[63]

The leadership development programs at the Banff Centre in Alberta focus on building leadership capability in five crucial areas that make up the leadership system. These are self, team, business unit, organization, and community/society. Leading in increasingly complex situations requires a systematic approach to successfully understand and navigate the interdependencies and linkages among all parts of the system, from the self through to the greater community. For this reason, the Banff Centre uses an integrated approach to develop leaders.[64] The

FIGURE 9.4 | Banff Centre Competency Matrix Model

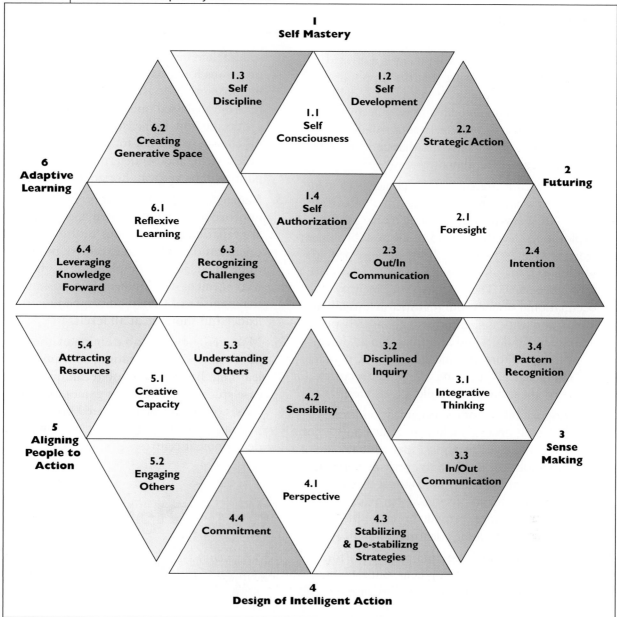

Source: Banff Centre Competency Matrix Model. © 2006. Banff AB: The Banff Centre. www.banffcentre.com/departments/leadership/ assessment_tools/competency_matrix/ (May 8, 2009). Reproduced with permission of The Banff Centre.

Banff Centre believes that the three basic requirements of successful leadership are knowledge, competency, and character. **Figure 9.4** illustrates the Banff Centre Competency Matrix Model, based on six categories of competencies—self mastery, futuring (vision), sense making (thinking), design of intelligent action, aligning people to action (leading), and adaptive learning.

Today it is critical that executive development be a strategic priority in order for organizations to successfully cope with the coming exodus of "boomer" executives. Without new executive talent that is trained and ready to assume senior-level responsibilities, Canadian companies will find it difficult to continue to compete successfully in the global economy.

Chapter | SUMMARY

1. Career planning and development is a critical strategic issue in ensuring that the supply of necessary talent is available. It involves the deliberate process through which a person becomes aware of personal career-related attributes, and the lifelong series of activities that contribute to his or her career fulfillment.

2. The first factor affecting career choice is to identify career stage. The main stages in a person's career are growth (roughly birth to age 14), exploration (roughly age 15 to 24), establishment (roughly age 24 to 44, the heart of most people's work lives), maintenance (45 to 65), and decline (pre-retirement). The next step is to identify occupational orientation: realistic, investigative, social, conventional, enterprising, and artistic. Then identify skills and aptitudes. Finally, identify career anchors: technical/functional, managerial competence, creativity, autonomy, security, service/dedication, pure challenge, or lifestyle.

3. The responsibilities of the organization in the career planning process include provide realistic job previews, avoid reality shock, provide challenging initial jobs, be demanding, provide periodic developmental job rotation, conduct career-oriented performance appraisals, provide career-planning workshops, provide opportunities for mentoring, and become a learning organization.

4. Transfers offer employees an opportunity for personal and career development, but they have become more difficult to manage because of spousal and family concerns. Thus career-transition programs for spouses are often provided. In making promotion decisions, firms have to (1) decide to promote based on seniority or competence, (2) decide how to measure competence, (3) choose between a formal or informal promotion system, and (4) determine whether career paths will be vertical, horizontal, or other.

5. Management development is any attempt to improve managerial performance and it is aimed at preparing employees for future jobs with the organization. When an executive position needs to be filled, succession planning is often involved. Management development is important because the majority of Canadian companies are facing a leadership shortage at all levels.

6. Managerial on-the-job training methods include developmental job rotation, coaching, and action learning. Basic off-the-job techniques include case studies, management games, outside seminars, college/university-related programs, role-playing, behaviour modelling, and in-house development centres.

PEARSON
myHRlab™
Test yourself on the material for this chapter at
www.pearsoned.ca/myhrlab

Key | TERMS

action learning *(p. 254)*
behaviour modelling *(p. 257)*
career anchor *(p. 244)*
career cycle *(p. 243)*
career planning and development *(p. 240)*
career-planning workshop *(p. 247)*
case study method *(p. 254)*
decline stage *(p. 243)*
developmental job rotation *(p. 253)*
establishment stage *(p. 243)*
exploration stage *(p. 243)*

growth stage *(p. 243)*
in-house development centre *(p. 258)*
learning organization *(p. 248)*
maintenance stage *(p. 243)*
management development *(p. 250)*
management game *(p. 255)*
mentoring *(p. 247)*
occupational orientation *(p. 243)*
role-playing *(p. 256)*
succession planning *(p. 251)*

Review and Discussion | QUESTIONS

1. Describe why career planning and development has become more strategically important. Give a brief outline of what organizations are doing to take a more strategic approach in this area.

2. Briefly describe each of the five stages in a typical career.

3. What are the six main types of occupational orientation?

4. What is a career anchor? For each of the five career anchors, why do you think it is important today?

5. Explain three different ways in which managers can assist in the career development of their employees.

6. Explain the four important decisions to be made in establishing a promotion policy.

7. Explain the three major on-the-job management development techniques.

Critical Thinking | QUESTIONS

1. Do you think developmental job rotation is a good method to use for developing management trainees? Why or why not?

2. Would you tell high-potential employees that they are on the "fast-track"? How might this knowledge affect their behaviour? How might the behaviour of employees who are disappointed at not being included in management development activities be affected?

3. How do you think employees are going to respond to the new focus on career planning, given the emphasis in recent years on "being in charge of your own career"?

4. What steps could a company take to reduce political behaviour in the succession planning process?

5. Discuss the six competencies in the Competency Matrix Model used at the Banff Centre. Do you think that any one of these is more important than the others? Why or why not? If you were asked to list them in order of importance, what order would you put them in and why?

Experiential | EXERCISES

1. Review the website of a provider of management-development seminars, such as the Canadian Institute of Management. Obtain copies of recent listings of seminar offerings. At what levels of management are the seminar offerings aimed? What seem to be the most popular types of development programs? Why do you think that is the case?

2. Find an older person who is web-challenged (perhaps a family friend or one of your professors who is having trouble setting up a website or getting full use of the email system). Offer to reverse mentor him or her on using the web for a short time (a few weeks) in return for some career mentoring for you. Prepare a short report on the benefits of this experience for both of you.

3. Using both the Strategic HR box and the Workforce Diversity box in this chapter, compare and contrast the approaches that firms are taking with respect to career development for younger and older workers. Based on your comparison, develop a career development policy statement for a financial institution that reflects the diverse needs of different groups of employees.

Running | CASE

Running Case: LearnInMotion.com

What to Do about Succession?

In the second year of operation of LearnInMotion. com, Jennifer was involved in a serious car accident and spent two months in the hospital and another four months in rehabilitation before she was able to return to work. During this six-month period, Pierre had to manage the entire business on his own. It proved to be impossible. Despite some new training, the sales effort continued to falter and sales revenues declined by 25 percent. Staff turnover at LearnIn-Motion.com increased, as employees found it very frustrating to encounter so much trouble to have even a brief conversation with Pierre. Employees who left were not replaced, as the decline in sales meant that costs had to be reduced. Thus, Pierre was spared the difficult job of downsizing—at least for now.

The first day that Jennifer returned to work, Pierre said, "We have to have a succession plan. This business will not survive unless we have other employees who can take over from us temporarily now and permanently in the long term."

Jennifer agreed. "Yes, it was difficult for me being unable to work and knowing that you were overwhelmed with every problem throughout the entire company," she said. "And maybe employees' performance in their current jobs would be enhanced if they knew they had been identified as having management potential and were provided with specific development opportunities. We'll have to establish a management development program as well."

"I agree," said Pierre, "but we can't afford to spend much money on this." So Pierre and Jennifer would like your help in establishing a succession plan and a management development plan. Here's what they've asked you to do.

QUESTIONS

1   Would the process of career and development planning assist Pierre and Jennifer?

2   If Jennifer and Pierre decide to use succession planning, what steps of this process should they follow to put such a program in place? Who should be involved in the process?

3   If they decide to promote from within, how should promotions or transfers be handled?

4   What management development techniques should be developed?

Case | INCIDENT

What Should Wilma and Frank Do?

Frank and Wilma Rogers live in the Toronto area. Frank is a product engineer in the automotive industry while Wilma is a professor for a local community college. Wilma has been working on her doctorate for the last five years and is scheduled to graduate with her Ph.D. in Business Administration shortly. Wilma has just received an interesting telephone call and can't wait to talk to Frank about it.

Over dinner that night Wilma tells Frank about a position she received a call about from a past boss of hers at a university in Nunavut. As Wilma excitedly discusses the associate professor of business position and the opportunities it will bring, Frank is thinking to himself what a great opportunity, but he doesn't find the location appealing. He subsequently tells her this. Nothing more is discussed however.

A week goes by and Wilma still finds herself yearning to know more about this position and finds herself wanting to apply. She calls Frank and explains this to him and he encourages her to apply. Wilma calls her former boss and applies. Eventually she gets offered the position. Wilma gives her notice at the college and within the next six months starts her new position. Wilma moves to Nunavut, however, Frank stays in Toronto until he can find another job in Nunavut. A few more months go by and Frank has not been able to find a comparable job, he pressures Wilma to consider moving back to Toronto and leaving her new position. Wilma is torn about what to do as she loves her new job but understands why Frank is so frustrated. Please help Wilma by answering the following questions.

QUESTIONS

1 What career stage do you feel Wilma is in when she decided to consider changing careers?

2 According to Edgar Schein what career anchors are driving Wilma's and Frank's careers at this point?

3 If Wilma wishes to stay in her new job how could her employer assist her with this dilemma?

4 Is there anything Frank and Wilma should have done differently in your opinion? If so, what?

PEARSON
myHRlab™

For additional cases and exercise material, go to
www.pearsoned.ca/myhrlab

CHAPTER 10

PERFORMANCE MANAGEMENT

REQUIRED PROFESSIONAL CAPABILITIES (RPC)

- Provides development information, support activities, and procedures for learners, supervisors, and managers to assist in achieving performance improvement

- Assists and coaches supervisors to help employees achieve required performance levels

THE STRATEGIC IMPORTANCE OF PERFORMANCE MANAGEMENT

performance management The process encompassing all activities related to improving employee performance, productivity, and effectiveness.

In any organization, achieving strategic objectives requires employee productivity above all else as organizations strive to create a high-performance culture by using a minimum number of employees. Thus, it has been suggested that better performance management represents a largely untapped opportunity to improve company profitability.[1] Many companies are still dealing with the reality that their performance management systems are ineffective—for example, they need to downsize poor performers, but performance appraisal records indicate that all employees are performing adequately.

Performance management is a process encompassing all activities related to improving employee performance, productivity, and effectiveness. It includes *goal setting*, *pay for performance*, *training and development*, *career management*, and *disciplinary action*. The performance management system must provide an integrated network of procedures across the organization that will direct all work behaviour.[2]

The foundation of performance management is the *performance appraisal* process. The primary purpose of appraising and coaching employees is to instill in them the desire for continuous improvement.[3] Appraisals provide a concrete basis for analysis of an employee's work performance and for any action taken to maintain, enhance, or change it. The other aspects of performance management are discussed in other chapters of this text.

THE PERFORMANCE MANAGEMENT PROCESS

Performance management is of considerable strategic importance to today's organizations because the most effective way for firms to differentiate themselves in a highly competitive, service-oriented, global marketplace is through the quality of their employees.[4] The performance management process contains five steps:[5]

1. *defining performance expectations and goals* to make sure that job duties and job standards are clear to all

2. *providing ongoing feedback and coaching* through open two-way communication

3. *conducting performance appraisal and evaluation discussions* at specific intervals by comparing an employee's actual performance to the standards that have been set (usually involving some type of rating form); the employee's performance and progress are discussed to reinforce the things that the employee is doing well and to develop a plan for correction of any deficiencies that the appraisal might have identified

4. *determining performance rewards/consequences* such as promotions, salary increases, and bonuses

5. *conducting development and career opportunities discussions* (usually annually) in order to review each employee's career plans in light of his or her exhibited strengths and weaknesses, and in light of the company's strategic plans

When performance management is ineffective, it is for reasons that parallel these steps. Some employees are not told ahead of time exactly what is expected of them in terms of good performance. Even if performance standards are defined, they may be irrelevant, subjective, or unrealistic.[6] In other cases, there may be problems with the forms or procedures used to actually appraise the performance; a lenient supervisor might rate all employees "high," for instance, although many are actually unsatisfactory. Still other problems, such as arguing and poor communications, arise during the feedback discussion. Failure to use appraisal results in human resource decision making and career development negates the primary purpose of performance evaluations. Effective performance management thus begins with defining the job and its performance standards, which will now be discussed.

STEP 1: DEFINING PERFORMANCE EXPECTATIONS

Defining performance expectations and goals is a critical step in employees' understanding of how their work makes a contribution to achieving business results. Performance expectations should be linked to current strategic objectives and implementation plans.[7] However, surveys indicate that this understanding is still limited for most employees.[8] Their "line of sight" from their own job duties to the achievement of strategic goals is blurred.[9] Most employees require much more clarification of their performance expectations and how these contribute to the organization's overall results.

In particular, the job description often is not sufficient to clarify what employees are expected to do and how their duties relate to strategic objectives. All sales associates in the firm might have the same job description, for instance, although each sales manager may have individual ideas about what his or her reporting sales associates are expected to do. For example, the job description may list such duties as "supervise support staff" and "be responsible for all customer liaisons." However, one particular sales associate may be expected to personally sell at least $600 000 worth of products per year by handling the division's two largest accounts, keeping the sales assistants happy, and keeping customers away from company executives.[10] With respect to strategic objectives, all the duties of sales associates contribute to increasing the revenue of the organization.

To clarify these expectations, measurable standards related to strategic objectives should be developed for each. The "personal selling" activity can be measured in terms of how many dollars of sales the associate is to generate personally. "Keeping the sales assistants happy" might be measured in terms of turnover (on the assumption that less than 10 percent of the sales assistants will quit in any given year if morale is high). "Keeping customers away from executives" can be measured with a standard of no more than ten customer complaints per year being the sales associate's target. In general, employees should always know ahead of time how and on what basis they will be appraised.

In global companies, performance appraisal criteria may need to be modified to be consistent with cultural norms and values. An interesting study found that some criteria are acceptable in many cultures, as discussed in the Global HRM box.

STEP 2: PROVIDING ONGOING COACHING AND FEEDBACK

Throughout the performance management process, managers and their reports should continue to discuss progress. **Figure 10.1** provides an example of a coaching worksheet that can be used to focus such discussions and facilitate ongoing

Global HRM

Performance Appraisal Criteria in China

Performance appraisal gradually has become more widely used in Chinese enterprises since 1978 when Deng Xiaoping's "open-door" policy began. The appraisal criteria used then were "good moral practice" (*de*), which refers to virtue or moral integrity; "adequate competence" (*neng*), which relates to one's educational background, physical condition, and ability to lead and manage; "positive working attitude" (*qing*), which covers diligence, attendance, and sense of responsibility; and "strong performance record" (*jie*), which refers mainly to work effectiveness, including work quality and quantity.

In the West, where individuals have an inalienable right to choose their own lifestyles and moralities, performance criteria cannot be based on personal character but instead focus on more objective criteria, such as job competences, abilities, and achievements. In China, however, the attitudes and moral character of a person have been regarded as highly relevant to performance. The Confucian view stresses that the most important aspect of an individual is the moral base of his or her character. Chinese culture tends to ascribe achievement more to effort (i.e. diligence, which reflects one's morality) than to ability (which, conceived as an inborn trait, requires no moral effort). For the Chinese, hard work reflects admirably on one's character, and achievement is thought to be closely related to moral character. These deeply rooted Confucian values in China thus lead to an emphasis on appraisals that are based upon personal attitudes and moral characteristics (a practice that is clearly antithetical to the appraisal practices in Western societies) that appear to reflect traditional Chinese values, such as being hard working, loyal, and respectful toward senior staff. Some specific examples are accepting overtime work; being punctual, careful, helpful, loyal, and respectful toward senior staff; as well as being persistent, adaptable, dedicated, and hard working.

Researchers Robert Taormina and Jennifer Gao from the University of Macau gave Chinese workers a list of appraisal items from both Western and Chinese sources and asked which of these would be acceptable. They found three performance appraisal factors that were very acceptable to Chinese employees: work dedication, work efficiency, and teamwork. Work dedication behaviours such as punctuality, loyalty, being hard working, and dedication toward one's work, exist in both Eastern and Western cultures. Employee efficiency has long been considered important to good job performance, as it is considered to be a means to achieve organizational goals. Chinese employees appear to recognize this managerial objective since they were willing to be evaluated on criteria that assess the efficiency of their work. Teamwork is a behavioural manifestation of the group orientation in Eastern cultures.

These findings indicate that relevant and carefully selected appraisal criteria can be applicable across cultures.

Source: Robert J. Taormina and Jennifer H. Gao (2009). Identifying acceptable performance appraisal criteria: An international perspective. *Asia Pacific Journal of Human Resources* 47(1), pp. 102–125. Copyright © 2009, Australian Human Resources Institute.

performance improvement. It is important to have open two-way communication, and both the employee and the manager need to check in frequently throughout the performance management process to talk about progression toward goals.

In some organizations, strategies and objectives change quickly. In such cases, managers and employees may need to change their goals to be consistent. Employees are responsible for monitoring their own performance and asking for help. This promotes employee ownership and control over the process.

STEP 3: PERFORMANCE APPRAISAL AND EVALUATION DISCUSSION

The appraisal itself is generally conducted with the aid of a predetermined and formal method, like one or more of those described in this section.

FIGURE 10.1 | Example of a Coaching Worksheet

Appraisal-Coaching Worksheet

Instructions: This form is to be filled out by supervisor and employee prior to each performance review period.

Employee: _____   Position: _____

Supervisor: _____   Department: _____

Date: _____ Period of Work under Consideration: from _____ to _____

1. What areas of the employee's work performance are meeting job performance standards?

2. In what areas is improvement needed during the next six to twelve months?

3. What factors or events that are beyond the employee's control may affect (positively or negatively) his or her ability to accomplish planned results during the next six to twelve months?

4. What specific strengths has the employee demonstrated on this job that should be more fully used during the next six to twelve months?

5. List two or three areas (if applicable) in which the employee needs to improve his or her performance during the next six to twelve months (gaps in knowledge or experience, skill development needs, behavior modifications that affect job performance, etc.).

6. Based on your consideration of items 1–5 above, summarize your mutual objectives:

A. What supervisor will do:

B. What employee will do:

C. Date for next progress check or to re-evaluate objectives:

D. Data/evidence that will be used to observe and/or measure progress.

_____
Employee Signature   Supervisor Signature

_____
Date

Formal Appraisal Methods

Graphic Rating Scale

graphic rating scale A scale that lists a number of traits and a range of performance for each. The employee is then rated by identifying the score that best describes his or her level of performance for each trait.

The **graphic rating scale** is the simplest and most popular technique for appraising performance. **Figure 10.2** shows a typical rating scale. It lists traits (such as reliability) and a range of performance values (from unsatisfactory to outstanding) for each one. The supervisor rates each employee by circling or checking the score that best describes his or her performance for each trait. The assigned values are then totalled.

FIGURE 10.2 | Sample Graphic Rating Scale Form

Sample Performance Rating Form

Employee's Name _____   Level: Entry-level employee

Manager's Name _____

Key Work Responsibilities   Results/Goals to be Achieved
1. _____   1. _____
2. _____   2. _____
3. _____   3. _____
4. _____   4. _____

Communication

1	2	3	4	5

Below Expectations	Meets Expectations	Role Model
Even with guidance, fails to prepare straightforward communications, including forms, paperwork, and records, in a timely and accurate manner; products require minimal corrections. Even with guidance, fails to adapt style and materials to communicate straightforward information.	With guidance, prepares straightforward communications, including forms, paperwork, and records, in a timely and accurate manner; products require minimal corrections. With guidance, adapts style and materials to communicate straightforward information.	Independently prepares communications, such as forms, paperwork, and records, in a timely, clear, and accurate manner; products require few, if any, corrections. Independently adapts style and materials to communicate information.

Organizational Know-How

1	2	3	4	5

Below Expectations	Meets Expectations	Role Model
<performance standards appear here>	<performance standards appear here>	<performance standards appear here>

Personal Effectiveness

1	2	3	4	5

Below Expectations	Meets Expectations	Role Model
<performance standards appear here>	<performance standards appear here>	<performance standards appear here>

Teamwork

1	2	3	4	5

Below Expectations	Meets Expectations	Role Model
<performance standards appear here>	<performance standards appear here>	<performance standards appear here>

Achieving Business Results

1	2	3	4	5

Below Expectations	Meets Expectations	Role Model
<performance standards appear here>	<performance standards appear here>	<performance standards appear here>

FIGURE 10.2 | (continued)

Results Assessment

Accomplishment 1: _____

	1		2		3		4		5	

Low Impact	Moderate Impact	High Impact
The efficiency or effectiveness of operations remained the same or improved only minimally. The quality of products remained the same or improved only minimally.	The efficiency or effectiveness of operations improved quite a lot. The quality of products improved quite a lot.	The efficiency or effectiveness of operations improved tremendously. The quality of products improved tremendously.

Accomplishment 2: _____

	1		2		3		4		5	

Low Impact	Moderate Impact	High Impact
The efficiency or effectiveness of operations remained the same or improved only minimally. The quality of products remained the same or improved only minimally.	The efficiency or effectiveness of operations improved quite a lot. The quality of products improved quite a lot.	The efficiency or effectiveness of operations improved tremendously. The quality of products improved tremendously.

Narrative

_____

_____

_____

_____

_____

Areas to be Developed	Actions	Completion Date

Manager's Signature _____ Date _____

Employee's Signature _____ Date _____

The above employee signature indicates receipt of, but not necessarily concurrence with, the evaluation herein.

Source: Adapted from Elaine Pulakos, Performance Management (SHRM Foundation, 2004) pp. 16–17. Reprinted by permission of Society for Human Resource Management via Copyright Clearance Center.

Instead of appraising generic traits or factors, many firms specify the duties to be appraised. For a payroll coordinator, these might include being the liaison with accounting and benefits staff, continual updating of knowledge regarding relevant legislation, maintenance of payroll records, data entry and payroll calculations, and ongoing response to employees' inquiries regarding payroll issues.

Alternation Ranking Method

alternation ranking method
Ranking employees from best to worst on a particular trait.

Ranking employees from best to worst on a trait or traits is another method for evaluating employees. Because it is usually easier to distinguish between the worst and best employees than to rank them, an **alternation ranking method** is most popular. First, list all employees to be rated, and then cross out the names of any not known well enough to rank. Then, on a form such as that in **Figure 10.3**, indicate the employee who is the highest on the characteristic being measured and also the one who is the lowest. Then choose the next highest and the next lowest, alternating between highest and lowest until all the employees to be rated have been ranked.

Paired Comparison Method

paired comparison method
Ranking employees by making a chart of all possible pairs of employees for each trait and indicating the better employee of the pair.

The **paired comparison method** helps to make the ranking method more precise. For every trait (quantity of work, quality of work, and so on), every employee is paired with and compared with every other employee.

Suppose that five employees are to be rated. In the paired comparison method, a chart is prepared, as in **Figure 10.4**, of all possible pairs of employees for each trait. Then, for each trait, indicate (with a + or −) who is the better

FIGURE 10.3 | Alternation Ranking Scale

ALTERNATION RANKING SCALE

For the Trait: _____

For the trait you are measuring, list all the employees you want to rank. Put the highest-ranking employee's name on line 1. Put the lowest-ranking employee's name on line 20. Then list the next highest ranking on line 2, the next lowest ranking on line 19, and so on. Continue until all names are on the scale.

Highest-ranking employee

1. _____   11. _____
2. _____   12. _____
3. _____   13. _____
4. _____   14. _____
5. _____   15. _____
6. _____   16. _____
7. _____   17. _____
8. _____   18. _____
9. _____   19. _____
10. _____   20. _____

Lowest-ranking employee

FIGURE 10.4 | Ranking Employees by the Paired Comparison Method

FOR THE TRAIT "QUALITY OF WORK"

Employee Rated:

As Compared with:	A Art	B Maria	C Chuck	D Diane	E José
A Art		+	+	–	–
B Maria	–		–	–	–
C Chuck	–	+		+	–
D Diane	+	+	–		+
E José	+	+	+	–	

↑ Maria Ranks Highest Here

FOR THE TRAIT "CREATIVITY"

Employee Rated:

As Compared with:	A Art	B Maria	C Chuck	D Diane	E José
A Art		–	–	–	–
B Maria	+		–	+	+
C Chuck	+	+		–	+
D Diane	+	–	+		–
E José	+	–	–	+	

↑ Art Ranks Highest Here

Note: "+" means "better than" and "–" means "worse than." For each chart, add up the number of + signs in each column to get the highest-ranked employee.

employee of the pair. Next, the number of times that an employee is rated better is added up. In Figure 10.4, employee Maria ranked highest (has the most + marks) for quality of work, while Art was ranked highest for creativity.

Forced Distribution Method

forced distribution method
Predetermined percentages of ratees are placed in various performance categories.

The **forced distribution method** places predetermined percentages of ratees in performance categories. For example, it may be decided to distribute employees as follows:

- 15 percent high performers
- 20 percent high-average performers
- 30 percent average performers
- 20 percent low-average performers
- 15 percent low performers

An Ethical | Dilemma

Is it ethical to use the forced distribution method, where some employees are classified as having low performance, when it is known that the company does not continue to employ workers whose performance really is poor?

Similar to bell-curve grading at school, this means that not everyone can get an A, and that one's performance is always rated relative to that of one's peers. This method has been criticized as being demotivating for the considerable proportion of the workforce that is classified as below average.[11]

Critical Incident Method

critical incident method Keeping a record of uncommonly good or undesirable examples of an employee's work-related behaviour and reviewing the list with the employee at predetermined times.

With the **critical incident method**, the supervisor keeps a log of desirable or undesirable examples or incidents of each employee's work-related behaviour. Then, every six months or so, the supervisor and employee meet to discuss the latter's performance by using the specific incidents as examples.

This method can always be used to supplement another appraisal technique, and in that role it has several advantages. It provides specific hard facts for explaining the appraisal. It also ensures that a manager thinks about the employee's

TABLE 10.1 | Examples of Critical Incidents for an Assistant Plant Manager

Continuing Duties	Targets	Critical Incidents
Schedule production for plant	Full utilization of employees and machinery in plant; orders delivered on time	Instituted new production scheduling system; decreased late orders by 10 percent last month; increased machine utilization in plant by 20 percent last month
Supervise procurement of raw materials and inventory control	Minimize inventory costs while keeping adequate supplies on hand	Let inventory storage costs rise 15 percent last month; overordered parts "A" and "B" by 20 percent; underordered part "C" by 30 percent
Supervise machinery maintenance	No shutdowns because of faulty machinery	Instituted new preventative maintenance system for plant; prevented a machine breakdown by discovering faulty part

appraisal throughout the year, because the incidents must be accumulated; therefore, the rating does not just reflect the employee's most recent performance. Keeping a running list of critical incidents should also provide concrete examples of what an employee can do to eliminate any performance deficiencies.

The critical incident method can be adapted to the specific job expectations laid out for the employee at the beginning of the year. Thus, in the example presented in **Table 10.1,** one of the assistant plant manager's continuing duties is to supervise procurement and to minimize inventory costs. The critical incident shows that the assistant plant manager let inventory storage costs rise 15 percent; this provides a specific example of what performance must be improved in the future.

The critical incident method is often used to supplement a ranking technique. It is useful for identifying specific examples of good and poor performance and for planning how deficiencies can be corrected. It is not as useful by itself for comparing employees nor, therefore, for making salary decisions.

Narrative Forms

Some employers use narrative forms to evaluate employees. For example, the form in **Figure 10.5** presents a suggested format for identifying a performance issue and presenting a *performance improvement plan.* The performance problem is described in specific detail, and its organizational impact is specified. The improvement plan identifies measurable improvement goals, provides directions regarding training and any other suggested activities to address the performance issue, and encourages the employee to add ideas about steps to be taken to improve performance. Finally, the outcomes and consequences, both positive and negative, are explicitly stated. A summary performance appraisal discussion then focuses on problem solving.[12]

Behaviourally Anchored Rating Scales

behaviourally anchored rating scale (BARS) An appraisal method that aims to combine the benefits of narratives, critical incidents, and quantified ratings by anchoring a quantified scale with specific narrative examples of good and poor performance.

A **behaviourally anchored rating scale (BARS)** combines the benefits of narratives, critical incidents, and quantified ratings by anchoring a series of quantified scales, one for each performance dimension, with specific behavioural

FIGURE 10.5 | Performance Improvement Plan

PERFORMANCE IMPROVEMENT PLAN

Employee Name: Brent Goldman   **Department:** Purchasing
Date Presented: August 8, 2007   **Supervisor:** Paul Reisman

Incident Description and Supporting Details: Include the following information: Time, Place, Date of Occurrence, and Persons Present as well as Organizational Impact.

Brent,

On August 1, you conducted a telephone conversation with Morris Kirschenbaum, a wholesaler, regarding the price of switchplates for an upcoming sale. Specifically, you told Mr. Kirschenbaum that the best bid that you currently had was $.20 each for a lot. Another wholesaler, Fred Schiller, whom we've worked with for the past two and a half years, learned of your disclosure to Mr. Kirschenbaum. Mr. Schiller later refused to honor our original bid and consequently severed our working relationship because you disclosed confidential information to a third party.

This disclosure of confidential pricing information violates policy 3.01, "Confidential Information," which states: "All sales price bids are to be strictly confidential. Release of prior sales or present bids is strictly prohibited."

Performance Improvement Plan

1. Measurable/Tangible Improvement Goals. Brent, I expect you to abide by all established policies and procedures. I also expect that you will never again display such a serious lack of judgment or discretion by sharing bid prices in advance of a sale.

2. Training or Special Direction to Be Provided: Policy 3.01 is attached. Please read this policy immediately and see me with any questions that you may have.

3. Interim Performance Evaluation Necessary? No

4. Our Employee Assistance Program (EAP) Provider, Prime Behavioral Health Group, can be confidentially reached to assist you at (800) 555-5555. This is strictly voluntary. A booklet regarding the EAP's services is available from Human Resources.

5. In addition, I recognize that you may have certain ideas to improve your performance. Therefore, I encourage you to provide your own Personal Improvement Plan Input and Suggestions:

_____
_____
_____

(Attach additional sheets if needed.)

Outcomes and Consequences

Positive: If you meet your performance goals, no further disciplinary action will be taken regarding this issue. In addition, you will help our company remain profitable by ensuring that our bids are competitive and that our relationships with our vendors remain solid.

Negative: If you ever again divulge confidential company information regarding pricing, bids, or any other protected areas of information, disciplinary action up to and including dismissal may result. A copy of this document will be placed in your personnel file.

Scheduled Review Date: None

Employee Comments and/or Rebuttal

_____
_____
_____

(Attach additional sheets if needed.)

X_____
Employee Signature

FIGURE 10.6 | Behaviourally Anchored Rating Scale

SALES SKILLS

Skilfully persuading customers to purchase products; using product benefits and opportunities effectively; closing skills; adapting sales techniques appropriately to different customers; effectively overcoming objections to purchasing products.

5 — If a customer insists on a particular brand name, the salesperson perseveres. Although products with this particular brand name are not available, the salesperson does not give up; instead, the salesperson persuades the customer that his or her needs could be better met with another product.

4 — The salesperson treats objections to purchasing the product seriously; works hard to counter the objections with relevant positive arguments regarding the benefits of the product.

3 — When a customer is deciding on which product to purchase, the salesperson tries to sell the product with the highest profit magin.

2 — The salesperson insists on describing more features of the product even though the customer wants to purchase it right now.

1 — When a customer states an objection to purchasing a product, the salesperson ends the conversation, assuming that the prospect must not be interested.

examples of good or poor performance. **Figure 10.6** provides an example of a BARS for one performance dimension, namely sales skill. The proponents of BARS claim that it provides better, more equitable appraisals than do the other tools that have been discussed.[13]

Developing a BARS typically requires five steps:[14]

Tips FOR THE FRONT LINE

1. *Generate critical incidents.* Persons who know the job being appraised (jobholders and/or supervisors) are asked to describe specific illustrations (critical incidents) of effective and ineffective performance.

2. *Develop performance dimensions.* These people then cluster the incidents into a smaller set of performance dimensions (say, five or ten). Each cluster (dimension) is then defined.

3. *Reallocate incidents.* Another group of people who also know the job then reallocate the original critical incidents. They are given the clusters' definitions and the critical incidents and are asked to reassign each incident to the cluster that they think it best fits. Typically, a critical incident is retained if some percentage (usually 50 percent to 80 percent) of this second group assigns it to the same cluster as did the group in Step 2.

4. *Scale the incidents.* This second group is generally asked to rate the behaviour described in the incident as to how effectively or ineffectively it represents performance on the appropriate dimension (seven- or nine-point scales are typical).

5. *Develop the final instrument.* A subset of the incidents (usually six or seven per cluster) is used as behavioural anchors for each dimension.

Advantages and Disadvantages: Developing a BARS can be more time-consuming than developing other appraisal tools, such as graphic rating scales. But BARS may also have important advantages:[15]

1. *A more accurate measure.* People who know the job and its requirements better than anyone else does develop BARS. The result should therefore be a good measure of performance on that job.

2. *Clearer standards.* The critical incidents along the scale help to clarify what is meant by extremely good performance, average performance, and so forth.

3. *Feedback.* The critical incidents may be more useful in providing feedback to appraisees than simply informing them of their performance rating and not providing specific behavioural examples.

4. *Independent dimensions.* Systematically clustering the critical incidents into five or six performance dimensions (such as "knowledge and judgment") should help to make the dimensions more independent of one another. For example, a rater should be less likely to rate an employee high on all dimensions simply because he or she was rated high in "conscientiousness."

5. *Consistency.* BARS evaluations also seem to be relatively consistent and reliable in that different raters' appraisals of the same person tend to be similar.[16]

Management by Objectives (MBO)

management by objectives (MBO)
Involves setting specific measurable goals with each employee and then periodically reviewing the progress made.

Stripped to its essentials, **management by objectives (MBO)** requires the manager to set specific measurable goals with each employee and then periodically discuss his or her progress toward these goals. A manager can implement a modest MBO program by jointly setting goals with employees and periodically providing feedback. However, the term "MBO" almost always refers to a comprehensive, *organization-wide, goal setting and appraisal program* that consists of six main steps:

1. *Set the organization's goals.* Establish an organization-wide plan for next year and set goals.

2. *Set departmental goals.* Here department heads and their superiors jointly set goals for their departments.

3. *Discuss departmental goals.* Department heads discuss the department's goals with all employees in the department (often at a department-wide meeting) and ask them to develop their own individual goals; in other words, how can each employee contribute to the department's attainment of its goals?

4. *Define expected results* (set individual goals). Here, department heads and employees set short-term performance targets.

5. *Performance reviews: Measure the results.* Department heads compare the actual performance of each employee with the expected results.

6. *Provide feedback.* Department heads hold periodic performance review meetings with employees to discuss and evaluate progress in achieving expected results.

Problems to Avoid: Using MBO has three problems. *Setting unclear, unmeasurable objectives* is the main one. Such an objective as "will do a better job of training" is useless. Conversely, "will have four employees promoted during the year" is a measurable objective. Second, MBO is *time-consuming*. Taking the time to set objectives, to measure progress, and to provide feedback can take several hours per employee per year, over and above the time already spent doing each person's appraisal. Third, setting objectives with an employee sometimes turns into a *tug of war*, with the manager pushing for higher goals and the employee pushing for lower ones. It is thus important to know the job and the person's ability. To motivate performance, the objectives must be fair and attainable.

Computerized and Web-Based Performance Appraisal

RPC

Provides development information, support activities, and procedures for learners, supervisors, and managers to assist in achieving performance improvement

Over the past few years, web-based performance management has moved from being a leading-edge approach adopted by only large companies to a mainstream practice that is quickly becoming an industry standard among medium and small organizations.[17] It enables managers to keep computerized notes on employees, combine these with ratings on several performance traits, and then generate written text to support each part of the appraisal.

But the true value in automating performance management goes beyond simply automating time-consuming, tedious tasks such as tracking down paper-based appraisal forms. They ultimately improve the overall performance management process, starting with higher completion rates, which can dramatically increase the value of performance management within organizations of all sizes. Performance management systems provide employees with a clear development path and a better understanding of how their goals are aligned with those of the organization, which in turn increases their support of the process. Managers have the information they need to ensure development plans are relevant and executed. Executives have a clear picture of the organization's talent strategy and how it ties into the bottom line.

Most web-based performance management systems provide advanced reporting capabilities, which allow managers to track the status of performance management initiatives easily. Goal management functions enable organizations to link individual goals to strategic corporate goals, meaning that executives have insight into the progress being made on corporate objectives. Succession planning tools provide executives with a clear plan to build a talent pool to meet the organization's business needs and address potential attrition.

In a relatively short time, employee performance management has undergone a rapid evolution with the development of powerful, web-based tools. HR professionals are no longer mired in paperwork and other mundane administrative tasks. They have more time to focus on meeting strategic objectives, better tools to implement best practices programs, and access to critical workforce metrics they can share with their executive team.

electronic performance monitoring (EPM) Having supervisors electronically monitor the amount of computerized data an employee is processing per day and thereby his or her performance.

Electronic performance monitoring is in some respects the ultimate in computerized appraising. Electronic performance monitoring (EPM) means having supervisors electronically observe the employee's output or whereabouts. This typically involves using computer networks and wireless audio or video links to monitor and record employees' work activities. It includes, for instance, monitoring a data clerk's hourly keystrokes, tracking via GPS the whereabouts of delivery drivers, and monitoring the calls of customer service clerks.

Mixing the Methods

Most firms combine several appraisal techniques. The form shown in Figure 10.1 is basically a graphic rating scale with behavioural incidents included to define values for the traits being measured. The quantifiable ranking method permits comparisons of employees and is therefore useful for making salary, transfer, and promotion decisions. The critical incidents provide specific examples of performance relative to expectations.[18]

Performance Appraisal Problems and Solutions

This food service supervisor is conducting a feedback session about an employee's performance during today's major banquet to keep communications open and build employee commitment.

Few of the things a manager does are fraught with more peril than appraising employees' performance. Employees in general tend to be overly optimistic about what their ratings will be, and they also know that their raises, career progress, and peace of mind may well hinge on how they are rated. Thus, an honest appraisal inevitably involves an emotional component, which is particularly difficult when managers are not trained in appraisal interview skills. The result is often dishonest appraisals or avoidance of appraisals.[19]

Even more problematic, however, are the numerous structural problems that can cast serious doubt on just how fair the whole process is. Fortunately, research shows that action by management to implement a more acceptable performance appraisal system can increase employee trust in management.[20] According to several studies, the majority of organizations view their performance management systems as ineffective. More focus on the execution of performance appraisal is required instead of searching for new techniques and methods.[21] Some of the main appraisal problems and how to solve them, as well as several other pertinent appraisal issues, will now be reviewed.

Validity and Reliability

Performance Measurement
Resources
www.zigonperf.com/resources.htm

Appraisal systems must be based on performance criteria that are valid for the position being rated and must be reliable, in that their application must produce consistent ratings for the same performance. Employee concerns about appraisal fairness are influenced by these characteristics of the performance appraisal system.

Criteria used in performance appraisal must be accurate, or valid, in order to produce useful results. Criteria must be (1) relevant to the job being appraised, (2) broad enough to cover all aspects of the job requirements, and (3) specific. For example, including a broad criterion, such as "leadership," may not be relevant to nonmanagement jobs and may be so vague that it can be interpreted in many different ways.

Effective appraisal criteria are precise enough to result in consistent measures of performance when applied across many employees by many different raters. This is difficult to achieve without quantifiable and measurable criteria.

Rating Scale Problems

Seven main problems can undermine appraisal tools such as graphic rating scales: unclear standards, the halo effect, central tendency, leniency or strictness, appraisal bias, the recency effect, and the similar-to-me bias.

TABLE 10.2 | A Graphic Rating Scale with Unclear Standards

	Excellent	Good	Fair	Poor
Quality of work				
Quantity of work				
Creativity				
Integrity				

Note: For example, what exactly is meant by "good," "quantity of work," and so forth?

unclear performance standards An appraisal scale that is too open to interpretation of traits and standards.

The problem of **unclear performance standards** is illustrated in **Table 10.2**. Although the graphic rating scale seems objective, it would probably result in unfair appraisals because the traits and degrees of merit are open to interpretation. For example, different supervisors would probably differently define "good" performance, "fair" performance, and so on. The same is true of traits, such as "quality of work" or "creativity." There are several ways in which to rectify this problem. The best way is to develop and include descriptive phrases that define each trait, as in Figure 10.1. There, the form specified what was meant by "outstanding," "very good," and "good" quality of work. This specificity results in appraisals that are more consistent and more easily explained.

halo effect In performance appraisal, the problem that occurs when a supervisor's rating of an employee on one trait biases the rating of that person on other traits.

The **halo effect** means that the rating of an employee on one trait (such as "gets along with others") biases the way that the person is rated on other traits (such as "reliability"). This problem often occurs with employees who are especially friendly (or unfriendly) toward the supervisor. For example, an unfriendly employee will often be rated unsatisfactory for all traits rather than just for the trait "gets along well with others." Being aware of this problem is a major step toward avoiding it. Supervisory training can also alleviate the problem.[22]

central tendency A tendency to rate all employees in the middle of the scale.

Many supervisors have a **central tendency** when filling in rating scales. For example, if the rating scale ranges from one to seven, they tend to avoid the highs (six and seven) and lows (one and two) and rate most of their employees between three and five. If a graphic rating scale is used, this central tendency could mean that all employees are simply rated "average." Such a restriction can distort the evaluations, making them less useful for promotion, salary, or counselling purposes. Ranking employees instead of using a graphic rating scale can avoid this central tendency problem, because all employees must be ranked and thus cannot all be rated average.

strictness/leniency The problem that occurs when a supervisor has a tendency to rate all employees either low or high.

Some supervisors tend to rate all of their employees consistently high (or low), just as some instructors are notoriously high graders, and others are not. Fear of interpersonal conflict is often the reason for leniency.[23] Conversely, evaluators tend to give more weight to negative attributes than to positive ones.[24] This **strictness/leniency** problem is especially serious with graphic rating scales, since supervisors are not necessarily required to avoid giving all of their employees low (or high) ratings. However, when ranking employees, a manager is forced to distinguish between high and low performers. Thus, strictness/leniency is not a problem with the ranking or forced distribution approaches.

Individual differences among ratees in terms of a wide variety of characteristics, such as age, race, and sex, can affect their ratings, often quite apart from each ratee's actual performance.[25] In fact, recent research shows that less than half of performance evaluation ratings are actually related to employee performance and

appraisal bias The tendency to allow individual differences, such as age, race, and sex, to affect the appraisal ratings that these employees receive.

Canadian Human Rights Commission
www.chrc-ccdp.ca

recency effect The rating error that occurs when ratings are based on the employee's most recent performance rather than on performance throughout the appraisal period.

similar-to-me bias The tendency to give higher performance ratings to employees who are perceived to be similar to the rater in some way.

that most of the rating is based on idiosyncratic factors.[26] This is known as **appraisal bias.** Not only does this bias result in inaccurate feedback, but it is also illegal under human rights legislation. Although age-related bias is typically thought of as affecting older workers, one study found a negative relationship between age and performance evaluation for entry-level jobs in public accounting firms.[27] A related issue is described in the Workforce Diversity box.

Interestingly, the friendliness and likeability of an employee have been found to have little effect on that person's performance ratings.[28] However, an employee's previous performance can affect the evaluation of his or her current performance.[29] The actual error can take several forms. Sometimes the rater may systematically overestimate improvement by a poor worker or decline by a good worker, for instance. In some situations—especially when the change in behaviour is more gradual—the rater may simply be insensitive to improvement or decline. In any case, it is important to rate performance objectively. Such factors as previous performance, age, or race should not be allowed to influence results.

The **recency effect** occurs when ratings are based on the employee's most recent performance, whether good or bad. To the extent that this recent performance does not exemplify the employee's average performance over the appraisal period, the appraisal is biased.

If a supervisor tends to give higher ratings to employees with whom he or she has something in common, the **similar-to-me bias** is occurring. This bias can be discriminatory if it is based on similarity in race, gender, or other prohibited grounds.

Workforce DIVERSITY

Watch for Cultural Biases in Assessing Employees

Canadian organizations are increasingly turning to immigrants as the supply of workers dries up in Canada. This demographic shift poses some unique challenges for organizations in integrating these new Canadians into the workplace, particularly when it comes to performance management.

Values, beliefs, and perspectives vary by culture. Typical group and individual behaviours in Canada may not be the norm for people from other cultures. The performance appraisal, with its goal-setting procedures and inherent feedback process, is a Western concept that can be a cultural disconnect for employees with different cultural roots. In Eastern cultures, appraisals are as likely to deal with attributes such as cooperation and sociability as they are with achievement of results. And because status is so important in Eastern cultures (it is crucial to an individual's sense of worth and contribution), it is important to ensure that the employee does not become insulted or lose face.

In some cultures, managers provide explicit directions and employees are more deferential to their superiors. Technical expertise is the proven path to promotion rather than taking initiative and seeking new responsibilities. Also, performance is more often assessed on a group basis, with recognition and rewards being assigned for strong group performance. The individual is expected to work for the good of the group. Typical performance criteria used in Canada are more individual-focused and may not value group-oriented performance.

Cultural diversity in the workplace provides an opportunity to maximize sales and profits while creating a work atmosphere appropriate for all cultures. Managers and executives in an economy becoming more dependent on the successful integration of highly skilled internationally trained professionals owe it to their organizations—and their futures as business leaders—to successfully manage the entire diverse workforce.

Source: Adapted from R. Singer, "Watch for Cultural Biases in Assessing Employees," *Canadian HR Reporter*, June 19, 2006.

TABLE 10.3 | Important Advantages and Disadvantages of Appraisal Tools

	Advantages	Disadvantages
Graphic rating scale	Simple to use; provides a quantitative rating for each employee.	Standards may be unclear; halo effect, central tendency, leniency, and bias can also be problems.
Alternation ranking	Simple to use (but not as simple as graphic rating scale). Avoids central tendency and other problems of rating scales.	Can cause disagreements among employees and may be unfair if all employees are, in fact, excellent.
Forced distribution method	End up with a predetermined number of people in each group.	Appraisal results depend on the adequacy of the original choice of cutoff points.
Critical incident method	Helps specify what is "right" and "wrong" about the employee's performance; forces supervisor to evaluate employees on an ongoing basis.	Difficult to rate or rank employees relative to one another.
Behaviourally anchored rating scale	Provides behavioural "anchors." BARS is very accurate.	Difficult to develop.
Management by objectives	Tied to jointly agreed-upon performance objectives.	Time consuming.

How to Avoid Appraisal Problems

There are at least three ways in which to minimize the impact of appraisal problems, such as bias and central tendency. First, raters must be familiar with the problems just discussed. Understanding the problem can help to prevent it.

Second, raters must choose the right appraisal tool. Each tool, such as the graphic rating scale or critical incident method, has its own advantages and disadvantages. For example, the ranking method avoids central tendency but can cause ill feelings when employees' performances are in fact all "high" (see **Table 10.3**).

Third, training supervisors to eliminate rating errors, such as halo, leniency, and central tendency, can help them to avoid these problems.[30] In a typical training program, raters are shown a videotape of jobs being performed and are asked to rate the worker. Ratings made by each participant are then placed on a flip chart and the various errors (such as leniency and halo) are explained. For example, if a trainee rated all criteria (such as quality, quantity, and so on) about the same, the trainer might explain that a halo error had occurred. Typically, the trainer gives the correct rating and then illustrates the rating errors made by the participants.[31] According to one study, computer-assisted appraisal training improved managers' ability to conduct performance appraisal discussions with their employees.[32]

Rater training will not eliminate all rating errors or ensure absolute accuracy. In practice, several factors—including the extent to which pay is tied to performance ratings, union pressure, employee turnover, time constraints, and the need to justify ratings—may be more important than training. This means that improving appraisal accuracy calls not only for training but also for reducing outside factors, such as union pressure and time constraints.[33] It has also been found that employee reaction to current performance reviews is affected by past appraisal feedback, which is beyond the control of the current manager.[34]

Legal and Ethical Issues in Performance Appraisal

Ethics should be the bedrock of a performance appraisal. Accurate, well-documented performance records and performance appraisal feedback are necessary to avoid legal penalties and to defend against charges of bias based on grounds prohibited under human rights legislation, such as age, sex, and so on. As one commentator puts it,

> The overall objective of high-ethics performance reviews should be to provide an honest assessment of performance and to mutually develop a plan to improve the individual's effectiveness. That requires that we tell people where they stand and that we be straight with them.[35]

Ashland Canada Ltd., an automotive products marketing company in British Columbia, was fined $20 000 for dismissing a sales employee based on an "unacceptable" performance rating even though the employee had exceeded his sales goals. The British Columbia Supreme Court found that the performance rating was unwarranted and undeserved and criticized Ashland's human resources department for a "reprehensible and substantial departure" from good faith dealings with the employee.[36] In another case, a worker in a government mental health facility was terminated for unsatisfactory performance after ten years of work with no performance evaluations and no disciplinary record. An adjudicator determined that the employer had failed to establish that the worker's job performance was unsatisfactory, that she had not been given a chance to improve, and that the employer did not have just cause for termination. The employer was required to pay compensation in lieu of reinstatement.[37]

Hints | **TO ENSURE LEGAL COMPLIANCE**

Guidelines for developing an effective appraisal process include the following:[38]

1. Conduct a job analysis to ascertain characteristics (such as "timely project completion") required for successful job performance. Use this information to create job performance standards.

2. Incorporate these characteristics into a rating instrument. (The professional literature recommends rating instruments that are tied to specific job behaviours, that is, BARS.)

3. Make sure that definitive performance standards are provided to all raters and ratees.

4. Use clearly defined individual dimensions of job performance (like "quantity" or "quality") rather than undefined, global measures of job performance (like "overall performance").

5. When using a graphic rating scale, avoid abstract trait names (such as "loyalty," "honesty") unless they can be defined in terms of observable behaviours.

6. Employ subjective supervisory ratings (essays, for instance) as only one component of the overall appraisal process.

7. Train supervisors to use the rating instrument properly. Give instructions on how to apply performance appraisal standards ("outstanding," "satisfactory," and so on) when making judgments. Ensure that subjective standards are not subject to bias.

The best performance appraisal systems are those in which the supervisor or manager makes an ongoing effort to coach and monitor employees instead of leaving evaluation to the last minute.

8. Allow appraisers regular contact with the employee being evaluated.

9. Whenever possible, have more than one appraiser conduct the appraisal, and conduct all such appraisals independently. This process can help to cancel out individual errors and biases.

10. Utilize formal appeal mechanisms and a review of ratings by upper-level managers.

11. Document evaluations and reasons for any termination decision.

12. Where appropriate, provide corrective guidance to assist poor performers in improving their performance.

Who Should Do the Appraising?

Who should actually rate an employee's performance? Several options exist.

Supervisors

Supervisors' ratings are still the heart of most appraisal systems. Getting a supervisor's appraisal is relatively easy and also makes a great deal of sense. The supervisor should be—and usually is—in the best position to observe and evaluate the performance of employees reporting to him or her and is responsible for their performance.

Peers

The appraisal of an employee by his or her peers can be effective in predicting future management success. There is a high correlation between peer and supervisor ratings.[39] Peers have more opportunity to observe ratees and to observe them at more revealing times than supervisors do.[40] From a study of military officers, for example, we know that peer ratings were quite accurate in predicting which officers would be promoted and which would not.[41] In another study that involved more than 200 industrial managers, peer ratings were similarly useful in predicting who would be promoted.[42] One potential problem is *logrolling*; here, all the peers simply get together to rate each other highly.

With more firms using self-managing teams, peer or team appraisals are becoming more popular. One study found that peer ratings had an immediate positive impact on perceptions of open communication, motivation, group cohesion, and satisfaction, and these were not dependent on the ratio of positive to negative feedback.[43] Thus, peer appraisals would appear to have great potential for work teams.

Committees

Many employers use rating committees to evaluate employees. These committees usually comprise the employee's immediate supervisor and three or four other supervisors. Using multiple raters can be advantageous. Although there may be a discrepancy in the ratings made by individual supervisors, the composite ratings tend to be more reliable, fair, and valid.[44] Using several raters can help cancel out problems like bias and the halo effect on the part of individual raters. Furthermore, when there are variations in raters' ratings, they usually stem from the fact that raters often observe different facets of an employee's performance; the appraisal ought to reflect these differences.[45] Even when a committee is not used, it is common to have the appraisal reviewed by the manager immediately above the one who makes the appraisal.

Self

Employees' self-ratings of performance are sometimes used, generally in conjunction with supervisors' ratings. Employees value the opportunity to participate in performance appraisal more for the opportunity to be heard than for the opportunity to influence the end result.[46] Nevertheless, the basic problem with self-ratings is that employees usually rate themselves higher than they are rated by supervisors or peers.[47] In one study, for example, it was found that when asked to rate their own job performance, 40 percent of the employees in jobs of all types placed themselves in the top 10 percent ("one of the best"), while virtually all remaining employees rated themselves either in the top 25 percent ("well above average") or at least in the top 50 percent ("above average"). Usually no more than 1 percent or 2 percent will place themselves in a below-average category and then almost invariably in the top below-average category. However, self-ratings have been found to correlate more highly with performance measures if employees know that this comparison will be made and if they are instructed to compare themselves with others.[48]

Supervisors requesting self-appraisals should know that their appraisals and their employees' self-appraisals may accentuate appraiser–appraisee differences, and rigidify positions.[49] Furthermore, even if self-appraisals are not formally requested, each employee will enter the performance review meeting with his or her own self-appraisal in mind, and this will usually be higher than the supervisor's rating.

Subordinates

Traditionally, supervisors feared that being appraised by their employees would undermine their management authority. However, with today's flatter organizations and empowered workers, much managerial authority is a thing of the past, and employees are in a good position to observe managerial performance.[50] Thus, more firms today are letting employees anonymously evaluate their supervisors' performance, a process many call *upward feedback*.[51] When conducted throughout the firm, the process helps top managers to diagnose management styles, identify potential "people" problems, and take corrective action with individual managers as required. Such employee ratings are especially valuable when used for developmental rather than evaluative purposes.[52] Managers who receive feedback from employees who identify themselves view the upward appraisal process more positively than do managers who receive anonymous feedback; however, employees (not surprisingly) are more comfortable giving anonymous responses, and those who have to identify themselves tend to provide inflated ratings.[53] Research comparing employee and peer ratings of managers found them to be comparable.[54]

Research | INSIGHT

Upward feedback from reporting employees is quite effective in terms of improving the supervisor's behaviour, according to the research evidence. One study examined data for 92 managers who were rated by one or more reporting employees in each of four administrations of an upward feedback survey over two and a half years. The reporting employees were asked to rate themselves and their managers in surveys that consisted of 33 behavioural statements. The feedback to the managers also contained results from previous administrations of the survey so that they could track their performance over time.

According to the researchers, "managers whose initial level of performance (defined as the average rating from reporting employees) was low improved between administrations one and two, and sustained this improvement two years later." Interestingly, the results also suggest that it is not necessarily the specific feedback that caused the performance improvement, because low-performing managers seemed to improve over time even if they did not receive any feedback. Instead, learning what the critical supervisory behaviours were (as a result of themselves filling out the appraisal surveys) and knowing that they might be appraised may have been enough to result in the improved supervisory behaviours. In a sense, therefore, it is the existence of the formal upward feedback program rather than the actual feedback itself that may signal and motivate supervisors to get their behaviours in line with what they should be.[55]

360-Degree Appraisal

360-degree appraisal A performance appraisal technique that uses multiple raters including peers, employees reporting to the appraisee, supervisors, and customers.

Many Canadian firms are now using what is called **360-degree appraisal,** or "multisource feedback." Here, as shown in **Figure 10.7**, performance information is collected "all around" an employee, from his or her supervisors, subordinates, peers, and internal or external customers.[56] This feedback was originally used only for training and development purposes, but it has rapidly spread to the management of performance and pay.[57] The 360-degree approach supports the activities of performance feedback, coaching, leadership development, succession planning, and rewards and recognition.[58]

There are a number of reasons for the rapid growth of the 360-degree appraisal, despite the significant investment of time required for it to function successfully. Today's flatter organizations employ a more open communicative climate conducive to such an approach, and 360-degree appraisal fits closely with the goals of organizations committed to continuous learning, as highlighted in the Strategic HR box. A multiple-rater system is also more meaningful in today's reality of complex jobs, with matrix and team reporting relationships. A 360-degree appraisal can be perceived as a jury of peers, rather than the supervisor as a single judge, which enhances perceptions of fairness.[59]

Most 360-degree appraisal systems contain several common features (including Internet-based 360-degree feedback systems, as described in Chapter 3). They are usually applied in a confidential and anonymous manner. Appropriate parties—peers, superiors, employees, and customers, for instance—complete survey questionnaires about an individual. The questionnaires must be custom-designed and linked to the organization's strategic direction, vision, and values.[60] All this information is then compiled into individualized reports. When the information is being used for self-development purposes only, the report is presented to the person being rated, who then meets with his or her own supervisor, and information pertinent for the purpose of developing a self-improvement plan is shared. When the information is being used for management of performance or pay, the information is also provided to the ratee's supervisor, and a supportive and facilitative process to follow up is required to ensure that the behavioural change required for performance improvement is made.[61]

There is a limited amount of research data on the effectiveness of 360-degree feedback. Some organizations have abandoned it for appraisal purposes because

Research | INSIGHT

FIGURE 10.7 | 360-Degree Performance Appraisals

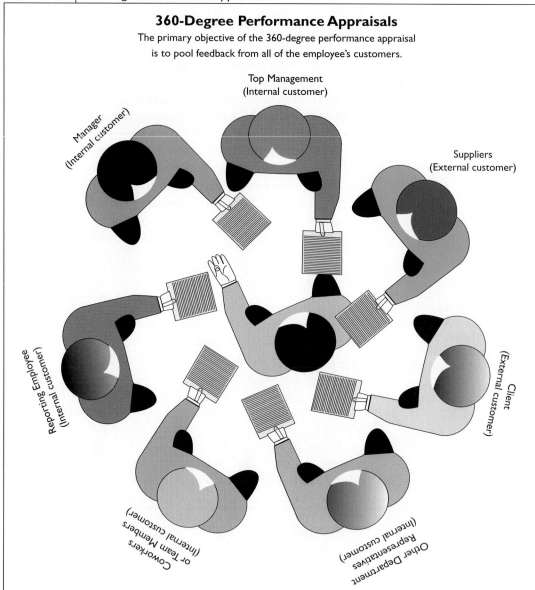

360-Degree Performance Appraisals

The primary objective of the 360-degree performance appraisal
is to pool feedback from all of the employee's customers.

Top Management
(Internal customer)

Manager
(Internal customer)

Suppliers
(External customer)

Reporting Employee
(Internal customer)

Client
(External customer)

Coworkers
or Team Members
(Internal customer)

Other Department
Representatives
(Internal customer)

Source: J.F. Milliman, R.A. Zawacki, C. Norman, L. Powell, and J. Kerksey, "Companies Evaluate Employee from All
Perspectives," *Personnel Journal*, November 1994, Vol. 73, No. 11, p. 100. Illustration by Tim Barker, copyright
November 1994. Used with permission. All rights reserved.

of negative attitudes from employees and inflated ratings.[62] Some studies have
found that the different raters often disagree on performance ratings.[63] A recent
study by researchers at Concordia University in Montreal
found that 360-degree feedback is popular among Canadian employers, despite such problems as the amount of
time and effort involved, lack of trust in the system by
employees, and lack of fit with strategic goals and other
HR practices. The results showed that organizations that
successfully implemented 360-degree feedback were those that had the most
clarity on what their initial objectives were. Organizations that rely exclusively

An Ethical | Dilemma

Is it fair to factor in employee self-ratings in 360-degree performance appraisal, when we know that these appraisals tend
to be inflated?

Strategic HR

360-Degree Feedback at PACCAR of Canada Ltd.

The PACCAR of Canada Ltd. plant, located in Sainte-Thérèse, Quebec, is a truck assembly plant with 800 unionized production workers. The company's corporate values include mutual respect, communication, teamwork, and continuous improvement.

A few years ago, PACCAR decided to adopt a 360-degree feedback process for plant managers and co-ordinators, to be used strictly for development or skills improvement at the managerial level. The union was not comfortable with using this feedback for evaluative purposes.

Initially designed as an in-house feedback process, PACCAR later decided to hire industrial psychologists to manage the 360-degree feedback system. These consultants designed questions aligned with PACCAR's values and established numerous precautions to protect the confidentiality of the evaluations. A psychologist now conducts development sessions with small groups of managers to explain their 360-degree feedback reports.

PACCAR developed an action plan for each manager to be assessed. The plan was submitted to his or her immediate superior in advance of a developmental meeting where opportunities for skills development were proposed. The superior then monitored the achievement of the action plan objectives and offered regular feedback during the year.

The 360-degree feedback process at PACCAR has been very successful. Managers were open to participating from the start because results were being used for development purposes only, not evaluative purposes. Now other employees have been asking to be included. The process has facilitated the communication of corporate values to managers on a regular basis and has helped to align managers' behaviour and skills with these values. It has also facilitated opportunities for career management and development.

The HR department received a list of overall strengths and weaknesses attributed to the managers involved. Recently the feedback revealed that managers offered too little positive recognition to employees, and information sessions were held to assist managers in this regard.

The keys to successful 360-degree feedback to align managerial behaviour with corporate values at PACCAR have been confidentiality and anonymity; training of both assessors and the managers being evaluated; and customization of the program for PACCAR. In fact, PACCAR executives would like to implement a simplified version of 360-degree feedback with all plant employees.

Source: B. Bannille and S. St-Onge, "360-Degree Feedback at PACCAR of Canada Ltd.," *Workplace Gazette*, Summer 2004, Vol. 7, No. 2, pp. 63–68.

on external consultants to establish 360-degree appraisal have less success than organizations that are more sensitive to contextual factors, such as the readiness of employees and the culture of the organization.[64]

Some experts suggest that 360-degree feedback be used for developmental purposes only.[65] In general, it is advisable to use 360-degree feedback for developmental/career-planning purposes initially and then to determine whether the organization is ready to use it for evaluative appraisal purposes. A pilot test in one department is often recommended. Once a decision to use 360-degree appraisal has been made, organizations should consider the following advice:[66]

Tips | FOR THE FRONT LINE

- Have the performance criteria developed by a representative group that is familiar with each job.
- Be clear about who will have access to reports.
- Provide training for all supervisors, raters, and ratees.
- Assure all raters that their comments will be kept anonymous.
- Plan to evaluate the 360-degree feedback system for fine-tuning.

Appraisal Interviews

The essence of a performance appraisal is the feedback provided in a one-on-one conversation called the **appraisal interview.** This is an interview in which the supervisor and employee review the appraisal and make plans to remedy deficiencies and reinforce strengths. Unfortunately, surveys show that less than half of companies describe their performance appraisal systems as effective or very effective because of weak execution due to managers abdicating their responsibility for screening out poor performers.[67] This discussion is often avoided by supervisors and managers who have not been trained to provide constructive feedback and to deal with defensive employees. Ultimately, feedback should be ongoing, making the formal appraisal interview one of many performance discussions.

appraisal interview An interview in which the supervisor and employee review the appraisal and make plans to remedy deficiencies and reinforce strengths.

Types of Interviews

There are three basic types of appraisal interviews, each with its own objectives:[68]

Appraisal Interview Type	Appraisal Interview Objective
(1) Satisfactory performance— Promotable employee	(1) Make development plans
(2) Satisfactory performance— Nonpromotable employee	(2) Maintain performance
(3) Unsatisfactory performance— Correctable	(3) Plan correction

If the employee's performance is unsatisfactory and the situation uncorrectable, there is usually no need for any appraisal interview because the person's performance is not correctable anyway. Either the person's poor performance is tolerated for now, or he or she is dismissed.

Satisfactory—Promotable

Here, the person's performance is satisfactory and there is a promotion ahead. This is the easiest of the three appraisal interviews. The objective is to discuss the person's career plans and to develop a specific action plan for the educational and professional development that the person needs in order to move to the next job.

Satisfactory—Not Promotable

This interview is for employees whose performance is satisfactory but for whom promotion is not possible. Perhaps there is no more room in the company. Some employees are happy where they are and do not want a promotion.[69] The objective here is not to improve or develop the person but to maintain satisfactory performance.

This situation is not easy. The best option is usually to find incentives that are important to the person and enough to maintain satisfactory performance. These might include extra time off, a small bonus, additional authority to handle a slightly enlarged job, and verbal reinforcement in the form of "Well done!"

Unsatisfactory—Correctable

When the person's performance is unsatisfactory but correctable, the interview objective is to lay out an *action plan* (as explained later) for correcting the unsatisfactory performance.

Preparing for the Appraisal Interview

RPC

Assists and coaches supervisors to help employees achieve required performance levels

There are three things to do in preparation for the interview.[70] First, assemble the data. Study the person's job description, compare the employee's performance to the standards, and review the files of the employee's previous appraisals. Next, prepare the employee. Give the employee at least a week's notice to review his or her own work, read over his or her job description, analyze problems he or she may be dealing with, and gather questions and comments for the interview. Finally, find a mutually agreeable time and place and allow plenty of time for the interview. Interviews with nonsupervisory staff should take no more than an hour. Appraising management employees often takes two or three hours. Be sure that the interview is conducted in a private place where there will be no interruptions. **Figure 10.8** provides a discussion checklist for appraisers.

FIGURE 10.8 | Checklist During the Appraisal Interview

CHECKLIST DURING THE APPRAISAL INTERVIEW

Yes No

- Did you discuss each goal or objective established for this employee?
- Are you and the employee clear on the areas of agreement? disagreement?
- Did you and the employee cover all positive skills, traits, accomplishments, areas of growth, etc.? Did you reinforce the employee's accomplishments?
- Did you give the employee a sense of what you thought of his or her potential or ability?
- Are you both clear on areas where improvement is required? expected? demanded? desired?
- What training or development recommendations did you agree on?
- Did you indicate consequences for noncompliance, if appropriate?
- Did you set good objectives for the next appraisal period?
  - Objective?
  - Specific?
  - Measurable?
- Did you set a standard to be used for evaluation?
  - Time frame?
- Did you set a time for the next evaluation?
- Did you confirm what your part would be? Did the employee confirm his or her part?
- Did you thank the employee for his or her efforts?

Source: Reprinted from www.HR.BLR.com with permission of the publisher *Business and Legal Reports, Inc.*, 141 Mill Rock Road East, Old Saybrook, CT © 2004

How to Conduct the Interview

There are four things to keep in mind when conducting an appraisal interview:[71]

1. *Be direct and specific.* Talk in terms of objective work data. Use examples, such as absences, tardiness, quality records, inspection reports, scrap or waste, orders processed, productivity records, material used or consumed, timeliness of tasks or projects, control or reduction of costs, numbers of errors, costs compared with budgets, customers' comments, product returns, order processing time, inventory level and accuracy, accident reports, and so on.

2. *Do not get personal.* Do not say, "You are too slow in producing those reports." Instead, try to compare the person's performance with a standard ("These reports should normally be done within ten days"). Similarly, do not compare the person's performance with that of other people ("He is quicker than you are").

3. *Encourage the person to talk.* Stop and listen to what the person is saying; ask open-ended questions, such as, "What do you think we can do to improve the situation?" Use a phrase such as, "Go on," or "Tell me more." Restate the person's last point as a question, such as, "You do not think that you can get the job done?"

4. *Develop an action plan.* Do not get personal but do make sure that by the end of the interview you have (a) provided specific examples of performance that does and does not need attention or improvement, (b) made sure the person understands how he or she should improve his or her performance, (c) obtained an agreement from the person that he or she understands the reasons for the appraisal, and (d) developed an action plan that shows steps to achieving specified goals and the results expected. Be sure that a timeline is included in the plan. **Figure 10.9** provides a good example of an action plan.

FIGURE 10.9 | Example of an Action Plan

ACTION PLAN

Date: May 18, 2007

For: John, Assistant Plant Manager
Problem: Parts inventory too high
Objective: Reduce plant parts inventory by 10% in June

Action Steps	When	Expected Results
Determine average monthly parts inventory	6/2	Establish a base from which to measure progress
Review ordering quantities and parts usage	6/15	Identify overstock items
Ship excess parts to regional warehouse and scrap obsolete parts	6/20	Clear stock space
Set new ordering quantities for all parts	6/25	Avoid future overstocking
Check records to measure where we are now	7/1	See how close we are to objective

How to Handle Criticism and Defensive Employees

When criticism is required, it should be done in a manner that lets the person maintain his or her dignity and sense of worth. Specifically, criticism should be provided constructively, in private, and immediately following poor performance. Provide examples of critical incidents and specific suggestions of what could be done and why. Finally, ensure that criticism is objective and free of any personal biases.

When poor performance by an employee is described, the first reaction will often be denial. By denying the fault, the person avoids having to question his or her own competence. Others react to criticism with anger and aggression. This helps them to let off steam and postpones confronting the immediate problem until they are able to cope with it. Still others react to criticism by retreating into a shell.

Understanding and dealing with defensiveness is an important appraisal skill that requires the following:[72]

1. Recognize that defensive behaviour is normal.

2. Never attack a person's defences. Do not try to "explain someone" to himself or herself by saying things like, "You know the real reason you are using that excuse is that you cannot bear to be blamed for anything." Instead, try to concentrate on the act itself ("sales are down") rather than on the person ("you are not selling enough").

3. Postpone action. Sometimes it is best to do nothing at all. People frequently react to sudden threats by instinctively hiding behind their "masks." Given sufficient time, however, a more rational reaction usually takes over.

4. Recognize human limitations. Do not expect to be able to solve every problem that comes up, especially the human ones. More important, remember that a supervisor should not try to be a psychologist. Offering employees understanding is one thing; trying to deal with deep psychological problems is another matter entirely.

Ensuring That the Appraisal Interview Leads to Improved Performance

It is important to clear up performance problems by setting goals and a schedule for achieving them. However, even if you have obtained agreement from your employees about the areas for performance improvement, they may or may not be satisfied with their appraisal. In one study, researchers found that whether or not employees expressed satisfaction with their appraisal interview depended mostly on three factors: (1) not feeling threatened during the interview, (2) having an opportunity to present their ideas and feelings and to influence the course of the interview, and (3) having a helpful and constructive supervisor conduct the interview.[73]

In the end, it is not enough for employees to be satisfied with their appraisal interviews. The main objective is to get them to improve their subsequent performance. Legal experts suggest following these seven steps:

1. Let the employee know that his or her performance is unacceptable and explain your minimum expectations.

2. Ensure that your expectations are reasonable.

3. Let employees know that warnings play a significant role in the process of establishing just cause; employees must be warned and told that discharge will result if they continue to fail to meet minimum standards.

4. Ensure that you take prompt corrective measures when required; failure to do so could lead to a finding that you condoned your employee's conduct.

5. Avoid sending mixed messages, such as a warning letter together with a "satisfactory" performance review.

6. Provide the employee with a reasonable amount of time to improve performance.

7. Be prepared to provide your employees with the necessary support to facilitate improvement.[74]

How to Handle a Formal Written Warning

There will be times when an employee's performance is so poor that a formal written warning is required. Such written warnings serve two purposes: (1) They may serve to shake the employee out of his or her bad habits, and (2) they can help the manager to defend his or her rating of the employee, both to his or her boss and (if needed) to a court or human rights commission.

Written warnings should identify the standards under which the employee is judged, make it clear that the employee was aware of the standard, specify any violation of the standard, indicate that the employee has had an opportunity to correct his or her behaviour, and specify what the employee must now do to correct his or her behaviour.

Hints | **TO ENSURE LEGAL COMPLIANCE**

STEP 4: DETERMINE PERFORMANCE REWARDS/CONSEQUENCES

Some time after the performance review has taken place, the manager should utilize the salary planning guidelines to determine the appropriate rewards and/or consequence that compares actual performance against the defined levels. Performance rewards are given through merit pay or extra payment such as cash bonus. The two most important aspects used to determine the appropriate reward/consequence are achievement of goals and how the employee meets the defined standards. Further detail on compensation and rewards are provided in Chapters 11 and 12.

STEP 5: CAREER DEVELOPMENT DISCUSSION

During this discussion, the manager and employee discuss opportunities for development to strengthen or improve the employee's knowledge, skills, and abilities. Business needs must be balanced with the employee's preferences. These opportunities may focus on actions to boost performance in the area of current goals or to develop new knowledge aimed at a future career plan. Further detail on career planning and development is provided in Chapter 9.

THE FUTURE OF PERFORMANCE MANAGEMENT

Effective appraisals are the basis for successful performance management. Although performance appraisal is a difficult interpersonal task for managers, it cannot be eliminated.

Managers still need some way to review employees' work-related behaviour, and no one has offered any concrete alternative. Despite the difficulties involved, performance management is still the basis for fostering and managing employee skills and talents, and it can be a key component of improved organizational effectiveness. Performance management techniques in high- and low-performing organizations are essentially the same, but managers in high-performing organizations tend to conduct and implement appraisals and manage performance on a daily basis more effectively.[75]

Recent research indicates that effective performance management involves

- linking individual goals and business strategy
- showing leadership and accountability at all levels of the organization
- ensuring close ties among appraisal results, rewards, and recognition outcomes
- investing in employee development planning
- having an administratively efficient system with sufficient communication support.[76]

The key success factor for effective performance appraisal that will lead to optimum employee performance is the quality of the performance appraisal dialogue between a manager and an employee.[77] Managers need to engage in training on an ongoing basis in order to ensure that they are in a position to engage in high-quality appraisal interviews.

Overall, the solution is to create more effective appraisals, as described in this chapter. Effective appraisals are essential to managing the performance required of an organization's employees in order to achieve that organization's strategic objectives.

Chapter | SUMMARY

1. The five steps in the performance management process are (1) *defining performance expectations and goals* to make sure that job duties and job standards are clear to all; (2) *providing ongoing feedback and coaching* through open two-way communication; (3) *conducting performance appraisal and evaluation discussions* at specific intervals by comparing an employee's actual performance to the standards that have been set (usually involving some type of rating form); the employee's performance and progress are discussed to reinforce the things that the employee is doing well, and to develop a plan for correction of any deficiencies that the appraisal might have identified; (4) *determining performance rewards/ consequences* such as promotions, salary increases, and bonuses; and (5) *conducting development and career opportunities discussions* (usually annually) in order to review each employee's career plans in light of his or her exhibited strengths and weaknesses and in light of the company's strategic plans.

2. There are a number of performance appraisal methods. Graphic rating scales are simple to use and facilitate comparison of employees, but the performance standards are often unclear, and

bias can be a problem. Alternation ranking is a simple method that avoids central tendency, but it can be unfair if most employees are doing well. Paired comparison ensures that all employees are compared with each other, but it can also be unfair if most employees are performing similarly. Narrative forms provide concrete information to the employee but are time-consuming and can be subjective. The forced distribution method ensures differentiation of performance ratings but can be demotivating for employees classified as less than average. The critical incident method is very specific about the employee's strengths and weaknesses and forces the supervisor to evaluate employees on an ongoing basis, but it makes it difficult to compare employees. BARS is very accurate but is difficult and time-consuming to develop. MBO ties performance ratings to jointly agreed-on performance objectives, but it is time-consuming to administer.

3. Appraisal problems to be aware of include unclear standards, the halo effect, central tendency, leniency or strictness, appraisal bias, the recency effect, and the similar-to-me bias.

4. The use of 360-degree feedback has grown rapidly. Performance information is collected from the individual being appraised, his or her supervisor, other employees reporting to the person being appraised, and customers. This approach supports the activities of performance appraisal, coaching, leadership development, succession planning, and employee rewards and recognition.

5. There are three types of appraisal interview. When performance is unsatisfactory but correctable, the objective of the interview is to set out an action plan for correcting performance. For employees whose performance is satisfactory but for whom promotion is not possible, the objective of the interview is to maintain satisfactory performance. Finally, the satisfactory-and-promotable interview has the main objective of discussing the person's career plans and developing a specific action plan for the educational and professional development that the person needs in order to move on to the next job.

6. Although appraisals can be a difficult interpersonal task for managers, they cannot be eliminated. There is no alternative method for assessing employee performance, which is essential for talent management and improved organizational effectiveness. The key success factor is the quality of the performance appraisal dialogue between managers and employees. More training on how to effectively conduct these discussions is required.

PEARSON
myHRlab™
Test yourself on material for this chapter at
www.pearsoned.ca/myhrlab

Key | TERMS

alternation ranking method   (p. 271)
appraisal bias   (p. 280)
appraisal interview   (p. 288)
behaviourally anchored rating scale
    (BARS)   (p. 273)
central tendency   (p. 279)
critical incident method   (p. 272)
electronic performance monitoring
    (EPM)   (p. 277)
forced distribution method   (p. 272)

graphic rating scale   (p. 268)
halo effect   (p. 279)
management by objectives (MBO)   (p. 276)
paired comparison method   (p. 271)
performance management   (p. 265)
recency effect   (p. 280)
similar-to-me bias   (p. 280)
strictness/leniency   (p. 279)
360-degree appraisal   (p. 285)
unclear performance standards   (p. 279)

Review and Discussion | QUESTIONS

1. Describe the five steps in the performance appraisal process.

2. Explain how to ensure that the performance appraisal process is carried out ethically and without violating human rights laws.

3. Discuss the pros and cons of using different potential raters to appraise a person's performance.

4. What are the four key actions in conducting an appraisal interview?

5. Explain how to handle a defensive employee in a performance appraisal interview.

Critical Thinking | QUESTIONS

1. Given the numerous problems with performance appraisal and the negative consequences that often ensue, should performance appraisal be abolished? Why or why not?

2. How can the problem of inconsistency between managers who are rating workers be solved or at least diminished? Make two or more suggestions.

3. Given the difficulty with providing traditional performance standards for jobs that are quite flexible, what sort of "standards" could be developed for these flexible jobs?

4. BARS is not commonly used because it is so time-consuming to develop.

How could the development steps be streamlined?

5. Do you agree with the use of forced distribution methods to rate employees? Why or why not?

6. How might a supervisor handle a situation in which negative appraisals in the past have caused an employee to undervalue his or her performance?

7. Discuss how employees might respond to the proposed implementation of electronic performance management systems, such as call monitoring, etc. How might an organization deal with employees' reactions?

Experiential | EXERCISES

1. Working individually or in groups, develop a graphic rating scale for a retail sales associate and a fast-food restaurant manager.

2. Working individually or in groups, develop, over a week, a set of critical incidents covering the classroom performance of one of your instructors.

3. Working in groups, using the NOC job description for professors and the example of a management rating form in Figure 10.1, develop a graphic rating scale with behavioural incidents for the job of professor. You may also want to consider your own classroom experience when constructing your form.

Once you have drafted your form, exchange forms with another student or group. Critique and suggest possible improvements to the forms. Then with your revised form in hand, develop statements of behavioural incidents for two of your rating scale items to address the following circumstances:

- the professor has achieved outstanding results
- the professor meets acceptable standards
- the professor has performed very poorly in this aspect of the job

Be prepared to share and critique statements developed by other students. Debrief the exercise as directed.

Running | CASE

Running Case: LearnInMotion.com

The Performance Appraisal

Jennifer and Pierre disagree over the importance of having performance appraisals. Pierre says it's quite clear whether any particular LearnInMotion.com employee is doing his or her job. It's obvious, for instance, if the salespeople are selling, if the web designer is designing, if the web surfer is surfing, and if the content management people are managing to get the customers' content up on the website in a timely fashion. Pierre's position, like that of many small-business managers, is that "we have 1000 higher-priority things to attend to," such as boosting sales and creating the calendar. And in any case, he says, the employees already get plenty of day-to-day feedback from him or Jennifer regarding what they're doing right and what they're doing wrong.

This informal feedback notwithstanding, Jennifer believes that a more formal appraisal approach is required. For one thing, they're approaching the end of the 90-day "introductory" period for many of these employees, and the owners need to make decisions about whether they should go or stay. And from a practical point of view, Jennifer simply believes that sitting down and providing formal, written feedback is more likely to reinforce what employees are doing right and to get them to modify things they may be doing wrong. "Maybe this is one reason we're not getting enough sales," she says. They've been debating this for about an hour. Now, they want you, their management consultant, to advise them on what to do.

QUESTIONS

1. What performance appraisal problems will LearnInMotion encounter if they continue on the course of not using formalized performance appraisals?

2. What guidelines would you recommend to Pierre and Jennifer for developing an effective appraisal system?

Case | INCIDENT

A Performance Dilemma

Brenda Jackson, a newly hired human resources manager, has been on the job for approximately six months and is in the process of trying to create a new performance appraisal system for her employer, Starbrite Manufacturing Systems. Brenda has reviewed the company's current employee files and has noted that no performance appraisals exist in the files. This situation is of great concern to Brenda.

In response, Brenda schedules a meeting with the CEO to discuss her concerns and to gain his support to ultimately recommend the designing of a new performance appraisal system. After the meeting, Brenda is happy at gaining the CEO's approval but starts to feel overwhelmed at the large task she has in pulling the new performance management system together. This is where you come in to help Brenda by answering the following questions.

QUESTIONS

1. Discuss the performance management process highlighted in the chapter and how it will aid Brenda in creating this new performance appraisal system for her employer.

2. Discuss and suggest the type of appraisal methods that Brenda should recommend the company utilize.

3. Discuss the rating errors that Brenda must be aware of and how these can be avoided.

For additional cases and exercise material, go to
www.pearsoned.ca/myhrlab

To view the CBC Videos, read a summary, and answer discussion questions, go to MyHRLab at
www.pearsoned.ca/myhrlab

CHAPTER 11

STRATEGIC PAY PLANS

LEARNING OUTCOMES

AFTER STUDYING THIS CHAPTER, YOU SHOULD BE ABLE TO

EXPLAIN the strategic importance of total rewards.

EXPLAIN in detail each of the three stages in establishing pay rates.

DISCUSS competency-based pay.

DESCRIBE the five basic elements of compensation for managers.

DEFINE pay equity and **EXPLAIN** its importance today.

REQUIRED PROFESSIONAL CAPABILITIES (RPC)

- Monitors the competitiveness of the total compensation strategy on an ongoing basis

- Monitors the competitiveness of the compensation program relative to comparable organizations

- Provides for delivery of payroll services in compliance with applicable legislation and

company policy and advises the organization on related matters

- Ensures compliance with legally required programs

- Ensures accurate and timely delivery of pay

- Ensures pay records are accurate and complete

THE STRATEGIC IMPORTANCE OF TOTAL REWARDS

total rewards An integrated package of all rewards (monetary and nonmonetary, extrinsic and intrinsic) gained by employees arising from their employment.

Compensation and rewards management is extremely important to every employee. **Total rewards** refers to an integrated package of all rewards (monetary and nonmonetary, extrinsic and intrinsic) gained by employees arising from their employment. Total rewards encompasses everything that employees value in the employment relationship.[1]

The total rewards approach, as opposed to the previous approach of managing different elements of compensation in isolation, has arisen from the changing business environment of the last several decades. The economies of developed nations, such as Canada, have evolved from a largely industrialized base to become far more virtual, knowledge-based, and service-based, where employees are increasingly regarded as drivers of productivity. A total rewards approach considers individual reward components as part of an integrated whole in order to determine the best mix of rewards that are aligned with business strategy and that provide employee value, all within the cost constraints of the organization. Alignment is the extent to which rewards support outcomes that are important to achieving the organization's strategic objectives. For example, when competitive advantage relies on relentless customer service, this behaviour should be reinforced. Employee value is created when rewards are meaningful to employees and influence their affiliation with the organization.[2]

Originally, total rewards were conceptualized as having three broad categories: *compensation*, *benefits*, and *work experience*. Recently, research conducted by WorldatWork has clarified the work experience category by splitting it into three parts—work/life programs, performance and recognition, and development and career opportunities—resulting in five categories of total rewards, as shown in **Figure 11.1**.

The Five Components of Total Rewards

1. *Compensation*. This category includes direct financial payments in the form of wages, salaries, incentives, commissions, and bonuses. Wages and salaries are discussed in this chapter and other direct financial payments are discussed in Chapter 12.

2. *Benefits*. This category includes indirect payments in the form of financial benefits, like employer-paid insurance and vacations. It also includes employee services, as discussed in Chapter 13.

3. *Work/life programs*. This category of rewards relates to programs that help employees do their jobs effectively, such as flexible scheduling, telecommuting, childcare, and so on. These programs are discussed in Chapter 4 and Chapter 13.

4. *Performance and recognition*. This category includes pay-for-performance and recognition programs. These programs are discussed in Chapter 12.

5. *Development and career opportunities*. This category of reward focuses on planning for the advancement and/or change in responsibilities to best suit individual skills, talents, and desires. Tuition assistance, professional development, sabbaticals, coaching and mentoring opportunities, succession planning, and apprenticeships are all examples of career-enhancing programs.

FIGURE 11.1 | The Total Rewards Model

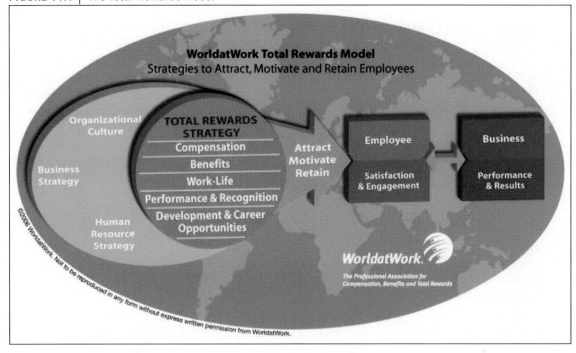

Source: Total Rewards: WorldatWork Introduces a New View 2006. Reprinted with permission of WorldatWork, Scottsdale, AZ. www.worldatwork.org.

The world's Most Admired Companies excel at taking a total rewards approach, as discussed in the Strategic HR box.

Impact of Rewards

Towers Perrin
www.towersperrin.com

The purposes of rewards are to attract, retain, and motivate/engage employees. *Engagement* refers to a positive emotional connection to the employer and a clear understanding of the strategic significance of the job, which results in discretionary effort on the part of the employee. The *2007–2008 Global Workforce Study* by Towers Perrin consultants found that, for Canadians, competitive base pay was the number one factor in attracting employees to an organization; having excellent career opportunities was the most important factor in retaining employees; and senior management's interest in employee well-being was the top factor influencing employee engagement. The results also showed that although only 23 percent of Canadians are engaged at work, fully 52 percent of them plan to stay with their current employer.[3]

BASIC CONSIDERATIONS IN DETERMINING PAY RATES

Four basic considerations influence the formulation of any pay plan: legal requirements, union issues, compensation policy, and equity.

Strategic HR

Rewards Program Effectiveness at the World's Most Admired Companies

Every year, the world's Most Admired Companies (MACs) are featured in *Fortune* magazine. In 2009, these companies excelled in six key areas related to reward program effectiveness:

1. focusing on excellence in the execution of rewards programs

2. ensuring their rewards programs are aligned with organizational goals, strategy, and culture

3. promoting a total rewards view across the organization and effectively leveraging intangible rewards

4. having stronger programs for developing talent from within, resulting in lower base salaries than that of their peers

5. better leveraging their managers' skills in rewards program implementation

6. reinforcing HR's role in helping their managers to succeed at putting reward programs in to action

One key reason MACs are more successful at aligning their rewards programs with their organizational goals is that they tend to take a more global, centralized approach to managing rewards strategy, compensation structures, and performance management programs. They also excel at communicating their business strategies to managers and employees. The emphasis on communication also extends to the rewards arena.

MACs understand that employees are motivated by much more than money. They are more likely to take a total rewards approach, covering not just tangible rewards like base salary, incentives and other monetary benefits, but also intangible rewards such as career-growth opportunities, quality of work, recognition, and work climate.

MACs generally pay lower base salaries than their peers. On average, MACs pay approximately 5 percent less in base pay for management and professional roles than other organizations. This is most likely the result of the emphasis that MACs place on intangible rewards like career development. They have a stronger pool of homegrown talent to choose from when job vacancies arise, so they are less reliant on hiring expensive external talent.

Organizations tend to fuss and fret about the design of their rewards programs, but these companies exemplify what research has indicated: Impressive design is not why rewards programs generally work well. It is the way they are put into action and then sustained by the organization that drives their effectiveness.

Legal Considerations in Compensation

All of the 14 jurisdictions regulating employment in Canada (ten provinces, three territories, and the federal jurisdiction) have laws regulating compensation. Thus, HR managers must pay careful attention to which legislation affects their employees. Further, these laws are constantly changing and require continual monitoring to ensure compliance. Legislation affecting compensation administration is discussed below.

Employment/Labour Standards Acts (Canada Labour Code)

Employment/labour laws set minimum standards regarding pay, including minimum wage, maximum hours of work, overtime pay, paid vacation, paid statutory holidays, termination pay, record keeping of pay information, and more. There are variations in some of the minimum standards for students, trainees, domestics, nannies, seasonal agricultural workers, and others. Executive, administrative, and professional employees are generally exempt from the overtime pay requirements.

Pay Equity Acts

Pay equity laws were enacted to redress the historical undervaluation of "women's work" by providing equal pay for work of equal (or comparable) value performed by men and women. Employers are required to identify male- and female-dominated jobs, and then use a gender-neutral job evaluation system based on specific compensable factors (such as skill, effort, responsibility, and working conditions) to evaluate the jobs. Pay for female-dominated jobs that are equivalent in value to male-dominated jobs must be increased to the pay level of the comparable male-dominated job. Not all Canadian jurisdictions have pay equity laws, as will be discussed later in this chapter.

Human Rights Acts

All jurisdictions have enacted human rights laws to protect Canadians from discrimination on a number of grounds in employment and other areas. These grounds differ somewhat among jurisdictions, but most prohibit discrimination in employment (such as in compensation and promotion) on the basis of age, sex, colour, race/ancestry/place of origin, religion/creed, marital/family status, and physical or mental disability.

Canada/Quebec Pension Plan

All employees and their employers must contribute to the Canada/Quebec Pension Plan throughout the employee's working life. Pension benefits based on the employee's average earnings are paid during retirement. Details of these and other benefits are provided in Chapter 13.

RPC

Ensures compliance with legally required programs

Association of Workers'
Compensation Boards of Canada
www.awcbc.org

Other Legislation Affecting Compensation

Each province and territory, as well as the federal government, has its own *workers' compensation laws*. The objective of these laws is to provide a prompt, sure, and reasonable income to victims of work-related accidents and illnesses. The Employment Insurance Act is aimed at protecting Canadian workers from total economic destitution in the event of employment termination that is beyond their control. Employers and employees both contribute to the benefits provided by this act. This act also provides up to 45 weeks of compensation for workers unemployed through no fault of their own (depending on the unemployment rate in the claimant's region and other factors). Maternity leave, parental leave, and compassionate care leave benefits are also provided under the Employment Insurance Act.[4]

Union Influences on Compensation Decisions

Unions and labour relations laws also influence how pay plans are designed. Historically, wage rates have been the main issue in collective bargaining. However, other issues—including time off with pay, income security (for those in industries with periodic layoffs), cost-of-living adjustments, and pensions—are also important.[5]

The Canada Labour Relations Board and similar bodies in each province and territory oversee employer practices and ensure that employees are treated in accordance with their legal rights. Their decisions underscore the need to involve union officials in developing the compensation package.

Work stoppages may reflect employee dissatisfaction with pay plans and other forms of compensation, such as benefits.

Union Attitudes toward Compensation Decisions

Several classic studies shed light on union attitudes toward compensation plans and on commonly held union fears.[6] Many union leaders fear that any system used to evaluate the worth of a job can become a tool for management malpractice. They tend to believe that no one can judge the relative value of jobs better than the workers themselves. In addition, they believe that management's usual method of using several compensable factors (like "degree of responsibility") to evaluate and rank the worth of jobs can be a manipulative device for restricting or lowering the pay of workers. One implication is that the best way in which to gain the cooperation of union members in evaluating the worth of jobs is to get their active involvement in this process and in assigning fair rates of pay to these jobs. However, management has to ensure that its prerogatives—such as the right to use the appropriate job evaluation technique to assess the relative worth of jobs—are not surrendered.

Compensation Policies

An employer's compensation policies provide important guidelines regarding the wages and benefits that it pays. A number of factors are taken into account when developing a compensation policy, including whether the organization wants to be a leader or a follower regarding pay, business strategy, and the cost of different types of compensation. Important policies include the basis for salary increases, promotion and demotion policies, overtime pay policy, and policies regarding probationary pay and leaves for military service, jury duty, and holidays. Compensation policies are usually written by the HR or compensation manager in conjunction with senior management.[7]

Equity and Its Impact on Pay Rates

A crucial factor in determining pay rates is the need for equity, specifically *external equity* and *internal equity*. Research has indicated that employee perceptions of fairness are one of the three key conditions for effective reward programs.[8] Externally, pay must compare favourably with rates in other organizations or an employer will find it hard to attract and retain qualified employees. Pay rates must also be equitable internally: Each employee should view his or her pay as equitable given other pay rates in the organization.

ESTABLISHING PAY RATES

In practice, the process of establishing pay rates that are both externally and internally equitable requires three stages:

1. Determine the worth of jobs within the organization through job evaluation (to ensure internal equity), and group jobs with similar worth into pay grades.
2. Conduct a wage/salary survey of what other employers are paying for comparable jobs (to ensure external equity).
3. Combine the job evaluation (internal) and salary survey (external) information to determine pay rates for the jobs in the organization.

Each of these stages will now be explained in turn.

Stage 1: Job Evaluation

job evaluation A systematic comparison to determine the relative worth of jobs within a firm.

Job evaluation is aimed at determining a job's relative worth. It is a formal and systematic comparison of jobs within a firm to determine the worth of one job relative to another, and it eventually results in a job hierarchy. The basic procedure is to compare the content of jobs in relation to one another, for example in terms of their effort, responsibility, skills, and working conditions. Job evaluation usually focuses on **benchmark jobs** that are critical to the firm's operations, or are commonly found in other organizations. Rohm and Haas, a multinational chemical company, ensure that its benchmark jobs represent all the various business units and departments in the organization; are drawn from all levels of the organization; have large numbers of incumbents; are clear and well-known in the industry; are stable and easily understood in terms of purpose and work content; and are visible and well understood by all employees.[9] The resulting evaluations of benchmark jobs are used as reference points around which other jobs are arranged in order of relative worth.

benchmark job A job that is critical to the firm's operations or commonly found in other organizations.

Compensable Factors

compensable factor A fundamental, compensable element of a job, such as skill, effort, responsibility, and working conditions.

Jobs can be compared intuitively by deciding that one job is "more important" or "of greater value or worth" than another without digging any deeper into why in terms of specific job-related factors. This approach, called the *ranking method*, is very hard to defend to employees or others who may not agree with the resulting job hierarchy. As an alternative, jobs can be compared by focusing on certain basic factors that they have in common. In compensation management, these basic factors are called **compensable factors.** They are the factors that determine the definition of job content, establish how the jobs compare with one another, and set the compensation paid for each job.

Some employers develop their own compensable factors. However, most use factors that have been popularized by packaged job evaluation systems or by legislation. For example, most of the pay equity acts in Canada focus on four compensable factors: *skill*, *effort*, *responsibility*, and *working conditions*. As another example, the job evaluation method popularized by the Hay Group consulting firm focuses on four compensable factors: *know-how*, *problem solving*, *accountability*, and *working conditions*. Often, different job evaluation systems are used for different departments, employee groups, or business units.

Identifying compensable factors plays a pivotal role in job evaluation. All jobs in each employee group, department, or business unit are evaluated *using the same compensable factors*. An employer thus evaluates the same elemental components for each job within the work group and is then better able to compare jobs—for example, in terms of the degree of skill, effort, responsibility, and working conditions present in each.[10]

Job Evaluation Committee

Job evaluation is largely a judgmental process and one that demands close co-operation among supervisors, compensation specialists, and the employees and their union representatives. The main steps involved include identifying the need for the program, getting cooperation, and choosing an evaluation committee; the committee then carries out the actual job evaluation.[11]

A *job evaluation committee* is established to ensure the representation of the points of view of various people who are familiar with the jobs in question, each of whom may have a different perspective regarding the nature of the jobs. The committee may include employees, HR staff, managers, and union representatives.

The evaluation committee first identifies 10 or 15 key benchmark jobs. These will be the first jobs to be evaluated and will serve as the anchors or

The job evaluation committee typically includes at least several employees and has the important task of evaluating the worth of each job using compensable factors.

benchmarks against which the relative importance or value of all other jobs can be compared. Then the committee turns to its most important function—actually evaluating the worth of each job. For this, the committee will probably use either the job classification method or the point method.

Classification Method

The **classification/grading method** involves categorizing jobs into groups. The groups are called **classes** if they contain similar jobs or **grades** if they contain jobs that are similar in difficulty but otherwise different.

This method is widely used in the public sector. The federal government's UT (University Teaching) job group is an example of a job class because it contains similar jobs involving teaching, research, and consulting. Conversely, the AV (Audit, Commerce, and Purchasing) job group is an example of a job grade because it contains dissimilar jobs, involving auditing, economic development consulting, and purchasing.

There are several ways in which to categorize jobs. One is to draw up class descriptions (similar to job descriptions) and place jobs into classes based on their correspondence to these descriptions. Another is to draw up a set of classifying rules for each class (for instance, the amount of independent judgment, skill, physical effort, and so on that the class of jobs requires). Then the jobs are categorized according to these rules.

The usual procedure is to choose compensable factors and then develop class or grade descriptions that describe each class in terms of amount or level of compensable factor(s) in jobs. The federal government's classification system, for example, employs different compensable factors for various job groups. Based on these compensable factors, a **grade/group description** (like that in **Figure 11.2**) is written. Then, the evaluation committee reviews all job descriptions and slots each job into its appropriate class or grade.

The job classification method has several advantages. The main one is that most employers usually end up classifying jobs anyway, regardless of the job evaluation method that they use. They do this to avoid having to work with and develop pay rates for an unmanageable number of jobs; with the job classification method, all jobs are already grouped into several classes. The disadvantages are that it is difficult to write the class or grade descriptions and that considerable judgment is required in applying them. Yet many employers use this method with success.

Point Method

The **point method** is widely used in the private sector and requires identifying several compensable factors. The extent/degree to which each factor is present in the job is evaluated; a corresponding number of points is assigned for each factor; and the number of points for each factor is summed to arrive at an overall point value for the job.

1. *Preliminary steps.* In order to use the point method, it is necessary to have current job descriptions and job specifications based on a thorough job analysis. The foundation of the job evaluation plan is a number of compensable factors which must be agreed upon. In Canada, four compensable factors are commonly used: skill, effort, responsibility, and working conditions. These factors are general and can mean different things in different workplaces. Therefore sub-factors of each one may also

FIGURE 11.2 | Example of Group Definition in the Federal Government

Correctional Services (CX) Group Definition

The Correctional Services Group comprises positions that are primarily involved in the custody, control and correctional influence of inmates in the institutions of Correctional Service Canada and the training of staff engaged in custodial and correctional work at a Staff College of Correctional Service Canada.

Inclusions

Notwithstanding the generality of the foregoing, for greater certainty, it includes positions that have as their primary purpose, responsibility for one or more of the following activities:

1. the custody and control of inmates and the security of the institution;
2. the custody and control of detainees being held under Immigration and Refugee Protection Act (IRPA) Security Certificates;
3. the correctional influence of inmates with the continuing responsibility to relate actively and effectively to inmates;
4. the admission and discharge of inmates, and the control of inmate visits and correspondence;
5. the organization and implementation of recreational activities, the surveillance and control of inmates engaged in these activities and the custody and issue of recreational equipment;
6. the training of staff in custodial and correctional procedures and techniques; and
7. the leadership of any of the above activities.

Exclusions

Positions excluded from the Correctional Services Group are those whose primary purpose is included in the definition of any other group or those in which one or more of the following activities is of primary importance:

1. the operation of heating plant, sewage facilities and water supplies and the provision of maintenance services;
2. the provision of patient care that requires the application of a comprehensive knowledge of or specialized expertise in physical and mental health care;
3. the provision of services and supplies to inmates; and
4. the instruction of inmates in workshops, crafts and training programs.

Source: Correctional Services (CX) Classification Standard. www.tbs-sct.gc.ca/cla/def/cx-eng.asp, Treasury Board of Canada Secretariat, 2009. Reproduced with the permission of the Minister of Public Works and Government Services Canada, 2009.

be determined in order to clarify the specific meaning of each factor, as shown below.

Factor	Sub-Factors
Skill	Education and Experience
	Interpersonal Skill
Effort	Physical Effort
	Mental Effort
Responsibility	Supervision of Others
	Planning
Working Conditions	Physical Environment
	Travel

Each sub-factor must be carefully defined to ensure that the evaluation committee members will apply them consistently. An example of a sub-factor definition is presented in **Figure 11.3**.

2. *Determine factor weights and degrees.* The next step is to decide on the maximum number of points (called weight) to assign to each factor. Assigning factor weights is generally done by the evaluation committee. The committee members carefully study each factor and determine the relative value of the factors. For example,

Skill	30 percent
Effort	30 percent
Responsibility	30 percent
Working conditions	10 percent
	100 percent

FIGURE 11.3 | Sub-Factor Definition

Responsibility for Others

This sub-factor is used to measure the responsibility that the incumbent of the position assumes for the direction and/or supervision of volunteers, external suppliers/contractors and staff. The following characteristics of the work are to be considered in selecting a level: the nature of supervision given, based either on accountability for results or functional guidance (how-to), and the number of employees or others directed/supervised. Occasional supervision, such as that performed during the absence of the supervisor on vacation or sick leaves, is not to be considered. **This sub-factor does NOT include the academic supervision of students or the activities of others outside of an employee-type relationship.**

Source: McMaster University CAW local 555 Job Evaluation Plan. www.workingatmcmaster.ca/jjesc (March 23, 2009)

Then definitions of varying amounts (called degrees or levels) of each sub-factor (or overall factor if no sub-factors are used) are prepared so that raters can judge the degree of a sub-factor/factor existing in a job. Thus, sub-factor "physical environment" for the factor "working conditions" might have three degrees—occasional, frequent, continuous—defined as follows:

Degree 1: Occasional—less than 30 percent of the time on an annual basis. Typically occurs once in a while, but not every day, or every day for less than 30 percent of the day.

Degree 2: Frequent—30 percent to 60 percent of the time on an annual basis. A regular feature of the job that occurs during any given day, week, or season.

Degree 3: Continuous—More than 60 percent of the time on an annual basis. Typically occurs for most of the regular work day, all year round (on average).

The number of degrees usually does not exceed five or six, and the actual number depends mostly on judgment. It is not necessary to have the same number of degrees for each factor, and degrees should be limited to the number necessary to distinguish among jobs.

3. *Assign points for each degree of each sub-factor.* Now, points are assigned to each factor, as in **Table 11.1.** For example, suppose that it is decided to use a total

TABLE 11.1 | Point Method Job Evaluation Plan

Factor	Sub-Factors	Degrees 1	2	3	4	Maximum Weight Points	
Skill	Education and Experience	50	100	150	200	200	
	Interpersonal Skill	25	50	75	100	100	
						300	30%
Effort	Physical Effort	25	50	75	100	100	
	Mental Effort	50	100	150	200	200	
						300	30%
Responsibility	Supervision of Others	50	100	150		150	
	Planning	50	100	150		150	
						300	30%
Working Conditions	Physical Environment	20	40	60		60	
	Travel	10	20	30	40	40	
						100	10%
						1000	100%

number of 1000 points in the point plan. Then, since the factor "skill" had a weight of 30 percent, it would be assigned a total of 30 percent × 1000 = 300 points. This automatically means that the highest degree for each sub-factor of the skill factor would be 300 points. Points are then assigned to the other degrees for this factor, in equal amounts from the lowest to the highest degree. This step is repeated for each factor and its sub-factors, resulting in the final job evaluation plan, as shown in Table 11.1. All these decisions are recorded in a job evaluation manual to be used by the job evaluation committee.

4. *Evaluate the jobs.* Once the manual is complete, the actual evaluations can begin. Each job is evaluated factor by factor to determine the number of points that should be assigned to it. First, committee members determine the degree (first degree, second degree, and so on) to which each factor is present in the job. Then, they note the corresponding points (see Table 11.1) that were assigned to each of these degrees. Finally, they add up the points for all factors, arriving at a total point value for the job. Raters generally start by rating benchmark jobs and obtaining consensus on these, and then they rate the rest of the jobs.

Point systems involve a quantitative technique that is easily explained to and used by employees. However, it can be difficult and time-consuming to develop a point plan and to effectively train the job evaluation user group. This is one reason that many organizations adopt a point plan developed and marketed by a consulting firm. In fact, the availability of a number of ready-made plans probably accounts in part for the wide use of point plans in job evaluation.

If the committee assigned pay rates to each individual job, it would be difficult to administer, since there might be different pay rates for hundreds or even thousands of jobs. Even in smaller organizations, there is a tendency to try to simplify wage and salary structures as much as possible. Therefore, the committee will probably want to group similar jobs (in terms of their number of points, for instance) into grades for pay purposes. Then, instead of having to deal with pay rates for hundreds of jobs, it might only have to focus on pay rates for 10 or 12 groupings of jobs.

pay grade Comprises jobs of approximately equal value.

A **pay grade** comprises jobs of approximately equal value or importance as determined by job evaluation. If the point method was used, the pay grade consists of jobs falling within a range of points. If the classification system was used, then the jobs are already categorized into classes or grades. The next stage is to obtain information on market pay rates by conducting a wage/salary survey.

Stage 2: Conduct a Wage/Salary Survey

wage/salary survey A survey aimed at determining prevailing wage rates. A good salary survey provides specific wage rates for comparable jobs. Formal written questionnaire surveys are the most comprehensive.

Compensation or **wage/salary surveys** play a central role in determining pay rates for jobs.[12] An employer may use wage/salary surveys in three ways. First, survey data are used to determine pay rates for benchmark jobs that serve as reference points or anchors for the employer's pay scale, meaning that other jobs are then paid based on their relative worth compared to the benchmark jobs. Second, an increasing number of positions are paid solely based on the marketplace (rather than relative to the firm's benchmark jobs).[13]

As a result of the current shift away from long-term employment, compensation is increasingly shaped by market wages and less by how it fits into the hierarchy of jobs in one organization. Finally, surveys also collect data on employee benefits, work–life programs, pay-for-performance plans, recognition plans, and so on, to provide a basis on which to make decisions regarding other types of rewards.

There are many ways to conduct a salary survey, including

- informal communication with other employers
- reviewing newspaper and Internet job ads
- surveying employment agencies
- buying commercial or professional surveys
- reviewing online compensation surveys
- conducting formal questionnaire-type surveys with other employers

RPC

Monitors the competitiveness of the compensation program relative to comparable organizations

Data from the Hay Group consulting firm indicate that large organizations participate in an average of 11 compensation surveys and use information from 7 of them to administer their own compensation practices.[14]

Upward bias can be a problem regardless of the type of compensation survey. At least one compensation expert argues that the way in which most surveys are constructed, interpreted, and used leads almost invariably to a situation in which firms set higher wages than they otherwise might. For example, "companies like to compare themselves against well-regarded, high-paying, and high-performing companies," so that baseline salaries tend to be biased upward. Similarly, "companies that sponsor surveys often do so with an implicit (albeit unstated) objective: to show the company [is] paying either competitively or somewhat below the market, so as to justify positive corrective action." For these and similar reasons, it is probably wise to review survey results with a skeptical eye and to acknowledge that upward bias may exist and should perhaps be considered when making decisions.[15]

Tips | **FOR THE FRONT LINE**

Whatever the source of the survey, the data must be carefully assessed for accuracy before they are used to make compensation decisions. Problems can arise when the organization's job descriptions only partially match the descriptions contained in the survey, the survey data were collected several months before the time of use, the participants in the survey do not represent the appropriate labour market for the jobs being matched, and so on.[16]

Formal and Informal Surveys by the Employer

Most employers rely heavily on formal or informal surveys of what other employers are paying.[17] Informal telephone surveys are good for collecting data on a relatively small number of easily identified and quickly recognized jobs, such as when a bank's HR director wants to determine the salary at which a newly opened customer service representative's job should be advertised. Informal discussions among human resources specialists at regular professional association meetings are other occasions for informal salary surveys. Some employers use formal questionnaire surveys to collect compensation information from other employers, including things like number of employees, overtime policies, starting salaries, and paid vacations.

TABLE 11.2 | Average Weekly Earnings by Industry 2003–2007

	2003	2004	2005 $	2006	2007
All industries excluding unclassified enterprises	**688.11**	**702.61**	**725.26**	**746.89**	**770.82**
Forestry, logging and support	855.94	891.16	916.51	959.30	975.97
Mining and oil and gas extraction	1,185.86	1,251.77	1,314.54	1,350.71	1,409.12
Utilities	1,068.89	1,061.59	1,065.65	1,087.82	1,126.58
Construction	831.48	841.18	872.70	895.09	935.81
Manufacturing	846.09	862.57	886.82	906.09	938.14
Wholesale trade	792.24	803.81	831.25	874.41	913.00
Retail trade	443.57	454.34	471.45	481.78	486.01
Transportation and warehousing	762.37	757.03	775.95	784.71	800.02
Information and cultural industries	822.71	833.66	881.17	933.13	972.61
Finance and insurance	876.37	897.76	932.91	962.04	998.11
Real estate and rental and leasing	607.83	627.99	651.86	676.11	708.65
Professional, scientific and technical services	914.61	928.10	951.39	962.75	983.78
Management of companies and enterprises	859.07	863.11	907.21	948.43	944.54
Administrative and support, waste management and remediation services	542.33	560.65	578.83	601.91	637.97
Educational services	735.43	761.02	787.81	815.80	833.20
Health care and social assistance	612.15	636.54	654.94	678.91	703.04
Arts, entertainment and recreation	427.29	422.60	429.47	436.62	453.65
Accommodation and food services	270.11	279.59	291.47	304.36	324.34
Public administration	855.15	872.05	899.05	930.85	969.04
Other services	527.67	546.85	565.48	583.34	608.45

Source: Statistics Canada, CANSIM database, Table 281-0027 and from Catalogue no. 72-002-X, 2008, available for free at the following URL: www40.statcan.gc.ca/101/cst01/labr73a-eng.htm.

Commercial, Professional, and Government Salary Surveys

Many employers also rely on surveys published by various commercial firms, professional associations, or government agencies. For example, Statistics Canada provides monthly data on earnings by geographic area, by industry, and by occupation. **Table 11.2** provides an example of earnings data by industry and occupation.

The Toronto Board of Trade conducts five compensation surveys annually, covering executive; management; professional, supervisory, and sales; information technology; and administrative and support positions. The surveys include information from small, medium, and large employers in the Greater Toronto Area. A separate survey of employee benefits and employment practices is also conducted.

Private consulting and/or executive recruiting companies, such as Watson Wyatt, Mercer Human Resources Consulting, and Hewitt Associates, annually publish data covering the compensation of senior and middle managers and members of boards of directors. Professional organizations, like the Certified General Accountants Association and Professional Engineers Ontario, conduct surveys of compensation practices among members of their associations.

For some jobs, salaries are determined directly based on formal or informal salary surveys such as those available from Monster.ca. In most cases, though, surveys are used to price benchmark jobs around which other jobs are then slotted based on their relative worth as determined through job evaluation. Now all

Monster.ca Salary Centre
http://salary.monster.ca

the information necessary to move to the next stage—determining pay for jobs—has been obtained.

Stage 3: Combine the Job Evaluation and Salary Survey Information to Determine Pay for Jobs

The final stage is to assign pay rates to each pay grade. (Of course, if jobs were not grouped into pay grades, individual pay rates would have to be assigned to each job.) Assigning pay rates to each pay grade (or to each job) is usually accomplished with a **wage curve.**

wage curve A graphic description of the relationship between the value of the job and the average wage paid for this job.

The wage curve graphically depicts the market pay rates currently being paid for jobs in each pay grade, relative to the job evaluation points for each job or grade. An example of a wage curve is presented in **Figure 11.4**. Note that pay rates are shown on the vertical axis, while the points for pay grades are shown along the horizontal axis. The purpose of the wage curve is to show the relationship between the value of the job as determined by one of the job evaluation methods and the current average pay rates for each job or grade.

There are several steps in determining pay for pay grades using a wage curve. First, *find the average pay for each pay grade*, since each of the pay grades consists of several jobs. Next, *plot the pay rates* for each pay grade, as was done in Figure 11.4. Then fit a line (called a *wage line*) through the points just plotted. This can be done either freehand or by using a statistical method known as regression analysis. Finally, *determine pay for jobs*. Wages along the wage line are the target wages or salary rates for the jobs in each pay grade.

An Ethical | Dilemma

What should employers do when there is a shortage of a certain type of skills and they cannot attract any workers unless they pay a market rate above the maximum of their salary range for that job? How should other jobs in the same salary range be paid?

Developing Rate Ranges

pay ranges A series of steps or levels within a pay grade, usually based on years of service.

Most employers do not just pay one rate for all jobs in a particular pay grade. Instead, they develop **pay ranges** for each grade so that there might, for instance,

FIGURE 11.4 | Plotting a Wage Curve

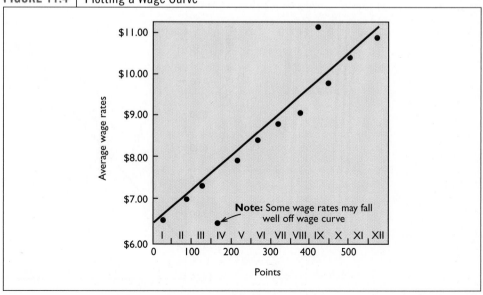

Note: The average market pay rate for jobs in each grade (Grade I, Grade II, Grade III, etc.) is plotted, and the wage curve is fitted to the resulting points.

TABLE 11.3 | Federal Government Pay Schedules CX-1 and CX-2

Rate Levels within Grade					
Grade	1	2	3	4	5
CX-1	$52 604	55 761	59 107	62 652	66 413
CX-2	$55 826	59 176	62 726	66 489	70 477

Source: CX - Correctional Services Group Annual Rates of Pay 2009, www.tbs-sct.gc.ca/pubs_pol/hrpubs/coll.agre/cx/cx08-eng.asp, Treasury Board of Canada Secretariat, 2009. Reproduced with the permission of the Minister of Public Works and Government Services Canada, 2009.

be ten levels or "steps" and ten corresponding pay rates within each pay grade. This approach is illustrated in **Table 11.3**, which shows the pay rates and levels for some of the federal government pay grades. As of the time of this pay schedule, for instance, employees in positions that were classified in grade CX-1 could be paid annual salaries between $52 604 and $66 413, depending on the level at which they were hired into the grade, the amount of time they were in the grade, and their merit increases (if any). Another way to depict the rate ranges for each grade is with a wage structure, as in **Figure 11.5**. The wage structure graphically depicts the range of pay rates (in this case, per hour) to be paid for each grade.

The use of pay ranges for each pay grade has several benefits. First, the employer can take a more flexible stance with respect to the labour market; for example, some flexibility makes it easier to attract experienced, higher-paid employees

FIGURE 11.5 | Wage Structure

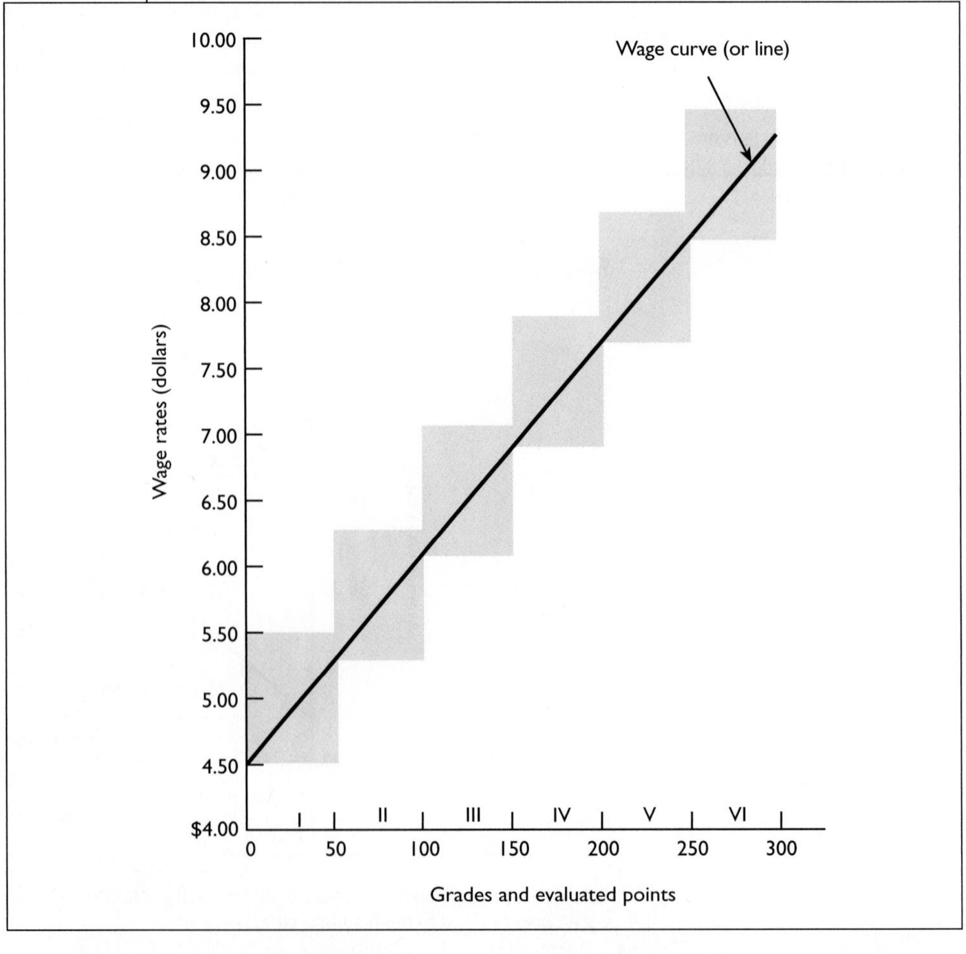

into a pay grade where the starting salary for the lowest step may be too low to attract such experienced people. Pay ranges also allow employers to provide for performance differences between employees within the same grade or between those with differing seniority. As in Figure 11.5, most employers structure their pay ranges to overlap a bit so that an employee with greater experience or seniority may earn more than an entry-level person in the next higher pay grade.

Broadbanding

The trend today is for employers to reduce their salary grades and ranges from ten or more down to three to five, a process that is called **broadbanding.** Broadbanding means combining salary grades and ranges into just a few wide levels or "bands," each of which then contains a relatively wide range of jobs and salary levels (see **Figure 11.6**).

Broadbanding a pay system involves several steps. First, the number of bands is decided on and each is assigned a salary range. The bands usually have wide salary ranges and also overlap substantially. As a result, there is much more flexibility to move employees from job to job within bands and less need to "promote" them to new grades just to get them higher salaries.

Broadbanding's basic advantage is that it injects greater flexibility into employee compensation.[18] The new, broad salary bands can include both supervisors and those reporting to them. Broadbanding also facilitates less specialized, boundaryless jobs and organizations. Less specialization and more participation in cross-departmental processes generally mean enlarged duties or capabilities and more possibilities for alternative career tracks.

Correcting Out-of-Line Rates

The actual wage rate for a job may fall well off the wage line or well outside the rate range for its grade, as shown in Figure 11.5. This means that the average pay for that job is currently too high or too low relative to other jobs in the firm. If a point falls well below the line, a pay raise for the job may be required. If the plot falls well above the wage line, pay cuts or a pay freeze may be required.

Underpaid employees should have their wages raised to the minimum of the rate range for their pay grade, assuming that the organization wants to retain the employees and has the funds. This can be done either immediately or in one or two steps.

FIGURE 11.6 | Broadbanding

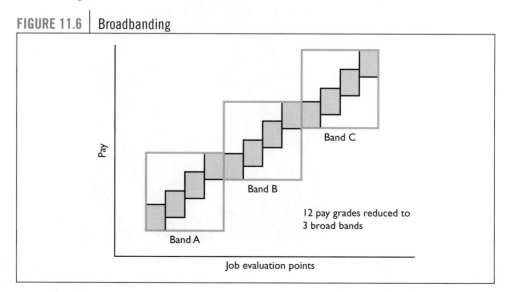

red circle pay rate A rate of pay that is above the pay range maximum.

Pay rates of overpaid employees are often called **red circle pay rates,** and there are several ways to cope with this problem. One is to freeze the rate paid to employees in this grade until general salary increases bring the other jobs into line with it. A second alternative is to transfer or promote some or all of the employees involved to jobs for which they can legitimately be paid their current pay rates. The third alternative is to freeze the rate for six months, during which time attempts are made to transfer or promote the overpaid employees. If this is not possible, then the rate at which these employees are paid is cut to the maximum in the pay range for their grade.

PAY FOR KNOWLEDGE

Pay-for-knowledge systems are known as *competency-based pay* (for management and professional employees) and *skill-based pay* (for manufacturing employees). These plans pay employees for the range, depth, and types of knowledge that they are capable of using, rather than for the job that they currently hold. Competencies are individual knowledge, skills, and behaviours that are critical to successful individual or corporate performance based on their relation to the organization's visions, values, and business strategy.[19]

Core competencies describe knowledge and behaviours that employees throughout the organization must exhibit for the organization to succeed, such as "customer service orientation" for all hotel employees. *Functional competencies* are associated with a particular organizational function, such as "negotiation skills" for salespeople, or "safety orientation" for pilots. *Behavioural competencies* are expected behaviours, such as "always walking a customer to

Construction workers today are often compensated for their work through the method of skill-based pay.

the product they are looking for rather than pointing."[20] A pay-for-knowledge program should include the following:

- Competencies and skills—directly important to job performance—that can be defined in measurable and objective terms. Skills tend to be easier to define and measure than competencies.
- New and different competencies that replace obsolete competencies or competencies that are no longer important to job performance. If additional competencies are needed, the obsolete competency should be removed from the program.
- On-the-job training, not "in the classroom." Those who possess the competencies or skills should teach them. Also include on-the-job assessment, which can be supplemented by paper-and-pencil exams administered on the job.[21]

As an example, in a manufacturing plant setting, workers would be paid based on their attained skill levels. In a three-level plan,

1. Level 1 would indicate limited ability, such as knowledge of basic facts and ability to perform simple tasks without direction.
2. Level 2 would mean that the employee has attained partial proficiency and could, for instance, apply technical principles on the job.
3. Level 3 would mean that the employee is fully competent in the area and could, for example, analyze and solve production problems.

Increased workforce flexibility is one of the most significant advantages of pay for knowledge. Employees rotate between different jobs or production areas to encourage the learning of new competencies and skills. This process fosters flexibility by encouraging workers to learn multiple competencies and skills and to willingly switch tasks.[22]

Experience has shown that competency-based pay is more efficient in the first years of its existence. The greatest challenge is measurement of competencies. As time goes on, employees often become dissatisfied if these measurements are not valid or if the people responsible for assessing competencies are considered incompetent or biased.[23]

Another major employee concern is that pay be linked sufficiently to performance as well as competencies. Some compensation consultants suggest that firms should not pay for competencies at the exclusion of rewards for high-performance results. For example, competencies could be linked to the determination of base salary combined with bonuses that are based on performance.[24] One final issue for many Canadian companies is that pay for knowledge systems do not meet pay equity requirements.[25]

Although only about 15 to 20 percent of workplaces use pay for knowledge at present, experts predict that the viewpoint that people, rather than jobs, provide advantage to organizations will continue to grow in popularity. They foresee the emergence of new pay systems combining competencies and market values.[26]

PAY FOR EXECUTIVE, MANAGERIAL, AND PROFESSIONAL JOBS

Developing a compensation plan to pay executive, managerial, and professional employees is similar in many respects to developing a plan for other employees.[27] The basic aims of the plan are the same in that the goal is to attract good employees and maintain their commitment. Yet for executive, managerial, and professional jobs, job evaluation provides only a partial answer to the question of how to pay these employees. Executives, managers, and professionals are almost always paid based on their performance as well as on the basis of static job demands, like working conditions.

Compensating Executives and Managers

There are five elements in an executive/managerial compensation package: salary, benefits, short-term incentives, long-term incentives, and perquisites.[28] The amount of salary paid usually depends on the value of the person's work to the organization and how well the person is discharging his or her responsibilities. Salary is the cornerstone of executive compensation, because it is the element on which the others are layered, with benefits, incentives, and perquisites often awarded in some proportion to base pay.

Executive compensation tends to emphasize performance incentives more than other employees' pay plans do, since organizational results are likely to reflect the contributions of executives more directly than those of other employees. The heavy incentive component of executive compensation can be illustrated by using some of Canada's best-paid executives.[29] In 2008, Tom Glocer, CEO of Thomson Reuters Corp., received total compensation of $39 010 519, of which the base salary was $1 598 223. Ted Rogers, CEO of Rogers Communications Inc., received total compensation of $21 484 708, of which the base salary was $1 592 067. George Cope, CEO of BCE Inc., received total compensation of $19 551 345, of which the base salary was $959 327.

An Ethical | Dilemma

Is it right that CEOs earn enormous amounts of money when most employees are getting small increases each year (sometimes even less than inflation)?

Research | INSIGHT

A major review of the results of many previous studies of CEO pay determined that firm size accounts for 40 percent in the variance of total CEO pay, while firm performance accounts for less than 5 percent of the variance.[30]

There has been considerable debate regarding whether top executives are worth what they are paid. Some argue that the job of an executive is increasingly difficult. The stakes are high and job tenure is often short. Expectations are getting higher, the questions from shareholders are more direct, and the challenge of navigating an organization through difficult economic times has never been so great. However, shareholder activism regarding executive pay has attempted to tighten the restrictions on what firms pay their top executives.

Some believe that pay for performance is taking hold, with companies now making stronger links between company performance and CEO total compensation. Others believe that linking pay to performance is still inadequate in the majority of companies. Most agree that better disclosure of executive pay is required, and such groups as the Canadian Securities Administrators and the Canadian Coalition for Good Governance are pressing for dramatic changes in executive compensation disclosure.[31]

Compensating Professional Employees

Compensating non-supervisory professional employees, like engineers and scientists, presents unique problems. Analytical jobs require creativity and problem solving, compensable factors not easily compared or measured. Furthermore, the professional's economic impact on the firm is often related only indirectly to the person's actual efforts; for example, the success of an engineer's invention depends on many factors, like how well it is produced and marketed.

In theory, the job evaluation methods explained previously can be used for evaluating professional jobs.[32] The compensable factors here tend to focus on problem solving, creativity, job scope, and technical knowledge and expertise. The job classification method is commonly used—a series of grade descriptions are written, and each position is slotted into the grade having the most appropriate definition.

In practice, traditional methods of job evaluation are rarely used for professional jobs since it is so difficult to identify compensable factors and degrees of factors that meaningfully capture the value of professional work. "Knowledge and the skill of applying it," as one expert notes, "are extremely difficult to quantify and measure."[33]

As a result, most employers use a *market-pricing approach* in evaluating professional jobs. They price professional jobs in the marketplace to the best of their ability to establish the values for benchmark jobs. These benchmark jobs and the employer's other professional jobs are then slotted into a salary structure. Specifically, each professional discipline (like mechanical engineering or electrical engineering) usually ends up having four to six grade levels, each of which requires a fairly broad salary range. This approach helps ensure that the employer remains competitive when bidding for professionals whose attainments vary widely and whose potential employers are found literally worldwide.[34]

PAY EQUITY

Historically, the average pay for Canadian women has been considerably lower than that for men. In 1967, women's average wages were 46.1 percent of men's average wages. This "wage gap" of 53.9 percent meant that for every dollar earned by a man, a woman earned 46.1 cents. **Table 11.4** shows the most recent wage gap statistics. Some of this gap is due to the fact that women do more part-time work than men, but even when full-year, full-time workers are compared,

TABLE 11.4 | Male/Female Average Earnings Ratio* for Full-Year, Full-Time Workers

Year	Women ($)	Men ($)	Earnings ratio (%)
1997	36,100	52,800	68.3
1998	38,700	53,800	71.9
1999	37,200	54,400	68.4
2000	38,400	54,400	70.6
2001	38,800	55,500	69.9
2002	39,000	55,600	70.2
2003	38,900	55,400	70.2
2004	40,100	57,400	69.9
2005	40,000	56,800	70.5
2006	41,300	57,400	71.9

*Earnings stated in constant year 2006 dollars.
Source: Statistics Canada CANSIM Table 202-0102. www40.statcan.gc.ca/l01/cst101/labor01b-eng.htm (March 23, 2009).

Workforce DIVERSITY

Women Work for Free as of September 17

For women in Ontario, the middle of September means more than the end of summer. It is a stark reminder of the gender pay gap that persists in the province. As of September 17, the year is 71 percent of the way through, and with women in Ontario earning an average of 71 cents for every dollar men earn; it also marks the day women start working for free, according to the Equal Pay Coalition.

With an overall 29 percent gender pay gap, women are effectively denied their fair pay from now until the end of the year while men get their full pay, states the coalition. Ontario's Pay Equity Act, which turned 20 years old in 2008, was supposed to end this devaluation by requiring employers to pay women's and men's jobs the same when they were of comparable value. The pay gap has decreased from 38 percent in 1988 to 29 percent today, but that is still too high, according to the coalition.

Canada ranks 17th among 22 Organization for Economic Cooperation and Development countries and is behind the United States, which has a 23 percent wage gap. The World Economic Forum's *2007 Global Gender Pay Gap Report* highlighted the key role gender "remuneration gaps" play in preventing economies from realizing their full potential. Businesses, communities, and governments all benefit from pay equity enforcement.

Discriminatory pay affects women throughout their lives, beginning with their first jobs and continuing into retirement. Young women graduating from high school earn 27 percent less than male high-school graduates. Young women graduating from university earn 16 percent less than male graduates, but this pay gap widens as their careers progress. The median income of retired women is almost half that of older men. Over a lifetime these pay gaps add up to enormous financial losses with Working Women in the United States estimating the total for each woman to be between US$700 000 and US$2 million, depending on education level.

Source: Adapted from "Women Work for Free as of Sept. 17," *Canadian HR Reporter*, September 18, 2008; and M. Cornish, "Much Work to Be Done on Pay Equity," *Canadian HR Reporter*, February 28, 2008.

---

the gap has stalled at approximately 30 percent since 1995, to the disappointment of pay equity proponents, as discussed in the Workforce Diversity box. The wage gap is narrower for single women than for those who are married and for younger women compared with those who are older.[35]

Moreover, the gap persists even when women have the same qualifications and do the same type of work as men. A 2004 study showed that, two years after graduation, female university graduates in the Maritime provinces working full-time earned 78 percent of the weekly wage of males, even after accounting for differences in field of study, occupation, location, and hours worked.[36]

pay equity Providing equal pay to male-dominated job classes and female-dominated job classes of equal value to the employer.

Although such factors as differences in hours worked, experience levels, education levels, and level of unionization contribute to the wage gap, systemic discrimination is also present.[37] The purpose of pay equity legislation is to redress systemic gender discrimination in compensation for work performed by employees in female-dominated job classes. **Pay equity** requires that equal wages be paid for jobs of equal value or "worth" to the employer, as determined by gender-neutral (i.e., free of any bias based on gender) job evaluation techniques.

The legal process involved can be lengthy. A final decision is still pending in a pay equity complaint filed against Canada Post in 1983 claiming that six thousand clerical workers had been subjected to systemic discrimination.[38] In 2006, the Supreme Court of Canada ruled against a Canadian Human Rights Tribunal decision that female Air Canada flight attendants' jobs could not be compared with those of mainly male mechanics and pilots and sent the case back to the tribunal. The Court condemned Air Canada's use of legal technicalities to delay the case, which began in 1991.[39]

Saskatchewan workers demonstrate for pay equity.

Six provinces (Ontario, Quebec, Manitoba, Nova Scotia, New Brunswick, and Prince Edward Island) have created separate proactive legislation that specifically requires that pay equity be achieved. Ontario and Quebec require pay equity in both the public and the private sectors, whereas the legislation in the other four provinces applies only to the public sector. In the federal jurisdiction and the Yukon (public sector only), human rights legislation requires equal pay for work of equal value.

The wage gap has narrowed since the introduction of pay equity legislation, but there is still no explanation other than systemic discrimination for much of the 30 percent gap that still persists.[40] In the long term, the best way to remove the portion of the wage gap resulting from systemic discrimination is to eliminate male- and female-dominated jobs by ensuring that women have equal access to and are equally represented in all jobs.

Chapter | SUMMARY

1. A total rewards approach considers individual reward components as part of an integrated whole in order to determine the best mix of rewards that are aligned with business strategy and provide employee value, all within the cost constraints of the organization. Alignment is the extent to which rewards support outcomes that are important to achieving the organization's strategic objectives. For example, when competi-

tive advantage relies on relentless customer service, this behaviour should be reinforced. Employee value is created when rewards are meaningful to employees and influence their affiliation with the organization.

2. Establishing pay rates involves three stages: job evaluation (to ensure internal equity), conducting wage/salary surveys (to ensure external equity), and combining job evaluation and salary survey

results to determine pay rates. Job evaluation is aimed at determining the relative worth of jobs within a firm. It compares jobs with one another based on their content, which is usually defined in terms of compensable factors, such as skill, effort, responsibility, and working conditions. Jobs of approximately equal value are combined into pay grades for pay purposes. Salary surveys collect data from other employers in the marketplace who are competing for employees in similar kinds of positions. The wage curve shows the average market wage for each pay grade (or job). It illustrates what the average wage for each grade should be and whether any present wages or salaries are out of line.

3. Competency-based pay plans provide employee compensation based on the skills and knowledge that they are capable of using, rather than the job that they currently hold.

4. The five basic elements of compensation for managers are salary, benefits, short-term incentives, long-term incentives, and perquisites.

5. Pay equity is intended to redress systemic gender discrimination as measured by the wage gap, which indicates that full-time working women make about 70 cents for every dollar made by full-time working men. Pay equity requires equal pay for female-dominated jobs of equal value to male-dominated jobs (where value is determined through job evaluation).

PEARSON
myHRlab™

Test yourself on the material for this chapter at
www.pearsoned.ca/myhrlab

Key | TERMS

benchmark job   *(p. 303)*
broadbanding   *(p. 313)*
classes   *(p. 305)*
classification/grading method   *(p. 305)*
compensable factor   *(p. 303)*
grade/group description   *(p. 305)*
grades   *(p. 305)*
job evaluation   *(p. 303)*

pay equity   *(p. 318)*
pay grade   *(p. 308)*
pay ranges   *(p. 311)*
point method   *(p. 305)*
red circle pay rate   *(p. 314)*
total rewards   *(p. 298)*
wage curve   *(p. 311)*
wage/salary survey   *(p. 308)*

Review and Discussion | QUESTIONS

1. What are the five components of total rewards?

2. Describe what is meant by the term "benchmark job."

3. Identify and briefly describe the three stages in establishing pay rates.

4. What are the pros and cons of the following methods of job evaluation: ranking, classification, factor comparison, point method?

5. Explain the term "competencies," and explain the differences among core, functional, and behavioural competencies.

6. Explain what is meant by the market-pricing approach in evaluating professional jobs.

7. Explain what pay equity legislation is intended to accomplish, what action is required by the legislation in order to accomplish it, and how effective the legislation has been in accomplishing its objectives.

Critical Thinking | QUESTIONS

1. Do you think that transactional or relational rewards have more impact on overall organizational performance?

2. Why do companies pay for compensation surveys where job matching may be difficult rather than conducting their own surveys?

3. It was recently reported in the news that the base pay for Canadian bank CEOs range in the millions of dollars, and the pay for the governor of the Bank of Canada is less than half of that of the lowest paid bank CEO. How do you account for this difference? Should anything be done about this? Why or why not?

4. Do you agree with paying people for competencies and skills that they are rarely required to use on the job?

5. What are some of the potential reasons that gender-based pay discrimination is so hard to eradicate?

6. Why do you think there is such a discrepancy between the pay rates of executives and employees? Is this fair? Why or why not?

Experiential | EXERCISES

1. Working individually or in groups, conduct salary surveys for the positions of entry-level accountant and entry-level chemical engineer. What sources did you use, and what conclusions did you reach? If you were the HR manager for a local engineering firm, what would you recommend that each job be paid?

2. Obtain information on the pay grades and rate ranges for each grade at your college or university. Do they appear to be broadbands? If not, propose specific broadbands that could be implemented.

3. You have been asked by the owner of your medium-sized import and export company (200 + people) to develop a way to standardize pay ranges for different jobs in the company. He says he is tired of employees complaining about the pay they get compared to others and is concerned that if he does nothing someone will complain about inequitable pay practices. Outline the steps you will follow to do this. Make sure to give a rationale for the type of job evaluation system you propose as well as for the method you suggest to obtain comparable salary data. The jobs he is most concerned about are

   - sales representative
   - shipping and receiving manager
   - multilingual contract negotiator
   - accounts receivable clerk
   - shipping clerk.

4. You are the HR manager in a large construction firm headquartered in Edmonton. Most administrative staff are also in Edmonton. You have regional and local site offices across the country. Draft a memo to employees about your company's new pay for knowledge and skills policy. Make sure to document at least one fully complete section on how this policy will be administered. Your professor may give you some ideas on what might be considered or you may create your own circumstances under which pay for knowledge and skills will be applied.

Running | CASE

Running Case: LearnInMotion.com

The New Pay Plan

LearnInMotion.com does not have a formal wage structure, nor does it have rate ranges or use compensable factors. Jennifer and Pierre base wage rates almost exclusively on those prevailing in the surrounding community, and they temper these by trying to maintain some semblance of equity among what workers with different responsibilities are paid. As Jennifer says, "Deciding what to pay dot-com employees is an adventure: Wages for jobs like web designer and online salesperson are always climbing dramatically, and there's not an awful lot of loyalty involved when someone else offers you 30 percent or 40 percent more than you're currently making." Jennifer and Pierre are therefore continually scanning various sources to see what others are paying for positions like theirs. They peruse the want ads almost every day and conduct informal surveys among their friends in other dot-coms. Once or twice a week, they also check compensation websites, like Monster.ca.

Although the company has taken a somewhat unstructured, informal approach to establishing its compensation plan, the firm's actual salary schedule is guided by several basic pay policies. For one thing, the difficulty they had recruiting and hiring employees caused them to pay salaries 10 to 20 percent above what the market would seem to indicate. Jennifer and Pierre write this off to the need to get and keep good employees. As Jennifer says, "If you've got ten web designers working for you, you can afford to go a few extra weeks without hiring another one, but when you need one designer and you have none, you've got to do whatever you can to get that one designer hired." Their somewhat informal approach has also led to some potential inequities. For example, the two salespeople—one a man, the other a woman—are earning different salaries, and the man is making about 30 percent more. If everything were going fine—for instance, if sales were up, and the calendar was functional— perhaps they wouldn't be worried. However, the fact is that the two owners are wondering if a more structured pay plan would be a good idea. Now they want you, their management consultant, to help them decide what to do.

QUESTIONS

1 Describe the total rewards model and its five components and whether it would benefit LearnInMotion.

2 What are some basic considerations in determining pay rates that LearnInMotion must be aware of?

3 Utilizing the three stages of establishing pay rates, provide recommendations to LearnInMotion in regard to job evaluation, wage/salary surveys, and how to combine the first two steps to determine pay rates for LearnInMotion's jobs.

Case | INCIDENT

Salary Inequities at Acme Manufacturing

Joe Blackenship was trying to figure out what to do about a problem salary situation that he had in his plant. Blackenship recently took over as president of Acme Manufacturing. The founder, Bill George, had been president for 35 years. The company is family-owned and located in a small eastern Manitoba town. It has approximately 250 employees and is the largest employer in the community. Blackenship is a member of the family that owns Acme, but he had never worked for the company prior to becoming president. He has an MBA and a law degree, plus 15 years of management experience with a large manufacturing organization, where he was senior vice-president of human resources when he made his move to Acme.

A short time after joining Acme, Blackenship started to notice that there was considerable inequity in the pay structure for salaried employees. A discussion with the HR director led him to believe that salaried employees' pay was very much a matter of individual bargaining with the past president. Hourly paid factory workers were not part of the problem because they were unionized and their wages were set by collective bargaining. An examination of the salaried payroll showed that there were 25 employees, whose pay ranged from that of the president to that of the receptionist. A closer examination showed that 14 of the salaried employees were female. Three of these were front-line factory supervisors, and one was the HR director. The rest were non-management employees.

This examination also showed that the HR director appeared to be underpaid and that the three female supervisors were paid somewhat less than any of the male supervisors. However, there were no similar supervisory jobs in which there were both male and female incumbents. When asked, the HR director said that she thought the female supervisors may have been paid at a lower rate mainly because they were women, and perhaps George did not think that women needed as much money because they had working husbands. However, she added the thought that they might be paid less because they supervised lesser-skilled employees than did male supervisors. Blackenship was not sure that this was true.

The company from which Blackenship had moved had a good job evaluation system. Although he was thoroughly familiar and capable with this compensation tool, Blackenship did not have time to make a job evaluation study at Acme. Therefore, he decided to hire a compensation consultant from a nearby university to help him. Together, they decided that all 25 salaried jobs should be in the same job evaluation cluster, that a modified ranking system of job evaluation should be used, and that the job descriptions recently completed by the HR director were current, accurate, and usable in the study.

The job evaluation showed that there was no evidence of serious inequities or discrimination in the nonmanagement jobs, but that the HR director and the three female supervisors were being underpaid relative to comparable male salaried employees.

Blackenship was not sure what to do. He knew that if the underpaid supervisors took their case to

the local pay equity commission, the company could be found guilty of sex discrimination and then have to pay considerable back wages. He was afraid that if he gave these women an immediate salary increase large enough to bring them up to where they should be, the male supervisors would be upset and the female supervisors might comprehend the total situation and want back pay. The HR director told Blackenship that the female supervisors had never complained about pay differences, and they probably did not know the law to any extent.

The HR director agreed to take a sizable salary increase with no back pay, so this part of the problem was solved. Blackenship believed that he had four choices relative to the female supervisors:

- to do nothing

- to increase the female supervisors' salaries gradually

- to increase their salaries immediately

- to call the three supervisors into his office, discuss the situation with them, and jointly decide what to do.

QUESTIONS

1   What would you do if you were Blackenship?

2   How do you think the company got into a situation like this in the first place?

3   Why would you suggest that Blackenship pursue your suggested alternative?

Source: Based on a case prepared by Professor James C. Hodgetts of the Fogelman College of Business and Economics at the University of Memphis. All names are disguised. Used with permission.

For additional cases and exercise material, go to **www.pearsoned.ca/myhrlab**

CHAPTER 12

LEARNING OUTCOMES

DISCUSS how piecework, standard hour, and team or group incentive plans are used.

EXPLAIN how to use short-term and long-term incentives for managers and executives.

ANALYZE the main advantages and disadvantages of salary plans and commission plans for salespeople.

EXPLAIN why money is somewhat less important as an incentive for professional employees than it is for other employees.

COMPARE the three types of organization-wide incentive plans.

EXPLAIN under what conditions it is best to use an incentive plan.

ANALYZE the emerging emphasis on employee recognition.

PAY-FOR-PERFORMANCE AND FINANCIAL INCENTIVES

REQUIRED PROFESSIONAL CAPABILITIES (RPC)

- Monitors the competitiveness of the total compensation strategy on an ongoing basis

MONEY AND MOTIVATION

variable pay Any plan that ties pay to productivity or profitability.

RPC

Monitors the competitiveness of the total compensation strategy on an ongoing basis

The use of financial incentives—financial rewards paid to workers whose production exceeds some predetermined standard—is not new; it was popularized by Frederick Taylor in the late 1800s. As a supervisory employee of the Midvale Steel Company, Taylor had become concerned with the tendency of employees to work at the slowest pace possible and produce at the minimum acceptable level. What especially intrigued him was the fact that some of these same workers still had the energy to run home and work on their cabins, even after a 12-hour day. Taylor knew that if he could find some way to harness this energy during the workday, huge productivity gains would be achieved.

Today's efforts to achieve the organization's strategy through motivated employees include financial incentives, pay-for-performance, and variable compensation plans. These types of compensation are now commonly called **variable pay**, meaning any plan that links pay with productivity, profitability, or some other measure of organizational performance. Employers continue to increase their use of variable pay plans while holding salary increases to modest levels. More than 80 percent of Canadian employers have one or more types of variable pay plans in place.[1] Of those, many have more than one type of plan, as shown in **Figure 12.1.**

Variable pay facilitates management of total compensation by keeping base pay inflation controlled. The fundamental premise of variable pay plans is that top performers must get top pay in order to secure their commitment to the organization. Thus, accurate performance appraisal or measurable outcomes is a precondition of effective pay-for-performance plans. Another important prerequisite for effective variable pay plans is "line of sight," or the extent to which an employee can relate his or her daily work to the achievement of overall corporate goals. Employees need to understand corporate strategy and how their work as individual employees is important to the achievement of strategic objectives.[2]

The entire thrust of such programs is to treat workers like partners and get them to think of the business and its goals as their own. It is thus reasonable to pay them more like partners, too, by linking their pay more directly to performance. For example, the owners of a Surrey, B.C.–based trucking company handed out bonus cheques totalling more than $400 000 to more than 400 employees in August 2005. Over the preceding five years, the owners had

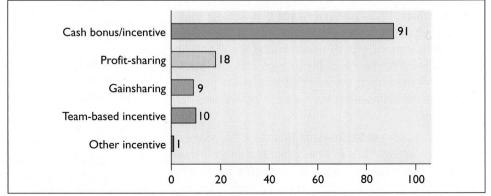

FIGURE 12.1 | Variable Pay Programs, 2008 (n = 320; per cent; based on organizations with at least one annual variable pay plan in place)

Note: Figures do not add to 100 because some respondents have more than one plan.

Source: A. Cowan, *Compensation Planning Outlook 2009.* (Ottawa: Conference Board of Canada, 2008), p. 7. Reprinted by permission of The Conference Board of Canada, Ottawa.

grown Coastal Pacific Xpress (CPX) by 500 percent and decided to reward their employees for their hard work.[3]

Types of Incentive Plans

There are several types of incentive plans. Individual incentive programs give income over and above base salary to individual employees who meet a specific individual performance standard. Informal incentives may be awarded, generally to individual employees, for accomplishments that are not readily measured by a standard, such as "to recognize the long hours that this employee put in last month," or "to recognize exemplary customer service this week." Group incentive programs are like individual incentive plans, but they provide payments over and above base salary to all team members when the group or team collectively meets a specified standard for performance, productivity, or other work-related behaviour. Organization-wide incentive plans provide monetary incentives to all employees of the organization. Examples are profit-sharing plans that provide employees with a share of the organization's profits in a specified period, and gainsharing programs designed to reward employees for improvements in organizational productivity. Finally, non-monetary recognition programs motivate employees through praise and expressions of appreciation for their work.

It is important to ensure that whatever incentive is being provided is appealing to the individual receiving it. Demographic factors can have an impact on what is appealing, as discussed in the Workforce Diversity box.

Workforce DIVERSITY

Targeting Incentives for Life Stage

In developing incentive programs, which are targeted to job function and performance level, employers should also consider the demographics of their workforce. For instance, what motivates a Generation X employee may not have an impact on a baby boomer in the same company. Understanding each employee's life stage will help employers determine the most effective incentive program approach, which results in a workforce that is satisfied, engaged, and more likely to perform better and remain with the company.

Traditionalists (1922–1946): Rewards that work for traditionalists include flexible schedules that allow them to work seasonally or as time permits; health and fitness rewards that help them enjoy this life stage; and entertainment rewards that they would not purchase for themselves, such as computers and cell phones.

Boomers (1946–1965): Rewards that work for boomers include recognition and being appreciated for their work; travel rewards, such as adventure travel; and luxury and health-related awards, such as spas, high-end fitness equipment, and personal chefs.

Generation X (1966–1980): Rewards that work for this generation include gadgets and high-tech rewards that are state-of-the-art technology; work/life balance rewards, such as extra vacation days and onsite daycare; and flexibility to allow time for family, friends, and meaningful life experiences.

Generation Y (1981+): Rewards that work for this group include relationship enhancers, such as electronic communications equipment, home entertainment items, and dining experiences; personalized rewards where they can choose colours and accessories; and charitable rewards, like time off to volunteer for non-profit organizations and charitable donations made in their names.

Motivation is highly personal. Companies that provide rewards and recognition that are meaningful to employees based on their stage in the life cycle will be more successful in creating the right environment for maximum performance.

Source: Adapted from R. Stotz, "Targeting Employee Incentives for Maximum Performance," *Workspan*, June 2006, pp. 46–48. Reprinted with permission of WorldatWork, Scottsdale, AZ. www.worldatwork.org.

For simplicity, these plans will be discussed as follows: incentives for operations employees; incentives for senior managers and executives; incentives for salespeople; incentives primarily for other managers and professional employees (merit pay); and organization-wide incentives.

INCENTIVES FOR OPERATIONS EMPLOYEES

Piecework Plans

piecework A system of pay based on the number of items processed by each individual worker in a unit of time, such as items per hour or items per day.

Several incentive plans are particularly well suited for use with operations employees, such as those doing production work.[4] **Piecework** is the oldest incentive plan and still the most commonly used. Earnings are tied directly to what the worker produces; the person is paid a piece rate for each unit that he or she produces. Thus, if Tom Smith gets $0.40 per piece for stamping out door jambs, then he would make $40 for stamping out 100 a day and $80 for stamping out 200.

Developing a workable piece-rate plan requires both job evaluation and (usually) industrial engineering. Job evaluation enables firms to assign an hourly wage rate to the job in question. The crucial issue in piece-rate planning is the production standard, however, and this standard is usually developed by industrial engineers. Production standards are stated in terms of a standard number of minutes per unit or a standard number of units per hour. In Tom Smith's case, the job evaluation indicated that his door-jamb stamping job was worth $10 per hour. The industrial engineer determined that 20 jambs per hour was the standard production rate. Therefore, the piece rate (for each door jamb) was $10 ÷ 20 = $0.50 per door jamb.

straight piecework plan A set payment for each piece produced or processed in a factory or shop.

With a **straight piecework plan,** Tom Smith would be paid on the basis of the number of door jambs that he produced; there would be no guaranteed minimum wage. However, after passage of employment/labour standards legislation, it became necessary for most employers to guarantee their workers a minimum wage. With a **guaranteed piecework plan,** Tom Smith would be paid the minimum wage whether or not he stamped out the number of door jambs required to make minimum wage—for example, 18 pieces if minimum wage is $9 per hour. As an incentive he would, however, also be paid at the piece rate of $0.50 for each unit that he produced over the number required to make minimum wage.

guaranteed piecework plan The minimum hourly wage plus an incentive for each piece produced above a set number of pieces per hour.

Piecework generally implies straight piecework, a strict proportionality between results and rewards regardless of the level of output. Thus, in Smith's case, he continues to get $0.50 apiece for stamping out door jambs, even if he stamps out many more than planned (say, 500 per day). Other types of piecework incentive plans call for a sharing of productivity gains between worker and employer such that the worker does not receive full credit for all production above normal.[5]

Advantages and Disadvantages

Piecework incentive plans have several advantages. They are simple to calculate and easily understood by employees. Piece-rate plans appear equitable in principle, and their incentive value can be powerful since rewards are directly tied to performance.

Piecework also has some disadvantages. A main one is its somewhat unsavoury reputation among many employees, based on some employers' habits of arbitrarily raising production standards whenever they found their workers earning "excessive" wages. In addition, piece rates are stated in monetary terms (like $0.50 per piece). Thus, when a new job evaluation results in a new hourly wage rate, the piece rate must also be revised; this can be a big clerical chore. Another disadvantage is more subtle: Since the piece rate is quoted on a per-piece basis, in workers' minds production standards become tied inseparably to the amount of money earned. When an attempt is made to revise production standards, it meets considerable worker resistance, even if the revision is fully justified.[6]

In fact, the industrial-engineered specificity of piecework plans represents the seeds of piecework's biggest disadvantage these days. Piecework plans tend to be tailor-made for relatively specialized jobs in which employees do basically the same narrow set of tasks over and over again many times a day. This, in turn, fosters a certain rigidity: Employees become preoccupied with producing the number of units needed and are less willing to concern themselves with meeting quality standards or switching from job to job (since doing so could reduce the person's productivity).[7] Employees tend to be trained to perform only a limited number of tasks. Similarly, attempts to introduce new technology or innovative processes may be more likely to fail, insofar as they require major adjustments to engineered standards and negotiations with employees. Equipment tends not to be as well maintained, since employees are focusing on maximizing each machine's output.

Such problems as these have led some firms to drop their piecework plans (as well as their standard hour plans, discussed next) and to substitute team-based incentive plans or programs, such as gainsharing, which will also be discussed later in this chapter.

Standard Hour Plan

standard hour plan A plan by which a worker is paid a basic hourly rate plus an extra percentage of his or her base rate for production exceeding the standard per hour or per day. It is similar to piecework payment but is based on a percentage premium.

The **standard hour plan** is like the piece-rate plan, with one major difference. With a piece-rate plan, the worker is paid a particular rate for each piece that he or she produces. With the standard hour plan, the worker is rewarded by a *premium that equals the percentage by which his or her performance exceeds the standard*. The plan assumes the worker has a guaranteed base rate.

As an example, suppose that the base rate for Smith's job is $10 per hour. (The base rate may, but need not, equal the hourly rate determined by the job evaluation.) Assume also that the production standard for Smith's job is 20 units per hour, or 3 minutes per unit. Suppose that in one day (8 hours) Smith produces 200 door jambs. According to the production standard, this should have taken Smith 10 hours (200 divided by 20 per hour); instead it took him 8 hours. He produced at a rate that was 25 percent higher than the standard rate. The standard rate would be 8 hours times 20 (units per hour) = 160: Smith actually produced 40 more, or 200. He will, therefore, be paid at a rate 25 percent (40/160) above his base rate for the day. His base rate was $10 per hour times 8 hours, which equals $80, so he will be paid 1.25 times $80, or $100 for the day.

The standard hour plan has most of the advantages of the piecework plan and is fairly simple to compute and easy to understand. The incentive is expressed in units of time instead of in monetary terms (as it is with the piece-rate system). Therefore, there is less tendency on the part of workers to link their production standard with their pay. Furthermore, the clerical job of re-computing piece rates whenever hourly wage rates are re-evaluated is avoided.

Team or Group Incentive Plans

team or group incentive plan
A plan in which a production standard is set for a specific work group and its members are paid incentives if the group exceeds the production standard.

There are several ways in which to implement **team or group incentive plans**.[8] One is to set work standards for each member of the group and maintain a count of the output of each member. Members are then paid based on one of three formulas: (1) All members receive the pay earned by the highest producer; (2) all members receive the pay earned by the lowest producer; or (3) all members receive payment equal to the average pay earned by the group.

The second approach is to set a production standard based on the final output of the group as a whole; all members then receive the same pay, based on the piece rate that exists for the group's job. The group incentive can be based on either the piece rate or standard hour plan, but the latter is somewhat more prevalent.

A third option is to choose a measurable definition of group performance or productivity that the group can control. For instance, broad criteria, such as total labour-hours per final product, could be used; piecework's engineered standards are thus not necessarily required here.[9]

There are several reasons to use team incentive plans. Sometimes, several jobs are interrelated, as they are on project teams. Here, one worker's performance reflects not only his or her own effort but that of co-workers as well; thus, team incentives make sense. Team plans also reinforce group planning and problem solving and help to ensure that collaboration takes place. In Japan, employees are rewarded as a group in order to reduce jealousy, make group members indebted to one another (as they would be to the group), and encourage a sense of cooperation. There tends to be less bickering among group members over who has "tight" production standards and who has loose ones. Group incentive plans also facilitate on-the-job training, since each member of the group has an interest in getting new members trained as quickly as possible.[10]

A group incentive plan's chief disadvantage is that each worker's rewards are no longer based solely on his or her own effort. To the extent that the person does not see his or her effort leading to the desired reward, a group plan may be less effective at motivating employees than an individual plan is.

Group incentive plans have been found to be more effective when there are high levels of communication with employees about the specifics of the plan, when there is strong worker involvement in the plan's design and implementation, and when group members perceive the plan as fair.[11]

INCENTIVES FOR SENIOR MANAGERS AND EXECUTIVES

Most employers award their senior managers and executives a bonus or an incentive because of the role they play in determining divisional and corporate profitability.[12]

Short-Term Incentives: The Annual Bonus

More than 90 percent of firms in Canada with variable pay plans provide an *annual bonus*.[13] Unlike salaries, which rarely decline with reduced performance, short-term incentive bonuses can easily result in an increase or decrease of 25 percent or more in total pay relative to the previous year. Three basic issues should be considered when awarding short-term incentives: eligibility, fund-size determination, and individual awards.

Jim Balsillie, co-CEO of Research In Motion, receives very high bonuses in addition to his regular compensation.

Eligibility

Eligibility is usually decided in one of three ways. The first criterion is *key position*. Here, a job-by-job review is conducted to identify the key jobs (typically only line jobs) that have a measurable impact on profitability. The second approach to determining eligibility is to set a *salary-level* cutoff point; all employees earning over that threshold amount are automatically eligible for consideration for short-term incentives. Finally, eligibility can be determined by *salary grade*. This is a refinement of the salary cutoff approach and assumes that all employees at a certain grade or above should be eligible for the short-term incentive program. The simplest approach is just to use salary level as a cutoff.[14]

The size of the bonus is usually greater for top-level executives. Thus, an executive earning $150 000 in salary may be able to earn another 80 percent of his or her salary as a bonus, while a manager in the same firm earning $80 000 can earn only another 30 percent. Similarly, a supervisor might be able to earn up to 15 percent of his or her base salary in bonuses. Average bonuses range from a low of 10 percent to a high of 80 percent or more: a typical company might establish a plan whereby executives could earn 45 percent of base salary, managers 25 percent, and supervisors 12 percent.

How Much to Pay Out (Fund Size)

Next, a decision must be made regarding the fund size—the total amount of bonus money that will be available—and there are several formulas to do this. Some companies use a *nondeductible formula*. Here a straight percentage (usually of the company's net income) is used to create the short-term incentive fund. Others use a *deductible formula* on the assumption that the short-term incentive fund should begin to accumulate only after the firm has met a specified level of earnings.

In practice, what proportion of profits is usually paid out as bonuses? There are no hard-and-fast rules, and some firms do not even have a formula for developing the bonus fund. One alternative is to reserve a minimum amount of the profits, say 10 percent, for safeguarding shareholders' investments, and then to establish a fund for bonuses equal to 20 percent of the corporate operating profit before taxes in excess of this base amount. Thus, if the operating profits were $100 000, then the management bonus fund might be 20 percent of $90 000, or $18 000. Other illustrative formulas used for determining the executive bonus fund are as follows:

- 10 percent of net income after deducting 5 percent of average capital invested in the business
- 12.5 percent of the amount by which net income exceeds 6 percent of shareholders' equity
- 12 percent of net earnings after deducting 6 percent of net capital.[15]

Determining Individual Awards

The third issue is determining the *individual awards* to be paid. In some cases, the amount is determined on a discretionary basis (usually by the employee's boss), but typically a target bonus is set for each eligible position and adjustments are then made for greater or less than targeted performance. A maximum amount, perhaps double the target bonus, may be set. Performance ratings are obtained for each manager and preliminary bonus estimates are computed. Estimates for the total amount of money to be spent on short-term incentives are thereby made and compared with the bonus fund available. If necessary, the individual estimates are then adjusted.

A related question is whether managers will receive bonuses based on individual performance, team performance, corporate performance, or some combination of these. Keep in mind that there is a difference between a profit-sharing plan and a true individual incentive bonus. In a profit-sharing plan, each person gets a bonus based on the company's results, regardless of the person's actual effort. With a true individual incentive, it is the manager's individual effort and performance that are rewarded with a bonus.

An Ethical | Dilemma

Is it ethical to provide potentially large bonuses to managers and executives on a purely discretionary basis, not necessarily related to performance?

Here, again, there are no hard-and-fast rules. Top-level executive bonuses are generally tied to overall corporate results (or divisional results if the executive is, say, the vice-president of a major division). The assumption is that corporate results reflect the person's individual performance. However, as one moves further down the chain of command, corporate profits become a less accurate gauge of a manager's contribution. For supervisory staff or the heads of functional departments, the person's individual performance, rather than corporate results, is a more logical determinant of his or her bonus.

Many experts argue that, in most organizations, managerial and executive-level bonuses should be tied to both organizational and individual performance, and there are several ways to do this.[16] Perhaps the simplest is the *split-award method*, which breaks the bonus into two parts. Here, the manager actually gets two separate bonuses, one based on his or her individual effort and one based on the organization's overall performance. Thus, a manager might be eligible for an individual performance bonus of up to $10 000 but receive an individual performance bonus of only $8000 at the end of the year, based on his or her individual performance evaluation. In addition, though, the person might also receive a second bonus of $8000 based on the company's profits for the year. Thus, even if there were no company profits, the high-performing manager would still get an individual performance bonus.

One drawback to this approach is that it pays too much to the marginal performer, who, even if his or her own performance is mediocre, at least gets that second, company-based bonus. One way to get around this problem is to use the *multiplier method*. For example, a manager whose individual performance was "poor" might not even receive a company-performance-based bonus, on the assumption that the bonus should be a *product* of individual *and* corporate performance. When either is very poor, the product is zero.

Whichever approach is used, outstanding performers should get substantially larger awards than do other managers. They are people that the company cannot afford to lose, and their performance should always be adequately rewarded by the organization's incentive system. Conversely, marginal or below-average performers should never receive awards that are normal or average, and poor performers should be awarded nothing. The money saved on those people should be given to above-average performers.[17]

Long-Term Incentives

Long-term incentives are intended to motivate and reward top management for the firm's long-term growth and prosperity and to inject a long-term perspective into executive decisions. If only short-term criteria are used, a manager could, for instance, increase profitability in one year by reducing plant maintenance;

this tactic might, however, reduce profits over the next two or three years. This issue of long- versus short-term perspective has received considerable attention in the past several years as shareholders have become increasingly critical of management focus on short-term returns at the expense of long-term increase in stock price. The deep economic recession that began in late 2008 following the sub-prime mortgage lending crisis resulted in increasing regulatory focus on this type of compensation.

Long-term incentives are also intended to encourage executives to stay with the company by giving them the opportunity to accumulate capital (in the form of company stock) based on the firm's long-term success. Long-term incentives or **capital accumulation programs** are most often reserved for senior executives but have more recently begun to be extended to employees at lower organizational levels.[18] Approximately 60 percent of Canadian private sector organizations provide long-term incentives. They are rarely provided to public sector employees.[19]

Some of the most common long-term incentive plans (for capital accumulation) in Canada are stock options, performance share unit plans, restricted share unit plans, and deferred share unit plans.[20] The popularity of these plans changes over time because of economic conditions and trends, internal company financial pressures, changing attitudes toward long-term incentives, and changes in tax law, as well as other factors. **Figure 12.2** illustrates the popularity of various long-term incentive plans.

> **capital accumulation programs** Long-term incentives most often reserved for senior executives.

Stock Options

> **stock option** The right to purchase a stated number of shares of a company stock at today's price at some time in the future.

The **stock option** is the most popular long-term incentive in Canada, but its use is decreasing. Fifty-three percent of organizations using long-term incentives provided stock options in 2008, compared with 57 percent in 2005 and 72 percent in 2002.[21] A stock option is the right to purchase a specific number of shares of company stock at a specific price during a period of time. Sometimes a vesting (waiting) period is required to ensure that the employee has contributed to any increase in stock price. The executive thus hopes to profit by exercising his or her

FIGURE 12.2 | Long-Term Incentive Plans, 2008 (n = 170; per cent; based on organizations with at least one LTIP in place)

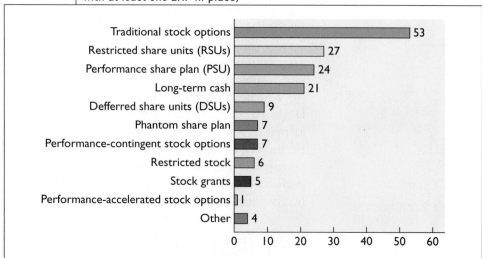

Note: Figures do not add to 100 because some respondents have more than one plan.

Source: A. Cowan, *Compensation Planning Outlook 2009.* (Ottawa: Conference Board of Canada, 2008), p. 11. Reprinted by permission of The Conference Board of Canada, Ottawa.

FIGURE 12.3 | Stock Options

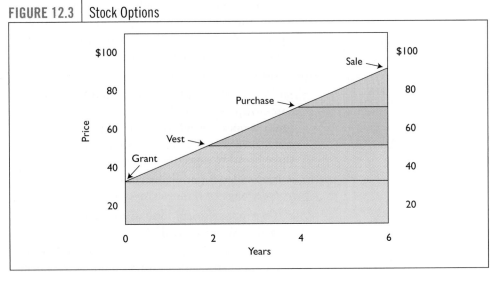

Source: B.R. Ellig, "Executive Pay: A Primer," *Compensation and Benefits Review*, January/February 2003, p. 48. © 2003. Reprinted with permission of Sage Publications, Inc.

option to buy the shares in the future but at today's price. The assumption is that the price of the stock will go up, rather than going down or staying the same. As shown in **Figure 12.3**, if shares provided at an option price of $20 per share are exercised (bought) later for $20 when the market price is $60 per share and sold on the stock market when the market price is $80 per share, a cash gain of $60 per share results. Often, part of the gain is needed to meet income tax liabilities that are triggered when the options are exercised. Stock options are attractive from a taxation perspective in Canada, as only 75 percent of the gain on exercising the options is taxable. Thus, stock option plans are often seen as a cash windfall with no downside risk but unlimited upside potential.[22]

Unfortunately, stock price depends to a significant extent on considerations outside the executive's control, such as general economic conditions and investor sentiment. An executive performing valiantly in a declining market or troubled industry may receive nothing, since stock options are worthless if share prices don't rise. This is a particularly important concern in today's volatile stock market.[23] However, stock price is affected relative to the overall stock market by the firm's profitability and growth, and to the extent that the executive can affect these factors, the stock option can be an incentive.

One of the interesting trends in stock options as long-term incentives is that, increasingly, they are not just for high-level managers and executives—or even just managers and executives—anymore. PepsiCo, Starbucks, Telus, and many other companies have broad-based stock option plans that include employees below the executive level. The trend toward broad-based plans is aimed at providing support for the competitive strategies being pursued by many firms today. Such companies have been asking more from employees than ever before, but employees often feel that they are corporate "partners" in name only, working harder but receiving little in return. In response,

> [c]ompanies are increasingly interested in drawing employees into the new deal by implementing broad-based stock option plans. By giving stock options to non-executives, companies make good the promise of letting employees share in the company's success.[24]

Proposals have been made to require that stock options be shown as an expense on company financial statements because the excessive issuing of options dilutes share values for shareholders and creates a distorted impression of the true value of a company. Guidelines used by the Canada Pension Plan Investment Board state the following:

> Stock options are a less effective and less efficient form of compensation than direct share ownership in aligning the interests of directors with those of shareholders, (and) it does not motivate the executive to enhance long-term corporate performance. Stock-based compensation is superior to option-based compensation plans for three broad reasons:
>
> • It provides better alignment of interest of employees with shareholders (across a wide range of future share prices);
>
> • It is a more efficient form of compensation (in terms of the perceived value received by the executive); and
>
> • It alters the capital structure in a more predictable way (with less potential dilution and more straightforward accounting treatment).[25]

Plans Providing Share "Units"

Although the use of stock options persists, a new approach based on providing "units" instead of stock has become increasingly common.[26] Executives are granted a specified number of units whose value is equal to (and fluctuates with) a company's share price, subject to certain conditions. A *performance share unit plan* provides units subject to the achievement of pre-determined financial targets, such as profit or growth in earnings per share (often over a multi-year period). If the performance goals are met, then the value of the units is paid to the executive in cash or stock. The units have no value if the pre-established performance criteria are not met. In a *restricted share unit plan*, units are promised to the executive but will be forfeited if an executive leaves the company before a vesting period (typically three years). If the executive is still employed at the company after the vesting period, the full value of the units based on the current stock price is payable in cash or stock. In a *deferred share unit plan*, units are promised to the executive but are only payable when the executive leaves the company.

Relating Strategy to Executive Compensation

Executive compensation is more likely to be effective if it is appropriately linked to corporate strategy.[27] Few HR practices have as much connection to strategy as does how the company crafts its long-term incentives. Whether expanding sales through joint ventures abroad, consolidating operations and downsizing the workforce, or some other tactic, few strategies can be accomplished in just one or two years. As a result, the long-term signals that are sent to executives regarding the results and activities that will (or will not) be rewarded can have an impact on whether or not the firm's strategy is implemented effectively. For example, a strategy to boost sales by expanding abroad might suggest linking incentives to increased sales abroad. A cost-reduction strategy might instead emphasize linking incentives to improved profit margins.

Compensation experts therefore suggest defining the strategic context for the executive compensation plan before creating the compensation package itself, as follows:[28]

1. Define the internal and external issues that face the company and its business objectives—boosting sales abroad, downsizing, and so on.

Strategic HR

Bank CEOs Take a Pay Cut

Top executives at some of Canada's biggest banks are taking pay cuts in the face of falling stock prices and profits. At RBC, CEO Gordon Nixon voluntarily turned down nearly $5 million in deferred shares and stock options. Before giving up these rewards, Nixon would have taken home $8.75 million in salary, bonus, and equity-based rewards in 2008. This is down from $10.9 million in 2007. RBC failed to meet most of its 2008 financial goals and its annual profits dropped by 17 percent.

The Bank of Nova Scotia slashed CEO Rick Waugh's compensation package by 20 percent from $10.1 million in 2007 to $7.5 million in 2008. His base salary remained the same at $1 million, but his bonus was cut by nearly 70 percent to $500 000, which he took in deferred stock units. The bank's earnings per share fell by nearly one-quarter and revenue dropped by 5.6 percent in 2008.

Bank of Montreal CEO William Downs received $6.38 million in total compensation in 2008, a 9.4 percent increase from 2007, but announced on February 2 that he was giving up both mid-term and long-term compensation worth $4.1 million.

The three banks are facing a proposal that would give shareholders a vote on executive compensation and a separate resolution calling for a comprehensive review of executive pay.

Source: Adapted from "Bank CEOs take a pay cut," *Canadian HR Reporter*, February 3, 2009.

2. Based on the strategic aims, shape each component of the executive compensation package and then group the components into a balanced whole. Include a stock option plan to give the executive compensation package the special character it needs to meet the unique needs of the executives and the company.

3. Check the executive compensation plan for compliance with all legal and regulatory requirements and for tax effectiveness.

4. Install a process for reviewing and evaluating the executive compensation plan whenever a major business change occurs.

The Strategic HR box illustrates changes made in executive compensation at three of Canada's major banks as a result of the unexpected economic recession that began in late 2008.

INCENTIVES FOR SALESPEOPLE

Sales compensation plans have typically relied heavily on incentives (sales commissions), although this varies by industry. In the real estate industry, for instance, salespeople are paid entirely via commissions, while in the pharmaceutical industry, salespeople tend to be paid a salary. However, the most prevalent approach is to use a combination of salary and commissions to compensate salespeople.[29]

Sales Compensation
www.davekahle.com/article/getem.htm

The widespread use of incentives for salespeople is due to three factors: tradition, the unsupervised nature of most sales work, and the assumption that incentives are needed to motivate salespeople. The pros and cons of salary, commission, and combination plans follow.

Salary Plan

In a salary plan, salespeople are paid a fixed salary, although there may be occasional incentives in the form of bonuses, sales contest prizes, and the like. There are several reasons to use straight salary. It works well when the main sales objective is prospecting (finding new clients) or when the salesperson is mostly involved in account servicing, such as developing and executing product training programs for a distributor's sales force or participating in national and local trade shows.[30] Jobs like these are often found in industries that sell technical products. This is one reason why the aerospace and transportation equipment industries have a relatively heavy emphasis on salary plans for their salespeople.

There are advantages to paying salespeople on a straight salary basis. Salespeople know in advance what their income will be, and the employer also has fixed, predictable sales force expenses. Straight salary makes it simple to switch territories or quotas or to reassign salespeople, and it can develop a high degree of loyalty among the sales staff. Commissions tend to shift the salesperson's emphasis to making the sale rather than to prospecting and cultivating long-term customers. A long-term perspective is encouraged by straight salary compensation.

The main disadvantage is that salary plans do not depend on results.[31] In fact, salaries are often tied to seniority rather than to performance, which can be demotivating to potentially high-performing salespeople who see seniority—not performance—being rewarded.

Commission Plan

Commission plans pay salespeople in direct proportion to their sales: They pay for results and only for results. The commission plan has several advantages. Salespeople have the greatest possible incentive, and there is a tendency to attract high-performing salespeople who see that effort will clearly lead to rewards. Sales costs are proportional to sales rather than fixed, and the company's selling investment is reduced. The commission basis is also easy to understand and compute.

The commission plan also has drawbacks, however. Salespeople focus on making a sale and on high-volume items; cultivating dedicated customers and

An Ethical | Dilemma

Is it fair to compensate sales employees on a 100-percent commission basis with no financial security?

working to push hard-to-sell items may be neglected. Wide variances in income between salespeople may occur; this can lead to a feeling that the plan is inequitable. More serious is the fact that salespeople are encouraged to neglect other duties, like servicing small accounts. In addition, pay is often excessive in boom times and very low in recessions.

Recent research evidence presents further insights into the impact of sales commissions. One study addressed whether paying salespeople on commission "without a financial net" might induce more salespeople to leave. The participants in this study were 225 field sales representatives from a telecommunications company. Results showed that paying salespersons a commission accounting for 100 percent of pay was the situation with by far the highest turnover of salespersons. Turnover was much lower in the situation in which salespersons were paid a combination of a base salary plus commissions.[32] These findings suggest that although 100 percent commissions can drive higher sales by focusing the attention of strong-willed salespeople on maximizing sales, without a financial safety net, it can also undermine the desire of sales people to stay.

The effects on the salesperson of a commission pay plan could also depend on that person's personality. A second study investigated 154 sales representatives who were responsible for contacting and renewing existing members and for identifying and adding new members. A number of the sales reps in this study were more extroverted than were the others—they were more sociable, outgoing, talkative, aggressive, energetic, and enthusiastic.[33] It might be expected that extroverted salespeople would usually generate higher sales than less extroverted ones, but in this study, extroversion was positively associated with higher performance (in terms of percentage of existing members renewing their memberships and the count of new members paying membership fees) *only when the salespeople were explicitly rewarded for accomplishing these tasks.* Thus, being extroverted did not always lead to higher sales; extroverts only sold more than those less extroverted when their rewards were contingent on their performance.

Combination Plan

There has been a definite movement away from the extremes of straight commission or fixed salary to combination plans for salespeople. Combination plans provide some of the advantages of both straight salary and straight commission plans and also some of their disadvantages. Salespeople have a floor to their earnings. Furthermore, the company can direct its salespeople's activities by detailing what services the salary component is being paid for, while the commission component provides a built-in incentive for superior performance.

However, the salary component is not tied to performance, and the employer is therefore trading away some incentive value. Combination plans also tend to become complicated, and misunderstandings can result. This might not be a problem with a simple "salary plus commission" plan, but most plans are not so simple. For example, there is a "commission plus drawing account" plan, whereby a salesperson is paid basically on commissions but can draw on future earnings to get through low sales periods. Similarly, in the "commission plus bonus" plan, salespeople are again paid primarily on the basis of commissions. However, they are also given a small bonus for directed activities, like selling slow-moving items.

An example can help to illustrate the complexities of the typical combination plan. In one company, for instance, the following three-step formula is applied:

- Step 1: Sales volume up to $18 000 a month. Base salary plus 7 percent of gross profits plus 0.5 percent of gross sales.
- Step 2: Sales volume from $18 000 to $25 000 a month. Base salary plus 9 percent of gross profits plus 0.5 percent of gross sales.
- Step 3: Sales volume more than $25 000 a month. Base salary plus 10 percent of gross profits plus 0.5 percent of gross sales.

In all cases, base salary is paid every two weeks, while the earned percentage of gross profits and gross sales is paid monthly. It should be remembered that setting sales goals or targets is complex and requires careful planning and analysis. Answers to such questions as why $18 000 and $25 000 were chosen as break points must be available.[34]

Tips | FOR THE FRONT LINE
The sales force also may get various special awards.[35] Trips and high-tech items such as BlackBerrys and iPhones are commonly used as sales prizes.

Sales Compensation in the E-commerce Era

Traditional product-based sales compensation focuses on the amount of product sold. In the Internet age, an integrated team of individuals works together to position the company with prospects, make sales, and service accounts. All sales team members work to deepen customer relationships. This new approach is due to the fact that for customers who know what they want, rapid low-cost purchases can be made over the Internet. Face-to-face sales are now reserved for high-volume customers and higher-margin services.

Sales incentive plans now need to encourage the sales force to focus on the customer, integrate with e-commerce, and support rapid change. Cross-selling incentives (making multiple sales of different product lines to the same customer) are more important, along with incentives for relationship management and customer satisfaction. Experts recommend setting sales salaries at 50 to 75 percent of total expected compensation, plus incentives. A portion of the incentive should be tied to team-based sales results, in order to encourage sharing, handoffs, and peer pressure.[36]

INCENTIVES FOR OTHER MANAGERS AND PROFESSIONALS

merit pay (merit raise) Any salary increase awarded to an employee based on his or her individual performance.

Merit pay or a **merit raise** is any salary increase that is awarded to an employee based on his or her individual performance. It is different from a bonus in that it usually represents a continuing increment, whereas the bonus represents a one-time payment. Although the term "merit pay" can apply to the incentive raises given to any employees—office or factory, management or nonmanagement—the term is more often used with respect to white-collar employees and particularly professional, office, and clerical employees.

Merit pay has both advocates and detractors and is the subject of much debate.[37] Advocates argue that only pay or other rewards tied directly to performance can motivate improved performance. They contend that the effect of awarding identical pay raises to all employees (without regard to individual performance) may actually detract from performance by showing employees that they will be rewarded the same regardless of how they perform.

Conversely, merit pay detractors present good reasons why merit pay can backfire. One is that the usefulness of the merit pay plan depends on the validity of the performance appraisal system, because if performance appraisals are viewed as unfair, so too will the merit pay that is based on them. Second, supervisors often tend to minimize differences in employee performance when computing merit raises. They give most employees about the same raise, either because of a reluctance to alienate some employees, or a desire to give everyone a raise that will at least help them to stay even with the cost of living. A third problem is that almost every employee thinks that he or she is an above-average performer; being paid a below-average merit increase can thus be demoralizing. Finally, some believe that merit pay pits employees against each other and harms team spirit.[38]

However, although problems like these can undermine a merit pay plan, the consensus of opinion is that merit pay can and does improve performance. It is critical, however, that performance appraisals be carried out effectively.[39]

Traditional merit pay plans have two basic characteristics: (1) Merit increases are usually granted to employees at a designated time of the year in the form of a higher base salary (or *raise*); and (2) the merit raise is usually based exclusively on individual performance, although the overall level of company profits may affect the total sum available for merit raises.[40] In some cases, merit raises are awarded in a single lump sum once a year, without changing base salary. Occasionally, awards are tied to both individual and organizational performance.

Incentives for Professional Employees

Professional employees are those whose work involves the application of learned knowledge to the solution of the employer's problems. They include lawyers, doctors, economists, and engineers. Professionals almost always reach their positions through prolonged periods of formal study.[41]

Pay decisions regarding professional employees involve unique problems. One is that, for most professionals, money has historically been somewhat less important as an incentive than it has been for other employees. This is true partly because professionals tend to be paid well anyway and partly because they are already driven—by the desire to produce high-calibre work and receive recognition from colleagues.

However, that is not to say that professionals do not want financial incentives. For example, studies in industries like pharmaceuticals and aerospace consistently show that firms with the most productive research and development groups have incentive pay plans for their professionals, usually in the form of bonuses. However, professionals' bonuses tend to represent a relatively small portion of their total pay. The time cycle of the professionals' incentive plans also tends to be longer than a year, reflecting the long time spent in designing, developing, and marketing a new product.

There are also many nonsalary items that professionals must have to do their best work. Not strictly incentives, these items range from better equipment and facilities and a supportive management style to support for professional journal publications.

ORGANIZATION-WIDE INCENTIVE PLANS

Many employers have incentive plans in which virtually all employees can participate. These include profit sharing, employee stock ownership, and Scanlon plans.

Profit-Sharing Plans

profit-sharing plan A plan whereby most or all employees share in the company's profits.

In a **profit-sharing plan,** most or all employees receive a share of the company's profits. Fewer than 20 percent of Canadian organizations offer profit sharing plans.[42] These plans are easy to administer and have a broad appeal to employees and other company stakeholders. The main weakness of profit-sharing plans is "line of sight." It is unlikely that most employees perceive that they personally have the ability to influence overall company profit. It has been found that these plans produce a one-time productivity improvement but no change thereafter. Another weakness of these plans is that they typically provide an annual payout, which is not as effective as more frequent payouts.[43]

There are several types of profit-sharing plans. In *cash plans*, the most popular, a percentage of profits (usually 15 to 20 percent) is distributed as profit shares at regular intervals. One example is Atlas-Graham Industries Limited in Winnipeg. A profit-sharing pool is calculated by deducting 2 percent of sales from pre-tax profit and then taking 30 percent of the result. The pool is distributed equally among all employees. Other plans provide cash and deferred benefits. Fisheries Products International Limited in St. John's, Newfoundland, contributes 10 percent of pre-tax income to a profit-sharing pool that is divided up, just before Christmas, based on each employee's earnings. The first 75 percent of each employee's share is paid in cash, and the remaining 25 percent is allocated to pension plan improvements.[44]

There are also *deferred profit-sharing plans*. Here, a predetermined portion of profits is placed in each employee's account under the supervision of a trustee. There is a tax advantage to such plans, since income taxes are deferred, often until the employee retires and is taxed at a lower rate.

Employee Share Purchase/Stock Ownership Plan

Employee share purchase/stock ownership plans (ESOPs) are in place at approximately 60 percent of Canadian organizations with publicly traded stock.[45] A trust is established to purchase shares of the firm's stock for employees by using cash from employee (and sometimes employer) contributions. Employers may also issue treasury shares to the trust instead of paying cash for a purchase on the open market. The trust holds the stock in individual employee accounts and distributes it to employees, often on retirement or other separation from service. Some plans distribute the stock to employees once a year.

The corporation receives a tax deduction equal to the fair market value of the shares that are purchased by the trustee by using employer contributions but not for any treasury shares issued. The value of the shares purchased with employer contributions, and of any treasury shares issued, is a taxable benefit to the employees in the year of purchase of the shares. This tax treatment can create two problems. First, if the plan requires employees to complete a certain period of service before taking ownership of the shares and the employee leaves before being eligible for ownership, the employee has paid tax on the value of shares that he or she never owns. Therefore, most plans have immediate vesting.[46] Second, if the value of the shares drops, employees may have paid tax on a greater amount than they receive when they eventually sell the shares.

ESOPs can encourage employees to develop a sense of ownership in and commitment to the firm, particularly when combined with good communication, employee involvement in decision making, and employee understanding of the business and the economic environment.[47] For example, one employee at Creo, a digital products company in Burnaby, British Columbia, that offers an ESOP said, "It's not just the shares. It's the way of thinking. I'm extremely happy here."[48] Don White, owner of Apex Distribution Company in Calgary, sees it as an important way to keep good people. Of the company's 250 employees, 130 participate in their ESOP and have benefited from a rise in stock price from 80 cents in 2001 to $6 in 2007. Apex has had zero turnover in top

employee share purchase/stock ownership plans (ESOPs) A trust is established to hold shares of company stock purchased for or issued to employees. The trust distributes the stock to employees on retirement, separation from service, or as otherwise prescribed by the plan.

National Centre for Employee Ownership
www.nceo.org

management and sales positions, which has contributed to year-over-year revenue growth of 100 percent in 2006 and 50 percent in 2005.[49]

Scanlon Plan

Scanlon plan An incentive plan developed in 1937 by Joseph Scanlon and designed to encourage cooperation, involvement, and sharing of benefits.

Aligning the organization's strategic goals with those of its employees is a powerful way of ensuring commitment. One technique that has been widely implemented with considerable success is the **Scanlon plan,** developed in 1937 by Joseph Scanlon, a United Steelworkers Union official.[50]

The Scanlon plan is remarkably progressive, considering that it was developed over 70 years ago. As currently implemented, Scanlon plans have the following basic features. The first is the *philosophy of cooperation* on which it is based. This philosophy assumes that managers and workers have to rid themselves of the "us" and "them" attitudes that normally inhibit employees from developing a sense of ownership in the company. A pervasive philosophy of cooperation must exist in the firm for the plan to succeed.[51]

A second feature of the plan is what its practitioners refer to as *identity*. This means that to focus employee involvement, the company's mission or purpose must be clearly articulated and employees must fundamentally understand how the business operates in terms of customers, prices, and costs, for instance.

Competence is a third basic feature. The plan assumes that hourly employees can competently perform their jobs as well as identify and implement improvements and that supervisors have leadership skills for the participative management that is crucial to a Scanlon plan.

The fourth feature of the plan is the *involvement system*.[52] Productivity-improving suggestions are presented by employees to the appropriate departmental-level committees, the members of which transmit the valuable ones to the executive-level committee. The latter group then decides whether to implement the suggestion.

The fifth element of the plan is the *sharing of benefits formula*. Basically, the Scanlon plan assumes that employees should share directly in any extra profits resulting from their cost-cutting suggestions. If a suggestion is implemented and successful, all employees usually share in 75 percent of the savings. For example, assume that the normal monthly ratio of payroll costs to sales is 50 percent. (Thus, if sales are $600 000, payroll costs should be $300 000.) Assume that suggestions are implemented and result in payroll costs of $250 000 in a month when sales were $550 000 and payroll costs would otherwise have been $275 000 (50 percent of sales). The saving attributable to these suggestions is $25 000 ($275 000 – $250 000). Workers would typically share in 75 percent of this ($18 750), while $6250 would go to the firm. In practice, a portion, usually one-quarter of the $18 750, is set aside for the months in which labour costs exceed the standard.

The Scanlon plan has been quite successful at reducing costs and fostering a sense of sharing and cooperation among employees. Yet Scanlon plans do fail, and there are several conditions required for their success. They are usually more effective when there are a relatively small number of participants, generally fewer than 1000. They are more successful when there are stable product lines and costs, since it is important that the labour costs/sales ratio remain fairly constant. Good supervision and healthy labour relations also seem essential. In addition, it is crucial that there be strong commitment to the plan on the part of management, particularly during the confusing phase-in period.[53]

Gainsharing Plans

gainsharing plan An incentive plan that engages employees in a common effort to achieve productivity objectives and share the gains.

The Scanlon plan is actually an early version of what today is known as a **gainsharing plan,** an incentive plan that engages many or all employees in a common effort to achieve a company's productivity objectives; any resulting incremental cost-saving gains are shared among employees and the company.[54] In addition to the Scanlon plan, other popular types of gainsharing plans include the Rucker and Improshare plans.

The basic difference among these plans is in the formula used to determine employee bonuses.[55] The Scanlon formula divides payroll expenses by total sales. The Rucker formula uses sales value minus materials and supplies, all divided into payroll expenses. The Improshare plan creates production standards for each department. The Scanlon and Rucker plans include participative management systems that use committees. Improshare does not include a participative management component but instead considers participation an outcome of the bonus plan.

The financial aspects of a gainsharing program can be quite straightforward. Assume that a supplier wants to boost quality. Doing so would translate into fewer customer returns, less scrap and rework, and therefore higher profits. Historically, $1 million in output results in $20 000 (2 percent) scrap, returns, and rework. The company tells its employees that if next month's production results in only 1 percent scrap, returns, and rework, the 1 percent saved would be a gain, to be split 50/50 with the workforce, less a small amount for reserve for months in which scrap exceeds 2 percent. Awards are often posted monthly but allocated quarterly.[56]

Gainsharing works well in stable organizations with predictable goals and measures of performance but is less flexible and useful in dynamic industries that require rapid business adjustment. In general, most of their cost savings are generated in the early years.[57] For example, in 2006 the Insurance Corporation of British Columbia province-wide and Canadian Office and Professional Employees' Union agreed to a plan which could pay out a maximum of 4 percent of annual salary if three quantitative corporate goals are met and exceeded in any year. Payments are made April 30 of each year based on corporate performance for the previous calendar year. Employees who retire during a gainsharing year are eligible for a pro-rated payment for the period they worked during that year.[58]

DEVELOPING EFFECTIVE INCENTIVE PLANS

There are two major practical considerations in developing an effective incentive plan—when to use it and how to implement it.

When to Use Incentives

Before deciding to implement an incentive plan, it is important to remember several points:

1. *Performance pay cannot replace good management.* Performance pay is supposed to motivate workers, but lack of motivation is not always the culprit. Ambiguous instructions, lack of clear goals, inadequate employee selection and training, unavailability of tools, and a hostile workforce (or management) are just a few of the factors that impede performance.

2. *Firms get what they pay for.* Psychologists know that people often put their effort where they know they will be rewarded. However, this can backfire. An incentive plan that rewards a group based on how many pieces are produced could lead to rushed production and lower quality. Awarding a plant-wide incentive for reducing accidents may simply reduce the number of reported accidents.

3. *"Pay is not a motivator."*[59] Psychologist Frederick Herzberg makes the point that money only buys temporary compliance; as soon as the incentive is removed, the "motivation" disappears too. Instead, Herzberg says, employers should provide adequate financial rewards and then build other motivators, like opportunities for achievement and psychological success, into their jobs.

4. *Rewards rupture relationships.* Incentive plans have the potential for reducing teamwork by encouraging individuals (or individual groups) to blindly pursue financial rewards for themselves.

5. *Rewards may undermine responsiveness.* Since the employees' primary focus is on achieving some specific goal, like cutting costs, any changes or extraneous distractions mean that achieving that goal will be harder. Incentive plans can, therefore, mediate against change and responsiveness.

Research | INSIGHT

Nelson Motivation Inc.
www.nelson-motivation.com

Recent research by two professors at the University of Alberta focused on resolving a longstanding debate about whether extrinsic rewards can backfire by reducing intrinsic motivation, or whether extrinsic rewards boost performance and enhance intrinsic motivation. The authors concluded that *careful* management of rewards does enhance performance. Common problem areas to be avoided include not tying rewards to performance, not delivering on all rewards initially promised, and delivering rewards in an authoritarian style or manner.[60]

Potential pitfalls like these do not mean that financial incentive plans cannot be useful or should not be used. They do suggest, however, that goals need to be reasonable and achievable but not so easily attained that employees view incentives as entitlements.[61] In general, any incentive plan is more apt to succeed if implemented with management support, employee acceptance, and a supportive culture characterized by teamwork, trust, and involvement at all levels.[62] This probably helps to explain why some of the longest-lasting incentive plans, like the Scanlon and Rucker plans, depend heavily on two-way communication and employee involvement in addition to incentive pay.

Therefore, in general, it makes more sense to use an incentive plan when units of output can be measured, the job is standardized, the workflow is regular, and delays are few or consistent. It is also important that there be a clear relationship between employee effort and quantity of output, that quality is less important than quantity, or, if quality is important, that it is easily measured and controlled.

How to Implement Incentive Plans

There are several specific common-sense considerations in establishing any incentive plan. Of primary importance is "line of sight." The employee or group must be able to see their own impact on the goals or objectives for which incentives are being provided.[63]

Recent research indicates that there are seven principles that support effective implementation of incentive plans that lead to superior business results:[64]

1. Pay for performance—and make sure that performance is tied to the successful achievement of critical business goals.

2. Link incentives to other activities that engage employees in the business, such as career development and challenging opportunities.

3. Link incentives to measurable competencies that are valued by the organization.

4. Match incentives to the culture of the organization—its vision, mission, and operation principles.

5. Keep group incentives clear and simple—employee understanding is the most important factor differentiating effective from ineffective group incentive plans.

6. Overcommunicate—employees become engaged when they hear the message that they are neither faceless nor expendable.

7. Remember that the greatest incentive is the work itself. For example, highly skilled engineers at MacDonald Detweiler and Associates Ltd. in Richmond, B.C., feel valued and appreciated when they are chosen by their peers to work on project teams, to work on the Canada space arm, or to work on a project to save the rainforest, and they don't require large financial incentives to work hard.

EMPLOYEE RECOGNITION PROGRAMS

In today's fast-changing environment, recognition is emerging as a critical component of the total rewards mix.[65] Why? Because lack of recognition and praise is the number-one reason that employees leave an organization. The traditional role of recognition plans has been to reward employees for long service, but today's employees value being appreciated by an employer throughout their career. In fact, recent Japanese research has shown that people get as excited about receiving a compliment as they do about receiving a cash reward because both activate the same reward centre in the brain (the striatum).[66]

An employee's introduction to a corporate recognition culture needs to start on the day he or she is hired. For example, the employee could receive a welcome note, a nameplate, and a personalized gift pack that includes a company t-shirt and coffee mug. These things are all very easy to do, and they send a very clear message to a new employee.[67] Recognition and other simple incentives are particularly effective in smaller entrepreneurial companies, as explained in the Entrepreneurs and HR box.

Employees consistently say that they receive little recognition. One study found that only 50 percent of managers give recognition for high performance, and that up to 40 percent of workers feel that they never get recognized for outstanding performance. Nurses are one group of employees that has long suffered from lack of respect. They feel ignored and undervalued as subservient assistants to doctors. The shortage of nurses in Canada has forced employers to consider treating nurses with the respect and recognition they deserve as invaluable contributors of knowledge and skills to the health-care system.[68]

Some believe that this lack of recognition occurs because expressing generous appreciation means talking about feelings in public, which may make managers feel vulnerable. However, when lack of recognition and praise is resulting

Entrepreneurs and HR

Recognition and Incentives for Entrepreneurs

Entrepreneurs may not have the time or money to provide many formal incentive programs. But there are many other approaches they can use to motivate employees toward achieving the strategic objectives of the organization. There are three guides to follow.

First, the best option for motivating employees is also the simplest—make sure the employee has a doable goal and that he or she agrees with it. It makes little sense to try to motivate employees in other ways (such as with financial incentives) if they don't know their goals or don't agree with them. Psychologist Edwin Locke and his colleagues have consistently found that specific, challenging goals lead to higher task performance than specific, unchallenging goals, or vague goals, or no goals. The best goals are SMART goals—Specific, Measurable, Attainable, Relevant, and Timely.

Second, recognizing an employee's contribution is a simple and powerful motivational tool. Studies show that recognition has a positive impact on performance, either alone or in combination with financial rewards. For example, in one study, combining financial rewards with recognition produced a 30 percent performance in service firms, almost twice the effect of using each rewards alone.

Third, there are numerous positive reinforcement rewards that can be used on a day-to-day basis, independent of formal incentive plans. A short list would include the following:

- challenging work assignments
- freedom to choose own work activity
- having fun built into work
- more of preferred task
- role as boss' stand-in when he or she is away
- role in presentations to top management
- job rotation
- encouragement of learning and continuous improvement
- being provided with ample encouragement
- being allowed to set own goals
- compliments
- expression of appreciation in front of others
- note of thanks
- employee-of-the-month award
- special commendation
- bigger desk
- bigger office or cubicle

Source: E. A. Locke & G.P. Latham, *A Theory of Goal Setting and Task Performance* (Englewood Cliffs NJ: Prentice Hall, 1990); R. Nelson, *1001 Ways to Reward Employees* (New York: Workmen Publishing, 1994), p. 19; S.J. Peterson & F. Luthans, "The Impact of Financial and Nonfinancial Incentives on Business Unit Outcomes Over Time," *Journal of Applied Psychology*, 2006, Vol. 91, No. 1, pp. 156–165.

Recognition Plus
www.recognitionplusinc.com
National Association for Employee Recognition
www.recognition.org
O.C. Tanner Recognition Co.
www.octanner.com
Rare Method
www.kudosnow.com

in the loss of valued employees, managers need to confront such apprehension and start recognizing their employees for their achievements. Why? Because employees favour recognition from supervisors and managers by a margin of two-to-one over recognition from other sources.[69] Thus line managers are critical to the success of recognition programs.

Recognition is also cost-effective. It takes 5 to 15 percent of pay to have an impact on behaviour when a cash reward is provided, but only 3 to 5 percent when a noncash form of reward is used (such as recognition and modest gifts).[70] Company DNA, an incentives provider, offers an online points system where recognition points can be spent on merchandise with merchant partners, such as Eddie Bauer, La Senza, Canadian Tire, and Future Shop.[71] There appears to be a growing interest by employees in having recognition awards linked to "green" or charitable causes, such as time off for volunteering.[72] The most common recognition awards are shown in **Figure 12.4.**

Effective recognition is specific, immediate, personal, and spontaneous. Making time to recognize the individual in front of his or her colleagues is critical to the success of the program. Personal attention and public celebration create recognition that is personal in nature and that addresses the deep needs that we all have for belonging and contributing to something worthwhile. By making

FIGURE 12.4 | Common Recognition Awards

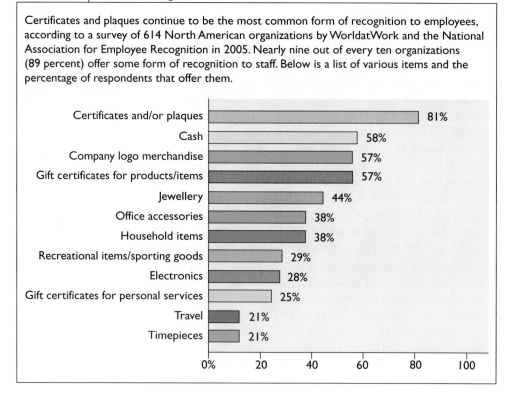

Certificates and plaques continue to be the most common form of recognition to employees, according to a survey of 614 North American organizations by WorldatWork and the National Association for Employee Recognition in 2005. Nearly nine out of every ten organizations (89 percent) offer some form of recognition to staff. Below is a list of various items and the percentage of respondents that offer them.

Item	Percentage
Certificates and/or plaques	81%
Cash	58%
Company logo merchandise	57%
Gift certificates for products/items	57%
Jewellery	44%
Office accessories	38%
Household items	38%
Recreational items/sporting goods	29%
Electronics	28%
Gift certificates for personal services	25%
Travel	21%
Timepieces	21%

Source: WorldatWork's Trends in Employee Recognition 2005. Reprinted with permission of WorldatWork, Scottsdale, AZ. www.worldatwork.org.

it memorable, the recognition experience will continue to evoke emotion and make the employee feel that his or her individual effort made a difference.

Recognition programs are more effective than cash in achieving improved employee attitudes, increased workloads and hours of work, and productivity (speed of work/intensity of work). They can build confidence, create a positive and supportive environment, build a sense of pride in accomplishments, inspire people to increase their efforts, and help people feel valued. Recognition can act as a strategic change effort if recognition criteria are aligned with business strategy, employee input is solicited regarding program design and implementation, and a recognition culture is created.[73]

Recognition is also important for high performers, who focus on what needs to be done to exceed expectations. These employees are driven by internal motivation, and look to reward programs to add fuel to their achievements. Recognition satisfies "wants" rather than "needs" (where cash bonuses often go); such programs eliminate guilt about owning luxury items, provide bragging rights, and create a lasting impression in the employees' memory.[74]

Finally, recognition programs are key corporate communication tools that can achieve several goals—saying thank you, encouraging good workers, and encouraging behaviour that supports strategic objectives.[75] RBC Financial Group, Fairmont Hotels and Resorts, Research In Motion, Procor Limited, Montana's Cookhouse, Minto Developments Inc., Alberta Milk, Southland Transportation, and Snow Valley Edmonton are just some of the Canadian companies that are reaping the benefits of employee recognition programs.[76]

Chapter | SUMMARY

1. Piecework is the oldest type of incentive plan. Here, a worker is paid a piece rate for each unit that he or she produces. The standard hour plan rewards workers by a premium that equals the percentage by which their performance is above standard. Group incentive plans are useful when the workers' jobs are highly interrelated.

2. Most management employees receive a short-term incentive, usually in the form of an annual bonus linked to company or divisional profits. Long-term incentives are intended to motivate and reward top management for the firm's long-term growth and prosperity and to inject a long-term perspective into executive decisions.

3. Salary plans for salespeople are effective when the main sales objective is finding new clients or servicing accounts. The main disadvantage of salary plans is that pay is not tied to performance. Commission plans attract high-performing salespeople who see that performance will clearly lead to rewards. The problem with straight commission plans is that there is a tendency to focus on "big-ticket" or "quick-sell" items and to disregard long-term customer relationships.

4. Money is somewhat less important as an incentive for professional employees than it is for other employees; professionals are already driven by the desire to produce high-calibre work, and the time cycle of professionals' incentive plans tends to be longer than one year, reflecting time for research, design, and development of new products and services. Professionals seek recognition and support in the form of the latest equipment and support for journal publications.

5. Profit-sharing plans, employee share purchase/stock ownership plans, and gainsharing plans, such as the Scanlon plan, are examples of organization-wide incentive plans. Profit-sharing plans provide a share of company profits to all employees in the organization. The problem with such plans is that sometimes the link between a person's efforts and rewards is unclear. Stock purchase plans provide a vehicle for employees to purchase company stock with their own and sometimes employer contributions. Gainsharing plans engage employees in a common effort to achieve a company's productivity objectives, and incremental cost-savings are shared among employees and the company. All these plans are intended to increase employee commitment to the organization and motivate workers.

6. Incentive plans are particularly appropriate when units of output are easily measured, employees can control output, the effort–reward relationship is clear, work delays are under employees' control, and quality is not paramount.

7. Employee recognition plans are growing in popularity as a cost-effective method of retaining employees by praising their achievements. Recognition has the most impact when it is sincerely and meaningfully provided by the supervisor in a public presentation format.

PEARSON
myHRlab

Test yourself on material for this chapter at
www.pearsoned.ca/myhrlab

Key | TERMS

Review and Discussion | QUESTIONS

1. Describe why it is important to consider employee life stage when developing incentive plans.

2. Describe the three basic issues to be considered when awarding short-term management bonuses.

3. Explain how stock options work. What are some of the reasons that stock options have been criticized in recent years?

4. When and why should a salesperson be paid a salary? A commission? Salary and commission combined?

5. What is a Scanlon plan? What are the five basic features of this plan?

6. Explain five reasons why incentive plans fail.

7. Why are recognition plans useful for motivating high performers? Identify the possible reasons why the top forms of recognition shown in Figure 12.4 are the most frequently used.

Critical Thinking | QUESTIONS

1. A university recently instituted a "Teacher Incentive Program" (TIP) for its faculty. Basically, faculty committees within each of the university's colleges were told to award $5000 raises (not bonuses) to about 40 percent of their faculty members based on how good a job they did in teaching undergraduates and how many of these students they taught per year. What are the potential advantages and pitfalls of such an incentive program? How well do you think it was accepted by the faculty? Do you think that it had the desired effect?

2. Is it ethical for companies to only offer incentive bonuses to top mangers? Why or why not? What are the pros and cons of making such bonuses available to all employees who meet performance criteria?

3. Do you think that it is a good idea to award employees with merit raises? Why or why not? If not, what approach would you take to incentive compensation?

4. In this chapter, we listed a number of reasons that experts give for not instituting a pay-for-performance plan in a vacuum (such as "rewards rupture relationships"). Do you think that these points (or any others) are valid? Why or why not?

5. Recognition can take many forms. Prepare a list of some forms of recognition that would be particularly motivational for Generation Y employees and explain why you have chosen them.

6. Think of organizations that have been in the news in the last few years because of scandals. Which of these involved incentives? What were the problems and how could they have been avoided?

Experiential | EXERCISES

1. Working individually or in groups, develop an incentive plan for each of the following positions: web designer, hotel manager, and used-car salesperson. What factors had to be taken into consideration?

2. Explain why employee recognition plans are growing in popularity. How would you go about recognizing your favourite professor?

3. Express Automotive, an automobile mega-dealership with more than 600 employees that represents 22 brands, has just received a very discouraging set of survey results. It seems its customer satisfaction scores have fallen for the ninth straight quarter. Customer complaints included the following:

Team	Responsibility	Current Compensation Method
Sales force	Persuade buyers to purchase a car.	Very small salary (minimum wage) with commissions; commission rate increases with every 20 cars sold per month.
Finance office	Help close the sale; persuade customer to use company finance plan.	Salary, plus bonus for each $10 000 financed with the company.
Detailing	Inspect cars delivered from factory, clean them, and make minor adjustments.	Piecework paid on the number of cars detailed per day.
Mechanics	Provide factory warranty service, maintenance, and repair.	Small hourly wage, plus bonus based on (1) number of cars completed per day and (2) finishing each car faster than the standard estimated time to repair.
Receptionists/ phone service personnel	Act as primary liaison between customer and sales force, finance, and mechanics.	Minimum wage.

- It was hard to get prompt feedback from mechanics by phone.
- Salespeople often did not return phone calls.
- The finance people seemed "pushy."
- New cars were often not properly cleaned or had minor items that needed immediate repair or adjustment.
- Cars often had to be returned to have repair work redone.

The table above describes Express Automotive's current compensation system.

The class is to be divided into five groups. Each group is assigned to one of the five teams in column one. Each group should analyze the compensation package for its team. Each group should be able to identify the ways in which the current compensation plan (1) helps company performance and/or (2) impedes company performance. Once the groups have completed their analyses, the following questions are to be discussed as a class:

(a) In what ways might your group's compensation plan contribute to the customer service problems?

(b) Do the rewards provided by your department impede the work of other departments?

(c) What recommendations would you make to improve the compensation system in a way that would likely improve customer satisfaction?

4. Working in groups, brainstorm ways in which a company that previously provided generous incentive pay and bonuses might provide less costly incentives to encourage employee commitment and productivity in recessionary times when company revenues are falling. Create a communications plan to announce the changes to employees who may have come to expect and rely on these incentives. Critique your plan from the employee perspective.

Running | CASE

The Incentive Plan

Of all its HR programs, those relating to pay for performance and incentives are LearnInMotion.com's most fully developed. For one thing, the venture capital firm that funded it was very explicit about reserving at least 10 percent of the company's stock for employee incentives. The agreement with the venture capital firm also included very explicit terms and conditions regarding LearnInMotion.com's stock option plan. The venture fund agreement included among its 500 or so pages the specific written agreement that LearnInMotion.com would have to send to each of its employees, laying out the details of the company's stock option plan.

Although there was some flexibility, the stock option plan details came down to this:

1. Employees would get stock options (the right to buy shares of LearnInMotion.com stock) at a price equal to 15 percent less than the venture capital fund paid for those shares when it funded LearnInMotion.com.

2. The shares will have a vesting schedule of 36 months, with one-third of the shares vesting once the employee has completed 12 full months of employment with the company, and one-third vesting on successful completion of each of the following two full 12-month periods of employment.

3. If an employee leaves the company for any reason before his or her first full 12 months with the firm, the person is not eligible for stock options.

4. If the person has stock options and leaves the firm for any reason, he or she must exercise the options within 90 days of the date of leaving the firm or lose the right to exercise them.

5. The actual number of options an employee gets depends on the person's bargaining power and on how much Jennifer and Pierre think the person brings to the company. The options granted generally ranged from options to buy 10 000 shares for some employees up to 50 000 shares for others, but this has not raised any questions to date.

When a new employee signs on, he or she receives a letter of offer. This provides minimal details regarding the option plan; after the person has completed the 90-day introductory period, he or she receives the five-page document describing the stock option plan, which Jennifer or Pierre, as well as the employee, signs.

6. Beyond that, the only incentive plan is the one for the two salespeople. In addition to their respective salaries, both salespeople receive about 20 percent of any sales they bring in, whether those sales are from advertising banners or course listing fees. It's not clear to Jennifer and Pierre whether this incentive is effective. Each salesperson gets a base salary regardless of what he or she sells (one gets about $50 000, the other about $35 000). However, sales have simply not come up to the levels anticipated. Jennifer and Pierre are not sure why. It could be that Internet advertising has dried up. It could be that their own business model is no good, or there's not enough demand for their company's services. They may be charging too much or too little. It could be that the salespeople can't do the job because of inadequate skills or inadequate training. Or, of course, it could be the incentive plan. ("Or it could be all of the above," as Pierre somewhat dejectedly said late one Friday evening.) They want to try to figure out what the problem is. They want you, their management consultant, to help them figure out what to do.

QUESTIONS

1 Is LearnInMotion's current compensation program motivating their staff? Or is it hindering employee performance?

2 Should LearnInMotion utilize a mix of individual, team, and organizational incentives? If so, recommend specific incentives that the company should use and discuss why.

3 Do you think changing the compensation strategy will positively affect this firm and, if so, specifically how so?

Case | INCIDENT

A New Compensation Program to Motivate Performance

Marilyn Brown started her chain of ten wedding boutiques approximately five years ago. She presently operates within southwestern Ontario and has been enjoying record profits. Marilyn's wedding boutiques provide full service amenities to future brides, including wedding planning services, custom fittings, and locating hard-to-find wedding dresses.

Marilyn's customer service philosophy is that the customer is number one and must be satisfied with their purchases. However, recently there has been a rise in complaints regarding the lack of friendly service being provided, and three longstanding employees have threatened to leave unless their compensation is adjusted in response to servicing Marilyn's very demanding clients. Currently Marilyn pays all of her staff the same base salary of $10 per hour without any benefits. Marilyn feels that this approach promotes equity and eliminates any perceptions of favouritism between employees regarding compensation.

Since receiving the negative complaints and the threats of some of her staff leaving, Marilyn has decided she needs to rethink her compensation philosophy and needs your help. Please answer the following questions for her.

QUESTIONS

1 What are the specific problems with Marilyn's current compensation program?

2 Discuss the types of compensation programs and plans available to Marilyn to motivate and retain her existing staff.

3 Should Marilyn use only one type of compensation plan or a combination plan for her employees? Discuss your recommendation in detail.

For additional cases and exercise material, go to
www.pearsoned.ca/myhrlab

CHAPTER 13

EMPLOYEE BENEFITS AND SERVICES

LEARNING OUTCOMES

AFTER STUDYING THIS CHAPTER, YOU SHOULD BE ABLE TO

EXPLAIN the strategic role of employee benefits.

DESCRIBE six government-sponsored benefits.

EXPLAIN why the cost of health insurance benefits is increasing and how employers can reduce these costs.

DESCRIBE the two categories of pension plans and the shift that is occurring in their relative popularity.

DISCUSS three types of personal employee services and six types of job-related services offered to employees.

EXPLAIN how to set up a flexible benefits program.

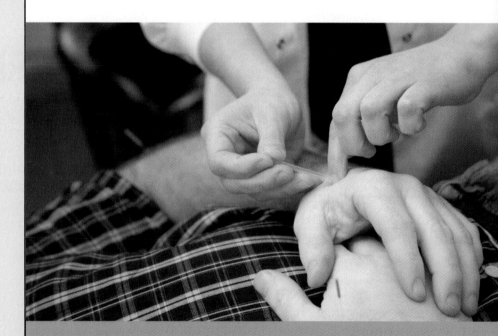

REQUIRED PROFESSIONAL CAPABILITIES (RPC)

- Integrates the basic benefits program with disability management

- Performs an analysis of organizational and employee needs related to benefit plans

- Administers the reporting, funding, and fiduciary aspects of the plan

- Provides information and counselling to pension plan participants

THE STRATEGIC ROLE OF EMPLOYEE BENEFITS

employee benefits Indirect financial payments given to employees. They may include supplementary health and life insurance, vacation, pension, education plans, and discounts on company products.

Employee benefits and services can be defined as all the indirect financial payments that an employee receives during his or her employment with an employer.[1] Benefits are generally provided to all of a firm's employees and include such things as time off with pay, supplementary health and life insurance, and employee assistance plans. Employee services, traditionally a minor aspect of compensation, are becoming more sought after by today's employees in the post-job-security era. Research indicates that benefits do matter to employees and that, if they are aligned with business strategy, they can help to attract and retain the right people to achieve business objectives.[2] Alberta's AltaGas uses benefits to help them compete for talented workers in the ultra-competitive Alberta labour market, as described in the Strategic HR box.

Employee benefits are an important part of most employees' compensation, particularly given today's reality of modest salary increases.[3] For the aging workforce, health-care benefits are becoming increasingly important. Employee

Strategic HR

AltaGas Benefits Drive Successful Competition for Talent

Time off has been a big focus at AltaGas in the past year. The Calgary-based energy company changed its vacation policy for the third time in eight years and reduced its workday from 8 hours to 7.5. It also gives employees eight "corporate" days off and workers enjoy provincial statutory holidays from outside their jurisdiction.

"We tried to listen to employees in terms of what's important and certainly time off stood out," says Kent Stout, vice-president of corporate resources at AltaGas. "Time off, quality of life, work/life balance are the issues we're taking to centre stage. And fun, we're trying to inject that as well."

AltaGas's range of generous benefits is typical of employers on Canada's Top 100 Employers list, published by Mediacorp Canada. To join the prestigious clan, organizations typically provide ample vacation, maternity leave top-ups, retirement savings options, bonuses, tuition subsidies, and health benefits, along with fitness incentives and flexible work arrangements.

"We have a highly competitive, challenging labour market in Calgary, particularly in the industry we operate in, so there's lots of competition out there, lots of big oil and gas producers that have very attractive compensation packages, including benefits, so somehow—we're not that large—we have to distinguish ourselves and attract and retain employees."

AltaGas offers three weeks' vacation to new employees but decided to steer away from flex days and instead offers five pre-designated corporate days aligned with long weekends, so employees can take a four-day break. Three other corporate days are given at Christmas, usually making for a ten-day break.

"Employees really like it because they don't have to feel guilty, worrying about others working, because the office shuts down, so they can relax more," says Stout.

Employees also enjoy quarterly events, contingent on financial success, that include scavenger hunts, cross-country skiing, or dinners, with prizes such as WestJet certificates.

On the financial side, the 357-employee company provides signing bonuses, year-end bonuses up to $57 400, a share-purchase plan, a pension plan with employer contributions up to 6 percent, life and disability insurance, and discounts on home computers.

AltaGas also pays 100 percent of health premiums and employees receive full family coverage. Family-friendly benefits include maternity leave top-up to 100 percent of salary for six weeks, emergency short-term daycare, and compassionate top-up payments to 10 percent for one week.

"It's a very competitive marketplace, but we seem to be attracting good-quality employees," Stout says.

Source: S. Dobson, "Top Benefits Go Beyond Financials," *Canadian HR Reporter*, September 8, 2008.

benefits are in the midst of an evolution, based on the aging population, the looming labour shortage in Canada, and advances in health care. Each of these factors is expected to increase the cost of benefits, which is already at an all-time high.[4]

Benefits Interface
www.benefits.org
Employee Benefit Research Institute
www.ebri.org
Benefits Link
www.benefitslink.com
Benefits Canada
www.benefitscanada.ca

Administering benefits today represents an increasingly specialized task, because workers are more financially sophisticated and demanding and because benefit plans must comply with a wide variety of laws. Providing and administering benefits is also an increasingly expensive task. Benefits as a percentage of payroll (for public and private sectors combined) are approximately 37 percent today (compared with about 15 percent in 1953). Most employees do not realize the market value and high cost to the employer of their benefits.

Certain benefits are mandated by law, and most Canadian companies voluntarily provide additional employee benefits such as group life insurance and health and dental care insurance and retirement benefits. In the remainder of this chapter, government-sponsored benefits, voluntary employer-sponsored benefits, employee services, flexible benefits, and benefits administration will be discussed.

GOVERNMENT-SPONSORED BENEFITS

Canada has one of the world's finest collections of social programs to protect its citizens when they cannot earn income. Employers and employees provide funding for these plans, along with general tax revenues.

Employment Insurance (EI)

employment insurance A federal program that provides income benefits if a person is unable to work through no fault of his or her own.

Employment insurance is a federal program that provides weekly benefits if a person is unable to work through no fault of his or her own. It does not apply to workers who are self-employed. EI provides benefits for employees who are laid off, terminated without just cause, or who quit their job for a justifiable reason, such as harassment. EI benefits are not payable when an employee is terminated for just cause—for example, for theft of company property—or when an employee quits for no good reason. Workers may also be eligible for special EI benefits in cases of illness (once the employer's sickness or disability benefits, if any, have been exhausted), maternity/parental leave, and compassionate care leave.

To receive benefits, an employee must first have worked a minimum number of hours during a minimum number of weeks called a *qualifying period* (the number of hours and weeks varies among regions of the country). Then there is a waiting period from the last day of work until benefits begin. The waiting period varies but is often two weeks. If the employee was provided with severance pay or holiday pay at the time of losing the job, these payments must run out before the waiting period begins.

Income Security Programs
**www.hrsdc.gc.ca/eng/
oas-cpp/index.shtml**

The EI benefit is generally 55 percent of average earnings during the last 14 to 26 weeks of the qualifying period, depending on the regional unemployment rate. The benefit is payable for up to 45 weeks, depending on the regional unemployment rate and other factors. To receive EI benefits, individuals must demonstrate that they are actively seeking work. Claimants are encouraged to work part-time, as they can earn up to 25 percent of their EI benefit amount before these earnings will be deducted from the benefit. Compassionate care benefits are payable for up to 6 weeks, illness benefits for up to 15 weeks, and maternity/parental leave benefits can be taken by one or split between both parents for up to 50 weeks.[5]

Hints | TO ENSURE LEGAL
        | COMPLIANCE

The EI program is funded by contributions from eligible employees and their employers. Employee contributions are collected by payroll deduction, and employers pay 1.4 times the employee contribution. Employer contributions can be reduced if the employer provides a wage loss replacement plan for employee sick leave.

A supplemental unemployment benefit (SUB) plan is an agreement between an employer and the employees (often the result of collective bargaining) for a plan that enables employees who are eligible for EI benefits to receive additional benefits from an SUB fund created by the employer. SUB plans help employees to maintain their standard of living during periods of unemployment (most often maternity leave) by receiving a combined benefit closer to their actual working wage. Most SUBs provide benefits of 90 percent of the working wage or greater.[6] Work-sharing programs are a related arrangement in which employees work a reduced workweek and receive EI benefits for the remainder of the week. The EI Commission must approve SUB plans and work-sharing programs.

Canada/Quebec Pension Plan (C/QPP)

Canada/Quebec Pension Plan (C/QPP) Programs that provide three types of benefits: retirement income; survivor or death benefits payable to the employee's dependants regardless of age at time of death; and disability benefits payable to employees with disabilities and their dependants. Benefits are payable only to those individuals who make contributions to the plans and/or available to their family members.

The **Canada/Quebec Pension Plans (C/QPP)** were introduced in 1966 to provide working Canadians with a basic level of financial security on retirement or disability. Four decades later, these benefits do indeed provide a significant part of most Canadians' retirement income. Almost all employed Canadians between the ages of 18 and 65 are covered, including self-employed individuals. Casual and migrant workers are excluded, as are people who are not earning any employment income, such as homemakers. The benefits are portable, meaning that pension rights are not affected by changes in job or residence within Canada. Both contributions and benefits are based only on earnings up to the "year's maximum pensionable earnings" (intended to approximate the average industrial wage) as defined in the legislation. Benefits are adjusted based on inflation each year in line with the consumer price index. Contributions made by employees (4.95 percent of pensionable earnings) are matched by employers.

Canada Pension Plan
www.hrsdc.gc.ca/eng/isp/cpp/cpptoc.shtml

Three types of benefits are provided: retirement pensions, disability pensions, and survivor benefits. The *retirement pension* is calculated as 25 percent of the average earnings (adjusted for inflation up to the average inflation level during the last five years before retirement) over the years during which contributions were made. Plan members can choose to begin receiving benefits at any time between the ages of 60 and 70. Benefits are reduced on early retirement before age 65 and are increased in the case of late retirement after age 65. *Disability benefits* are only paid for severe disabilities that are expected to be permanent or to last for an extended period. The disability benefit is 75 percent of the pension benefit earned at the date of disability, plus a flat-rate amount per child. *Survivor benefits* are paid on the death of a plan member. A lump sum payment is made to the plan member's estate, and a monthly pension is also payable to the surviving spouse and each dependent child.

Workers' Compensation

Workers' compensation laws are aimed at providing sure, prompt income and medical benefits to victims of work-related accidents or illnesses and/or their dependants, regardless of fault. Every province and territory, and the federal jurisdiction, has its own workers' compensation law. These laws impose compulsory collective liability for workplace accidents and work-related illnesses. This means that employees and employers cannot sue each other regarding the costs of workplace accidents or illnesses. Workers' compensation is, in effect, a "no fault" insurance plan designed to help injured or ill workers get well and return to work. For an injury or illness to be covered by workers' compensation, one must only prove that it arose while the employee was on the job. It does not matter that the employee may have been at fault; if he or she was on the job when the injury or illness occurred, he or she is entitled to workers' compensation. For example, suppose all employees are instructed to wear safety goggles when working at their machines, and one does not and is injured. Workers' compensation benefits will still be provided. The fact that the worker was at fault in no way waives his or her claim to benefits.

Employers collectively pay the full cost of the workers' compensation system, which can be an onerous financial burden for small businesses. The cost varies by industry and with actual employer costs. Employer premiums are tax-deductible. Workers' Compensation Boards (or equivalent bodies) exist in each jurisdiction to determine and collect payments from employers, determine rights to compensation, and pay workers the amount of benefit to which they are entitled under the legislation in their jurisdiction. Employers and employees have some representation on these boards, but usually both parties believe they should have more control.

Association of Workers' Compensation Boards of Canada **www.awcbc.org**

Workers' compensation benefits include payment of expenses for medical treatment and rehabilitation, and income benefits during the time in which the worker is unable to work (temporarily or permanently) because of his or her disability (partial or total). Survivor benefits are payable if a work-related death occurs. All benefits are nontaxable.

Controlling Workers' Compensation Costs

All parties agree that a renewed focus on accident prevention is the best way to manage workers' compensation costs over the long term. Minimizing the number of workers' compensation claims is an important goal for all employers. Although the Workers' Compensation Board pays the claims, the premiums for most employers depend on the number and amount of claims that are paid. Minimizing such claims is thus important.

In practice, there are two basic approaches to reducing workers' compensation claims. First, firms try to reduce accident- or illness-causing conditions in facilities by instituting effective *safety and health programs* and complying with government safety standards. Second, since workers' compensation costs increase the longer an employee is unable to return to work, employers have become involved in instituting *rehabilitation programs* for injured or ill employees. These include physical therapy programs and career counselling to guide such employees into new, less strenuous or stressful jobs to reintegrate recipients back into the workforce. Workers are required to cooperate with return-to-work initiatives, such as modified work.[7] When Purolator Courier's workers' compensation costs came to $13 million, it decided to use both of these approaches to reduce costs. The company hired occupational nurses, conducted physical demands analysis of many of its jobs, strengthened its return-to-work program, tied injury reduction to managers' bonuses, and increased its interaction with doctors.[8]

Vacations and Holidays

Labour/employment standards legislation sets out a minimum amount of paid vacation that must be provided to employees, usually two weeks per year, but the requirements vary by jurisdiction. The actual number of paid employee vacation days also varies considerably from employer to employer. Even within the same organization, the number of vacation days usually depends on how long the employee has worked at the firm. Thus, a typical vacation policy might call for

- two weeks for the first 5 years of service
- three weeks for 6 to 10 years of service
- four weeks for 11 to 15 years of service
- five weeks for 16 to 25 years of service
- six weeks after 25 years of service

The number of paid holidays similarly varies considerably from one jurisdiction to another, from a minimum of five to a maximum of nine. The most common paid holidays include New Year's Day, Good Friday, Canada Day, Labour Day, and Christmas Day. Other common holidays include Victoria Day, Thanksgiving Day, and Remembrance Day. Additional holidays may be observed in each province, such as Saint Jean-Baptiste Day in Quebec.

Leaves of Absence

All the provinces and territories, and the federal jurisdiction, require unpaid leaves of absence to be provided to employees in certain circumstances. Maternity/parental leave is provided in every jurisdiction (usually after one year of service). The amount of maternity leave is 17 or 18 weeks in each jurisdiction (15 weeks in Alberta), but parental and adoption leaves range from 34 to 52 weeks. Employees who take these leaves of absence are guaranteed their old job or a similar job when they return to work.

Bereavement leave on the death of a family member is provided for employees in some, but not all, jurisdictions. The amount of time off varies by jurisdiction and depends on the closeness of the relationship between the employee and the deceased. Bereavement leave is usually unpaid, but in some cases it can be partially or fully paid. All jurisdictions except Alberta provide compassionate care leave for employees who are caring for a critically or terminally ill relative (six weeks of EI is payable during these leaves).[9] Quebec has extended compassionate leave to cover in situations where close family members are victims of criminal acts, commit suicide, or where a child disappears.[10]

Having a clear procedure for any leave of absence is essential. An application form, such as the one in **Figure 13.1**, should be the centrepiece of any such procedure. In general, no employee should be given a leave until it is clear what the leave is for. If the leave is for medical or family reasons, medical certification should be obtained from the attending physician or medical practitioner. A form like this also places on record the employee's expected return date and the fact that, without an authorized extension, his or her employment may be terminated.

FIGURE 13.1 | Sample Application for Leave of Absence

APPLICATION FOR LEAVE
(SUPPORT STAFF)

This form is used by all Support Staff employees to record applications for leave of one-half day duration or longer.

UNIVERSITY OF
NEW BRUNSWICK

HR USE ONLY

LAST NAME [　　　]   **FIRST NAME** [　　　]   **DATATEL / EMPLOYEE ID#** [　　　]

DEPARTMENT [　　　]   ○ **UNBF**   ○ **UNBSJ**

TYPE OF LEAVE	DATES (use separate forms for each year) Specify first and last day of leave for those longer than 1 day. Show A.M. or P.M. for half days.	# OF WORK DAYS
VACATION		
SICK		

	START DATE	END DATE	HR USE ONLY
MATERNITY			
PARENTAL			

	START DATE	END DATE	# of DAYS	
BEREAVEMENT				Relative:
EMERGENCY				Reason:
LEAVE WITHOUT PAY if over 30 days needs VP approval				Reason:
OTHER				Reason:

ADDITIONAL DETAILS:

EMPLOYEE SIGNS HERE _____   09-07-14
DATE

APPROVAL

_____   _____   _____
RECOMMENDED   POSITION   DATE

_____   _____   _____
APPROVED   POSITION   DATE

FORWARD COMPLETED FORMS TO: **UNBF** HUMAN RESOURCES ROOM 102 I.U.C. COMPLEX   **UNBSJ** FINANCIAL & ADMINISTRATIVE SERVICES ROOMS 114,115 OLAND HALL

HR USE ONLY   POSTED ON:

Source: Prepared by University of New Brunswick Human Resources. Used by permission.

Although these leaves are unpaid, it is incorrect to assume that the leave is costless to the employer. For example, one study concluded that the costs associated with recruiting new temporary workers, training replacement workers, and compensating for the lower level of productivity of these workers could represent a substantial expense over and above what employers would normally pay their full-time employees.[11]

Pay on Termination of Employment

Employment/labour standards legislation requires that employees whose employment is being terminated by the employer be provided with termination pay when they leave. The amount to be paid varies among jurisdictions and with the circumstances, as follows.

Pay in Lieu of Notice

An employee must be provided with advance written notice if the employer is going to terminate his or her employment (unless the employee is working on a short-term contract or is being fired for just cause). The amount of advance notice that is required increases with the length of employment of the employee (often one week per year of employment to a specified maximum) and varies among jurisdictions. Many employers do not provide advance written notice. Instead, they ask the employee to cease working immediately and provide the employee with a lump sum equal to their pay for the notice period. This amount is called "pay in lieu of notice."

Severance Pay

Employees in Ontario and the federal jurisdiction may be eligible for severance pay in addition to pay in lieu of notice in certain termination situations. In Ontario, employees with five or more years of service may be eligible for severance pay if (1) the employer's annual Ontario payroll is $2.5 million or more, or (2) the employer is closing down the business and 50 or more employees will be losing their jobs within a six-month period. The amount of the severance pay is one week's pay for each year of employment (maximum 26 weeks). In the federal jurisdiction, employees who have been employed for 12 months or more receive the greater of two days' wages per year of employment or five days' wages.

Pay for Mass Layoffs

The provinces of British Columbia, Manitoba, Ontario, New Brunswick, and Newfoundland and Labrador require that additional pay be provided when a layoff of 50 or more employees occurs. In Nova Scotia and Saskatchewan, additional pay is required if 10 or more employees are being laid off. The amount of additional pay ranges from 6 weeks to 18 weeks, depending on the province and the number of employees being laid off.

VOLUNTARY EMPLOYER-SPONSORED BENEFITS

Although they are not required to do so, employers often provide many other employee benefits. Several of the most common types of employee benefits will now be described.

Life Insurance

Virtually all employers provide **group life insurance** plans for their employees. As a group, employees can obtain lower rates than if they bought such insurance as individuals. In addition, group plans usually contain a provision for coverage of all employees—including new ones—regardless of health or physical condition.

In most cases, the employer pays 100 percent of the base premium, which usually provides life insurance equal to about two years' salary. Additional life insurance coverage is sometimes made available to employees, on an optional, employee-paid basis. *Accidental death and dismemberment* coverage provides a fixed lump-sum benefit in addition to life insurance benefits when death is accidental. It also provides a range of benefits in case of accidental loss of limbs or sight and is often paid for by the employer.

Critical illness insurance provides a lump-sum benefit to an employee who is diagnosed with and survives a life-threatening illness. This benefit bridges the gap between life insurance and disability insurance by providing immediate funds to relieve some the financial burden associated with the illness (such as paying for out-of-country treatment or experimental treatment) or enabling employees to enjoy their remaining time by pursuing activities that would normally be beyond their financial means.[12]

Supplementary Health-Care/Medical Insurance

Most employers provide their employees with supplementary health-care/medical insurance (over and above that provided by provincial health-care plans). Along with life insurance and long-term disability, these benefits form the cornerstone of almost all benefit programs.[13] Supplementary health-care insurance is aimed at providing protection against medical costs arising from off-the-job accidents or illness.

Most supplementary health insurance plans provide insurance at group rates, which are usually lower than individual rates and are generally available to all employees—including new ones—regardless of health or physical condition. Supplementary health-care plans provide major medical coverage to meet medical expenses not covered by government health-care plans, including prescription drugs, private or semi-private hospital rooms, private duty nursing, physiotherapy, medical supplies, ambulance services, and so on. In most employer-sponsored drug plans, employees must pay a specified amount of **deductible** expense (typically $25 or $50) per year before plan benefits begin. Many employers also sponsor health-related insurance plans that cover expenses like vision care, hearing aids, and dental services, often with deductibles. In a majority of cases, the participants in such plans have their premiums paid for entirely by their employers.[14]

Reducing Health Benefit Costs

Dramatic increases in health-care costs are the biggest issue facing benefits managers in Canada today. **Figure 13.2** shows how increases in medical and dental plan costs have continued to escalate at double-digit rates since 2005. The main reasons for these increases are increased use of expensive new drugs and rising drug utilization by an aging population.[15] Despite government health-care plans, Canadian employers pay about 30 percent of all health-care expenses in Canada, most of this for prescription drugs.[16]

FIGURE 13.2 | Increases in Health Plan Costs 2005–2009

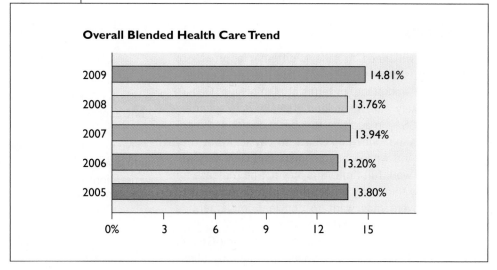

Overall Blended Health Care Trend

Year	Percentage
2009	14.81%
2008	13.76%
2007	13.94%
2006	13.20%
2005	13.80%

Source: Canadian Health Care Trend Survey Results 2009. Toronto ON: Buck Consultants, 2009, p. 2. Reprinted with permission of Buck Consultants, an ACS Company.

Tips | **FOR THE FRONT LINE**

coinsurance The percentage of expenses (in excess of the deductible) that are paid for by the insurance plan.

Public Health Agency of Canada
www.publichealth.gc.ca

Many Canadian managers now find controlling and reducing health-care costs topping their to-do lists. The simplest approach to reducing health-benefit costs is to *increase the amount of health-care costs paid by employees*. This can be accomplished by increasing employee premiums, increasing deductibles, reducing company **coinsurance** levels, instituting or lowering annual maximums on some services, or even eliminating coverage for spouses, private hospital rooms, and other benefits. An Angus Reid poll of 1500 Canadians found that three-quarters of the respondents were willing to pay higher premiums to cover the high cost of prescription drugs.[17]

Another cost-reduction strategy is to publish a *restricted list of drugs* that will be paid for under the plan to encourage the use of generic rather than more expensive brand-name drugs. New drugs may not be covered if equally effective, cheaper alternatives are available. This approach should be combined with employee education to effectively manage the demand for drugs.[18]

A third approach is *health promotion*. In-house newsletters can caution workers to take medication properly and advertise programs on weight management, smoking cessation, exercise classes, on-site massage therapy, nutrition counselling, and other wellness programs. After ten years of providing an on-site exercise program for employees, Canada Life Insurance Company found that absenteeism dropped 24 percent for employees who exercised two to three times per week.[19] Employee assistance programs can help to combat alcohol and drug addiction and provide stress-management counselling.

A fourth approach is to implement *risk-assessment* programs. Such programs are being used by the Canadian Imperial Bank of Commerce and other companies. A third party conducts a confidential survey of the health history and lifestyle choices of employees in order to identify common health risk factors, such as those associated with heart disease or mental health, so that problem-specific programs can be implemented.[20]

An on-site employee fitness centre

Workforce DIVERSITY

Y's Benefits

Employers will need to take a different approach to their benefits plans to accommodate the latest generation in their workplace. In terms of plan design, Gen Ys will most likely want some kind of health care spending account (HCSA) in addition to a basic dental and medical plan so that they don't have to pay for what they won't use. And while baby boomers and Gen Xers will continue to work full time, this may not be the case for Gen Y. Many think they'll hold three part-time jobs, and thus employers may want to consider implementing benefits for part-time workers.

Unfortunately, the health picture for many Gen Ys isn't rosy. Twice as many young people are obese now as compared to 30 years ago. Roughly 15 percent suffer from at least one chronic disease such as diabetes, cancer, mental illness, and bone and joint disorders. In terms of prescription drugs, a study by Green Shield Canada found that, after oral contraceptives, the most-used drug type was antidepressants.

No matter what the composition of the benefits plan, online access is critical for this technologically savvy generation. Plan sponsors will want to ensure that benefits information is available online, accessible 24/7.

Source: Adapted from B. Smith, "Y's Benefits," *Benefits Canada*, July 2008, p. 9.

Finally, *health care spending accounts* (HCSA) are offered by more than 90 percent of Canadian employers, either alone or in combination with a standard health-care plan.[21] The employer establishes an annual account for each employee containing a certain amount of money (determined by the employer to control costs). Then the employee can spend the money on health-care costs as he or she wants. This provides flexibility for the employee. These accounts are governed by the Income Tax Act, which allows expenses not normally covered under employer-sponsored health-care plans (such as laser eye surgery) and defines dependants more broadly than most employer plans.[22] HCSAs are very popular with employees, particularly those in Generation Y, as discussed in the Workforce Diversity box.

Retiree Health Benefits

Another concern is the cost of health benefits provided to retirees. These benefits typically include life insurance, drugs, and private/semi-private hospital coverage. Some continue coverage to a surviving spouse. Retiree benefit costs are already exceeding the costs for active employees in some organizations, in part because many early retirees between the ages of 50 and 65 are not yet eligible for government health benefits that start at age 65. Employers are required to disclose liabilities for retiree benefits in their financial statements. These liabilities are not required to be prefunded and thus are at risk in the case of business failure.[23]

An Ethical | Dilemma

Should it be the employer's responsibility to cover health-care costs for early retirees until they become eligible for government health-care benefits at age 65?

Employers can cut costs by increasing retiree contributions, increasing deductibles, tightening eligibility requirements, and reducing maximum payouts.[24] The last few years have seen a trend away from employer-provided retiree health benefits. This trend is expected to continue as a result of rising health-care costs, growing retiree populations, uncertain business profitability, and federal regulations that provide only limited opportunities for funding retiree medical benefits.[25]

Short-Term Disability Plans and Sick Leave Plans

Short-term disability plans (also known as salary continuation plans) provide a continuation of all or part of an employee's earnings when the employee is absent from work because of non-work-related illness or injury. Usually a medical certificate is required if the absence extends beyond two or three days. These plans typically provide full pay for some period (often two or three weeks) and then gradually reduce the percentage of earnings paid as the period of absence lengthens. The benefits cease when the employee returns to work or when the employee qualifies for long-term disability. These plans are sometimes provided through an insurance company.

Sick leave plans operate quite differently from short-term disability plans. Most sick leave policies grant full pay for a specified number of permissible sick days—usually up to about 12 per year (often accumulated at the rate of one day per month of service). Most jurisdictions require a few days of sick leave (unpaid) as a minimum standard. Sick leave pay creates difficulty for many employers. The problem is that, although many employees use their sick days only when they are legitimately sick, others simply use their sick leave as extensions to their vacations, whether they are sick or not. Also, seriously ill or injured employees get no pay once their sick days are used up.

Some now buy back unused sick leave at the end of the year by paying their employees a daily equivalent pay for each sick leave day not used. The drawback is that the policy can encourage legitimately sick employees to come to work despite their illness. Others have experimented with holding monthly lotteries in which only employees with perfect monthly attendance are able to participate; those who participate are eligible to win a cash prize. Still others aggressively investigate all absences, for instance by calling the absent employees at their homes when they are off sick.

Long-Term Disability

Long-term disability insurance is aimed at providing income protection or compensation for loss of income because of long-term illness or injury that is not work-related. The disability payments usually begin when normal short-term disability or sick leave is used up and may continue to provide income to age 65 or beyond. The disability benefits usually range from 50 to 75 percent of the employee's base pay.

The number of long-term disability claims in Canada is rising sharply. This trend is expected to accelerate as the average age of the workforce continues to increase because the likelihood of chronic illness, such as arthritis, heart disease, and diabetes, increases with age. Therefore, disability management programs with a goal of returning workers safely back to work are becoming a priority in many organizations.[26] For example, employers are beginning to put more effort into managing employees with episodic disabilities, which are chronic illnesses such as HIV, lupus, multiple sclerosis, arthritis, and some cancers and mental illnesses that are unpredictable. These employees may have long periods of good health followed by unpredicted episodes of poor health.[27]

Disability management is a proactive, employer-centred process that coordinates the activities of the employer, the insurance company, and health-care providers in an effort to minimize the impact of injury, disability, or disease on a worker's capacity to successfully perform his or her job. Maintaining contact with a worker who is ill or injured is imperative in disability management so that the worker can be involved in the return-to-work process from the beginning. Ongoing contact also allows the employer to monitor the employee's emotional well-being, which is always affected by illness and/or injury.[28]

Effective disability management programs include prevention, early assessment and intervention regarding employee health problems, monitoring and management of employee absences, and early and safe return-to-work policies.[29] The three most common approaches to returning a worker with a disability to work are reduced work hours, reduced work duties, and workstation modification.[30] Evaluating the physical capabilities of the worker is an important step in designing work modifications to safely reintegrate injured workers. In many cases, the cost of accommodating an employee's disability can be quite modest.

Mental Health Benefits

Mental health issues continue to be the leading cause of short- and long-term disability claims in Canada. Psychiatric disabilities are the fastest growing of all occupational disabilities, with depression being the most common (even though only 32 percent of those afflicted seek treatment, as they do not want to admit it to their employer).[31]

Depression has been described as a "clear and present danger" to business, as it manifests itself in alcoholism, absenteeism, injury, physical illness, and lost productivity. Estimates suggest that an employee with depression who goes untreated costs the company twice what treatment costs per year. A Harvard University study projects that, by 2020, depression will become the biggest source of lost workdays in developed countries; the World Health Organization predicts that depression will rank second as a cause of disability on a global basis by the same year.[32] Young workers (15 to 24) are at most risk.[33]

For Canadian employers, the cost of mental health benefits is about $51 billion annually.[34] Despite the staggering costs, depression is not being addressed in a systematic way, and employers are unprepared to deal with stress, depression, and anxiety in the workplace. Some of the challenges involved in improving this situation are shown in **Figure 13.3.** Only one-third of employers have

World Federation for Mental Health
www.wfmh.org

FIGURE 13.3 | The Top Challenges in Improving How Mental Health Issues Are Addressed in the Workplace

1. Employee perceptions and stigma related to mental health issues	60%
2. Lack of front line manager awareness	54%
3. Inability to identify suitable modified work	40%
4. Inability to introduce significant flexibility options	39%
5. Lack of tools and supports	29%
6. Lack of funds/budget for program enhancements	23%
7. Lack of senior management buy-in	20%
8. Don't know where to start	14%
9. Other	8%

Source: "What are the top challenges you face in improving how mental health issues are addressed in your workplace?" *2008 Mental Health in the Workplace National Survey* (Toronto, ON: Mercer and Canadian Alliance on Mental Illness and Mental Health, 2008), p. 22. Reprinted with permission of Mercer.

implemented return-to-work programs specific to mental health. Such companies as Bell Canada, Alcan, and Superior Propane are trying to help reduce costs with prevention and early intervention programs, including psychiatric counselling and peer-support groups.[35]

Additional Leaves of Absence

Some employers provide full or partial pay for all or part of legally required unpaid leaves by "topping up" what employees receive from EI so the total amount they receive more closely matches their regular salary. For example, in some cases bereavement leave may be partially or fully paid by the employer.

A few employers provide sabbatical leaves for employees who want time off to rejuvenate or to pursue a personal goal. Sabbatical leaves are usually unpaid, but some employers provide partial or full pay. Sabbaticals can help to retain employees and to avoid employee burnout.

Additional Paid Vacations and Holidays

Many employers provide additional paid holidays and paid vacation over and above the amount required by law. For example, long-service employees typically receive more vacation time than legally required.

Retirement Benefits

pension plans Plans that provide income when employees reach a predetermined retirement age.

Employer-sponsored **pension plans** are intended to supplement an employee's government-sponsored retirement benefits, which on average make up 50 percent of the average Canadian's retirement income.[36] Unlike government-provided retirement benefits, employer-sponsored pension plans are prefunded. Money is set aside in a pension fund to accumulate with investment income until it is needed to pay benefits at retirement. Pension fund assets have grown rapidly over the past 40 years. Much of this money is invested in Canadian stocks and bonds because of laws restricting the investment of these assets in foreign securities.

Two Categories of Pension Plans

defined benefit pension plan
A plan that contains a formula for determining retirement benefits.

defined contribution pension plan
A plan in which the employer's contribution to the employees' retirement fund is specified.

Pension plans fall into two categories—defined benefit pension plans and defined contribution pension plans. A **defined benefit pension plan** contains a formula for determining retirement benefits so that the actual benefits to be received are defined ahead of time. For example, the plan might include a formula, such as 2 percent of final year's earnings for each year of service, which would provide a pension of 70 percent of final year's earnings to an employee with 35 years of service.

A **defined contribution pension plan** specifies what contribution the employer will make to a retirement fund set up for the employee. The defined contribution plan does not define the eventual benefit amount, only the periodic contribution to the plan. In a defined benefit plan, the employee knows ahead of time what his or her retirement benefits will be on retirement. With a defined contribution plan, the employee cannot be sure of his or her retirement benefits until retirement, when his or her share of the money in the pension fund is used to buy an annuity. Thus, benefits depend on both the amounts contributed to the fund and the retirement fund's investment earnings. The prevalence of these two types of plans is shown in **Table 13.1**.

Canadian Association for Retired Persons
www.fifty-plus.net
Benefits and Pensions Monitor
www.bpmmagazine.com
Association of Canadian Pension Management
www.acpm.com

TABLE 13.1 | Registered Pension Plans 2008

Type of Plan	Number of Plans	Percentage of Plans Registered	Number of Canadians Covered	Percentage of Total Plan Membership
Defined benefit	11 539	60.2	4 538 192	76.8
Defined Contribution	7 165	37.3	935 236	15.8
Combination	403	2.1	369 926	6.3
Other	78	.4	65 279	1.1
Total	19 185	100	5 908 633	100

Source: Statistics Canada, "Registered Pension Plans and Members, by Type of Plan and Sector." www40.statcan.gc.ca/l01/cst01/famil120a-eng.htm (July 12, 2009).

Defined contribution plans are often considered ideal for the growing number of today's businesses with a relatively young workforce of highly skilled professional and technical people who expect to work with several employers during their careers. Defined contribution plan sponsors benefit from predictable employer costs, and employees find the plan easier to understand.[37]

Employees in defined contribution plans make decisions about the investment of the pension fund assets, which means that member communication is one of the most critical challenges facing defined contribution plan sponsors. Surveys show that many employees are not comfortable with making their own investment decisions, given their relative inexperience in that area. Fluctuating returns in the stock market over the last few years have highlighted the importance of sound investment decisions and of employers' responsibility for educating their employees about investment choices.[38]

Employers must pay careful attention to their obligation to educate and inform (but not advise) plan members about pension investments. There have been cases where plan members who were unhappy with the information provided by the employer and surprised by small benefits have sued their employers and won. Conversely, the University of Western Ontario plan converted to defined contribution in 1970, and faculty members are retiring with incomes greater than their working salaries.[39]

As shown in **Figure 13.4**, the number of defined contribution plans has been increasing over the past 15 years, due to the cost and complexity of sponsoring a defined benefit plan in an increasingly fragmented legislative environment. Correspondingly, the number of Canadian employees who are defined benefit plan members dropped 30 percent between 1991 and 2006.[40] Nevertheless it should be remembered that the vast majority of pension plan members are still in defined benefit plans.

The severe economic recession that began in late 2008 resulted in major shrinkage in the value of pension funds and highlighted issues with both types of plan. For defined benefit plans, the recession necessitated major increases in contributions to pension funds in order to maintain their required funding levels.[41] Although some jurisdictions eased the funding rules temporarily to allow more time to repay funding shortfalls, defined benefit plans began to be called an "endangered species."[42] For defined contribution plans, many plan members

FIGURE 13.4 | Defined Contribution Pension Plan Participants 1991–2006

Source: Statistics Canada, Pension Plans in Canada Survey.

nearing retirement saw no other option but to defer retirement and continue working until the markets recovered and their pension fund account balance recovered to an amount that would provide them with the retirement income they need.[43] These issues created considerable debate about the adequacy of retirement savings for future generations.

There are two other types of defined contribution arrangements. Under a *group registered retirement savings plan (Group RRSP)*, employees can have a portion of their compensation (which would otherwise be paid in cash) put into an RRSP by the employer. The employee is not taxed on those set-aside dollars until after he or she retires (or removes the money from the plan). Most employers do not match all or a portion of what the employee contributes to the Group

Workers rally in Windsor, Ontario, after the provincial government refuses to expand pension guarantees.

deferred profit-sharing plan A plan in which a certain amount of company profits is credited to each employee's account, payable at retirement, termination, or death.

RRSP because employer contributions are considered taxable income to employees. Instead, the employer often establishes a **deferred profit-sharing plan (DPSP)** and contributes a portion of company profits into the DPSP fund, where an account is set up for each employee. No employee contributions to a DPSP are allowed under Canadian tax law. Group RRSP/DPSP combinations are popular in Canada because no tax is paid until money is received from the plans at the time of the employee's death or termination of employment (at retirement or otherwise).

The entire area of pension planning is complicated, partly because of the laws governing pensions. For example, companies want to ensure that their pension contributions are tax deductible and must therefore adhere to the Income Tax Act. The provincial and the federal jurisdictions also have laws governing employer-sponsored pension plans. Sometimes the complicated and overlapping federal and provincial legislation can make employers question whether or not to sponsor a pension plan.[44] Legislation regarding pension plans varies around the world, and Canada's regulators can learn important lessons from other countries' successes and failures, as described in the Global HRM box.

Global HRM

Defined Benefit Pension Problems and Solutions Around the World

Many countries designed generous defined benefit social security programs between 1950 and 1970 based on fertility rates that created a stable population. The actual experience of declining populations in many countries, particularly Japan, created serious intergenerational inequity as younger employees were subsidizing older ones. Solutions included increasing contribution rates (Belgium, Canada), raising the normal retirement age to 67 (E.U.), both of these (Germany), moving to defined contribution plans (Australia, France, Switzerland, U.K.), and even more complex protective legislation (Netherlands). Japan first permitted defined contribution plans in 2001, and they have slowly become more prevalent.

Unfortunately, none of these national actions seem to be the optimal solution to the global defined benefits plan issue. The numerous retirement savings plans known as "provident funds" in Asia and defined contribution plans in Australia seem to be doing fairly well. The E.U. encourages the creation of pan-European pension plans where an employer can create a plan in one location and cover all European employees under that single plan. This encourages employee mobility and reduces administrative costs. The plans must comply with the rules from the plan's home country, while still respecting some of the pension laws of other countries where employees reside or have retired. Countries such as Luxembourg, Ireland, and Belgium have tried to create the best tax and legal environment to attract these plans, but it is too early to tell if a leader will emerge.

The E.U. situation is very similar to our Canadian system with its patchwork of legislation. Given Canada's population of 33 million versus 700 million in Europe, it is clear that our pension landscape should have been more straightforward from the outset and desperately needs to be simplified. There is some hope for the future as three expert commissions in Ontario, Nova Scotia, and, jointly, in Alberta and British Columbia are undertaking reviews of the pension legislation in those provinces. Perhaps they will find the right balance between regulation and governance, and perhaps other provinces will also align to their findings.

But until we find better ways to enhance and preserve defined benefit plans, employers will have to make some difficult decisions. Country by country, they must choose between assuming the risks and higher administrative costs of sponsoring defined benefit plans or moving to defined contribution plans, which typically do not produce the same retirement value to each dollar spent and are less flexible as an HR tool.

Source: Adapted from F. Letourneau, "Around the World in Six Pages," *Benefits Canada*, August 2008, pp. 14–19. Reprinted with permission.

When designing a pension plan, there are several legal and policy issues to consider:[45]

- *Membership requirements.* For example, at what minimum number of years of service do employees become eligible to join the plan?
- *Benefit formula* (defined benefits plans only). This usually ties the pension to the employee's final earnings, or an average of his or her last three to five years' earnings.
- *Retirement age.* Traditionally, the normal retirement age in Canada has been 65. However, since mandatory retirement is now prohibited by human rights laws across the country, employees cannot be required to retire at age 65. Some plans call for "30 and out." This permits an employee to retire after 30 years of continuous service, regardless of the person's age.
- *Funding.* The question of how the plan is to be funded is another key issue. One aspect is whether the plan will be contributory or noncontributory. In the former, contributions to the pension fund are made by both employees and the employer. In a noncontributory fund, only the employer contributes.

vesting Provision that employer money placed in a pension fund cannot be forfeited for any reason.

- *Vesting.* Employee **vesting** rights is another critical issue in pension planning. Vesting refers to the money that the employer has placed in the pension fund that cannot be forfeited for any reason. The employees' contributions can never be forfeited. An employee is vested when he or she has met the requirements set out in the plan, whereby, on termination of employment, he or she will receive future benefits based on the contributions made to the plan by the *employer* on behalf of the employee. In most provinces, pension legislation requires that employer contributions be vested once the employee has completed two years of service. Plans may vest more quickly than required by law. If the employee terminates employment before being vested, he or she is only entitled to a refund of his or her own contributions, plus interest (unless the employer has decided to be more generous). Once an employee is vested, all contributions are "locked in" and cannot be withdrawn by the employee on termination of employment; that is, employees must wait until retirement to receive a pension from the plan. Most plans permit the employee to transfer the amount into a locked-in RRSP (see the discussion on portability below), but the money cannot be accessed until retirement.

An Ethical | Dilemma

Should an employer with a pension plan that covers employees in several provinces give each group the minimum vesting and portability benefits for their province, or take the most generous of these and provide it to all employees?

- *Portability.* Canadian employers today are being required by pension legislation to make their pensions more "portable" for employees on termination of employment. **Portability** means that employees in defined contribution plans can take the money in their company pension account to a new employer's plan or roll it over into a locked-in RRSP. For defined benefit plans, the lump-sum value of the benefit earned can be transferred.

portability A provision that employees who change jobs can transfer the lump-sum value of the pension they have earned to a locked-in RRSP or their new employer's pension plan.

Phased Retirement

The labour shortage is resulting in employers seeking to retain older employees. At the same time, many Canadians wishing to retire early are finding that they are not in a financial position to do so and that they need to continue working to age 60, 65, or even later.[46] The idea of **phased retirement,** whereby employees gradually ease into retirement using reduced workdays and/or shortened workweeks has been increasing in Canada, as shown in **Figure 13.5.** Constraints

phased retirement An arrangement whereby employees gradually ease into retirement by using reduced workdays and/or shortened workweeks.

FIGURE 13.5 | Prevalence of Phased Retirement Programs

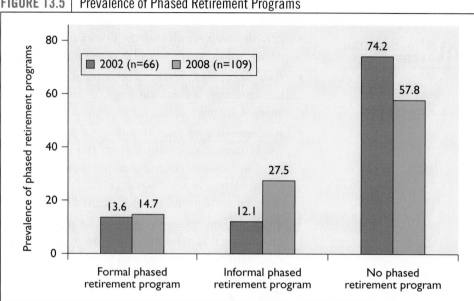

Source: K. Thorpe, *Harnessing the Power: Recruiting, Engaging, and Retaining Mature Workers* (Ottawa: The Conference Board of Canada, October 2008), 23. Reprinted by permission of The Conference Board of Canada, Ottawa.

under the Income Tax Act and pension legislation in some jurisdictions are slowly being loosened, and it is now possible for older workers to receive some benefits from their pension plan while they are being paid to continue to work.[47]

Supplemental Employee Retirement Plans (SERPs)

The Income Tax Act has not changed the maximum pension benefit permissible under the Income Tax Act (for tax-deductibility of plan contributions) since 1976. Thus many Canadians have their pension benefits capped at less than what their defined benefit plan formula would otherwise provide. Originally this situation only created problems for highly paid executives, but in recent years, more and more employees have been affected. **Supplemental employee retirement plans (SERPs)** are intended to provide the difference in pension benefit and thus restore pension adequacy for high earners.

A Towers Perrin survey found that nearly three-quarters of employers provide SERPs (including about two-thirds of small employers with fewer than 500 employees). The survey also found that 53 percent of SERP sponsors cover employees below the executive level in "broad-based" plans. Most SERPs are "pay-as-you-go" plans; that is, they do not have a fund established to accumulate money to pay the benefits (because contributions are not tax-deductible). However, the security of SERP benefits has been improving, as 41 percent of plans are now secured in some manner.[48]

supplemental employee retirement plans Plans that provide the additional pension benefit required for employees to receive their full pension benefit in cases where their full pension benefit exceeds the maximum allowable benefit under the Income Tax Act.

EMPLOYEE SERVICES

Although an employer's time off and insurance and retirement benefits account for the largest portion of its benefits costs, many employers also provide a range of services, including personal services (such as counselling), job-related services (such as childcare facilities), and executive perquisites (such as company cars and planes for executives).

Personal Services

First, many companies provide personal services that most employees need at one time or another. These include credit unions, counselling, employee assistance plans, and social and recreational opportunities.

Credit Unions

Credit unions are usually separate businesses established with the assistance of the employer. Employees usually become members of a credit union by purchasing a share of the credit union's stock for $5 or $10. Members can then deposit savings that accrue interest at a rate determined by the credit union's board of directors. Perhaps more important to most employees, loan eligibility and the rate of interest paid on the loan are usually more favourable than those found in banks and finance companies.

Counselling Services

Employers are also providing a wider range of counselling services to employees. These include *financial counselling* (e.g., in terms of how to overcome existing indebtedness problems), *family counselling* (for marital problems and so on), *career counselling* (in terms of analyzing one's aptitudes and deciding on a career), *job placement counselling* (for helping terminated or disenchanted employees find new jobs), and *pre-retirement counselling* (aimed at preparing retiring employees for what many find is the trauma of retiring). Many employers also make available to employees a full range of *legal counselling* through legal insurance plans.[49]

Employee Assistance Plans (EAPs)

employee assistance plan (EAP)
A company-sponsored program to help employees cope with personal problems that are interfering with or have the potential to interfere with their job performance, as well as issues affecting their well-being and/or that of their families.

Family Services Employee Assistance Programs
www.familyserviceseap.com
Shepell.fgi
www.shepellfgi.com

An **employee assistance plan (EAP)** is a formal employer program that provides employees (and very often their family members) with confidential counselling and/or treatment programs for problems such as mental health issues, marital/family problems, work/life balance issues, stress, legal problems, substance abuse, and other addictions such as gambling. They are particularly important for helping employees who suffer workplace trauma—ranging from harassment to physical assault. There was a significant increase in EAP usage during the economic recession that began in late 2008, particularly in the areas of financial problems and stress.[50]

The number of EAPs in Canada is growing because they are a proactive way for organizations to reduce absenteeism and disability costs. A very general estimate is that 10 percent of employees use EAP services. With supervisory training in how to identify employees who may need an EAP referral, usage can be expanded to more employees who need help.[51]

EAP counsellors can be employed in-house, or the company can contract with an external EAP firm.[52] It is important to assess the services provided by external EAP providers before using them, as quality levels vary. Whatever the model, an EAP provider should be confidential, accessible to employees in all company locations, and timely in providing service, and should offer highly educated counsellors and provide communication material to publicize the plan to employees. They should also provide utilization reports on the number of employees using the service and the types of services being provided, without compromising confidentiality.[53]

Other Personal Services

Finally, some employers also provide various social and recreational opportunities for their employees, including company-sponsored athletic events, dances, annual summer picnics, craft activities, and parties. In practice, the benefits offered are limited only by creativity in thinking up new benefits. For example, pharmaceutical giant Pfizer Inc. provides employees with free drugs made by the company, including Viagra![54]

Job-Related Services

Job-related services aimed directly at helping employees perform their jobs, such as educational subsidies and daycare centres, constitute a second group of services.

Subsidized Childcare

Eighty percent of Canadian families with young children have both parents working.[55] Subsidized daycare is offered to assist in balancing these work and life responsibilities. Many employers simply investigate the daycare facilities in their communities and recommend certain ones to interested employees, but more employers are setting up company-sponsored daycare facilities themselves, both to attract young parents to the payroll and to reduce absenteeism. In this case, the centre is a separate, privately run venture, paid for by the firm. IKEA, Husky Injection Moldings, IBM, and the Kanata Research Park have all chosen this option. Where successful, the hours of operation are structured around parents' schedules, the daycare facility is close to the workplace (often in the same building), and the employer provides 50 to 75 percent of the operating costs. Two emerging benefits are daycare for mildly ill children and emergency backup childcare.[56]

Subsidizing daycare facilities for children of employees has many benefits for the employer, including lower employee absenteeism.

To date, the evidence regarding the actual effects of employer-sponsored childcare on employee absenteeism, turnover, productivity, recruitment, and job satisfaction is positive, particularly with respect to reducing obstacles to coming to work and improving workers' attitudes.[57]

Eldercare

With the average age of the Canadian population rising, eldercare is increasingly a concern for many employers and individuals. It is a complex, unpredictable, and exhausting process that creates stress for the caregiver, the family, and co-workers. Eldercare is expected to become a more common workplace issue than childcare as the 21st-century progresses.[58]

Company eldercare programs are designed to assist employees who must help elderly parents or relatives who are not fully able to care for themselves, up to and including palliative care of the dying. Eldercare benefits include flexible hours, support groups, counselling, free pagers, and adult daycare programs. Referral services to help employees connect with the wide variety of services for the elderly are particularly helpful for employees with eldercare responsibilities.[59] For example, BMO's EAP can be used to find nursing homes by entering a postal code and utilizing the list of questions provided to assist in selecting the best one. BMO employee Yasmin Meralli says, "It helped me with my work because it reduced the amount of time I had to spend outside of work doing other stuff. . . . It really felt to me that I worked for a company that cared."[60]

Subsidized Employee Transportation

Some employers also provide subsidized employee transportation. An employer can negotiate with a transit system to provide free year-round transportation to its employees. Other employers facilitate employee car-pooling, perhaps by acting as the central clearinghouse to identify employees from the same geographic areas who work the same hours.

Food Services

Food services are provided in some form by many employers; they allow employees to purchase meals, snacks, or coffee usually at relatively low prices. Even employers that do not provide full dining facilities generally make available food services, such as coffee wagons or vending machines, for the convenience of employees.

Educational Subsidies

Educational subsidies, such as tuition refunds, have long been a popular benefit for employees seeking to continue or complete their education. Payments range from all tuition and expenses to some percentage of expenses to a flat fee per year of, say, $500 to $600. Most companies pay for courses directly related to an employee's present job. Many also reimburse tuition for courses that are not job-related (such as a secretary taking an accounting class) that pertain to the company business and those that are part of a degree or diploma program. In-house educational programs include remedial work in basic literacy and training for improved supervisory skills.

Family-Friendly Benefits

One of the top drivers of workforce commitment in Canada is management's recognition of personal and family life. Ninety percent of responding employees in one survey said work/life benefits were "important" or "very important" to them.[61] Recognition of the pressures of balancing work and family life have led many employers to bolster what they call their "family-friendly" benefits. Examples include flexible work hours, on-site daycare, and eldercare benefits.

Family-friendly benefits are intended to reduce the extent to which work–family conflicts spill over to the employee's job and undermine the person's job satisfaction and performance. Research has found that "the relationship between job satisfaction and various [work–family] conflict measures is strong and negative across all samples; people with high levels of [work–family] conflict tend to be less satisfied with their jobs."[62] Similarly, there was a strong negative correlation between work–family conflict and the extent to which the employees were satisfied with their lives in general. Managers should therefore understand that providing their employees with family-friendly benefits can apparently have very positive effects on the employees, one of which is making them more satisfied with their work and their jobs.

Boomers are the "Sandwich Generation" caring for both children and elderly parents.

Executive Perquisites

Perquisites (perks, for short) are usually given to only a few top executives. Perks can range from the substantial to the almost insignificant. A bank chairperson may have a chauffeur-driven limousine and use of a bank-owned property in the Caribbean. Executives of large companies often use a corporate jet for business travel. At the other extreme, perks may entail little more than the right to use a company car.[63]

An Ethical | Dilemma

Is it ethical for executive perquisites to continue if the company is facing financial problems?

A multitude of popular perks fall between these extremes. These include management loans (which typically enable senior officers to use their stock options); salary guarantees (also known as *golden parachutes*) to protect executives if their firms are the targets of acquisitions or mergers; financial counselling (to handle top executives' investment programs); and relocation benefits, often including subsidized mortgages, purchase of the executive's current house, and payment for the actual move. A potpourri of other executive perks include outplacement assistance, company cars, chauffeured limousines, security systems, company planes and yachts, executive dining rooms, legal services, tax assistance, liberal expense accounts, club memberships, season tickets, credit cards, and subsidized education for their children. Perks related to wellness and quality of life (such as physical fitness programs) are highly valued in today's stressful environment. An increasingly popular new perk offered at KPMG, Telus, and Ernst & Young is concierge service, intended to carry out errands, such as grocery shopping or organizing a vacation, for busy executives.[64] Employers have many ways of making their hard-working executives' lives as pleasant as possible!

FLEXIBLE BENEFITS PROGRAMS

flexible benefits program
Individualized benefit plans to accommodate employee needs and preferences.

Research conducted more than 30 years ago found that an employee's age, marital status, and sex influenced his or her choice of benefits.[65] For example, preference for pensions increased significantly with employee age, and preference for the family dental plan increased sharply as the number of dependants increased. Thus, benefits that one worker finds attractive may be unattractive to another. In the last 25 years in Canada, there has been a significant increase in **flexible benefits programs** that permit employees to develop individualized benefits packages for themselves by choosing the benefits options they prefer. In 1980 there were no flex plans in Canada, but by 2005, 41 percent of employers offered flex benefits plans. Benefit consultants Hewitt Associates report that 85 percent of Canadian employers either have a flex plan in place or expect to implement one at some point. Fifty-three percent either have a full flex plan now or are in the process of doing so.[66]

RPC

Performs an analysis of organizational and employee needs related to benefit plans.

Employers derive several advantages from offering flexible benefit plans, the two most important being cost containment and the ability to meet the needs of an increasingly diverse workforce. Hewitt Associates' surveys have found that over the years, the most important advantage of implementing flexible benefits has been meeting diverse employee needs. However, in 2005, for the first time in survey history, the concern about containing benefit cost increases surpassed meeting diverse employee needs as the most significant reason to implement

Benefits Design Inc.
www.benefitsdesign.com
International Foundation of
Employee Benefit Plans
www.ifebp.org

flexible plans. In the 2006 survey, 100 percent of respondents reported that their flex plans were meeting or exceeding their expectations regarding meeting employee needs, and the level of satisfaction with flex plans as a cost containment measure was 78 percent.[67]

Flexible benefits plans empower the employee to put together his or her own benefit package, subject to two constraints. First, the employer must carefully limit total cost for each total benefits package. Second, each benefit plan must include certain items that are not optional. These include, for example, Canada/Quebec Pension Plan, workers' compensation, and employment insurance. Subject to these two constraints, employees can pick and choose from the available options. Thus, a young parent might opt for the company's life and dental insurance plans, while an older employee opts for an improved pension plan. The list of possible options that the employer might offer can include many of the benefits discussed in this chapter—vacations, insurance benefits, pension plans, educational services, and so on.

Advantages and disadvantages of flexible benefit programs are summarized in **Figure 13.6.** The flexibility is, of course, the main advantage. Although most employees favour flexible benefits, some do not like to spend time choosing among available options, and some choose inappropriate benefits. Communication regarding the choices available in a flexible plan is considered the biggest challenge for employers. A majority of flex plan sponsors provide a plan website. However, even with new technology, employers still find face-to-face communication is the preferred method for providing initial information about a new flex plan.[68] The recent rapid increase in the number of flexible plans in Canada indicates that the pros outweigh the cons.

FIGURE 13.6 | Advantages and Disadvantages of Flexible Benefit Programs

ADVANTAGES

1. Employees choose packages that best satisfy their unique needs.
2. Flexible benefits help firms meet the *changing* needs of a *changing* workforce.
3. Increased involvement of employees and families improves understanding of benefits.
4. Flexible plans make introduction of new benefits less costly. The new option is added merely as one among a wide variety of elements from which to choose.
5. Cost containment—the organization sets the dollar maximum. Employee chooses within that constraint.

DISADVANTAGES

1. Employees make bad choices and find themselves not covered for predictable emergencies.
2. Administrative burdens and expenses increase.
3. Adverse selection—employees pick only benefits they will use. The subsequent high benefit utilization increases its cost.

Source: G.T. Milkovich, J.M. Newman, N.D. Cole, *Compensation,* Canadian 3rd ed. Toronto: McGraw Hill Ryerson © 2010. Reprinted with permission of McGraw-Hill Ryerson Ltd.

BENEFITS ADMINISTRATION

Canadian Pension and Benefits Institute
www.cpbi-icra.ca

Whether it is a flexible benefits plan or a more traditional one, benefits administration is a challenge. Even in a relatively small company with 40 to 50 employees, the administrative problems of keeping track of the benefits status of each employee can be a time-consuming task as employees are hired and separated and as they use or want to change their benefits. However, software is available to assist with this challenge. Many companies make use of some sort of benefits spreadsheet software to facilitate tracking benefits and updating information. Another approach is outsourcing benefits administration to a third-party expert. The major advantages are greater efficiency and consistency and enhanced service.[69]

Keeping Employees Informed

RPC

Administers the reporting, funding, and fiduciary aspects of the plan
Provides information and counselling to pension plan participants

Benefits communication, particularly regarding pension plans and flexible benefits, is increasingly important as a large number of people are approaching retirement. Correct information must be provided in a timely, clear manner. Pension legislation across Canada specifies what information must be disclosed to plan members and their spouses. Court challenges concerning information on benefits plans are on the rise as people's awareness of their right to information grows.[70]

Increasingly, organizations are utilizing new technology, such as intranets, to ensure that up-to-date information is provided in a consistent manner. Some companies are now using real-time e-statements. At Hewlett Packard (Canada) Ltd., an electronic pension booklet is available on the company's intranet, and a pension-modelling tool can be accessed through the web. The modelling software allows employees to fill in their personal information to calculate various "what if" scenarios.[71]

Chapter | SUMMARY

1. The strategic importance of employee benefits is increasing in the post-job-security era. When benefits are aligned with business strategy, they can help to attract and retain the right people to achieve business objectives.

2. Six government-sponsored benefits are employment insurance, Canada/Quebec Pension Plan, workers' compensation, vacations and holidays, leaves of absence, and pay on termination of employment.

3. Health insurance costs are rising because of expensive new drugs, rising drug utilization by an aging population, and reductions in coverage under provincial health-care plans. These costs can be reduced by increasing the amount of health-care costs paid by employees, publishing a restricted list of the drugs that will be paid for

under the plan, implementing health and wellness promotion plans, using risk assessment programs, and offering health services spending accounts.

4. The two categories of pension plans are defined benefit plans and defined contribution plans. Defined benefit plans provide a benefit based on a formula related to years of service, and the employer assumes the investment risk associated with the pension fund assets. Defined contribution plans provide for specified contributions to a pension fund by the employer, and the benefit will vary depending on the rate of return on the pension fund assets (employees assume the investment risk). Defined contribution plans have been gaining in popularity due to the cost and complex rules associated with defined benefit plans.

5. Three types of personal employee services offered by many organizations include credit unions, counselling services, and employee assistance plans. Six types of job-related services offered by many employers include subsidized childcare, eldercare, subsidized employee transportation, food services, educational subsidies, and family-friendly benefits.

6. The flexible benefits approach allows the employee to put together his or her own benefit plan, subject to total cost limits and the inclusion of certain compulsory items. The employer first determines the total cost for the benefits package. Then a decision is made as to which benefits will be compulsory (such as Canada/Quebec Pension Plan, workers' compensation, and employment insurance). Then other benefits are selected for inclusion in the plan, such as life insurance, health and dental coverage, short- and long-term disability insurance, and retirement plans. Sometimes vacations and employee services are included as well. Then employees select the optional benefits they prefer with the money they have available to them under the total plan.

PEARSON
myHRlab™

Test yourself on the material for this chapter at
www.pearsoned.ca/myhrlab

Key | TERMS

Canada/Quebec Pension Plan (C/QPP)   *(p. 355)*
coinsurance   *(p. 361)*
deductible   *(p. 360)*
deferred profit-sharing plan (DPSP)   *(p. 368)*
defined benefit pension plan   *(p. 365)*
defined contribution pension plan   *(p. 365)*
disability management   *(p. 363)*
employee assistance plan (EAP)   *(p. 371)*
employee benefits   *(p. 353)*
employment insurance   *(p. 354)*

flexible benefits program   *(p. 375)*
group life insurance   *(p. 360)*
pension plans   *(p. 365)*
phased retirement   *(p. 369)*
portability   *(p. 369)*
short-term disability   *(p. 363)*
sick leave plans   *(p. 363)*
supplemental employee retirement plans   *(p. 370)*
vesting   *(p. 369)*
workers' compensation   *(p. 356)*

Review and Discussion | QUESTIONS

1. Explain two main approaches to reducing workers' compensation claims.

2. Explain what companies are doing to reduce health-benefit costs.

3. Explain the difference between sick leave plans and short-term disability plans.

4. Explain why many organizations are changing from a defined benefit to a defined contribution pension plan.

5. Why are long-term disability claims increasing so rapidly in Canada?

6. Outline the kinds of services provided by EAPs.

7. Explain the pros and cons of flexible benefits from both an employer and employee perspective.

8. Answer or complete the following questions from the information in this chapter.

   • What company gives their employees a 10-day break at Christmas?

   • What are the six government-sponsored or legislated benefits?

   • A ____ _____ is the amount the employee must pay on a yearly basis before supplementary health-care benefits begin.

   • _____ _____ includes such things as newsletters, fitness centres, and nutrition counselling.

   • The __ Generation wants their benefits information online.

   • The difference between a group pension plan and a group registered retirement savings plan is _____.

- _____ rights mean that the employee with the required length of service has a nonforfeitable right to the money contributed to the pension plan by the employer.
- There are two types of employee services, _____ and _____. One example of each is _____ and _____.
- Tuition reimbursement is an example of an _____ _____.
- The most preferred way to communicate initial flexible benefits plan information to employees is _____.

Critical Thinking | QUESTIONS

1. You are applying for a job as a manager and are at the point of negotiating salary and benefits. What questions would you ask your prospective employer concerning benefits? Describe the benefits package that you would try to negotiate for yourself.
2. What are pension "vesting" and "portability"? Why do you think these are (or are not) important to a recent university or college graduate?
3. You are the HR consultant to a small business with about 40 employees. Currently, the business offers only the legal minimum number of days for vacation and paid holidays and the legally mandated benefits. Develop a list of other benefits that you believe should be offered, along with your reasons for suggesting them.
4. If you were designing a retirement benefit for a mid-sized organization that had not previously offered one, what type of plan would you recommend to them and why?
5. What questions might an employee who currently has no benefits or a minimal coverage standard benefits plan have about flexible benefits? How can an organization address these questions and concerns? List suggested topics for a new flexible benefits plan communication plan and include at least suggestions about the appropriate media to be used.

Experiential | EXERCISES

1. Working individually or in groups, compile a list of the perks available to the following individuals: the head of your local public utilities commission, the president of your college or university, and the president of a large company in your area. Do they all have certain perks in common? What do you think accounts for any differences?
2. Working individually or in groups, contact your provincial Workers' Compensation Board (or equivalent in your province/territory) and compile a list of its suggestions for reducing workers' compensation costs. What seem to be the main recommendations?

Running | CASE

Running Case: LearnInMotion.com

The New Benefits Plan
LearnInMotion.com provides only legislatively required benefits for all its employees. These include participation in employment insurance, Canada Pension Plan, and workers' compensation. No employee services are provided.

Jennifer can see several things wrong with the company's policies regarding benefits and services. First, she wants to determine whether similar companies' experiences with providing health and life insurance benefits make hiring easier and/or reduces employee turnover. Jennifer is also concerned that the company has no policy regarding vacations or sick leave. Informally, at least, it is understood that employees get a one-week vacation after one year's work. However, the policy regarding pay for such days as New Year's and Thanksgiving has been inconsistent. Sometimes employees on the job only two or three weeks are paid fully for one of these holidays; sometimes employees who have been with the firm for six months or more get paid for only half a day. No one really knows what the company's chosen "paid" holidays are. Jennifer knows these policies must be more consistent.

She also wonders about the wisdom of establishing some type of retirement plan for the firm. Although everyone working for the firm is still in their 20s, she believes a defined contribution plan in which employees contribute a portion of their pre-tax salary, to be matched up to some limit by a contribution by LearnInMotion.com, would contribute to the sense of commitment she and Pierre would like to create among their employees. However, Pierre isn't so sure. His position is that if they don't get sales up pretty soon, they're going to burn through their cash. Now they want you, their management consultant, to help them decide what to do.

QUESTIONS

1   Which benefit and services policy would you recommend LearnInMotion change first and why?

2   What changes would you recommend to Jennifer regarding their lack of a vacation policy?

3   As most of LearnInMotion's staff are in their mid-20s, what type of pension plan would appeal to this employee demographic and why?

Case | INCIDENT

Technology Plus's Benefit Dilemma

In order to stay competitive, many organizations today are choosing to restructure their benefit programs. Technology Plus is an example of such a company. Technology Plus employs 150 employees including upper management, skilled tradespersons, sales representatives, and customer service representatives. Five years ago, this company was enjoying huge profits and could afford their current benefits program; however, times have changed and now they need to find cost savings without laying off any of their staff.

Technology Plus to this point has offered all of their staff a premium benefits program, including much more than government-required benefits of employment insurance, Canada Pension Plan, worker's compensation, standard vacation of two weeks per year, and access to legislated leaves of absence. They offer group life insurance of three times salary, accidental death and dismemberment insurance of three times salary, extended health-care benefits (with vision care, dental care, hearing aids, and more), long-term disability of 75 percent of salary (employer-paid), and a defined benefit pension plan.

They also provide a wellness program, an employee assistance plan, and many other services such as subsidized childcare and assistance with eldercare. However, now they need your help in deciding how to restructure their benefit plan to find significant cost savings but still provide meaningful benefit coverage for their employees.

QUESTIONS

1   What voluntary employer-sponsored benefits should this company maintain and which ones should they not maintain in your opinion, and why?

2   Would a flexible benefit program save this organization money if administered properly?

For additional cases and exercise material, go to
www.pearsoned.ca/myhrlab

 To view the CBC Videos, read a summary, and answer discussion questions, go to MyHRLab at
www.pearsoned.ca/myhrlab

CHAPTER 14

LEARNING OUTCOMES

AFTER STUDYING THIS CHAPTER, YOU SHOULD BE ABLE TO

ANALYZE the responsibilities and rights of employees and employers under occupational health and safety legislation.

EXPLAIN WHMIS legislation.

ANALYZE in detail three basic causes of accidents.

DESCRIBE how accidents at work can be prevented.

EXPLAIN why employee wellness programs are becoming increasingly popular.

DISCUSS six major employee health issues at work and **RECOMMEND** how they should be handled.

OCCUPATIONAL HEALTH AND SAFETY

REQUIRED PROFESSIONAL CAPABILITIES (RPC)

- Prepares organizational health and safety files for investigation and/or for litigation

- Responds to any refusals to perform work believed to be unsafe

- Establishes a joint Health and Safety committee as required by law

- Provides information to employees and managers on available programs

- Ensures that policies for required medical testing fall within the limits of statute and contract

- Ensures compliance with legislated reporting requirements

- Ensures adequate accommodation, modified work, and graduated return-to-work programs are in place

- Ensures that modifications to the work environment are consistent with worker limitations

STRATEGIC IMPORTANCE OF OCCUPATIONAL HEALTH AND SAFETY

Ceremonies are held across Canada every April 28 to mark the National Day of Mourning for workers killed or injured on the job. In Moncton, New Brunswick, Pauline Farrell lays roses in memory of her late husband, Bill Kelly, who was killed more than 30 years ago.

Health and safety initiatives are part of a strategic approach to human resources management. Service provided to clients and customers is a function of how employees are treated, and employee health, safety, and wellness management are important determinants of employee perceptions regarding fair treatment by the organization. Further, investment in disability management and proactive wellness programs create measurable bottom-line returns.[1]

Another reason that safety and accident prevention concerns managers is that the work-related accident figures are staggering. According to the Association of Workers' Compensation Boards of Canada, in 2007 there were 1055 deaths and 317 524 injuries resulting from accidents at work. Thus, on average, more than three Canadian workers die each working day.[2] On April 28 each year, a day of mourning is observed for Canadian workers killed or injured on the job. These figures do not include minor injuries that do not involve time lost from work beyond the day of the accident. Moreover, these figures do not tell the full story. They do not reflect the human suffering incurred by injured or ill workers and their families.

Workplace health concerns are also widespread. Surveys have shown that 61 percent of Canadians believe that workplace accidents are inevitable.[3] This statistic is particularly disturbing, because workplace accidents can be prevented.

BASIC FACTS ABOUT OCCUPATIONAL HEALTH AND SAFETY LEGISLATION

occupational health and safety legislation Laws intended to protect the health and safety of workers by minimizing work-related accidents and illnesses.

All provinces, territories, and the federal jurisdiction have **occupational health and safety legislation** based on the principle of joint responsibility shared by workers and employers to maintain a hazard-free work environment and to enhance the health and safety of workers.[4]

Purpose

These laws fall into three categories: general health and safety rules, rules for specific industries (e.g., mining), and rules related to specific hazards (e.g., asbestos). In some jurisdictions, these are combined into one overall law with regulations for specific industries and hazards, while in others they remain separate. The regulations are very complex and cover almost every conceivable hazard in great detail, as shown in **Figure 14.1**. Provisions of occupational health and safety legislation differ significantly across Canada but most have certain basic features in common.

FIGURE 14.1 | Ontario Occupational Health and Safety Act—Construction Regulations

O.REG.213/91

68. A sign used to direct traffic,

(a) shall be diamond shaped, 450 millimetres wide and 450 millimetres long, with the diamond mounted at one corner on a pole 1.2 metres long; (b) shall be made of material that has at least the rigidity of six millimetres thick plywood; (c) shall be reflective fluorescent and coloured, (i) red-orange on one side with the corner areas coloured black, so that the red-orange area forms a regular eight-sided figure, with the word "STOP" written in legible white letters 150 millimetres high in a central position on the sign, and (ii) chartreuse on one side, with the word "SLOW" written in legible black letters 150 millimetres high in a central position on the sign; and (d) shall be maintained in a clean condition.

Responsibilities and Rights of Employers and Employees

In all jurisdictions, employers are responsible for taking every reasonable precaution to ensure the health and safety of their workers. This is called the "due diligence" requirement. Specific duties of the employer include filing government accident reports, maintaining records, ensuring that safety rules are enforced, and posting safety notices and legislative information.[5] A recent Ontario court decision suggests that employers must enforce safe work procedures through the progressive discipline process in order to establish a defense of due diligence when workers do not follow safety rules and are injured on the job.[6]

Employees are responsible for taking reasonable care to protect their own health and safety and, in most cases, that of their co-workers. Specific requirements include wearing protective clothing and equipment and reporting any contravention of the law or regulations. Employees have three basic rights under the joint responsibility model: (1) the right to know about workplace safety hazards, (2) the right to participate in the occupational health and safety process, and (3) the right to refuse unsafe work if they have "reasonable cause" to believe that the work is dangerous. "Reasonable cause" usually means that a complaint about a workplace hazard has not been satisfactorily resolved, or a safety problem places employees in immediate danger. If performance of a task would adversely affect health and safety, a worker cannot be disciplined for refusing to do the job.

RPC
Responds to any refusals to perform work believed to be unsafe

Joint Health and Safety Committees

The function of joint health and safety committees is to provide a nonadversarial atmosphere where management and labour can work together to ensure a safe and healthy workplace. Most jurisdictions require a joint health and safety committee to be established in each workplace with a minimum number of workers (usually 10 or 20). In the other jurisdictions, the government has the power to require a committee to be formed. Committees are usually required to consist of between 2 and 12 members, at least half of whom must represent workers. In small workplaces, one health and safety representative may be required.

RPC
Establishes a joint health and safety committee as required by law

The committee is generally responsible for making regular inspections of the workplace in order to identify potential health and safety hazards, evaluate the hazards, and implement solutions. Hazard control can be achieved by addressing safety issues before an accident or injury happens, identifying ways in which a hazardous situation can be prevented from harming workers, and establishing procedures to ensure that a potential hazard will not recur. Health and safety committees are also responsible for investigating employee complaints, accident investigation, development and promotion of measures to protect health and safety, and dissemination of information about health and safety laws and regulations. In Ontario, at least one management and one labour representative must be certified in occupational health and safety through a provincial training program. Committees are often more effective if the company's health and safety manager acts as an independent expert rather than as a management representative.[7]

Enforcement of Occupational Health and Safety Laws

In all Canadian jurisdictions, occupational health and safety law provides for government inspectors to periodically carry out safety inspections of workplaces. Health and safety inspectors have wide powers to conduct inspections any place at any time without a warrant or prior notification and may engage in any examination and inquiry that they believe necessary to ascertain whether the workplace is in compliance with the law. Safety inspectors may order a variety of actions on the part of employers and employees, including orders to stop work, stop using tools, install first aid equipment, and stop emission of contaminants. Governments have been criticized for weak enforcement of health and safety laws, and several provinces have recently strengthened their inspection services.[8]

Penalties consist of fines and/or jail terms. Governments across Canada are increasingly turning to prosecutions as a means of enforcing health and safety standards. In 2008, Alberta imposed a record $5 million in penalties against companies for health and safety violations.[9] Other provinces are increasing the number of charges laid against both individual managers and organizations.[10]

Canadian corporate executives and directors may be held directly responsible for workplace injuries, and corporate officers have been convicted and received prison sentences for health and safety violations.[11] The Criminal Code includes a criminal offence commonly known as "corporate killing," which imposes criminal liability on "all persons" who direct the work of other employees and fail to ensure an appropriate level of safety in the workplace. Criminal Code convictions can be penalized by incarceration up to life in prison and unlimited fines. The first company to be charged with and plead guilty to criminal negligence causing death of a worker was Transpavé, a concrete block manufacturer in Quebec. The company was fined $110 000.[12]

Control of Toxic Substances

Most occupational health and safety laws require basic precautions with respect to toxic substances, including chemicals, biohazards (such as HIV/AIDS and

SARS), and physical agents (such as radiation, heat, and noise). An accurate inventory of these substances must be maintained, maximum exposure limits for airborne concentrations of these agents adhered to, the substances tested, and their use carefully controlled.

Workplace Hazardous Materials Information System (WHMIS) A Canada-wide, legally mandated system designed to protect workers by providing information about hazardous materials in the workplace.

The **Workplace Hazardous Materials Information System (WHMIS)** is a Canada-wide, legally mandated system designed to protect workers by providing crucial information about hazardous materials or substances in the workplace. WHMIS was the outcome of a cooperative effort among the federal, provincial, and territorial governments, together with industry and organized labour. The WHMIS legislation has three components:[13]

1. Labelling of hazardous material containers to alert workers that there is a potentially hazardous product inside (see **Figure 14.2** for examples of hazard symbols).

2. Material safety data sheets (MSDS) to outline a product's potentially hazardous ingredients and the procedures for safe handling of the product (see **Figure 14.3** for a sample MSDS).

3. Employee training to ensure that employees can identify WHMIS hazard symbols, read WHMIS supplier and workplace labels, and read and apply the information on an MSDS.

WHMIS Training
www.whmis.net

Occupational Health and Safety and Other Legislation

Health and safety, human rights, labour relations, and employment standards laws are in force in every jurisdiction in Canada in an interlaced web of legislation. Situations arise in which it is difficult to know which law is applicable, or which one takes precedence over another. For example, are the human rights of one employee to wear a ceremonial knife related to a religion more important than the safety of other employees? How much discipline is acceptable to labour arbitrators for health and safety violations? Should fights in the workplace be considered a safety hazard? Is sexual harassment a safety hazard? And how long does an employer have to tolerate poor performance from an alcoholic employee whose attempts at treatment fail? In Saskatchewan, human rights and occupational health and safety legislation overlap because sexual harassment is considered to be a workplace hazard.[14]

The Supervisor's Role in Safety

Most jurisdictions impose a personal duty on supervisors to ensure that workers comply with occupational health and safety regulations. They place a specific obligation on supervisors to advise and instruct workers about safety, to ensure that all reasonable precautions have been taken to provide for the safety of all employees, and to minimize risk of injuries or illness.

Safety-minded managers must aim to instill in their workers the desire to work safely. Minimizing hazards (by ensuring that spills are wiped up, machine guards are adequate, and so forth) is important, but no matter how safe the workplace is, there will be accidents unless workers want to and do act safely. Of course, supervisors try to watch each employee closely, but most managers know that this will not work. In the final analysis, the best (and perhaps only) alternative is to get workers to want to work safely. Then, when needed, safety rules should be enforced.[15]

FIGURE 14.2 | WHMIS Symbols

 Health   Santé
Canada Canada

Canada

Do You Know These Vital Signs?

THE HAZARD SYMBOLS OF WHMIS

CLASS A
Compressed Gas

CLASS D-2
Poisonous and Infectious Material (material causing other toxic effects)

CLASS B
Flammable and Combustible Material

CLASS D-3
Poisonous and Infectious Material (Biohazardous Infectious Material)

CLASS C
Oxidizing Material

CLASS E
Corrosive Material

CLASS D-1
Poisonous and Infectious Material (material causing immediate and serious effects)

CLASS F
Dangerously Reactive Material

WHMIS provides you with information on the safe use, storage, handling and disposal of hazardous materials at Canadian workplaces.

 Workplace
Hazardous Materials
Information System

For more information, consult the MSDS, and visit the Health Canada WHMIS Web site:
http://www.hc–sc.gc.ca/whmis

Source: The Hazard Symbols of WHMIS. www.hc-sc.gc.ca/whmis. Health Canada 2009 ©. Adapted and reproduced with the permission of the Minister of Public Works and Government Services Canada, 2009.

FIGURE 14.3 | Material Safety Data Sheet (MSDS)

NORTH ATLANTIC REFINING LTD.
MATERIAL SAFETY DATA SHEET

PREPARED: July 26, 2008

SECTION 1. PRODUCT INFORMATION

Product Identifier: **Propane**

Application and Use: Multiple use fuel gas.

Product Description: A colourless gas composed primarily of C3 hydrocarbons and handled as a liquid under pressure.

REGULATORY CLASSIFICATION
W.H.M.I.S.
CLASS A: COMPRESSED GAS
CLASS B1: FLAMMABLE GAS

MANUFACTURER/SUPPLIER:
NORTH ATLANTIC REFINING LTD.   CONTACT BETWEEN
COME BY CHANCE, NFLD. A0B 1N0   07:30–1600 HRS N.S.T.
TEL: (709) 463-8811 (24 hrs.)   Plant Industrial Hygienist
FAX: (709) 463-8076
AFTER HOURS: Plant Security

USE IN CASE OF A DANGEROUS GOODS EMERGENCY:
CANUTEC: (613) 996 6666

SECTION 2. REGULATED COMPONENT
THE FOLLOWING ARE DEFINED IN ACCORDANCE WITH SUBPARAGRAPH 13 (a)(I) TO (iv) OR PARAGRAPH 14(a) OF THE HAZARDOUS PRODUCTS ACT:

Name	%	CAS #
CONTROLLED INGREDIENTS		
PROPANE	90 to 95 v/v	74-98-6
ETHANE	0 to 5 v/v	74-84-0
PROPYLENE	0 to 5 v/v	115-07-1
BUTANE	1 to 2.5 v/v	106-97-8

Manufacturer recommended TWA: 1000 ppm

SECTION 3. HAZARDS IDENTIFICATION

Potential Acute Health Effects:
Inhalation: Low toxicity. This gas may displace oxygen and cause suffocation (asphyxiant)
Eye Contact: Exposure to rapidly expanding gases may cause frostbite and permanent eye injury.
Skin Contact: Exposure to rapidly expanding gases may cause frostbite.
Ingestion: Not considered a hazard.

Potential Chronic Health Effects:
None established

SECTION 4. TYPICAL PHYSICAL AND CHEMICAL PROPERTIES

Physical state:	Gas
Odour and appearance:	Colourless gas; may be odorized
Odour threshold:	Not available
Density:	0.51 g/cc @ 15 °C
Vapour pressure	92000 kPa @ 16 °C
Vapour density:	1.52 (Air = 1)
Evaporation rate:	>1
Boiling point:	−42 °C
Freezing/melting point:	Not available
pH:	Not applicable
Coefficient of water/oil distribution:	Not available
Solubility in water:	0 %

SECTION 5. FIRST AID MEASURES

EYE CONTACT:
In case of cold burns or frostbite of the eye, get prompt medical attention.

SKIN CONTACT:
In case of cold burns or frostbite to the skin, get prompt seek medical attention.

INGESTION:
First aid is not applicable.

INHALATION:
In emergence situations, use proper respiratory protection to remove the victim from the hazard. Allow the victim to rest in a well-ventilated area. If victim is not breathing, perform mouth-to-mouth resuscitation. Seek immediate medical attention.

SECTION 6. FIRE AND EXPLOSION DATA

Fire Fighting Instructions: Flammable gas, insoluble in water. Use water spray to cool fire-exposed surfaces and to protect personnel. Shut off fuel to fire if it is possible to do so without hazard. If a leak or spill has not ignited, use water spray to disperse the vapours. Remotely disconnect or shut off the power sources. Either, allow the fire to burn out under controlled conditions or extinguish with foam, dry chemicals or other approved extinguishing medium. Try to cover spilled liquid with foam. Respiratory, eye and body protection is required for fire fighting personnel. Response to small fire with extinguishers will usually be done upwind and only if considered safe. Personal protective equipment is usually not required when using portable extinguishers. Response to larger (catastrophic) fires should only be attempted by trained fire fighters.

Flammability:	Extremely flammable
Auto-Ignition Temperature:	432 °C
Flammable Limits:	Approx. 2.4 LEL, 9.5 UEL
Products of Combustion:	CO_X, and Smoke
Conditions of Flammability:	Heat and ignition source, flame or electric spark.
Explosion Hazards:	Not believed to be sensitive to mechanical agitation. May accumulate static charge.
Auto-refrigerant:	Rapidly expanding gases may cause ice to form. Drains and valves may become inoperable due to ice formation.

SECTION 7. ACCIDENTAL RELEASE MEASURES

Small Spill: Eliminate sources of ignition. Keep people away. Prevent additional discharge. Warn downwind occupant of hazard.

continued

FIGURE 14.3 | *continued*

Large Spill: Eliminate sources of ignition. Keep people away. Prevent additional discharge. Warn downwind occupant of hazard. Seek advice from the appropriate authorities.

SECTION 8. REACTIVITY DATA

Stability:	Product is stable.
Conditions for instability:	Not available.
Conditions to avoid:	Avoid excessive heat, sources of ignition product extremely flammable
Incompatibility:	Highly reactive with oxidising agents such as peroxides, perchlorates.
Decomposition products:	CO_X, and Smoke.

SECTION 9. PREVENTATIVE MEASURES

Personal Protective Equipment: A full-face shield is recommended to protect eyes and face. Chemically resistant gloves (with a thermal liner) and impervious clothing should be worn at all times while handling the product. When eye or skin contact may occur during short and/or periodic events, long sleeves, chemical-resistant gloves (thermal liner) and a face shield are required. A full-face respirator may be necessary to prevent overexposure by inhalation.

Engineering Controls: Highly recommended for all indoor situations to control fugitive emissions. Electrical and mechanical equipment should be explosion proof Concentrations should be maintained below the lower explosion limit at all times or below the recommended threshold limit value if unprotected personnel are involved. For personnel entry into a confined space (i.e. bulk storage tanks), a proper confined space entry must be followed, including ventilation and testing of tank atmosphere. Make up air should always be supplied to balance air exhausted.

Land Spill: Allow gases to dissipate. Eliminate any sources of ignition. Keep the public away. Prevent additional discharge of material if possible to do so without hazard. Consult an expert on disposal of recovered material. Ensure disposal is performed in compliance with government regulations. Notify the appropriate authorities. For spills over 70L in Canada contact the Canadian Coast Guard, 1-800-563-2444. Take additional action to prevent and remedy the adverse effects of the spill.

Water Spill: Allow gases to dissipate. Eliminate all sources of ignition. Prevent additional discharge of material. Consult an expert on disposal of recovered material. Ensure disposal is performed in compliance with government regulations. Notify the appropriate authorities. For all spills in Canada contact the Canadian Coast Guard, 1-800-563-2444. Take additional action to prevent and remedy the adverse effects of the spill.

Storage and handling: Combustible, store in a cool, dry, well ventilated area away from heat sources.

Keep containers closed. Handle and open propane containers with care.

The information contained herein is based on the data available to us and is believed to be correct. However, North Atlantic Refining Limited makes no warranty, expressed or implied regarding the accuracy of these data or results to be obtained from the use thereof. North Atlantic Refining Limited assumes no responsibility for injury from the use of the product described herein.

Prepared by:
Paul Sullivan
North Atlantic Refining Limited
P.O. Box 40
Come By Chance, Newfoundland, Canada
A0B 1N0
Phone: 709-463-8811 ext 306
FAX: 709-463-3489

At DuPont, safety is the company's highest value, and its accident rate worldwide has been much lower than that of the chemical industry as a whole. As the DuPont safety philosophy states, "Safety management is an integral part of our business and is built on the belief that all injuries and occupational illnesses are preventable; that we are all responsible for our safety and also that of our fellow employees; and that managers are responsible for the safety of those in their organizations."[16]

Without full commitment at all levels of management, any attempts to reduce unsafe acts by workers will meet with little success. The first-line supervisor is a critical link in the chain of management. If the supervisor does not take safety seriously, it is likely that those under him or her will not either.

WHAT CAUSES ACCIDENTS?

Workplace accidents have three basic causes: (1) chance occurrences, (2) unsafe conditions, and (3) unsafe acts on the part of employees.

Chance Occurrences

Chance occurrences (such as walking past a plate-glass window just as someone hits a ball through it) contribute to accidents but are more or less beyond management's control. We will therefore focus on *unsafe conditions* and *unsafe acts*.

Unsafe Conditions

Unsafe conditions are one main cause of accidents. They include such factors as

Safety Council
www.safety-council.org

- improperly guarded equipment
- defective equipment
- hazardous procedures in, on, or around machines or equipment
- unsafe storage (congestion, overloading)
- improper illumination (glare, insufficient light)
- improper ventilation (insufficient air change, impure air source)[17]

The basic remedy here is to eliminate or minimize the unsafe conditions. Government standards address the mechanical and physical conditions that cause accidents. Furthermore, a checklist of unsafe conditions can be used to conduct a job hazard analysis. Common indicators of job hazards include increased numbers of accidents, employee complaints, poor product quality, employee modifications to workstations, and higher levels of absenteeism and turnover.[18]

In addition to unsafe conditions, three other work-related factors contribute to accidents: the *job itself*, the *work schedule*, and the *psychological climate* of the workplace. Certain *jobs* are inherently more dangerous than others. According to one study, for example, the job of crane operator results in about three times more accident-related hospital visits than does the job of supervisor. Similarly, some departments' work is inherently safer than that of others. An accounting department usually has fewer accidents than a shipping department.

Work schedules and fatigue also affect accident rates. Accident rates usually do not increase too noticeably during the first five or six hours of the workday. Beyond that, however, the accident rate increases quickly as the number of hours worked increases. This is due partly to fatigue. It has also been found that accidents occur more often during night shifts.

Many experts believe that the *psychological climate* of the workplace affects the accident rate. For example, accidents occur more frequently in plants with a high seasonal layoff rate and those where there is hostility among employees, many garnished wages, and blighted living conditions. Temporary stress factors, such as high workplace temperature, poor illumination, and a congested workplace, are also related to accident rates. It appears that workers who work under stress or who consider their jobs to be threatened or insecure have more accidents than those who do not work under these conditions.[19]

Unsafe Acts

Most safety experts and managers know that it is impossible to eliminate accidents just by improving unsafe conditions. People cause accidents, and no one has found a sure-fire way to eliminate *unsafe acts* by employees, such as

- throwing materials
- operating or working at unsafe speeds (either too fast or too slow)

- making safety devices inoperative by removing, adjusting, or disconnecting them
- using unsafe equipment or using equipment unsafely
- using unsafe procedures in loading, placing, mixing, combining
- taking unsafe positions under suspended loads
- lifting improperly
- distracting, teasing, abusing, startling, quarrelling, and instigating horseplay

Such unsafe acts as these can undermine even the best attempts to minimize unsafe conditions, and the progressive discipline system should be used in such situations.

Personal Characteristics

A model summarizing how personal characteristics are linked to accidents is presented in **Figure 14.4**. Personal characteristics (personality, motivation, and so on) can serve as the basis for certain behaviour tendencies, such as the tendency to take risks, and undesirable attitudes. These behaviour tendencies in turn result in unsafe acts, such as inattention and failure to follow procedures. It follows that such unsafe acts increase the probability of someone having an accident.[20]

Years of research have failed to unearth any set of traits that accident repeaters seemed to have in common. Instead, the consensus is that the person who is accident prone on one job may not be that way on a different job—that accident proneness is situational. For example, *personality traits* (such as emotional stability) may distinguish accident-prone workers on jobs involving risk; and *lack of motor skills* may distinguish accident-prone workers on jobs involving coordination. In fact, many human traits *have* been found to be related to accident repetition *in specific situations*, as the following discussion illustrates.[21]

FIGURE 14.4 | How Personal Factors May Influence Employee Accident Behaviour

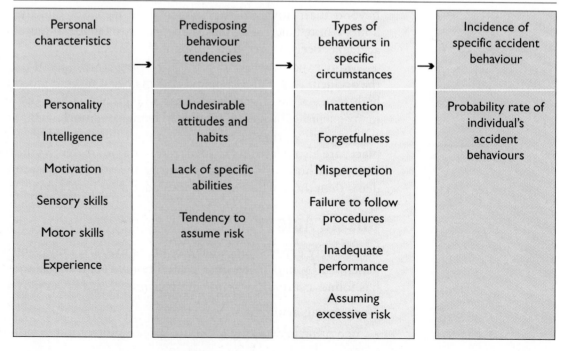

Personal characteristics	Predisposing behaviour tendencies	Types of behaviours in specific circumstances	Incidence of specific accident behaviour
Personality	Undesirable attitudes and habits	Inattention	Probability rate of individual's accident behaviours
Intelligence		Forgetfulness	
Motivation	Lack of specific abilities	Misperception	
Sensory skills		Failure to follow procedures	
Motor skills	Tendency to assume risk	Inadequate performance	
Experience		Assuming excessive risk	

Vision

Vision is related to accident frequency for many jobs. For example, passenger car drivers, intercity bus drivers, and machine operators who have high visual skills have fewer injuries than those who do not.[22]

Literacy

The risk of accidents is higher for employees who cannot read and understand machinery operating instructions, safety precautions, equipment and repair manuals, first aid instructions, or organizational policies on workplace health and safety. Low literacy skills potentially put workers and their co-workers in harm's way and increase the likelihood of work stoppages due to accidents or errors.[23] This situation is complicated by the fact that most workers with low literacy skills believe that their skills are good or excellent.[24]

A report by the Conference Board of Canada concluded that employers can reduce accidents by improving employees' literacy skills. They found an inverse relationship between industries requiring a high level of health and safety and investment in literacy skills.[25] This finding, together with the reality that people with lower levels of literacy often end up in more dangerous occupations like trucking, manufacturing, or construction where literacy requirements are low compared to more intellectual jobs, clearly indicates the need for action to heighten literacy skills of workers.

Age

Accidents are generally most frequent among people between the ages of 17 and 28, declining thereafter to reach a low in the late 50s and 60s. Although different patterns might be found with different jobs, this age factor repeats year after year. Across Canada, young workers between the ages of 15 and 24 (often students in low-paying summer jobs) are over five times more likely to be injured during their first four weeks on the job than others, which raises questions

Managing Young Workers
www.youngworker.ca
Canadian LifeQuilt
www.youngworkerquilt.ca

Jessica DiSabatino, with a picture of her 18-year-old brother David Ellis, who was killed on his second day on the job in 1999, wants employers to take young worker safety seriously.

Guiding Young Workers in Health and Safety

The Canadian Centre for Occupational Health and Safety suggests that in order to reduce the likelihood of accidents and injuries to young workers, the following basic steps should be observed:

1. *Assign suitable work.* Avoid assigning jobs that require long training times, a high degree of skill, or a lot of responsibility, critical or risky tasks, or working alone.

2. *Understand young workers.* Young workers think differently than older and more experienced employees do. Young workers tend to take risks and are unrealistic about their own mortality; they may be reluctant to ask questions for fear of appearing unknowledgeable; and because of a lack of understanding, they may decide to make changes to the job in unexpected and possibly risky ways.

3. *Provide training.* Tell young workers not to perform any task until they have been properly trained; not to

leave their work area unless they are told to do so, as other work sites may have special hazards; and to ask someone if they are unsure of anything. Make sure that any young worker who must use hazardous equipment is given detailed training on safety features. If young workers must wear protective equipment, make sure they know when they need to wear it, where to find it, how to use it, and how to care for it. Finally, provide training on what to do in case of emergency.

4. *Supervise.* Effective supervision of young workers requires that supervisors be qualified to organize and direct work; that they know the laws and regulations that apply to the job; and that they know the actual and potential hazards in the workplace.

Source: Canadian Centre for Occupational Health and Safety (CCOHS), Employers: Guiding Young Workers in Health and Safety, www.ccohs.ca/youngworkers/employers.html. Reproduced with the permission of CCOHS (2009).

about the supervision and training of young workers.[26] Suggestions regarding training of young workers are provided in the Workforce Diversity box.

Perceptual versus Motor Skills

If a worker's perceptual skill is greater than or equal to his or her motor skill, the employee is more likely to be a safe worker than another worker whose perceptual skill is lower than his or her motor skill.[27] In other words, a worker who reacts more quickly than he or she can perceive is more likely to have accidents.

In summary, these findings provide a partial list of the human traits that have been found to be related to higher accident rates, and they suggest that, for specific jobs, it seems to be possible to identify accident-prone individuals and to screen them out. Overall, it seems that accidents can have multiple causes. With that in mind, accident prevention will be discussed.

HOW TO PREVENT ACCIDENTS

In practice, accident prevention involves reducing unsafe conditions and reducing unsafe acts.

Reducing Unsafe Conditions

Reducing unsafe conditions is an employer's first line of defence. Safety engineers can design jobs to remove or reduce physical hazards. In addition, supervisors and managers play a role in reducing unsafe conditions by ensuring that employees wear personal protective equipment, an often difficult chore. However, only 4 percent of accidents stem from unsafe working conditions, and therefore more attention will be paid to accident prevention methods that focus on changing behaviours.

Reducing Unsafe Acts

Reducing unsafe acts is the second basic approach, and there are five specific actions that can help to reduce unsafe acts.

Selection Testing

Certain selection tests can help to screen out accident-prone persons before they are hired. For example, measures of muscular coordination can be useful because coordination is a predictor of safety for certain jobs. Tests of visual skills can be important because good vision plays a part in preventing accidents in many occupations, including operating machines and driving. A test called the Employee Reliability Inventory (ERI), that measures reliability dimensions, such as emotional maturity, conscientiousness, safe job performance, and courteous job performance, can also be helpful in selecting employees who are less likely to have accidents.

A Canadian study conducted in a major industrial plant compared injury costs for a group of employees that was subjected to post-offer screening to assess their physical capability to perform job duties and another group that did not receive post-offer screening. Injury costs over five years for the screened group were $6500 and for the non-screened group were $2 073 000—a highly significant difference.[28]

Many employers would like to inquire about applicants' workers' compensation history before hiring, in part to avoid habitual workers' compensation claimants and accident-prone individuals. However, inquiring about an applicant's workers' compensation injuries and claims can lead to allegations of discrimination based on disability. Similarly, applicants cannot be asked whether they have a disability, nor can they be asked to take tests that tend to screen out those with disabilities.

Employers can ask each applicant whether he or she has the ability to perform the essential duties of the job and ask, "Do you know of any reason why you would not be able to perform the various functions of the job in question?" Candidates can also be asked to demonstrate job-related skills, provided that every applicant is required to do so. Any selection test that duplicates the physical requirements of the job at realistic levels and type of work expected does not violate human rights law, as long as it is developed and imposed honestly and in good faith to test whether or not the applicant can meet production requirements.[29]

Top-Management Commitment

Studies consistently find that successful health and safety programs require a strong management commitment. An example of the importance of top-management commitment is provided in the Strategic HR box. This commitment manifests itself in senior managers being personally involved in safety activities on a routine

Employee Reliability Inventory
www.ramsaycorp.com/products/
eriphone.asp

Research INSIGHT

Hints TO ENSURE LEGAL COMPLIANCE

Strategic HR

Top Management Commitment to Safety at Steelcase Canada Pays Off

"Quite exceptional." That's how Tony Grech, a field consultant for the Industrial Accident Prevention Association (IAPA), describes the lost-time injury rates at Steelcase Canada's facility in Markham, Ontario, where their 460 employees manufacture office furniture. The company's lost-time injury rates were 79 percent to 87 percent lower than its associated rate group from 2001 to 2005.

The high scores were the result of a reinvigorated commitment to health and safety at the company, according to Mike Fenuta, manager of health and safety. "The key was ownership from our leadership," said Fenuta. "They really started integrating that and made it an accountability across the board, not only from senior executives but right down to the shop-floor employee, where safety was discussed on a daily basis."

Steelcase set up a joint health and safety committee, as required by law, but decided to go beyond that in establishing safety teams that met weekly for each area of responsibility. These then developed into safety and quality teams that "have now become part of the business," said Fenuta.

"We've always believed people are our most important asset and we have to invest in them, just like we would in hard assets like equipment. We've been establishing standards that not only meet the requirements but are one step beyond. Most of the time we are ahead of the curve."

Consequently morale has improved because of the safer environment and employees feel more appreciated. New employees are also given an extensive orientation so they "get on board a lot quicker with quality issues and adherence to safety issues," said Steve Taylor, environmental and plant engineer at Steelcase.

And, "if you take care of people, they produce good quality products, which in return are delivered to customers on time, and that takes care of your financials," said Fenuta.

There are definite savings, both tangible and intangible, from improved health and safety, said Taylor. For one, Steelcase has received significant rebates every year through an experience rating system run by Ontario's Workplace Safety and Insurance Board. Taylor said Steelcase has averaged more than $250 000 in annual savings. The better health and safety conditions have also reduced the absentee rate, so additional "floater" labour hired to cover routine absence is no longer needed, meaning two fewer employees and no need for extra staff.

Over the past ten years, health and safety has become a fundamental part of the company's culture. "It's a major cultural shift and it takes years to develop this," said Grech. "It's not done overnight."

Source: S. Dobson, "Good Health and Safety Brings Enviable Rewards," *Canadian HR Reporter*, February 12, 2007.

basis, giving safety matters high priority in company meetings and production scheduling, giving the company safety officer high rank and status, and including safety training in new workers' training. For example, linking managers' bonuses to safety improvements can reinforce a firm's commitment to safety and encourage managers to emphasize safety. HR managers have an important role to play in communicating the importance of health and safety to senior management, by demonstrating how it affects the bottom line.

Training and Education

RPC

Provides information to employees and managers on available programs

Safety training is another technique for reducing accidents. The Canadian Centre for Occupational Health and Safety and several safety associations, such as the Industrial Accident Prevention Association (IAPA), are available to partner in training efforts. The Canadian Federation of Independent Business offers online training leading to a Small Business Health and Safety (SBHS) certificate.

Industrial Accident Prevention
Association
www.iapa.ca

All employees should be required to participate in occupational health and safety training programs, and opportunities for employee input into the content and design of such programs is advisable. The training should include a practical evaluation process to ensure that workers are applying the acquired knowledge and following recommended safety procedures. Such training is especially appropriate for new employees.

Safety posters can also help reduce unsafe acts. However, posters are no substitute for a comprehensive safety program; instead, they should be combined with other techniques, like screening and training, to reduce unsafe conditions and acts. Posters with pictures may be particularly valuable for immigrant workers if their first language is not the language of the workplace.

Positive Reinforcement

Safety programs based on positive reinforcement can improve safety behaviour at work. Employees often receive little or no positive reinforcement for performing safely. One approach is to establish and communicate a reasonable goal (in terms of observed incidents performed safely) so that workers know what is expected of them in terms of good performance. Employees are encouraged to increase their performance to the new safety goal, for their own protection and to decrease costs for the company. Various observers (such as safety coordinators and senior managers) walk through the plant regularly, collecting safety data. The results are then posted on a graph charting the percentage of incidents performed safely by the group as a whole, thus providing workers with feedback on their safety performance. Workers can compare their current safety performance with their assigned goal. In addition, supervisors should praise workers when they perform selected activities safely.[30]

For example, UPS Canada honours drivers who have achieved 25 years or more of safe driving with a special badge to add to their uniform. The drivers are part of UPS's prestigious Circle of Honour, the company's highest level of driving recognition.[31]

An Ethical | Dilemma

Is it ethical to provide safety training in English to immigrant workers who speak little English, in order to reduce costs?

Controlling Workers' Compensation Costs

Workers' compensation costs are often the most expensive benefit provided by an employer. For example, the average workplace injury in Ontario costs more than $59 000 in workers' compensation benefits. Indirect costs are estimated to be about four times the direct costs.[32] Each firm's workers' compensation premiums are proportional to its workers' compensation experience rate. Thus, the more claims a firm has, the more the firm will pay in premiums. A new online tool is available for small businesses in Ontario to calculate the true costs of a workplace injury, as explained in the Entrepreneurs and HR box.

Before the Accident

Association of Workers'
Compensation Boards of Canada
www.awcbc.org
Canadian Injured Workers Alliance
www.ciwa.ca

The appropriate time to begin "controlling" workers' compensation claims is before the accident happens, not after. This involves taking all the steps previously summarized. For example, firms should remove unsafe conditions, screen out employees who might be accident-prone for the job in question (without violating human rights legislation), and establish a safety policy and loss control goals.

Entrepreneurs and HR

Small Business Safety Calculator

Statistics from Ontario's Workplace Safety and Insurance Board (WSIB) show that the job fatality rates of small businesses are 6.7 times higher than those for larger businesses and lost-time injury rates are 10 percent higher. When a worker in Ontario is injured on the job, the WSIB pays for costs associated with the injury claim, including health, rehabilitation, and disability costs. However, injuries cost small businesses in many other areas not covered by WSIB insurance. The Industrial Accident Prevention Association (IAPA)'s free Small Business Safety Calculator will help businesses identify and quantify these costs, including the following:

- **Incident Costs**—time to provide first aid; time for transportation to hospital/clinic/home; lost productivity of all affected workers; time to make area safe; cost of first aid supplies and equipment used; cost of ambulance or taxi

- **Investigation Costs**—time to investigate the accident; time spent to complete an accident investigation report; time to complete related paperwork for the company; time taken to report the incident to the WSIB and meet with WSIB officers; follow-up meetings to discuss the accident

- **Damage Costs**—time to assess the damage; time to repair or replace equipment; time to coordinate repair work; clean-up time; cost of outside contractors and materials for clean up; cost to dispose of damaged equipment; cost of replacement parts, equipment, or lost product

- **Replacement Costs**—time to hire or relocate replacement worker; relocation or rescheduling of another worker; trainer time for new or relocated worker; trainee time for new or relocated worker; cost to hire a replacement worker

- **Productivity Costs**—lost productivity due to disruption; time spent managing the injury claim; reduced productivity of injured worker after they return to work

The IAPA Small Business Safety Calculator is modelled after one created by WorkSafe BC. It was reengineered for use in Ontario and specifically for those companies that fall within one of IAPA's 12 industry groups: Glass, Stone, and Ceramics; Chemical and Plastics; Food and Beverage; Agri-Business; High-Tech; Industrial Auto Sales; Leather, Rubber, and Tanners; Metal Trades; Office and Relate Services; Printing Trades; Textile and Allied Trades; and Woodworking. The calculator is available online at www.iapa.ca/sbc.

Source: "Calculating the Costs of Workplace Injuries," *Canadian HR Reporter*, April 9, 2007.

Tips | **FOR THE FRONT LINE**

RPC

Ensures compliance with legislated reporting requirements

Ensures adequate accommodation, modified work, and graduated return-to-work programs are in place

Ensures that modifications to the work environment are consistent with worker limitations

After the Accident—Facilitating the Employee's Return to Work

Employers should provide first aid, make sure that the worker gets quick medical attention, make it clear that they are interested in the injured worker and his or her fears and questions, document the accident, file any required accident reports, and encourage a speedy return to work. Perhaps the most important and effective thing an employer can do to reduce costs is to develop an aggressive return-to-work program.

The National Institute of Disability Management and Research (NIDMAR) in Victoria, British Columbia, recommends following the three Cs: (1) *commitment* to keeping in touch with the worker and ensuring his or her return to work; (2) *collaboration* among the parties involved, including medical, family, and workers' compensation; and (3) *creativity* in focusing on how to use the worker's remaining abilities on the job.[33]

Specific actions to encourage early return to work can be internal and/or external to the organization. Internally, an employer can set up rehabilitation committees to identify modified work, including relevant stakeholders, such as the employee and his or her colleagues, HR professionals, union representatives, and managers.

Functional abilities evaluations (FAEs) are an important step in facilitating the return to work. The FAE is conducted by a health-care professional, in order to

- improve the chances that the injured worker will be safe on the job
- help the worker's performance by identifying problem areas of work that can be addressed by physical therapy or accommodated through job modification
- determine the level of disability so that the worker can either go back to his or her original job or be accommodated[34]

Externally, the employer can work with the employee's family to ensure that they are supportive, mobilize the resources of the EAP to help the employee, ensure that physical and occupational therapists are available, and make the family physician aware of workplace accommodation possibilities.

EMPLOYEE WELLNESS PROGRAMS

employee wellness program
A program that takes a proactive approach to employee health and well-being.

Strength-Tek Fitness and Wellness Consultants
www.strengthtek.com
Healthy Workplace Month
www.healthyworkplacemonth.ca

There are three elements in a healthy workplace: the physical environment, the social environment, and health practices. **Employee wellness programs** take a proactive approach to all these areas of employee well-being (as opposed to EAPs, which provide reactive management of employee health problems). Wellness should be viewed as a management strategy to achieve measurable outcomes related to productivity, cost reduction, recruitment/retention, and profit, as shown in **Figure 14.5**. Telus has a 50-year-old wellness program in which managers are held accountable—if absenteeism increases in their department, their bonus decreases![35] The company believes that a focus on wellness and

FIGURE 14.5 | Benefits for Employers from Action on the Determinants of Health

PRODUCTIVITY
- Reduced absenteeism
- Reduced distractions
- Improved performance
- Improved skills

COST REDUCTION
- Reduced workplace accidents and injuries
- Reduced compensation claims
- Reduced benefits costs

RECRUITMENT AND RETENTION
- Improved retention rates
- Improved employee engagement

PROFIT
- Reduced turnover costs
- Improved customer service and retention
- Improved recruitment competitiveness

Source: Daniel Munro, *Healthy People, Healthy Performances, Healthy Profits: The Case for Business Action on the Socio-Economic Determinants of Health* (Ottawa: Conference Board of Canada, 2008). Reprinted by permission of The Conference Board of Canada, Ottawa.

enhancing corporate competitiveness are one and the same. Its long-term experience has netted a savings of three dollars for every dollar spent on wellness.

Experience has shown that wellness programs are very effective; there is overwhelming evidence that money invested in a wellness program is returned many times over.[36] For example, Seven Oaks Hospital in Winnipeg, which has a 10-year-old Wellness Institute, reports a turnover rate of 4.5 percent, well under half of the industry average in Winnipeg of 11.9 percent.[37] A study of heart health wellness initiatives reported a return on investment of 415 percent.[38] NCR Canada saved $600 000 in direct and indirect costs during the first year of its wellness program, and absenteeism was cut by more than half after 12 months and was still one-third lower after 36 months.[39]

One expert predicts that, over the next 25 years, prevention and wellness will be the next great leap forward in health care, as employees become more broadly recognized as the most important assets of organizations. A focus on wellness will also be driven by the shrinking workforce, an increase in postponed retirement, increased awareness of mental health, and medical and technological advances.[40]

Wellness initiatives often include stress management, nutrition and weight management, smoking cessation programs, tai chi, heart health (such as screening cholesterol and blood pressure levels), physical fitness programs, and workstation wellness through ergonomics. Even simple things like providing safe bicycle lockup and change rooms or making fresh fruit and water available can make a difference.[41] Wellness and prevention efforts need to be understood and undertaken as a process—a long-term commitment to a holistic focus on the total person.

OCCUPATIONAL HEALTH AND SAFETY ISSUES AND CHALLENGES

A number of health-related issues and challenges can undermine employee performance at work. These include alcoholism and substance abuse, stress and burnout, repetitive strain injuries, workplace toxins, workplace smoking, influenza pandemics, and workplace violence.

Substance Abuse

The effects of substance abuse on the employee and his or her work are severe. Both the quality and quantity of work decline sharply, and safety may be compromised. When dealing with alcohol and substance abuse on the job, employers must balance conflicting legal obligations. On the one hand, under human rights laws, alcoholism and drug addiction are considered to be disabilities. On the other hand, under occupational health and safety legislation, employers are responsible for maintaining due diligence. As a result, employers worry that, when they accommodate an employee with an addiction, they may not be ensuring a safe work environment for other employees.[42]

Further, drug and alcohol testing in Canada is only legal in situations where three conditions determined by the Supreme Court are met, as follows:

1. The test is rationally connected to the performance of the job.

2. The test is adopted in an honest and good-faith belief that it is necessary for the fulfillment of a legitimate work-related purpose.

Hints TO ENSURE LEGAL COMPLIANCE

3. The test is reasonably necessary to the accomplishment of the work-related purpose.[43]

Random drug tests do not measure actual impairment and are therefore unjustifiable. Arbitrary alcohol testing of one or more employees but not others is not usually justifiable, but for employees in safety-sensitive positions, such as airline pilots, it may be justifiable. "For cause" and "post-incident" testing for either alcohol or drugs may be acceptable in specific circumstances. Positive test results should generally result in accommodation of the employee. Immediate dismissal is not generally justifiable.[44]

Recognizing the substance abuser on the job can pose a problem. The early symptoms can be similar to those of other problems and thus hard to classify. Problems range from tardiness to prolonged, unpredictable absences in later stages of addiction. Supervisors should be the company's first line of defence in combating substance abuse in the workplace, but they should not try to be company detectives or medical diagnosticians. Guidelines for supervisors should include the following:[45]

Tips | **FOR THE FRONT LINE**

- If an employee appears to be under the influence of drugs or alcohol, ask how the employee feels and look for signs of impairment, such as slurred speech. An employee judged to be unfit for duty may be sent home but not fired on the spot.

- Make a written record of observed behaviour and follow up each incident. In addition to issuing a written reprimand, managers should inform workers of the number of warnings that the company will tolerate before requiring termination. Regardless of any suspicion of substance abuse, concerns should be focused on work performance, expected changes, and available options for help.

- Troubled employees should be referred to the company's employee assistance program.

The four traditional techniques for dealing with substance abuse are discipline, discharge, in-house counselling, and referral to an outside agency. Discharge is used to deal with alcoholism and drug problems only after repeated attempts at rehabilitation have failed. In-house counselling can be offered by the employer's medical staff or the employee assistance plan. External agencies such as Alcoholics Anonymous can also be utilized.

Bellwood Health Services Inc.
www.bellwood.ca
Shepell-fgi
www.shepellfgi.com

In Grande Prairie, Alberta, a clinic was established by the Alberta Alcohol and Drug Abuse Commission as a result of requests from the business community for a treatment centre that could deal with workplace-specific issues. It offers quick enrollment in its 30-day alcohol treatment program, or the 50-day cocaine treatment program, for $175 per day, plus months of follow-up, helping 180 clients a year return to work as soon as possible.[46]

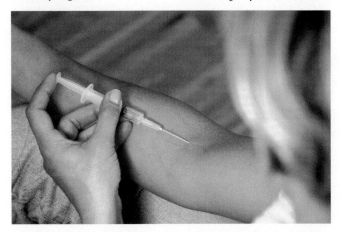

The use of drugs, especially in the workplace, is a growing concern for Canadian companies and has led to increased numbers of alcohol and drug abuse counselling programs.

Substance Abuse Policies

In general, a clear, well-communicated substance abuse policy that is reasonably and consistently enforced is the employer's best approach. The Centre for Addiction and Mental Health recommends that the policy components should include the following:[47]

- the prohibition of alcohol and drug use (or coming to work drugged or drunk) during work hours and company special events, with clearly defined business circumstances, if any, in which alcohol consumption is considered appropriate
- clearly defined roles and responsibilities of workers and management in meeting company expectations regarding alcohol and drug use, and seeking help if problems arise
- disciplinary measures for infractions (these must meet human rights legal requirements that addictions be considered a disability)
- communication procedures to ensure that all employees know and understand the policy
- preventive education to ensure that employees are knowledgeable about alcohol and drug abuse
- training to ensure that front-line supervisors and union stewards can identify employees with suspected substance abuse problems, complete thorough documentation of job performance problems, and refer the employees to a company-sponsored or external treatment program
- provision for confidential assistance and treatment programs for employees with drug and alcohol problems

Finally, organizations should remember that health promotion and drug education programs can help to prevent employee drug and alcohol problems from developing in the first place.

Job Stress

Workplace stress is a pervasive problem that is getting worse. Job stress has serious consequences for both the employee and the organization. The human consequences of job stress include anxiety, depression, anger, and various physical consequences, such as cardiovascular disease, headaches, and accidents. In Canada, the total cost of mental health problems approximates 17 percent of payroll, and the overall economic impact of work-related mental health problems is estimated to be $51 billion annually.[48] Stress also has serious consequences for the organization, including reductions in productivity and increased absenteeism and turnover.[49] Lost productivity at work due to health-related issues can cost the average Canadian organization up to $10 million each year.[50] Mental health issues are the leading cause of both short- and long-term disability claims.[51] Many organizations make physical safety a priority, but too often work environments that clearly have the potential for serious consequences from stress are simply tolerated.[52] Perhaps this reflects the fact that two-thirds of companies underestimate the prevalence of mental illness in the workplace, and only 13 percent of senior executives have a strong awareness of the impact of mental health on their workplaces.[53]

Organizations begin to suffer when too many employees feel that the relentless pace of work life is neither sustainable nor healthy. Why is this happening? Employees are being asked to do more with less, creating work overload, increased time pressures, and tighter deadlines (almost one-third of Canadian workers consider themselves workaholics).[54] More people are working in "precarious" employment such as temporary or part-time work with no benefits.[55] The sheer volume of email imposes terrific amounts of pressure and distraction on employees, taking a toll on their emotional equilibrium. Psychopathic bosses with no conscience, called "snakes in suits," can wreak havoc with other employees, and the result is a corporate climate characterized by fatigue, depression, and anxiety.[56]

Job stress has two main sources: environmental factors and personal factors. First, a variety of external, *environmental factors* can lead to job stress. Two factors are particularly stress-inducing. The first is a high-demand job, such as one with constant deadlines coupled with low employee control. The second is high levels of mental and physical effort combined with low reward in terms of compensation or acknowledgement.[57] Health-care workers, whose jobs typically include these factors, are more stressed than any other group.[58] However, no two people react to the same job in an identical way, since *personal factors* also influence stress. For example, Type A personalities—people who are workaholics and who feel driven to always be on time and meet deadlines—normally place themselves under greater stress than do others. Similarly, one's patience, tolerance for ambiguity, self-esteem, health and exercise, and work and sleep patterns can also affect how one reacts to stress. Add to job stress the stress caused by non-job-related problems like divorce, postpartum depression, seasonal affective disorder, and work/family time conflict, and many workers are problems waiting to happen.

Yet stress is not necessarily dysfunctional. Too little stress creates boredom and apathy. Performance is optimal at a level of stress that energizes but does not wear someone out.[59] Others find that stress may result in a search that leads to a better job or to a career that makes more sense, given the person's aptitudes. A modest level of stress may even lead to more creativity if a competitive situation results in new ideas being generated.

Reducing Job Stress

There are things that a person can do to alleviate stress, ranging from common-sense remedies, such as getting more sleep, eating better, and taking vacation time, to more exotic remedies, such as biofeedback and meditation. Finding a more suitable job, getting counselling through an EAP or elsewhere, and planning and organizing each day's activities are other sensible responses.[60]

An Ethical | Dilemma

Is it ethical for an organization to ignore the issue of job stress entirely?

Research | INSIGHT

The organization and its HR specialists and supervisors can also play a role in identifying and reducing job stress. Offering an EAP is a major step toward alleviating the pressure on managers to try to help employees cope with stress. About 40 percent of EAP usage is related to stress at work. For the supervisor, important activities include monitoring each employee's performance to identify symptoms of stress and then informing the person of the organizational remedies that may be available, such as EAPs, job transfers, or other counselling. Also important are fair treatment and permitting the employee to have more control over his or her job.[61]

The importance of control over a job was illustrated by the results of a study in which the psychological strain caused by job stress was reduced by the amount of control that employees had over their job. The less stressful jobs did have high demands in terms of quantitative workload, the amount of attention that the employees had to pay to their work, and work pressure; however, they also ranked high in task clarity, job control, supervisory support, and employee skill utilization. The researchers conclude that "to achieve a balanced system, that is, to reduce psychological strain, [job] demands and [ambiguity regarding the future of the job] need to be lowered, while skill utilization, task clarity, job control, and supervisor support need to be increased."[62]

HR executives need to become advocates for employee mental health within the senior management team. Today's highly valued employees who are driving corporate productivity, innovation, and performance tend to be young knowledge workers, precisely the type of worker most prone to depression and stress.[63]

Burnout

burnout The total depletion of physical and mental resources caused by excessive striving to reach an unrealistic work-related goal.

Many people fall victim to **burnout**—the total depletion of physical and mental resources—because of excessive striving to reach an unrealistic work-related goal. Burnout begins with cynical and pessimistic thoughts and leads to apathy, exhaustion, withdrawal into isolation, and eventually depression.[64] Burnout is often the result of too much job stress, especially when that stress is combined with a preoccupation with attaining unattainable work-related goals. Burnout victims often do not lead well-balanced lives; virtually all of their energies are focused on achieving their work-related goals to the exclusion of other activities, leading to physical and sometimes mental collapse. This need not be limited to upwardly mobile executives: For instance, social-work counsellors caught up in their clients' problems are often burnout victims.

Tips | FOR THE FRONT LINE

What can a candidate for burnout do? Here are some suggestions.

Break patterns. First, survey how you spend your time. Are you doing a variety of things, or the same thing over and over? The more well-rounded your life is, the better protected you are against burnout. If you have stopped trying new activities, start them again—for instance, travel or new hobbies.

Get away from it all periodically. Schedule occasional periods of introspection during which you can get away from your usual routine, perhaps alone, to seek a perspective on where you are and where you are going.

Reassess goals in terms of their intrinsic worth. Are the goals that you have set for yourself attainable? Are they really worth the sacrifices that you will have to make?

Think about work. Could you do as good a job without being so intense or while also pursuing outside interests?

Reduce stress. Organize your time more effectively, build a better relationship with your boss, negotiate realistic deadlines, find time during the day for detachment and relaxation, reduce unnecessary noise around your office, and limit interruptions.

Workers' Compensation and Stress-Related Disability Claims

All Canadian jurisdictions provide benefits for post-traumatic stress caused by a specific and sudden workplace incident. However, when it comes to chronic stress, there is very limited or no coverage, depending on the jurisdiction.[65] The rationale is that stress has multiple causes, including family situations and personal disposition. Research suggests, however, that a significant portion of chronic stress is often work-related. In particular, high-demand/low-control jobs (such as an administrative assistant with several demanding bosses) are known to be "psychotoxic." Consequently, employees who are denied workers' compensation benefits for chronic stress that they believe to be work-related are suing their employers. The courts are recognizing these claims and holding employers responsible for actions of supervisors who create "poisoned work environments" through harassment and psychological abuse. Courts are finding that a fundamental implied term of any employment relationship is that the employer will treat the employee fairly and with respect and dignity and that the due diligence requirement includes protection of employees from psychological damage as well as physical harm.[66]

Repetitive Strain Injuries

repetitive strain injuries (RSIs) Activity-related soft-tissue injuries of the neck, shoulders, arms, wrist, hands, back, and legs.

RSI Clinic
www.treatpain.ca/RSI_CLINIC. html
Human Systems Inc.
www.humansys.com
Human Factors and Ergonomics Society
www.hfes.org

Repetitive strain injuries (RSIs) are rapidly becoming the most prevalent work-related injury because of the increasing number of "knowledge" workers who use computers. RSI is an umbrella term for a number of "overuse" injuries affecting muscles, tendons, and nerves of the neck, back, chest, shoulders, arms, and hands. Typically arising as aches and pains, these injuries can progress to become crippling disorders that prevent sufferers from working and from leading normal lives. Warning signs of RSI include tightness or stiffness in the hands, elbow, wrists, shoulder, and neck; numbness and tingling in the fingertips; hands falling asleep; and frequent dropping of tools.[67]

A variety of workplace factors can play a role in the development of RSIs, including repetition, work pace, awkward or fixed positions, forceful movements, vibration, cold temperatures, and insufficient recovery time. RSIs are costly for employers in terms of compensation claims, overtime, equipment modification, retraining, and lost productivity. As with any other workplace safety issue, employers are required under occupational health and safety law to put controls in place to prevent RSIs. British Columbia has the most rigorous requirements regarding protection of workers against RSIs, and unions are calling for other provinces to follow suit. Employers must advise and train workers about the risk of RSIs from workplace activity, identify and assess job-related RSI risk factors, encourage workers to report RSI symptoms early, and use ergonomic interventions.[68]

Ergonomics

ergonomics The art of fitting the workstation and work tools to the individual.

Poorly designed workstations, bad posture, and long periods of time working on computers are common conditions leading to RSIs, and these are easily preventable. **Ergonomics** is the art of fitting the workstation and work tools to the individual, which is necessary because there is no such thing as an average body. **Figure 14.6** illustrates ergonomic factors at a computer workstation. The most important preventive measure is to have employees take short breaks every half-hour or hour to do simple stretches at their workstations.[69]

Ergonomically designed workstations have been found to increase productivity and efficiency, as well as reduce injuries. The Institute for Work and Health studied 200 tax collectors who were in sedentary, computer-intensive jobs. Workers who were given a highly adjustable chair combined with a 90-minute ergonomics training session reported less musculoskeletal pain over

FIGURE 14.6 | Computer Ergonomics

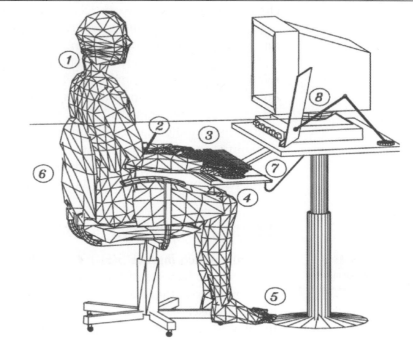

Note: This diagram is just an example. Workstation set ups will vary according to the particular desk style, monitor, tray mount or other accessories used.

1) The monitor should be set at a height so that your neck will be straight.

2) Your elbow joints should be at about 90 degrees, with the arms hanging naturally at the sides.

3) Keep your hands in line with the forearms, so the wrists are straight, not bending up, down or to either side.

4) Thighs should be roughly parallel to the floor, with your feet flat on the floor or footrest.

5) If necessary, use a footrest to support your feet.

6) Your chair should be fully adjustable (i.e., for seat height, backrest height and seat pan tilt, and, preferably, armrests). It should have a well-formed lumbar (lower back) support to help maintain the lumbar curve.

7) There should be enough space to use the mouse. Use a wrist rest or armrest so that your wrist is straight and your arm muscles are not overworked.

8) Use an adjustable document holder to hold source documents at the same height, angle and distance as the monitor.

Source: Computer Ergonomics: Workstation Layout and Lighting (Toronto: Ontario Ministry of Labour Health and Safety Guidelines, 2004). © Queen's Printer for Ontario, 2004. Reproduced with permission.

their workday, compared with workers who received just the training or nothing at all. Productivity increased nearly 18 percent because of the reduction in pain and more effective use of workspaces.[70]

Ergonomics will become more and more important as the workforce ages, and the physical demands of work will need to be adapted to accommodate some of the many physical changes typically associated with aging, including changes in muscular strength, hand function, cardiovascular capacity, vision, and hearing.

Video Display Terminals

The physical demands of new technologies have brought a new set of RSIs. The fact that many workers today must spend hours each day working with video display terminals (VDTs) is creating new health problems at work. Short-term eye problems, like burning, itching, and tearing, as well as eyestrain and eye soreness are common complaints among video display operators. Backaches and neck aches are also widespread among display users. These often occur because employees try to compensate for display problems like glare and immovable keyboards by manoeuvring into awkward body positions.

Researchers also found that employees who used VDTs and had heavy workloads were prone to psychological distress, like anxiety, irritability, and fatigue. There is also a tendency for computer users to suffer from RSIs, such as *carpal tunnel syndrome* (a tingling or numbness in the fingers caused by the narrowing of a tunnel of bones and ligaments in the wrist) caused by repetitive use of the hands and arms at uncomfortable angles.[71]

General recommendations regarding the use of VDTs include giving employees rest breaks every hour, designing maximum flexibility into the workstation so that it can be adapted to the individual operator, reducing glare with devices, such as shades over windows and terminal screens, and giving VDT workers a complete pre-placement vision exam to ensure that vision is properly corrected to reduce visual strain.[72]

Tips | **FOR THE FRONT LINE**

Workplace Toxins

The leading cause of work-related deaths around the world is cancer. Hundreds of Canadian workers die from occupational cancer each year.[73] There is an erroneous perception that cancer-causing agents in the workplace are disappearing. Employers often face significant costs in order to eliminate carcinogens in the workplace, and unions are often so preoccupied with wage and benefit increases that they don't bring the issue to the bargaining table (although the Canadian Labour Congress has launched an initiative to reduce work-related cancers by releasing an information kit for workers on cancer-causing materials on the job).[74] In addition to known carcinogens, such as asbestos and benzene, new chemicals and substances are constantly being introduced into the workplace without adequate testing.[75] Workers' compensation laws in several provinces have been amended to provide benefits to firefighters who develop specific job-related cancers.[76]

Workplace Smoking

Smoking is a serious problem for employees and employers. Employers face higher costs for health-care and disability insurance, as smoking is associated with numerous health problems. Employees who smoke have reduced productivity and a significantly greater risk of occupational accidents than do non-smokers. Employees who smoke also expose nonsmoking co-workers to toxic second-hand smoke.

Smokers who are also exposed to other carcinogens in the workplace, such as asbestos, have dramatically higher rates of lung cancer. The effects of on-the-job exposure to radon on lung cancer rates were found to last up to 14 years, and the cancer rates were greatly increased for smokers.[77]

Most Canadian jurisdictions have banned smoking in workplaces. Health Canada is urging employers to implement smoking cessation programs for employees to achieve better health for employees, better business results, legislative compliance, increased employee satisfaction (especially for the 80 percent of Canadians who do not smoke), and avoidance of litigation.[78]

Influenza Pandemic

Recent major outbreaks of influenza have alarmed people around the world and reminded everyone that a major influenza pandemic is inevitable at some time in the future. Despite estimates that one-third to one-half of the population will be sick at some point in an influenza pandemic, a sense of urgency regarding organizational planning for such an event is lacking.[79] A 2006 study by the Conference Board of Canada found that although almost 80 percent of executives are concerned about the impact of a pandemic on their organization, only 4 percent of their organizations had developed a pandemic preparedness plan.[80] Another survey at the end of 2008 found that half of Canadian companies with more than 500 employees had no plan for an influenza pandemic.[81]

The first organizational impact of a pandemic will be absenteeism, estimated at 35 percent in the influenza plan for the Government of Canada.[82] HR will be a key player in responding to a pandemic as most employers are planning to continue their business operations using the existing workforce—in other words, with substantially fewer employees. Immediate decisions will be required regarding telecommuting and working at remote work sites, compensation for absent employees, and maintenance of occupational health for employees who are working on company premises.[83] Even in the plans that do exist, there is little detail on the status of quarantined employees, compensating employees who cover for absent co-workers, responding to employee refusals to work in an unsafe environment, and business shutdown if health and safety officers declare the entire workplace to be unsafe.[84]

A pandemic preparedness plan should address prevention, containment, response to employee work refusals, creation of a pandemic preparation and response team, viability of continuing company operations, security of company premises, sickness/disability coverage, leaves to care for sick family members or children at home if schools are closed, and visitors to company premises.[85] Communication will be a critical component of pandemic management (likely using email, intranet, and hot lines), particularly if travel bans are imposed.[86] Unionized organizations will also need to consult their collective agreements and may wish to consult with the union when making pandemic preparedness plans.[87]

Recently amended Ontario legislation provides that if an emergency is declared by the government, then ten unpaid days of leave will be available to employees who need to care for sick family members, in addition to the already existing ten unpaid days available in these circumstances.[88]

Although the risk of a pandemic occurring in any one year may be small, the potential consequences are so serious that business leaders are well advised to prepare their organizations.[89]

Violence at Work

Workplace violence is defined by the International Labour Organization (ILO) as incidents in which an employee is abused, threatened, or assaulted in circumstances relating to work, and it includes harassment, bullying, intimidation,

Canada Influenza Pandemic Site
www.influenza.gc.ca/index_e.html
World Health Organization
www.who.int/en
Quebec Pandemic Web Site
**www.pandemiequebec.gouv.qc.ca/
en/index.aspx.html**

Health Minister Leona Aglukkaq speaks at a news conference in Ottawa about the swine flu outbreak. Employers that lack pandemic plans should start putting them together now, according to experts.

physical threats, assaults, and robberies. Most workplace violence arises from members of the public—customers or strangers—rather than co-workers. Canada is the fourth-worst country in the world for workplace violence (the United States is seventh) according to ILO data.[90]

The first-ever Statistics Canada report on criminal victimization in the workplace, released in 2007, indicated that one in every five violent incidents in Canada (such as physical and sexual assault, armed robbery) occurred in the workplace. Physical assault was the most common violent incident, representing 71 percent of all incidents of workplace violence.[91] Violence against employees at work is particularly prevalent for women in health-care professions. More than one-third of nurses are physically assaulted and almost half suffer emotional abuse.[92] Reports of abuse of nurses by clinical area of practice are shown in **Figure 14.7.**

Workplace Violence and the Law

Most Canadian jurisdictions now have workplace violence legislation in place covering physical violence, and some include psychological/emotional violence as well. Human rights laws across the country prohibit various forms of harassment and bullying. Employers may be found vicariously liable for the violent acts of their employees on the basis that the employer negligently hired or negligently retained someone whom the employer should reasonably have known could cause the violent act; employers may also be found liable when they are aware of violent incidents and fail to respond.[93]

Hints | TO ENSURE LEGAL COMPLIANCE

FIGURE 14.7 | Reports of Abuse by Clinical Area of Practice

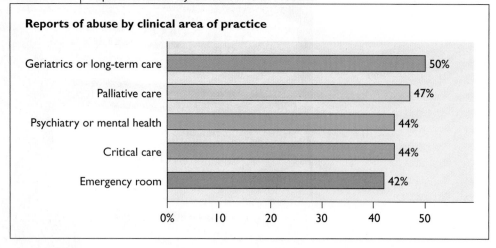

Reports of abuse by clinical area of practice

Clinical area	Percentage
Geriatrics or long-term care	50%
Palliative care	47%
Psychiatry or mental health	44%
Critical care	44%
Emergency room	42%

Source: Statistics Canada, Factors related to on-the-job abuse of nurses by patients, *Health Reports,* Vol. 20, No. 2, pp. 7–19, 2009.

Prevention and Control of Workplace Violence

Canadian Initiative on Workplace Violence
www.workplaceviolence.ca

There are several concrete steps that employers can take to reduce the incidence of workplace violence. These include identifying jobs with high risk of violence, enhancing security arrangements, instituting a workplace violence policy, creating a healthy work environment, heightening security measures, training for violence reduction, and improving employee screening.

Identify Jobs with High Risk of Violence Kevin Kelloway, a researcher at Saint Mary's University in Halifax, has identified job characteristics that are reliable predictors of workplace violence, shown in **Figure 14.8.** Identifying and redressing these hazards and risk factors, such as installing safety shields for taxi drivers and bus drivers, can help to reduce victimization.

Institute a Workplace Violence Policy Firms should develop, support, and communicate a workplace violence policy that clearly communicates management's

FIGURE 14.8 | Job Characteristics That Increase the Risk of Workplace Violence

1. Being responsible for the physical/emotional care of others.
2. Making decisions that influence other people's lives/denying a service or request.
3. Working alone during the day/night/evening.
4. Handling valuables, guns, weapons, or dispensing drugs.
5. Exercising security functions of physical control of others.
6. Supervising/disciplining others.
7. Interacting with frustrated individuals.
8. Working evenings or nights.
9. Working in clients' homes.
10. Having contact with individuals under the influence of alcohol, illegal drugs, or medication.

Source: E.K. Kelloway, "Predictors and Outcomes of Workplace Violence," *HR Professional*, February/March 2003, p. 52.

commitment to preventing violent incidents. The policy should state that no degree or type of violence is acceptable in the workplace; provide definitions of prohibited conduct; specify consequences of violating the policy; encourage reporting of violent incidents; include prohibitions and sanctions for retaliation or reprisal; and specify that all physical assaults will be reported to police.[94]

Create a Healthy Work Environment   According to Julian Barling, a researcher at Queen's University, a healthy work environment with professional supervision is the best way to reduce violence on the part of employees. Leaders, managers, and supervisors should express real concern for employees and treat people fairly, as acts of revenge typically occur in response to perceived injustice.[95]

Heighten Security Measures   Security precautions to reduce the risk of workplace violence include improving external lighting; using drop safes to minimize cash on hand and posting signs noting that only a limited amount of cash is on hand; installing silent alarms and surveillance cameras; increasing the number of staff members on duty; and closing establishments during high-risk hours late at night and early in the morning. In workplaces serving members of the public, some important precautions for employee safety include providing staff training in conflict resolution and defusing anger; having security staff to refuse admittance to anyone who appears intoxicated, visibly angry, or threatening; and instituting a recognizable "help" signal to alert other staff members that assistance is required.[96]

Provide Workplace Violence Training   Workplace violence training explains what workplace violence is, identifies its causes and signs, and offers tips on how to prevent it and what to do when it occurs. Supervisors can also be trained to identify the typical perpetrator—male, aged 25 to 40, bad at handling stress, a constant complainer, has a tendency to make verbal threats and physical or verbal outbursts, harbours grudges, and brandishes weapons to gain attention.[97]

Improve Employee Screening   Screening out potentially violent applicants means instituting a sound pre-employment investigation of all information provided. Sample interview questions to ask might include "What frustrates you?" and "Who was your worst supervisor and why?"[98] As sensible as it is to try to screen out potentially violent employees, doing so incurs the risk of liability and lawsuits. Human rights legislation limits the use of criminal records in hiring decisions.

Chapter | SUMMARY

1. Employers and employees are held jointly responsible for maintaining the health and safety of workers, including participation on joint health and safety committees. Employers are responsible for "due diligence"—taking every reasonable precaution to ensure the health and safety of their workers. Employees are responsible for protecting their own health and safety and that of their co-workers. Employees have the right to know about workplace safety hazards, the right to participate in the occupational health and safety process, and the right to refuse unsafe work.

2. The Workplace Hazardous Materials Information System (WHMIS) law is a Canada-wide legally mandated system designed to protect workers by providing crucial information about hazardous materials and substances in the workplace. WHMIS requires labelling of hazardous material containers, material safety data sheets, and employee training.

3. There are three basic causes of accidents—chance occurrences, unsafe conditions, and unsafe acts on the part of employees. In addition, three other work-related factors—the job itself, the work schedule, and the psychological climate—also contribute to accidents.

4. One approach to preventing accidents is to reduce unsafe conditions by identifying and removing potential hazards. Another approach to improving safety is to reduce unsafe acts—for example, through selection and placement, education and training, positive reinforcement, top-management commitment, and monitoring work overload and stress.

5. Employee wellness programs aim to improve employees' health and reduce costs for sickness and disability claims, workers' compensation, and absenteeism. Wellness initiatives include physical fitness programs, smoking cessation programs, relaxation classes, and heart-health monitoring.

6. Substance abuse is an important and growing health problem among employees. Techniques to deal with this challenge include disciplining, discharge, in-house counselling, and referrals to an outside agency. Stress, depression, and burnout are other potential health problems at work. Job stress can be reduced by ensuring that employees take breaks each day, providing access to counselling, and giving employees more control over their jobs. Repetitive strain injuries occur as a result of repetitive movements, awkward postures, and forceful exertion. Ergonomics is very effective at reducing RSIs. Workplace toxins can be carcinogenic, and some governments are providing workers' compensation benefits to workers with job-related cancer. Employees who smoke have reduced productivity and greater health costs. Governments across Canada have increasingly banned workplace smoking. Violence against employees is a serious problem at work. Steps that can reduce workplace violence include improved security arrangements, better employee screening, and workplace violence training.

PEARSON
myHRlab™

Test yourself on the material for this chapter at
www.pearsoned.ca/myhrlab

Key | TERMS

burnout   *(p. 402)*
employee wellness program   *(p. 397)*
ergonomics   *(p. 403)*
occupational health and safety legislation   *(p. 382)*

repetitive strain injuries (RSIs)   *(p. 403)*
Workplace Hazardous Materials Information System (WHMIS)   *(p. 385)*

Review and Discussion | QUESTIONS

1. Discuss the purpose of occupational health and safety legislation and how it is enforced.

2. Explain the supervisor's and the employee's roles and responsibilities in safety.

3. Explain what causes unsafe acts.

4. Describe how to reduce workers' compensation costs, both before and after an accident.

5. Explain the four traditional techniques for dealing with substance abuse.

6. Analyze the legal and safety issues concerning workplace toxins.

7. Explain how to reduce violence at work.

Critical Thinking | QUESTIONS

1. What is your opinion on the following question: "Is there such a thing as an accident-prone person?"

2. Young people have a disproportionate number of workplace accidents. Why do you think this is so? What can be done to reduce them?

3. What guidelines would you suggest for determining the point at which to terminate an employee who shows signs of being prone to violence?

4. What do you think are the most important things to include in a wellness program, and why?

5. Given the disappointing progress in reducing workplace injuries and deaths, do you think that the "corporate killing" law should be used more aggressively?

6. Assume that you have an employee working in your company who has been treated several times already for substance abuse through the company counselling program. Today, the manager found him "stoned" again, trying to operate a piece of equipment in an unsafe manner. The manager just came to you and said "Fire him! I've had enough! He's not only endangering himself, but other workers." The company has a no substance use while at work and zero tolerance for arriving at work in an impaired state policy that all employees are aware of and have signed off on as part of the Code of Conduct. What steps can/should your company take in this circumstance?

Experiential | EXERCISES

1. In a group of four to six students, spend about 30 to 45 minutes in and around one of the buildings on your campus identifying health and safety hazards. Research whether or not these unsafe conditions violate the applicable health and safety legislation.

2. Review a workplace-violence consulting website and contact a workplace-violence consultant. Gather information on what advice is provided to clients on preventing workplace violence, and ask for a sample workplace-violence policy. Prepare a brief presentation to the class on your findings.

3. On your own, identify the workplace hazards that might be present in the following list:

   car repair and auto body shop

   home renovations supplies and equipment storage area

   live concert venue

   health clinic dealing with homeless people

   office with many employees working on computers and paper files

   chemical plant finished product storage area.

   Then think about what such companies can and should do to ensure that their employees are safe at work. Once you have completed your own list of answers, work with a group of four or five students to compare your lists. Brainstorm other hazards and solutions.

4. Conduct an internet search on Canadian websites to find a Material Safety Data Sheet (MSDS) for chlorine laundry bleach for home use. Compare the information on this sheet to the information shown in the MSDS for propane in Figure 14.3 on pages 387–88. Have all of the same areas been covered and to the same depth? Compare this information to the information found on the label of a bottle of bleach. What is different? What have you learned that you did not know? Bring the results of your research to class for a discussion on the importance of MSDS information to employees in different types of organizations.

Running | CASE

Running Case: LearnInMotion.com

The New Health and Safety Program

At first glance, a dot-com is one of the last places you would expect to find potential health and safety hazards—or so Jennifer and Pierre thought. There is no danger of moving machinery, no high-pressure lines, no cutting or heavy lifting, and certainly no forklift trucks. However, there are health and safety problems.

In terms of unsafe conditions, for instance, two things dot-com companies have lots of are cables and wires. There are cables connecting the computers to each other and to the servers, and in many cases separate cables running from some computers to separate printers. There are ten telephones in the office, all on five-metre phone lines that always seem to be snaking around chairs and tables. There is, in fact, an astonishing amount of cable considering that this is an office with fewer than ten employees. When the installation specialists wired the office (for electricity, high-speed DSL, phone lines, burglar alarms, and computers), they estimated that they used more than five kilometres of cable of one sort or another. Most of the cables are hidden in the walls or ceilings, but many of them snake their way from desk to desk and under and over doorways.

Several employees have tried to reduce the nuisance of having to trip over wires whenever they get up by putting their plastic chair pads over the wires closest to them. However, that still leaves many wires unprotected. In other cases, they brought in their own packing tape and tried to tape down the wires in those spaces where they are particularly troublesome, such as across doorways.

The cables and wires are one of the more obvious potential accident-causing conditions. The firm's programmer, before he left the firm, had tried to repair the main server while the unit was still electrically alive. To this day, they are not exactly sure where he stuck the screwdriver, but the result was that he was "blown across the room," as Pierre puts it. He was all right, but it was still a scare.

And although the company has not received any claims yet, every employee spends hours at his or her computer, so carpal tunnel syndrome is a risk, as are eyestrain and strained backs. One recent incident particularly scared them. The firm uses independent contractors to deliver the firm's book- and CD-ROM–based course in Toronto and two other cities. A delivery person was riding his bike at the corner of King and Bay Streets in Toronto, where he was struck by a car. Luckily he was not hurt, but the bike's front wheel was wrecked, and the close call got Pierre and Jennifer thinking about their lack of a safety program.

It's not just the physical conditions that concern the company's two owners. They also have some concerns about potential health problems such as job stress and burnout. Although the business may be (relatively) safe with respect to physical conditions, it is also relatively stressful in terms of the demands it makes in hours and deadlines. It is not at all uncommon for employees to get to work by 7:30 or 8 A.M. and to work through until 11 P.M. or midnight, at least five and sometimes six or seven days per week. Getting the company's new calendar fine-tuned and operational requires 70-hour workweeks for three weeks from five of LearnInMotion's employees. The bottom line is that both Jennifer and Pierre feel quite strongly that they need to do something about implementing a health and safety plan. Now they want you, their management consultant, to help them to actually do it.

QUESTIONS

1   If LearnInMotion happened to receive a visit from the Ministry of Labour, what specific areas do you feel they would be ordered to change and why?

2   Do Jennifer and Pierre as owners of LearnInMotion have specific responsibilities for ensuring their employees' health and safety is maintained and for having a health and safety policy in place which is subsequently enforced?

3   What unsafe conditions and acts were described in this case?

Case | **INCIDENT**

Ramona's Health and Safety Nightmare

Ramona McKenzie was on her way to work on a cloudy Monday morning when she got the call on her cellphone that no human resources manager wants to receive—an employee had just been injured at her workplace. While turning into the company driveway, Ramona sees an ambulance, the injured worker, and a number of other employees surrounding the injured worker. Ramona parks her call, rushes over to where the employee is laying, and inquires about what had happened.

The injured employee informs Ramona that she fell on the way into the building because no salt had been laid earlier in the morning to melt the ice on the parking lot. At this point, the ambulance takes the injured employee to the hospital and Ramona asks to speak to the plant manager in his office. Shaken by everything that had occurred, Ramona asks the plant manager to find out why no salt had been put on the parking lot, as this was the norm after a significant snowfall. The plant manager informs Ramona that he would do this

but also that the injured worker was wearing high-heeled shoes while on her way into the building.

Now that you know the facts of this scenario, please assist Ramona by answering the following questions.

QUESTIONS

1   How could this accident have been prevented?

2   Is the employee or employer responsible for this accident happening?

3   What does Ramona have to do to ensure a smooth return to work for the injured worker after the accident?

CHAPTER 15

LEARNING OUTCOMES

AFTER STUDYING THIS CHAPTER, YOU SHOULD BE ABLE TO

DEFINE employee engagement and **DISCUSS** the drivers and outcomes of employee engagement.

EXPLAIN various techniques for ensuring effective employee communication in organizations.

ANALYZE important HR considerations in ensuring fairness in downsizings and mergers.

DISCUSS the three foundations of a fair and just disciplinary process.

DEFINE wrongful dismissal and constructive dismissal.

EXPLAIN the six steps in the termination interview.

FAIR TREATMENT:
The Foundation of Effective Employee Relations

REQUIRED PROFESSIONAL CAPABILITIES (RPC)

- Uses communication strategies to advance organizational objectives
- Develops and implements programs for employee involvement
- Develops and maintains the trust and support of collaborators including the immediate supervisor, subordinates, and internal clients
- Gathers and analyzes information on organizational context (climate, culture) in order to highlight key issues
- Recommends or initiates actions in response to known or suspected incidents of misconduct
- Participates in the termination process by preparing termination notices, conducting

exit interviews, and arranging outplacement services
- Monitors and reports on the progress of major change initiatives
- Develops processes to engage and involve employees in achieving the objectives of the organization
- Provides advice on issues relating to labour and employee relations including hiring, discipline, and termination
- Contributes to development of an environment that fosters effective working relationships

THE STRATEGIC IMPORTANCE OF EFFECTIVE EMPLOYEE RELATIONS

Today more than ever it is important to build a strategic, competitive advantage through an organization's human resources. Consequently, management of employee relations has been shifting from its traditional focus on handling disciplinary matters and dismissals to a new focus on achieving the strategic benefits of "employee engagement." It is important to keep the employees that companies have spent time and money recruiting, selecting, and training continually motivated and engaged in pursuing the goals of the organization.

distributive justice Fairness of a decision outcome.

procedural justice Fairness of the process used to make a decision.

interactional justice Fairness in interpersonal interactions by treating others with dignity and respect.

The most important aspect of managing employee relations is ensuring that employees are treated fairly, ethically, and legally. Over 25 years of organizational research clearly indicates that employees are sensitive to the treatment they receive, and that they have strong perceptions regarding the fairness of their experiences at work.[1] With respect to employee relations, experts generally define organizational justice in terms of three components—distributive justice, procedural justice, and interactional justice. **Distributive justice** refers to the fairness and justice of the outcome of a decision (for instance, did I get an equitable pay raise?). **Procedural justice** refers to the fairness of the process (for instance, is the process my company uses to allocate merit raises fair?). **Interactional justice** refers to the manner in which managers conduct their interpersonal dealings with employees and, in particular, to the degree to which they treat employees with dignity and respect as opposed to abuse or disrespect (for instance, does my supervisor treat me with respect?).

This chapter will review how managers can enhance employee engagement and ensure effective employee relations by ensuring fair treatment.

EMPLOYEE ENGAGEMENT

employee engagement A positive, fulfilling, work-related state of mind characterized by vigour, dedication, and absorption.

Employee engagement is a positive, fulfilling, work-related state of mind characterized by vigour, dedication, and absorption.[2] It is a heightened emotional and intellectual connection that an employee has for his or her job, organization, manager, or coworkers that in turn influences the employee to apply additional discretionary effort.[3] Engaged employees feel a vested interest on the company's success and are both willing and motivated to perform to levels that exceed the stated job requirements.[4]

Drivers of Engagement

Engagement is heightened by several factors that vary across different countries and cultures, according to a recent major study of nearly 90 000 workers in 18 countries around the world by consultants Towers Perrin.[5] Further details are provided in the **Global HRM** box.

Also, the factors that enhance engagement are different from those that enhance attraction to an organization and retention of employees.[6] Organizational factors such as senior leadership, opportunities for learning and development, and company image and reputation are the primary influencers of engagement. The top drivers of attraction, retention and engagement for Canadian workers in the Towers Perrin study are shown in **Figure 15.1**.

The Towers Perrin study found that only 21 percent of employees around the world are highly engaged at work and that 38 percent are highly disengaged, creating an "engagement gap." Three recommendations were provided for companies

Global HRM

Engagement Drivers Vary Around the World

The Towers Perrin Global Workforce Study of 2007–2008 reported on employee engagement levels and the top drivers of engagement in numerous countries around the world. Overall, the top drivers of engagement were:

1. senior management sincerely interested in employee well-being

2. improved my skills and capabilities over the last year; and

3. organization's reputation for social responsibility.

However, there was considerable variation between countries, meaning that approaches to managing engagement in one country may not be appropriate in another. The top drivers for 10 of these countries are displayed in the following chart.

Country	#1 Driver	#2 Driver	#3 Driver
Brazil	Organization rewards outstanding customer service	Improved my skills and capabilities over the last year	Senior management sincerely interested in employee well-being
China	Have excellent career advancement opportunities	Organization encourages innovative thinking	Organization's reputation for financial stability
Germany	Senior management sincerely interested in employee well-being	Appropriate amount of decision making authority to do my job well	Organization's reputation for social responsibility
India	Input into decision making in my department	Senior management's actions consistent with our values	Organization's reputation for social responsibility
Italy	Senior management communicates openly and honestly	Input into decision making in my department	Understand potential career track within organization
Japan	Have excellent career advancement opportunities	Organization's reputation for social responsibility	Set high professional standards
Mexico	Appropriate amount of decision making authority to do my job well	Enjoy challenging work assignments that broaden skills	Manager handles performance reviews fairly and effectively
Russia	Senior management sincerely interested in employee well-being	Organization's reputation for social responsibility	Set high professional standards
South Korea	Senior management acts to ensure organization's long term success	Unit has skills needed to succeed	Organization supports work-life balance
Switzerland	Senior management supports new ideas	Input to decision making in my department	Organization quickly resolves customer concerns

Source: Adapted from *Closing the Engagement Gap: A Road Map for Driving Superior Business Performance.* Towers Perrin Global Workforce Study 2007–2008. Copyright 2009 Towers Perrin. Used with permission.

RPC

Develops processes to engage and involve employees in achieving the objectives of the organization

that wish to increase engagement. First, employees need their senior leaders to demonstrate inspiration, vision, and commitment. Leadership matters at every level, and therefore management development programs also matter. Second, employees have a strong desire to learn and grow. Learning and development programs have never been more important. It is very important to develop a culture of learning and growing. Third, employees want to work for a company with a good reputation, which is seen as a leader, and which strives for excellence.

A closer look at the drivers of employee engagement reveals the importance of fair treatment. Senior management that are concerned about the well-being of

FIGURE 15.1 | Top Drivers of Attraction, Retention, and Engagement in Canada

TOP FIVE DRIVERS		
Top Attraction Drivers	**Top Retention Drivers**	**Top Engagement Drivers**
Competitive base pay	Have excellent career advancement opportunities	Senior management sincerely interested in employee well-being
Vacation/paid time off	Satisfaction with the organization's people decisions	Organization's reputation for social responsibility
Competitive health care benefits	Ability to balance my work/personal life	Input into decision making in my department
Challenging work	Fairly compensated compared to others doing similar work in my organization	Improved my skills and capabilities over the last year
Career advancement opportunities	Understand potential career track within organization	Understand potential career track within organization

Source: *Closing the Engagement Gap: A Road Map for Driving Superior Business Performance.* Towers Perrin Workforce Study 2007–2008 (page 21). Copyright 2009 Towers Perrin. Used with permission.

their employees, tell the truth, and communicate difficult messages well are treating employees with dignity and respect, the cornerstones of interactional justice. Opportunities for growth and development, including increased autonomy and participation in day-to-day decision making, are manifestations of procedural justice. Organizations that strive for excellence by ensuring that career tracks are clear to employees and by paying for performance are ensuring distributive justice.

Outcomes of Engagement

There is clear and mounting evidence that employee engagement is strongly correlated to a number of individual, group, and corporate performance outcomes, including improvements in recruiting, retention, turnover, individual productivity, customer service, and customer loyalty, as well as growth in operating margins, increased profit margins, and revenue growth rates.[7] A study conducted by Hewitt Associates went a step further and found evidence of a causal link. Over a five-year period, Hewitt studied engagement and financial indicators and discovered that when employee engagement levels increased, there was a corresponding increase in financial performance indicators that followed. This evidence supports the contention that employee engagement results in an increase in a company's overall financial performance.[8]

Employee engagement fosters and drives discretionary behaviour, eliciting the employees' highest productivity, their best ideas, and their genuine commitment to the success of the organization. Engagement contributes significantly to an organization's performance, leading to improvements in service quality, customer satisfaction, and long-term financial results. All other factors being equal, it also serves the individual, fulfilling a basic human need to be connected to worthwhile endeavours and make a significant contribution. In short, engagement is good for the company and good for the employee.[9]

EFFECTIVE EMPLOYEE COMMUNICATION

One of the important drivers of employee engagement is good communication, because an engaged employee is an informed employee who feels valued and critical to success.[10] It is important for managers not to confuse information (facts) with communication that conveys both the rational and emotional components of a message to maximize employee engagement. It is also important to maximize face-to-face opportunities when delivering information from members of the senior management team.[11]

In order to increase employee engagement, many firms give employees extensive data on the performance of and prospects for their operations.[12] It must be remembered that employee communication requires careful consideration, as Chrysler found out in early 2009 when it sent a letter to unionized employees outlining the serious challenges the company was facing and the need to reduce labour costs. Within hours, workers in Windsor, Ontario, spilled out of the plant to burn the letter in protest. The union called the letter a "clear attempt to sidestep and undermine" them.[13]

Suggestion Programs

RPC

Develops and implements programs for employee involvement

Uses communication strategies to advance organizational objectives

Employees can often offer well-informed, thoughtful, and creative suggestions regarding issues ranging from malfunctioning vending machines to unlit parking lots to a manager's spending too much of the department's money on travel. Dofasco Inc.'s suggestion program has been a success story for decades. Employees can receive cash awards of up to $50 000, depending on the savings realized by implementing the suggestion. Suggestion programs like these have several benefits. They let management continually monitor employees' feelings and concerns, they make it clear that employees have several channels through which to communicate concerns and get responses, and the net effect is that there is less likelihood that small problems will grow into big ones.

Employee Opinion Surveys

employee opinion surveys Communication devices that use questionnaires to ask for employees' opinions about the company, management, and work life.

Employee Feedback System
**www.brocku.ca/buwi/tools/pdf/
WHRL_EFS_Fact_Sheet.pdf**

Many firms also administer periodic anonymous **employee opinion surveys.** For maximum benefit, surveys should be conducted regularly and the results must be provided to participants.[14] An employee satisfaction survey, called the Employee Feedback System (EFS), has been developed by the National Quality Institute and the Workplace Health Research Unit at Brock University.[15] The EFS examines 16 areas ranging from job satisfaction and co-worker cohesion to quality focus and employee commitment.

RPC

Develops and maintains the trust and support of collaborators including the immediate supervisor, subordinates, and internal clients

Gathers and analyzes information on organizational context (climate, culture) in order to highlight key issues

Recently, employees began to use blogs to express opinions about their employers, and employer concerns arose about damage to their reputation and possible disclosure of confidential company information. Some corporations, such as IBM, Cisco, and Sun Microsystems, have chosen to trust their employees and have suggested guidelines and specific tactics so that employees can blog without causing themselves or their employers any grief.[16] However, there are also cases where employees have been terminated for posting negative opinions about their employer, and arbitration boards have upheld the terminations, finding that postings about managers, coworkers, and the work environment are sufficient grounds for discharge.[17] A blogging policy is recommended by legal experts and should include directions to refrain from disclosing any confidential company information or embarrassing or demeaning information about the company and its employees.[18]

Communication from Management

In order to increase employee engagement, many firms give employees extensive data on the performance of and prospects for their operations. Traditionally, newsletters and verbal presentations were the methods used to disseminate information from the company to employees. More recently, organizations have utilized videos, email, and intranets.[19] Blogs can also be used by senior managers to connect with employees. When Jim Estill sold his company and became CEO of the larger combined operation, he found employees of the acquiring company "treated me like I was some sort of Martian." He started a blog (80 percent company-related content and 20 percent personal) and soon overcame the problem—staff even sent him pictures from their kids' birthday parties! In addition, staff sent the blog to vendors and customers, which elevated him in their eyes as well.[20] One Canadian company used improved management communication to drive huge increases in employee engagement as well as a turnaround in financial results, as described in the **Strategic HR** box.

Strategic HR

Forensic Technology: Improved Engagement Fuels Company Turnaround

When Horatio Caine from CSI: Miami studies a digital image of a gun's spent cartridge case looking for clues to this week's puzzling murder, he is using a real-life analysis system built by Montreal-based Forensic Technology (FT). The firm is a leader in ballistics and firearms identification technologies.

The company was barely making a profit in 2004 and had to downsize by 25 percent. In 2005, salaries were frozen and the generous employee profit-sharing plan was discontinued. In 2006 the company was for sale. Turnover hit 20 percent and stayed there.

"High turnover is a particularly painful experience in most companies, but it is excruciating and very costly in high-tech companies," said Elisabeth Lecavalier, FT vice-president of human resources. "Not only were we losing valued employees with high levels of education and technical skills and knowledge that are tough to find in a very competitive market in Montreal, but replacement costs, time spent in retraining and reintegrating, added to the burden. Add to that the demoralizing impact of losing friends and facing additional workload on the employees who stayed, we were faced with a situation that just had to turn around, and turn around fast."

The turnaround began in the fall of 2006 with an internal effort to improve employee engagement and increase retention. They began with the recognition of a need for strategic alignment of people, processes and technology. With the support of top management, the role of human resources became one of a catalyst, conducting research, suggesting new strategies and programs, training, coordinating and supporting business initiatives. Using focus groups, they developed a new company tag line: "Work that matters." Surveys and focus group discussions identified the key drivers of engagement as career development, recognition, internal communications, and work environment issues (flexibility and social responsibility). Each of these areas was addressed.

A new management development program emphasizing employee engagement encouraged managers to listen to their employees, understand their career aspirations, and provide training and development that would move them toward achieving those aspirations. The President's Award for Excellence recognition program was established, along with a new intranet site with the latest in corporate news. A new community involvement event was instituted where FT employees organize and conduct a learning event for high-school students in high-risk areas of the city to show them the value of pursuing their education.

By 2008, FT's turnover fell to less than 4 percent and employee engagement levels rose from 30 percent to close to 65 percent. Employees now have great pride in the company, with one field technician commenting "there is a moral value to what we do."

Source: B. King, "Revised Total Rewards Package Leads Forensic Technology Company Turnaround, Increases Engagement," *Workspan*. Contents © 2009. Reprinted with permission from WorldatWork. No part of this article may be reproduced, excerpted or redistributed in any form without express written permission from WorldatWork.

RESPECTING EMPLOYEE PRIVACY

Today's employers are grappling with the problem of how to balance employee privacy rights with their need to monitor the use of technology-related activities in the workplace. Employers must maintain the ability to effectively manage their employees and prevent liability to the company, which can be held legally liable for the actions of its employees.[21] They want to eliminate time wastage (on web surfing, playing computer games, and so on) and abuse of company resources (such as use of the internet and email at work for personal and possibly illegal uses, such as gambling or visiting pornographic sites).[22] For example, one employee used workplace computers to access hundreds of pornographic websites, to surf internet dating sites for hours at a time, and to maintain personal files with sexually explicit images. The employee was dismissed and an arbitrator upheld the decision, stating that the employee had engaged in serious culpable misconduct.[23] Another concern is employee blogging, as a posting meant to be seen by a few friends that includes confidential company information or comments about management can easily make its way to a national media outlet without the author even knowing it.[24]

Employees are concerned with privacy—their control over information about themselves and their freedom from unjustifiable interference in their personal life. The Personal Information Protection and Electronic Documents Act (PIPEDA) governs the collection, use, and disclosure of personal information across Canada, including employers' collection and dissemination of personal information about employees. Any information beyond name, title, business address, and telephone number is regarded as personal and private, including health-related information provided to insurers. Employers must obtain consent from employees whenever personal information is collected, used, or disclosed.[25]

Some employers have resorted to electronic monitoring, which is becoming easier and less expensive as new software is developed that can track websites visited by workers and the time spent on each.[26] In general, courts in Canada have permitted electronic surveillance as long as there is proper balancing of opposing interests. Employers are given substantial leeway in monitoring their employees' use of the internet and email. Employers are in an even stronger position if there is a written policy in place. The policy should be updated regularly to reflect changes in technology and should address the use of all company technological equipment away from the employer's premises, including laptops, cellphones, BlackBerrys and so on.[27] **Figure 15.2** provides a sample company internet and email usage policy.

Video Surveillance

Some employers install video surveillance of employees to prevent theft and vandalism and to monitor productivity. Employees must be made aware of the surveillance. Unions often file grievances against video surveillance, and arbitrators have been reluctant to support it because of privacy concerns. Courts typically assess whether the surveillance was reasonable and whether there were reasonable alternatives available. Generally, they have decided that video surveillance is not reasonable and that other means could be used.[28] The Federal, British Columbia, and Alberta Privacy Commissioners have jointly issued video surveillance guidelines, which are shown in **Figure 15.3**.

Hints | TO ENSURE LEGAL COMPLIANCE

An Ethical | Dilemma

Is it ethical to use video surveillance of employees?

FIGURE 15.2 | Sample Company E-mail and Internet Usage Policy

1. Employees shall not use the Internet or email in any manner that may harm the business interests of the employer, subject the employer to liability or be offensive to other employees.
2. Employees may use the Internet and email for reasonable limited personal use providing such use does not interfere with job performance or employee productivity.
3. Employee personal email shall include a disclaimer that the views expressed therein are not the views, representations, or position of the company.
4. Employees shall not send, retrieve, or archive any material that may be considered discriminatory, harassment, or creates a hostile work environment.
5. Employees shall post no junk mail or spam.
6. Employees shall not access, attach, or store any information that may compromise the bandwidth of the employer's system.
7. Employees acknowledge the employer has the right and does monitor both Internet and email use.
8. Employees acknowledge that the employer has the right to keep and store any information resulting from this monitoring.
9. Employees acknowledge the employer has the right to block access and filter any material that the employer determines to be inappropriate, offensive or a threat to the security of the employer Internet and email system.
10. Employer shall consent to employees the right to store personal information in "personal" files provided said files do not violate any provisions of this Internet and email policy.
11. Employee agrees that the employer may access any email or computer storage file, including personal files, to protect the interests of the employer.
12. Employer shall disclose to all employees the extent of monitoring, the type of reports, the level of detail, and who will receive these reports.
13. Employer shall disclose to all employees who is responsible for enforcement of email and Internet policy, clarifying interpretation of policy, granting employee use exceptions, and resolving disputes.
14. Employer shall disclose to all employees the penalties for violation of the Internet and email acceptable use policy.
15. Employer and employees shall establish a procedure for both parties involvement in design and implementation of the company's Internet and email policy, including a system for continual evaluation of that policy and procedure for making changes to it as necessary.

Source: Journal of organizational culture, communication and conflict. Online by Arnesen and Weis. Copyright 2007 by ALLIED ACADEMIES. Reproduced with permission of ALLIED ACADEMIES.

FIGURE 15.3 | Video Surveillance Guidelines

1. Determine whether a less privacy-invasive alternative to video surveillance would meet your needs
2. Establish the business reason for conducting video surveillance and use video surveillance only for that reason
3. Develop a policy on the use of video surveillance
4. Limit the use and viewing range of cameras as much as possible.
5. Inform the public that video surveillance is taking place
6. Store any recorded images in a secure location, with limited access, and destroy them when they are no longer required for business purposes
7. Be ready to answer questions from the public. Individuals have the right to know who is watching them and why, as well as that information is being captured and what is being done with recorded images.
8. Give individuals access to information about themselves. This includes video images.
9. Educate camera operators about the obligation to protect the privacy of individuals.
10. Periodically evaluate the need for video surveillance.

Source: "Ten Things To Do." Office of the Privacy Commissioner of Canada, Guidelines for Overt Video Surveillance in the Private Sector (March 2008). Reprinted with permission. www.priv.gc.ca/information/guide/2008/gl_vs0803063.pdf.

PRESERVING DIGNITY IN THE RETIREMENT PROCESS

With Canada's rapidly aging population, management of the employee retirement experience will become an increasingly common task.[29] By 2025, more than 20 percent of the Canadian population will be over age 65, and the labour force will shrink dramatically. For many years, the trend has been toward earlier retirement—the average retirement age dropped from 65 in 1979 to 61 in 2005. However, with a labour shortage approaching as baby boomers retire over the next two decades, it is expected that this trend will reverse as organizations promote later retirement as a key strategy for dealing with the labour shortage.[30]

The Retirement Education Centre
www.iretire.org
Financial Knowledge Inc.
www.financialknowledgeinc.com
T.E. Financial Consultants
www.tefinancial.com

At any age, retirement for most employees is bittersweet. For some, it is the culmination of their careers, a time when they can relax and enjoy the fruits of their labour without worrying about the problems of work. For others, it is the retirement itself that is the trauma, as the once-busy employee tries to cope with suddenly being "non-productive." For many retirees, in fact, maintaining a sense of dignity and self-worth without a full-time job is the single most important task they will face. It is one that employers are increasingly trying to help their retirees cope with as a logical last step in the employee relations process.

Pre-Retirement Counselling

pre-retirement counselling Counselling provided to employees some months (or even years) before retirement, which covers such matters as benefits advice, second careers, and so on.

Most employers provide some type of formal **pre-retirement counselling** aimed at easing the passage of their employees into retirement.[31] Court decisions have confirmed that employers do have some legal responsibility to help employees prepare for retirement.[32] Retirement education and planning firms provide services to assist upcoming retirees with such issues as lifestyle goals (including part-time or volunteer work and/or moving to another country), financial planning, relationship issues, and health issues. Both individual and group transition counselling are offered in seminars and workshops featuring workbooks, questionnaires, discussions, group exercises, and software products. In the end, employees who are taking control of their retirement plans often have reduced absenteeism and health-care costs.[33]

The Future of Retirement

A recent Statistics Canada report entitled New Frontiers of Research on Retirement identified some of the major changes expected in the management of the retirement process.[34] First, there are gender differences in retirement patterns. Boomers are the first group to include a generation of women who have worked in the labour force for most of their lives, and they are expected to change retirement norms. Women are more likely to take early retirement for lifestyle reasons and they find the psychological transition to retirement easier than men do. These women will treat retirement as "amorphous and fluid," opting in and out of the workforce after retirement, based on caregiving demands. They are also more likely to seek out new experiences and challenges after retirement.

Second, joint retirement is becoming an issue for many dual-income couples. Retirement planning is becoming much more complex as two sets of financial and personal circumstances must be considered when making retirement decisions. Third, maintaining a standard of living in retirement will be a concern for those without substantial personal savings.

An employee contemplating different retirement options

Finally, flexibility in retirement arrangements is expected to increase dramatically. Currently, many retirees return to paid work on a contract or part-time basis, and about half participate in volunteer activities. Employers will encourage later retirement and more gradual transitions to retirement by making more flexible retirement options available to older workers: one study found almost 70 percent of HR managers are planning to provide alternate work arrangements for older employees.[35] Reduced work schedules with continued pension accrual may be very attractive to retirement-age workers. HR policies that are older-worker-friendly and an end to age discrimination will be necessary for more flexible retirement options to succeed.

FAIR TREATMENT IN LAYOFFS AND DOWNSIZING

Fair treatment of employees whose jobs are lost in layoffs and downsizing is very important for them and for maintaining employee engagement on the part of the "survivors" who continue to come to work in these difficult circumstances. Communicating the news of impending layoffs or downsizing is a difficult task, but ensuring interactional justice when doing so is critical to maintaining engagement on the part of the employees who will continue working for the organization.

Layoffs

layoff The temporary withdrawal of employment to workers for economic or business reasons.

A **layoff,** in which workers are sent home for a period of time (often indefinite), is a situation in which three conditions are present: (1) There is no work available for the employees, (2) management expects the no-work situation to be temporary and probably short term, and (3) management intends to recall the employees when work is again available.[36] A layoff is therefore not a termination, which is a permanent severing of the employment relationship. Layoffs almost always involve unionized employees and are based on "bumping" procedures outlined in the collective agreement. These procedures are almost always based on seniority.

Alternatives to Layoffs

Many employers today recognize the enormous investments that they have in recruiting, screening, and training their employees. As a result, they are more hesitant to lay off employees at the first signs of business decline. Instead, they are using new approaches to either blunt the effects of the layoff or eliminate the layoffs entirely.

There are several alternatives to layoff. With the voluntary reduction in pay plan, all employees agree to reductions in pay in order to keep everyone working. Other employers arrange to have all or most of their employees accumulate their vacation time and to concentrate their vacations during slow periods. Other employees agree to take voluntary time off, which again has the effect of reducing the employer's payroll and avoiding the need for a layoff. Another way to avoid layoffs is the use of contingent employees hired with the understanding that their work is temporary and they may be laid off at any time.[37] Finally, the Work Sharing Program available through Human Resources and Social Development Canada allows employers to reduce the workweek by one to three days and employees can claim employment insurance for the time not worked.

Downsizing

downsizing Refers to the process of reducing, usually dramatically, the number of people employed by the firm.

group termination laws Laws that require an employer to notify employees in the event that an employer decides to terminate a group of employees.

Downsizing refers to the process of reducing, usually dramatically, the number of people employed by the firm. The employees who lose their jobs and those remaining must all be treated fairly. **Group termination laws** require employers who are terminating a large group of employees to give them more notice than that required on termination of an individual employee. The laws are intended to assist employees in situations of plant closings and large downsizings. Most jurisdictions in Canada require employers who are terminating a group of employees (some specify 10 or more, others 25 or more) within a short time to give advance notice to employees and sometimes to their union. The amount of notice varies by jurisdiction and with the number of employees being terminated, but it generally ranges from 6 weeks to 18 weeks. The laws do not prevent the employer from closing down, nor do they require saving jobs; they simply give employees time to seek other work or retraining by giving them advance notice of the termination.

Research INSIGHT

Recent research has found that employees who receive bad news delivered face-to-face feel more fairly treated and are more willing to accept the news than are employees who receive the same news through email or word of mouth. The use of personal face-to-face communication leads to greater perceptions of fair treatment and acceptance of the news because the employees feel that they are being treated with dignity and respect, thanks to the genuine and sincere manner of the people who give them the bad news.[38]

RPC

Monitors and reports on the progress of major change initiatives

A critical responsibility of human resources managers in any downsizing is to ensure that the bad news is delivered in a humane manner.[39] Department managers need to be trained in how to deliver unwelcome news effectively (by participating in role-plays for practice) and in how to listen to and observe other managers. The responsibility for delivering tough news humanely, treating people with dignity and respect, and advising people of all support services available to them must be emphasized. It helps if managers work with a partner who acts as a coach when preparing for a termination interview and debriefs them on the experience when it is over. Finally, every effort should be made to deliver downsizing news in a one-on-one manner and to anticipate the emotional reactions from everyone involved, including the manager.

For remaining employees, the message should answer three questions: Why is this happening? What effect will the decision have? What is the long term view?[40] If no further reductions are anticipated at that time, workers can be reassured accordingly. If it is expected that more reductions will probably take place, be honest with those who remain, explaining that while future downsizings will probably occur, they will be informed of these reductions as soon as possible.

Downsizing in a Merger/Acquisition Downsizings in the case of mergers or acquisitions are usually one-sided, with either the acquiring company or the larger merger partner dominating the process. The employees in the non-dominant firm will be hypersensitive to mistreatment of their colleagues. Thus, managers should ensure that employees whose employment is terminated are treated with dignity and respect. Seeing former colleagues downsized is bad enough for morale; seeing their employment terminated under conditions that seem unfair can reduce employee engagement on the part of the remaining employees for years to come. In order to create a solid foundation for future employee engagement, managers should avoid the appearance of power and domination and remain businesslike and professional in all dealings.[41]

FAIRNESS IN DISCIPLINE AND DISMISSALS

RPC

Recommends or initiates actions in response to known or suspected incidents of misconduct

Employee discipline and termination of employment are two of the most common situations in which employees perceive that they are treated unfairly. This reaction is not surprising given the negative ramifications in each case. Thus, it is very important for all managers and HR professionals to be aware of how to discipline employees fairly and how to ensure that employee terminations are conducted legally and fairly.

Employee Discipline

discipline A procedure intended to correct an employee's behaviour because a rule or procedure has been violated.

The purpose of **discipline** is to encourage employees to adhere to rules and regulations. Courts have repeatedly articulated the rights of employees to fair treatment, not only during the term of employment but also during the disciplinary and termination process.[42] A fair and just disciplinary process is based on three foundations: rules and regulations, a system of progressive penalties, and an appeals process.

A set of clear rules and regulations is the first foundation. These rules should address serious matters such as theft, destruction of company property, drinking on the job, and insubordination. The purpose of these rules is to inform employees ahead of time as to what is and is not acceptable behaviour. Employees must be told, preferably in writing, what is not permitted. This is usually done during the employee's orientation.

A system of progressive penalties is a second foundation of effective discipline. Penalties may range from verbal warnings to written warnings to suspension (paid or unpaid) from the job to dismissal. The severity of the penalty is usually a function of the type of offence and the number of times the offence has occurred. For example, most companies issue warnings for the first instance of

An Ethical | Dilemma

Is it ethical to apply disciplinary action in cases of ongoing absenteeism and tardiness because of family responsibilities? What other approach could be used?

unexcused lateness. However, for chronic lateness, dismissal is the more usual disciplinary action.

Finally, there should be an appeals process as part of the disciplinary process; this helps to ensure procedural fairness in the employee discipline process.

Dismissal for Just Cause

dismissal Involuntary termination of an employee's employment.

Dismissal is the most drastic disciplinary step that can be taken toward an employee and one that must be handled with deliberate care. Specifically, the dismissal should be fair in that just cause exists for it. Furthermore, the dismissal should occur only after all reasonable steps to rehabilitate or salvage the employee have failed. However, there are undoubtedly times when dismissal is required, and in these instances it should be carried out forthrightly.[43]

There is no clear definition of what behaviour constitutes "just cause" for dismissal.[44] Any allegation of just cause must be considered using a contextual approach, looking at not only the alleged behaviour but the entirety of the employment relationship.[45] If an employer is considering making an allegation of just cause, it is crucial to investigate fully and fairly before any decision is made. The fundamental question is whether or not the employee has irreparably harmed the relationship to the point that it would be unreasonable to expect the employer to continue the employment relationship.[46]

Just cause can often be demonstrated in cases of disobedience, incompetence, dishonesty, insubordination, fighting, and persistent absence or lateness.[47] However, just cause cannot be assessed in isolation and may vary depending on the possible consequences of the misconduct, the status of the employee, and the circumstances of the case. The burden of proof rests with the employer. In Canada, courts often do not accept the assertion of just cause by the employer, and unions almost never do—one union alleged that a death threat made by an employee to his supervisor was "mild insubordination."[48]

Employee misconduct (including theft, expense account fraud, abuse of sick leave, and so on) is a fundamental violation of the employment relationship and can constitute just cause.[49] Unfortunately, the prevalence of theft behaviour is alarming. For example, a recent Ernst & Young study estimated that 47 percent of retail "inventory shrinkage" is attributable to employees, and the Retail Council of Canada estimates that employee theft costs Canadian businesses about $1 billion per year.[50] Air Canada estimates that it loses up to 9 percent of its cabin stock each year to employee theft, or about $9 per day per employee.[51]

insubordination Wilful disregard or disobedience of the boss's authority or legitimate orders; criticizing the boss in public.

Insubordination is a form of misconduct that often provides grounds for just cause dismissal, although it may be relatively difficult to describe and to prove. To that end, it is important to communicate to employees that some acts are considered insubordinate whenever and wherever they occur. These generally include the following:[52]

1. Direct disregard of the boss' authority. Refusal to obey the boss' reasonable instructions—particularly in front of others.
2. Deliberate defiance of clearly stated company policies, rules, regulations, and procedures.
3. Public criticism of the boss; contradicting or arguing with him or her.
4. Contemptuous display of disrespect: making insolent comments, for example, and, more important, portraying these feelings in the attitude shown while on the job.

RPC

Provides advice on issues relating to labour and employee relations including hiring, discipline and termination

5. Disregard for the chain of command, shown by going around the immediate supervisor or manager with a complaint, suggestion, or political manoeuvre.

6. Participation in (or leadership of) an effort to undermine and remove the boss from power.

A recent example of dismissal for just cause based on insubordination involved a Calgary stockbroker who was fired after he brought a prostitute to his office after hours and left her there alone following a dispute about payment. The woman was left alone in the reception area where she could have accessed confidential client and company data after he left. She showed up at the office the next day demanding payment. The court said the stockbroker's conduct exhibited contempt for his employer, his coworkers, and their reputation in the business community.[53]

Figure 15.4 provides guidelines on insubordination used by the Saskatchewan government to assist managers and supervisors in dealing with insubordination.

Dismissal Without Just Cause: Providing Reasonable Notice

In Canada, the employer–employee relationship is governed by an employment contract—a formal agreement (in writing or based on mutual understanding) made between the two parties. If the contract is for a specific length of time, the contract ends at the expiration date, and the employee cannot be prematurely dismissed without just cause.

More commonly, employees are hired under an implied contract where the understanding is that employment is for an indefinite period of time and may be terminated by either party only when reasonable notice is given.[54] Employers cannot hire and fire employees at will, as is the case in the United States. Canadian employers can only terminate an employee's employment without reasonable notice when just cause exists. If there is no employment contract and just cause is not present, then a termination without reasonable notice is considered unfair and is known as **wrongful dismissal.** Although it is rare for employees to be accused of not providing reasonable notice, a manager in British Columbia was ordered to compensate his former employer for lost profits when he left without providing any notice and went to work for a competitor.[55]

Often, the amount of notice considered reasonable is beyond the minimum notice requirements of employment/labour standards legislation. A rule of thumb for reasonable notice is about three to four weeks per year of service. The employee sometimes continues to work during the period of notice given but usually ceases work at the time that the notice of termination is given. In the latter case, the employee receives a lump sum of money equal to his or her pay for the period of notice. Payments are often conditional on the employees signing a general release of all legal claims against their employer.

The employee can accept the notice given (and sign any required release form) or can sue for wrongful dismissal if the notice is considered unacceptable. The court will review the circumstances of the dismissal and make a final decision on the amount of notice to be provided. The courts generally award a period of notice based on their assessment of how long it will take the employee to find alternative employment, taking into account the employee's age, salary, length of service, the level of the job, and other factors. Rarely have notice periods exceeded 24 months.[56]

wrongful dismissal An employee dismissal that does not comply with the law or does not comply with a written or implied contractual arrangement.

RPC

Participates in the termination process by preparing termination notices, conducting exit interviews, and arranging outplacement services

FIGURE 15.4 | Saskatchewan Public Service Commission Corrective Discipline Guidelines for Insubordination

Saskatchewan Public Service Commission	**Human Resource Manual** www.gov.sk.ca/psc/hrmanual

Section: PS 803–Guidelines

Corrective Discipline Guidelines
Part E: Insubordination

Date issued: 1982 11 17

Revision date: 1990 09 30

The following sets out guidelines to assist managers and supervisors in dealing with the discipline situation.

1. Insubordination - A Special Case

Insubordination is defined as the refusal of an employee to carry out the order of a supervisor. Employees are required, under the Public Service Employment Regulations Section 15.1, to carry out such orders. Employees may disagree with such orders. However, the proper employee response is to obey the order and seek redress via grievance action. The rule of "obey now - grieve later" is well founded in arbitration decisions.

Note however, that the "obey now - grieve later" rule does not apply to all orders given by supervisors. Some exceptions are as follows:

- where the order given is not related to work, e.g., deliver my personal mail as opposed to deliver departmental mail, etc. An employee may be directed and is required to perform work duties not found in his job description. However, the employee may later grieve the assignment of these duties.

- where the employee has reasonable grounds for believing that obeying the order given would endanger health and/or safety.

- where the order given is illegal.

- where the order is given by someone without authority. Note however that all orders need not be given by one's immediate supervisor. Where the employee knows that the order is being given by his supervisor's superior, such orders must be followed.

- where the order interferes with personal appearance or privacy, e.g., a search of one's personal effects where there is suspected theft, that one shave a beard, cut ones hair, wear certain clothes, etc. Note however that appearance or clothing rules may apply where they are a direct job requirement, e.g., uniforms for regulatory staff, cleanliness when preparing food, etc. The refusal of an employee to submit himself to a search of personal effects when management has reasonable grounds for such a request should be recorded. Inform the employee discipline action may be taken; consult with your personnel advisor on how to proceed.

- where the employee has a reasonable personal excuse, e.g., the employee was provoked into refusing the order, where the employee has a legitimate and reasonable personal excuse and gives it at the time of refusal - personal illness, death in the family, etc. Note however that mere personal inconvenience is not acceptable, e.g., I'm on my break, it's my bowling night, etc.

2. Insubordination - How to Handle

Among disciplinary offenses, insubordination is common. To have an employee refuse an order can be unsettling for a supervisor. As a result, the following approach is suggested:

- give the order in the normal manner, e.g., would you be kind enough to help out. The employee refuses.

- determine the employee's reason for refusal.

- determine if the employee's refusal is valid.

- if not, inform the employee you will give a formal order and failure to comply could result in disciplinary action.

- if feasible, inform the employee you will give him three (3) to five (5) minutes to consider his response to the order you will give.

- on return or when you give the order, it is desirable to be accompanied by another supervisory representative or employee if possible. This person will act as a witness.

- clearly repeat the order, e.g., as your supervisor I am ordering you to help out; failure could result in disciplinary action.

- if the employee continues to refuse, inform him that the matter will be investigated further and disciplinary action could result.

- record all of the above in writing immediately after the event; note complete details, i.e., the exact order you gave, the exact words of refusal, the time of the order, etc. Have your witness add his comments.

- initiate the employer's policy of Corrective Discipline.

Source: Human Resources Manual, Saskatchewan Public Service Commission. www.psc.gov.sk.ca/Default.aspx?DN=6acee10d-6c70-4392-a536-9aac55f273e5 (July 17, 2009).

Another important factor in determining notice periods is whether the dismissed employee was induced or lured away from stable employment elsewhere and then terminated because of a business downturn. For example, a senior marketing manager who had worked for Bell Canada for 20 years was urged by two former coworkers to join them at Alcatel. She joined Alcatel with a 50 percent salary increase to offset her pension loss at Bell. She was terminated after 21 months, sued for wrongful dismissal, and was awarded nine months' notice due to the inducement.[57]

Bad-Faith Damages In 1997, "bad-faith conduct" on the part of the employer in dismissing an employee was added as another factor considered by the courts in determining the period of reasonable notice.[58] At a minimum, employers are required to be candid, reasonable, honest, and forthright with their employees in the course of dismissal and should refrain from engaging in conduct that is unfair or in bad faith, such as being untruthful, misleading, or unduly insensitive. The resulting additional periods of notice were unpredictable, often around three to four months, but sometimes considerably higher.[59] A significant change to the assessment of bad-faith damages was established by a 2008 decision by the Supreme Court of Canada, who ruled that bad-faith damages apply to only the most extreme conduct and that damages should not be provided by extending the notice period but by compensation for actual damages suffered by the employee.[60] Nevertheless, it is still clear that employers must treat employees with dignity and respect at all times, especially at the time of dismissal.[61]

Punitive Damages In extreme cases, employers may also be ordered to pay punitive damages for harsh and vindictive treatment of an employee and/or damages for aggravated or mental distress if the employee suffered undue distress from not being given adequate notice of termination.[62] In 2005, the largest punitive damage award in Canadian history was handed down when Honda Canada was ordered to pay $500 000 in punitive damages to a terminated employee for its mistreatment of the employee, who was disabled due to chronic fatigue syndrome.[63] The amount was later reduced to $100 000 by an appeal court and eliminated entirely by the Supreme Court of Canada, who ruled in 2008 that punitive damages should only apply in exceptional cases with wrongful acts by the employer that are truly malicious and outrageous.[64]

Avoiding Wrongful Dismissal Suits

There are several steps that can be taken in order to avoid wrongful dismissal suits:[65]

1. Use employment contracts with a termination clause and with wording clearly permitting the company to dismiss without cause during the probationary period.
2. Document all disciplinary action.
3. Do not allege just cause for dismissal unless it can be proven.
4. Time the termination so that it does not conflict with special occasions, such as birthdays or holidays.
5. Use termination letters in all cases, clearly stating the settlement offer.
6. Schedule the termination interview in a private location at a time of day that will allow the employee to clear out belongings with a minimal amount of contact with other employees.
7. Include two members of management in the termination meeting.

If a wrongful dismissal suit is made against the company, the firm should[66]

- review the claim carefully before retaining an employment lawyer, and investigate for other improper conduct; ask for a legal opinion on the merits of the case; work with the lawyer and provide all relevant facts and documentation; and discuss any possible letter of reference with the lawyer

- never allege cause if none exists, and avoid defamatory statements

- consider mediation as an option, or offer to settle in order to save time and money.

Constructive Dismissal

constructive dismissal The employer makes unilateral changes in the employment contract that are unacceptable to the employee, even though the employee has not been formally terminated.

Constructive dismissal can be considered to occur when the employer makes unilateral changes in the employment contract that are unacceptable to the employee, even though the employee has not been formally terminated.[67] The most common changes in employment status that are considered to constitute constructive dismissal are demotion, reduction in pay and benefits, forced resignation, forced early retirement, forced transfer, and changes in job duties and responsibilities. An employee who believes that he or she has been constructively dismissed can sue the employer for wrongful dismissal. If the judge agrees that constructive dismissal occurred, then a period of notice to be provided to the employee will be determined.

For example, a long-term employee of Ontario Power Generation was affected by a shift on the company's focus that largely eliminated his responsibilities for business development. He was told that he would be "underutilized for the foreseeable future" and that if he didn't like the changes he could resign or retire. He resigned shortly thereafter and sued for constructive dismissal. The court found that the essential terms of his employment had been substantially changed, that the company had no plan to provide him with work, and that he had been constructively dismissed. He was awarded 24 months' pay.[68]

The definition of constructive dismissal was expanded in a recent case where an employee was given two years' notice of a change to his written employment agreement that would reduce the amount in the termination pay clause. The employee disagreed with the change and was told two years later that he had to accept the new terms or "we do not have a job for you." The employee left the company and successfully sued for constructive dismissal.[69]

Fairness in Dismissal Procedures

A recent study of 996 recently fired or laid-off workers found that wrongful dismissal claims were strongly correlated with the way workers felt they had been treated at the time of termination. They also found a "vendetta effect" where the instances of wrongful dismissal claims became stronger as negative treatment became extreme, as shown in **Figure 15.5.** The researchers concluded that many wrongful dismissal lawsuits could be avoided if effective human resource practices, specifically treating employees fairly, were employed. Providing clear, honest explanations of termination decisions and handling the termination in a way that treats people with dignity and respect can be especially effective.[70]

FIGURE 15.5 | Fair Treatment and Wrongful Dismissal Claims: The Vendetta Effect

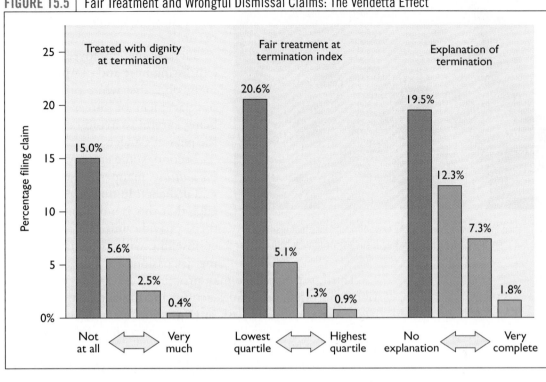

Source: E.A. Lind, J. Greenberg, K.S. Scott, and T.D. Welchans, "The Winding Road from Employee to Complainant: Situational and Psychological Determinants of Wrongful-Termination Claims," *Administrative Science Quarterly*, September 2000, pp. 557–590. Used by permission of Cornell University Johnson School.

The Termination Interview

termination interview The interview in which an employee is informed of the fact that he or she has been dismissed.

Dismissing an employee is one of the most difficult tasks that a manager will face at work.[71] The dismissed employee, even if warned many times in the past, will often still react with total disbelief or even violence. Guidelines for the **termination interview** itself are as follows.

Step 1: Plan the Interview Carefully schedule the meeting on a day early in the week, and try to avoid Fridays, pre-holidays, and vacation times. Have the employee agreement, human resources file, and release announcement (internal and external) prepared in advance. Be available at a time after the interview in case questions or problems arise, and have phone numbers ready for medical or security emergencies.

Step 2: Get to the Point As soon as the employee arrives, give the person a moment to get comfortable and then inform him or her of the decision.

Step 3: Describe the Situation Briefly, in three or four sentences, explain why the person is being let go. For instance, "Production in your area is down 4 percent, and we are continuing to have quality problems. We have talked about these problems several times in the past three months, and the solutions are not being followed through. We have to make a change."[72] Remember to describe the situation rather than attacking the employee personally.

Step 4: Listen It is important to continue the interview until the person appears to be talking freely and reasonably calmly about the reasons for his or her termination and the severance package that he or she is to receive. Behavioural indications

Termination interviews are among the most difficult tasks that managers face, but there are guidelines for making them less painful for both parties.

can be used to help gauge the person's reaction and to decide how best to proceed. Five major reactions often occur.

First, some employees will be *hostile and angry*, expressing hurt and disappointment. In such case, remain objective while providing information on any outplacement or career counselling to be provided, being careful to avoid being defensive or confronting the person's anger.

Second, some employees may react in a *defensive, bargaining* manner, based on their feelings of fear and disbelief. In this case, it is important to acknowledge that this is a difficult time for the employee and then provide information regarding outplacement counselling without getting involved in any bargaining discussions.

Third, the employee may proceed in a *formal, controlled* manner, indicative of a suppressed, vengeful reaction, and the potential for legal action. In this case, allow the employee to ask any questions pertaining to his or her case (avoiding side issues) in a formal tone while leading into information about the outplacement counselling to be provided.

Fourth, some employees will maintain a *stoic* façade, masking their shock, disbelief, and numbness. In this case, communicate to the employee that his or her shock is recognized and that the details can be handled later if the employee prefers. Answer any questions arising at that point and provide information on outplacement counselling.

A fifth reaction is an *emotional* one involving tears and sadness, indicating grief and worry on the part of the employee. Allow the person to cry and provide tissues. When the person regains his or her composure, explain the outplacement counselling process.

An Ethical | Dilemma

Is it ethical to "buy out" an undesirable employee with severance pay and a good letter of reference in order to avoid prolonged wrongful dismissal litigation, even if you know the letter is misleading to potential future employers?

Step 5: Review All Elements of the Severance Package Describe severance payments, benefits, and the way in which references will be handled. However, under no conditions should any promises or benefits beyond those already in the severance package be implied. The termination should be complete when the person leaves.

Step 6: Identify the Next Step The terminated employee may be disoriented, so explain where he or she should go on leaving the interview. Remind the person whom to contact at the company regarding questions about the severance package or references.

Outplacement Counselling

outplacement counselling A systematic process by which a terminated person is trained and counselled in the techniques of self-appraisal and securing a new position.

Outplacement counselling provides career counselling and job search skills training for terminated employees. The counselling itself is done either by the employer's in-house specialist or by outside consultants. The outplacement counselling is considered part of the terminated employee's severance package.[73]

Outplacement counselling is usually conducted by outplacement firms, such as Drake Beam Morin and Right Management. Middle- and upper-level managers who are let go will typically have office space and secretarial services that they can use at local offices of such firms, in addition to the counselling services.

Chapter | SUMMARY

1. Employee engagement is a positive, fulfilling, work-related state of mind characterized by vigour, dedication, and absorption. Organizational factors such as senior leadership, opportunities for learning and development, and company image and reputation are the primary influencers of engagement. Outcomes of employee engagement include improvements in recruiting, retention, turnover, individual productivity, customer service, and customer loyalty, as well as growth in operating margins, increased profit margins and revenue growth rates.

2. Techniques for ensuring effective employee communication include suggestion programs, employee opinion surveys, and communication from management. Electronic forms of communication such as email, intranets and blogs are increasingly being used to implement all of these techniques.

3. HR considerations in adjusting to downsizings and mergers include avoiding the appearance of power and domination, remaining businesslike and professional in all dealings, and remembering that the degree to which the organization treats the acquired group with care and dignity will affect the confidence, productivity, and commitment of those remaining.

4. A fair and just disciplinary process is based on three prerequisites: rules and regulations, a system of progressive penalties, and an appeals process.

5. Employees who are dismissed without just cause must be provided with reasonable notice. This means paying them for several weeks or months in addition to the legally required notice period on termination. If the employee does not believe that the period of notice is reasonable, he or she may file a wrongful dismissal lawsuit. Constructive dismissal occurs when the employer makes unilateral changes in the employment contract that are unacceptable to the employee, even though the employee has not been formally terminated.

6. The six steps in the termination interview are to plan the interview carefully, get to the point, describe the situation, listen until the person has expressed his or her feelings, discuss the severance package, and identify the next step.

PEARSON
myHRlab™

Test yourself on material for this chapter at
www.pearsoned.ca/myhrlab

Key | TERMS

constructive dismissal   *(p. 430)*
discipline   *(p. 424)*
dismissal   *(p. 426)*
distributive justice   *(p. 415)*
downsizing   *(p. 424)*
employee engagement   *(p. 415)*
employee opinion surveys   *(p. 418)*
group termination laws   *(p. 424)*

insubordination   *(p. 426)*
interactional justice   *(p. 415)*
layoff   *(p. 423)*
outplacement counselling   *(p. 432)*
pre-retirement counselling   *(p. 422)*
procedural justice   *(p. 415)*
termination interview   *(p. 431)*
wrongful dismissal   *(p. 427)*

Review and Discussion | QUESTIONS

1. Explain why organizations today are concerned with employee engagement.

2. Describe specific techniques that you would use to foster top-down communication in an organization.

3. Explain how fairness in employee discipline can be ensured, particularly the prerequisites to discipline and discipline guidelines.

4. Describe the four main reasons for dismissal.

5. What are the techniques that can be used as alternatives to layoffs?

6. Discuss some of the issues that should be covered in a pre-retirement counselling program.

Critical Thinking | QUESTIONS

1. Should organizations today prohibit blogging that includes specific references to company information and practices, or adopt an approach similar to that adopted by IBM, Cisco, and Sun Microsystems (page 418)? Why or why not?

2. Is it worth the time and expense to monitor employees' use of the internet if employee performance is generally good? How is this any different from monitoring telephone usage for personal calls? What should be done about personally owned communications devices in the workplace?

3. Should a company consider providing termination packages to employees who have ongoing disciplinary problems rather than taking the time and effort to go through the progressive discipline process?

4. Many people are now working past the age of 65. Identify the career concerns that new graduates will have if more older people continue working. What do you think companies should do about managing the career aspiration of those who wish to continue working and those entering the workforce?

5. Discuss the options presented as alternative to layoffs. Which of these would appeal to you, your family members, and friends? Why? What challenges does this pose to organizations?

Experiential | EXERCISES

1. Looking at the various drivers of employee engagement in the Towers Perrin study (see the Global HRM box, page 416), determine which of these would be a driver for you. Form a group of four or five students to explore similarities and differences in your employee engagement drivers.

2. Working individually or in groups, obtain copies of the student handbook for a college or university and determine to what extent there is a formal process through which students can air grievances. Would you expect the process to be effective? Why or why not? Based on contacts with students who have used the grievance process, has it been effective?

3. Working individually or in groups, determine the nature of the academic discipline process in a college or university. Does it appear to be an effective one? Based on this chapter, should any modification be made to the student discipline process?

4. A computer department employee made an entry error that ruined an entire run of computer reports. Efforts to rectify the situation produced a second batch of improperly run reports. As a result of the series of errors, the employer incurred extra costs of $2400, plus a weekend of overtime work by other computer department staffers. Management suspended the employee for three days for negligence and also revoked a promotion for which the employee had previously been approved.

   Protesting the discipline, the employee stressed that she had attempted to correct her error in the early stages of the run by notifying the manager of computer operations of her mistake. Maintaining that the resulting string of errors could have been avoided if the manager had followed up on her report and stopped the initial run, the employee argued that she had been treated unfairly in being severely punished because the manager had not been disciplined at all, even though he had compounded the problem. Moreover, citing her "impeccable" work record and management's acknowledgement that she had always been a "model employee," the employee insisted that the denial of her previously approved promotion was "unconscionable."

(a) In groups, determine what your decision would be if you were the arbitrator. Why? (Your instructor will inform you of the actual arbitrator's decision when you discuss this exercise in class.)

(b) Do you think that the employer handled the disciplinary situation correctly? Why? What would you have done differently?

5. Working with a partner, review the following scenario and discuss your responses.

Maggie sat there stunned. Her boss had just told her that, as a result of the merger with the ABC Company, she would be reporting to the vice president of customer service and that her title would be associate vice president of customer service. "This can't be. My job is the VP of customer service. How can I report to another VP?"

Has Maggie been demoted? Constructively dismissed? Discuss your rationale for your answer.

6. You are the HR manager in a small company that has just bought another company in your field. You only learned of the purchase when you were asked to attend a meeting this morning. Somehow, between now and tomorrow at noon, you must come up with a plan to communicate the purchase to your and the other organization's employees. What do you think will be the main concerns of employees in each company? Describe your first steps and the plan for the transition period between now and the closing date of the purchase.

Running | CASE

Running Case: LearnInMotion.com

Fair Treatment in Disciplinary Action

Because the employees used high-cost computer equipment to do their jobs, Jennifer and Pierre have always felt strongly about not allowing employees to eat or drink at their desks. Jennifer was therefore surprised to walk into the office one day to find two employees eating lunch at their desks. There was a large pizza in its box, and the two of them were sipping soft drinks and eating slices of pizza and submarine sandwiches from paper plates. Not only did it look messy, but there were also grease and soft drink spills on their desks, and the office smelled of onions and pepperoni. In addition to looking unprofessional, the mess on the desks increased the possibility that the computers could be damaged. One of the employees continued to use his computer with greasy fingers between bites.

Although this was a serious matter, neither Jennifer nor Pierre believes that what the employees were doing is grounds for immediate dismissal, partly because there is no written policy on eating at the workstations. They just assumed that people would use their common sense. The problem is that they do not know what to do. It seems to them that the matter calls for more than just a warning but less than dismissal. As their management consultant, how would you answer the following questions?

QUESTIONS

1 What is a progressive discipline policy and should LearnInMotion put one in place formally in writing within their human resources policy manual?

2 If LearnInMotion puts a progressive disciplinary policy in place and these two employees choose to eat at their desks again, would this constitute "just cause" termination?

3 If LearnInMotion chooses to terminate these two employees right now, would they face any legal ramifications?

Case | INCIDENT

An Inappropriate Email

Roger Miller, the Director of Human Resources for Virtual Reality Media, was returning to his office after a half-day training session on how to retain and engage today's top talent when he received a disturbing phone call. Randy, the manager of the multimedia lab, had called to let Roger know about an email he had just been copied on.

One of Randy's salespeople, John, had sent all of his fellow staff within the multimedia lab department a very derogatory email describing how Randy was a useless supervisor who should not be in a management position as he does not know what he is doing and should be fired. Randy is very upset and wants Roger to terminate John. This is where you come in to help Roger by answering the following questions.

QUESTIONS

1. Assume you are Roger. Specifically, what should you do now?
2. How should you do it?
3. Is this a just-cause termination?

For additional cases and exercise material, go to
www.pearsoned.ca/myhrlab

CHAPTER 16

LABOUR RELATIONS

REQUIRED PROFESSIONAL CAPABILITIES (RPC)

- Provides advice on the interpretation of the collective agreement
- Collects and presents information required for decision making in the bargaining process
- Effectively handles disagreements and conflicts
- Analyzes and provides advice on employment rights and responsibilities

INTRODUCTION TO LABOUR RELATIONS

labour union (union) An officially recognized association of employees practising a similar trade or employed in the same company or industry who have joined together to present a united front and collective voice in dealing with management.

labour–management relations The ongoing interactions between labour unions and management in organizations.

collective agreement (union contract) A formal agreement between an employer and the union representing a group of its employees regarding terms and conditions of employment.

collective bargaining Negotiations between a union and an employer to arrive at a mutually acceptable collective agreement.

bargaining unit The group of employees in a firm, a plant, or an industry that has been recognized by an employer or certified by a Labour Relations Board (LRB) as appropriate for collective bargaining purposes.

Canadian Labour and Business Centre
www.clbc.ca
Ontario Ministry of Labour, Labour Management Services
www.labour.gov.on.ca
Canada LabourWatch Association
www.labourwatch.com

A **labour union** (or **union**) is an officially recognized body representing a group of employees who have joined together to present a collective voice in dealing with management. The purposes of unionization are to influence HR policies and practices that affect bargaining unit members, such as pay and benefits; to achieve greater control over the jobs being performed, greater job security, and improved working conditions; and to increase job satisfaction and meet employees' affiliation needs. The term **labour–management relations** refers to the ongoing interactions between labour unions and management in organizations.

The presence of a labour union alters the relationship between employees and the firm and has implications for planning and implementing a business strategy. Managerial discretion and flexibility in dealing with employees and in implementing and administering HR policies and procedures are reduced. For example, union seniority provisions in the **collective agreement** (**union contract**), negotiated through **collective bargaining**, govern the selection of employees for transfers, promotions, and training programs and specify the order in which employees can be laid off and recalled. Many other terms and conditions of employment for **bargaining unit** members are determined and standardized through collective bargaining, rather than being left to management's discretion.

An organization's *labour relations (LR) strategy*, one component of its HR strategy, is its overall plan for dealing with unions, which sets the tone for its union–management relationship. The decision to accept or avoid unions is the basis of an organization's LR strategy.[1]

Managers in firms choosing a *union acceptance strategy* view the union as the legitimate representative of the firm's employees. Such a relationship can lead to innovative initiatives and win–win outcomes. Managers select a *union avoidance strategy* when they believe that it is preferable to operate in a non-unionized environment. Wal-Mart is well known for its preference to remain non-union (and has even closed stores that have attempted to unionize).[2] To avoid unions, companies can either adopt a *union substitution approach*, in which they become so responsive to employees' needs that there is no incentive for them to unionize (as is the case at Dofasco) or adopt a *union suppression approach* when there is a desire to avoid a union at all costs (Wal-Mart challenged the constitutionality of Saskatchewan's labour laws all the way to the Supreme Court of Canada, but lost).[3]

Chrysler workers at the company's assembly plant in Windsor, Ontario, burn letters they received from management. The letters outlined a number of concessions the company is requesting of employees.

Canada's Labour Laws

Canadian labour laws have two general purposes:

1.   to provide a common set of rules for fair negotiations

2.   to protect the public interest by preventing the impact of labour disputes from inconveniencing the public.

As with other employment-related legislation, there are 13 provincial/territorial jurisdictions, as well as federal labour relations legislation for employees subject to federal jurisdiction. There are a number of common characteristics in the LR legislation across Canada, which can be summarized as follows:

- procedures for the certification of a union
- the requirement that a collective agreement be in force for a minimum of one year
- procedures that must be followed by one or both parties before a strike or lockout is legal
- the prohibition of strikes or lockouts during the life of a collective agreement
- the requirement that disputes over matters arising from interpretation of the collective agreement be settled by final and binding arbitration
- prohibition of certain specified "unfair practices" on the part of labour and management
- establishment of a Labour Relations Board or the equivalent; Labour Relations Boards are tripartite—made up of representatives of union and management, as well as a neutral chair or a vice-chair, typically a government representative.

Labour relations legislation attempts to balance employees' rights to engage in union activities with employers' rights to manage. For example, managers are prohibited from interfering with and discriminating against employees who are exercising their rights under the LR legislation. One restriction on unions is that they are prohibited from calling or authorizing an unlawful strike.

The Labour Movement in Canada Today

The primary goal of the labour unions active in Canada is to obtain economic benefits and improved treatment for their members. It may involve lobbying for legislative changes pertaining to these issues. This union philosophy, with its emphasis on economic and welfare goals, has become known as **business unionism**. Unions strive to ensure *job security* for their members and to attain *improved economic conditions* and *better working conditions* for their members. Most unions today also become involved in broader political and social issues affecting their members. Activities aimed at influencing government economic and social policies are known as **social (reform) unionism**. For example, unions have recognized the special circumstances of Aboriginal workers, as outlined in the **Workforce Diversity** box.

Types of Unions

The labour unions in Canada can be classified according to the following characteristics:

1. *Type of worker eligible for membership.* All the early trade unions in Canada were **craft unions**—associations of persons performing a certain type of skill or trade (e.g., carpenters or bricklayers). Examples in today's workforce include the British Columbia Teachers' Federation and the Ontario Nurses' Association. An **industrial union** is a labour organization comprising all the workers eligible for union membership in a particular company or industry, irrespective of the type of work performed.

RPC

Analyzes and provides advice on employment rights and responsibilities

business unionism The activities of labour unions focusing on economic and welfare issues, including pay and benefits, job security, and working conditions.

social (reform) unionism Activities of unions directed at furthering the interests of their members by influencing the social and economic policies of governments at all levels, such as speaking out on proposed legislative reforms.

craft union Traditionally, a labour organization representing workers practising the same craft or trade, such as carpentry or plumbing.

industrial union A labour organization representing all workers eligible for union membership in a particular company or industry, including skilled tradespersons.

Workforce DIVERSITY

Collective Agreement Puts Aboriginals First

It's not every day a union agrees to a contract that puts some members behind outside applicants for a job opening or to a collective agreement that has little to offer when it comes to the privileges of seniority. But the collective agreement at Voisey's Bay Nickel Company is one such rarity. At this mine, located 350 kilometres north of Happy Valley-Goose Bay in Labrador, the Innu and Inuit people, regardless of whether or not they're employees, are always first in line whenever a position, a training opportunity, or a promotion comes up.

That's one of the implications of the two Impacts and Benefits Agreements (IBAs) that the nickel company, a subsidiary of Inco, signed with the Innu Nation and the Labrador Inuit Association. Innu and Inuit people are on top of this order of preference, starting with those in the bargaining unit, followed by those already employed by Voisey's Bay and by Innu and Inuit outside candidates. Among non-Aboriginals, priority goes to Labrador residents. Those with union membership rank first, followed by Voisey's Bay employees, and then those in the community.

Inco's IBAs with the Innu and Inuits of Labrador aren't unique. Agreements have been signed in many other resource projects, including Xstrata's Raglan

nickel mine in Quebec, BHP Billiton's Ekati diamond mine in the Northwest Territories, and De Beers Canada's Victor Project in Ontario.

The union also negotiated other benefits not stipulated in the IBAs to reflect the fact that Aboriginals make up more than half of the bargaining unit. For example, National Aboriginal Day on June 21 is now a paid holiday under the collective agreement.

The IBAs also impose obligations on the employer to provide training opportunities for Aboriginals. The training initiatives go back 10 years, when the company first sought out candidates by providing information about the work conditions and kinds of careers available in mining. When the project was under construction, the company drew up its workforce plans, identified areas where the skilled workers were already available and where there were gaps. Then, with funding support from the federal government, the company offered skilled trades training for occupations such as heavy equipment operator and millwright.

"Once they graduated, we then looked for opportunities where we could employ them during the construction phase to give them actual experience," said Wayne Scott, Manager of HR.

Source: U. Vu, "Collective Agreement puts Aboriginals First," *Canadian HR Reporter*, November 6, 2006.

2. *Geographical scope.* Labour unions with their head offices in the United States that charter branches in both Canada and the United States are known as *international unions*. Labour unions that charter branches in Canada only and have their head office in this country are known as *national unions*. A small number of employees belong to labour unions that are purely *local* in geographical scope.

3. *Labour congress affiliation.* A third way of distinguishing among labour unions is according to affiliation with one or another central labour organization. These central organizations include

- *Canadian Labour Congress (CLC).* The CLC is the major central labour organization in Canada and has over 3 million affiliated union members. Most international and national unions belong, as well as all directly chartered local unions, local/district labour councils, and provincial/territorial federations of labour.

- *Confédération des syndicats nationaux (CSN)*—in English, Confederation of National Trade Unions (CNTU). This organization is the Quebec counterpart of the CLC and has more than 300 000 members.

- *American Federation of Labor—Congress of Industrial Organizations (AFL–CIO).* The American counterpart of the CLC is the AFL–CIO. The two organizations operate independently, but since most international

Construction Labour Relations
www.clra.org
International Labour News
www.labourstart.org
Canadian Labour Congress (CLC)
www.canadianlabour.ca
Ontario Federation of Labour
www.ofl.ca
American Federation of
Labor–Congress of Industrial
Organizations (AFL–CIO)
www.aflcio.org

unions in the CLC are also members of the AFL–CIO, a certain degree of common interest exists.

The basic unit of the labour union movement in Canada is the **local**, formed in a particular location. For HR managers and front-line supervisors, the union locals are generally the most important part of the union structure. Key players within the local are the elected officials known as **union stewards**, who are responsible for representing the interests and protecting the rights of bargaining unit employees in their department or area.

local A group of unionized employees in a particular location.

union steward A union member elected by workers in a particular department or area of a firm to act as their union representative.

Membership Trends

As of 2008, just over 30 percent of Canadian employees were unionized. The membership in unions as a percentage of the labour force has been slowly decreasing since the 1980s, as shown in **Figure 16.1**. Various factors are responsible for membership decline, including a dramatic increase in service-sector and white-collar jobs, combined with a decrease in employment opportunities in the industries that have traditionally been highly unionized, such as manufacturing. More effective HR practices in non-unionized firms are another contributing factor.[4]

Current Challenges Facing the Canadian Labour Movement

As with employers, global competition and technological advances pose challenges for the union movement. Unions also have to deal with challenges pertaining to global competition, unionization of white-collar employees, managers, and professionals, and innovative work practices that have the potential to decrease employee interest in unionization.

FIGURE 16.1 | Union Membership in Canada, 1991–2008

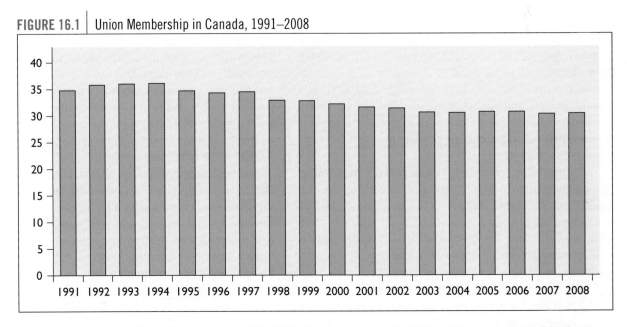

Source: Statistics Canada, The Labour Force Survey, 1991–2006, www.hrsdc.gc.ca/eng/lp/wid/um/pdf/union_membership06.pdf; and Union Membership in Canada 2008, The Labour Force Survey, Table 1, Statistics Canada, 2008, www.hrsdc.gc.ca/eng/labour/labour_relations/info_analysis/union_membership/index.shtml.

Global Competition

Globalization is transforming the dynamics of labour relations in Canada. Global competition is forcing employers to become more militant, and unions are struggling to maintain their influence at the bargaining table.[5] Some unions face the difficult choice of negotiating concessions or watching jobs go to lower-cost countries. Some companies even face being unable to compete and having to go out of business, particularly in the manufacturing sector. The recent crisis in the automobile manufacturing sector is a good example.[6] Citing the view that the traditional, confrontational model of labour relations is unproductive and wastes energy that would be better focused on creating the conditions that would be fair to employees and would ensure that Magna remains competitive in the global automotive industry, Magna Chairman Frank Stronach reached a historic agreement with the CAW called the "Framework of Fairness." Magna, mostly union-free for more than 50 years, will facilitate unionization of 18 000 employees at 45 Magna plants in Ontario under one collective agreement. Workers will not have the right to strike and management will be prohibited from locking them out. Disputes will be settled through binding arbitration.[7] Further details are described in the **Strategic HR** box.

Strategic HR

Magna and Canadian Auto Workers Sign Historic "Framework of Fairness" Agreement

We come from opposite sides of the labour relations street. A manufacturing executive and a union leader. And we've had our share of battles and confrontations over the years. But, in recent years, we've noticed there are a surprising number of issues on which we now see eye to eye.

We're both passionate about Canada. We both love autos. Not just to drive, but because of the immense economic and social benefits a healthy auto industry can generate. Yet, we both recognize that Canada's auto industry and our entire manufacturing base face a moment of truth. New challenges in global competition mean that our industry must change, or else it will continue to wither away.

Through this agreement, Magna accepts the CAW as a genuine partner, with a crucial role to safeguard the interests of Magna's workers as the company grows and changes. And the CAW accepts Magna's culture of "fair enterprise," and the unique structures we've put in place over the years to make decisions and resolve concerns with maximum worker participation.

We think we are combining the best of both worlds: The best traditions of union protection and security and the best features of Magna's fair enterprise corporate culture. Indeed, economic studies have suggested that companies that pair union representation with extensive mechanisms for worker involvement and participation attain the best possible combination of high productivity and high morale.

This is an experimental approach to labour relations, We believe it will enhance our shared effort to build a successful competitive industry, but in a manner that respects and invests in working people, their families, and their communities.

Magna is Canada's largest automotive player. The CAW is Canada's largest private-sector union. Both our organizations have demonstrated incredible innovation over the years, as we've evolved to perform our respective functions to the fullest. In our own ways, we've put a unique Canadian stamp on our auto industry. What we make, how we make it, and how we share the fruits of what we've produced.

Our new system of labour relations, we believe, will also be uniquely Canadian—melding North American and European aspects, with a homegrown emphasis on fairness, mutual respect, and hard work. We enter this new phase in our relationship optimistic that it will make a significant contribution to the future success of Canada's most important industry.

Source: Adapted from Frank Stronach and Buzz Hargrove, "For the Sake of the Auto Industry, We've Put Aside Our Differences," *Canadian HR Reporter*, October 18, 2007.

Demographics

The aging of the workforce and pending labour shortage affects unions as well as HR managers.[8] It has been suggested that unions and management may need to work together to attract and retain workers. Retention concerns may make employers more willing to offer job security in exchange for promises of productivity and flexibility from unions. Pensions and benefits for older workers and retirees has also become more of a union priority.

Unionization of White-Collar Employees

Difficulties in attempting to resolve grievances and lack of job security has led to increased interest in unionization among white-collar workers. Service sector workers, such as those in retail stores, fast-food chains, and government agencies, as well as managers and professionals (including university/college faculty), have been targeted for organizing campaigns. Since these jobs tend to have more women and young people than manufacturing jobs, unions are now focusing more on work/family issues and the health and safety risks associated with white-collar jobs, such as the potential for repetitive strain injury from working at video display terminals.[9] In 2007, women outnumbered men in Canadian unions for the first time ever.[10]

THE LABOUR RELATIONS PROCESS

As illustrated in **Figure 16.2**, the labour relations process consists of five steps:

1. Employees decide to seek collective representation.
2. The union organizing campaign begins.
3. The union receives official recognition.
4. Union and management negotiate a collective agreement.
5. Day-to-day contract administration begins.

Each of these five steps will now be reviewed in detail.

Step 1: Desire for Collective Representation

Based on numerous research studies, a number of factors can clearly be linked to the desire to unionize:[11]

Research | INSIGHT

- job dissatisfaction, especially with pay, benefits, and working conditions
- lack of job security
- unfair or biased administration of policies and practices
- perceived inequities in pay
- lack of opportunity for advancement
- lack of a desired amount of influence or participation in work-related decisions
- the belief that unions can be effective in improving pay and working conditions.

Given the fact that unionized employees in Canada earn 8 percent more than non-unionized workers, these expectations seem quite justifiable. Being a union

FIGURE 16.2 | An Overview of the Labour Relations Process

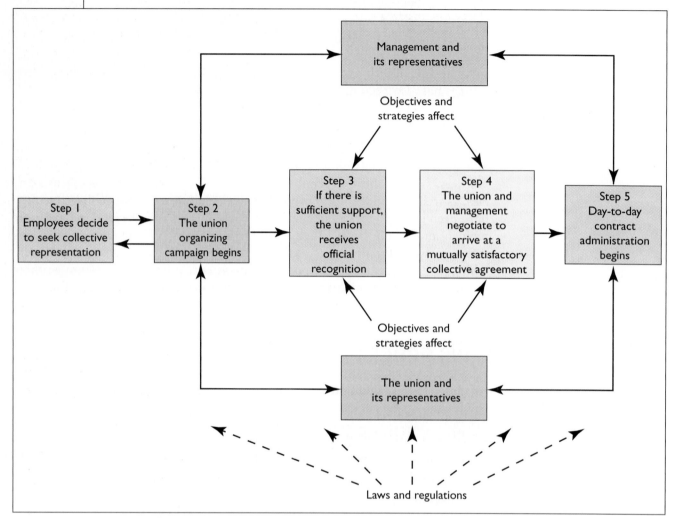

member also has an impact on female workers' ability to achieve pay equity. On average, full-time female unionized workers earned 93 percent of the hourly wages of their male counterparts.[12]

However, research studies have made it clear that dissatisfaction alone will not lead to unionization. More important seems to be the employees' belief that it is only through unity that they can protect themselves from the arbitrary whims of management. *In other words, it is only when workers are dissatisfied and believe that they are without the ability to change the factors causing dissatisfaction, except through collective action, that they become interested in unionizing.*[13]

Promoting the benefits of unionization.

Step 2: Union Organizing Campaign

Once interest in joining a union has been aroused, the union organizing process begins. There are five steps typically involved in this process:

1. *Employee/union contact.* A formal organizing campaign may be initiated by a union organizer or by employees acting on their

own behalf. Most organizing campaigns are begun by employees who get in touch with an existing union.[14] However, large unions have a number of *union organizers* on staff, who are responsible for identifying organizing opportunities and launching organizing campaigns. During these initial discussions, employees investigate the advantages of union representation, and the union officials start to gather information about the employees' sources of dissatisfaction.

2. *Initial organizational meeting.* The union organizer then schedules an initial meeting with the individuals who first expressed an interest in unionization and co-workers who subsequently express their support. The aim is to identify employees who would be willing to help the organizer direct the campaign.

3. *Formation of an in-house organizing committee.* This committee comprises a group of employees who are dedicated to the goal of unionization and who are willing to assist the union organizer.

4. *The organizing campaign.* Members of the in-house committee then contact employees, present the case for unionization, and encourage as many employees as possible to sign an **authorization card** that indicates their willingness to be represented by the union in collective bargaining with their employer.

5. *The outcome.* There are a number of possible outcomes to a unionization campaign, including rejection by the majority of eligible employees. For a union to become the bargaining unit for a group of employees, it must be certified by an LRB or receive official recognition from the employer.

authorization card A card signed by an employee that indicates his or her willingness to have the union act as his or her representative for purposes of collective bargaining.

Signs of Organizing Activity

Managers who suspect that a unionization attempt may be underway should watch for a number of the following signs:[15]

- disappearance of employee lists or directories
- more inquiries than usual about benefits, wages, promotions, and other HR policies and procedures
- questions about their opinions of unions
- an increase in the number or nature of employee complaints or grievances
- a change in the number, composition, and size of informal groups at lunch and coffee breaks
- the sudden popularity of certain employees (especially if they are the informal leaders)
- the sudden cessation of employee conversation when a member of management approaches or an obvious change in employees' behaviour toward members of management, expressed either formally or informally
- the appearance of strangers in the parking lot
- the distribution of cards, flyers, or pro-union buttons.

Tips | **FOR THE FRONT LINE**

Employer Response to an Organizing Campaign

If the employer prefers that the group seeking unionization retain its non-union status, a careful campaign is usually mounted to counteract the union drive. Normally, HR department staff members head up the campaign, although they

Labour Management Services (Ontario)
www.labour.gov.on.ca

may be assisted by a consultant or labour lawyer. Absolutely critical to the success of a company's counter-campaign is supervisory training. Supervisors need to be informed about what they can and cannot do or say during the organizing campaign to ensure that they do not violate LR legislation and avoid actions that might inadvertently provide fuel for the union's campaign.

An Ethical | Dilemma

Knowing that head office plans to close your facility should a unionization bid be successful, how should you, as a manager, respond to inquiries from employees about the impact of a union?

As much information about the union as possible should be obtained pertaining to dues, strike record, salaries of officers, and any other relevant facts that might cause employees to question the benefits of unionization. Communication strategies can be planned, with the aim of reminding employees about the company's good points, pointing out disadvantages of unionization, and refuting any misleading union claims. The employer's case for remaining non-union should be presented in a factual, honest, and straightforward manner.

Under the law, employers are granted the right to do the following:

Hints | TO ENSURE LEGAL COMPLIANCE

- express their views and opinions regarding unions
- state their position regarding the desirability of remaining non-union
- prohibit distribution of union literature on company property on company time
- increase wages, make promotions, and take other HR actions, as long as they would do so *in the normal course of business*. In most jurisdictions, however, once an application for certification is received by the LRB, wages, benefits, and working conditions are frozen until the application is dealt with.
- assemble employees during working hours to state the company's position, as long as employees are advised of the purpose of the meeting in advance, attendance is optional, and threats and promises are avoided (employers have no obligation to give the union the same opportunity).

Step 3: Union Recognition

A union can obtain recognition as a bargaining unit for a group of workers in three basic ways: (1) voluntary recognition, (2) the regular certification process, and (3) a pre-hearing vote. Bargaining rights can also be terminated in various ways.

Voluntary Recognition

An employer in every Canadian jurisdiction, except Quebec, can voluntarily recognize a union as the bargaining agent for a group of its employees. Although fairly rare, this may occur if an employer has adopted a union acceptance strategy and believes that employees want to be represented by that union.

Regular Certification

certification The procedure whereby a labour union obtains a certificate from the relevant LRB declaring that the union is the exclusive bargaining agent for a defined group of employees in a bargaining unit that the LRB considers appropriate for collective bargaining purposes.

The normal union **certification** procedure is for the union to present evidence of at least a minimum level of membership support for a bargaining unit that they have defined, in the form of signed authorization cards, to the appropriate LRB, along with an application for certification. The minimum level of support required to apply for certification varies by jurisdiction, from 25 percent of the bargaining unit in Saskatchewan to 65 percent in Manitoba.[16] The LRB then determines whether the bargaining unit defined by the union is appropriate for collective bargaining purposes.

In most jurisdictions, LRBs can grant *automatic certification* without a vote if the applicant union can demonstrate a high enough level of support for the proposed bargaining unit (generally 50 or 55 percent). Automatic certification may also be granted in some jurisdictions if the employer has engaged in unfair practices. If the level of support is not sufficient for automatic certification, but is above a specified minimum level (between 25 and 45 percent, depending on jurisdiction), the LRB will order and supervise a **representation vote**.[17] Eligible employees have the opportunity to cast a secret ballot, indicating whether or not they want the union to be certified. In some jurisdictions, to gain certification, the voting results must indicate that *more than 50 percent of the potential bargaining unit members* are in support of the union. In other jurisdictions, the standard is the support of *more than 50 percent of those voting*.[18] If the union loses, another election cannot be held among the same employees for at least one year. Only about 20 percent of certifications are the result of a vote—roughly four out of five certifications are the result of authorization cards alone.[19]

Pre-hearing Votes

In most jurisdictions, a **pre-hearing vote** may be conducted where there is evidence of violations of fair labour practices early in an organizing campaign. In such a case, the LRB may order a vote before holding a hearing to determine the composition of the bargaining unit. The intent is to determine the level of support for the union as quickly as possible, before the effect of any irregularities can taint the outcome. The ballot box is then sealed until the LRB determines whether the bargaining unit is appropriate and, if so, which employees are eligible for membership. If the bargaining unit is deemed appropriate by the LRB, only the votes of potential bargaining unit members are counted, and if the majority of the ballots cast support the union, it is certified.

Termination of Bargaining Rights

All LR acts provide procedures for workers to apply for the **decertification** of their unions. Generally, members may apply for decertification if the union has failed to negotiate a collective agreement within one year of certification, or if they are dissatisfied with the performance of the union. The LRB holds a secret-ballot vote, and if more than 50 percent of the ballots cast (or bargaining unit members, depending on jurisdiction) are in opposition to the union, the union will be decertified. A labour union also has the right to notify the LRB that it no longer wants to continue to represent the employees in a particular bargaining unit. This is known as "termination on abandonment." Once the LRB has declared that the union no longer represents the bargaining unit employees, any collective agreement negotiated between the parties is void.

Step 4: Collective Bargaining

Collective bargaining is the process by which a formal collective agreement is established between labour and management. The collective agreement is the cornerstone of the Canadian LR system. Both union and management representatives are required to bargain in good faith. This means that they must communicate

representation vote A vote conducted by the LRB in which employees in the bargaining unit indicate, by secret ballot, whether or not they want to be represented, or continue to be represented, by a labour union.

pre-hearing vote An alternative mechanism for certification, used in situations in which there is evidence of violations of fair labour practices early in the organizing campaign.

decertification The process whereby a union is legally deprived of its official recognition as the exclusive bargaining agent for a group of employees.

An Ethical | Dilemma

As the HR manager, how would you handle a situation in which a supervisor has knowingly violated the collective agreement when scheduling overtime?

Collective Bargaining
www.labour.gov.on.ca/english/lr/cbis

International Labour Organization
www.ilo.org

and negotiate, that proposals must be matched with counter-proposals, and that both parties must make every reasonable effort to arrive at an agreement.

Steps typically involved in the collective bargaining process include (1) preparation for bargaining, (2) face-to-face negotiations, and (3) obtaining approval for the proposed contract. There are two possible additional steps. First, when talks break down, third-party assistance is required by law in every jurisdiction except Saskatchewan.[20] The second additional step is a strike/lockout or interest arbitration if the parties arrive at a bargaining impasse. Each of these steps will be described next.

Preparation for Negotiations

Good preparation leads to a greater likelihood that desired goals will be achieved. Preparation for negotiations involves planning the bargaining strategy and process and assembling data to support bargaining proposals. Both union and management will gather data on general economic trends, analyze other collective agreements and trends in collective bargaining, conduct an analysis of grievances, review the existing contract or the union's organizing campaign promises, conduct wage and salary surveys at competitor organizations, prepare cost estimates of monetary proposals, and make plans for a possible strike or lockout. In addition, management negotiators will obtain input from supervisors. Union negotiators will obtain input from union stewards, obtain the company's financial information (if it is a public company), gather demographic information on their membership, and obtain input from members.

Once these steps are completed, each side forms a negotiating team and an initial bargaining plan/strategy is prepared. Initial proposals are then finalized and presented for approval by either senior management or the union membership.

Face-to-Face Negotiations

Negotiating a collective agreement.

caucus session A session in which only the members of one's own bargaining team are present.

Under LR legislation, representatives of either union or management can give written notice to the other party of their desire to negotiate a first collective agreement or renew an existing one. Early in the negotiating process, demands are exchanged—often before the first bargaining session. Then both negotiating teams can make a private assessment of the other team's demands. Usually, each team finds some items with which they can agree quite readily and others on which compromise seems likely. Tentative conclusions are also made regarding which items, if any, are potential strike or lockout issues.

Location, Frequency, and Duration of Meetings Negotiations are generally held at a neutral, off-site location, such as a hotel meeting room, so that there is no psychological advantage for either team and so that interruptions and work distractions can be kept to a minimum. Each side generally has another room in which intra-team meetings, known as **caucus sessions,** are held.

Generally, meetings are held as often as either or both parties consider desirable, and they last as long as progress is being made. Marathon bargaining sessions, such as those lasting all night, are not typical until conciliation has been exhausted and the clock is ticking rapidly toward the strike/lockout deadline.

Initial Bargaining Session The initial meeting of the bargaining teams is extremely important in establishing the climate that will prevail during the negotiating sessions that follow. A cordial attitude can help to relax tension and ensure that negotiations proceed smoothly. Generally, the first meeting is devoted to an exchange of demands (if this has not taken place previously) and the establishment of rules and procedures that will be used during negotiations.

Subsequent Bargaining Sessions In traditional approaches to bargaining, each party argues for its demands and resists those of the other at each negotiating session. At the same time, both are looking for compromise alternatives that will enable an agreement to be reached. Every proposal submitted must be either withdrawn temporarily or permanently, accepted by the other side in its entirety, or accepted in a modified form. Ideally, both sides should come away from negotiations feeling that they have attained many of their basic bargaining goals and confident that the tentative agreement reached will be acceptable to senior management and the members of the bargaining unit.

For each issue on the table to be resolved satisfactorily, the point at which agreement is reached must be within limits that the union and employer are willing to accept, often referred to as the **bargaining zone**. As illustrated in **Figure 16.3**, if the solution desired by one party exceeds the limits of the other party, then it is outside of the bargaining zone. Unless that party modifies its demands sufficiently to bring them within the bargaining zone, or the other party extends its limits to accommodate such demands, a bargaining deadlock is the inevitable result.

Distributive bargaining is an approach often typified as "win–lose" bargaining, because the gains of one party are normally achieved at the expense of the other.[21] It is appropriately involved when the issues being discussed pertain to the distribution of things that are available in fixed amounts, such as wage increases and benefits improvements. However, it may also be used when there is a history of distrust and adversarial relations, even when dealing with issues on which a more constructive approach is possible.

RPC

Collects and presents information required for decision making in the bargaining process

bargaining zone The area defined by the bargaining limits (resistance points) of each side, in which compromise is possible, as is the attainment of a settlement satisfactory to both parties.

distributive bargaining A win–lose negotiating strategy, such that one party gains at the expense of the other.

FIGURE 16.3 | The Bargaining Zone and Characteristics of Distributive Bargaining

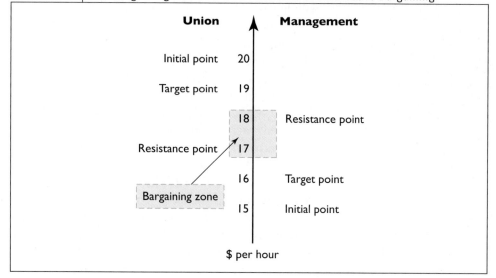

As indicated in Figure 16.3, distributive bargaining is characterized by three distinct components: the initial point, the target point, and the resistance point. The initial point for the union is usually higher than what the union expects to receive from management. The union target point is next, and represents the negotiating team's assessment of what is realistically achievable from management. The union's bargaining zone limit is its resistance point, which represents its minimally acceptable level.

These points are essentially reversed for management. The management team's initial point is its lowest level, which is used at the beginning of negotiations. Next is its target point, the desired agreement level. Management's resistance point forms the other boundary of the bargaining zone.

Integrative bargaining is an approach that assumes that a win–win solution can be found but also acknowledges that one or both sides can be losers if the bargaining is not handled effectively.[22] Integrative bargaining strategies require that both management and union negotiators adopt a genuine interest in the joint exploration of creative solutions to common problems.

Issues pertaining to work rules, job descriptions, and contract language can often be handled effectively by using an integrative approach, in situations in which management negotiators are not intent on retaining management rights and both sides are committed to seeking a win–win solution. Wage rates and vacation entitlements are more likely to be fixed-sum issues that are handled by a distributive approach.

The objective of integrative bargaining is to establish a creative negotiating relationship that benefits labour and management. Becoming increasingly popular these days is a relatively new integrative approach, known as mutual gains or interest-based bargaining.

Mutual gains (interest-based) bargaining is another win–win approach to LR issues. All key union and management negotiators are trained in the fundamentals of effective problem solving and conflict resolution. Such training is often extended to other employees in order to ensure that the principles of mutual gains (interest-based) bargaining are incorporated into the organization's value system and that co-operation becomes a year-round corporate objective.[23]

Solutions must take the interests of each party into account. A joint sense of accountability is fostered and ongoing joint union/management initiatives can result from the negotiating process. In addition, the tools that are used at the bargaining table can be applied to the resolution of all workplace issues. Although mutual gains (interest-based) bargaining has been put into practice in about 40 percent of Canadian negotiations, experts warn that implementation is difficult, as it requires a grassroots culture change.[24]

Thus, the negotiating process is far more complex than it may appear to a casual observer. There are different types of bargaining strategies involved, and each side arrives at the bargaining table with political and organizational interests at stake.

The Contract Approval Process

As mentioned previously, collective agreements must be written documents. However, the parties do not normally execute a formal written document until some time after the bargaining process has been completed. Instead, the terms and conditions agreed to by the parties are usually reduced to a

integrative bargaining A negotiating strategy in which the possibility of win–win, lose–win, win–lose, and lose–lose outcomes is recognized, and there is acknowledgement that achieving a win–win outcome will depend on mutual trust and problem solving.

mutual gains (interest-based) bargaining A win–win approach based on training in the fundamentals of effective problem solving and conflict resolution, in which the interests of all stakeholders are taken into account.

memorandum of settlement A summary of the terms and conditions agreed to by the parties that is submitted to the constituent groups for final approval.

ratification Formal approval by secret-ballot vote of the bargaining unit members of the agreement negotiated between union and management.

memorandum of settlement and submitted to the constituent groups for final approval.

Generally, final approval for the employer rests with the senior management team. In most cases, the union bargaining team submits the memorandum of settlement to the bargaining unit members for **ratification**. In some jurisdictions, ratification is required by law, and all members of the bargaining unit must be given ample opportunity to cast a secret-ballot vote indicating approval or rejection of the proposed contract. If the majority of bargaining unit members vote in favour of the proposal, it goes into effect. If the proposed collective agreement is rejected, union and management negotiators must return to the bargaining table and seek a more acceptable compromise. In such instances, third-party assistance is often sought.

Once approval has been received from the constituent groups, the bargaining team members sign the memorandum of settlement. Once signed, this memorandum serves as the collective agreement until the formal document is prepared and contract administration begins.

Third-Party Assistance and Bargaining Impasses

Legislation in all Canadian jurisdictions provides for conciliation and mediation services. Although the terms *conciliation* and *mediation* are often used interchangeably, they have quite distinct and different meanings.

conciliation The use of a neutral third party to help an organization and the union representing a group of its employees to come to a mutually satisfactory collective agreement.

Conciliation is the intervention of a neutral third party whose primary purpose is to bring the parties together and keep them talking to enable them to reach a mutually satisfactory collective agreement. The only means available to a conciliator to bring the parties to agreement is persuasion; he or she is not permitted to have any direct input into the negotiation process or to impose a settlement. Conciliation is typically requested after the parties have been negotiating for some time and are starting to reach a deadlock or after talks have broken down. The aim of conciliation is to try to help the parties avoid the hardship of a strike or lockout.

Conciliation and Mediation
www.labour.gov.on.ca/english/lr/

In all jurisdictions except Saskatchewan, strikes and lockouts are prohibited until third-party assistance has been undertaken. (Conciliation is required in all but two jurisdictions.) In most jurisdictions in which third-party assistance is mandatory, strikes/lockouts are prohibited until conciliation efforts have failed and a specified time period has elapsed.[25]

mediation The use (usually voluntary) of a neutral third party to help an organization and the union representing its employees to reach a mutually satisfactory collective agreement.

Mediation is the intervention of a neutral third party whose primary purpose is to help the parties to fashion a mutually satisfactory agreement. Mediation is usually a voluntary process, typically occurring during the countdown period prior to a strike or lockout or during the strike or lockout itself. The mediator's role is an active one. It often involves meeting with each side separately and then bringing them together in an attempt to assist them in bridging the existing gaps. He or she is allowed to have direct input into the negotiation process but cannot impose a settlement.

When the union and management negotiating teams are unable to reach an agreement, and once the conciliation process has been undertaken (where required), the union may exercise its right to strike or request interest arbitration, and the employer may exercise its right to lock out the bargaining unit members. Alternatively, bargaining unit members may continue to work without a collective agreement once the old one has expired, until talks resume and an agreement is reached.

strike The temporary refusal by bargaining unit members to continue working for the employer.

strike vote Legally required in some jurisdictions, it is a vote seeking authorization from bargaining unit members to strike if necessary. A favourable vote does not mean that a strike is inevitable.

picket Stationing groups of striking employees, usually carrying signs, at the entrances and exits of the struck operation to publicize the issues in dispute and discourage people from entering or leaving the premises.

boycott An organized refusal of bargaining unit members and supporters to buy the products or use the services of the organization whose employees are on strike in an effort to exert economic pressure on the employer.

Striking members of the Canadian Union of Public Employees, local 3903, picket at York University in Toronto.

Strikes A **strike** can be defined as a temporary refusal by bargaining unit members to continue working for the employer. When talks are reaching an impasse, unions will often hold a **strike vote**. Legally required in some jurisdictions, such a vote seeks authorization from bargaining unit members to strike if necessary. A favourable vote does not mean that a strike is inevitable. In fact, a highly favourable strike vote is often used as a bargaining ploy to gain concessions that will make a strike unnecessary. The results of a strike vote also help the union negotiating team members to determine their relative bargaining strength. Unless strike action is supported by a substantial majority of bargaining unit members, union leaders are rarely prepared to risk a strike and must therefore be more willing to compromise, if necessary, to avoid a work stoppage.

Since a strike can have serious economic consequences for bargaining unit members, the union negotiating team must carefully analyze the prospects for its success. Striking union members receive no wages and often have no benefits coverage until they return to work, although they may draw some money from the union's strike fund. Work stoppages are also costly for employers, customers, and suppliers.

When a union goes on strike, bargaining unit members often **picket** the employer. To ensure as many picketers as possible, the union may make strike pay contingent on picket duty. Picketers stand at business entrances, carrying signs advertising the issues in dispute, and attempt to discourage people from entering or leaving the premises.

Another economic weapon available to unions is a **boycott**, which is a refusal to patronize the employer. A boycott occurs when a union asks its members, other union members, the employer's customers/clients, and supporters in the general public not to patronize the business involved in the labour dispute. Such action can harm the employer if the union is successful in gaining a large number of supporters. As with a strike, a boycott can have long-term consequences if former customers/clients develop a bias against the employer's products

or services or make a change in buying habits or service provider that is not easily reversed.

The duration and ultimate success of a strike depends on the relative strength of the parties. Once a strike is settled, striking workers return to their jobs. During a labour dispute many people are put under remarkable pressure, and relationships essential to effective post-settlement work dynamics can be tarnished—especially in firms that rely heavily on teamwork. Post-settlement work environments are often riddled with tension, derogatory remarks, and hostility.

lockout Temporary refusal of a company to continue providing work for bargaining unit employees involved in a labour dispute, which may result in closure of the establishment for a time.

Lockout Although not a widely used strategy in Canada, a **lockout** is legally permissible. This involves the employer prohibiting the bargaining unit employees from entering the company premises as a means of putting pressure on the union to agree to the terms and conditions being offered by management. Sometimes the employer chooses to close operations entirely, which means that nonstriking employees are also affected. Most employers try to avoid this option, since doing so means that the well-being of innocent parties is threatened, and a lockout may damage the firm's public image. Employees at forest products company Stora Enso in Port Hawkesbury, Nova Scotia, were locked out in 2006 after 20 months of bargaining when the union refused to accept a wage rollback of 10 percent, contracting out, and loss of seniority rights. An agreement was ratified five months later, just before the mill closure deadline set by the company.[26]

An Ethical | Dilemma

Is it ethical for a firm to close the establishment during a labour dispute if that results in nonstriking employees being laid off?

Unlawful Strikes and Lockouts An unlawful strike is one that contravenes the relevant LR legislation and lays the union and its members open to charges and possible fines and/or periods of imprisonment if found guilty. For example, it is illegal for a union to call a strike involving employees who do not have the right to strike because of the essential nature of their services, such as nurses or police officers. In all jurisdictions, it is illegal to call a strike during the term of an existing collective agreement.

wildcat strike A spontaneous walkout, not officially sanctioned by the union leadership, which may be legal or illegal, depending on its timing.

A **wildcat strike** is a spontaneous walkout, not officially sanctioned by the union leaders, that is illegal if it occurs during the term of a collective agreement. For example, hotel workers at a Holiday Inn in Toronto, many of them new Canadians in low-end jobs, staged a wildcat walkout for about 45 minutes in November 2007 to protest lagging contract talks.[27]

arbitration The use of an outside third party to investigate a dispute between an employer and union and impose a settlement.

Arbitration
www.psab.gov.on.ca/english/psgb/Arbitration.htm

interest arbitration The imposition of the final terms of a collective agreement.

interest dispute A dispute between an organization and the union representing its employees over the terms of a collective agreement.

Interest Arbitration Arbitration involves the use of an outside third party to investigate a dispute between an employer and union and impose a settlement. A sole arbitrator or three-person arbitration board may be involved. Arbitrators listen to evidence, weigh it impartially and objectively, and make a decision based on the law and/or the contract language. An arbitrator is not a judge, however. First, arbitration hearings tend to be much more informal than courtroom proceedings. Second, the arbitrator is not bound by precedents to the extent that a judge is usually held.[28] Third, both the law and court decisions have given the arbitration function considerable power and freedom. Arbitration decisions are final and binding and cannot be changed or revised.

Interest arbitration may be used to settle an **interest dispute** regarding the terms of a collective agreement by imposing the terms of the collective agreement. The right to interest arbitration is legally mandated for workers who are not permitted to strike, such as hospital and nursing home employees, police officers and firefighters in most jurisdictions, and some public servants.[29] Interest arbitration is also involved when special legislation is passed, ordering striking or locked-out parties back to work because of public hardship.

The Collective Agreement: Typical Provisions

The eventual outcome of collective bargaining, whether negotiated by the parties or imposed by an arbitrator, is a formal, written, collective agreement.

Union Recognition Clause A *union recognition clause* clarifies the scope of the bargaining unit by specifying the employee classifications included therein or listing those excluded.

Union Security/Checkoff Clause All Canadian jurisdictions permit the inclusion of a **union security clause** in the collective agreement to protect the interests of the labour union. This clause deals with the issue of membership requirements and, often, the payment of union dues. There are various forms of union security clauses:[31]

- A *closed shop* is the most restrictive form of union security. Only union members in good standing may be hired by the employer to perform bargaining unit work. This type of security clause is common in the construction industry.

- In a *union shop*, membership and dues payment are mandatory conditions of employment. Although individuals do not have to be union members at the time that they are hired, they are required to join the union on the day on which they commence work or on completion of probation.

- In a *modified union shop*, the individuals who were bargaining unit members at the time of certification or when the collective agreement was signed are not obliged to join the union, although they must pay dues, but all subsequently hired employees must do both.

- Under a *maintenance-of-membership arrangement*, individuals voluntarily joining the union must remain members during the term of the contract. Membership withdrawal is typically permitted during a designated period around the time of contract expiration. Dues payment is generally mandatory for all bargaining unit members.

- The *Rand formula* is the most popular union security arrangement. It does not require union membership, but it does require that all members of the bargaining unit pay union dues. It is a compromise arrangement that recognizes the fact that the union must represent all employees in the bargaining unit and should therefore be entitled to their financial support but also provides the choice to join or not join the union.

- An *open shop* is a type of security arrangement whereby union membership is voluntary and nonmembers are not required to pay dues.

No-Strike-or-Lockout Provision There must be a clause in every contract in Canada forbidding strikes or lockouts while the collective agreement is in effect. The intent is to guarantee some degree of stability in the employment relationship during the life of the collective agreement, which must be at least one year. Saskatchewan and Quebec are the only jurisdictions that impose a maximum duration of three years.[30] In general, the duration of collective agreements in Canada is increasing.[31] Halifax police accepted a 12-year agreement in 2003.[32]

union security clause The contract provisions protecting the interests of the labour union, dealing with the issue of membership requirements and, often, the payment of union dues.

An Ethical | Dilemma

Given the fact that some workers have religious or other objections to unions, is the Rand formula ethical?

Management Rights Clause The management rights clause clarifies the areas in which management may exercise its exclusive rights without agreement from the union and the issues that are not subject to collective bargaining. It typically refers to the rights of management to operate the organization, subject to the terms of the collective agreement. Any rights not limited by the clause are reserved to management.

Arbitration Clause All Canadian jurisdictions require that collective agreements contain a clause providing for the final and binding settlement, by arbitration, of all disputes arising during the term of a collective agreement. Such disputes may relate to the application, interpretation, or administration of the agreement, as well as alleged contraventions by either party.

Step 5: Contract Administration

After a collective agreement has been negotiated and signed, the contract administration process begins. Both union and management are required to abide by the contract provisions. It is also in day-to-day contract administration that the bulk of labour–management relations occurs. Regardless of the amount of time and effort put into the wording of the contract, it is almost inevitable that differences of opinion will arise regarding the application and interpretation of the agreement. Seniority and discipline issues tend to be the major sources of disagreement between union and management.

Seniority

seniority Length of service in the bargaining unit.

Unions typically prefer to have employee-related decisions determined by **seniority**, which refers to length of service in the bargaining unit. In many collective agreements, seniority is the governing factor in layoffs and recalls (the most senior employees are the last to be laid off and the first to be recalled), and a determining factor in transfers and promotions. In some collective agreements, seniority is also the determining factor in decisions pertaining to work assignments, shift preferences, allocation of days off, and vacation time.

Unions prefer the principle of seniority as an equitable and objective decision-making criterion, ensuring that there is no favouritism. Managers often prefer to place greater weight on ability or merit.

Discipline

Almost all collective agreements give the employer the right to make reasonable rules and regulations governing employees' behaviour and to take disciplinary action if the rules are broken. In every collective agreement, bargaining unit members are given the right to file a grievance if they feel that any disciplinary action taken was too harsh or without just cause.

Most collective agreements restrict an employer's right to discipline employees by requiring proof of just cause for the disciplinary action imposed. Since just cause is open to different interpretations, disciplinary action is a major source of grievances. Thus, disciplinary issues must be handled in accordance with the terms of the collective agreement and backed by carefully documented evidence. Even when disciplinary action is handled carefully, the union may argue that there were extenuating circumstances that should be taken into consideration. Supervisors have to strike a delicate balance between fairness and consistency.

When discipline cases end up at arbitration, two independent decisions are made. The first is whether the employee actually engaged in some form of misconduct. Then, if that question is answered in the affirmative, an assessment must be made of whether such misconduct warrants the particular discipline imposed, as well as whether such disciplinary action violated the collective agreement.

Grievance Resolution and Rights Arbitration

grievance A written allegation of a contract violation, filed by an individual bargaining unit member, the union, or management.

A **grievance** is a written allegation of a contract violation relating to a disagreement about its application or interpretation. When such alleged violations or disagreements arise, they are settled through the grievance procedure. A multistep grievance procedure, the last step of which is final and binding arbitration, is found in virtually all collective agreements. Such procedures have been very effective in resolving day-to-day problems arising during the life of the collective agreement.

The primary purpose of the grievance procedure is to ensure the application of the contract with a degree of justice for both parties. Secondary purposes include providing the opportunity for the interpretation of contract language, such as the meaning of "sufficient ability"; serving as a communications device through which managers can become aware of employee concerns and areas of dissatisfaction; and bringing to the attention of both union and management those areas of the contract requiring clarification or modification in subsequent negotiations.

Steps in the Grievance Procedure The grievance procedure involves systematic deliberation of a complaint at progressively higher levels of authority in the company and union, and most provide for arbitration as a final step. Grievances are usually filed by individual bargaining unit members. If the issue in contention is one that may affect a number of union members, either at that time or in the future, the union may file a *policy grievance*. Management also has the right to use the grievance procedure to process a complaint about the union, although such use is rare. Although the number of steps and people involved at each vary, **Figure 16.4** illustrates a typical grievance procedure.

As illustrated in Figure 16.4, the typical first step of the grievance procedure is the filing of a written complaint with the employee's immediate supervisor. If the problem is not resolved to the satisfaction of the employee at the first step, he or she may then take the problem to the next higher managerial level designated in the contract, and so on through all the steps available. Time limits are typically provided for resolution at each step. Failure to respond within the specified time limit may result in the grievance being automatically processed at the next step or being deemed to have been withdrawn or resolved. Ninety percent or more of all grievances are settled, abandoned, or withdrawn before arbitration.

rights dispute A disagreement between an organization and the union representing its employees regarding the interpretation or application of one or more clauses in the current collective agreement.

rights arbitration The process involved in the settlement of a rights dispute.

Rights Arbitration Grievances relating to the interpretation or administration of the collective agreement are known as **rights disputes**. If these cannot be resolved internally, they must be referred to arbitration for a final and binding decision. The process involved in resolving such issues is known as **rights arbitration**.

A written arbitration award is issued at the conclusion of most rights arbitration cases, indicating that the grievance has been upheld or overturned. In disciplinary cases, it is also possible for an arbitration award to substitute a penalty that is more or less severe than the one proposed by union or management.

FIGURE 16.4 | A Typical Grievance Procedure

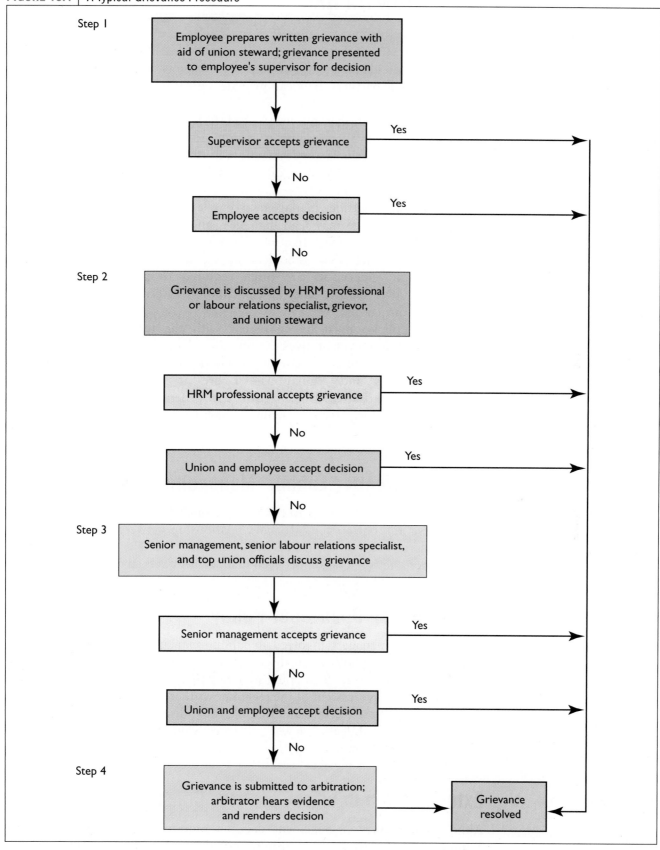

THE IMPACT OF UNIONIZATION ON HRM

Unionization results in a number of changes relating to HRM, all relating back to the requirements of the collective agreement. A union does have an impact on the way in which managers perform their HR responsibilities; when union leaders are treated as partners, they can provide a great deal of assistance with HR functions.

Once an organization is unionized, the HR department is typically expanded by the addition of an LR specialist or section. In a large firm with a number of bargaining units, human resources and labour relations may form two divisions within a broader department, often called industrial relations or labour relations.

In a unionized setting, management has less freedom to make unilateral decisions. This change may lead managers and supervisors to feel that they have lost some of their authority, which can cause resentment, especially since they inevitably find that unionization results in an increase in their responsibilities. Supervisors are often required to produce more written records than ever before, since documentation is critical at grievance and arbitration hearings.

All HR policies must be consistent with the terms of the collective agreement. Union representatives are often involved in the formulation of any policies that affect bargaining unit members—such as those pertaining to disciplinary rules and regulations—or are at least consulted as such policies are being drafted. Unionization also generally results in greater centralization of employee record keeping, which helps to ensure consistency and uniformity.

Building Effective Labour–Management Relations

Tips | FOR THE FRONT LINE

One of the biggest challenges to HRM in unionized organizations is to build a co-operative and harmonious working relationship between management and union leaders. The result can be a win–win situation. There are a number of ways to promote cooperation between management and labour.

Instituting an Open-Door Policy

When the key managers involved in labour–management relations welcome employees into their offices to discuss any problems or concerns, and when employees feel comfortable in doing so, many issues can be resolved informally. For example, if the president of the local knows that he or she can approach the LR manager "off the record" and that anything discussed in such sessions will be kept strictly confidential, fewer grievances and more trusting and harmonious relationships often result.

Extending the Courtesy of Prior Consultation

Although not every management decision requires union approval, if any actions that might affect union members are discussed with the union executive first, the likelihood of grievances is greatly reduced.

Demonstrating Genuine Concern for Employee Well-Being

When managers are genuinely concerned about employee well-being and demonstrate that concern, mutual trust and respect are often established. This involves fair treatment and communication going well above and beyond the requirements of the collective agreement.

Forming Joint Committees and Holding Joint Training Programs

Forming labour–management committees to investigate and resolve complex issues can lead to innovative and creative solutions, as well as to a better relationship. When a contract is first signed, it can be beneficial to hold a joint training program to ensure that supervisors and union stewards are familiar with the terms and conditions specified therein and that they understand the intent of the negotiating teams. Such training can reduce misunderstandings and the likelihood of disagreement regarding interpretation of contract language.

Meeting Regularly

Whether required by the collective agreement or voluntarily instituted, regularly scheduled union–management meetings can result in more effective communication and the resolution of problems/concerns before they become formal grievance issues.

Using Third-Party Assistance

To build a better relationship, it is often beneficial to bring in a consultant or a government agency representative to help identify common goals and objectives and ways in which trust and communication can be strengthened.

Chapter | SUMMARY

1. Canada's labour laws provide a common set of rules for fair negotiations and ensure the protection of public interest by preventing the impact of labour disputes from inconveniencing the public. Tripartite Labour Relations Boards across the country administer labour relations laws. These laws try to balance employees' rights to engage in union activity with employers' management rights.

2. There are five steps in the LR process: (i) employees' decision to seek collective representation, (ii) the union organizing campaign, (iii) official recognition of the union, (iv) negotiation of a collective agreement, and (v) day-to-day contract administration.

3. The union organizing process involves five steps, which typically include (i) employee/union contact, (ii) an initial organizational meeting, (iii) the formation of an in-house organizing committee, (iv) an organizing campaign, and (v) the outcome—certification, recognition, or rejection.

4. There are three basic ways in which a union can obtain recognition as a bargaining unit for a group of workers: voluntary recognition, the regular certification process, and a pre-hearing vote.

5. The three steps in the collective bargaining process are preparation for negotiations, face-to-face negotiations, and obtaining approval for the proposed contract. Two possible additional steps are third-party assistance if talks break down and a strike/lockout or interest arbitration if the parties arrive at a bargaining impasse.

6. Typical steps in a grievance procedure involve presenting a written grievance to the worker's immediate supervisor, then to an HR/LR specialist, then to senior management, and finally to an arbitrator for final and binding rights arbitration.

PEARSON
myHRlab™

Test yourself on the material for this chapter at
www.pearsoned.ca/myhrlab

Key | TERMS

arbitration   *(p. 453)*
authorization card   *(p. 445)*
bargaining unit   *(p. 438)*
bargaining zone   *(p. 449)*
boycott   *(p. 452)*
business unionism   *(p. 439)*
caucus session   *(p. 448)*
certification   *(p. 446)*
collective agreement (union contract)   *(p. 438)*
collective bargaining   *(p. 438)*
conciliation   *(p. 451)*
craft union   *(p. 439)*
decertification   *(p. 447)*
distributive bargaining   *(p. 449)*
grievance   *(p. 456)*
industrial union   *(p. 439)*
integrative bargaining   *(p. 450)*
interest arbitration   *(p. 453)*
interest dispute   *(p. 453)*
labour–management relations   *(p. 438)*

labour union (union)   *(p. 438)*
local   *(p. 441)*
lockout   *(p. 453)*
mediation   *(p. 451)*
memorandum of settlement   *(p. 451)*
mutual gains (interest-based) bargaining   *(p. 450)*
picket   *(p. 452)*
pre-hearing vote   *(p. 447)*
ratification   *(p. 451)*
representation vote   *(p. 447)*
rights arbitration   *(p. 456)*
rights dispute   *(p. 456)*
seniority   *(p. 455)*
social (reform) unionism   *(p. 439)*
strike   *(p. 452)*
strike vote   *(p. 452)*
union security clause   *(p. 454)*
union steward   *(p. 441)*
wildcat strike   *(p. 453)*

Review and Discussion | QUESTIONS

1. Cite three examples of unfair labour practices on the part of management and three on the part of unions.

2. Explain three of the challenges facing the union movement in Canada today.

3. Describe five signs to which managers should be alert in order to detect an organizing campaign.

4. Explain the bargaining zone and draw a diagram to illustrate this concept.

5. Explain the six common forms of union security clause.

6. Explain how arbitration differs from conciliation and mediation and differentiate between interest arbitration and rights arbitration.

Critical Thinking | QUESTIONS

1. Discuss why Dofasco, a company that has remained union-free for many years, allowed the United Steelworkers access to its workers in Hamilton to try to sign them up as union members. In your opinion, why was this attempt by the union unsuccessful?

2. "If supervisors communicate effectively with employees, deal with their concerns, and treat them fairly, employees are far less likely to be interested in forming or joining a union." Do you agree or disagree with this statement? Why?

3. Two possible approaches to labour relations are union acceptance and union avoidance. Determine which of these strategies seems to have been adopted in a firm in which you have been employed or with which you are familiar. Provide evidence to back up your answer.

4. As the LR specialist, what steps would you take in order to prepare the firm and management team if you believed that a strike was a possible outcome of the upcoming negotiations?

5. Review the Magna/CAW example in the Strategic HRM box (page 442). Compare and contrast the steps taken by Magna and the CAW to build such a relationship with the guidelines provided in this chapter.

Experiential | EXERCISES

1. Assume that you are the vice-president of HR at a relatively new non-union firm that has been experiencing rapid growth. In view of the management team's desire to remain non-union, you have been asked to prepare a report to the other senior management team members, making specific recommendations regarding strategies that the firm should adopt to help to ensure that the employees will have no desire to unionize.

2. Working with two or three classmates, devise a management counter-campaign to a unionization attempt, ensuring that all recommended courses of action are legal.

3. Working with several of your classmates, use role-playing to differentiate between distributive and integrative bargaining.

4. Obtain a copy of two collective agreements. Compare and contrast the following provisions: union recognition, management rights, union security, grievance procedures, and arbitration clauses.

5. Read the following scenario and then, based on the role your team has been assigned by your professor and the preparation time allowed, develop a negotiating strategy, including your bargaining zone that you think will enable you to reach a fair and reasonable outcome for all parties. Before coming to the bargaining table, pick a chief negotiator for your team. Negotiate a settlement.

Scenario

ABC manufacturing is a large multinational machinery and heavy equipment manufacturer. The last two years have been very difficult, with more competition coming from offshore companies whose labour costs are much lower than those in Canada. The company is losing money and is considering whether to lay off people in one or more of its Canadian plants, perhaps opening a new plant in Mexico or somewhere else in Central America. The union contract is up and negotiations will begin soon.

6. Research past issues of Canadian HR publications and find at least two labour arbitration awards, one that finds in favour of the organization and the other in favour of the union. Prepare a brief presentation on what you find fair/unfair in these settlements. Be prepared to discuss why you think this.

Running | CASE

LearnInMotion.com

The Grievance

When coming in to work one day, Pierre was surprised to be taken aside by Jason, one of their original employees, who met him as he was parking his car. "Jennifer told me I was suspended for two days without pay because I came in late last Thursday," said Jason. "I'm really upset, but around here Jennifer's word seems to be law, and it sometimes seems like the only way anyone can file a grievance is by meeting you like this in the parking lot."

Pierre was very disturbed by this revelation and promised the employee that he would discuss the situation with Jennifer. He began mulling over possible alternatives.

QUESTIONS

1   Does LearnInMotion run the potential risk of becoming unionized through its reactive managerial policy by one instead of both owners?

2   What are the primary reasons why people unionize?

3   Should a union wish to organize LearnInMotion employees, what are the five steps in the labour relations process a union must go through?

Case | INCIDENT

Strategy

"They want what?" the mayor exclaimed.

"Like I said," the town clerk replied, "17 percent over two years."

"There is no way that the taxpayers will accept a settlement anywhere near that," reiterated the mayor. "I don't care if the garbage doesn't get collected for a century. We can't do more than 8 percent over the next two years."

The town clerk looked worried. "How much loss of service do you think the public will accept? Suppose they do go on strike? I'm the one who always gets the complaints. Then there's the health problem with rats running all over the place! Remember over in Neibringtown, when that little kid was bitten? There was a hell of an outcry."

The mayor agreed. "Garbage collectors always have strong bargaining power, but, if I don't fight this, I'll be voted out in the next election. I say we offer 6 percent over 18 months. Then we can go either way— 6 percent over 12 months or 8 percent over two years."

"I wonder if we have any other options?" worried the town clerk.

"Well, we could threaten not to hire any more union personnel and to job out the collection service to private contractors if the union wasn't co-operative," mused the mayor.

"That's a good idea!" The town clerk sounded enthusiastic. "Also, we can mount a newspaper advertising campaign to get the public behind us. If we play on the fear of massive tax increases, the garbage collectors won't have much public sympathy."

"What about asking the union to guarantee garbage collection for old people during a strike? If they refuse, they'll look bad in the public eye; if they accept, we are rid of a major problem. Most people can bring their trash to a central collection point. Not all old people can," chuckled the mayor. "We can't lose on that issue!"

"Okay then," said the town clerk. "It looks like we have the beginning of a bargaining strategy here. Actually, I feel better now. I think we're in a rather strong position."

QUESTIONS

1   Discuss the plight of public sector unions faced with the reality of a limited tax base and public pressure to lower taxes.

2   Is the town clerk right? Is the town in a good bargaining position? Explain your answer.

3   What strengths does the union have in its position?

4   If you were a labour relations consultant, would you agree with the present strategy? What alternatives, if any, would you propose?

Source: R.W. Mondy, R.M. Noe, S.R. Premeaux, and R.A. Knowles, *Human Resource Management,* Second Canadian Edition. Toronto: Pearson Education Canada, 2001, p. 386.

For additional cases and exercise material, go to
www.pearsoned.ca/myhrlab

   To view the CBC Videos, read a summary, and answer discussion questions, go to MyHRLab at
www.pearsoned.ca/myhrlab

CHAPTER 17

LEARNING OUTCOMES

AFTER STUDYING THIS CHAPTER, YOU SHOULD BE ABLE TO

EXPLAIN how intercountry differences have an impact on HRM.

EXPLAIN how to improve global assignments through employee selection.

DISCUSS the major considerations in formulating a compensation plan for international employees.

DESCRIBE the main considerations in repatriating employees from abroad.

EXPLAIN why it is or is not "realistic for a company to try to institute a standardized HR system in all or most of its facilities around the world."

MANAGING HUMAN RESOURCES IN A GLOBAL BUSINESS

REQUIRED PROFESSIONAL CAPABILITIES (RPC)

- Contributes to an environment that fosters effective working relationships

THE GLOBALIZATION OF BUSINESS AND STRATEGIC HR

expatriate Employees who are citizens of the country where the parent company is based, who are sent to work in another country.

The globalization of business is now the norm. European market unification is ongoing and the economies of Brazil, Russia, India, and China are burgeoning. Huge Canadian companies like Noranda, Alcan, and Molson have long had extensive overseas operations, but today the vast majority of companies are finding that their success depends on their ability to market and manage overseas. Thousands of Canadian corporations with international operations are now relocating employees overseas on a regular basis. These employees, called **expatriates**, are citizens of the country where the parent company is based who are sent to work in another country.

Strategic HR involvement in the design and implementation of a global expansion strategy is required right from the start. Extensive research may be required with regard to local hiring practices, the availability of skilled labour, and employment regulations. Drivers of employee engagement vary across countries, but one company found that an engagement strategy based on communication drove spectacular growth in their emerging-markets division, as described in the Strategic HR box.

Strategic HR

Employee Engagement Program Drives Business Results at DHL

Employees form the backbone of any successful organization. Valued members of staff can make, or break, a company's success, so it is essential that employers do their best to keep them happy. However, one of the most effective ways to create and maintain staff satisfaction is arguably one of the least practised. Communication is the key to employee engagement. On a practical level, internal communications help employees to understand a company's vision, values, and culture, while on a more subliminal level, good internal communication is one of the most effective ways to build strong relationships and forge a sense of fulfillment.

DHL's emerging markets division was one of the first to realize this. Started as a separate region in 2000, the division serves 93 countries across a 14-hour time zone. The countries are grouped by area: Russia and the Commonwealth of Independent States; southeast Europe and north Africa; the Middle East, sub-Saharan Africa and Turkey. "By aligning these countries according to similar needs, issues, potential and expectations, we made our venture into new territory more manageable," said David Wild, general manager, DHL United Arab Emirates. "However, we were determined to be aware and to acknowledge that all the countries are diverse in culture, language, and standards. This was the key to our

success in these emerging markets." The emerging markets division now contributes some 200 000 customers to the company's 4.2 million across the globe.

In 2006, Maverick Events Worldwide developed a method under which all messages within the emerging markets division of DHL could be delivered across the entire workforce. It created the Mission Possible brand, based on the Mission Impossible movie, as it considered film to be one to the few media capable of translation across a culturally diverse region.

A movie, filmed in 14 countries, was produced featuring DHL senior managers delivering their messages. All staff were "agents" taking part in a mission to make the emerging-markets division the fastest growing and most profitable in DHL. They were issues with "agent packs" containing the tools they needed to complete their mission.

Mission Possible was directly responsible for additional revenue of €16 million in 12 months. The emerging-markets division saw 18 percent annual growth using Mission Possible as its internal focus. The campaign was subsequently taken forward in other regions of the DHL group.

Source: Adapted from C. Edmonds, "Delivering an international HR strategy at DHL," *Human Resources Management International Digest* 17(1) 2009, pp. 32–34. Copyright © 2009, Emerald Group Publishing Limited.

A strategic approach is also required to manage the current talent shortage, which is a global phenomenon. The working population is aging in both developed and emerging economies, while lower birth rates mean a reduced supply of workers in coming decades.[1] Although China and India, with more than a billion people each, have no labour shortage, they have major shortages of talent. For example, although India's universities deliver as many as 350 000 engineering graduates every year, no more than 25 percent of those engineers are considered employable by multinational companies. The problem is that many of India's university programs fall well below global standards and far below the basic expectations of most multinational companies.[2] Similar problems with finance graduates led China to take advantage of layoffs in the financial sector in London, Chicago, and New York to recruit 170 positions for institutions such as the Bank of Shanghai, the Pudong Development Bank, and the Shanghai Stock Exchange.[3]

Relocation specialists are becoming strategic partners in determining the need for an assignment or relocation, identifying who is best suited to go, and making sure that all supports are in place to make that assignment a success.[4] According to Roger Herod, senior vice-president of global relocation consultants ORC Worldwide,[5]

> In order to be truly competitive, companies must begin to recognize the value of mobility in terms of talent development, using assignments as a means to strengthen leadership development and facilitate a diffusion of talent throughout the organization. Linked to this goal is the repositioning of the global mobility function within organizations as a strategic business partner. In today's business environment, addressing these global mobility imperatives is vital to achieving a true competitive advantage.

In the 21st century, workforce mobility programs have a direct impact on company profits. Research by Runzheimer International shows that organizations can improve profitability by 1 percent to 4 percent simply by making workforce mobility management a strategic priority and by managing mobility programs in a more integrated way. This is because disjointed management of mobility programs often results in employee confusion, aggravation, frustration, and disengagement.[6]

Global Relocation

The number of expatriates working abroad is continuing to increase. One survey showed that the number of expatriates doubled between 2005 and 2008. The number of "global nomads" (employees who continuously move from country to country on multiple assignments) has also increased.[7] In addition, there has been a gradual increase in the number of female expatriates, who have long been underrepresented in the expatriate ranks.[8] Expatriates may be not only invaluable but also irreplaceable in the near future as the global labour pool contracts in most Western countries as well as Japan and China.[9] Overall, relocation policies are becoming more flexible, as the majority of all services are provided on a case-by-case basis.[10]

Family issues rank as the number one concern when it comes to employee relocations, and many employees are reluctant to accept expatriate assignments for this reason.[11] Employees who are considering an international assignment will also want to know how working and living in another country will affect their compensation, benefits, and taxes, and what kind of relocation assistance they will receive. From a practical perspective, some of the most pressing challenges are techniques used to recruit, select, train, compensate, and provide family support for employees who are based abroad, such as the following:

1. Candidate identification, assessment, and selection. In addition to the required technical and business skills, key traits to consider for global assignments include cultural sensitivity, interpersonal skills, and flexibility.

2. Cost projections. The average cost of sending an employee and family on an overseas assignment is reportedly between three and five times the employee's pre-departure salary; as a result, quantifying total costs for a global assignment and deciding whether to use an expatriate or a local employee are essential in the budgeting process.

3. Assignment letters. The assignee's specific job requirements and remuneration, vacation, home leave, and repatriation arrangements will have to be documented and formally communicated in an assignment letter.[12]

4. Compensation, benefits, and tax programs. There are many ways in which to compensate employees who are transferred abroad, given the vast differences in living expenses around the world. Some common approaches to international pay include home-based pay plus a supplement and destination-based pay.

5. Relocation assistance. The assignee will probably have to be assisted with such matters as maintenance of a home and automobiles, shipment and storage of household goods, and so forth. The average cost of a permanent international relocation for a Canadian employee is between $50 000 and $100 000.[13]

6. Family support. Cultural orientation, educational assistance, and emergency provisions are just some of the matters to be addressed before the family is moved abroad.

The last two issues relate to the heightened focus on the spouse and family, who are so necessary in today's climate of relocation refusals because of concerns about a mother-in-law's homecare, the children's education, a spouse's career, and the difficulty of adjusting to new surroundings while juggling family responsibilities at the same time as focusing on the job. Although the typical expatriate has traditionally been a male with a non-working spouse, dual career families are now the norm. Major work/life balance relocation challenges thus include career assistance for the spouse and education and school selection assistance for the children.[14] Cross-cultural and language training programs will probably be required. Policies for repatriating the expatriate when he or she returns home are another matter that must be addressed. Sending employees abroad and managing HR globally is complicated by the nature of the countries into which many firms are expanding. Today's expatriates are heading to China (now the most likely destination for a foreign assignment) and other emerging economies.[15]

WHY EXPATRIATE ASSIGNMENTS FAIL

expatriate assignment failure
Early return of an expatriate from a global assignment

Global mobility management is important because the cost of **expatriate assignment failure**—early return from an expatriate assignment—can result in costs up to a million dollars.[16] There is some evidence that the rate of early departures, at least, is declining. This appears to be because more employers are taking steps to reduce expatriates' problems abroad. For example, they are selecting expatriates more carefully, helping spouses to get jobs abroad, and providing more ongoing support to the expatriate and his or her family.[17] As another example, some companies have formal "global buddy" programs. Here local managers assist new expatriates with advice on things such as office politics, norms of behaviour, and where to receive emergency medical assistance.[18]

Discovering why expatriate assignments fail is an important research task, and experts have made considerable progress. Personality is one factor. For example, in a study of 143 expatriate employees, extroverted, agreeable, and emotionally stable individuals were less likely to want to leave early.[19] Furthermore, the person's intentions are important. For example, people who want expatriate careers try harder to adjust to such a life.[20] Non-work factors like family pressures usually loom large in expatriate failures. In one study, managers listed, in descending order of importance for leaving early, inability of spouse to adjust, managers' inability to adjust, other family problems, managers' personal or emotional immaturity, and inability to cope with larger overseas responsibility.[21] Managers of European firms emphasized only the inability of the manager's spouse to adjust as an explanation for the expatriate's failed assignment. Other studies similarly emphasize dissatisfied spouses' effects on the international assignment.[22]

A truism regarding selection for international assignments is that it is usually not inadequate technical competence but family and personal problems that undermine the international assignee.[23] As one expert puts it,

> The selection process is fundamentally flawed. Expatriate assignments rarely fail because the person cannot accommodate to the technical demands of the job. The expatriate selections are made by line managers based on technical competence. They fail because of family and personal issues and lack of cultural skills that haven't been part of the process.[24]

Family Issues

Given the fact that family issues are the number one cause of expatriate assignment failure, it is important that the employer understand just how unhappy and cut off the expatriate manager's spouse can feel in a foreign environment. One study involved analyzing questionnaire data from 221 international assignee couples working in 37 countries.[25] Perhaps the most poignant finding concerned the degree to which many spouses often felt cut off and adrift:

> It's difficult to make close friends. So many expats have their guard up, not wanting to become too close. Too many have been hurt, too many times already, becoming emotionally dependent on a friend only to have the inevitable happen—one or the other gets transferred. It's also difficult to watch your children get hurt when their best friend gets transferred. Although I have many acquaintances, I have nowhere near the close friends I had in the States. My spouse therefore has become my rock.[26]

Male spouses of female expatriates face the greatest challenge when it comes to isolation. Because there are so few of them, it is difficult for them to find other men facing the same challenges.[27]

What Employers Can Do

One study identified three things that helped make it easier for the spouse to adjust. First is language fluency. Since spouses will obviously feel even more cut off from their new surroundings if they can't make themselves understood, the employer should provide the spouse—not just the employee—with language training. Second, having preschool-age children (rather than school-age children or no children) seemed to make it easier for the spouse to adjust. "This suggests that younger children, perhaps because of their increased dependency, help spouses retain that part of their social identities: As parents, their responsibilities for these children remain the same."[28] Third, it also clearly helps that there be a strong bond of closeness and mutual sharing between spouse and expat partner, to provide the continuing emotional and social support many spouses find lacking abroad.

There are other useful steps the employer can take. Providing realistic previews of what to expect, careful screening, improved orientation, and improved benefits packages are some obvious solutions. A less obvious solution is to institute procedures that ensure your firm treats its employees fairly—treating them with respect, providing an appeal process, and so on.[29] In one study of international assignees, non-work problems were "significantly less pronounced when the organization's procedures were judged to be more fair."[30] For example, providing lots of information to the family before they leave, providing assistance in initial adjustment, and helping spouses get started on to find personal, social, and employment networking all aided in making a smooth transition to life in a foreign country.[31]

Many employers have tried to eliminate family issues as a problem by shortening the assignment length and having the family remain at home. Expatriate assignments have traditionally been for a term of three to five years, but recently there has been a trend toward short-term global assignments instead of permanent relocations.[32] A recent survey by global consulting firm KPMG found that short term assignments of less than 12 months are almost as prevalent as long term assignments, as shown in **Figure 17.1**.

FIGURE 17.1 | Prevalence of International Assignment Types

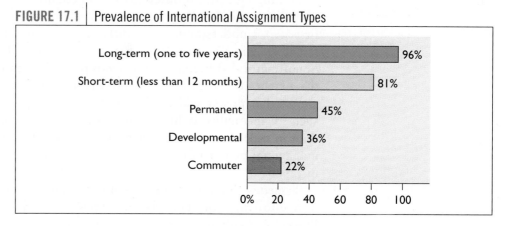

Source: KPMG's *Survey 2007 Global Assignment Policies and Practices*, p. 14. http://www.kmpg.com/SiteCollectionDocuments/GAPP-survey-2008.pdf. Reprinted with permission of KPMG International Executive Services.

Short-term assignment alternatives include frequent extended business trips with corresponding time spent back at home, short-term assignments of between three months and a year with frequent home leave (once every 12 weeks on average), and the dual household arrangement where the employee's family remains at home and the employee sets up a small household for himself or herself in the foreign country. Often, firms neglect to prepare employees for short-term assignments in the same way as they do for the long-term variety, which leads to problems such as lack of cross-cultural awareness, extreme loneliness, and feeling undervalued on returning to the home office.[33] Companies that provide strong support to expatriate employees stand a higher chance of success.[34]

HOW INTERCOUNTRY DIFFERENCES AFFECT HRM

To a large extent, companies operating only within Canada's borders have the luxury of dealing with a relatively limited set of economic, cultural, and legal variables. However, a company that is operating multiple units abroad does not operate in an environment of such relative homogeneity with respect to HRM. For example, minimum legally mandated holidays may range from none in the United States to five weeks per year in Luxembourg. In addition, although there are no formal requirements for employee participation in Italy, employee representatives on boards of directors are required in companies with more than 30 employees in Denmark.

Another troubling issue is the need for tight security and terrorism awareness training for employees sent to such countries as Colombia, where kidnapping of foreign executives is commonplace.[35] And two-thirds of the world's nations are corrupt places to conduct business.[36] The point is that the management of the HR functions in multinational companies is complicated enormously by the need to adapt HR policies and procedures to the differences among countries in which each subsidiary is based. The following are some intercountry differences that demand such adaptation.[37]

Cultural Factors

Wide-ranging cultural differences from country to country demand corresponding differences in HR practices among a company's foreign subsidiaries. The first step is understanding the differences in underlying cultural values in different societies. Major studies have clarified some basic dimensions of international cultural differences. For example, societies differ in power distance—the extent to which the less powerful members of institutions accept and expect that power will be distributed unequally.[38] The institutionalization of such an inequality is higher in some countries (such as Mexico and Japan) than in others (such as Sweden and the Netherlands). For example, abuse of managerial power in the form of bullying and harassment is widely tolerated in Japan.[39]

Societies also differ when it comes to individualism versus collectivism—the degree to which ties between individuals are normally loose rather than close. In more individualistic countries such as Canada and the United States, individuals look out for themselves and their immediate families. However, in more collectivist countries such as China and Pakistan, an individual's identity is very

A worker walks past a broken electricity transformer in Lagos, Nigeria. Despite having one of the world's great energy reserves, corruption and mismanagement have left Africa's oil giant chronically short of electricity.

strongly linked to their extended family group, and sometimes even to their work group. Interestingly, the one-child policy in China has resulted in a younger generation that is much more individualistic, known for job-hopping and lack of company loyalty.[40]

A recent major worldwide study of cultural dimensions found that societies differ in their attitudes to gender egalitarianism. Global competition has produced an interesting change in male-dominated mining operations in Australia, as described in the Workforce Diversity box.

Workforce DIVERSITY

Women Rule in Monster Trucks

Bigger than a house and tipping the scales, fully loaded, at more than 400 tons, it seems an unlikely vehicle to smash the old stereotype that women are bad drivers. But mining bosses in Australia are realizing that the growing number of women in charge of the industry's massive dump trucks are often better behind the wheel than their male counterparts. Not only do they drive more carefully, but their superior skills reduce wear and tear on the huge, three-metre high tires. "Mining companies are finding that women operate equipment in ways that make it last longer," says Michael Roche, chief executive at the Queensland Resource Council.

Surprised by the extent of the sudden, China-led commodity boom, Australian companies have spent the best part of the 21st century tackling a chronic shortage of skilled workers. With the supply of traditional talent almost exhausted, they turned to the group that made up the other half of the potential general workforce. Numerous initiatives have been introduced to attract women. The aim is to increase the number of females from today's 6 percent to 15 percent.

It might seem a modest goal, but in reality it is a huge task. Australian mines are typically sited in unforgiving outback or bush locations where searing heat and choking dust merely intensify the sense of extreme isolation. Three years ago, a dearth of drivers prompted a forward-thinking mining company in northern Queensland to introduce shorter, six-hour day shifts between nine and three o' clock. The new recruits quickly became known as the "Mummy Crew." Each day a bus drops their children at school and day care centres before taking the mothers to work at the Xstrata copper mine, 40 kilometres away. "It certainly has been a success story for us," says Andrew Uphill, the mine's employee services and community relations superintendent.

Source: Adapted from B. Adams, "Women Rule in Monster Trucks," Sunday Morning Post, December 23, 2007, p. 10. Reprinted with permission of South China Post Publishers.

Such intercountry cultural differences have several HR implications. First, they suggest the need for adapting HR practices, such as training and pay plans, to local cultural norms. They also suggest that HR staff members in a foreign subsidiary should include host-country citizens. A high degree of sensitivity and empathy for the cultural and attitudinal demands of co-workers is always important when selecting expatriate employees to staff overseas operations. Such sensitivity is especially important when the job is HRM and the work involves "human" jobs like interviewing, testing, orienting, training, counselling, and (if need be) terminating.

Economic Systems

Differences in economic systems among countries also translate into inter-country differences in HR practices. In free enterprise systems, for instance, the need for efficiency tends to favour HR policies that value productivity, efficient workers, and staff cutting where market forces dictate. Moving along the scale toward more socialist systems, HR practices tend to shift toward preventing unemployment, even at the expense of sacrificing efficiency. For example, in communist Vietnam, workplace culture involves a siesta after lunch for workers, and managers spending a lot time out of the office enhancing personal and social relationships.[41]

Legal Systems

Labour laws vary considerably across the world. China continues to update its labour laws, which now include many similarities to those in the West. Discrimination is prohibited on most of the grounds commonly found in Western countries, with the exception of age. However, enforcement of labour laws is haphazard.[42]

When it comes to employee termination, the amount of notice with pay to be provided, continuation of benefits, notification of unions, and minimum length of service to qualify for severance payments vary significantly and can in some cases have a major impact on labour costs.[43]

Health and safety laws vary from non-existent in many African states to Britain's new Corporate Manslaughter and Corporate Homicide Act, which tightens liability of senior management for health and safety offences.[44] In other countries such as China, worker health and safety laws exist but are largely unenforced.[45]

Labour Cost Factors

Differences in labour costs may also produce differences in HR practices. In order to maintain the competitive advantage of lower labour costs in China, the concept of investing in employees through training and development is seen as an unnecessary cost.[46] High labour costs can require a focus on efficiency and on HR practices (like pay for performance) aimed at improving employee performance.

Industrial Relations Factors

Industrial relations, and specifically the relationship among the workers, the union, and the employer, vary dramatically from country to country and have an enormous impact on HRM practices. In Germany, for instance, codetermination is the rule. Here, employees have the legal right to a voice in setting company policies. In this and several other countries, workers elect their own representatives to the supervisory board of the employer, and there is also a vice-president for labour at the top management level.[47] Conversely, in many other countries, the state interferes little in the relations between employers and unions. In China, for instance, company unions fall under the administration of the local Communist Party committee, which often shares long-term goals with the company. Thus unions seldom play an effective role in labour disputes.[48]

Summary

In summary, intercountry variations in culture, economic systems, labour costs, and legal and industrial relations systems complicate the task of selecting, training, and managing employees abroad. These variations result in corresponding differences which make the job of expatriate managers much more complex and difficult than when at home. International assignments thus run a relatively high risk of failing unless these differences are taken into account when selecting, training, and compensating international assignees.

SELECTION FOR GLOBAL ASSIGNMENTS

International managers can be expatriates, locals (citizens of the countries where they are working), or third-country nationals (citizens of a country other than the parent or the host country) such as a British executive working in a Tokyo subsidiary of a Canadian multinational bank.[49] Expatriates represent a minority of managers. Most managerial positions are filled by locals rather than expatriates in both headquarters and foreign subsidiary operations.

An Ethical | Dilemma

How ethical is it for a multinational organization to recruit expatriate staff for managerial positions when similarly qualified staff can be identified in the host country?

There are several reasons to rely on local, host-country management talent for filling the foreign subsidiary's management ranks. Many people simply prefer not to work in a foreign country, and in general the cost of using expatriates is far greater than the cost of using local management talent. The multinational corporation may be viewed locally as a "better citizen" if it uses local management talent, and indeed some governments actually press for the localization of management. There may also be a fear that expatriates, knowing that they are posted to the foreign subsidiary for only a few years, may overemphasize short-term projects rather than focus on perhaps more necessary long-term tasks.

There are also several reasons for using expatriates—either parent-country or third-country nationals—for staffing subsidiaries. The major reason is technical competence. In other words, employers may be unable find local candidates with the required technical qualifications. Multinationals also increasingly view a successful stint abroad as a required step in leadership development. Control is another important reason. Multinationals sometimes assign expatriates from their headquarters staff abroad on the assumption that these managers are more steeped in the firm's policies and culture and more likely to unquestioningly implement headquarters' instructions.

Global Staffing Policy

Canadian Employee Relocation Council
www.cerc.ca
Transition Dynamics
www.transition-dynamics.com
The Expatriate Group
www.expat.ca

There are three international staffing policies. An ethnocentric staffing policy is based on the attitude that home-country managers are superior to those in the host country, and all key management positions are filled by parent-country nationals. At Royal Dutch Shell, for instance, virtually all financial controllers around the world are Dutch nationals. Reasons given for ethnocentric staffing policies include lack of qualified host-country senior management talent, a desire to maintain a unified corporate culture and tighter control, and the desire to transfer the parent firm's core competencies (e.g., a specialized manufacturing skill) to a foreign subsidiary more expeditiously.

A polycentric staffing policy is based on the belief that only host-country managers can understand the culture and behaviour of the host-country market, and therefore foreign subsidiaries would be staffed with host-country nationals and its home-office headquarters with parent-country nationals. This may reduce the local cultural misunderstandings that expatriate managers may exhibit. It will also almost undoubtedly be less expensive. One expert estimates that an expatriate executive can cost a firm up to three times as much as a domestic executive because of transfer expenses and other expenses such as schooling for children, annual home leave, and the need to pay income taxes in two countries.

A geocentric staffing policy assumes that management candidates must be searched for globally, on the assumption that the best manager for any specific position anywhere on the globe may be found in any of the countries in which the firm operates. This allows the global firm to use its human resources more efficiently by transferring the best person to the open job, wherever he or she may be. It can also help to build a stronger and more consistent culture and set of values among the entire global management team. Team members here are continually interacting and networking with one another as they move from assignment to assignment around the globe and participate in global development activities.

Selecting Global Managers

Wherever an employee is to be posted, he or she will need the technical knowledge and skills to do the job and the intelligence and people skills to be a successful manager. In addition, foreign assignments make demands on expatriate assignees that are different from what the manager would face if simply assigned to a management post in his or her home country. There is the need to cope with a workforce and management colleagues whose cultural inclinations may be drastically different from one's own and the considerable stress that being alone in a foreign land can bring to bear on the manager.

If the employee's spouse and children share the assignment, there are also the complexities and pressures that the family will have to confront, from learning a new language to shopping in strange surroundings, to finding new friends and attending new schools. Perceived organizational support and fairness regarding family issues can reduce intentions to return home early.[50]

Selecting managers for expatriate assignments, therefore, means screening them for traits that predict success in adapting to what may be dramatically new environments. A research study of 338 international assignees from many countries and organizations identified five factors perceived by international assignees to contribute to success in a foreign assignment. They were job knowledge and motivation, relational skills, flexibility/adaptability, extracultural openness, and family situation. Specific items—including managerial ability, organizational ability, administrative skills, and creativity—were statistically combined into a single "job knowledge and motivation" factor. Respect, courtesy and tact, display of respect, and kindness were some of the items composing the "relational skills" factor. "Flexibility/adaptability" included such items as resourcefulness, ability to deal with stress, flexibility, and emotional stability. "Extracultural openness" included a variety of outside interests, interest in foreign countries, and openness. Finally, several items (including adaptability of spouse and family, spouse's positive opinion, willingness of spouse to live abroad, and stable marriage) compose the "family situation" factor.[51]

The five factors were not equally important in the foreign assignee's success, according to the responding managers. Family situation was generally found to be the most important factor, a finding consistent with other research on international assignments and transfers. Therefore, although all five factors were perceived to be important to the foreign assignee's success, the company that ignores the candidate's family situation does so at its own peril.

A study of 838 managers from 6 international firms and 21 countries studied the extent to which personal characteristics (such as "sensitive to cultural differences") could be used to distinguish between managers who had high potential as international executives and those whose potential was not as high. Results showed that personal characteristics successfully distinguished the managers identified by their companies as "high potential." Consistent with such results as those mentioned previously, the characteristics—such as flexibility, integrity, the courage to take a stand, seeking and using feedback, business knowledge, bringing out the best in people, taking risks, and openness to criticism—reflect a blend of technical expertise, openness, and flexibility in dealing with people and getting things done.[52]

Adaptability Screening

Adaptability screening is generally recommended as an integral part of the expatriate selection process. Generally conducted by a professional psychologist or psychiatrist, adaptability screening aims to assess the family's probable success in handling the foreign transfer and to alert them to personal issues (such as the impact on children) that the foreign move may involve.

Past experience is often the best predictor of future success, and some companies look for overseas candidates whose work and nonwork experience, education, and language skills already demonstrate a commitment to and facility in living and working with different cultures. Even several summers spent successfully travelling overseas or participating in foreign student programs would seem to provide some concrete basis for believing that the potential transferee can accomplish the required adaptation when he or she arrives overseas.

Realistic job previews at this point are also crucial. Again, both the potential assignee and his or her family require all the information that can be provided on the problems to expect in the new job (such as mandatory private schooling for the children), as well as any information obtainable about the cultural benefits, problems, and idiosyncrasies of the country in question. A pre-assignment visit to the new location by the employee and his or her family can provide an opportunity to make an informed decision about a potential relocation assignment. Mobility managers speak about avoiding culture shock in much the same way as we discussed using realistic job previews to avoid reality shock among new employees.[53]

There are also paper-and-pencil tests that can be used to more effectively select employees for overseas assignments. The Overseas Assignment Inventory is one such assessment tool. Based on many years of research with more thousands of candidates, the test's publisher contends that it is useful in identifying characteristics and attitudes that such candidates should have.[54]

Success of Canadian Expatriates

Canadian companies have reported low failure rates for expatriates relative to other countries, particularly the United States, which has a failure rate of 40 to 50 percent.[55] Canadians may be more culturally adaptable than their foreign counterparts because they are already familiar with bilingualism and multiculturalism. In fact, Canadian executives are in demand across the globe. The country's diverse ethnic makeup has produced a generation of business leaders who mix easily with different cultures.[56]

MAINTAINING GLOBAL EMPLOYEES

Careful screening is just the first step in ensuring that the foreign assignee is successful. The employee may then require special training and, additionally, international HR policies must be formulated for compensating the firm's overseas managers and maintaining healthy labour relations.

Orienting and Training Employees for Global Assignments

Cross-cultural training is very important for creating realistic expectations, which in turn are strongly related to cross-cultural adjustment.[57]A four-step approach to cross-cultural training is often used. Level 1 training focuses on the impact of cultural differences and on raising trainees' awareness of such differences and their impact on business outcomes. Even transfers to the United States from Canada can involve culture shock. Level 2 training focuses on attitudes and aims at getting participants to understand how attitudes (both negative and positive) are formed and how they influence behaviour. (For example, unfavourable stereotypes may subconsciously influence how a new manager responds to and treats his or her new foreign employees.) Level 3 training provides factual knowledge about the target country, while Level 4 provides skill building in areas like language and adjustment and adaptation skills. The depth of training is of the utmost importance. If firms are going to provide cross-cultural training, it needs

Orientation and training for international assignments can help employees (and their families) to avoid "culture shock" and better adjust to their new surroundings.

to be in-depth and done with care. For example, language training must include nonverbal communication awareness, as it varies so widely across the world.[58]

In addition to cross-cultural training, leadership development opportunities are often an important learning component of expatriate assignment.[59] At IBM, for instance, such development includes the use of a series of rotating assignments that permits overseas managers to grow professionally. At the same time, IBM and other major firms have established management development centres around the world where executives can go to hone their skills. Beyond that, classroom programs (such as those at the London Business School, or at INSEAD in France) provide overseas executives with the opportunities that they need to hone their functional and leadership skills.

International Compensation

The whole area of international compensation management presents some tricky problems. Compensation programs throughout a global firm must be integrated for overall effectiveness, yet differentiated to effectively motivate and meet the specific needs of the various categories and locations of employees. On the one hand, there is certain logic in maintaining company-wide pay scales and policies so that, for instance, divisional marketing directors throughout the world are all paid within the same narrow range. This reduces the risk of perceived inequities and dramatically simplifies the job of keeping track of disparate country-by-country wage rates. However, most multinational companies have recognized the need to make executive pay decisions on a global level, and executive pay plans are gradually becoming more uniform.[60]

On the other hand, the practice of not adapting pay scales to local markets can present an HR manager with more problems than it solves. The fact is that living in Tokyo is many times more expensive than living in Calgary, while the cost of living in Bangalore, India, is considerably lower than that in Toronto.[61] If these cost-of-living differences are not considered, it may be almost impossible to get managers to accept assignments in high-cost locations. One way to handle the problem is to pay a similar base salary company-wide and then add on various allowances according to individual market conditions.[62]

Compensation professionals also face the challenge of designing programs that motivate local employees in each country as well as internationally mobile employees of all nationalities. Some multinational companies deal with this problem for local managers by conducting their own annual compensation surveys. Others use a global career progression framework that includes the flexibility to accommodate local practices and still maintain organization-wide consistency.[63]

balance sheet approach Expatriate pay based on equalizing purchasing power across countries.

The Balance Sheet Approach

The most common approach to formulating expatriate pay is to equalize purchasing power across countries, a technique known as the **balance sheet approach.** The basic idea is that each expatriate should enjoy the same standard of living that he or she would have had at home. The employer estimates the cost of major expenses such as housing would be in the expatriate's home country, and the cost of each in the expatriate's host country. Any differences—such as higher housing expenses—are then paid by the employer.

In practice, this involves building the expatriate's total compensation around five or six separate components, as shown in **Figure 17.2.** For example, base salary will normally be in the same range as the manager's home-country salary. In addition, however, there might be a mobility premium. This is paid as a percentage of the executive's base salary, in part to compensate the manager for the cultural and physical adjustments that he or she will have to make.[64] There may also be several allowances, including a housing allowance and an education allowance for the expatriate's children.

An Ethical | Dilemma

Is it ethical to pay expatriates using the balance sheet approach when local staff at the same level receive far less compensation?

Variable Pay

As organizations around the world have shifted their focus to individual performance differentiation, there has been a rise in the prevalence of individual performance rewards, although the widespread use of team awards remains in a few Asian countries.[65] Across the globe, over 85 percent of companies offer at least one type of broad-based variable pay program, as shown in **Figure 17.3.** In addition, variable pay spending in emerging and high-growth markets has come to match the levels in more mature markets. Target bonuses for management and professional employees, as a percentage of base salary, have become quite similar globally.

Historically, there have been lower levels of eligibility for general staff roles, but this is no longer the case. Broad-based variable pay has gone global and is now an integral part of the compensation landscape for management and professional employees in every region. There has been a convergence in variable pay plan eligibility to encompass general staff as well, as shown in **Figure 17.4.**

International EAPs

EAPs are going global, helping expatriates to take care of their mental health, which is often affected by the stressful relocation process. A 2007 worldwide survey found that more than half of expatriates are weighed down by added stress caused by longer hours, extended workdays/workweeks, and cultural differences, among other factors. Two-thirds feel the strain of managing the demands of work and the well-being of family.[66] The proactive approach is to contact employees before departure to explain the program's services; then about three months after arrival, families are contacted again. By this time, they have usually run into some challenges from culture shock and will welcome some assistance. The expatriates and their families have then established a connection with the EAP to use for ongoing support.[67]

FIGURE 17.2 | Balance Sheet Approach

Net Compensation Package in Singapore by Home Country of Expatriate

Management level (IPE 56): Standard

Net amounts in SGD	AUS	FRA	DEU	IND	JPN	SWE	CHE	GBR	USA	Local +
Home net base salary	131,779	128,384	146,512	48,859	117,142	99,223	190,564	132,182	115,500	134,565
COLA	6,168	0	2,655	15,506	2,615	2,352	0	5,202	16,570	0
Mobility premium	19,111	17,671	22,270	6,916	15,628	15,789	26,743	19,276	16,570	0
Acommodation	115,500	115,500	115,500	115,500	115,500	115,500	115,500	115,500	115,500	92,400
Car benefit	14,400	14,400	14,400	14,400	14,400	14,400	14,400	14,400	14,400	0
Education	33,177	21,075	24,120	7,410	8,025	20,100	17,010	28,888	33,600	20,100
Total	**320,135**	**297,030**	**325,457**	**208,591**	**273,310**	**267,364**	**364,217**	**315,448**	**312,140**	**247,065**
Home net base salary	41.2	43.2	45.0	23.4	42.9	37.1	52.3	41.9	37.0	54.5
COLA	1.9	0.0	0.8	7.4	1.0	0.9	0.0	1.6	5.3	0.0
Mobility premium	6.0	5.9	6.8	3.3	5.7	5.9	7.3	6.1	5.3	0.0
Acommodation	36.1	38.9	35.5	55.4	42.3	43.2	31.7	36.6	37.0	37.4
Car benefit	4.5	4.8	4.4	6.9	5.3	5.4	4.0	4.6	4.6	0.0
Education	10.4	7.1	7.4	3.6	2.9	7.5	4.7	9.2	10.8	8.1
Total	**100**	**100**	**100**	**100**	**100**	**100**	**100**	**100**	**100**	**100**

FIGURE 17.3 | Overall Prevalence of Broad-Based Variable Pay Programs

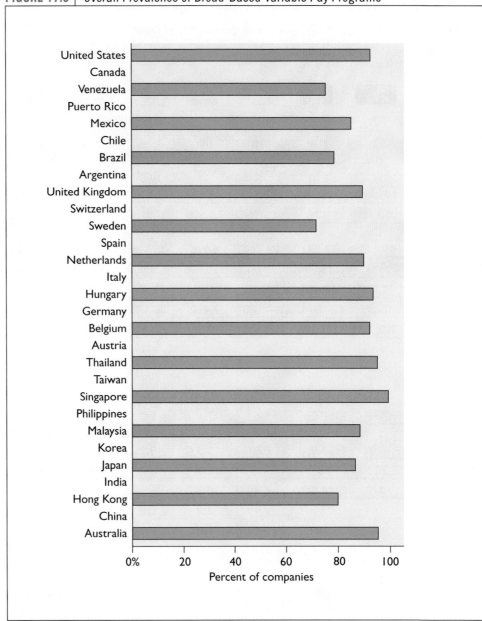

Source: K. Abosch, J. Schermerhorn and L. Wisper, "Broad-Based Variable Pay Goes Global," *Workspan* (May 2008), pp. 56–62. Reprinted with permission of WorldatWork, Scottsdale, AZ.

Problems, such as homesickness, boredom, withdrawal, depression, compulsive eating and drinking, irritability, marital stress, family tension, and conflict, are all common reactions to culture shock. Employees on short-term assignment without their families can experience extreme loneliness. Treatment for psychiatric illnesses varies widely around the world, as do the conditions in government-run mental health institutions, and consultation with an EAP professional having extensive cross-cultural training may be critical in ensuring that appropriate medical treatment is obtained.[68]

FIGURE 17.4 | Broad-Based Variable Pay Eligibility by Job Level and Region, 2007

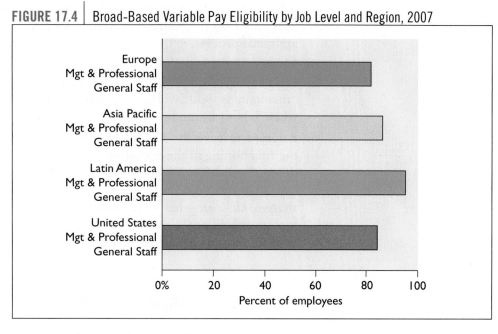

Source: K. Abosch, J. Schermerhorn and L. Wisper, "Broad-Based Variable Pay Goes Global," *Workspan* (May 2008), pp. 56–62. Reprinted with permission of WorldatWork, Scottsdale, AZ.

Performance Appraisal of Global Managers

Several issues complicate the task of appraising an expatriate's performance. The question of who actually appraises the expatriate is crucial. Local management must have some input, but the appraisal may then be distorted by cultural differences. Thus, an expatriate manager in India may be evaluated somewhat negatively by his host-country bosses, who find the use of participative decision making or other behaviour on the part of the expatriate to be inappropriate in their culture. However, home-office managers may be so geographically distanced from the expatriate that they cannot provide valid appraisals because they are not fully aware of the situation that the manager actually faces. Therefore, problems can arise if the expatriate is measured by objective criteria, such as profits and market share, but local events, such as political instability, undermine the manager's performance while remaining "invisible" to home-office staff.

Suggestions for improving the expatriate appraisal process include the following:[69]

1. Stipulate the assignment's difficulty level. For example, being an expatriate manager in China is generally considered to be more difficult than working in England, and the appraisal should take such difficulty-level differences into account.

2. Weight the evaluation more toward the on-site manager's appraisal than toward the home-site manager's distant perceptions of the employee's performance.

3. If, however (as is usually the case), the home-site manager does the actual written appraisal, he or she should use a former expatriate from the same

overseas location to provide background advice during the appraisal process. This can help to ensure that unique local issues are considered during the appraisal process.

4. Modify the normal performance criteria used for that particular position to fit the overseas position and characteristics of that particular locale. For example, "maintaining positive labour relations" might be more important in Chile, where labour instability is more common, than it would be in Canada.

5. Attempt to give the expatriate manager credit for relevant insights into the functioning of the operation and specifically the interdependencies of the domestic and foreign operations. In other words, do not just appraise the expatriate manager in terms of quantifiable criteria, like profits or market share. His or her recommendations regarding how home-office/ foreign-subsidiary communication might be enhanced and other useful insights should also affect the appraisal.

International Labour Relations

Firms opening subsidiaries abroad will find substantial differences in labour relations practices among the world's countries and regions. For example, Wal-Mart, which has successfully resisted unionization in most of the world, had to accept unions in many of its stores in China.[70] In Eastern Europe, unionization rates have plummeted since the fall of the Iron Curtain, resulting in a competitive advantage, with wages averaging only one-third of those in Western Europe.[71]

Some important differences between labour relations practices in Europe and North America include the following:[72]

• Centralization. In general, collective bargaining in Europe is likely to be industry-wide or regionally oriented, whereas North American collective bargaining generally occurs at the enterprise or plant level.

• Employer organization. Because of the prevalence of industry-wide bargaining, the employer's collective bargaining role tends to be performed primarily by employer associations in Europe; individual employers in North America generally (but not always) represent their own interests when bargaining collectively with unions.

• Union recognition. Union recognition for collective bargaining in Europe is much less formal than in North America. For example, in Europe there is no legal mechanism requiring an employer to recognize a particular union; even if a union claims to represent 80 percent of an employer's workers, another union can try to organize and bargain for the other 20 percent.

• Content and scope of bargaining. North American labour–management agreements tend to focus on wages, hours, and working conditions. European agreements tend to be brief and simple and to specify minimum wages and employment conditions.

• Worker participation. Worker participation has a long and relatively extensive history in Europe. In many countries, works councils are required. A works council is a committee in which plant workers consult with management about certain issues or share in the governance of the workplace.[73]

Personal Safety Abroad

Many employers are sending employees into regions with high business potential that are also plagued by endemic economic and political turmoil and disease risks, extending concerns about employee safety beyond the typical work environment. Regional conflicts, terrorist attacks, and difficult social and medical conditions are common problems for employees in high-risk areas.[74] As one security executive at an oil company put it, "It's crucial for a company to understand the local environment, local conditions, and what threat exists." For example, in 2009, Port Harcourt, Nigeria (the centre of foreign oil operations in the country), tied with Baghdad as the world's most dangerous city for foreign workers.[75] For some time now, kidnapping of foreign executives has been a common money-making business in some countries in Central and South America; it can also be a problem in Africa and parts of Asia-Pacific.[76]

Even in France, executives have been taken hostage (the country has a long history of confrontational labour relations). For example, workers at a Nortel Networks research centre that was being closed threatened to blow up the facility if they did not receive more severance pay, and managers at Caterpillar, 3M, and Sony were taken hostage by workers demanding more severance pay after layoffs were announced.[77]

Kidnap and ransom insurance is a rapidly growing benefit, given that between 10 000 and 15 000 kidnappings of foreigners for ransom occur each year, with about 80 percent in Latin America. The insurance policy usually covers[78]

- ransom money and coverage on the money while in transit
- professional negotiators
- consultants to handle media, law, and family communications
- bodily injury of abductee
- security company fees
- extortion against company property, product contamination, and computer systems
- travel expenses for negotiator, family, and employee
- lost salary of abductee
- psychological counselling for employee and family.

Keeping business travellers out of crime's way is a specialty all its own, and employers sending employees to dangerous locations should consult with a firm specializing in global security. General suggestions for any foreign executive (and in some cases their family members) include the following:

- Provide expatriates with general training about travelling and living abroad and specific information about the place that they are going to, so they are better oriented when they get there.
- Have travellers arrive at airports as close to departure time as possible and wait in areas away from the main flow of traffic where they are not as easily observed.
- Equip the expatriates' car and home with adequate security systems.
- Tell employees to vary their departure and arrival times and take different routes to and from work.

- Keep employees current on crime and other problems by regularly checking travel advisory service and consular information sheets; these provide up-to-date information on possible threats in almost every country of the world.

- Advise employees to remain confident at all times. Body language can attract perpetrators, and those who look like victims often become victimized.[79]

REPATRIATION

repatriation Process of moving the expatriate and his or her family back home from the foreign assignment.

Repatriation is the process of moving the expatriate and his or her family back home from the foreign assignment. Repatriation can be more difficult than going abroad. [80] Up to half of expatriates leave their organization following a repatriation, usually because they are not able to use their newly developed skills and capabilities in their roles on their return.[81] Their expert knowledge and international expertise often ends up with the competition.

Several repatriation problems are very common. One is the expatriate's fear that he or she has been "out of sight, out of mind" during an extended foreign stay and has thus lost touch with the parent firm's culture, top executives, and those responsible for the firm's management selection processes. Indeed, such fears can be well founded: Many repatriates are temporarily placed in mediocre or makeshift jobs. Ironically, the company often undervalues the cross-cultural skills acquired abroad, and the international posting becomes a career-limiting, rather than career-enhancing, move. Many are shocked to find that the executive trappings of the overseas job (private schools for the children and a company car and driver, for instance) are lost on return and that the executive is again just a small fish in a big pond. Perhaps more exasperating is the discovery that some of the expatriate's former colleagues have been more rapidly promoted while he or she was overseas. Even the expatriate's family may undergo a sort of reverse culture shock, as the spouse and children face the often-daunting task of picking up old friendships and habits or starting schools anew on their return.[82]

Progressive multinationals anticipate and avoid these problems by taking a number of sensible steps. These can be summarized as follows:[83]

1. Writing repatriation agreements. Many firms use repatriation agreements, which guarantee in writing that the international assignee will not be kept abroad longer than some period (such as five years) and that on return he or she will be given a mutually acceptable job.

2. Assigning a sponsor. The employee should be assigned a sponsor/mentor (such as a senior manager at the parent firm's home office). This person's role is to look after the expatriate while he or she is away. This includes keeping the person apprised of significant company events and changes back home, monitoring his or her career interests, and nominating the person to be considered for key openings when the expatriate is ready to come home.

3. Providing career counselling. Provide formal career counselling sessions to ensure that the repatriate's job assignments on return will meet his or her needs.

4. Keeping communication open. Keep the expatriate "plugged in" to home-office business affairs through management meetings around the world and frequent home leave combined with meetings at headquarters. Only 18 percent of companies in a 2006 Watson Wyatt global survey had a global

communication plan in place to keep employees around the world informed about what the company was doing.

5. Offering financial support. Many firms pay real estate and legal fees and help the expatriate to rent or in some other way to maintain his or her residence so that the repatriate and his or her family can actually return "home."

6. Developing reorientation programs. Provide the repatriate and his or her family with a reorientation program to facilitate the adjustment back into the home culture.

7. Building in return trips. Expatriates can benefit from more frequent trips to the home country to ensure that they keep in touch with home-country norms and changes during their international assignment.

HOW TO IMPLEMENT A GLOBAL HR SYSTEM

global HR system A standardized HR system in all company locations around the world.

Given cross-cultural differences like these in HR practices around the world, the question is whether it is realistic for a company to try to institute a **global HR system**, meaning a standardized HR system in all company locations around the world. A recent study suggests that the answer is "yes." It shows that the employer may have to defer to local managers on some specific issues. However, in general, the fact that there are currently global differences in HR practices doesn't mean that these differences are necessary or even advisable. The important thing is knowing how to create and implement the global HR system.

In this study, the researchers interviewed HR professionals from six global companies—Agilent, Dow, IBM, Motorola, Procter & Gamble, and Shell Oil—as well as international HR consultants.[84] Their overall conclusion was that employers who successfully implement global HR systems apply various international HR best practices in doing so. This enables them to create global HR systems that are globally acceptable, that they can develop more effectively, and that their HR staffs can then implement more effectively.

Making the Global HR System More Acceptable

First, employers engage in three best practices so that the global HR systems they eventually develop will be acceptable to their local managers around the world.

1. Remember that global systems are more accepted in truly global organizations. Truly global organizations require their managers to work on global teams, and they identify, recruit, and place the employees they hire globally. This makes it easier for managers everywhere to accept the global imperative for having a more standardized HR system.

2. Investigate pressures to differentiate and determine their legitimacy. HR managers seeking to standardize selection, training, appraisal, compensation, or other HR practices worldwide will always meet resistance from local managers who insist "you can't do that here, because we are different culturally and in other ways." It is important to carefully assess whether the local culture or other differences might in fact undermine the new

A global HR team

system, become knowledgeable about local legal issues, and be willing to differentiate where necessary. Then the new HR tool should be market-tested.

3. Try to work within the context of a strong corporate culture. A strong corporate culture helps override geographical differences. Companies that create a strong corporate culture find it easier to obtain agreement among far-flung employees when it comes time to implement standardized practices worldwide. For example, Procter & Gamble has a strong corporate culture. Because of how P&G recruits, selects, trains, and rewards them, its managers have a strong sense of shared values. Because all P&G managers worldwide tend to share these values, they are in a sense more similar to each other than they are geographically different. Having such global unanimity makes it easier to develop and implement standardized HR practices worldwide.

Developing a More Effective Global HR System

Similarly, researchers found that these companies engaged in several best practices in developing effective worldwide HR systems do the following:

1. Form global HR networks. The firm's HR managers around the world should feel that they're not merely local HR managers but are part of a greater whole, namely, the firm's global HR network. In developing global HR systems, the most critical factor for success is "creating an infrastructure of partners around the world that you use for support, for buy-in, for organization of local activities, and to help you better understand their own systems and their own challenges." Treat the local HR managers as equal partners, not just implementers.

2. Remember that it's more important to standardize ends and competencies than specific methods. For example, with regard to screening applicants, the researchers concluded, "while companies may strive to standardize tools globally, the critical point is [actually] to standardize what is assessed but to be flexible in how it is assessed." Thus, IBM uses a more or less standardized recruitment and selection process worldwide, but "details such as who conducts the interview (hiring manager versus recruiter) or whether the pre-screen is by phone or in person, differ by country."

Implementing the Global HR System

Finally, in actually implementing the global HR systems, several best practices can help ensure a more effective implementation:

1. Remember, you can't communicate enough. For example, there's a need for constant contact with the decision makers in each country, as well as the people who will be implementing and using the system.

2. Dedicate adequate resources for the global HR effort. For example, do not expect local HR offices to suddenly start implementing the new job analysis procedures unless the head office provides adequate resources for these additional activities.

Chapter | SUMMARY

1. Intercountry differences include cultural factors (such as power distance, individualism versus collectivism, and gender egalitariansim), economic systems, labour cost factors, and industrial relations factors. These affect HRM in a variety of ways.

2. Selecting managers for expatriate assignments means screening them for traits that predict success in adapting to dramatically new environments. Such expatriate traits include adaptability and flexibility, job knowledge and motivation, relational skills, extracultural openness, and family situation. Adaptability screening that focuses on the family's probable success in handling the foreign transfer can be an especially important step in the expatriate selection process.

3. The most common approach to formulating expatriate pay is to equalize purchasing power across countries, a technique known as the balance sheet approach. With this approach, the employer estimates expenses for income taxes, housing, goods and services, and reserve, and pays supplements to the expatriate in such a way

as to maintain the same standard of living that he or she would have had at home.

4. Repatriation problems are very common but can be minimized. They include the often well-founded fear that the expatriate is "out of sight, out of mind" and difficulties in re-assimilating the expatriate's family back into home-country culture. Suggestions for avoiding these problems include using repatriation agreements, assigning a sponsor/mentor, offering career counselling, keeping the expatriate plugged in to home-office business, building in return trips, providing financial support to maintain the expatriate's home-country residence, and offering reorientation programs to the expatriate and his or her family.

5. Employers who successfully implement global HR systems apply various international HR best practices in doing so. These enable them to create global HR systems that are globally acceptable, that they can develop more effectively, and that their HR staffs can then implement more effectively.

Key | TERMS

balance sheet approach   *(p. 478)*
expatriate   *(p. 465)*
expatriate assignment failure   *(p. 467)*

global HR system   *(p. 485)*
repatriation   *(p. 484)*

Review and Discussion | QUESTIONS

1. Specifically, what are some of the uniquely international activities that an international HR manager typically engages in?

2. Explain three broad global HR challenges.

3. What special training do overseas candidates need? In what ways is such training similar to and different from traditional diversity training?

4. Discuss the reasons why expatriate assignments fail and what is being done to reduce the failure rate.

5. How does appraising an expatriate's performance differ from appraising that of a home-office manager? How can some of the unique problems of appraising the expatriate's performance be avoided?

6. Describe five actions that can be taken by expatriate managers in other countries to increase their personal safety.

Critical Thinking | QUESTIONS

1. You are president of a small business. In what ways do you expect that being involved in international business activity will affect HRM in your business?

2. A firm is about to send its first employees overseas to staff a new subsidiary. The president asks why such assignments fail and what can be done to avoid such failures. Write a memo in response to these questions.

3. What can an organization do to ensure that the skills acquired on an international assignment are utilized when the employee returns to his or her home country?

4. How would you implement a geocentric staffing policy?

5. Using the DHL example in the Strategic HR box (page 465), identify and consider other movies that organizations could use as a base of common understanding to launch similar programs.

Experiential | EXERCISES

1. Choose three traits that are useful for selecting international assignees, and create a straightforward test (not one that uses pencil and paper) to screen candidates for these traits.

2. Describe the most common approach to formulating expatriate pay. Use a library source to determine the relative cost of living in five countries as of this year, and explain the implications of such differences for drafting a pay plan for managers being sent to each country.

3. Either in pairs or groups of four or five students, develop an outline for an initial four-hour cross-cultural training program. What training resources, tools, and processes might you use? Be prepared to give a rationale for your program.

4. Check online and find at least two websites that deal with or otherwise discuss the expatriate experience, and note the concerns and suggestions expressed. Compare to the text discussion. How do the actual expatriate experiences you found influence your current attitude towards working overseas? What are you major concerns? What excites you?

Running | CASE

Running Case: LearnInMotion.com

Going Abroad

According to its business plan and in practice, LearnInMotion.com "acquires content globally but delivers it locally." In other words, all the content and courses and other material that it lists on its site come from content providers all over the world. However, the "hard copy" (book and CD-ROM) courses are delivered, with the help of independent contracting delivery firms, locally in Ontario and Quebec.

Now the company is considering an expansion. Although the most logical strategic expansion would probably entail adding cities in Canada, one of LearnInMotion.com's major content providers—a big training company in England—believes there is a significant market for LearnInMotion.com services in England, and particularly in London, Oxford, and Manchester (all of which are bustling business centres, and all of which have well-known universities). The training company has offered to finance and co-own a branch of LearnInMotion.com in London. They want it housed in the training firm's new offices in Mayfair, near Shepherds Market. This is an easily accessible (if somewhat expensive) area, within easy walking distance of Hyde Park and not far from the London Underground Piccadilly line, which runs directly through the city to Heathrow airport.

Everyone concerned wants to make sure the new operation can "hit the ground running." This means either Jennifer or Pierre will have to move to London almost at once and take one salesperson and one of the content management people along. Once there, this small team could hire additional employees locally, and then, once the new operation is running successfully, return to Ottawa, probably within three or four months.

Jennifer and Pierre have decided to go ahead and open the London office, but this is not a decision they've taken lightly, since there are many drawbacks to doing so. The original, Ottawa-based site is not generating anywhere near the sales revenue it was supposed to at this point, and being short three key employees is not going to help. Neither the board of directors nor the representatives of the venture capital fund were enthusiastic about the idea of expanding abroad. However, they went along with it, and the deciding factor was probably the cash infusion that the London-based training firm was willing to make. It basically provided enough cash to run not just the London operation but the one in Ottawa for an additional six months.

Having made the decision to set up operations abroad, Jennifer and Pierre now need to turn to the multitude of matters involved in the expansion—for instance, obtaining the necessary licences to open the business in England and arranging for phone lines (all carried out with the assistance of the London-based training firm). However, it's also obvious to Jennifer and Pierre that there are considerable human resource management implications involved in moving LearnInMotion.com employees abroad, and in staffing the operation once they're there. Now, they want you, their management consultant, to help them actually do it.

QUESTIONS

1   What intercountry differences will affect the human resource management practices of LearnInMotion?

2   Should LearnInMotion use a global selection policy to source talent for their London operation?

3   How should LearnInMotion implement a global HR system?

Case | INCIDENT

"Boss, I Think We Have a Problem"

Central Steel Door Corporation has been in business for about 20 years, successfully selling a line of steel industrial-grade doors, as well as the hardware and fittings required for them. Focusing mostly in the United States and Canada, the company had gradually increased its presence from the New York City area, first into New England and then down the Atlantic Coast, then through the Midwest and West, and finally into Canada. The company's basic expansion strategy was always the same: Choose an area, open a distribution center, hire a regional sales manager, then let that regional sales manager help staff the distribution center and hire local sales reps.

Unfortunately, the company's traditional success in finding sales help has not extended to its overseas operations. With the introduction of the new European currency in 2002, Mel Fisher, president of Central Steel Door, decided to expand his company abroad, into Europe. However, the expansion has not gone smoothly at all. He tried for three weeks to find a sales manager by advertising in the *International Herald Tribune,* which is read by business people in Europe and by American expatriates living and working in Europe. Although the ads placed in the *Tribune* also run for about a month on the *Tribune*'s Web site, Mr. Fisher so far has received only five applications. One came from a possibly viable candidate, whereas four came from candidates whom Mr. Fisher refers to as "lost souls"—people who seem to have spent most of their time traveling aimlessly from country to country sipping espresso in sidewalk cafés. When asked what he had done for the last three years, one told Mr. Fisher he'd been on a "walkabout."

Other aspects of his international HR activities have been equally problematic. Fisher alienated two of his U.S. sales managers by sending them to Europe to temporarily run the European operations, but neglecting to work out a compensation package that would cover their relatively high living expenses in Germany and Belgium. One ended up staying the better part of the year, and Mr. Fisher was rudely surprised to be informed by the Belgian government that his sales manager owed thousands of dollars in local taxes. The managers had hired about 10 local people to staff each of the two distribution centers. However, without full-time local European sales managers, the level of sales was disappointing, so Fisher decided to fire about half the distribution center employees. That's when he got an emergency phone call from his temporary sales manager in Germany: "I've just been told that all these employees should have had written employment agreements and that in any case we can't fire anyone without at least one year's notice, and the local authorities here are really up in arms. Boss, I think we have a problem."

QUESTIONS

1   Based on this chapter and the case incident, compile a list of 10 international HR mistakes Mr. Fisher has made so far.

2   How would you have gone about hiring a European sales manager? Why?

3   What would you do now if you were Mr. Fisher?

For additional cases and exercise material, go to
www.pearsoned.ca/myhrlab

To view the CBC Videos, read a summary, and answer discussion questions, go to MyHRLab at
www.pearsoned.ca/myhrlab

Chapter 1

1. O. Parker, *The Strategic Value of People: Human Resource Trends and Metrics* (Ottawa: The Conference Board of Canada, July 2006); E. Andrew, "Most Canadian Companies Are Still Not Treating Human Resources as a Serious Strategic Issue," *Workspan Focus Canada* (February 2006), pp. 14–16; S. Prashad, "All Aligned: How to Get HR on Board with Business," *HR Professional* (February/March 2005), pp. 19–29.

2. O. Parker, *It's the Journey That Matters: 2005 Strategic HR Transformation Study Tour*. Ottawa: The Conference Board of Canada, March 2006.

3. N. Bontis, "Made to Measure: Linking human capital metrics with organizational performance," *HR Professional* (August/September 2007), pp. 16–20; B. Becker, M. Huselid, P.S. Pickus, and M.F. Spratt, "HR as a Source of Shareholder Value: Research and Recommendations," *Human Resource Management* 36, no. 1 (Spring 1997), pp. 39–47; B. Becker and B. Gerhart, "The Impact of Human Resource Management on Organizational Performance: Progress and Prospects," *Academy of Management Journal* 39, no. 4 (August 1996), pp. 779–801; M. Huselid, "The impact of human resources management practices on turnover, productivity, and corporate performance," *Academy of Management Journal*, 38, pp. 635–672; P. Wright, Gary McMahan, B. McCormick, and S. Sherman, "Strategy, core competence, and HR involvement as determinants of HR effectiveness and refinery," *Human Resource Management, 37*(37), 1998, pp. 17–31.

4. R.D. Banker, S-Y Lee, G. Potter, and D. Srinivasan, "Contextual Analysis of Performance impacts of Outcome-Based Incentive Compensation," *Academy of Management Journal*, 39(4), 1996, pp. 920–948

5. J.E. Delery and D.H. Doty, "Modes of Theorizing in Strategic Human Resource Management: Tests of Universalistic, Contingency, and Configurational Performance Predictions," *Academy of Management Journal*, 39(4), 1996, pp. 802–835.

6. M. Huselid, "The impact of human resources management practices on turnover, productivity, and corporate performance," *Academy of Management Journal*, 38, pp. 635–672.

7. *Watson Wyatt 2005 Human Capital Index Report* (Watson Wyatt, 2005); *Watson Wyatt Human Capital Index: Human Capital as a Lead Indicator of Shareholder Value* (Watson Wyatt, 2002).

8. D. Ulrich and W. Brockbank, *The HR Value Proposition* (Boston: Harvard University Press, 2005); D.M. Cox and C.H. Cox, "At the Table: Transitioning to Strategic Business Partner," *Workspan* (November 2003), pp. 20–23; D. Brown, "HR Pulled in Two Directions at Once," *Canadian HR Reporter* (February 23, 2004), pp. 1, 6; R. Morgan and M. Serino, "Mapping Human Capital DNA," *WorldatWork Journal* (Third Quarter 2002), pp. 42–51.

9. J. Miller, "HR Outsourcing and the Bottom Line," *Workspan* (October 2008), pp. 76–81; Jamieson, "People Skills Required," *National Post* (October 19, 2005).

10. S. Singh, "Exulted Expectations," *HR Professional* (August/September 2004), pp. 21–24; D. Brown, "Calgary Health Outsources HR," *Canadian HR Reporter* (February 23, 2004), pp. 1, 7; "CIBC Extends HR Outsourcing Deal," *Canadian HR Reporter* (December 15, 2003), p. 2; "Air Canada Plans to Outsource HR," *Canadian HR Reporter* (May 17, 2004), p. 2); D. Brown, "After Experiment with Outsourcing, RBC Brought Recruitment Back In-House," *Canadian HR Reporter* (April 19, 2004), pp. 8–9; J. Melnitzer, "Locating the Ouch Source," *Workplace News* (August 2005), pp. 12–13.

11. T. Belford, "HR Focusing on How It Can Add Value," *Globe & Mail* (March 25, 2002), p. B11.

12. O. Parker, *The Strategic Value of People: Human Resource Trends and Metrics* (Ottawa: The Conference Board of Canada, July 2006).

13. *CCHRA Awareness Study*. Toronto: CCHRA and Ekos Research Associates, 2008.

14. B.E. Becker, M.A. Huselid, and D. Ulrich, *The HR Scorecard: Linking People, Strategy and Performance* (Boston: Harvard Business School Press, 2001);

D. Brown, "Measuring the Value of HR," *Canadian HR Reporter* (September 24, 2001), pp. 1, 5. See also E. Beaudan, "The Failure of Strategy: It's All in the Execution, *Ivey Business Journal* (January/February 2001).

15. "CEOs Talk," *Canadian HR Reporter* (March 11, 2002), p. 19.

16. D.S. Cohen, "Behaviour-Based Interviewing," *Human Resources Professional* (April/May 1997), p. 29.

17. R. Wright, *Measuring Human Resources Effectiveness Toolkit* (Ottawa: The Conference Board of Canada, 2004); U. Vu, "The HR Leader's Contribution in an Engaged Organization," *Canadian HR Reporter* (May 22, 2006); D. Brown, "Measuring Human Capital Crucial, ROI Isn't, Says New Think-Tank Paper," *Canadian HR Reporter* (October 25, 2004), pp. 1, 4; J. Douglas and T. Emond, "Time to Pop the Question: Are Your Employees Engaged?" *WorldatWork Canadian News* (Third Quarter 2003), pp. 12–14.

18. R. Baumruk, "The Missing Link: The Role of Employee Engagement in Business Success," *Workspan* (November 2004), pp. 48–52; N. Winter, "Tuned in and Turned On," *Workspan* (April 2003), pp. 48–52.

19. O. Parker, *The Strategic Value of People: Human Resource Trends and Metrics* (Ottawa: The Conference Board of Canada, July 2006).

20. O. Parker, *The Strategic Value of People: Human Resource Trends and Metrics* (Ottawa: The Conference Board of Canada, July 2006).

21. R. Kaplan and D. Norton, *The Strategy-Focused Organization: How Balanced Scorecard Companies Thrive in the New Business Environment* (Boston: Harvard Business School Press, 1996); S. Mooraj, D. Oyon, and D. Hostettler, "The Balanced Scorecard: A Necessary Good or an Unnecessary Evil?" *European Management Journal* 17, no. 5 (October 1999), pp. 481–491; B. Becker, M. Huselid, and D. Ulrich, *The HR Scorecard: Linking People, Strategy and Performance* (Boston: Harvard Business School Press, 2001); M. Huselid, B. Becker, and R. Beatty, *The Workforce Scorecard: Managing Human Capital to Execute Strategy* (Boston: Harvard Business School Press, 2006).

22. G. Ferris, D. Frink, and M.C. Galang, "Diversity in the Workplace: The Human Resources Management Challenge," *Human Resource Planning* 16, no. 1 (1993), p. 42.

23. "Study: Canada's Visible Minority Population in 2017," *The Daily*, Statistics Canada (March 2005); *Canada's Ethnocultural Portrait: The Changing Mosaic*, Statistics Canada, Catalogue No. 96 F0030 XIE 2001 0082004.

24. "Wives as Primary Breadwinners," *Perspectives* (August 2006), p. 3. Statistics Canada Catalogue # 75-001-XIE; Labour force characteristics by age and sex, CANSIM Table 282-0087, Statistics Canada. www.statcan.gc.ca/subjects-sujets/labour-travail/lfs-epa/t090710al-eng.htm (July 31, 2009).

25. M. Hutchinson, *Aboriginal Workforce Poised to Replace Retiring Baby Boomers*, www.aboriginaltimes.com/science/immigration-baby-boom/view (August 17, 2006).

26. C. Williams, "Disability in the Workplace," *Perspectives on Labour and Income* 18, no. 1 (February 2006), pp. 16–24.

27. S. Dobson, "Passing the knowledge baton from one generation to the next," *Canadian HR Reporter* (October 20, 2008).

28. S.P. Eisner, "Managing Generation Y," *S.A.M. Advanced Management Journal* 70(4), 2005, pp. 4–15; "Canadians plan to work past traditional retirement age, survey finds," www.worldatwork.org/waw/adimComment?id=3085&printable (March 11, 2009); :More than half of Canadians plan to work in retirement," *Canadian HR Reporter* (January 8, 2007).

29. S. Dobson, "Age-free culture goal of top employers," *Canadian HR Reporter* (January 12, 2009).

30. A. Glass, "Understanding generational differences for competitive success," *Industrial and Commercial Training* 39(2), 2007, pp. 98–103.

31. N. Spinks and C. Moore, "Compassionate Care Leave Takes Effect," *WorldatWork Canadian News* (Second Quarter 2004), pp. 1, 21; U. Vu,

"'Sandwich Generation' Challenges Big, and Getting Bigger," *Canadian HR Reporter* (October 25, 2004), pp. 1, 8.

32. Based on material cited in "News and Views: Flex Appeal," compiled by M. Griffin, *HR Professional* (February/March 1999), p. 10; research reported by P.L. Nyhof in "Managing Generation X: The Millennial Challenge," *Canadian HR Reporter* (May 22, 2000), pp. 7–8; R. Berry, "Observations on Generational Diversity," *Profiles in Diversity Journal* 4, no. 3 (2002).

33. A. Glass, "Understanding generational differences for competitive success," *Industrial and Commercial Training* 39(2), 2007, pp. 98–103.

34. Jean-Philippe Naud, "Generation Y at Work," *WorldatWork Canadian News* (Second Quarter 2005), pp. 6–8; D. Piktialis, "The Generational Divide in Talent Management," *Workspan* (March 2006), pp. 10–12; G. Kovary and A. Buahene, "Recruiting the Four Generations," *Canadian HR Reporter* (May 23, 2005), p. R6.

35. *Managing Tomorrow's People: The Future of Work to 2020*. London UK: PricewaterhouseCoopers, 2007.

36. Jean-Michel Caye, Andrew Dyer, Michael Leicht, Anna Minto, and Rainer Strack, *Creating People Advantage: How to Address HR Challenges Worldwide Through 2015*. Boston: The Boston Consulting Group and World Federation of Personnel Management Associations, 2008.

37. A. Belanger, L. Martel, and E. Caron-Malenfant, *Population Projections for Canada, Provinces and Territories: 2005-2031*, Statistics Canada Catalogue No. 91-520-XIE, (December 2005), pp. 16–17; *Canada's Demographic Revolution: Adjusting to an Aging Population* (Ottawa: The Conference Board of Canada, March 2006).

38. M. Birchall-Spencer, "University of Toronto Economics Professor, Consultant and Author of Boom, Bust and Echo, David K. Foot Forecasts Global Demographic Trends and Their Effect on Canadian Workplaces," *HR Professional* (February/March 2009), pp. 570–64; "Canada's Demographic Revolution: Adjusting to an Aging Population," *Conference Board of Canada Executive Action*, March 2006.

39. P. Benimadhu, "Startling Business Shifts Causing a Rethink of Work," *InsideEdge* (Summer 2008), The Conference Board of Canada.

40. M. Armstrong-Stassen, "Organisational practices and the post-retirement employment experience of older workers," *Human Resource Management Journal*, 18(1), 2008, pp. 36–53.

41. Statistics Canada. *Labour Force Historical Review*. Ottawa: Statistics Canada, 2007 (Cat. No.71F0004XCB).

42. A. Campbell and N. Gagnon, *Literacy, Life and Employment: An Analysis of Canadian International Adult Literacy Survey (IALS) Microdata*. Ottawa: Conference Board of Canada, January 2006.

43. P. Bleyer, "Let's Make Productivity Work for Canadians," Canadian Council on Social Development, 2005, www.ccsd.ca/pr/2005/ccsd_prebudget.htm (January 6, 2007).

44. J. Bernier, *The Scope of Federal Labour Standards and Nontraditional Work Situations* (Submission to the Federal Labour Standards Review), October 2005, pp. 5–13.

45. J. Bernire, *The Scope of Federal Labour Standards and Nontraditional Work Situations*, October 2005, pp. 5–13; M. Townson, *Women in Non-Standard Jobs: The Public Policy Challenge*. Ottawa: Status of Women Canada, 2003; M. Townson, "The Impact of Precarious Employment," in L.O. Stone (ed.), *New Frontiers of Research on Retirement,* Statistics Canada, Catalogue No. 75-511-XIE, 2006, pp. 355–382; R.P. Chaykowski, *Non-standard Work and Economic Vulnerability*, Canadian Policy Research Network, Vulnerable Workers Series, No. 3 (March 2005); G. Valeé, *Towards Enhancing the Employment Conditions of Vulnerable Workers: A Public Policy Perspective,* Canadian Policy Research Network, Vulnerable Workers Series, No. 2 (March 2005).

46. M. Vartiainen, M. Hakonen, S. Koivisto, P. Mannonen, M. P. Nieminen, V. Ruohomaki, and A. Vartola, *Distributed and Mobile: Places, People ad Technology*. Helsinki Finland: Oy Yliopistokustannus University Press, 2007, p. 75.

47. C. Clark, "The World is Flat: Work-Life Trends to Watch," *Workspan* (January 2009), pp. 17–19.

48. K. Williams, "Privacy in a Climate of Electronic Surveillance," *Workplace News* (April 2005), p. 10.

49. P. Benimadhu, "Startling Business Shifts Causing a Rethink of Work," *InsideEdge*, Summer 2008, p. 10.

50. "Multinational Corporation," http://en.wikipedia.org/wiki/Multinational_corporation (August 17, 2006).

51. S. Nolen, "Step 1: Keep Workers Alive," *Globe & Mail* (August 5, 2006), pp. B4–B5.

52. U. Vu, "Climate change sparks attitude shift," *Canadian HR Reporter* (March 26, 2007), p. 11.

53. S. Dobson, "Fairmont finds it's easy being green," *Canadian HR Reporter* (March 26, 2007).

54. R. Stringer, *Leadership and Organizational Climate* (Upper Saddle River, NJ: Prentice-Hall, 2002).

55. F.W. Taylor, "The Principles of Scientific Management," in J.M. Sharfritz and J.S. Ott (eds.), *Classics of Organization Theory*, 2nd ed. (Chicago: The Dorsey Press, 1987), pp. 66–81.

56. D.G. Nickels, J.M. McHugh, S.M. McHugh, and P.D Berman, *Understanding Canadian Business*, 2nd ed. (Toronto: Irwin, 1997), p. 220.

57. This discussion is based on E.E. Lawler III, "Human Resources Management," *Personnel* (January 1988), pp. 24–25.

58. R.J. Cattaneo and A.J. Templer, "Determining the Effectiveness of Human Resources Management," T.H. Stone (ed.), *ASAC: Personnel and Human Resources Division Proceedings* (Halifax: St. Mary's University, June 1988), p. 73.

59. J. Pfeffer, *Competitive Advantage Through People* (Boston: Harvard Business School Press, 1994); E.E. Lawler, *Treat People Right* (San Francisco: Jossey-Bass, 2003); O. Parker, *It's the Journey That Matters: 2005 Strategic HR Transformation Tour* (Ottawa: The Conference Board of Canada, 2005).

60. E. Lawler III, "Becoming a Key Player in Business Strategy," *Workspan* (January 2006), pp. 10–13.

61. A. Aijala, B. Walsh and J. Schwartz, *Aligned at the Top: How Business and HR Executives View Today's Most Significant People Challenges—And What They're Doing About It.* Deloitte Development LLC, 2007.

62. *Canada's Demographic Revolution: Adjusting to an Aging Population* (Ottawa: The Conference Board of Canada, March 2006).

63. This section is based on www.cchra.ca.

64. C. Balthazard, "The difference between a professional association and a regulatory body," *Canadian HR Reporter* (August 11, 2008); C. Balthazard, "Regulatory agenda at HRPA," *Canadian HR Reporter* (November 3, 2008).

65. This section is based on www.cchra.ca.

66. S. Klie, "Senior HR designation unveiled," *Canadian HR Reporter* (July 7, 2009).

67. D. McDougall, "Employees Want an Ethical Work Environment," *Canadian HR Reporter* (April 10, 2000), p. 4.

68. S. Klie, "Most HR professionals have been coerced," *Canadian HR Reporter* (June 16, 2008).

69. "KPMG's Ethics Survey 2000—Managing for Ethical Practice," cited in L. Young, "Companies Not Doing Right," *Canadian HR Reporter* (April 10, 2000), p. 17.

70. Based on Walker Information Canada Inc. study, cited in J. Martin, "Studies Suggest a Link between Employees' Perception of a Firm's Ethics—and Loyalty," *Recruitment & Staffing*, Supplement to *Canadian HR Reporter* (September 20, 1999), p. G7; D. McDougall, "Employees Want an Ethical Work Environment," *Canadian HR Reporter* (April 10, 2000), p. 4.

71. Mountain Equipment Coop. www.mec.ca (July 29, 2009)

Chapter 2

1. "CIBC facing another $360-million class-action suit," *Canadian HR Reporter* (October 29, 2008); "KPMG to pay employees for unpaid overtime," *Canadian HR Reporter* (February 21, 2008); J.R. Smith, "Scotiabank becomes the latest target of unpaid overtime suit," *Canadian HR Reporter* (December 11, 2007); "KPMG faces $20 million overtime suit," *Canadian*

HR Reporter (September 5, 2007); S. Klie, "CIBC hit with $600-million lawsuit," *Canadian HR Reporter* (July 16, 2007); S. Dobson, "Plenty of exceptions to overtime rules," *Canadian HR Reporter* (July 16, 2007); "CIBC hit with overtime class-action lawsuit," *Canadian HR Reporter* (June 6, 2007).

2. S. Klie, "Feds discriminated against nurses," *Canadian HR Reporter* (February 25, 2008).

3. *Canadian Charter of Rights and Freedoms*, as part of the Constitution Act of 1982.

4. *Canadian Charter of Rights and Freedoms*, Section 15(1).

5. *Annual Report of the Canadian Human Rights Commission* (Ottawa: Government of Canada, 1991), p. 65.

6. Ontario Human Rights Commission, *Human Rights at Work* (Toronto: Government of Ontario, 1999), pp. 63–64.

7. S. Rudner, "Just cause—back from the dead?" *Canadian HR Reporter* (September 22, 2008); M. Bélanger and R. Ravary, "Supreme Court of Canada Sets Limits on Employer's Duty to Accommodate," *McCarthy Tétrault e-Alert* (July 24, 2008), D. Elenbaas, "Undue Hardship: Supreme Court of Canada Clarifies the Standard—or Does it?" *Ultimate HR Manual*, 39 (August 2008), pp. 1–3.

8. J.R. Smith, "Bipolar employee awarded $80,000" *Canadian HR Reporter* (April 7, 2008); C. Hall, "Just Because You Can't See Them Doesn't Mean They're Not There: 'Invisible Disabilities'," *Ultimate HR Manual*, 34 (March 2008), pp. 1–3; "Duty to Accommodate Mental Helath Disability Upheld in Landmark Ontario Human Rights Decision," *Ultimate HR Manual*, 33 (February 2008), p. 6.

9. A.P. Aggarwal, *Sex Discrimination: Employment Law and Practices* (Toronto: Butterworths Canada, 1994).

10. H.J. Jain, "Human Rights: Issues in Employment," *Human Resources Management in Canada* (Toronto: Prentice-Hall Canada, 1995), p. 50.

11. "Construction Firms Fight B.C. Human Rights Ruling," *HR Professional* (April/May 2009), p. 13.

12. "Key Provisions of Ottawa's Same-Sex Legislation," *Canadian HR Reporter* (March 27, 2000), p. 11.

13. Canadian Human Rights Commission, www.chrc-ccdp.ca/adr/settlements/archives2/page5-en.asp (August 13, 2006).

14. Canadian Human Rights Commission, www.chrc-ccdp.ca/discrimination/age-en.asp (August 13, 2006).

15. Ontario Human Rights Commission, www.ohrc.on.ca/english/publicatoins/age-policy_5.shtml (June 2, 2006).

16. S. Klie, "Muslims Face Discrimination in Workplace," *Canadian HR Reporter* (February 27, 2006).

17. H. Levitt and L-K Hum, "Accommodating family status," *Canadian HR Reporter* (January 12, 2009).

18. L. Corrente, "Accommodating Family Status," Torkin Maines Presentation (June 8, 2005).

19. S. Klie, "Harassment twice as bad for minority women," *Canadian HR Reporter* (April 10, 2006).

20. S. Dobson, "Tackling the bullies," *Canadian HR Reporter* (March 9, 2009).

21. B. Kuretzky, "When Push Comes to Shove," *Workplace News* (November/December 2005), p. 22; U. Vu, "Employers Waiting for Courts to Define Bullying," *Canadian HR Reporter* (September 12, 2005), pp. 1, 13.

22. "Saskatchewan's anti-bullying law now in effect," *Canadian HR Reporter* (October 4, 2007); S. Rudner, "Psychological harassment hurts employees, productivity," *Canadian HR Reporter* (October 21, 2007).

23. J.R. Smith, "Employers: Don't let workplace harassment catch you off guard," *Canadian HR Reporter* (October 22, 2007); *Anti-Harassment Policies for the Workplace: An Employer's Guide* (Canadian Human Rights Commission, March 2006), p. 3.

24. J.R. Smith, "Employer's damage control leads to big-time damages," *Canadian HR Reporter* (June 1, 2009); "Employer Vicariously Liable for Supervisor's Abusive Conduct," *Ultimate HR Manual*, 49 (June 2009), p. 7.

25. A.P. Aggarwal, *Sexual Harassment in the Workplace*, 2nd ed. (Toronto: Butterworths Canada, 1992), pp. 10–11.

26. N.C. MacDonald, "Keeping the bedroom out of the boardroom," *Canadian HR Reporter* (October 22, 2007).

27. *Anti-Harassment Policies for the Workplace: An Employer's Guide* (Canadian Human Rights Commission, March 2006), pp. 16–25.

28. *The Bottom Line: Corporate Performance and Women's Representation on Boards*. New York: Catalyst, 2007; *Women Matter: Gender diversity, a corporate performance driver*. New York: McKinsey & Company, 2007; *Groundbreakers*. New York: Ernst & Young, 2009.

29. *Women in Canada: Work Chapter Updates*, Statistics Canada, Catalogue No. 89F0133XIE, 2006.

30. K.A. Zavitz, "Intolerance costly problem for employers," *Canadian HR Reporter* (December 15, 2008).

31. C. Williams, "Disability in the Workplace," *Perspectives on Labour and Income* 7, no. 2 (February 2006), pp. 16–23.

32. D. Zietsma, *The Canadian Immigrant Labour Market in 2006: First Results from Canada's Labour Force Survey*. Statistics Canada Catalogue # 71-606-XWE2007001, September 2007; A. Sharpe, J-F Arsenault, S. Lapointe and F. Cowan, *The Effect of Increasing Aboriginal Educational Attainment on the Labour Force, Output and the Fiscal Balance*. (Ottawa: Centre for the Study of Living Standards, May 2009).

33. W. Cukier and M. Yap, *DiverseCity Counts: A Snapshot of Diversity in the Greater Toronto Area*. (Toronto: The Diversity Institute, Ryerson University, May 2009).

34. S. Klie, "Toronto losing out on diversity: Report," *Canadian HR Reporter* (December 15, 2008).

35. R.S. Abella, *Equality in Employment: A Royal Commission Report* (Ottawa: Supply and Services Canada, 1984).

36. A.B. Bakan and A. Kobyashi, *Employment Equity Policy in Canada: An Interprovincial Comparison* (Ottawa: Status of Women Canada, March 2000), pp. 9–10.

37. M.B. Currie, "Destined for Equity," *Human Resources Professional* (July/August 1993), pp. 7–8.

38. S. Klie, "Hail the new chief," *Canadian HR Reporter* (July 14, 2008).

39. B. Taylor, "Canoe trip with minister ripples across the ranks," *Toronto Star* (February 19, 2009), p. B6.

40. S. Klie, "Firms short on diversity practices: Report," *Canadian HR Reporter* (March 23, 2009).

41. D. Harder, "Diversity takes flight at Air Canada," *Canadian HR Reporter* (May 5, 2008).

42. S. Klie, "Aboriginal inclusion benefits all," *Canadian HR Reporter* (December 15, 2008).

43. L. Young, "Diversity drives KPMG to top," *Canadian HR Reporter* (March 24, 2008).

44. M. Swartz, "Employers Are Learning to Embrace Diversity," *Toronto Star* (January 8, 2004).

45. S. Klie, "Top employers know diversity is 'good business'," *Canadian HR Reporter* (May 5, 2008).

46. S. Klie, "Diversity makes employers more attractive to candidates," *Canadian HR Reporter* (April 20, 2009); S. Klie, "Top employers know diversity is 'good business'," *Canadian HR Reporter* (May 5, 2008).

47. S. Klie, "Top employers know diversity is 'good business'," *Canadian HR Reporter* (May 5, 2008).

48. S. Klie, "Firms short on diversity practices: Report," *Canadian HR Reporter* (March 23, 2009).

49. U. Vu, "FedEx Holds Managers Accountable for Diversity," *Canadian HR Reporter* (November 8, 2004), p. 3.

50. S. Parris, A.P. Cowan and N. Huggett, *Report on Diversity: Priorities, Practices and Performance in Canadian Organizations*. (Ottawa: The Conference Board of Canada, November 2006).

Chapter 3

1. "Companies Continue to Invest in HR Technology to Manage Workforce, Towers Perrin Reports." www.hrtools.com/training_performance/companies_continue_to_invest_in_hr_technology_to_manage_workforce

_towers_perrin_reports.aspx (August 26, 2008); Towers Perrin, www.towersperrin.com (August 20, 2008)

2. S. Shrivastava and J.B. Shaw, "Liberating HR Through Technology," *Human Resource Management* (Fall 2003), p. 201.

3. W.J. Jones and R.C. Hoell, "Human Resource Information System Courses: An Examination of Instructional Methods," *Journal of Information Systems Education* (Fall 2005), p. 321.

4. A.S. Targowski and S.P. Deshpande, "The Utility and Selection of an HRIS," *Advances in Competitiveness Research* (Autumn 2001), p. 42.

5. S. Shrivastava and J.B. Shaw, "Liberating HR Through Technology," *Human Resource Management* (Fall 2003), p. 201.

6. R. Zampetti and L. Adamson, "Web-Based Employee Self-Service: A Win–Win Proposition for Organizations and Employees," in A.J. Walker (ed.), *Web-Based Human Resources.* (New York NY: McGraw-Hill, 2001, p. 15.)

7. P. Vernon, "Delivering on the promise of HR transformation," (November 29, 2004). www.humanresourcesmagazine.com.au/articles/CB/0C0293CB.asp?Type=61&Category=872 (August 20, 2009).

8. P. Vernon, "Delivering on the promise of HR transformation," (November 29, 2004). www.humanresourcesmagazine.com.au/articles/CB/0C0293CB.asp?Type=61&Category=872 (August 20, 2009).

9. J. Schramm, "HR Technology Competencies: New Roles for HR Professionals," *2006 SHRM Research Quarterly,* p. 2.

10. P. Vernon, "Delivering on the promise of HR transformation," (November 29, 2004). www.humanresourcesmagazine.com.au/articles/CB/0C0293CB.asp?Type=61&Category=872 (August 20, 2009).

11. J. Collison, "2005 HR Technology Survey Report," *SHRM Research*, p. vii.

12. "HRIS for the HRIS Professional: What You Need to Know," *HR Focus* (June 2005), pp. 10–11.

13. E.E. Lawler III, "From Human Resource Management to Operational Effectiveness," *Human Resource Management* (Summer 2005), pp. 165–169.

14. W. Brockbank, "If HR Were Really Strategically Proactive: Present and Future Directions in HR's Contribution to Competitive Advantage," *Human Resource Management* (Winter 1999), pp. 337–352.

15. "2008 HR Service Delivery Report." www.towersperrin.com/tp/getwebcachedoc?web=USA/2008/200810/HRSDExecutiveReport2008.pdf (September 2008).

16. S. Shrivastava and J.B. Shaw, "Liberating HR Through Technology," *Human Resource Management* (Fall 2003), p. 201.

17. J. Johnston, "What Does It Take to Put in an HRMS?" *Canadian HR Reporter* (October 22, 2001), p. G3.

18. A. Doran, "HRMS in the New Millenium: What will the next 10 years bring us and what is the international perspective?" in *21 Tomorrows New Formula: Concept-Driven Innovation through Strategic HR* (2000) pp. 29–35.

19. W.J. Jones and R.C. Hoell, "Human Resource Information System Courses: An Examination of Instructional Methods," *Journal of Information Systems Education* (Fall 2005), pp. 321–329

20. A.R. Hendrickson, "Human Resource Information Systems: Backbone Technology of Contemporary Human Resources," *Journal of Labor Research* (Summer 2003), p. 381.

21. M.J. Kavanaugh and M. Thite, *Human Resource Information Systems.* (Thousand Oaks, CA: Sage Publications, 2009.)

22. M.J. Kavanaugh and M. Thite, *Human Resource Information Systems.* (Thousand Oaks, CA: Sage Publications, 2009.)

23. E.W.T. Ngai and F.K.T. Wat, "Human Resource Information Systems: A Review and Empirical Analysis," Department of Management and Marketing, The Hong Kong Polytechnic University (July 7, 2004), p. 297.

24. R. Zampetti and L. Adamson, "Web-Based Employee Self-Service: A Win–Win Proposition for Organizations and Employees," in A.J. Walker (ed.), *Web-Based Human Resources.* (New York NY: McGraw-Hill, 2001, p. 15).

25. M. Mayfield, "Human Resource Information Systems: A Review and Model Development," *Advances in Competitiveness Research* (January 1, 2003), pp. 139–152.

26. A.R. Hendrickson, "Human Resource Information Systems: Backbone Technology of Contemporary Human Resources," *Journal of Labor Research* (Summer 2003), p. 381.

27. A.S. Targowski and S.P. Deshpande, "The Utility and Selection of an HRIS," *Advances in Competitiveness Research* (Autumn 2001), p. 42.

28. M.J. Kavanaugh and M. Thite, *Human Resource Information Systems.* California: Sage Publications, 2009.

29. M. Mayfield, "Human Resource Information Systems: A Review and Model Development," *Advances in Competitiveness Research* (January 1, 2003), pp. 139–152.

30. Human Resources and Social Development Canada, "Employment Equity Computerized Reporting System (EECRS) Software," www.hrsdc.gc.ca/asp/gateway.asp?hr=en/lp/lo/lswe/we/ee_tools/software/eecrs/index-we.shtml&hs=wzp (August 17, 2006).

31. J. Sullivan, "The Six Levels of HRIS Technology," in R.H. Stambaugh (ed.), *21 Tomorrows: HR Systems in the Emerging Workplace of the 21st Century*, pp. 79–86 (Dallas: Rector Duncan & Associates, 2000).

32. W.J. Jones and R.C. Hoell, "Human Resource Information System Courses: An Examination of Instructional Methods," *Journal of Information Systems Education* (Fall 2005), p. 326.

33. J.W. Boudreau, "Talentship and HR Measurement and Analysis: From ROI to Strategic Organizational Change," *Human Resource Planning* (2006), p. 30.

34. G. Safran, "Getting the I out of your HRZIS," *Canadian HR Reporter* (Feb 26, 2001), p. 21.

35. J. Schramm, "HR Technology Competencies: New Roles for HR Professionals," *2006 SHRM Research Quarterly*, p. 2.

36. J. Johnston, "What Does It Take to Put in an HRMS?" *Canadian HR Reporter* (October 22, 2001), p. G3.

37. S. Shrivastava and J.B. Shaw, "Liberating HR Through Technology," *Human Resource Management* (Fall 2003), pp. 201–215.

38. A.R. Hendrickson, "Human Resource Information Systems: Backbone Technology of Contemporary Human Resources," *Journal of Labor Research* (Summer 2003), p. 381.

39. J.G. Meade, *The Human Resources Software Handbook* (San Francisco, CA: Jossey-Bass/Pfeiffer, 2003) p. 85.

40. "Bridgefield Group ERP/Supply Chain Glossary," http://bridgefieldgroup.com/bridgefieldgroup/glos2.htm (June 29, 2006).

41. A.R. Hendrickson, "Human Resource Information Systems: Backbone Technology of Contemporary Human Resources," *Journal of Labor Research* (Summer 2003), p. 381–394; J.G. Meade, *The Human Resources Software Handbook* (San Francisco: Jossey-Bass/Pfeiffer, 2003) p. 85.

42. SAP AG, www.en.wikipedia.org/wiki/SAP_(company) (June 17, 2006); SAP Canada, www.sap.com (January 8, 2007).

43. PeopleSoft, http://en.wikipedia.org/ciki/PeopleSoft (June 17, 2006); Oracle, www.oracle.com (June 17, 2006).

44. V. Gerson, "CIBC Taps PeopleSoft HR System," *Bank Systems 1 Technology* (February 2002), p. 16.

45. Halogen Software. www.halogensoftware.com (June 29, 2006).

46. S. Shrivastava and J.B. Shaw, "Liberating HR Through Technology," *Human Resource Management* (Fall 2003), pp. 201–215; J.G. Meade, *The Human Resources Software Handbook* (San Francisco: Jossey-Bass/Pfeiffer, 2003) p. 85.

47. J.G. Meade, *The Human Resources Software Handbook* (San Francisco, CA: Jossey-Bass/Pfeiffer, 2003) p. 85.

48. J.C. Hubbard, K.A. Forcht, and D.S. Thomas, "Human Resource Information Systems: An Overview of Current Ethical and Legal Issues," *Journal of Business Ethics* (September 1998), pp. 1320–1321.

49. K.A. Kovach, A.A. Hughes, P. Fagan, and P.G. Maggitti, "Administrative and Strategic Advantages of HRIS," *Employment Relations Today* (Summer 2002), p. 46.

50. J. Caplan, "eHR in Greater China: The Future of HR Takes Flight," *China Staff* (March 2004), p. 3.

51. B. Jorgensen, "eHR Is Playing a Larger Role in Corporate Communications: But Companies Must Make a Business for Additional Spending," *Electronic Business* (August 2002), p. 36.

52. "Which HRIS Technologies Best Support the Vital Workplace?" *HR Focus* (February 2000), p. 6.

53. "Glossary of Distance Education Terms," www.tamu.edu/ode/glossary.html (January 8, 2007).

54. G. Downey, "Use of Self-Service HR Skyrockets," *Computing Canada* (February 1, 2002), pp. 1–2.

55. R. Zampetti and L. Adamson, "Web-Based Employee Self-Service: A Win–Win Proposition for Organizations and Employees," in A.J. Walker (ed.), *Web-Based Human Resources.* (New York: McGraw-Hill, 2001), p. 15; H.C. Gueutal and D.L. Stone, *The Brave New World of eHR* (San Francisco: Jossey-Bass, 2005), p. 192.

56. R. Zampetti and L. Adamson, "Web-Based Employee Self-Service: A Win–Win Proposition for Organizations and Employees," in A.J. Walker (ed.), *Web-Based Human Resources.* (New York NY: McGraw-Hill, 2001, p. 15).

57. Interactive Voice Response, www.hr-software.net/pages/216.htm (June 8, 2006).

58. "Do More to Get More from HR Systems," *HR Focus* (Jun 2006), p. 3.

59. P. MacInnis, "Toronto Police Services Ramps Up for Self-Serve HR," *Computing Canada* (October 11, 2002), p. 10.

60. D. Robb, "Unifying Your Enterprise with a Global HR Portal," *HRMagazine* (March 2006), p. 110.

61. "Do More to Get More from HR Systems," *HR Focus* (Jun 2006), p. 3.

62. "Do More to Get More from HR Systems," *HR Focus* (Jun 2006), p. 3.

63. Industry Canada, "Strategis: Canada's Business and Consumer Site," http://strategis.ic.gc.ca (January 8, 2007).

64. 2008 HR Service Delivery Report. www.towersperrin.com/tp/getwebcachedoc?web=USA/2008/200810/HRSDExecutiveReport2008.pdf (September 2008).

65. J.G. Meade, *The Human Resources Software Handbook* (San Francisco: Jossey-Bass/Pfeiffer, 2003) p. 85.

66. "What's New," *HRMagazine* (January 2005), p. 107.

67. ExecuTRACK Solutions, www.execctrack.com (June 29, 2006).

68. Organizational Charts by Human Concepts, www.orgplus.com (June 29, 2006).

69. Companies Aim to Transform HR Delivery Strategy to Meet New Employee Needs, Watson Wyatt Study Finds. www.watsonwyatt.com/news/press.asp?ID=17525 (August 20, 2009).

70. T.J. Keebler and D.W. Rhodes, "E-HR Becoming the 'Path of Least Resistance'," *Employment Relations Today* (Summer 2002), pp. 57–58.

71. D. Brown, "eHR—Victim of Unrealistic Expectations," *Canadian HR Reporter* (March 11, 2002), p. 2.

72. J. Collison, "2005 HR Technology Survey Report," *SHRM Research*, pp. 3–4.

73. S. Shrivastava and J.B. Shaw, "Liberating HR Through Technology," *Human Resource Management* (Fall 2003), p. 205

74. J. Sullivan, "The Six Levels of HRIS Technology," in R.H. Stambaugh (ed.), *21 Tomorrows: HR Systems in the Emerging Workplace of the 21st Century*, pp. 79–86 (Dallas: Rector Duncan & Associates, 2000).

75. National Center for Education Statistics, US Department of Education, Institute of Education Sciences, Technology @ Your Fingertips Glossary. http://nces.ed.gov/pubs98/tech/glossary.asp (June 29, 2006)

76. J. Sullivan, "The Six Levels of HRIS Technology," in R.H. Stambaugh (ed.), *21 Tomorrows: HR Systems in the Emerging Workplace of the 21st Century*, (Dallas, TX: Rector Duncan & Associates, 2000), pp. 79–86.

77. R. Henson, "HR 20/20: Clarifying the View of HR in Year 2020," in R.H. Stambaugh (ed.), *21 Tomorrows: HR Systems in the Emerging Workplace of the 21st Century*, (Dallas, TX: Rector Duncan & Associates, 2000), pp. 11–16.

78. Hackett Group, *World-Class HR Metrics: World-Class Spend Less Yet Achieve Higher effectiveness.* (July 25, 2006).

79. R. Zampetti and L. Adamson, "Web-based Employee Self-Service: A Win–Win Proposition for Organizations and Employees," in A. J. Walker (ed.), *Web-Based Human Resources.* (New York NY: McGraw-Hill, 2001, p. 15).

80. "HRIS in 2010 (or Sooner!): Experts Predict Use of Wrist Mounted Devised, Virtual HR Access, and HR Voice Recognition," *Managing HR Information Systems* (February 2002), pp. 1–4.

81. Companies Aim to Transform HR Delivery Strategy to Meet New Employee Needs, Watson Wyatt Study Finds. www.watsonwyatt.com/news/press.asp?ID=17525 (August 20, 2009).

82. J. Sullivan Ph.D., "The Six Levels of HRIS Technology," in R.H. Stambaugh (ed.), *21 Tomorrows: HR Systems in the Emerging Workplace of the 21st Century,* (Dallas, TX: Rector Duncan & Associates, 2000), pp. 79–86.

83. L.A. Weatherly, "HR Technology: Leveraging the Shift to Self-Service—It's Time to Go Strategic," *HRMagazine* (March 2005), p. A1.

84. "Human Resource Outsourcing Gains Traction, Says Aberdeen Group; Report Cites Growing Use of Outsourcing," *Business Wire* (January 23, 2006), p. 1.

Chapter 4

1. C. Babbage, *On the Economy of Machinery and Manufacturers* (London: Charles Knight, 1832), pp. 169–76; reprinted in Joseph Litterer, *Organizations* (New York: John Wiley and Sons, 1969), pp. 73–75.

2. F. Herzberg, "One More Time, How Do You Motivate Employees?" *Harvard Business Review* 46 (January–February 1968), pp. 53–62.

3. G.M. Parker, *Cross-Functional Teams: Working with Allies, Enemies and Other Strangers* (San Francisco: Jossey-Bass, 2003), p. 68.

4. "Collaboration for Virtual Teams," *HR Professional* (December 2002/January 2003), p. 44.

5. J.A. Veitch, K.E. Charles, and G.R. Newsham, "Workstation Design for the Open-Plan Office," *Construction Technology Update*, 61 (October 2004), http://irc.nrc-cnrc.gc.ca/pubs/ctus/61_e.html (May 31, 2009).

6. J. Heerwagen, K. Kelly, and K. Kampschroer, "The Changing Nature of Organizations, Work, and Workplace," *Whole Building Design Group (WBDG), National Institute of Building Sciences* (February 2006).

7. R. I. Henderson, *Compensation Management in a Knowledge-Based World* (Upper Saddle River, NJ: Prentice-Hall, 2003), pp. 135–138. See also P.W. Wright and K. Wesley, "How to Choose the Kind of Job Analysis You Really Need," *Personnel* 62 (May 1985), pp. 51–55; C.J. Cranny and M.E. Doherty, "Importance Ratings in Job Analysis: Note on the Misinterpretation of Factor Analyses," *Journal of Applied Psychology* (May 1988), pp. 320–322.

8. Note that the PAQ (and other quantitative techniques) can also be used for job evaluation.

9. E. Cornelius III, F. Schmidt, and T. Carron, "Job Classification Approaches and the Implementation of Validity Generalization Results," *Personnel Psychology* 37 (Summer 1984), pp. 247–260; E. Cornelius III, A. DeNisi, and A. Blencoe, "Expert and Naïve Raters Using the PAQ: Does It Matter?" *Personnel Psychology* 37 (Autumn 1984), pp. 453–464; L. Friedman and R. Harvey, "Can Raters with Reduced Job Description Information Provide Accurate Position Analysis Questionnaire (PAQ) Ratings?" *Personnel Psychology* 34 (Winter 1986), pp. 779–789; R. J. Harvey et al., "Dimensionality of the Job Element Inventory, A Simplified Worker-oriented Job Analysis Questionnaire," *Journal of Applied Psychology* (November 1988), pp. 639–646; S. Butler and R. Harvey, "A Comparison of Holistic versus Decomposed Rating of Position Analysis Questionnaire Work Dimensions," *Personnel Psychology* (Winter 1988), pp. 761–772.

10. This discussion is based on H. Olson et al., "The Use of Functional Job Analysis in Establishing Performance Standards for Heavy Equipment Operators," *Personnel Psychology* 34 (Summer 1981), pp. 351–364.

11. Human Resources Development Canada, *National Occupation Classification Career Handbook*, 2006.

12. R. Reiter-Palmon et al., "Development of an O*NET Web-Based Job Analysis and Its Implementation in the U.S. Navy: Lessons Learned," *Human Resource Management Review* 16, 2006, pp. 294–309.

13. R. J. Plachy, "Writing Job Descriptions That Get Results," *Personnel* (October 1987), pp. 56–58. See also M. Mariani, "Replace with a Database," *Occupational Outlook Quarterly* 43 (Spring 1999), pp. 2–9.

14. J. Evered, "How to Write a Good Job Description," *Supervisory Management* (April 1981), p. 16.

15. J. Evered, "How to Write a Good Job Description," *Supervisory Management* (April 1981), p. 18.

16. P.H. Raymark, M.J. Schmidt, and R.M. Guion, "Identifying Potentially Useful Personality Constructs for Employee Selection," *Personnel Psychology* 50 (1997), pp. 723–726.

17. Next two sections based on Jeffrey Shippmann et al., "The Practice of Competency Modeling," *Personnel Psychology* 53, no. 3 (2000), p. 703; P. Singh, "Job analysis for a changing workplace," *Human Resource Management Review*, 18, 2008, pp. 87–99.

18. Adapted from Richard Mirabile, "Everything You Wanted to Know About Competency Modeling," *Training and Development* 51, no. 8 (August 1997), pp. 73–78.

19. Dennis Kravetz, "Building a Job Competency Database: What the Leaders Do," Kravetz Associates (Bartlett, Illinois, 1997).

Chapter 5

1. S. Klie, "Guesses just don't cut it anymore," *Canadian HR Reporter* (March 24, 2008).

2. O. Parker, *Too Few People, Too Little Time: The Employer Challenge of an Aging Workforce* (Conference Board of Canada Executive Action, July 2006).

3. *Are Canadian Firms Prepared for the Boomer Exodus from the Workforce?* Toronto: Life's Next Steps and Human Resources Professionals Association, 2008; S. Armstrong, "Employers unprepared for boomers retirements," *Canadian HR Reporter* (December 1, 2008); "Most Canadian Companies Not Prepared for Baby Boomer Retirement," *Workspan* (December 2008).

4. J.W. Walker, "Human Resource Planning, 1990s Style," *Human Resource Planning* 13, no. 4 (1990), pp. 229–240; D. Ulrich, "Strategic and Human Resource Planning: Linking Customers and Employees," *Human Resource Planning* 15, no. 2 (1992), pp. 47–62.

5. S.Klie, "Canada needs national solution to health HR planning: Report," *Canadian HR Reporter* (December 3, 2007); L. Young, "Government's Unique Incentive Plan Falls Short of Retention Mark, Nurses Contend," *Canadian HR Reporter* (March 13, 2000), p. 8.

6. S. Klie, "Nursing grads can't find jobs: association," *Canadian HR Reporter* (June 18, 2007).

7. U.Vu, "Aging Nurses Spell Trouble," *Canadian HR Reporter* (January 17, 2005), pp. 1–2; U. Vu, "Nursing Needs Mending: Reports," *Canadian HR Reporter* (June 6, 2005), pp. 1, 3.

8. L. Young, "Supply of workers drying up fast," *Canadian HR Reporter* (January 28, 2008).

9. J. Langton, "Accountants Offer Two Cents on Aging Workforce," *Canadian HR Reporter* (February 28, 2005).

10. G. Milkovich, A.J. Annoni, and T.A. Mahoney, "The Use of Delphi Procedures in Manpower Forecasting," *Management Science* (1972), pp. 381–388.

11. A.L. Delbecq, A.H. Van DelVen, and D.H. Gustafson, *Group Techniques for Program Planning: A Guide to Nominal and Delphi Processes* (Glenview, IL: Scott Foresman, 1975).

12. "Federal retirements on the rise: StatsCan," *Canadian HR Reporter* (May 16, 2008).

13. This is a modification of a definition found in P. Wallum, "A Broader View of Succession Planning," *Personnel Management* (September 1993), pp. 43–44.

14. G. Lowe, "Retiring Baby Boomers Open to Options, But Get Them Before They Leave," *Canadian HR Reporter* (March 10, 2003), p. 6.

15. A. Shaw, "Immigrants fill construction gaps in B.C.," *Canadian HR Reporter* (January 29, 2007); S.Klie, "Service sector turns to foreign workers," *Canadian HR Reporter* (January 15, 2007); B. Cheadle, "High-Skill Immigrants Drive Labour Force Growth but Job Prospects Still Grim," *Canadian Press Newswire* (February 11, 2003).

16. "Canada expects up to 265,000 new immigrants in 2009," *Canadian HR Reporter* (December 10, 2008); "BC creates employment council to address challenges for immigrant workers," *Workplace* (November/December 2008); "Manitoba hires first fairness commissioner for qualifications recognition," *Workplace* (November/December 2008); J. Yang, "Help aimed at foreign workers," *The Edmonton Journal* (July 11, 2008); D. Harder, "Rules eased in B.C., Alberta, for temp foreign workers," *Canadian HR Reporter* (November 5, 2007); S. Klie, "Immigrant employment model goes national," *Canadian HR Reporter* (October 22, 2007); K. Allen, "Engineering a better way," *Canadian HR Reporter* (June 18, 2007); "Provincial nominee programs from coast to coast," *Canadian HR Reporter* (March 26, 2007).

17. C. Fleming, "Program bridges transitions for skilled immigrants," *Workplace* (May/June 2007).

18. G. Nixon, "The Immigrant Imperative: Why Canada Can't Afford to Continue to Waste the Skills of Newcomers," *Canadian HR Reporter* (July 18, 2005), p. 19.

19. A. Coughlin, *Alberta's Labour Shortage Just the Tip of the Iceberg* (Conference Board of Canada Executive Action, 2006); G. Hodgson and G. McGowan, "Taking Sides: Is Alberta's Labour Shortage a Doomsday Scenario?" *Canadian HR Reporter* (July 17, 2006); P. Brethour, "Oil Patch Labour Crisis Seen Spreading to Rest of Country; Husky Head Raises Alarm Over Rising Costs, Saying Projects at Risk," *Globe and Mail* (April 20, 2006).

20. "Mining industry needs 80,000 workers," *Canadian HR Reporter* (March 26, 2007), p. 2; S. Klie, "Construction demand outpaces labour growth," *Canadian HR Reporter* (September 10, 2007); "Non-profits facing labour shortage," *Canadian HR Reporter* (July 9, 200&); U. Vu, "Mounties prepare for recruiting spree," *Canadian HR Reporter* (October 23, 2006); "Manufacturing Sector Labours to Address Human Resources Issues," Conference Board of Canada *InsideEdge* (Spring 2008), p. 18; S. Klie, "Short circuiting labour supply," *Canadian HR Reporter* (December 15, 2008).

21. *Canadian Perspectives on ICT Outsourcing and Offshoring*. Toronto ON: IDC, 2007; S. Klie, "IT offshoring growing," *Canadian HR Reporter* (October 22, 2007); L. Young, "IT university enrolment plunges," *Canadian HR Reporter* (December 3, 2007); S; Klie, "Price tag of IT shortage: $10 billion per year," *Canadian HR Reporter* (February 11, 2008); S. Klie, "Women could solve IT worker shortage," *Canadian HR Reporter* (October 20, 2008).

22. H. Sokoloff, "Legal Exodus," *National Post* (March 17, 2005), p. FP3; "Baby Boomers an HR Problem for Funeral Services," *Canadian HR Reporter* (January 16, 2006), p. 2; "Today's Forecast: Meteorologist Shortage," *Canadian HR Reporter* (December 5, 2005), p. 2; "Engineers in Short Supply," *Canadian HR Reporter* (November 21, 2005), p. 2; S. Klie, "Fewer Accountants Is a Bad Thing—Really," *Canadian HR Reporter* (February 13, 2006), p. 3; "Alberta Labour Shortage Draining Civil Service," *Canadian HR Reporter* (January 30, 2006), p. 2.

23. "Stripper shortage forces Ontario clubs to get creative," *Canadian HR Reporter* (June 10, 2008).

24. "Feds help employers avoid layoffs," *HR Professional* (June/July 2009), p. 12.

25. M. MacKillop, "Ballpark Justice," *Human Resources Professional* (September 1994), pp. 10–11.

26. W.F. Cascio and C.E. Young, "Financial Consequences of Employment Change Decisions in Major U.S. Corporations: 1982–2000," in K.P. DeMeuse and M.L. Marks (eds.), *Resizing the Organization*, pp. 131–156 (San Francisco: Jossey-Bass, 2003).

27. O. Parker, *Too Few People, Too Little Time: The Employer Challenge of an Aging Workforce* (Conference Board of Canada Executive Action, July 2006).

28. D. Brown, "Training Older Workers Can Offset Shortages Due to Aging: Report," *Canadian HR Reporter* (September 13, 2004), pp. 3, 13; M. Potter, "A Golden Opportunity: Older Workers Step Up to the Plate," *WorldatWork Canadian News* (Third Quarter 2005), pp. 8–11; V. Galt, "Firms See Value in Putting Retirees Back to Work," *Globe & Mail* (September 8, 2004), p. B7; G. Lowe, "Are You Ready to Tap Older Workers' Talents?" *Canadian HR Reporter* (February 27, 2006); S. Klie, "Poor Health Thinning Ranks of Older Workers," *Canadian HR Reporter* (March 27, 2006).

29. S. Klie, "People with disabilities a labour solution," *Canadian HR Reporter* (November 5, 2007); S. Klie, "Cities Face Off over Talent," *Canadian HR Reporter* (February 13, 2006), pp. 1, 4; S. Klie, "Nunavut Trade School Will Tackle Labour Shortage," *Canadian HR Reporter* (April 24, 2006); "B.C. Sets Aside $400 Million for Training and Skills," *Canadian HR Reporter* (March 13, 2006), p. 2; K. Howlett, "Ontario Expands College Apprentice Programs," *Globe & Mail* (August 27, 2005), p. A9.

30. S. Klie, "Sask. Turns on the charm," *Canadian HR Reporter* (April 20, 2009); S. Klie, "Hot economy keeps grads in Saskatchewan," *Canadian HR Reporter* (September 24, 2007).

31. G. Lowe, "Are You Ready to Tap Older Workers' Talents?" *Canadian HR Reporter* (February 27, 2006).

32. K. Eckler and B. Kofman, "Handling the next generation of leaders' demand for work–life balance," *Canadian HR Reporter* (November 6, 2006).

33. H. Sokoloff, "Legal Exodus," *National Post* (March 17, 2005), p. FP3; S. Klie, "Work–Life Balance Elusive for Most Lawyers," *Canadian HR Reporter* (January 16, 2006), pp. 1, 3.

34. "Work Pressure Is Top Cause of Stress," *Workplace Today* (January 2001), p. 6.

35. L. Duxbury, *Dealing with Work–Life Issues in the Workplace: Standing Still Is Not an Option*, 2004, Don Wood Lecture in Industrial Relations, Industrial Relations Centre, Queen's University.

36. L.F. Thompson and K.R. Aspinwall, "The recruitment value of work/life benefits," *Personnel Review*, 38(2), 2009, pp. 195–210; B. Parus, "Pump Up Your Flexibility Quotient," *Workspan* (August 2004), pp. 47–53; J.T. Bond, E. Galinsky, and E.J. Hill, "Flexibility: A Critical Ingredient in Creating an Effective Workplace," *Workspan* (February 2005), pp. 17–20; F. Giancola, "Flexible Schedules: A Win–Win Reward," *Workspan* (July 2005), pp. 52–54.

37. P. Kulig, "Flextime Increasing in Popularity With Employers," *Canadian HR Reporter* (September 7, 1998), pp. 1, 3.

38. L. Cassiani, "Women Consider Leaving for Better Work–Life Balance," *Canadian HR Reporter* (August 13, 2001), pp. 1, 14.

39. S. Singh, "When the Going Gets Tough, the Tough Hold on to Top Employees," *Canadian HR Reporter* (January 13, 2003), p. 17.

40. C. Sladek and E. Hollander, "Where is Everyone? The Rise of Workplace Flexibility," *Benefits Quarterly*, 25(2), 2009, pp. 17–22; M. Madigan, J. Norton, and I. Testa, "The Quest for Work–Life Balance," *Benefits Canada* (November 1999), p. 113.

41. N. Verma, "Making the Most of Virtual Working," *WorldatWork Journal* (Second Quarter 2005), pp. 15–23.

42. S. Klie, "Mistrust 'number one barrier' to telework," *Canadian HR Reporter* (June 2, 2008).

43. D. Brown, "Telework Not Meeting Expectations—But Expectations Were 'Nonsense,'" *Canadian HR Reporter* (February 24, 2003), pp. 3, 11.

44. C. Sladek and E. Hollander, "Where is Everyone? The Rise of Workplace Flexibility," *Benefits Quarterly*, 25(2), 2009, pp. 17–22.

45. B. Aldrige, "Innovative Workplace Practices," *Workplace Gazette* (May 15, 2006).

Chapter 6

1. G. Bouchard, "Strong employer brand can tap scarce resource: Talent," *Canadian HR Reporter*, November 19, 2007, p. 10.

2. "Effective Recruiting Tied to Stronger Financial Performance," *WorldatWork Canadian News* (Fourth Quarter 2005), pp. 18–19.

3. K. Peters, "Public Image Ltd," *HR Professional*, December 2007/January 2008, pp. 24–30; S. Klie, "Getting employees to come to you," *Canadian HR Reporter*, November 19, 2007, pp. 9–10; S. Klie, "Tuning into TV's recruitment reach," *Canadian HR Reporter*, September 25, 2006.

4. G. Bouchard, "Strong employer brand can tap scarce resource: Talent," *Canadian HR Reporter*, November 19, 2007, p. 10.

5. K. Peters, "Public Image Ltd," *HR Professional*, December 2007/January 2008, pp. 24–30; G. Bouchard, "Strong employer brand can tap scarce resource: Talent," *Canadian HR Reporter*, November 19, 2007, p. 10; M. Morra, "Best in show," *Workplace News*, September/October 2006,

pp. 17–21; M. Shuster, "Employment branding: The law of attraction!" *Workplace*, January/February 2008, pp. 14–15.

6. M. Morra, "Best in show," *Workplace News*, September/October 2006, pp. 17–21.

7. G. Bouchard, "Strong employer brand can tap scarce resource: Talent," *Canadian HR Reporter*, November 19, 2007, p. 10.

8. S. Klie, "Getting employees to come to you," *Canadian HR Reporter*, November 19, 2007, pp. 9–10; M. Shuster, "Employment branding: The law of attraction!" *Workplace*, January/February 2008, pp. 14–15.

9. K. Peters, "Public Image Ltd," *HR Professional*, December 2007/January 2008, pp. 24–30; S. Dobson, "The little school bus company that could," *Canadian HR Reporter*, April 23, 2007.

10. M. Shuster, "Employment branding: The law of attraction!" *Workplace*, January/February 2008, pp. 14–15.

11. A. Watanabe, "From Brown to Green, What Colour is Your Employment Brand?" *HR Professional*, February/March 2008, pp. 47–49.

12. M. Morra, "Best in show," *Workplace News*, September/October 2006, pp. 17–21.

13. R. Milgram, "Getting the most out of online job ads," *Canadian HR Reporter*, January 28, 2008.

14. K. Peters, "Public Image Ltd," *HR Professional*, December 2007/January 2008, pp. 24–30; S. Klie, "Getting employees to come to you," *Canadian HR Reporter*, November 19, 2007, pp. 9–10.

15. S. Klie, "Getting employees to come to you," *Canadian HR Reporter*, November 19, 2007, pp. 9–10; M. Shuster, "Employment branding: The law of attraction!" *Workplace*, January/February 2008, pp. 14–15.

16. "Recruitment Tops HR Areas Expecting 'Enormous Change,'" *Canadian HR Reporter* (December 6, 2004), p. G3; *Hewitt Associates Timely Topic Survey* (February 2004).

17. D. Dahl and P. Pinto, "Job Posting, an Industry Survey," *Personnel Journal* (January 1977), pp. 40–41.

18. J. Daum, "Internal Promotion—Psychological Asset or Debit? A Study of the Effects of Leader Origin," *Organizational Behavior and Human Performance* 13 (1975), pp. 404–413.

19. See, for example, A. Harris, "Hiring Middle Management: External Recruitment or Internal Promotion?" *Canadian HR Reporter* (April 10, 2000), pp. 8–10.

20. U. Vu, "Security Failures Expose Resumes," *Canadian HR Reporter* (May 24, 2003); P. Lima, "Talent Shortage? That Was Yesterday. Online Recruiters Can Deliver More Candidates for Your Job Openings and Help You Find Keepers," *Profit: The Magazine for Canadian Entrepreneurs* (February/March 2002), pp. 65–66; "Online Job Boards," *Canadian HR Reporter* (February 11, 2002), pp. G11–G15.

21. U. Vu, "Security Failures Expose Resumes," *Canadian HR Reporter* (May 24, 2003).

22. S. Bury, "Face-based recruiting," *Workplace*, September/October 2008, pp. 19–21.

23. G. Stanton, "Recruiting Portals Take Centre Stage in Play for Talent," *Canadian HR Reporter* (September 25, 2000), pp. G1–G2.

24. A. da Luz, "Video enhances online job ads," *Canadian HR Reporter*, February 11, 2008.

25. D. Brown, "Canadian Government Job Boards Lag on Best Practices," *Canadian HR Reporter* (January 13, 2003), p. 2.

26. T. Martell, "Resume Volumes Push Firms to Web," *ComputerWorld Canada* (April 7, 2000), p. 45.

27. A. Altass, "E-Cruiting: A Gen X Trend or Wave of the Future?" *HR Professional* (June–July 2000), p. 33.

28. "Corporate Spending Millions on Ineffective Web Recruiting Strategies," *Canadian HR Reporter* (September 25, 2000), p. G5.

29. A. Snell, "Best Practices for Web Site Recruiting," *Canadian HR Reporter* (February 26, 2001), pp. G7, G10.

30. D. Brown, "Who's Looking Online? Most Firms Don't Know," *Canadian HR Reporter* (August 13, 2001), pp. 2, 12; "Corporate Spending Millions on

Ineffective Web Recruiting Strategies," *Canadian HR Reporter* (September 25, 2000), p. G5; A. Snell, "Best Practices for Web Site Recruiting," *Canadian HR Reporter* (February 26, 2001), pp. G7, G10.

31. S. Bury, "Face-based recruiting," *Workplace*, September/October 2008, pp. 19–21.

32. D. Harder, "Recruiting in age of social networking," *Canadian HR Reporter*, April 21, 2008.

33. L. Barrington and J. Shelp, "Looking for Employees in *All* the Right Places," *The Conference Board Executive Action Series* (December 2005).

34. A. Pell, *Recruiting and Selecting Personnel* (New York: Regents, 1969), pp. 16–34.

35. Statistics Canada, *The Daily* (April 8, 2005); Association of Canadian Search, Employment and Staffing Services (ACSESS), "Media Kit: Media Fact Sheet," www.acsess.org/NEWS/factsheet.asp (May 31, 2009).

36. J.A. Parr, "7 Reasons Why Executive Searches Fail," *Canadian HR Reporter* (March 12, 2001), pp. 20, 23.

37. Association of Canadian Search, Employment and Staffing Services (ACSESS), www.acsess.org (August 8, 2006).

38. A. Doran, "Technology Brings HR to Those Who Need It," *Canadian HR Reporter* (October 6, 1997), p. 8.

39. M. Sharma, "Welcome Back!" *HR Professional*, February/March 2006, pp. 38–40; E. Simon, "You're leaving the company? Well, don't be a stranger," *Globe and Mail*, December 22, 2006, p. B16.

40. U. Vu, "EnCana Builds Talent Pipeline into High School Classrooms," *Canadian HR Reporter* (April 11, 2005), p. 3.

41. Halifax Career Fair, www.halifaxcareerfairs.com (May 31, 2009).

42. Career Edge, www.careeredge.ca (May 31, 2009).

43. N. Laurie and M. Laurie, "No Holds Barred in Fight for Students to Fill Internship Programs," *Canadian HR Reporter* (January 17, 2000), pp. 15–16.

44. Service Canada, Job Bank, http://jb-ge.hrdc-drhc.gc.ca (May 31, 2009).

45. Human Resources Professionals Association of Ontario, www.hrpao.org (June 25, 2003).

46. D. Hurl, "Letting the Armed Forces Train Your Managers," *Canadian HR Reporter* (December 3, 2001), pp. 8–9.

47. L. MacGillivray, "Cashing in on the Canadian Forces," *Workplace Today* (October 2001), pp. 40–41.

48. L. Blake, "Ready-trained, untapped source of skilled talent—courtesy Canadian Forces," *Workplace*. www.workplace-mag.com (December 2, 2008).

49. T. Lende, "Workplaces Looking to Hire Part-Timers," *Canadian HR Reporter* (April 22, 2002), pp. 9, 11.

50. K. LeMessurier, "Temp Staffing Leaves a Permanent Mark," *Canadian HR Reporter* (February 10, 2003), pp. 3, 8.

51. A. Ryckman, "The 5 Keys to Getting Top Value from Contractors," *Canadian HR Reporter* (December 2, 2002), p. 25; S. Purba, "Contracting Works for Job Hunters," *Globe & Mail* (April 24, 2002).

52. "Flexible Staffing in the Aerospace Industry," *Airfinance Journal l Aircraft Economic Yearbook* (2001), pp. 14–17.

53. M. Potter, "A Golden Opportunity for Older Workers to Energize Firms," *Canadian HR Reporter* (April 25, 2005), p. 13.

54. L. Cassiani, "Looming Retirement Surge Takes on New Urgency," *Canadian HR Reporter* (May 21, 2001), pp. 1, 10.

55. O. Parker, *Too Few People, Too Little Time: The Employer Challenge of an Aging Workforce* (Ottawa: The Conference Board of Canada Executive Action, July 2006).

56. K. Thorpe, *Harnessing the Power: Recruiting, Engaging, and Retaining Mature Workers*. Ottawa: Conference Board of Canada, 2008.

57. S.B. Hood, "Generational Diversity in the Workplace," *HR Professional* (June/July 2000), p. 20.

58. G. Kovary and A. Buahene, "Recruiting the Four Generations," *Canadian HR Reporter* (May 23, 2005), p. R6.

59. S. Klie, "Firm asks students: What do you want?" *Canadian HR Reporter*, May 5, 2008.

60. Inclusion Network, www.inclusionnetwork.ca (May 31, 2009), and Aboriginal Human Resource Council, http://aboriginalhr.ca (May 31, 2009).

61. WORKlnk, www.workink.com (May 31, 2009).

62. Society for Canadian Women in Science and Technology, www.harbour.sfu.ca/scwist/index_files/Page1897.htm (May 31, 2009); C. Emerson, H. Matsui, and L. Michael, "Progress Slow for Women in Trades, Tech, Science," *Canadian HR Reporter* (February 14, 2005), p. 11.

63. F. Mael, M. Connerley and R. Morath, "None of Your Business: Parameters of Biodata Invasiveness," *Personnel Psychology* 49 (1996), pp. 613–650.

64. H.N. Chait, S.M. Carraher, and M.R. Buckley, "Measuring Service Orientation with Biodata," *Journal of Management Issues* (Spring 2000), pp. 109–120; V.M. Catano, S.F. Cronshaw, R.D. Hackett, L.L. Methot, and W.H. Weisner, *Recruitment and Selection in Canada*, 2nd ed. (Scarborough, ON: Nelson Thomson Learning, 2001), p. 307; J.E. Harvey-Cook and R.J. Taffler, "Biodata in Professional Entry-Level Selection: Statistical Scoring of Common-Format Applications," *Journal of Occupational and Organizational Psychology* (March 1, 2000), pp. 103–118; Y.Y. Chung, "The Validity of Biographical Inventories for the Selection of Salespeople," *International Journal of Management* (September 2001).

Chapter 7

1. D. Brown, "Waterloo Forced to Fire Top Bureaucrat Weeks after Hiring," *Canadian HR Reporter* (October 11, 2004), p. 3.

2. British Columbia Criminal Records Review Act; www.pssg.gov.bc.ca/criminal-records-review/index.htm (May 31, 2009).

3. C. Kapel, "Giant Steps," *Human Resources Professional* (April 1993), pp. 13–16.

4. S.A. Way and J.W. Thacker, "Selection Practices: Where Are Canadian Organizations?" *HR Professional* (October/November 1999), p. 34.

5. L.J. Katunich, "How to Avoid the Pitfalls of Psych Tests," *Workplace News Online* (July 2005), p. 5; *Testing and Assessment—FAQ/Finding Information About Psychological Tests*, APA Online, www.apa.org/science/faq-findtests.html (August 1, 2006).

6. M. McDaniel et al., "The Validity of Employment Interviews: A Comprehensive Review and Meta-analysis," *Journal of Applied Psychology* 79, no. 4 (1994).

7. "Hiring: Psychology and Employee Potential," *HR Professional*, August/September 2008, p. 16.

8. Ibid.

9. S. Bakker, "Psychometric Selection Assessments," *HR Professional*, April/May 2009, p. 21.

10. Canadian Psychological Association, *Guidelines for Educational and Psychological Testing*, www.cpa.ca/documents/PsyTest.html (May 31, 2009).

11. "Emotional Intelligence Testing," *HR Focus* (October 2001), pp. 8–9.

12. Results of meta-analyses in one recent study indicated that isometric strength tests were valid predictors of both supervisory ratings of physical performance and performance on work simulations. See B.R. Blakley, M. Quinones, M.S. Crawford, and I.A. Jago, "The Validity of Isometric Strength Tests," *Personnel Psychology* 47 (1994), pp. 247–274.

13. C. Colacci, "Testing Helps You Decrease Disability Costs," *Canadian HR Reporter* (June 14, 1999), p. G4.

14. K. Gillin, "Reduce Employee Exposure to Injury with Pre-Employment Screening Tests," *Canadian HR Reporter* (February 28, 2000), p. 10.

15. This approach calls for construct validation, which, as was pointed out, is extremely difficult to demonstrate.

16. Myers-Briggs Type Indicator (MBTI) Assessment, www.cpp.com/products/mbti/index.asp (May 31, 2009).

17. See, for example, D. Cellar et al., "Comparison of Factor Structures and Criterion Related Validity Coefficients for Two Measures of Personality Based on the Five-Factor Model," *Journal of Applied Psychology* 81, no. 6 (1996), pp. 694–704; J. Salgado, "The Five Factor Model of Personality and

Job Performance in the European Community," *Journal of Applied Psychology* 82, no. 1 (1997), pp. 30–43.

18. M.R. Barrick and M.K. Mount, "The Big Five Personality Dimensions and Job Performance: A Meta-Analysis," *Personnel Psychology* 44, (Spring 1991), pp. 1–26.

19. T. Judge, J. Martocchio, and C. Thorensen, "Five-Factor Model of Personality and Employee Absence," *Journal of Applied Psychology* 82 (1997), pp. 745–755.

20. E. Silver and C. Bennett, "Modification of the Minnesota Clerical Test to Predict Performance on Video Display Terminals," *Journal of Applied Psychology* 72, no. 1 (February 1987), pp. 153–155.

21. L. Siegel and I. Lane, *Personnel and Organizational Psychology* (Homewood, IL: Irwin, 1982), pp. 182–183.

22. J. Weekley and C. Jones, "Video-Based Situational Testing," *Personnel Psychology* 50 (1997), p. 25.

23. Ibid, pp. 26–30.

24. D. Chan and N. Schmitt, "Situational Judgment and Job Performance," *Human Performance* 15, no. 3 (2002), pp. 233–254.

25. S. Klie, "Screening Gets More Secure," *Canadian HR Reporter* (June 19, 2006).

26. Canadian Human Rights Commission, *Canadian Human Rights Commission Policy on Alcohol and Drug Testing* (June 2002).

27. M. McDaniel et al., "The Validity of Employment Interviews: A Comprehensive Review and Meta-analysis," *Journal of Applied Psychology* 79, no. 4 (1994), p. 599.

28. J.G. Goodale, *The Fine Art of Interviewing* (Englewood Cliffs, NJ: Prentice Hall Inc., 1982), p. 22. See also R.L. Decker, "The Employment Interview," *Personnel Administrator* 26 (November 1981), pp. 71–73.

29. M. Campion, E. Pursell, and B. Brown, "Structured Interviewing: Raising the Psychometric Properties of the Employment Interview," *Personnel Psychology* 41 (1988), pp. 25–42.

30. M. McDaniel et al., "The Validity of Employment Interviews: A Comprehensive Review and Meta-analysis," *Journal of Applied Psychology* 79, no. 4 (1994).

31. D.S. Chapman and P.M. Rowe, "The Impact of Video Conferencing Technology, Interview Structure, and Interviewer Gender on Interviewer Evaluations in the Employment Interview: A Field Experiment," *Journal of Occupational and Organizational Psychology*, 74 (September 2001), pp. 279–298.

32. M. McDaniel et al., "The Validity of Employment Interviews: A Comprehensive Review and Meta-analysis," *Journal of Applied Psychology* 79, no. 4 (1994), p. 601.

33. Ibid.

34. "Lights, camera...can I have a job?" *Globe and Mail*, March 2, 2007, p. C1; A. Pell, *Recruiting and Selecting Personnel* (New York: Regents, 1969), p. 119.

35. J.G. Goodale, *The Fine Art of Interviewing* (Englewood Cliffs, NJ: Prentice Hall Inc., 1982), p. 26.

36. See R.D. Arvey and J.E. Campion, "The Employment Interview: A Summary and Review of Recent Research," *Personnel Psychology* 35 (1982), pp. 281–322; M. Heilmann and L. Saruwatari, "When Beauty Is Beastly: The Effects of Appearance and Sex on Evaluation of Job Applicants for Managerial and Nonmanagerial Jobs," *Organizational Behavior and Human Performance* 23 (June 1979), pp. 360–722; C. Marlowe, S. Schneider, and C. Nelson, "Gender and Attractiveness Biases in Hiring Decisions: Are More Experienced Managers Less Biased?" *Journal of Applied Psychology* 81, no. 1 (1996), pp. 11–21; V. Galt, "Beauty Found Not Beastly in the Job Interview," *Globe & Mail* (April 15, 2002).

37. A. Pell, "Nine Interviewing Pitfalls," *Managers* (January 1994), p. 29; T. Dougherty, D. Turban, and J. Callender, "Confirming First Impressions in the Employment Interview: A Field Study of Interviewer Behavior," *Journal of Applied Psychology* 79, no. 5 (1994), p. 663.

38. See A. Pell, "Nine Interviewing Pitfalls," *Managers* (January 1994), p. 29; P. Sarathi, "Making Selection Interviews Effective," *Management and Labor Studies* 18, no. 1 (1993), pp. 5–7; J. Shetcliffe, "Who, and How, to Employ," *Insurance Brokers' Monthly* (December 2002), pp. 14–16.

39. G.J. Sears and P.M. Rowe, "A Personality-Based Similar-to-Me Effect in the Employment Interview: Conscientious, Affect-versus-Competence Mediated Interpretations, and the Role of Job Relevance," *Canadian Journal of Behavioural Sciences* 35 (January 2003), p. 13.

40. This section is based on E.D. Pursell, M.A. Campion, and S.R. Gaylord, "Structured Interviewing: Avoiding Selection Problems," *Personnel Journal* 59 (1980), pp. 907–912; G.P. Latham, L.M. Saari, E.D. Pursell, and M.A. Campion, "The Situational Interview," *Journal of Applied Psychology* 65 (1980), pp. 422–427. See also M. Campion, E. Pursell, and B. Brown, "Structured Interviewing: Raising the Psychometric Properties of the Employment Interview," *Personnel Psychology* 41 (1988), pp. 25–42, and J.A. Weekley and J.A. Gier, "Reliability and Validity of the Situational Interview for a Sales Position," *Journal of Applied Psychology* 72 (1987), pp. 484–487.

41. P. Lowry, "The Structured Interview: An Alternative to the Assessment Center?" *Public Personnel Management* 23, no. 2 (Summer 1994), pp. 201–215.

42. Steps two and three are based on the Kepner-Tregoe Decision-Making Model.

43. A. Pell, *Recruiting and Selecting Personnel* (New York: Regents, 1969), pp. 103–115.

44. W.H. Wiesner and R.J. Oppenheimer, "Note-Taking in the Selection Interview: Its Effect upon Predictive Validity and Information Recall," *Proceedings of the Annual Conference Meeting. Administrative Sciences Association of Canada* (Personnel and Human Resources Division, 1991), pp. 97–106.

45. V. Tsang, "No More Excuses," *Canadian HR Reporter* (May 23, 2005); L.T. Cullen, "Getting Wise to Lies," *TIME* (May 1, 2006), p. 27.

46. L. Fischer, "Gatekeeper," *Workplace News* (August 2005), pp. 10–11.

47. Ibid.

48. "Background Checks," *HR Professional*, June/July 2008, p. 16.

49. T. Humber, "Recruitment Isn't Getting Any Easier," *Canadian HR Reporter* (May 23, 2005).

50. C. Hall and A. Miedema, "But I thought you checked?" *Canadian HR Reporter*, May 21, 2007.

51. *Is Your Future Boss Researching You Online?* www.careerbuilder.ca/Article/CB-417-Interviewing-Is-Your-Future-Boss-Researching-You-Online/?sc_extcmp=cbca_9417&cblang=CAEnglish&pf=true&SiteId=cbca_9417&ArticleID=417&cbRecursionCnt=1&cbsid=02a1e103f09840968597bacd20a26d98-296480762-VG-4 (May 24, 2009).

52. J.R. Smith, "Damaging reference survives Alberta privacy challenge," *Canadian HR Reporter*, January 28, 2008.

53. A.C. Elmslie, "Writing a Reference Letter—Right or Wrong?" *Ultimate HR Manual*, Number 44, January 2009, pp. 1–3.

54. A. Moffat, "The danger of digging too deep," *Canadian HR Reporter*, August 11, 2008. See also P. Israel, "Providing References to Employees: Should You or Shouldn't You?" *Canadian HR Reporter* (March 24, 2003), pp. 5–6; T. Humber, "Name, Rank and Serial Number," *Canadian HR Reporter* (May 19, 2003), pp. G1, G7.

55. J.A. Breaugh, "Realistic Job Previews: A Critical Appraisal and Future Research Directions," *Academy of Management Review* 8, no. 4 (1983), pp. 612–619.

56. P. Buhler, "Managing in the '90s: Hiring the Right Person for the Job," *Supervision* (July 1992), pp. 21–23; S. Jackson, "Realistic Job Previews Help Screen Applicants and Reduce Turnover," *Canadian HR Reporter* (August 9, 1999), p. 10.

57. S. Jackson, "Realistic Job Previews Help Screen Applicants and Reduce Turnover," *Canadian HR Reporter* (August 9, 1999), p. 10.

58. B. Kleinmutz, "Why We Still Use Our Heads Instead of Formulas: Toward an Integrative Approach," *Psychological Bulletin* 107 (1990), pp. 296–310.

Chapter 8

1. B.W. Pascal, "The Orientation Wars," *Workplace Today* (October 2001), p. 4.

2. B. Pomfret, "Sound Employee Orientation Program Boosts Productivity and Safety," *Canadian HR Reporter* (January 25, 1999), pp. 17–19.

3. L. Shelat, "First Impressions Matter—A Lot," *Canadian HR Reporter* (May 3, 2004), pp. 11, 13.

4. For a recent discussion of socialization see, for example, G. Chao et al., "Organizational Socialization: Its Content and Consequences," *Journal of Applied Psychology* 79, no. 5 (1994), pp. 730–743.

5. S. Jackson, "After All That Work in Hiring, Don't Let New Employees Dangle," *Canadian HR Reporter* (May 19, 1997), p. 13.

6. A. Macaulay, "The Long and Winding Road," *Canadian HR Reporter* (November 16, 1998), pp. G1–G10.

7. R. Biswas, "Employee Orientation: Your Best Weapon in the Fight for Skilled Talent," *Human Resources Professional* (August/September 1998), pp. 41–42.

8. "Employee Onboarding Guides New Hires," *Workspan*, January 2009, p. 119.

9. D. Chhabra, "What Web-Based Onboarding Can Do For Your Company," *Workspan*, May 2008, pp. 111–114.

10. A. Macaulay, "The Long and Winding Road," *Canadian HR Reporter* (November 16, 1998), p. G1.

11. R. Harrison, "Onboarding: The First Step in Motivation and Retention," *Workspan*, September 2007, pp. 43–45.

12. D. Barnes, "Learning Is Key to Post-merger Success," *Canadian HR Reporter* (July 12, 1999), pp. 16–17.

13. C. Gibson, "Online Orientation: Extending a Welcoming Hand to New Employees," *Canadian HR Reporter* (November 30, 1998), pp. 22–23.

14. "Onboarding: Virtual Orientation at IBM," *HR Professional*, August/September 2008, p. 12.

15. D. Brown, "Execs Need Help Learning the Ropes Too," *Canadian HR Reporter* (April 22, 2002), p. 2.

16. Ibid.

17. "The Critical Importance of Executive Integration," *Drake Business Review* (December 2002), pp. 6–8.

18. S. Mingail, "Employers Need a Lesson in Training," *Canadian HR Reporter* (February 11, 2002), pp. 22–23.

19. U. Vu, "Trainers Mature into Business Partners," *Canadian HR Reporter* (July 12, 2004), pp. 1–2.

20. S. Klie, "Training Isn't Always the Answer," *Canadian HR Reporter* (December 5, 2005), pp. 13–14.

21. V. Galt, "Training Falls Short: Study," *Globe & Mail* (July 9, 2001), p. M1.

22. D. Harder, "Sierra Systems earns top marks for training," *Canadian HR Reporter*, February 2, 2009.

23. *Knowledge Matters: Skills and Learning for Canadians* (Government of Canada, 2002), p. 3, www11.sdc.gc.ca/sl-ca/doc/summary.shtml (June 7, 2006).

24. A. Tomlinson, "More Training Critical in Manufacturing," *Canadian HR Reporter* (November 4, 2002), p. 2.

25. D. Brown, "PM Calls for Business to Spend More on Training," *Canadian HR Reporter* (December 16, 2002), pp. 1, 11; D. Brown, "Budget Should Include More for Training: Critics," *Canadian HR Reporter* (March 10, 2003), pp. 1–2; D. Brown, "Legislated Training, Questionable Results," *Canadian HR Reporter* (May 6, 2002), pp. 1, 12.

26. N.L. Trainor, "Employee Development the Key to Talent Attraction and Retention," *Canadian HR Reporter* (November 1, 1999), p. 8.

27. Bank of Montreal. www.bmo.com (May 31, 2009).

28. L. Johnston, "Employees put high price on learning, development," Canadian HR Reporter, November 3, 2008; S. Klie, "Higher education leads to higher productivity," *Canadian HR Reporter*, December 3, 2007.

29. D. LaMarche-Bisson, "There's More than One Way to Learn," *Canadian HR Reporter* (November 18, 2003), p. 7.

30. M. Belcourt, P.C. Wright, and A.M. Saks, *Managing Performance Through Training and Development*, 2nd ed. (Toronto: Nelson Thomson Learning, 2000). See also A.M. Saks and R.R. Haccoun, "Easing the Transfer of Training," *Human Resources Professional* (July–August 1996), pp. 8–11.

31. J.A. Colquitt, J.A. LePine, and R.A. Noe, "Toward an Integrative Theory of Training Motivation: A Meta-analytic Path Analysis of 20 Years of Research," *Journal of Applied Psychology* 85 (2000), pp. 678–707.

32. M. Georghiou, "Games, simulations open world of learning," *Canadian HR Reporter* (May 5, 2008).

33. K.A. Smith-Jentsch et al., "Can Pre-Training Experiences Explain Individual Differences in Learning?" *Journal of Applied Psychology* 81, no. 1 (1986), pp. 100–116.

34. J.A. Cannon-Bowers et al., "A Framework for Understanding Pre-Practice Conditions and Their Impact on Learning," *Personnel Psychology* 51 (1988), pp. 291–320.

35. Based on K. Wexley and G. Latham, *Developing and Training Human Resources in Organizations* (Glenview, IL: Scott, Foresman, 1981), pp. 22–27.

36. G. Na, "An employer's right to train," *Canadian HR Reporter* (October 6, 2008).

37. B.M. Bass and J.A. Vaughan, "Assessing Training Needs," in C. Schneier and R. Beatty, *Personnel Administration Today*, p. 311 (Reading, MA: Addison-Wesley, 1978). See also R. Ash and E. Leving, "Job Applicant Training and Work Experience Evaluation: An Empirical Comparison of Four Methods," *Journal of Applied Psychology* 70, no. 3 (1985), pp. 572–576; J. Lawrie, "Break the Training Ritual," *Personnel Journal* 67, no. 4 (April 1988), pp. 95–77; T. Lewis and D. Bjorkquist, "Needs Assessment—A Critical Reappraisal," *Performance Improvement Quarterly* 5, no. 4 (1992), pp. 33–54.

38. See, for example, G. Freeman, "Human Resources Planning—Training Needs Analysis," *Human Resources Planning* 39, no. 3 (Fall 1993), pp. 32–34.

39. J.C. Georges, "The Hard Realities of Soft Skills Training," *Personnel Journal* 68, no. 4 (April 1989), pp. 40–45; R.H. Buckham, "Applying Role Analysis in the Workplace," *Personnel* 64, no. 2 (February 1987), pp. 63–55; J.K. Ford and R. Noe, "Self-Assessed Training Needs: The Effects of Attitudes towards Training, Management Level, and Function," *Personnel Psychology* 40, no. 1 (Spring 1987), pp. 39–54.

40. K. Wexley and G. Latham, *Developing and Training Human Resources in Organizations* (Glenview, IL: Scott, Foresman, 1981), p. 107.

41. "German Training Model Imported," *BNA Bulletin to Management* (December 19, 1996), p. 408; L. Burton, "Apprenticeship: The Learn While You Earn Option," *Human Resources Professional* (February/March 1998), p. 25; H. Frazis, D.E. Herz, and M.W. Harrigan, "Employer-Provided Training: Results from a New Survey," *Monthly Labor Review*, 118 (1995), pp. 3–17.

42. "Apprenticeship grant gets going," *Canadian HR Reporter*, January 25, 2007; "New Funding for Apprenticeships," *Canadian HR Reporter* (May 3, 2004), p. 2; "Ontario Boosts Apprenticeship Program with $37 Million Investment," *Canadian HR Reporter* (April 7, 2000); ThinkTrades (Alberta Aboriginal Apprenticeship Project) www.thinktrades.com/candidates.htm (June 13, 2006).

43. N. Day, "Informal Learning Gets Results," *Workforce* (June 1998), p. 31.

44. S. Williams, "'Classroom' training alive and changing," *Canadian HR Reporter*, October 6, 2008.

45. M. Emery and M. Schubert, "A Trainer's Guide to Videoconferencing," *Training* (June 1993), p. 60.

46. G.N. Nash, J.P. Muczyk, and F.L. Vettori, "The Role and Practical Effectiveness of Programmed Instruction," *Personnel Psychology* 24 (1971), pp. 397–418.

47. K. Wexley and G. Latham, *Developing and Training Human Resources in Organizations* (Glenview, IL: Scott, Foresman, 1981), p. 141. See also R. Wlozkowski, "Simulation," *Training and Development Journal* 39, no. 6 (June 1985), pp. 38–43.

48. "Pros and Cons of E-learning," *Canadian HR Reporter* (July 16, 2001), pp. 11, 15; D. Murray, *E-learning for the Workplace* (Ottawa: Conference Board of Canada, 2001). See also M. Rueda, "How to Make E-Learning Work for Your Company," *Workspan* (December 2002), pp. 50–53; U. Vu, "Technology-Based Learning Comes of Age," *Canadian HR Reporter* (April 21, 2003), pp. 3, 17.

49. S. Mingail, "Good e-Learning Built on Good Instructional Design," *Canadian HR Reporter* (March 22, 2004), p. 12.

50. S. Carliner, M. Ally, N. Zhao, L. Bairstow, S. Khoury, and L. Johnston, *A Review of the State of the Field of Workplace Learning: What We Need to Know About Competencies, Diversity, E-Learning, and Human Performance Impact* (Canadian Society for Training and Development, 2006).

51. G. Siemens, "5 things to watch in e-learning," *Canadian HR Reporter*, October 6, 2008.

52. See, for example, T. Falconer, "No More Pencils, No More Books!" *Canadian Banker* (March/April 1994), pp. 21–25.

53. M. Georghiou, "Games, simulations open world of learning," *Canadian HR Reporter*, May 5, 2008.

54. W. Powell, "Like Life?" *Training & Development* (February 2002), pp. 32–38. See also A. Macaulay, "Reality-Based Computer Simulations Allow Staff to Grow through Failure," *Canadian HR Reporter* (October 23, 2000), pp. 11–12.

55. S. Klie, "L'Oreal plays games with training," *Canadian HR Reporter*, October 6, 2008.

56. A. Czarnecki, "Interactive Learning Makes Big Dent in Time, Money Requirements for T&D," *Canadian HR Reporter* (November 18, 1996), pp. L30–L31.

57. L. Young "Self-Directed Computer-Based Training That Works," *Canadian HR Reporter* (April 24, 2000), pp. 7–8.

58. F. Manning, "The Misuse of Technology in Workplace Learning," *Canadian HR Reporter* (April 24, 2000), pp. 7, 10; T. Purcell, "Training Anytime, Anywhere," *Canadian HR Reporter* (July 16, 2001), pp. 11, 15; L. Cassini, "Student Participation Thrives in Online Learning Environments," *Canadian HR Reporter* (May 2, 2001), p. 2.

59. O. Diss, "Deploying a New E-Learning Program?" *HR Professional* (October–November 2005), p. 16.

60. P. Weaver, "Preventing E-Learning Failure," *Training & Development* (August 2002), pp. 45–50; K. Oakes, "E-Learning," *Training & Development* (March 2002), pp. 73–75. See also P. Harris, "E-Learning: A Consolidation Update," *Training & Development* (April 2002), pp. 27–33; C.R. Taylor, "The Second Wave," *Training & Development* (October 2002), pp. 24–31; E. Wareham, "The Educated Buyer," *Computing Canada* (February 18, 2000), p. 33; A. Tomlinson, "E-Learning Won't Solve All Problems," *Canadian HR Reporter* (April 8, 2002), pp. 1, 6.

61. P. Weaver, "Preventing E-Learning Failure," *Training & Development* (August 2002), pp. 45–50.

62. M. Belcourt, P.C. Wright, and A.M. Saks, *Managing Performance through Training and Development*, 2nd ed. (Toronto: Nelson Thomson Learning, 2002), pp. 188–202.

63. Ibid, p. 9.

64. D. Kirkpatrick, "Effective Supervisory Training and Development," Part 3, "Outside Programs," *Personnel* 62, no. 2 (February 1985), pp. 39–42. Among the reasons training might not pay off on the job are a mismatching of courses and trainees' needs, supervisory slip-ups (with supervisors signing up trainees and then forgetting to have them attend the sessions when the training session is actually given), and lack of help in applying skills on the job.

65. N.L. Trainor, "Evaluating Training's Four Levels," *Canadian HR Reporter* (January 13, 1997), p. 10.

66. C. Knight, "Awards for Literacy Announced," *Canadian HR Reporter* (December 29, 1997), p. 10.

67. *Reading the Future: Planning to Meet Canada's Future Literacy Needs.* Ottawa: Canadian Council on Learning, 2008.

68. S. Coulombe, J-F. Tremblay, and S. Marchand, *International Adult Literacy Study: Literacy Scores, Human Capital and Growth Across 14 OECD Countries*, Statistics Canada, Catalogue No. 89-552-MIE, 2004; S. Mingal, "Tackling Workplace Literacy a No-Brainer," *Canadian HR Reporter* (November 22, 2004), pp. G3, G10; D. Brown, "Poor Reading, Math Skills a Drag on Productivity, Performance," *Canadian HR Reporter* (February 28, 2005), pp. 1, 10.

69. U. Vu, "Workplace language training gets cash boost," *Canadian HR Reporter*, May 19, 2008; K. Wolfe, "Language Training for the Workplace," *Canadian HR Reporter* (June 6, 2005), pp. 1, 13.

70. B. Siu, "Cross-Cultural Training and Customer Relations: What Every Manager Should Know," *Canadian HR Reporter* (November 15, 1999), pp. G3, G15.

71. D. Roberts and B. Tsang, "Diversity Management Training Helps Firms Hone Competitive Edge," *Canadian HR Reporter* (June 19, 1995), pp. 17–18.

72. Handidactis, www.handidactis.com (May 31, 2009).

73. L. Young, "Retail Sector Seeks to Upgrade Education, Training to Solve Human Resource Woes," *Canadian HR Reporter* (February 8, 1999), p. 11. See also B. Nagle, "Superior Retail Training Blends Customer Service, Product Knowledge," *Canadian HR Reporter* (July 15, 2002), pp. 7–8; D. Brown, "Is Retail Ready to Buy Training?" *Canadian HR Reporter* (July 15, 2002), pp. 7–8.

74. Canadian Retail Institute, www.retaileducation.ca/cms/sitem.cfm/certification_&_training (May 31, 2009).

75. Based on J. Laabs, "Team Training Goes Outdoors," *Personnel Journal* (June 1991), pp. 56–63. See also S. Caudron, "Teamwork Takes Work," *Personnel Journal* 73, no. 2 (February 1994), pp. 41–49.

76. B. Donais, "Training managers in handling conflict," *Canadian HR Reporter*, March 12, 2007; A. Tomlinson, "A Dose of Training for Ailing First-Time Managers," *Canadian HR Reporter* (December 3, 2001), pp. 7, 10.

77. L.C. McDermott, "Developing the New Young Managers," *Training & Development* (October 2001), pp. 42–48; A. Tomlinson, "A Dose of Training for Ailing First-Time Managers," *Canadian HR Reporter* (December 3, 2001), pp. 7, 10.

78. S. Odenwald, "A Guide for Global Training," *Training & Development* (July 1993), pp. 22–31.

79. R. Rosen and P. Digh, "Developing Globally Literate Leaders," *Training & Development* (May 2001), pp. 70–81.

Chapter 9

1. Towers Perrin, *Talent Management: The State of the Art* (Toronto: Towers Perrin, 2005); E. Chadnick, "Is HR prepared to keep the keepers?" *Canadian HR Reporter*, January 29, 2007.

2. S. O'Neal and J. Gebauer, "Talent Management in the 21st Century: Attracting, Retaining and Engaging Employees of Choice," *WorldatWork Journal* (First Quarter 2006), pp. 6–17.

3. Quoted from F. Otte and P. Hutcheson, *Helping Employees Manage Careers* (Englewood Cliffs, NJ: Prentice Hall, 1992), pp. 5–6.

4. W. Enelow, *100 Ways to Recession-Proof Your Career* (Toronto: McGraw-Hill, 2002), p. 1.

5. P. Linkow, "Winning the Competition for Talent: The Role of the New Career Paradigm in Total Rewards," *Workspan*, October 2006, pp. 28–32.

6. M. Watters and L. O'Connor, *It's Your Move: A Personal and Practical Guide to Career Transition and Job Search for Canadian Managers, Professionals and Executives* (Toronto: HarperCollins, 2001).

7. For example, one survey of "baby boomers" concluded that "allowed to excel" was the most frequently mentioned factor in overall job satisfaction in an extensive attitude survey of Canadian supervisors and middle managers between 30 and 45 years old. J. Rogers, "Baby Boomers and Their Career Expectations," *Canadian Business Review* (Spring 1993), pp. 13–18.

8. E. Schein, *Career Dynamics: Matching Individual and Organizational Needs* (Reading, MA: Addison-Wesley, 1978).

9. J. Holland, *Making Vocational Choices: A Theory of Careers* (Englewood Cliffs, NJ: Prentice-Hall, 1973).

10. E. Schein, *Career Dynamics: Matching Individual and Organizational Needs* (Reading, MA: Addison-Wesley, 1978), pp. 128–129; E.H. Schein, *Career Anchors Revisited: Implications for Career Development in the 21st Century*, Society of Organizational Learning—Working Paper 10.009, 1996.

11. R. Bolles, *What Color Is Your Parachute?* (Berkeley, CA: Ten Speed Press, 1976), p. 86.

12. R. Payne, *How to Get a Better Job Quicker* (New York: New American Library, 1987).

13. J. Ross, *Managing Productivity* (Reston, VA: Reston, 1979).

14. H.G. Kaufman, *Obsolescence and Professional Career Development* (New York: AMACOM, 1974).

15. See, for example, T. Scandurg, "Mentorship and Career Mobility: An Empirical Investigation," *Journal of Organizational Behavior* 13, no. 2 (March 1992), pp. 169–174.

16. E. Schein, *Career Dynamics: Matching Individual and Organizational Needs* (Reading, MA: Addison-Wesley, 1978), p. 19. See also R. Jacobs and R. Bolton, "Career Analysis: The Missing Link in Managerial Assessment and Development," *Human Resource Management Journal* 3, no. 2 (1994), pp. 55–62.

17. F. Otte and P. Hutcheson, *Helping Employees Manage Careers* (Englewood Cliffs, NJ: Prentice Hall, 1992), pp. 15–16.

18. Ibid, p. 143.

19. B. Moses, "Implementing an Employee Career Development Program—Part Two: Tools to Support Career Development," *HR Professional* (December 1985), pp. 6–10.

20. A.M. Young and P.L. Perrewé, "What Did You Expect? An Examination of Career-Related Support and Social Support Among Mentors and Protégés," *Journal of Management* 20 (2000), pp. 611–632; "Mentoring Makes Better Employees," *Workplace Today* (June 2001), p. 12; S. Butyn, "Mentoring Your Way to Improved Retention," *Canadian HR Reporter* (January 27, 2003), pp. 13, 15.

21. S. Klie, "Mentoring accelerates leadership development," *Canadian HR Reporter*, March 23, 2009.

22. L. Young, "Potential of Mentoring Programs Untapped," *Canadian HR Reporter* (April 10, 2000), pp. 1–2; S. Butyn, "Mentoring Your Way to Improved Retention," *Canadian HR Reporter* (January 27, 2003), pp. 13, 15.

23. A.K. Buahene and G. Kovary, "Reversing the roles: Why Gen Ys can make great mentors," *Canadian HR Reporter*, May 4, 2009.

24. D.A. Garvin, "Building a Learning Organization," *Harvard Business Review* (July–August 1993), p. 80.

25. See, for example, R. Chanick, "Career Growth for Baby Boomers," *Personnel Journal* 71, no. 1 (January 1992), pp. 40–46.

26. R. Sheppard, "Spousal Programs and Communication Curb Relocation Rejections," *Canadian HR Reporter* (November 1, 1999), p. 17.

27. D. Quinn Mills, *Labor–Management Relations* (New York: McGraw-Hill, 1986), pp. 387–396.

28. G. Dessler, *Winning Commitment* (New York: McGraw-Hill, 1993), pp. 144–149.

29. See J. Famularo, *Handbook of Modern Personnel Administration* (New York: McGraw-Hill, 1972), p. 17.

30. For a discussion, see S. Schmidt, "The New Focus for Career Development Programs in Business and Industry," *Journal of Employment Counseling* 31 (March 1994), pp. 22–28.

31. R. Tucker, M. Moravee, and K. Ideus, "Designing a Dual Career-Track System," *Training and Development* 6 (1992), pp. 55–58; S. Schmidt, "The New Focus for Career Development Programs in Business and Industry," *Journal of Employment Counseling* 31 (March 1994), p. 26.

32. J. Swain, "Dispelling Myths about Leadership Development," *Canadian HR Reporter* (June 3, 2002), p. 27.

33. J. Cooper, "Succession Planning: It's Not Just for Executives Anymore," *Workspan* (February 2006), pp. 44–47.

34. Ibid.

35. P. Cantor, "Succession Planning: Often Requested, Rarely Delivered," *Ivey Business Journal* (January/February 2005).

36. R. Cheloha and J. Swain, "Talent Management System Key to Effective Succession Planning," *Canadian HR Reporter* (October 10, 2005), pp. 5, 8.

37. U. Vu, "Beware the Plan That's Led Too Much by HR," *Canadian HR Reporter* (October 10, 2005), pp. 6–7.

38. For discussions of the steps in succession planning see, for example, K. Nowack, "The Secrets of Succession," *Training and Development* (November 1994), pp. 49–55, and D. Brookes, "In Management Succession, Who Moves Up?" *Human Resources* (January/February 1995), pp. 11–13.

39. "Half of companies fail to update succession plans," *Workplace e-Newsletter*. www.workplace-mag.com/Half-of-companies-fail-to-update-succession-plans.html (May 31, 2009).

40. K. Spence, "The Employee's Role in Succession Planning," *Canadian HR Reporter* (February 14, 2000), p. 13.

41. J. Orr, "Job Rotations Give Future Leaders the Depth They Need," *Canadian HR Reporter* (January 30, 2006), pp. 17, 20.

42. "TDBFG Associate," TD Bank Financial Group, www.td.com/hr/CTA.jsp (June 14, 2006).

43. D. Yoder, H.G. Heneman, J. Turnbull, and C.H. Stone, *Handbook of Personnel Management and Labor Relations* (New York: McGraw Hill, 1958). See also Jack Phillips, "Training Supervisors Outside the Classroom," *Training and Development Journal* 40, no. 2 (February 1986), pp. 46–49.

44. K. Wexley and G. Latham, *Developing and Training Human Resources in Organizations* (Glenview, IL: Scott, Foresman, 1981), p. 207.

45. D. Brown, "Action Learning Popular in Europe, Not Yet Caught on in Canada," *Canadian HR Reporter* (April 25, 2005), pp. 1–17.

46. K. Wexley and G. Latham, *Developing and Training Human Resources in Organizations* (Glenview, IL: Scott, Foresman, 1981), p. 193.

47. J. Kay, "At Harvard on the Case," *National Post Business* (March 2003), pp. 68–78.

48. For a discussion of management games and other noncomputerized training and development simulations, see C.M. Solomon, "Simulation Training Builds Teams through Experience," *Personnel Journal* (June 1993), pp. 100–105; K. Slack, "Training for the Real Thing," *Training and Development* (May 1993), pp. 79–89; B. Lierman, "How to Develop a Training Simulation," *Training and Development* (February 1994), pp. 50–52.

49. Development Dimensions International, www.ddiworld.com (August 16, 2006).

50. IPM Management Training and Development, "Workplace.ca," www.workplace.ca (March 31, 2003).

51. L. Cassiani, "Taking Team Building to New Heights," *Canadian HR Reporter* (February 26, 2001), pp. 8, 17.

52. J. Famularo, *Handbook of Modern Personnel Administration* (New York: McGraw-Hill, 1972), pp. 21.7–21.8.

53. J. Hinrichs, "Personnel Testing," in M. Dunnette (ed.), *Handbook of Industrial and Organizational Psychology* (Chicago: Rand McNally, 1976), p. 855.

54. D. Swink, "Role-Play Your Way to Learning," *Training and Development* (May 1993), pp. 91–97; A. Test, "Why I Do Not Like to Role Play," *The American Salesman* (August 1994), pp. 7–20.

55. Based on A. Kraut, "Developing Managerial Skill via Modeling Techniques: Some Positive Research Findings—A Symposium," *Personnel Psychology* 29, no. 3 (Autumn 1976), pp. 325–361.

56. L. Morin and S. Renaud, "Corporate University Basics," *Workplace Gazette*, 7(4), pp. 61–71.

57. E. Lazarus, "Corporate University," *HR Professional*, June/July 2006, pp. 28–29; "City of Richmond Wins International Award." www.richmond.ca/__shared/printpages/page4754.htm (May 8, 2009).

58. D. Crisp, "Leadership values evolving," *Canadian HR Reporter*, September 8, 2008; S. Klie, "Holistic approach to developing leaders best," *Canadian HR Reporter*, October 27, 2008.

59. D. Brown, "Banking on Leadership Development," *Canadian HR Reporter* (January 17, 2005), pp. 7, 9.

60. Maple Leaf Foods, "Developing Leaders," www.mapleleaf.com/Working/YourDevelopment.aspx (June 13, 2006).

61. R.J.Kramer, Growing the New Business Leader," *The Conference Board Executive Action Series*, No. 208, September 2006.

62. E. Chadnick, "Is HR prepared to keep the keepers?" *Canadian HR Reporter*, January 29, 2007.

63. L. Finkelstein, "Coaching SaskEnergy to higher performance," *Canadian HR Reporter*, December 1, 2008.

64. Banff Centre, www.banffcentre.ca/departments/leadership/programs/framework.asp#model (May 31, 2009).

Chapter 10

1. J.T. Rich, "The Solutions for Employee Performance Management," *Workspan* (February 2002), pp. 32–37.

2. J.A. Rubino, "Aligning Performance Management and Compensation Rewards Successfully," *WorldatWork Canadian News* (Fourth Quarter 2004), pp. 12–16.

3. G. P. Latham, J. Almost, S. Mann, and C. Moore, "New Developments in Performance Management," *Organizational Dynamics* 34, no. 1, 2005, pp. 77–87.

4. D. Brown, "HR Improving at Performance Management," *Canadian HR Reporter* (December 2, 2002), pp. 1, 14.

5. "The Performance-Management Process," *Workspan* (October 2006), p. 96.

6. D. Brown, "HR Improving at Performance Management," *Canadian HR Reporter* (December 2, 2002), pp. 1, 14.

7. D. Brown, "Re-evaluating Evaluation," *Canadian HR Reporter* (April 8, 2002), p. 2.

8. A. Sung and E. Todd, "Line of Sight: Moving Beyond the Catchphrase," *Workspan* (October 2004), pp. 65–69.

9. R. Greenberg and L. Lucid, "Beyond Performance Management: Four Principles of Performance Leadership," *Workspan* (September 2004), pp. 42–45.

10. For a recent discussion see G. English, "Tuning Up for Performance Management," *Training and Development Journal* (April 1991), pp. 56–60.

11. C.L. Hughes, "The Bell-Shaped Curve That Inspires Guerrilla Warfare," *Personnel Administrator* (May 1987), pp. 40–41.

12. R. Girard, "Are Performance Appraisals Passé?" *Personnel Journal* 67, no. 8 (August 1988), pp. 89–90.

13. J. Ivancevich, "A Longitudinal Study of Behavioral Expectation Scales: Attitudes and Performance," *Journal of Applied Psychology* (April 1980), pp. 139–146.

14. U. Wiersma and G. Latham, "The Practicality of Behavioral Observation Scales, Behavioral Expectations Scales, and Trait Scales," *Personnel Psychology* 30, no. 3 (Autumn 1986), pp. 619–628.

15. J. Goodale and R. Burke, "Behaviorally Based Rating Scales Need Not Be Job Specific," *Journal of Applied Psychology* 60 (June 1975).

16. K.R. Murphy and J. Constans, "Behavioral Anchors as a Source of Bias in Rating," *Journal of Applied Psychology* 72, no. 4 (November 1987), pp. 573–577.

17. P. Loucks, "Plugging into performance management," *Canadian HR Reporter* (February 26, 2007).

18. M. Levy, "Almost-Perfect Performance Appraisals," *Personnel Journal* 68, no. 4 (April 1989), pp. 76–83.

19. C. Howard, "Appraise This!" *Canadian Business* (May 23, 1998), p. 96.

20. R.C. Mayer and J.H. Davis, "The Effect of the Performance Appraisal System on Trust for Management: A Field Quasi-Experiment," *Journal of Applied Psychology* 84 (1999), pp. 123–136.

21. J. Kochanski and A. Sorenson, "Managing Performance Management," *Workspan* (September 2005), pp. 20–27.

22. K.S. Teel, "Performance Appraisal: Current Trends, Persistent Progress," *Personnel Journal* 59, no. 4 (April 1980), pp. 296–316.

23. D. Brown, "Performance Management Systems Need Fixing: Survey," *Canadian HR Reporter* (April 11, 2005), pp. 1, 10; M. Waung and S. Highhouse, "Fear of Conflict and Empathic Buffering: Two Explanations for the Inflation of Performance Feedback," *Organizational Behavior and Human Decision Processes* 71 (1997), pp. 37–54.

24. Y. Ganzach, "Negativity (and Positivity) in Performance Evaluation: Three Field Studies," *Journal of Applied Psychology* 80 (1995), pp. 491–499.

25. T.J. Maurer and M.A. Taylor, "Is Sex by Itself Enough? An Exploration of Gender Bias Issues in Performance Appraisal," *Organizational Behavior and Human Decision Processes* 60 (1994), pp. 231–251. See also C.E. Lance, "Test for Latent Structure of Performance Ratings Derived from Wherry's (1952) Theory of Ratings," *Journal of Management* 20 (1994), pp. 757–771.

26. S.E. Scullen, M.K. Mount, and M. Goff, "Understanding the Latent Structure of Job Performance Ratings," *Journal of Applied Psychology* 85 (2001), pp. 956–970.

27. A.M. Saks and D.A. Waldman, "The Relationship Between Age and Job Performance Evaluations for Entry-Level Professionals," *Journal of Organizational Behavior* 19 (1998), pp. 409–419.

28. W.C. Borman, L.A. White, and D.W. Dorsey, "Effects of Ratee Task Performance and Interpersonal Factors in Supervisor and Peer Performance Ratings," *Journal of Applied Psychology* 80 (1995), pp. 168–177.

29. K. Murphy, W. Balzer, M. Lockhart, and E. Eisenman, "Effects of Previous Performance on Evaluations of Present Performance," *Journal of Applied Psychology* 70, no. 1 (1985), pp. 72–84. See also K. Williams, A. DeNisi, B. Meglino, and T. Cafferty, "Initial Decisions and Subsequent Performance Ratings," *Journal of Applied Psychology* 71, no. 2 (May 1986), pp. 189–195.

30. B. Davis and M. Mount, "Effectiveness of Performance Appraisal Training Using Computer Assistance Instruction and Behavior Modeling," *Personnel Psychology* 37 (Fall 1984), pp. 439–452.

31. J. Hedge and M. Cavanagh, "Improving the Accuracy of Performance Evaluations: Comparison of Three Methods of Performance Appraiser Training," *Journal of Applied Psychology* 73, no. 1 (February 1988), pp. 68–73.

32. B. Davis and M. Mount, "Effectiveness of Performance Appraisal Training Using Computer Assistance Instruction and Behavior Modeling," *Personnel Psychology* 37 (Fall 1984), pp. 439–452.

33. T. Athey and R. McIntyre, "Effect of Rater Training on Rater Accuracy: Levels of Processing Theory and Social Facilitation Theory Perspectives," *Journal of Applied Psychology* 72, no. 4 (November 1987), pp. 567–572.

34. M.M. Greller, "Participation in the Performance Appraisal Review: Inflexible Manager Behavior and Variable Worker Needs," *Human Relations* 51 (1998), pp. 1061–1083.

35. L. Axline, "Ethical Considerations of Performance Appraisals," *Management Review* (March 1994), p. 62.

36. M. McDougall and L. Cassiani, "HR Cited in Unfair Performance Review," *Canadian HR Reporter* (September 10, 2001), pp. 1, 6.

37. "Health Worker's Performance Review Unfair," *Workplace Today* (June 2001), p. 23.

38. G. Barrett and M. Kernan, "Performance Appraisal and Terminations: A Review of Court Decisions Since Brito v. Zia with Implications for Personnel Practices," *Personnel Psychology* 40, no. 3 (Autumn 1987), pp. 489–504.

39. M.M. Harris and J. Schaubroeck, "A Meta-Analysis of Self-Supervisor, Self-Peer, and Peer-Supervisor Ratings," *Personnel Psychology*, 41 (1988), pp. 43–62.

40. G.P. Latham and K.N. Wexley, *Increasing Productivity Through Performance Appraisal*, 2nd ed. (Reading, MA: Addison-Wesley, 1994).

41. J. Barclay and L. Harland, "Peer Performance Appraisals: The Impact of Rater Competence, Rater Location, and Rating Correctability on Fairness Perceptions," *Group and Organization Management* 20, no. 1 (March 1995), pp. 39–60.

42. M. Mount, "Psychometric Properties of Subordinate Ratings of Managerial Performance," *Personnel Psychology* 37, no. 4 (Winter 1984), pp. 687–702.

43. V.V. Druskat and S.B. Wolff, "Effects and Timing of Developmental Peer Appraisals in Self-Managing Work Groups," *Journal of Applied Psychology* 84 (1999), pp. 58–74.

44. M.M. Harris and J. Schaubroeck, "A Meta-analysis of Self–Supervisor, Self–Peer, and Peer–Supervisor Ratings," *Personnel Psychology* 41 (1988), pp. 43–62.

45. W.C. Borman, "The Rating of Individuals in Organizations: An Alternate Approach," *Organizational Behavior and Human Performance* 12 (1974), pp. 105–124.

46. B.D. Cawley, L.M. Keeping, and P.E Levy, "Participation in the Performance Appraisal Process and Employee Reactions: A Meta-analytic Review of Field Investigations," *Journal of Applied Psychology* 83 (1998), pp. 615–633.

47. J.W. Lawrie, "Your Performance: Appraise It Yourself!" *Personnel* 66, no. 1 (January 1989), pp. 21–33; includes a good explanation of how

self-appraisals can be used at work. See also A. Furnham and P. Stringfield, "Congruence in Job-Performance Ratings: A Study of 360° Feedback Examining Self, Manager, Peers, and Consultant Ratings," *Human Relations* 51 (1998), pp. 517–530.

48. P.A. Mabe III and S.G. West "Validity of Self-Evaluation of Ability: A Review and Meta-Analysis," *Journal of Applied Psychology* 67, no. 3 (1982), pp. 280–296.

49. J. Russell and D. Goode, "An Analysis of Managers' Reactions to Their Own Performance Appraisal Feedback," *Journal of Applied Psychology* 73, no. 1 (February 1988), pp. 63–67; M.M. Harris and J. Schaubroeck, "A Meta-analysis of Self–Supervisor, Self–Peer, and Peer–Supervisor Ratings," *Personnel Psychology* 41 (1988), pp. 43–62.

50. H.J. Bernardin and R.W. Beatty, "Can Subordinate Appraisals Enhance Managerial Productivity?" *Sloan Management Review* (Summer 1987), pp. 63–73.

51. M. London and A. Wohlers, "Agreement between Subordinate and Self-Ratings in Upward Feedback," *Personnel Psychology* 44 (1991), pp. 375–390.

52. Ibid, p. 376.

53. D. Antonioni, "The Effects of Feedback Accountability on Upward Appraisal Ratings," *Personnel Psychology* 47 (1994), pp. 349–355.

54. T.J. Maurer, N.S. Raju, and W.C. Collins, "Peer and Subordinate Performance Appraisal Measurement Equivalence," *Journal of Applied Psychology* 83 (1998), pp. 693–702.

55. R. Reilly, J. Smither, and N. Vasilopoulos, "A Longitudinal Study of Upward Feedback," *Personnel Psychology* 49 (1996), pp. 599–612.

56. K. Nowack, "360-Degree Feedback: The Whole Story," *Training and Development* (January 1993), p. 69. For a description of some of the problems involved in implementing 360-degree feedback, see M. Budman, "The Rating Game," *Across the Board* 31, no. 2 (February 1994), pp. 35–38.

57. C. Romano, "Fear of Feedback," *Management Review* (December 1993), p. 39. See also M.R. Edwards and A.J. Ewen, "How to Manage Performance and Pay With 360-Degree Feedback," *Compensation and Benefits Review* 28, no. 3 (May/June 1996), pp. 41–46.

58. G.P. Latham, J. Almost, S. Mann, and C. Moore, "New Developments in Performance Management," *Organizational Dynamics* 34, no. 1 (2005), pp. 77–87; R. Brillinger, "The Many Faces of 360-Degree Feedback," *Canadian HR Reporter* (December 16, 1996), p. 21.

59. J.F. Milliman, R.A. Zawacki, C. Norman, L. Powell, and J. Kirksey, "Companies Evaluate Employees from All Perspectives," *Personnel Journal* 73, no. 11 (November 1994), pp. 99–103.

60. R. Brillinger, "The Many Faces of 360-Degree Feedback," *Canadian HR Reporter* (December 16, 1996), p. 20.

61. Ibid.

62. D.A. Waldman, L.A. Atwater, and D. Antonioni, "Has 360-Degree Feedback Gone Amok?" *Academy of Management Executive* 12 (1998), pp. 86–94.

63. P.E. Levy, B.D. Cawley, and R.J. Foti, "Reactions to Appraisal Discrepancies: Performance Ratings and Attributions," *Journal of Business and Psychology* 12 (1998), pp. 437–455.

64. M. Derayeh and S. Brutus, "Learning from Others' 360-Degree Experiences," *Canadian HR Reporter* (February 10, 2003), pp. 18, 23.

65. A.S. DeNisi and A.N. Kluger, "Feedback Effectiveness: Can 360-Degree Appraisal Be Improved?" *Academy of Management Executive* 14 (2000), pp. 129–139.

66. T. Bentley, "Internet Addresses 360-Degree Feedback Concerns," *Canadian HR Reporter* (May 8, 2000), pp. G3, G15.

67. D. Brown, "Performance Management Systems Need Fixing: Survey," *Canadian HR Reporter* (April 1, 2005), pp. 1, 10.

68. See also J. Greenberg, "Using Explanations to Manage Impressions of Performance Appraisal Fairness," *Employee Responsibilities and Rights Journal* 4, no. 1 (March 1991), pp. 51–60.

69. R.G. Johnson, *The Appraisal Interview Guide*, Chapter 9 (New York: AMACOM, 1979).

70. J. Block, *Performance Appraisal on the Job: Making It Work* (New York: Executive Enterprises Publications, 1981), pp. 58–62. See also T. Lowe, "Eight Ways to Ruin a Performance Review," *Personnel Journal* 65, no. 1 (January 1986).

71. J. Block, *Performance Appraisal on the Job: Making It Work* (New York: Executive Enterprises Publications, 1981), pp. 58–62.

72. M. Feinberg, *Effective Psychology for Managers* (New York: Simon & Schuster, 1976).

73. J. Pearce and L. Porter, "Employee Response to Formal Performance Appraisal Feedback," *Journal of Applied Psychology* 71, no. 2 (May 1986), pp. 211–218.

74. D.B. Jarvis and R.E. McGilvery, "Poor Performers," *HR Professional* (June/July 2005), p. 32.

75. J. Kochnarski and A. Sorenson, "Managing Performance Management," *Workspan* (September 2005), pp. 20–37.

76. E.E. Lawler and M. McDermott, "Current Performance Management Practices," *WorldatWork Journal* 12, no. 2, pp. 49–60.

77. D. Bell, J. Blanchet, and N. Gore, "Performance Management: Making It Work Is Worth the Effort," *WorldatWork Canadian News* 12, no. 11 (Fourth Quarter 2004), pp. 1, 27–28.

Chapter 11

1. S. O'Neal, "Total Rewards and the Future of Work," *Workspan* (January 2005), pp. 18–26; S. Watson, "Total Rewards: Building a Better Employment Deal," *Workspan* (December 2003), pp. 48–51.

2. S. O'Neal, "Total Rewards and the Future of Work," *Workspan* (January 2005), pp. 18–26; L. Wright, "Total Rewards Can Mean More HR Work than You Think," *Canadian HR Reporter* (October 6, 2003), pp. 9, 12; K.D. Scott, D. Morajda, and J.W. Bishop, "Increase Company Competitiveness: 'Tune Up' Your Pay System," *WorldatWork Journal* (First Quarter 2002), pp. 35–42.

3. *Towers Perrin 2007–2008 Global Workforce Study* (Stamford CT:Towers Perrin, 2008).

4. 5.J. Dawe, "Compassionate Care Benefit: A New Alterative for Family Caregivers," *Workplace Gazette* (Summer 2004); S. Klie, "Feds Expand Eligibility For Compassionate Care," *Canadian HR Reporter* (July 17, 2006).

5. "GM, Daimler-Chrysler Workers Ratify Agreements," *Workplace Today* (December 1999), p. 11.

6. Harold Jones, "Union Views on Job Evaluations: 1971 vs. 1978," *Personnel Journal* 58 (February 1979), pp. 80–85.

7. R. Sahl, "Job Content Salary Surveys: Survey Design and Selection Features," *Compensation and Benefits Review* (May–June 1991), pp. 14–21.

8. M.A. Thompson, "Rewards, Performance Two Biggest Words in HR Future," *WorldatWork Canadian News* 10 (2002), pp. 1, 2, 11.

9. E. Sibray and J.B. Cavallaro, "Case Study: Market data and job evaluation equals the best of both worlds," *Workspan*, (July 2007), pp. 27–30.

10. Job analysis can be a useful source of information on compensable factors, as well as on job descriptions and job specifications. For example, a quantitative job analysis technique like the position analysis questionnaire generates quantitative information on the degree to which the following five basic factors are present in each job: having decision making/ communication/social responsibilities, performing skilled activities, being physically active, operating vehicles or equipment, and processing information. As a result, a job analysis technique like the PAQ is actually as appropriate as a job evaluation technique (or, some say, more), in that jobs can be quantitatively compared with one another on those five dimensions and their relative worth thus ascertained.

11. H. Risher, "Job Evaluation: Validity and Reliability," *Compensation and Benefits Review* 21 (January–February 1989), pp. 22–36.

12. S. Werner, R. Konopaske, and C. Touhey, "Ten Questions to Ask Yourself about Compensation Surveys," *Compensation and Benefits Review* 31 (May/June 1999), pp. 54–59.

13. P. Cappelli, *The New Deal at Work: Managing the Market-Driven Workforce* (Boston, MA: Harvard Business School Press, 1999).

14. "Compensation Surveys on the Internet," *Canadian HR Reporter* (February 10, 1997), p. 6.

15. F.W. Cook, "Compensation Surveys Are Biased," *Compensation and Benefits Review* (September–October 1994), pp. 19–22.

16. K.R. Cardinal, "The Art and Science of the Match, or Why Job Matching Keeps Me Up at Night," *Workspan* (February 2004), pp. 53–56; S. Werner, R. Konopaske, and C. Touhey, "Ten Questions to Ask Yourself about Compensation Surveys." See also U. Vu, "Know-how Pays in Comp Surveys," *Canadian HR Reporter* (April 7, 2003), p. 13.

17. S. Werner, R. Konopaske, and C. Touhey, "Ten Questions to Ask Yourself about Compensation Surveys," *Compensation and Benefits Review* 31 (May/June 1999), pp. 54–59.

18. D. Hofrichter, "Broadbanding: A 'Second Generation' Approach," *Compensation and Benefits Review* (September–October 1993), pp. 53–58. See also G. Bergel, "Choosing the Right Pay Delivery System to Fit Banding," *Compensation and Benefits Review* 26, (July–August 1994), pp. 34–38.

19. C. Bacca and G. Starzmann, "Clarifying Competencies: Powerful Tools for Driving Business Success," *Workspan* (March 2006), pp. 44–46.

20. Ibid.

21. P.K. Zingheim and J.R. Schuster, "Reassessing the Value of Skill-Based Pay," *WorldatWork Journal* (Third Quarter 2002).

22. R. Long, "Paying for Knowledge: Does It Pay?" *Canadian HR Reporter* (March 28, 2005), pp. 12–13.

23. S. St.-Onge, "Competency-Based Pay Plans Revisited," *Human Resources Professional* (August/September 1998), pp. 29–34; J. Kochanski and P. Leblanc, "Should Firms Pay for Competencies: Competencies Have to Help the Bottom Line," *Canadian HR Reporter* (February 22, 1999), p. 10.

24. F. Giancola, "Skill-Based Pay—Issues for Consideration," *Benefits & Compensation Digest*, 44(5) (May 2007), pp. 10–15.

25. D. Tyson, *Canadian Compensation Handbook*. Toronto: Aurora Professional Press, 2002.

26. P.K. Zingheim, J.R. Schuster, and M.G. Dertien, "Measuring the Value of Work: The 'People-Based' Pay Solution," *WorldatWork Journal* (Third Quarter 2005), pp. 42–49.

27. D. Yoder, *Personnel Management and Industrial Relations* (Englewood Cliffs, NJ: Prentice Hall, 1970), pp. 643–645.

28. B.R. Ellig, "Executive Pay: A Primer," *Compensation & Benefits Review* (January–February 2003), pp. 44–50.

29. "The Top 1000: Top 50 Highest Paid Executives 2007." www.reportonbusiness.com/v5/content/tp1000-2007/index.php?view-top_50_execs (November 26, 2008).

30. H.L. Tosi, S. Werner, J.P. Katz, and L.R. Gomez-Mejia, "How Much Does Performance Matter? A Meta-analysis of CEO Pay Studies," *Journal of Management* 26 (2000), pp. 301–339.

31. M.A. Thompson, "Investors Call for Better Disclosure of Executive Compensation in Canada," *Workspan Focus Canada 2006*, pp. 5–6.

32. P. Moran, "Equitable Salary Administration in High-Tech Companies," *Compensation and Benefits Review* 18 (September–October 1986), pp. 31–40.

33. R. Sibson, *Compensation* (New York: AMACOM, 1981), p. 194.

34. B. Bridges, "The Role of Rewards in Motivating Scientific and Technical Personnel: Experience at Egland AFB," *National Productivity Review* (Summer 1993), pp. 337–348.

35. M. Drolet, "The Male–Female Wage Gap," *Perspectives,* Statistics Canada, Spring 2002, pp. 29–37; E. Carey, "Gender Gap in Earnings Staying Stubbornly High," *Toronto Star* (March 12, 2003), p. A9.

36. "Female Grads Make Less Than Males," *Canadian HR Reporter* (April 19, 2004), p. 2.

37. D. Brown, "StatsCan Unable to Explain Gender Wage Gap," *Canadian HR Reporter* (January 31, 2000), p. 3.

38. "PSAC prepares for Federal Court of Appeal hearing on pay equity complaint at Canada Post," July 10, 2008. www.psac.com/news/2008/what/2080710-e.shtml (March 23, 2009)

39. "Air Canada Loses Pay Equity Decision, For Now," *Canadian HR Reporter* (February 13, 2006), p. 2.

40. D. Brown, "StatsCan Unable to Explain Gender Wage Gap," *Canadian HR Reporter* (January 31, 2000), p. 3.

Chapter 12

1. A. Cowan, *Compensation Planning Outlook 2009* (Ottawa: Conference Board of Canada, 2009).

2. P.K. Zingheim and J.R. Schuster, *Pay People Right!: Breakthrough Reward Strategies to Create Great Companies* (San Francisco, CA: Jossey-Bass, 2000); D. Brown, "Top Performers Must Get Top Pay," *Canadian HR Reporter* (May 8, 2000), pp. 7, 10; V. Dell'Agnese, "Performance-Based Rewards, Line-of-Sight Foster Ownership Behaviour in Staff," *Canadian HR Reporter* (October 8, 2001), p. 10.

3. S. Klie, "'Employees First' at CPX," *Canadian HR Reporter* (September 26, 2005), pp. 1, 3.

4. R. Henderson, *Compensation Management* (Reston, VA: Reston, 1979), p. 363. For a discussion of the increasing use of incentives for blue-collar employees, see, for example, R. Henderson, "Contract Concessions: Is the Past Prologue?" *Compensation and Benefits Review* 18, no. 5 (September–October 1986), pp. 17–30. See also A.J. Vogl, "Carrots, Sticks and Self-Deception," *Across-the-Board* 3, no. 1 (January 1994), pp. 39–44.

5. D. Belcher, *Compensation Administration* (Englewood Cliffs, NJ: Prentice Hall, 1973), p. 314.

6. For a discussion of these, see T. Wilson, "Is It Time to Eliminate the Piece Rate Incentive System?" *Compensation and Benefits Review* (March–April 1992), pp. 43–49.

7. Measured day work is a third type of individual incentive plan for production workers. See, for example, M. Fein, "Let's Return to MDW for Incentives," *Industrial Engineering* (January 1979), pp. 34–37.

8. A. Saunier and E. Hawk, "Realizing the Potential of Teams through Team-Based Rewards," *Compensation and Benefits Review* (July–August 1994), pp. 24–33; S. Caudron, "Tie Individual Pay to Team Success," *Personnel Journal* 73, no. 10 (October 1994), pp. 40–46.

9. Some other suggestions are equal payments to all members on the team; differential payments to team members based on their contributions to the team's performance; differential payments determined by a ratio of each group member's base pay to the total base pay of the group. See K. Bartol and L. Hagmann, "Team-Based Pay Plans: A Key to Effective Teamwork," *Compensation and Benefits Review* (November–December 1992), pp. 24–29.

10. J. Nickel and S. O'Neal, "Small Group Incentives: Gainsharing in the Microcosm," *Compensation and Benefits Review* (March–April 1990), p. 24. See also J. Pickard, "How Incentives Can Drive Teamworking," *Personnel Management* (September 1993), pp. 26–32; S. Caudron, "Tie Individual Pay to Team Success," *Personnel Journal* (October 1994), pp. 40–46. For an explanation of how to develop a successful group incentive program, see K. Dow Scott and Timothy Cotter, "The Team That Works Together Earns Together," *Personnel Journal* 63 (March 1984), pp. 59–67.

11. L.N. McClurg, "Team Rewards: How Far Have We Come?" *Human Resource Management* 40 (Spring 2001), pp. 73–86. See also A. Gostick, "Team Recognition," *Canadian HR Reporter* (May 21, 2001), p. 15.

12. W.E. Reum and S. Reum, "Employee Stock Ownership Plans: Pluses and Minuses," *Harvard Business Review* 55 (July–August 1976), pp. 133–143; R. Bavier, "Managerial Bonuses," *Industrial Management* (March–April 1978), pp. 1–5. See also J. Thompson, L. Murphy Smith, and A. Murray, "Management Performance Incentives: Three Critical Issues," *Compensation and Benefits Review* 18, no. 5 (September–October 1986), pp. 41–47.

13. A. Cowan, *Compensation Planning Outlook 2009* (Ottawa: Conference Board of Canada, 2009).

14. B.R. Ellig, "Incentive Plans: Short-Term Design Issues," *Compensation Review* 16, no. 3 (Third Quarter 1984), pp. 26–36; B. Ellig, *Executive Compensation—A Total Pay Perspective* (New York: McGraw-Hill, 1982), p. 187.

15. B. Ellig, *Executive Compensation—A Total Pay Perspective* (New York: McGraw-Hill, 1982), pp. 188–189; R. Bavier, "Managerial Bonuses," *Industrial Management* (March–April 1978), pp. 1–5. See also C. Tharp, "Linking Annual Incentive Awards to Individual Performance," *Compensation and Benefits Review* 17 (November–December 1985), pp. 38–43.

16. F.D. Hildebrand, Jr., "Individual Performance Incentives," *Compensation Review* 10 (Third Quarter 1978), p. 32.

17. Ibid., pp. 28–33.

18. P. Brieger, "Shareholders Target CEO Compensation," *Financial Post* (April 7, 2003), p. FP5. See also S.M. Van Putten and E.D. Graskamp, "End of an Era? The Future of Stock Options," *Compensation and Benefits Review* (September–October 2002), pp. 29–35; N. Winter, "The Current Crisis in Executive Compensation," *WorldatWork Canadian News* (Fourth Quarter 2002), pp. 1–3; R.M. Kanungo and M. Mendonca, *Compensation: Effective Reward Management* (1997), p. 237.

19. A. Cowan, *Compensation Planning Outlook 2009* (Ottawa: Conference Board of Canada, 2009).

20. R. Levasseur and D. D'Alessandro, "Preparing for changes in executive compensation," *Workspan* (Canada: Workspan Focus), January 2009, pp. 101–104.

21. A. Cowan, *Compensation Planning Outlook 2009* (Ottawa: Conference Board of Canada, 2009).

22. R. Murrill, "Executive Share Ownership," *Watson Wyatt Memorandum* 11, no. 1 (March 1997), p. 11.

23. R.J. Long, "Ensuring Your Executive Compensation Plan Is an Asset Rather Than a Liability," *Canadian HR Reporter* (October 19, 1998), pp. 15–16. See also D. Brown, "Bringing Stock Options back to the Surface," *Canadian HR Reporter* (May 7, 2001), p. 2.

24. I. Huss and M. Maclure, "Broad-Based Stock Option Plans Take Hold," *Canadian HR Reporter* (July 17, 2000), p. 18; J. Staiman and C. Thompson, "Designing and Implementing a Broad-Based Stock Option Plan," *Compensation and Benefits Review* (July–August 1998), p. 23.

25. *CPP Investment Board Proxy Voting Principles and Guidelines* (February 7, 2006).

26. R. Levasseur and D. D'Alessandro, "Preparing for changes in executive compensation," *Workspan* (Canada: Workspan Focus), January 2009, pp. 101–104.

27. P. Singh and N.C. Agarwal, "Executive Compensation: Examining an Old Issue from New Perspectives," *Compensation and Benefits Review* (March/April 2003), pp. 48–54.

28. R. Levasseur and D. D'Alessandro, "Preparing for changes in executive compensation," *Workspan* (Canada: Workspan Focus), January 2009, pp. 101–104.

29. J. Tallitsch and J. Moynahan, "Fine-Tuning Sales Compensation Programs," *Compensation and Benefits Review* 26, no. 2 (March–April 1994), pp. 34–37.

30. Straight salary by itself is not, of course, an incentive compensation plan as we use the term in this chapter; J. Steinbrink, "How to Pay Your Sales Force," *Harvard Business Review* 57 (July–August 1978), pp. 111–122.

31. T.H. Patten, "Trends in Pay Practices for Salesmen," *Personnel* 43 (January–February 1968), pp. 54–63. See also C. Romano, "Death of a Salesman," *Management Review* 83, no. 9 (September 1994), pp. 10–16.

32. D. Harrison, M. Virick, and S. William, "Working Without a Net: Time, Performance, and Turnover under Maximally Contingent Rewards," *Journal of Applied Psychology* 81 (1996), pp. 331–345.

33. G. Stewart, "Reward Structure as Moderator of the Relationship Between Extroversion and Sales Performance," *Journal of Applied Psychology* 81 (1996), pp. 619–627.

34. In the salary plus bonus plan, salespeople are paid a basic salary and are then paid a bonus for carrying out specified activities. For a discussion of how to develop a customer-focused sales compensation plan, see, for example, M. Blessington, "Designing a Sales Strategy with the Customer in Mind," *Compensation and Benefits Review* (March–April 1992), pp. 30–41;

S.S. Sands, "Ineffective Quotas: The Hidden Threat to Sales Compensation Plans," *Compensation and Benefits Review* (March/April 2000), pp. 35–42.

35. E. Maggio, "Compensation Strategies Pulling You in Different Directions?" *Canadian HR Reporter* (October 4, 1999), pp. 11, 19. See also B. Serino, "Non-cash Awards Boost Sales Compensation Plans, " *Workspan* (August 2002), pp. 24–27.

36. B. Weeks, "Setting Sales Force Compensation in the Internet Age," *Compensation and Benefits Review* (March/April 2000), pp. 25–34.

37. See, for example, W. Kearney, "Pay for Performance? Not Always," *MSU Business Topics* (Spring 1979), pp. 5–16. See also H. Doyel and J. Johnson, "Pay Increase Guidelines with Merit," *Personnel Journal* 64 (June 1985), pp. 46–50.

38. J. Pfeffer and R.I. Sutton, *Hard Facts, Dangerous Half-Truths, and Total Nonsense* (Boston MA: Harvard Business School Press, 2006).

39. W. Seithel and J. Emans, "Calculating Merit Increases: A Structured Approach," *Personnel* 60, no. 5 (June 1985), pp. 56–68; D. Gilbert and G. Bassett, "Merit Pay Increases Are a Mistake," *Compensation and Benefits Review* 26, no. 2 (March–April 1994), pp. 20–25.

40. S. Minken, "Does Lump Sum Pay Merit Attention?" *Personnel Journal* (June 1988), pp. 77–83; J. Newman and D. Fisher, "Strategic Impact Merit Pay," *Compensation and Benefits Review* (July–August 1992), pp. 38–45.

41. Based primarily on R. Sibson, *Compensation* (New York: AMACOM, 1981), pp. 189–207; C. Shelton and L. Shelton, "What HR Can Do about the 'Opt-Out' Revolution (Guest Commentary)," *Canadian HR Reporter* (May 8, 2006).

42. A. Cowan, *Compensation Planning Outlook 2009* (Ottawa: Conference Board of Canada, 2009).

43. B. Duke, "Are Profit-Sharing Plans Making the Grade?" *Canadian HR Reporter* (January 11, 1999), pp. 8–9.

44. D.E. Tyson, *Profit-Sharing in Canada: The Complete Guide to Designing and Implementing Plans That Really Work* (Toronto: Wiley, 1996), pp. 200–207.

45. C. Baarda, *Compensation Planning Outlook 2006* (Ottawa: Conference Board of Canada, 2006).

46. R. Murrill, "Executive Share Ownership," *Watson Wyatt Memorandum* 11, no. 1 (March 1997), p. 11.

47. P. Robertson, "Increasing Productivity through an Employee Share Purchase Plan," *Canadian HR Reporter* (September 20, 1999), pp. 7, 9.

48. C. Beatty, "Our Company: Employee Ownership May Sound Drastic, but It Can Work," *HR Professional*, June/July 2004, p. 20.

49. E. Beaton, "The lure of ESOPs," *PROFIT*, June 2007. http://rankings.canadianbusiness.com/profit100/article.asp?pageID=article&year=2007&content=esops&type=feature (July 8, 2009).

50. B. Moore and T. Ross, *The Scanlon Way to Improved Productivity: A Practical Guide* (New York: Wiley, 1978), p. 2.

51. Based in part on S. Markham, K. Dow Scott, and W. Cox, Jr., "The Evolutionary Development of a Scanlon Plan," *Compensation and Benefits Review* (March–April 1992), pp. 50–56; J.K. White, "The Scanlon Plan: Causes and Correlates of Success," *Academy of Management Journal* 22 (June 1979), pp. 292–312.

52. B. Moore and T. Ross, *The Scanlon Way to Improved Productivity: A Practical Guide* (New York: Wiley, 1978), pp. 1–2.

53. J.K. White, "The Scanlon Plan: Causes and Correlates of Success," *Academy of Management Journal* 22 (June 1979), pp. 292–312. For a discussion of the Improshare plan, see R. Kaufman, "The Effects of Improshare on Productivity," *Industrial and Labor Relations Review* 45, no. 2 (1991), pp. 311–322.

54. B.W. Thomas and M.H. Olson, "Gainsharing: The Design Guarantees Success," *Personnel Journal* (May 1988), pp. 73–79. See also "Aligning Compensation with Quality," *Bulletin to Management, BNA Policy and Practice Series* (April 1, 1993), p. 97.

55. See T.A. Welbourne and L. Gomez Mejia, "Gainsharing Revisited," *Compensation and Benefits Review* (July–August 1988), pp. 19–28.

56. Paraphrased from W. Imberman, "Boosting Plant Performance with Gainsharing," *Business Horizons* (November–December 1992), p. 77;

for other examples, see T. Ross and L. Hatcher, "Gainsharing Drives Quality Improvement," *Personnel Journal* (November 1992), pp. 81–89. See also J. McAdams, "Employee Involvement and Performance Reward Plans: Design, Implementation, and Results," *Compensation and Benefits Review* 27, no. 2 (March 1995), pp. 45–55.

57. P.K. Zingheim and J.R. Schuster, "Value Is the Goal," *Workforce* (February 2000), pp. 56–61.

58. *Innovative Workplace Practices 2006*. Human Resources and Social Development Canada, Workplace Information Labour Program. www.hrsdc.gc.ca/eng/lp/wid/win/2006_overview.shtml (July 8, 2009).

59. A. Kohn, "Why Incentive Plans Cannot Work," *Harvard Business Review* (September–October 1993), pp. 54–63.

60. J. Cameron and W.D. Pierce, *Rewards and Intrinsic Motivation: Resolving the Controversy* (Westport, CT: Bergin & Garvey, 2002). See also G. Bouchard, "When Rewards Don't Work," *Globe & Mail* (September 25, 2002), p. C3.

61. P.K. Zingheim and J.R. Schuster, *Pay People Right!: Breakthrough Reward Strategies to Create Great Companies* (San Francisco: Jossey-Bass, 2000).

62. S. Gross and J. Bacher, "The New Variable Pay Programs: How Some Succeed, Why Some Don't," *Compensation and Benefits Review* (January–February 1993), pp. 55–56; see also G. Milkovich and C. Milkovich, "Strengthening the Pay–Performance Relationship: The Research," *Compensation and Benefits Review* (November–December 1992), pp. 53–62; J. Schuster and P. Zingheim, "The New Variable Pay: Key Design Issues," *Compensation and Benefits Review* (March–April 1993), pp. 27–34.

63. D. Belcher, *Compensation Administration* (Englewood Cliffs, NJ: Prentice Hall, 1973), pp. 309–310.

64. C. Kapel and T. Kinsman-Berry, "Seven Key Factors for Effective Incentive Plans," *Canadian HR Reporter* (October 4, 1999), pp. 12–13.

65. A. Avalos, "Recognition: A Critical Component of the Total Rewards Mix," *Workspan*, July 2007, pp. 32–35.

66. K. Izuma, D.N. Saito, and N. Sadato, "Processing of Social and Monetary Rewards in the Human Striatum," *Neuron* 58(2) (April 24 2008), pp. 284–294.

68. J. Mills, "Gratitude à la carte," *Workplace News* (January 2005), p. 12; L. McKibbon-Brown, "Beyond the Gold Watch: Employee Recognition Today," *Workspan* (April 2003), pp. 44–46.

69. A. Welsh, "The Give and Take of Recognition Programs," *Canadian HR Reporter* (September 22, 1997), pp. 16–17, 22; J.M. Kouzas and B.Z. Posner, *Encouraging the Heart: A Leader's Guide to Rewarding and Recognizing Others* (San Francisco: Wiley, 2003); D. Brown, "Canada Wants Nurses Again, but Will Anyone Answer the Call?" *Canadian HR Reporter* (January 15, 2001), pp. 1, 14, 15.

70. J.M. Kouzas and B.Z. Posner, *Encouraging the Heart: A Leader's Guide to Rewarding and Recognizing Others* (San Francisco: Wiley, 2003). See also B. Nelson, "Why Managers Don't Recognize Employees," *Canadian HR Reporter* (March 11, 2002), p. 9; L. Cassiani, "Lasting Impressions through Recognition," *Canadian HR Reporter* (March 12, 2001), p. 7; J. Mills, "A Matter of Pride: Rewarding Team Success," *Canadian HR Reporter* (March 8, 1999), p. 16; L. Young, "How Can I Ever Thank You?" *Canadian HR Reporter* (January 31, 2000), pp. 7, 9.

71. E. Wright and K. Ryan, "Thanks a Million (More or Less)," *Canadian HR Reporter* (March 9, 1998), pp. 19, 21, 23. See also "How to Sell Recognition to Top Management," *Canadian HR Reporter* (June 1, 1998), p. 21; B. Nelson, "Cheap and Meaningful Better Than Expensive and Forgettable," *Canadian HR Reporter* (August 13, 2001), p. 22.

72. L. Davidson, "The Power of Personal Recognition," *Workforce* (July 1999), pp. 44–49. See also A. Gostick and C. Elton, "Show Me the Rewards," *Canadian HR Reporter* (March 12, 2001), pp. 7, 10; V. Scott and B. Phillips, "Recognition Program Links Achievement to Corporate Goals," *Canadian HR Reporter* (December 14, 1998), pp. 22–23. See also R. Clarke, "Building a Recognition Program: Alternatives and Considerations," *Canadian HR Reporter* (November 2, 1998), pp. 17, 19; E. Wright and K. Ryan, "Thanks a Million (More or Less)," *Canadian HR Reporter* (March 9, 1998), pp. 19, 21,

23; L. Davidson, "The Power of Personal Recognition," *Workforce* (July 1999), pp. 44–49; D. Brown, "Recognition an Integral Part of Total Rewards," *Canadian HR Reporter* (August 12, 2002), pp. 25, 27.

73. U. Vu, "Green recognition a mere whisper," *Canadian HR Reporter* (August 11, 2008); U. Vu, "What green recognition looks like," *Canadian HR Reporter* (Aug 11, 2008).

74. J. Jackson, "The Art of Recognition," *Canadian HR Reporter* (January 15, 2001), p. 22. See also B.P. Keegan, "Incentive Programs Boost Employee Morale," *Workspan* (March 2002), pp. 30–33; S. Nador, "Beyond Trinkets and Trash," *Canadian HR Reporter* (May 20, 2002), pp. 15, 19.

75. H. Hilliard, "How to Reward Top Performers When Money Is No Object," *Canadian HR Reporter* (August 13, 2001), pp. 21, 23.

76. A. Welsh, "The Give and Take of Recognition Programs," *Canadian HR Reporter* (September 22, 1997), pp. 16–17, 22; E. Wright and K. Ryan, "Thanks a Million (More or Less)," *Canadian HR Reporter* (March 9, 1998).

77. L.J. Blake, "Montana's Cookhouse serves up recognition," *Workplace* (September–October 2008), pp. 14–16; D. Irvine, "Bring back that lovin' feeling," *Canadian HR Reporter* (November 3, 2008); T. Humber, "Beyond the Gold Watch," *Canadian HR Reporter* (January 30, 2006), pp. 23, 29; S. Singh, "'Tis the Season for Recognition," *Canadian HR Reporter* (December 5, 2005), pp. 19–20.

Chapter 13

1. Based on F. Hills, T. Bergmann, and V. Scarpello, *Compensation Decision Making* (Fort Worth: The Dryden Press, 1994), p. 424. See also L.K. Beatty, "Pay and Benefits Break Away from Tradition," *HR Magazine* 39 (November 1994), pp. 63–68.

2. R.K. Platt, "A Strategic Approach to Benefits," *Workspan* (July 2002), pp. 23–24.

3. S. Beech and J. Tompkins, "Do Benefits Plans Attract and Retain Talent?" *Benefits Canada* (October 2002), pp. 49–53.

4. F. Holmes, "Talking about an Evolution," *Benefits Canada* (September 2001), pp. 30–32; J. Thomas and M. Chilco, "Coming of Age," *Benefits Canada* (March 2001), pp. 36–38.

5. J. Dawe, "Compassionate Care Benefit: A New Alterative for Family Caregivers," *Workplace Gazette* (Summer 2004); S. Klie, "Feds Expand Eligibility for Compassionate Care," *Canadian HR Reporter* (July 17, 2006).

6. "EI Top-ups Common—Survey," *Canadian HR Reporter* (February 23, 1998), p. 15.

7. H. Amolins, "Workers Must Cooperate in Return to Work," *Canadian HR Reporter* (November 3, 1997), p. 8; C. Knight, "Ontario Businesses Ready for New WCB," *Canadian HR Reporter* (November 17, 1997), p. 9.

8. U. Vu, "How Purolator Dealt with Skyrocketing Costs," *Canadian HR Reporter* (March 13, 2006).

9. S. Klie, "Feds Expand Eligibility for Compassionate Care," *Canadian HR Reporter* (July 17, 2006).

10. "Tragedy Leaves of Absence," *HR Professional* (October/November 2008), p.16.

11. D. Gunch, "The Family Leave Act: A Financial Burden?" *Personnel Journal* (September 1993), p. 49.

12. S. Pellegrini, "Considering Critical," *Benefits Canada* (April 2002), pp. 71–73.

13. "Employee Benefits in Small Firms," *BNA Bulletin to Management* (June 27, 1991), pp. 196–197.

14. "Employee Benefits," *Commerce Clearing House Ideas and Trends in Personnel* (January 23, 1991), pp. 9–11.

15. S. Dobson, "Health-care costs maintain dramatic rise," *Canadian HR Reporter* (July 13, 2009).

16. *Canadian Health Care Trend Survey Results 2009*. Toronto: Buck Consultants.

17. C. Kapel, "Unitel Asks Employees to Share Costs," *Canadian HR Reporter* (June 17, 1996), p. 17. See also J. Sloane and J. Taggart, "Runaway Drug Costs," *Canadian HR Reporter* (September 10, 2001), pp. 17–18; "Deductibles Could Be Making a Comeback," *Canadian HR Reporter* (February 26, 2001), pp. 2, 16.

18. J. Norton, "The New Drug Invasion," *Benefits Canada* (June 1999), pp. 29–32.

19. S. Felix, "Healthy Alternative," *Benefits Canada* (February 1997), p. 47; A. Dimon, "Money Well Spent," *Benefits Canada* (April 1997), p. 15.

20. A. Dimon, "Money Well Spent," *Benefits Canada* (April 1997), p. 15.

21. D. Jones, "Accounting for Health: The present and future of HCSAs and other consumer-driven health care products in Canada," *Benefits Canada* (January 2009), pp. 21–23.

22. J. Taggart, "Health Spending Accounts: A Prescription for Cost Control," *Canadian HR Reporter* (October 22, 2001), pp. 16, 18. See also "How Spending Accounts Work," *Canadian HR Reporter* (February 24, 2003), p. 16.

23. K. Gay, "Post-Retirement Benefits Costing Firms a Fortune," *Financial Post* (June 2, 1995), p. 18; S. Lebrun, "Turning a Blind Eye to Benefits," *Canadian HR Reporter* (February 24, 1997), p. 2; S. Pellegrini, "Keep Benefits Costs Low by Assessing Retiree Health," *Canadian HR Reporter* (June 14, 1999), pp. 9–10; M. Warren, "Uncovering the Costs," *Benefits Canada* (November 1996), p. 41; G. Dufresne, "Financing Benefits for Tomorrow's Retirees," *Canadian HR Reporter* (April 6, 1998), p. 11.

24. A. Khemani, "Post-Retirement Benefits Liability Grows," *Canadian HR Reporter* (November 4, 1996), p. 17. See also M. Warren, "Retiree Benefits Come of Age," *Benefits Canada* (May 2000), pp. 73–77.

25. *2008 Post-Retirement Trends.* Toronto: Mercer Human Resources Consulting.

26. W. Pyper, "Aging, Health and Work," *Perspectives on Labour and Income* (Spring 2006, p. 48); S. Klie, "Private Health Coverage Enters Benefits Realm," *Canadian HR Reporter* (September 12, 2005), pp. 1, 22.

27. "Managing episodic disabilities course," *HR Professional* (February/March 2009), p. 18.

28. A. Blake, "A New Approach to Disability Management," *Benefits Canada* (March 2000), pp. 58–64; P. Kulig, "Returning the Whole Employee to Work," *Canadian HR Reporter* (March 9, 1998), p. 20. See also A. Gibbs, "Gearing Disability Management to the Realities of Working Life," *Canadian HR Reporter* (December 2, 2002), p. G7.

29. J. Curtis and L. Scott, "Making the Connection," *Benefits Canada* (April 2003), pp. 75–79.

30. N. Rankin, "A Guide to Disability Management," *Canadian HR Reporter* (March 22, 1999), pp. 14–15.

31. *Staying@Work: Effective Presence at Work* (2007 Survey Report–Canada). Toronto: Watson Wyatt; "Mental Health Claims On the Rise in Canada," *WorldatWork Canadian News* (Third Quarter 2005), pp. 15–16; D. Brown, "Mental Illness a Top Concern but Only Gets Band-Aid Treatment," *Canadian HR Reporter* (May 9, 2005), pp. 1, 3; "Mental Health Biggest Workplace Barrier, Women Say," *Canadian HR Reporter* (January 17, 2005), p. 2.

32. P. Weiner, "A Mental Health Priority for Canada's Employers," *Workspan* (January 2009), pp. 91–95; L. Sussman, "An Executive Guide to Workplace Depression," *Academy of Management Executive* 14 (August 2000), pp. 103–114.

33. *Workplace Mental Health Indicators: An EAP's Perspective.* Shepell-fgi Research Group, 2005, Series 1, Vol. 1, Issue 1.

34. P. Weiner, "A Mental Health Priority for Canada's Employers," *Workspan* (January 2009), pp. 91–95.

35. J. Melnitzer, "Down and Out," *Workplace News* (September/October 2005), pp. 20–23; M. Burych, "Baby Blues," *Benefits Canada* (October 2000), pp 33–35.

36. B. Hayhoe, "The Case for Employee Retirement Planning," *Canadian HR Reporter* (May 20, 2002), p. 18.

37. M. Banks and M. Lowry, "Changing Workforce Requires Rethinking of Pension Plan," *Canadian HR Reporter* (March 10, 1997), p. 17; J. Pearce, "Switching from Defined Benefits to a Money Purchase Plan? Think Twice," *Canadian HR Reporter* (October 6, 1997), pp. 20, 23.

38. F. Giancola, "The Truth about Employee Investment Behavior," *Workspan* (April 2005), pp. 42–45; L. Maldonado, "You Decided to Convert. . . Now What?" *Canadian HR Reporter* (May 23, 2005), pp. 15, 17; F. Holden and S. Lewis, "The Rules Are Changing for Capital Accumulation Plans," *Canadian HR Reporter* (January 16, 2004), pp. 15–16.

39. J. Thompson and P.C. Statler, "Sound Options Make for Sound Choices," *Canadian HR Reporter* (February 9, 1998), p. 10; K. Press, "Top 10 Defined Contribution Pension Funds," *Benefits Canada* (August 1999), pp. 33–42.

40. P. Gougeon, "Shifting Pensions," *Perspectives* (May 2009). Statistics Canada Catalogue No. 75-001-X.

41. S. Klie, "Little guarantee for Ontario pensions," *Canadian HR Reporter* (May 4, 2009); S. Dobson, "Costs top list of concerns for DB plan sponsors: Survey," *Canadian HR Reporter* (March 24, 2008).

42. A. Scappatura, "DB plans endangered," *Canadian HR Reporter* (June 15, 2009); T. Humber, "The death of the DB pension," *Canadian HR Reporter* (March 23, 2009); S. Dobson, "Ottawa provides pension relief," *Canadian HR Reporter* (December 15, 2008); D. Birschel, "Alberta and British Columbia Provide Pension Solvency Relief," *Benefits Quarterly*, 25(2), 2009, p. 66.

43. S. Dobson, "Workers postpone retirement to save money," *Canadian HR Reporter* (May 18, 2009); "Canadians Delaying Retirement Due to Economic Slowdown," *Workspan* (January 2009), pp.106–107; S. Klie, "Workers delay retirement as economy tanks," *Canadian HR Reporter* (January 26, 2009).

44. J. Nunes, "Defined Benefit or Defined Contribution, It's Always Costly," *Canadian HR Reporter* (November 5, 2001), pp. 7, 9.

45. T. Piskorski, "Minimizing Employee Benefits Litigation through Effective Claims Administration Procedures," *Employee Relations Law Journal* 20, no. 3 (Winter 1994–95), pp. 421–431.

46. A. Rappaport, "Phased Retirement_An Important Part of the Evolving Retirement Scene," *Benefits Quarterly*, 25(2), 2009, pp. 38–50; R. Castelli, "Phased Retirement Plans, *HR Professional* (December 2008/January 2009), p. 23.

47. D. Brown, "New Brunswick Nurses Find Phased Retirement Solution," *Canadian HR Reporter* (September 22, 2003), pp. 1, 12; Y. Saint-Cyr, "Phased Retirement Agreements," *Canadian Payroll and Employment Law News*, www.hrpao.org/HRPAO/HRResourceCentre/LegalCentre/ (July 11, 2005).

48. *Towers Perrin 2004 SERP Report: Supplementary Pensions Under Pressure* (Toronto: Towers Perrin).

49. L. Burger, "Group Legal Service Plans: A Benefit Whose Time Has Come," *Compensation and Benefits Review* 18 (July–August 1986), pp. 28–34.

50. *Financial Distress Impacts Health and Productivity: Employees Turning to EAP for Help.* Shepell-fgi Research Group, 2009 Series, Vol. 5, Issue 1; A. Scappatura, "EAP use soars as economy tanks: Study," *Canadian HR Reporter* (March 23, 2009); "Requests for Help Through EAP Up Significantly," *Workspan* (February 2009), p. 13.

51. J. Hobel, "EAPs Flounder without Manager Support," *Canadian HR Reporter* (June 2, 2003), p. 7; P. Davies, "Problem Gamblers in the Workplace," *Canadian HR Reporter* (November 4, 2002), p. 17; A. Sharratt, "When a Tragedy Strikes," *Benefits Canada* (November 2002), pp. 101–105.

52. R. Csiernik, "The great EAP question_internal or external?" *Canadian HR Reporter* (August 20, 2007).

53. R. Csiernik, "What to Look for in an External EAP Service," *Canadian HR Reporter* (May 31, 2004), p. 7; D. Sharar, "With HR Chasing Lowest Price, EAPs Can't Improve Quality," *Canadian HR Reporter* (May 31, 2004), pp. 6, 8; A. Davis, "Helping Hands," *Benefits Canada* (November 2000), pp. 117–121.

54. "100 Best Companies to Work For," *Fortune* (January 2000).

55. C. Foster, "Workers don't leave problems at home," *Canadian HR Reporter* (May 7, 2007).

56. S. Dobson, "Is backup care worth the investment?" *Canadian HR Reporter* (November 3, 2008); D. Brown, "Bringing the Family to Work," *Canadian HR Reporter* (November 6, 2000), pp. 19–20.

57. "Employer-Sponsored Child Care Can Be Instrumental in Attraction and Retention," *Workspan* (January 2009), p. 10.

58. D. McCloskey, "Caregiving and Canadian Families," *Transition Magazine* (Summer 2005); B. Parus, "Who's Watching Grandma? Addressing the Eldercare Dilemma," *Workspan* (January 2004), pp. 40–43.

59. "Elder Care to Eclipse Child Care, Report Says," *Canadian HR Reporter* (August 14, 1995), p. 11; A. Vincola, "Eldercare—What Firms Can Do to Help," *Canadian HR Reporter* (June 5, 2000), p. G3.

60. S. Klie, "Employers can help with 'long goodbye'," *Canadian HR Reporter* (August 13, 2007).

61. D. Dyck, "Make Your Workplace Family-Friendly," *Canadian HR Reporter* (December 13, 1999), pp. G5, G10.

62. E.E. Kossek and C. Ozeki, "Work-Family Conflict, Policies, and the Job-Life Satisfaction Relationship: A Review and Direction for Organizational Behavior–Human Resources Research," *Journal of Applied Psychology* 83, (1998), pp. 139–149.

63. B. Ellig, *Executive Compensation—A Total Pay Perspective* (New York: McGraw-Hill, 1982), p. 141.

64. B. Jaworski, " 'I'll Have My People Call Your People. . . ,' " *Canadian HR Reporter* (March 27, 2006).

65. W. White and J. Becker, "Increasing the Motivational Impact of Employee Benefits," *Personnel* (January–February 1980), pp. 32–37; B. Olmsted and S. Smith, "Flex for Success!" *Personnel* 66, no. 6 (June 1989), pp. 50–55.

66. B. McKay, "The Flexible Evolution," *Workplace News* (January/February 2006), pp. 14–15.

67. R. Dawson and B. McKay, "The Flexibility of Flex," *WorldatWork Canadian News* (Fourth Quarter 2005), pp. 1, 6–13.

68. D. Brown, "Everybody Loves Flex," *Canadian HR Reporter* (November 18, 2002), pp. 1, 11; R. Dawson and B. McKay, "The Flexibility of Flex," *WorldatWork Canadian News* (Fourth Quarter 2005), pp. 1, 6–13

69. J. Tompkins, "Moving Out: A Look at Comprehensive Benefits Outsourcing," *Canadian HR Reporter* (May 5, 1997), p. 9.

70. N. Chaplick, "Enter at Your Own Risk," *Benefits Canada* (May 2000), pp. 37–39. See also M. Reid, "Legal Aid," *Benefits Canada* (June 2000), pp. 46–48; S. Deller, "Five Hot Survival Tips for Communicating Benefits," *Canadian HR Reporter* (July 13, 1998), pp. 9, 19.

71. C. Davenport, "Employers Twig to Value of Ongoing Pension Communication," *Canadian HR Reporter* (December 16, 1996), p. 33.

Chapter 14

1. D. Brown, "Wellness Programs Bring Healthy Bottom Line," *Canadian HR Reporter* (December 17, 2001), pp. 1, 14.

2. Association of Workers' Compensation Boards of Canada, www.awcbc.ca (July 15, 2009); "Working to Death—Millions Die Each Year Due to Work-Related Accidents and Diseases," *IAPA Press Release* (April 19, 2006), www.iapa.ca/about_iapa/2006_apr19_press.asp (June 20, 2006).

3. H. Bryan, "Attitude Is Everything," *WorkSafe Magazine* (October 2005), p. 18.

4. Based on T.A. Opie and L. Bates, *1997 Canadian Master Labour Guide* (CCH Canada Inc.), pp. 1015–1034.

5. C.A. Edwards and C.E. Humphrey, *Due Diligence Under the Occupational Health and Safety Act: A Practical Guide* (Toronto: Carswell/Thomson Canada, 2000).

6. N. Keith, "The Omniscient employer: the need to see the unforeseeable," *Workplace* (March/April 2008), pp. 16–19.

7. M. Pilger, "Conducting a Hygiene Assessment," *Canadian HR Reporter* (April 10, 2000), pp. G3, G4; J. Montgomery, *Occupational Health and Safety* (Toronto: Nelson Canada, 1996), p. 97; D. Brown, "Joint H&S Committees: An Opportunity, Not a Nuisance," *Canadian HR Reporter* (October 20, 2002), pp. 7, 10.

8. J. Grant and D. Brown, "The Inspector Cometh," *Canadian HR Reporter* (January 31, 2005), pp. 13, 17; "It's Time to Wake Up to Health and Safety: Ministry of Labour Increases Number of Inspectors," *Safety Mosaic* 8 (Spring 2005), pp. 5–6.

9. "Alberta imposes record penalties for oh&s violations," *Workplace*. www.workplace-mag.com/Alberta-imposes-record-penalties-for-ohs-violations.html (July 16, 2009).

10. S. Klie, "Individuals targeted under OHS," *Canadian HR Reporter* (March 12, 2007); R. Stewart, "Legal duties of the front line," *Canadian HR Reporter* (March 12, 2007).

11. "Employer Jailed for H&S Violation," *Canadian HR Reporter* (April 8, 2002), p. 2. See also T. Humber, "Putting the Boss Behind Bars?" *Canadian HR Reporter* (April 7, 2003).

12. "Quebec employer first to be criminally convicted in death of worker," *Canadian HR Reporter* (February 7, 2008); "C-45 conviction nets $110K fine," *Canadian HR Reporter* (April 7, 2008).

13. J. Montgomery, *Occupational Health and Safety* (Toronto: Nelson Canada, 1996), p. 34.

14. K. Prisciak, "Health, Safety & Harassment?" *OH&S Canada* (April/May 1997), pp. 20–21.

15. P. Strahlendorf, "What Supervisors Need to Know," *OH&S Canada* (January/February 1996), pp. 38–40; N. Tompkins, "Getting the Best Help from Your Safety Committee," *HR Magazine* 40, no. 4 (April 1995), p. 76.

16. Dupont Canada, www2.dupont.com/DuPont_Home/en_CA/index.html (June 20, 2006).

17. *A Safety Committee Man's Guide*, Aetna Life and Casualty Insurance Company, Catalog 872684.

18. J. Roughton, "Job Hazard Analysis," *OH&S Canada* (January/February 1996), pp. 41–44.

19. A. Fowler, "How to Make the Workplace Safer," *People Management* 1, no. 2 (January, 1995), pp. 38–39.

20. List of unsafe acts from *A Safety Committee Man's Guide*, Aetna Life and Casualty Insurance Company; E. McCormick and J. Tiffin, *Industrial Psychology* (Englewood Cliffs, NJ: Prentice Hall, 1974).

21. E. McCormick and J. Tiffin, *Industrial Psychology* (Englewood Cliffs, NJ: Prentice Hall, 1974), pp. 522–523; David DeJoy, "Attributional Processes and Hazard Control Management in Industry," *Journal of Safety Research* 16 (Summer 1985), pp. 61–71.

22. E. McCormick and J. Tiffin, *Industrial Psychology* (Englewood Cliffs, NJ: Prentice Hall, 1974), p. 523.

23. A. Campbell, *All Signs Point to Yes: Literacy's Impact on Workplace Health and Safety*. Ottawa: The Conference Board of Canada, 2008.

24. S. Dobson, "Evidence of link between literacy, safety," *Canadian HR Reporter* (December 1, 2008).

25. A. Campbell, *All Signs Point to Yes: Literacy's Impact on Workplace Health and Safety*. Ottawa: The Conference Board of Canada, 2008.

26. "IAPA wins first place at International Film and Multimedia Festival." *Workplace* e-newsletter (July 18, 2008).

27. M. Blum and J. Nayler, *Industrial Psychology* (New York: Harper & Row, 1968), p. 522.

28. L. Scott, "Measuring Employee Abilities," *Benefits Canada* (September 2002), pp. 41–49.

29. K. Gillin, "Reduce Employee Exposure to Injury with Pre-Employment Screening Tests," *Canadian HR Reporter* (February 28, 2000), p. 10.

30. M. Shaw, "Rewarding Health and Safety," *Canadian HR Reporter* (December 2, 2002), pp. 19–20.

31. "Rewarding Safety: 70 million kilometres and counting," *Workplace* (November/December 2008).

32. M. Morra, "Fun, with caution," *Workplace* (March/April 2008); L. Scott, "Measuring Employee Abilities," *Benefits Canada* (September 2002), pp. 41–49.

33. A. Dunn, "Back in Business," *Workplace News* (April 2005), pp. 16–17.

34. Ergomed Solutions. http://ergomedsolutions.com/functionalabilitiesevaluationsp17.php (July 15, 2009); C. Colacci, "Meet Your Return to Work Obligations with a Functional Abilities Evaluation," *Canadian HR Reporter* (April 10, 2000), p. G5.

35. L. Young, "Managers at B.C. Telus Held Accountable for Wellness," *Canadian HR Reporter* (February 28, 2000), p. 9.

36. J. Taggart and J. Farrell, "Where Wellness Shows Up on the Bottom Line," *Canadian HR Reporter* (October 20, 2003), pp. 12, 15.

37. S. Klie, "Seven Oaks hospital relies on healthy staff," *Canadian HR Reporter* (October 23, 2006).

38. E. Buffett, "Healthy employees translate into profits," *Canadian HR Reporter* (April 9, 2007).

39. A. Tomlinson, "Healthy Living a Remedy for Burgeoning Employee Absentee Rates," *Canadian HR Reporter* (March 25, 2002), pp. 3, 12.

40. S. Pellegrini, "The Next 25 Years: Wellness," *Benefits Canada* (June 2002), pp. 83–85.

41. C. Warren, "Healthy Competition Boosts Workplace Wellness," *Workplace News* (November/December 2007).

42. C. Hall, "Sobering Advice," *Workplace News* 11, no. 10 (November/December 2005), pp. 11–12.

43. *British Columbia (Public Service Employee Relations Commission) v. B.C.G.S.E.U.*, (1999) 176 D.L.R. (4th) 1 (S.C.C.) [*Meiorin*].

44. Policy on Drug and Alcohol Testing, Ontario Human Rights Commission. www.ohrc.on.ca/en/resources/Policies/PolicyDrugAlch (July 16, 2009).

45. D. McCutcheon, "Confronting Addiction," *HR Professional* (June/July 2009).

46. D. O'Meara, "Sober Second Chance," *Alberta Venture* 9, no. 2 (March 2005).

47. A. Chiu, "The Elements of Workplace Drug, Alcohol Policies," *Canadian HR Reporter* (March 13, 2000), p. 17.

48. A. Nicoll, *Time for Action: Managing Mental Health in the Workplace*. Toronto: Mercer Human Resources Consulting; L. Duxbury and C. Higgins, *Exploring the Link between Work–Life Conflict and Demands on Canada's Health Care System: Report Three* (Public Health Agency of Canada: March 2004).

49. *Mental Health at Work: Booklet 1.* IRSST (Laval University, 2005).

50. *Staying@Work: Effective Presence at Work_2007 Survey Report_Canada.* Toronto: Watson Wyatt.

51. Ibid.

52. D. Crisp, "Leaders make the difference," in A. Shaw, "Toxic workplaces as bad as unsafe ones, *Canadian HR Reporter* (April 21, 2008).

53. A. Nicoll, *Time for Action: Managing Mental Health in the Workplace*. Toronto: Mercer Human Resources Consulting.

54. "Study: Workaholics and Time Perception," *The Daily, Statistics Canada* (May 15, 2007).

55. "Is your job making you sick?" *Canadian HR Reporter* (September 17, 2008).

56. J.W. Simpson, "Psychopaths Wear Suits, Too," *National Post* (May 10, 2006), p. WK6; A. Gill, "The Psychopath in the Corner Office," *Globe & Mail* (May 27, 2006), p. F1; "Push for Productivity Taking its Toll," *Canadian HR Reporter* (November 6, 2001), p. 15; D. Brown, "Doing More with Less Hurts Employees and Productivity," *Canadian HR Reporter* (October 7, 2002), pp. 3, 13; A. Sharratt, "Silver Linings," *Benefits Canada* (March 2003), pp. 51–53.

57. J. Santa-Barbara, "Preventing the Stress Epidemic," *Canadian HR Reporter* (March 8, 1999), p. 19. See also A. Chiu, "Beyond Physical Wellness: Mental Health Issues in the Workplace," *Canadian HR Reporter* (February 26, 2001), p. 4; L. Hyatt, "Job Stress: Have We Reached the Breaking Point?" *Workplace Today* (January 2002), pp. 14, 15, 37.

58. "Health care workers most stressed," *Canadian HR Reporter* (November 15, 2007)

59. P. Crawford-Smith, "Stressed Out," *Benefits Canada* (November 1999), pp. 115–117.

60. *Stress at Work: Taking Control* (Industrial Accident Prevention Association, 2002); J. Newman and T. Beehr, "Personal and Organizational Strategies for Handling Job Stress: A Review of Research and Opinion," *Personnel Psychology* (Spring 1979), pp. 1–43. See also Bureau of National Affairs, "Work Place Stress: How to Curb Claims," *Bulletin to Management* (April 14, 1988), p. 120.

61. T. Humber, "Stress Attack," *Canadian HR Reporter* (February 10, 2002), pp. G1, G10; M. Shain, "Stress and Satisfaction," *OH&S Canada* (April/May 1999), pp. 38–47.

62. P. Carayon, "Stressful Jobs and Non-stressful Jobs: A Cluster Analysis of Office Jobs," *Ergonomics* 37, no. 2 (1994), pp. 311–323.

63. *Workplace Mental Health Indicators: An EAP's Perspective.* Shepell-fgi Research Group, 2005, Series 1, Vol.1, Issue 1.

64. A. Pihulyk, "When the Job Overwhelms," *Canadian HR Reporter* (January 14, 2002), p. 11.

65. P. Kishchuk, *Yukon Workers' Compensation Act Subsection 105.1 Research Series: Expansion of the Meaning of Disability* (March 2003).

66. M. Gibb-Clark, "The Case for Compensating Stress Claims," *Globe & Mail* (June 14, 1999), p. M1; L. Young, "Stressed Workers Are Suing Employers," *Canadian HR Reporter* (May 3, 1999), pp. 1, 6; D. Brown, "Liability Could Extend to Mental Damage," *Canadian HR Reporter* (October 9, 2000), pp. 1, 8.

67. OPSEU Online, "International RSI Awareness Day—February 28, 2006," www.opseu.org/hands/rsi2006.htm (May 18, 2006); J. Hampton, "RSIs: The Biggest Strain Is on the Bottom Line," *Canadian HR Reporter* (February 10, 1997), pp. 15, 19. See also G. Harrington, "Pushing Ergonomics into Place," *Canadian HR Reporter* (April 24, 1995), pp. 11–12.

68. "Prevent Workplace Pains and Strains! It's Time to Take Action!" Ontario Ministry of Labour, www.labour.gov.on.ca/english/hs/ergonomics/is_ergonomics.html (May 25, 2006).

69. S.B. Hood, "Repetitive Strain Injury," *Human Resources Professional* (June/July 1997), pp. 29–34.

70. "Ergonomic Intervention Improves Worker Health and Productivity," *Institute for Work and Health* (December 15, 2003), www.iwh.on.ca/media/ergonomic.php (July 8, 2006); "Ergonomic Intervention Improves Worker Health and Productivity," *Workplace News* (February 2004), p. 16.

71. J.A. Savage, "Are Computer Terminals Zapping Workers' Health?" *Business and Society Review* (1994).

72. "Office Ergonomics and Repetitive Strain Injuries: What You Need to Know," Ottawa Valley Physiotherapy, www.ovphysio.com (May 25, 2006); Occupational Health and Safety Agency for Healthcare in British Columbia, www.ohsah.bc.ca/templates/index.php?section_copy_id=5396 (May 25, 2006); S. Tenby, "Introduction to Ergonomics: How to avoid RSI—Repetitive Strain Injury," Disabled Women's Network Ontario, http://dawn.thot.net/cd/20.html (May 25, 2006).

73. U. Vu, "Steel union gathers workplace cancer data," *Canadian HR Reporter* (June 2, 2008).

74. "Unions Stress Cancer Prevention," *Canadian HR Reporter* (February 28, 2005), p. 2.

75. D. Brown, "Killer Toxins in the Workplace," *Canadian HR Reporter* (April 23, 2001), pp. 1, 12.

76. A. Scappatura, "Enhanced coverage for firefighters," *Canadian HR Reporter* (May 18, 2009).

77. "EI Granted in Second-Hand Smoke Case," *Canadian HR Reporter* (May 19, 2003), p. 3. See also M.M. Finklestein, "Risky Business," *OH&S Canada* (September/October 1996), pp. 32–34.

78. T. Humber, "Snuffing out Smoking," *Canadian HR Reporter* (April 11, 2005), p. 19, 23; *Towards Healthier Workplaces and Public Places* (Health Canada, 2004).

79. D. J. McKeown and K. Ford, "The importance of people-focused pandemic planning," *Workplace News* (September/October 2006).

80. C. Hallamore, *A State of Unpreparedness: Canadian Organizations' Readiness for a Pandemic.* Ottawa: The Conference Board of Canada, June 2006.

81. S. Dobson, "Employers prepare for the worst," *Canadian HR Reporter* (April 30, 2009).

82. Government of Canada, *The Canadian Pandemic Influenza Plan.* Ottawa: Government of Canada, February 2004.

83. C.C. Cavicchio, "Action Plan for Dealing with a Global Pandemic," *The Conference Board Executive Action Series* (May 2009).

84. C. Hallamore, *A State of Unpreparedness: Canadian Organizations' Readiness for a Pandemic.* Ottawa: The Conference Board of Canada, June 2006.

85. R. A. Macpherson, E. Ringsels and H. Singh, "Swine Influenza_Advice for Employers Preparing for a Pandemic," *McCarthy Tetrault e-Alert* (April 29, 2009). http://news.mccarthy.ca/en/news_template_full.asp?pub_code=4502&news_code=1066 (April 29, 2009).

86. C.C. Cavicchio, "Action Plan for Dealing with a Global Pandemic," *The Conference Board Executive Action Series* (May 2009).

87. D. J. McKeown and K. Ford, "The importance of people-focused pandemic planning," *Workplace News* (September/October 2006).

88. Ibid

89. C. Harden, "Preparing for a Pandemic: The Total Rewards Angle," *Workspan* (July 2006).

90. *Violence in the Workplace*, Canadian Association of University Teachers (October 4, 2004); W.H. Glenn, "Workplace Violence: An Employees' Survival Guide," *OH&S Canada* (April/May 2002), pp. 26–31.

91. S. De Leseleuc, *Criminal Victimization in the Workplace*. Canadian Centre for Justice Statistics (Catalogue No. 85F0033MIE – No. 013), 2004.

92. "Male nurses more likely to be assaulted by patients: StatsCan," *Canadian HR Reporter* (April 16, 2009).

93. S. Dobson, "Sexual assault prompts OHS charge," *Canadian HR Reporter* (December 15, 2008); L. De Piante, "Watch out for dangerous employees," *Canadian HR Reporter* (October 22, 2007); A. Feliu, "Workplace Violence and the Duty of Care: The Scope of an Employer's Obligation to Protect against the Violent Employee," *Employee Relations Law Journal* 20, no. 3 (Winter 1994/95), pp. 381–406; G. French and P. Morgan, "The Risks of Workplace Violence," *Canadian HR Reporter* (December 18, 2000), pp. 27–28.

94. L. De Piante, "Watch out for dangerous employees," *Canadian HR Reporter* (October 22, 2007).

95. S. Klie, "Screening New Hires Won't End Workplace Violence, Study Says," *Canadian HR Reporter* (November 21, 2005), pp. 1, 3; K. Acquino et al, "How Employees Respond to Personal Offense: The Effect of the Blame Attribution, Victim Status, and Offender Status on Revenge and Reconciliation in the Workplace," *Journal of Applied Psychology* 86(1), 2001, pp. 52–59.

96. A. Tomlinson, "Re-evaluating Your Workplace: Is It Safe and Secure?" *Canadian HR Reporter* (February 25, 2002), pp. 3, 12; L. Martin and D. Tona, "Before It's Too Late," *OH&S Canada* (April/May 2000), pp. 52–53.

97. P. Viollis and C. Mathers, "Companies Need to Re-engineer Their Cultural Thinking About Workplace Violence," *Canadian HR Reporter* (March 14, 2005), p. 19; D. Anfuso, "Workplace Violence," *Personnel Journal* (October 1994), p. 71. See also L. Martin and D. Tona, "Before It's Too Late," *OH&S Canada* (April/May 2000), pp. 52–53; H. Bloom, "Workplace Violence: The Myth That We're Helpless," *Workplace Today* (January 2002), pp. 36–37; W.H. Glenn, "Workplace Violence: An Employees' Survival Guide," *OH&S Canada* (April/May 2002), pp. 26–31.

98. D. Anfuso, "Workplace Violence," *Personnel Journal* (October 1994), pp. 66–77.

Chapter 15

1. Y. Cohen-Charash and P. E. Spector, "The Role of Justice in Organizations: A Meta-analysis," *Organizational Behavior and Human Decision Processes* 86 (November 2001), pp. 278–321.

2. A. Saks, "Engagement: The academic perspective," *Canadian HR Reporter* (January 26, 2009).

3. J. Gibbons, *Employee Engagement: A Review of Current Research and Its Implications*. New York: The Conference Board, 2006.

4. *Engaging employees to drive global business success: Insights from Mercer's What's WorkingTM research*. New York: Mercer, 2007.

5. *Towers Perrin Global Workforce Study 2007–2008*. New York: Towers Perrin.

6. S. O'Neal and J. Gebauer, "Talent Management in the 21st Century: Attracting, Retaining and Engaging Employees of Choice," *WorldatWork Journal*, 15(1), 2006, pp. 6–17.

7. J. Gibbons, *Employee Engagement: A Review of Current Research and Its Implications*. New York: The Conference Board, 2006; J.K. Harter, F.L. Schmidt, and T.L. Hayes, "Business-unit–level relationship between employee satisfaction, employee engagement and business outcomes: A meta-analysis," *Journal of Applied Psychology*, 87(2), 2002.

8. *Best Employers in Australia and New Zealand*, Hewitt Associates, 2004.

9. *Engaging employees to drive global business success: Insights from Mercer's What's WorkingTM research*. New York: Mercer, 2007.

10. S. O'Neal and J. Gebauer, "Talent Management in the 21st Century: Attracting, Retaining and Engaging Employees of Choice," *WorldatWork Journal*, 15(1), 2006, pp. 6–17.

11. "J. Shaffer, "Measurable Payoff: How Employee Engagement Can Boost Performance and Profits," *Communication World* (July–August 2004).

12. Based on D. McElroy, "High Tech with High Touch: A New Communication Contract," *Canadian HR Reporter* (April 7, 1997), p. G6.

13. "Chrysler workers furious over CEO`s letter," *Canadian HR Reporter* (May 4, 2009).

14. D. Jones, "What If You Held a Survey and No-One Came?" *Canadian HR Reporter* (July 16, 2001), pp. 19, 22.

15. D. Brown, "Getting the Hard Facts in Employee Attitude and Satisfaction," *Canadian HR Reporter* (November 1, 1999), p. 2.

16. A. Massey, "Blogging Phobia Hits Employers," *Canadian HR Reporter* (September 26, 2005), pp. 15, 17.

17. L. Harris, "Staffer fired after bad-mouthing colleagues, management in blog," *Canadian HR Reporter* (September 8, 2008); S.E. Sorenson, "Employee Blogging," *HR Professional* (April/May 2008), p. 16.

18. L. De Piante, "Blogging guidelines for employees: A necessity in the workplace," *Canadian HR Reporter* (April 23, 2007); S. Crossley and M. Torrance, "Indiscriminate blogging and the workplace," *Workplace News* (November/December 2007), pp. 12–13.

19. Based on D. McElroy, "High Tech with High Touch: A New Communication Contract," *Canadian HR Reporter* (April 7, 1997), p. G6.

20. S. Klie, "Blogs connect CEOs with employees, clients," *Canadian HR Reporter* (November 17, 2008).

21. P. Israel, "Employee Misconduct . . . Employer Responsibility?" *Canadian HR Reporter* (May 20, 2002), p. 5.

22. P. Israel, "Spying on Employees . . . and It's Perfectly Legal," *Canadian HR Reporter* (April 21, 2003), p. 5.

23. M. Draaisma, "Computer Use Policy in Workplace is a Must, Says Toronto Lawyer," *Ultimate HR Manual* (May 2009), pp. 1–4.

24. A.P. Cleek, "Six Steps to an Effective Workplace Blogging Policy," *Ultimate HR Manual* (August 2007), pp. 6–7.

25. E. Kuzz, "More Rules for Employee Information Protection," *Canadian HR Reporter* (September 9, 2002), p. 16; D. Brown, "10 Months to Get Ready," *Canadian HR Reporter* (February 24, 2003), pp. 1, 11.

26. D. Fallows, "Technology paves the way for Big Brother," *Canadian HR Reporter* (April 9, 2007).

27. M. Draaisma, "Computer Use Policy in Workplace is a Must, Says Toronto Lawyer," *Ultimate HR Manual* (May 2009), pp. 1–4; S. Rudner, "The High Cost of Internet, E-mail Abuse," *Canadian HR Reporter* (January 31, 2005), pp. R5–R6; N. MacDonald, "You've Got E-mail Problems," *Canadian HR Reporter* (March 10, 2003), pp. G5, G10.

28. K. Williams, "Privacy in a Climate of Electronic Surveillance," *Workplace News* (April 2005), p. 10; S. Hood, "What's Private, What's Not?" *HR Professional* (February/March 2006), pp. 20–28; P. Strazynski, "Falsely accused employee gets $2.1 million," *Canadian HR Reporter* (July 14, 2008).

29. S. Stephens, "When Two Worlds Collide," *HR Professional* (April/May 2000), pp. 27–35.

30. *Canada's Demographic Revolution: Adjusting to an Aging Population* (The Conference Board of Canada, 2006).

31. *1995 Canadian Dismissal Practices Survey* (Toronto: Murray Axmith & Associates).

32. G. Golightly, "Preparing Employees for Retirement Transitions," *HR Professional* (December 1999/January 2000), pp. 27–33.

33. Ibid.

34. *New Frontiers of Research on Retirement*, Statistics Canada, Catalogue No. 75-511-XPE, 2006, www.statcan.ca/bsolc/english/bsolc?catno= 75-511-XIE (July 11, 2006).

35. A. Templer and M. Armstrong-Stassen, "The Elder Effect," *HR Professional*, (December 2006/January 2007), p. 40.

36. Quoted from Commerce Clearing House, *Ideas and Trends in Personnel* (August 9, 1988), p. 133.

37. Commerce Clearing House, *Personnel Practices/Communications* (Chicago: CCH, 1992), p. 1410.

38. D. Patient and D. Skarlicki, "Don't Shoot the Messenger! How to Deliver Bad News," *HR Professional* (June/July 2003), pp. 48–49.

39. Based on *Mossop Cornelissen Report* (August 1996).

40. P. Block and G. Wilder, "What to do after the layoffs: Supporting those left behind," *Canadian HR Reporter* (November 17, 2008).

41. J. Emshoff, "How to Increase Employee Loyalty While You Downsize," *Business Horizons* (March–April 1994), pp. 49–57. See also R. Ford and P. Perrewé, "After the Layoff: Closing the Barn Door before All the Horses Are Gone," *Business Horizons* (July–August 1993), pp. 34–40.

42. P. Israel, "How to Tackle Poor Job Performance—and Bring Down Legal Costs," *Canadian HR Reporter* (February 10, 2003), pp. 5, 12.

43. J. Famularo, *Handbook of Modern Personnel Administration* (New York: McGraw-Hill, 1972), pp. 65.3–65.5.

44. N.C. MacDonald, "Progressing towards just cause," *Canadian HR Reporter* (September 22, 2008).

45. S. Rudner, "Just cause termination still not clearcut," *Canadian HR Reporter* (March 23, 2009).

46. D. Bambrough and M. Certosimo, "Worker fraud usually justifies dismissal," *Canadian HR Reporter* (October 23, 2006).

47. L. Cassiani, "Dishonesty Not Always Enough to Terminate," *Canadian HR Reporter* (August 13, 2001), pp. 3, 6; P. Israel, "Firing an Employee for Dishonesty? Put Things in Context First," *Canadian HR Reporter* (August 12, 2002), p. 5.

48. "Proving Cause for Termination Getting Harder," *Workplace Today* (January 2001), p. 17; L. Harris, "High Standards Allow Employer to Fire Threatening Employee," *Canadian HR Reporter* (October 22, 2001), pp. 8, 10.

49. D. Bambrough and M. Certosimo, "Worker fraud usually justifies dismissal," *Canadian HR Reporter* (October 23, 2006).

50. A. Britnell, "Stop Employee Theft," *Canadian Business Online*, July 16, 2003, www.canadianbusiness.com (May 29, 2006); J. Towler, "Dealing with Employees Who Steal," *Canadian HR Reporter* (September 23, 2002), p. 4.

51. "Air Canada Searches Employee Rooms," *Canadian HR Reporter* (February 10, 2003), p. 2.

52. J. Famularo, *Handbook of Modern Personnel Administration* (New York: McGraw-Hill, 1972), pp. 65.4–65.5.

53. "Good broker, bad decision," *Canadian HR Reporter* (July 17, 2006).

54. E.E. Mole, *Wrongful Dismissal Practice Manual*, Chapter 7 (Toronto: Butterworths Canada, 1993).

55. J.R. Smith, "Worker ordered to pay $41.5 million," *Canadian HR Reporter* (December 1, 2008).

56. K. Blair, "Sports Editor Scores 28-Month Severance," *Canadian HR Reporter* (April 7, 1997), p. 5.

57. M. Fitzgibbon, "Desperate for workers? Watch your step," *Canadian HR Reporter* (January 28, 2008).

58. J. McAlpine, "Don't Add Bad Faith to Wrongful Dismissal," *Canadian HR Reporter* (May 6, 2002), p. 7; P. Israel, "Cut Down on Lawsuits Just by Being Nice," *Canadian HR Reporter* (November 18, 2002), p. 5.

59. N.C. MacDonald, "Record-setting Wallace award overturned," *Canadian HR Reporter* (September 11, 2006).

60. J.R. Smith, "Top court strips out damages in *Keays*," *Canadian HR Reporter* (July 14, 2008); T. Giesbrecht, K. McDermott and K. McNeill, "*Keays v. Honda Canada Inc.*" www.mccarthy.ca/article_detail.aspx?id=4053 (June 27, 2008).

61. M.J. MacKillop, "The Perils of Dismissal: The Impact of the Wallace Decision on Reasonable Notice." Paper presented at the Human Resources Professionals Association of Ontario Employment Law Conference (October 1999), Toronto, p. 18.

62. K. Blair, "Pay in Lieu Just the Beginning," *Canadian HR Reporter* (July 14, 1997), p. 5. See also K. Blair, "Dismissal Damages, Thy Name Is Mitigation," *Canadian HR Reporter* (February 9, 1998), p. 5.

63. M. MacKillop and L. Jessome, "Manage Disability Claims with Care," *HR Professional* (August/September 2005), p. 30; J.M. Carvalho, "$500,000 Punitive Damages Award Shocks Honda," *McCarthy Tetrault Report on Canadian Labour and Employment Law* (September 2005).

64. N.C. MacDonald, "The *Keays* to punitive damages," Canadian HR Reporter (November 20, 2006); T. Giesbrecht, K. McDermott and K. McNeill, "*Keays v. Honda Canada Inc.*" www.mccarthy.ca/article_detail.aspx?id=4053 (June 27, 2008).

65. J. McApline, "10 Steps for Reducing Exposure to Wrongful Dismissal," *Canadian HR Reporter* (May 6, 2002), p. 8.

66. E. Caruk, "What to Do If a Wrongful Dismissal Action Hits," *Canadian HR Reporter* (May 6, 2002), p. 10.

67. E.E. Mole, *Wrongful Dismissal Practice Manual*, Chapter 3 (Toronto: Butterworths Canada, 1993).

68. H.A.Levitt and V. Michaelidis, "Ex-employee granted $800,000 in constructive dismissal case," *Workplace* (March/April 2008), p. 11.

69. H. Nieuwland, "Changing Employment Contracts," *HR Professional* (October/November 2008), p. 21.

70. E.A. Lind, J. Greenberg, K.S. Scott, and T.D. Welchans, "The Winding Road from Employee to Complainant: Situational and Psychological Determinants of Wrongful Dismissal Claims," *Administrative Science Quarterly* 45 (2000), pp. 557–590.

71. D. Bell, "No easy way to say 'You're fired'," *Canadian HR Reporter* (June 15, 2009); J. Coil, III and C. Rice, "Three Steps to Creating Effective Employee Releases," *Employment Relations Today* (Spring 1994), p. 92.

72. S. Milne, "The Termination Interview," *Canadian Manager* (Spring 1994), pp. 15–16.

73. Sonny Weide, "When You Terminate an Employee," *Employment Relations Today* (August 1994), pp. 287–293.

Chapter 16

1. T.T. Delaney, "Unions and Human Resource Policies," in K. Rowland and G. Ferris (eds.), *Research in Personnel and Human Resources Management* (Greenwich, CT: JAI Press, 1991).

2. S. Klie, "Wal-Mart closes union shop in Quebec," *Canadian HR Reporter* (November 3, 2008).

3. L. Harris, "Union-proof: How some employers avoid organized labour," *Canadian HR Reporter* (October 22, 2007).

4. R. Morissette, G. Shellenberg, and A. Johnson, "Diverging Trends in Unionization," *Perspectives on Labour and Income* 17, no. 2, Statistics Canada (Summer 2005); U. Vu, "Low Membership Keeps Unions on the Defensive," *Canadian HR Reporter* (February 13, 2006), pp. 4, 9.

5. C. Hallamore, "Globalization Shifts the Ground in Labour Relations," *Inside Edge* (Spring 2006), p. 14. See also C. Hallamore, *Industrial Relations Outlook 2006: Shifting Ground, Shifting Attitudes* (Ottawa: Conference Board of Canada).

6. S. Klie, "Auto bailout demands tie union's hands," *Canadian HR Reporter* (February 9, 2009); S. Klie. "Economic crisis changes union priorities," *Canadian HR Reporter* (December 1, 2008); A. Scappatura, "Role of unions evolves," *Canadian HR Reporter* (May 18, 2009).

7. L. Young, "Unlikely allies team up," *Canadian HR Reporter* (November 5, 2007).

8. C. Hallamore, *Industrial Relations Outlook 2007: Finding Common Ground Through the War for Workers*. Ottawa ON: The Conference Board of Canada, 2007; S. Klie, "Labour market should unite business, unions," *Canadian HR Reporter* (February 27, 2007).

9. L. Harris, "Unions taking up the mantle of women's issues," *Canadian HR Reporter* (August 11, 2008); L. Harris, "Youthful proposition from unions," *Canadian HR Reporter* (October 20, 2008).

10. S. Klie, "Women outnumber men in Canadian unions," *Canadian HR Reporter* (September 24, 2007).

11. W.C. Hamner and F. Schmidt, "Work Attitude as Predictor of Unionization Activity," *Journal of Applied Psychology* 63, no. 4 (1978), pp. 415–521; A. Okafor, "White Collar Unionization: Why and What to Do," *Personnel* 62, no. 8 (August 1985), pp. 17–20; M.E. Gordon and A. DiNisi, "A Re-examination of the Relationship between Union Membership and Job Satisfaction," *Industrial and Labor Relations Review* 48, no. 2 (January 1995), pp. 222–236.

12. L. Harris, "Unions taking up the mantle of women's issues," *Canadian HR Reporter* (August 11, 1008).

13. C. Fullager and J. Barling, "A Longitudinal Test of a Model of the Antecedents and Consequences of Union Loyalty," *Journal of Applied Psychology* 74, no. 2 (April 1989), pp. 213–227; A. Eaton, M. Gordon, and J. Keefe, "The Impact of Quality of Work-Life Programs and Grievance Systems Effectiveness on Union Commitment," *Industrial and Labor Relations Review* 45, no. 3 (April 1992), pp. 592–604.

14. L. Young, "Union Drives: Initiated Within, Prevented Within," *Canadian HR Reporter* (November 29, 1999), pp. 2, 14.

15. Based in part on L. Field, "Early Signs," *Canadian HR Reporter* (November 29, 1999), p. 14.

16. *Canadian Master Labour Guide*, 16th ed. (Toronto: CCH Canadian, 2002).

17. A.W.J. Craig and N.A. Solomon, *The System of Industrial Relations in Canada*, 5th ed. (Scarborough, ON: Prentice Hall Canada, 1996), p. 217.

18. Ibid, p. 218.

19. Ibid, p. 216.

20. J. Peirce, *Canadian Industrial Relations* (Scarborough, ON: Prentice Hall Canada, 2000), p. 431.

21. The section on distributive bargaining is based on R.E. Walton and R.B. McKersie, *A Behavioral Theory of Labor Negotiations* (New York: McGraw-Hill, 1965), pp. 4–6.

22. The section on integrative bargaining is based on R.E. Walton and R.B. McKersie, *A Behavioral Theory of Labor Negotiations* (New York: McGraw-Hill, 1965), pp. 4–6.

23. Based on C. Kapel, "The Feeling's Mutual," *Human Resources Professional* (April 1995), pp. 9–13. See also S.D. Smith, "Taking the Confrontation out of Collective Bargaining," *Canadian HR Reporter* (September 10, 2001), pp. 11, 13.

24. U. Vu, "Interest Wanes on Interest-Based?" *Canadian HR Reporter* (February 28, 2006), pp. 6, 9.

25. J. Peirce, *Canadian Industrial Relations* (Scarborough, ON: Prentice Hall Canada, 2000), p. 431.

26. C. Spurr, "A 'Perfect Storm': Stora Enso Lockout in Nova Scotia," *Shunpiking Online* 3, no. 4 (May 3, 2006), www.shunpiking.com/o10304/0304-AC-CS-perfectstrom.htm (June 1, 2006); "Keep Stora off Campaign Agenda: Mayor," *CBC News* (May 26, 2006), www.cbc.ca/ns/story/nsv-stora20060526.html (June 1, 2006).

27. L. Diebel, "45-minute job action staged for International Hotel Workers' Day," *Toronto Star*, November 11, 2007. www.thestar.com/printArticle/275447 (July 21, 2009).

28. See J.E. Grenig, "Stare Decisis, Re Judicata and Collecteral Estoppel in Labour Arbitration," *Labour Law Journal* 38 (April 1987), pp. 195–205.

29. Based on M. Gunderson and D.G. Taras, *Union–Management Relations in Canada* (Toronto: Pearson Education Canada, 2001), p. 429; J. Peirce, *Canadian Industrial Relations* (Scarborough, ON: Prentice Hall Canada, 2000), p. 431.

30. *Canadian Master Labour Guide*, 16th ed. (Toronto: CCH Canadian Ltd., 2002).

31. M. Hebert, "Length of Collective Agreements," *Workplace Gazette* 7, no. 4 (Winter 2004), p. 27.

32. G. Sova, "How Long a Contract Should You Sign?" *Canadian HR Reporter* (February 28, 2005), p. 9.

Chapter 17

1. "Global talent shortage persists despite recession," *Canadian HR Reporter* (May 29, 2009); N. M. Carter and E. Galinsky, *Leaders in a Global Economy:*
Talent Management in European Cultures. (New York: Catalyst and Families and Work Institute, November 2008); *Survey of Global HR Challenges: Yesterday, today and tomorrow.* (New York: PricewaterhouseCoopers and World Federation of Personnel Management Associations, 2005).

2. P. Alaganandan, "India's Human Capital Challenge," *Workspan* (November 2008), 111–114.

3. J. Wang, "China's Financial Industry Recruits Abroad," *New York Times* (December 25, 2008).

4. S. Cryne, "The Changing World of the Relocation Specialist," *Canadian HR Reporter* (March 8, 2004), pp. 13, 15.

5. "Companies Facing Major Challenges in Handling Increase in Global Mobility," *Workspan* (April 2008), pp. 11–12.

6. R. Runzheimer and G. Harper, "Workforce Mobility Management Saves Money and Increases Efficiency," *Workspan* (December 2007), pp. 76–81.

7. *2008/2009 Benefits Survey for Expatriates and Globally Mobile Employees.* (New York: Mercer).

8. M. Sim and L. Dixon, "Number of women expats increasing," *Canadian HR Reporter* (May 21, 2007).

9. T. Shelton, "A Best-of-Breed Approach: Addressing the ROI and Retention Challenges of Global Workforce Management," *Workspan* (April 2009), pp. 50–54.

10. D. Bergles and R. Peterman, "Selling Relocation Used to Be Easier Than This," *Canadian HR Reporter* (September 27, 2004), p. 8; S. Cryne, "Are Short-Term Gigs Better Than Permanent Moves?" *Canadian HR Reporter* (December 6, 2004), pp. 1–2.

11. S. Dobson, "Enticing employees to go on relocation," *Canadian HR Reporter* (May 18, 2009).

12. J. Head, "How Paper Can Protect International Relocations," *Canadian HR Reporter* (March 13, 2006).

13. *2005 Employee Relocation Survey: Domestic, Cross-Border & International Relocations* (Toronto: Canadian Employee Relocation Council, 2005).

14. Ibid.

15. *Global Relocation Trends: Survey Report 2008.* GMAC Global Relocation Services.

16. G. N. Abbott, B.W. Stening, P.W.B. Atkins, and A.M. Grant, "Coaching expatriate managers for success: Adding value beyond training and mentoring," *Asia-Pacific Journal of Human Resources,* 44, pp. 295–317.

17. G. Insch and J. Daniels, "Causes and Consequences of Declining Early Departures from Foreign Assignments," *Business Horizons* 46(6), (November–December 2002), pp. 39–48.

18. E. Krell, "Budding Relationships," *HR Magazine* 50(6), (June 2005), pp. 114–118.

19. P. Caliguri, "The Big Five Personality Characteristics as Predictors of Expatriates' Desire to Terminate the Assignment and Supervisor-Rated Performance," *Personnel Psychology* 53(1), (Spring 2000), pp. 67–88.

20. J. Selmer, "Expatriation: Corporate Policy, Personal Intentions and International Adjustment," *International Journal of Human Resource Management* 9(6), (December 1998), pp. 997–1007.

21. Discussed in C. Hill, *International Business: Competing in the Global Marketplace*, (Burr Ridge, IL: Irwin, 1994), pp. 511–515.

22. C. Solomon, "One Assignment, Two Lives," *Personnel Journal*, May 1996, pp. 36–47; M. Harvey, "Dual-Career Couples During International Relocation: The Trailing Spouse," *International Journal of Human Resource Management* 9(2), (April 1998), pp. 309–330.

23. B. Anderson, "Expatriate Selection: A Good Management Are Good Luck?" *International Journal of Human Resource Management* 16(4), April 2005, pp. 567–583.

24. M. Schell, quoted in C. Marmer Solomon, "Success Abroad Depends on More Than Job Skills," *Personnel Journal* (April 1994), p. 52.

25. M. Shaffer and D. Harrison, "Forgotten Partners of International Assignments: Development and Test of a Model of Spouse Adjustment," *Journal of Applied Psychology* 86(2), 2001, pp. 238–254.

26. Ibid., p. 251.

27. N.D. Cole, "Expatriate accompanying spouses: The males speak," paper presented at the Academy of International Business Conference, San Diego, 2009.

28. M. Shaffer and D. Harrison, "Forgotten Partners of International Assignments: Development and Test of a Model of Spouse Adjustment," *Journal of Applied Psychology* 86(2), 2001, p. 250.

29. For example, see S. Maurer and S. Li, "Understanding Expatriate Manager Performance: Effects of Governance Environments on Work Relationships in Relation-Based Economies," *Human Resource Management Review* 16(1), (March 2006), pp. 29–46.

30. R. Garonzik, J. Brockner and P. Siegel, "Identifying International Assignees at Risk for Premature Departure: The Interactive Effect of Outcome Favorability and Procedural Fairness," *Journal of Applied Psychology* 85(1), 2000, pp. 13–20. For a discussion of the importance of organizational support in expatriate adjustment, see, for example, M. Kraimer et al., "Sources of Support and Expatriate Performance: Mediating Role of Expatriate Adjustment," *Personnel Psychology* 54, 2001, pp. 71–99.

31. N.D. Cole, "Managing Global Talent: What do Expatriate Spouses Need?" *International Journal of Human Resources Management* (in press), 2009.

32. S. Cryne, "The Changing World of the Relocation Specialist," *Canadian HR Reporter* (March 8, 2004), pp. 13, 15; G. Reinhart, "Preparing for Global Expansion: A Primer," *Canadian HR Reporter* (March 14, 2005), pp. 14, 17.

33. Z. Fedder, "Short-Sighted Thinking Shortchanges Short-Term International Assignments," *Canadian HR Reporter* (September 25, 2000), p. 20.

34. S. Cryne, "The Changing World of the Relocation Specialist," *Canadian HR Reporter* (March 8, 2004), pp. 13, 15.

35. L. Grobovsky, "Protecting Your Workers Abroad with a Global Diversity Strategy," *Canadian HR Reporter* (November 1, 1999), pp. 15–16.

36. B. Best, "Battling bribery, corruption abroad," *Canadian HR Reporter* (April 9, 2007); "Expect Corruption Overseas," *Canadian HR Reporter* (September 23, 2002), p. 9; "Oil and Water," *Canadian Business* (November 8–21, 2004), pp. 14, 16.

37. "Oil and Water," *Canadian Business* (November 8–21, 2004), pp. 14, 16; "Expect Corruption Overseas," *Canadian HR Reporter* (September 23, 2002), p. 9.

38. R.J. House, P.J. Hanges, M. Javidan, P.W. Dorfman and V. Gupta, *Culture, Leadership, and Organizations: The GLOBE Study of 62 Societies.* (Thousand Oaks: Sage Publications, 2004); G. Hofstede, "Cultural Dimensions in People Management," in V. Pucik, N. Tichy and C. Barnett (eds.), *Globalizing Management*, (New York: John Wiley & Sons, 1992), p. 143.

39. "Abuse of power rampant in Japanese workplaces: Survey," *Canadian HR Reporter* (February 13, 2008).

40. S. Klie, "HR around the world," *Canadian HR Reporter* (November 6, 2006); K. King-Metters and R. Metters, "Misunderstanding the Chinese Worker," *The Wall Street Journal*, July 7, 2008, p. R11.

41. R. Little, "Foreigners explore pros and cons behind Vietnamese work ethic." http://vietnamnews.vnagency.com.vn/showarticle.php?num=)!SAY080808 (September 4, 2008).

42. A. Yeo, "A Brief Look at the PRC Employment Promotion Law," *Human Resources* (December 2007), pp. 29–31; J. Yan, "A snapshot of Chinese employment law," *Canadian HR Reporter* (November 6, 2006); "China's New Labor Contract Law," *Workspan* (March 2008), p. 12.

43. *Severance Practices Around the World.* (Philadelphia: Right Management, 2008); G. Avraam, A. Ishak and T. Appleyard, "Terminating employees around the world," *Canadian HR Reporter* (April 6, 2009).

44. "Britain introduces corporate manslaughter act," *Canadian HR Reporter* (April 16, 2008).

45. A. Macaulay, "Culture, safety and privacy norms abroad present challenges for HR," *Canadian HR Reporter* (November 6, 2006).

46. E. Kelly, "The New Frontier," *HR Professional* (August/September 2008), pp. 24–28.

47. Discussed in E. Gaugler, "HR Management: An International Comparison," *Personnel* (August 1988), p. 28.

48. Wharton School, "Made in China," *Human Resource Executive Online* (February 26, 2008).

49. J.D. Daniels and L.H. Radebaugh, *International Business* (Reading, MA: Addison-Wesley, 1994), p. 767; Arvind Phatak, *International Dimensions of Management* (Boston: PWS-Kent, 1989), pp. 106–107.

50. M.A. Shaffer, D.A. Harrison, K.M. Gilley, and D.M. Luk, "Struggling for Balance Amid Turbulence on International Assignments: Work–Family Conflict, Support and Commitment," *Journal of Management* 27 (2001), pp. 99–121; R. Garonzik, J. Brockner, and P.A. Siegel, "Identifying International Assignees at Risk for Premature Departure: The Interactive Effects of Outcome Favorability and Procedural Fairness," *Journal of Applied Psychology* 85 (2000), pp. 13–20; M.A. Shaffer and D.A. Harrison, "Forgotten Partners of International Assignments: Development and Test of a Model of Spouse Adjustment," *Journal of Applied Psychology,* 86 (2001), pp. 238–254.

51. W. Arthur, Jr. and W. Bennett, Jr., "The International Assignee: The Relative Importance of Factors Perceived to Contribute to Success," *Personnel Psychology* 48 (1995), pp. 99–114; table on pp. 106–107. See also E. Davison and B. J. Punnett, "International Assignments: Is There a Role for Gender and Race in Decisions?" *International Journal of Human Resource Management* 6, no. 2 (May 1995), pp. 411–441.

52. G. Spreitzer, M. McCall Jr., and J. Mahoney, "Early Identification of International Executive Potential," *Journal of Applied Psychology* 82 (1997), pp. 6–29.

53. P.M. Caligiuri and J.M. Phillips, "An Application of Self-Assessment Realistic Job Previews to Expatriate Assignments," *International Journal of Human Resource Management* 14, no. 7 (2003), pp. 1102–1116.

54. Discussed in M. Callahan, "Preparing the New Global Manager," *Training and Development Journal* (March 1989), p. 30. The publisher of the inventory is the New York consulting firm Moran, Stahl, and Boyer; T.S. Chan, "Developing International Managers: A Partnership Approach," *Journal of Management Development* 13, no. 3 (1994), pp. 38–46.

55. Based on B.J. Punnett, "International Human Resources Management," in A.M. Rugman (ed.), *International Business in Canada: Strategies for Management,* pp. 330–346 (Scarborough, ON: Prentice Hall Canada, 1989); L.G. Klaff, "Thinning the Ranks of the 'Career Expats,'" *Workforce Management* (October 2004), pp. 84–87.

56. V. Galt, "World Loves to Milk Canada's Executive Pool," *Globe & Mail* (September 5, 2005), p. B10.

57. A. Bross, A. Churchill, and J. Zifkin, "Cross-Cultural Training: Issues to Consider during Implementation," *Canadian HR Reporter* (June 5, 2000), pp. 10, 12.

58. A. Bross, A. Churchill, and J. Zifkin, "Cross-Cultural Training: Issues to Consider During Implementation," *Canadian HR Reporter* (June 5, 2000); C. Shick, "It Wasn't What You Said, It Was How You Said It," *Canadian HR Reporter* (February 28, 2000), p. 18.

59. E. M. Norman, "How Multinationals Doing Business in Asia can Develop Leadership Talent During a Recession," *Workspan* (May 2009), pp. 35–43.

60. "More Multinationals Embracing Centralized Compensation Structures," *Workspan* (November 2006), p. 10; C. Reynolds, "Global Compensation and Benefits in Transition," *Compensation and Benefits Review* (January/February 2000), pp. 28–28; J.E. Richard, "Global Executive Compensation: A Look at the Future," *Compensation and Benefits Review* (May/June 2000), pp. 35–38.

61. L. Laroche, "Negotiating Expatriate Packages," *Canadian HR Reporter* (November 20, 2000), pp. 15, 19.

62. J. Cartland, "Reward Policies in a Global Corporation," *Business Quarterly* (Autumn 1993), pp. 93–96; L. Mazur, "Europay," *Across-the-Board* (January 1995), pp. 40–43.

63. K. Bensky, "Developing a Workable Global Rewards System," *Workspan* (October 2002), pp. 44–48.

64. Arvind Phatak, *International Dimensions of Management* (Boston: PWS-Kent, 1989), p. 134. See also L. Laroche, "Negotiating Expatriate Packages," *Canadian HR Reporter* (November 20, 2000), pp. 15, 19.

65. K. Abosch, J. Schermerhorn, and L. Wisper, "Broad-Based Variable Pay Goes Global," *Workspan* (May 2008), pp. 56–62.

66. "Expatriates, Families Face Different Stressors Than Stateside Counterparts," *Workspan* (October 2008), p. 18.

67. V. Frazee, "Keeping Your Expats Healthy," *Global Workforce* (November 1998), pp. 18–23. See also B. Barker and D. Schulde, "Special EAP Helps Expatriates Face International 'Culture Shock,'" *Canadian HR Reporter* (November 29, 1999), p. 20; L. O'Grady, "Using Technology to De-stress on International Assignment," *Canadian HR Reporter* (September 24, 2001), pp. 8, 12; R. Melles, "Lost in Translation," *Canadian HR Reporter* (March 8, 2004), p. 14; E.C. Heher, "Anticipating the Psychological Effects of Expatriate Life," *Workspan* (May 2006), pp. 54–56.

68. A. Bross and G. Wise, "Sustaining the Relocated Employee with an International EAP," *Canadian HR Reporter* (November 29, 1999), pp. 18, 19, 21.

69. M. Mendenhall and G. Addou, *International Human Resource Management* (Boston: PWS-Kent Publishing, 1991), p. 366. See also Maddy Janssens, "Evaluating International Managers' Performance: Parent Company Standards as Control Mechanism," *The International Journal of Human Resource Management* 5, no. 4, (December 1994), pp. 853–873.

70. A. Lauffs, "Labor Relations in China," presentation to South China Morning Post Conference: Human Capital in Greater China, Hong Kong, December 2007.

71. M. Higginson, "Hungary's Low Labor Costs Still Lure Big Investors," *Budapest Business Journal* (April 10, 2006).

72. R. Sauer and K. Voelker, *Labor Relations: Structure and Process* (New York: Macmillan, 1993), pp. 510–525.

73. Quoted from R. Sauer and K. Voelker, *Labor Relations: Structure and Process* (New York: Macmillan, 1993), p. 519.

74. M. Penrose, "Safety extends to employees abroad," *Canadian HR Reporter* (May 5, 2008).

75. D. Mbachu, "Nigeria's Kidnap Capital Forces Shell, Chevron to Cut Output." www.bloomberg.com/apps/news?pid=20601116&sid=aKxpQiFk9AkM&refer=africa (August 13, 2009); D. Gauthier-Villars and L. Abboud, "In France, the Bosses can Become Hostages," *Wall Street Journal* (April 3, 2009);

"Kidnapped_Bosses are Taken Hostage in France," *The Economist*, 390(8623), p. 68; D. Jolly, "French Workers Ratchet Up Threats," *New York Times* (July 15, 2009).

76. G. Pitts, "Kidnap Consultants Always Have Room for Negotiation," *Globe & Mail* (October 25, 2003), p. B3.

77. "French workers hold bosses hostage for severance," *Canadian HR Reporter* (April 2, 2009).

78. S. Merkling and E. Davis, "Kidnap and Ransom Insurance: A Rapidly Growing Benefit," *Compensation and Benefits Review* (November/December 2001), pp. 40–45; T. Appleby, "Kidnap Insurers Stay Shrouded in Secrecy," *Globe & Mail* (September 27, 2004), p. A9.

79. B. Belisle and W. Cuthbertson, "Anticipate Expat Crises Instead of Responding," *Canadian HR Reporter* (March 10, 2003); S. Greengard, "Mission Possible: Protecting Employees Abroad," *Workforce* (August 1997), p. 32.

80. C. Storti, *The Art of Coming Home*. (Boston: Nicholas Brealey Publishing, 2001); S. Cryne, "Homeward bound," *Canadian HR Reporter* (March 9, 2009).

81. "Views of Employees and Companies Differ on International Assignments," *Workspan Focus Canada 2006*, pp. 22–24; Linda Stroh, "Predicting Turnover among Repatriates: Can Organizations Affect Retention Rates?" *International Journal of Human Resource Management* 6, no. 2, (May 1995), pp. 443–456.

82. J. Keogh, "A Win–Win, from Start to Finish," *Workspan* (February 2003), pp. 36–39; D. Brown, "Companies Undervaluing Skills Learned during Relocation," *Canadian HR Reporter* (February 28, 2000), pp. 15, 21; J. Hobel, "The Expatriate Employee Homecoming," *Canadian HR Reporter* (June 1, 1998), pp. G5, G11.

83. D. McCutcheon, "Repatriation: Bringing Home the Troops," *HR Professional* (April/May 2009), pp. 33–34; P. Stanoch and G. Reynolds, "Relocating Career Development," *Canadian HR Reporter* (May 5, 2003), pp. 13, 15; "Global Talk," *HR Professional* (June/July 2006), p. 12.

84. Based on Ann Marie Ryan et al., "Designing and Implementing Global Staffing Systems: Part 2—Best Practices," *Human Resource Management* 42, no. 1 (Spring 2003), pp. 85–94.

360-degree appraisal A performance appraisal technique that uses multiple raters including peers, employees reporting to the appraisee, supervisors, and customers.

A

accommodation measures Strategies to assist designated group members.

achievement tests Tests used to measure knowledge and/or proficiency acquired through education, training, or experience.

action learning A training technique by which management trainees are allowed to work full-time, analyzing and solving problems in other departments.

alternation ranking method Ranking employees from best to worst on a particular trait.

appraisal bias The tendency to allow individual differences, such as age, race, and sex, to affect the appraisal ratings that these employees receive.

appraisal interview An interview in which the supervisor and employee review the appraisal and make plans to remedy deficiencies and reinforce strengths.

aptitude tests Tests that measure an individual's aptitude or potential to perform a job, provided he or she is given proper training.

arbitration The use of an outside third party to investigate a dispute between an employer and union and impose a settlement.

attrition The normal separation of employees from an organization because of resignation, retirement, or death.

authorization card A card signed by an employee that indicates his or her willingness to have the union act as his or her representative for purposes of collective bargaining.

B

Baby Boomers Individuals born between 1946 and 1964.

balance sheet approach Expatriate pay based on equalizing purchasing power across countries.

balanced scorecard A measurement system that translates an organization's strategy into a comprehensive set of performance measures.

bargaining unit The group of employees in a firm, a plant, or an industry that has been recognized by an employer or certified by a Labour Relations Board (LRB) as appropriate for collective bargaining purposes.

bargaining zone The area defined by the bargaining limits (resistance points) of each side, in which compromise is possible, as is the attainment of a settlement satisfactory to both parties.

behaviour modelling A training technique in which trainees are first shown good management techniques, then asked to play roles in a simulated situation, and finally given feedback regarding their performance.

behavioural or behaviour description interview (BDI) A series of job-related questions that focus on relevant past job-related behaviours.

behaviourally anchored rating scale (BARS) An appraisal method that aims to combine the benefits of narratives, critical incidents, and quantified ratings by anchoring a quantified scale with specific narrative examples of good and poor performance.

benchmark job A job that is critical to the firm's operations or commonly found in other organizations.

biographical information blank (BIB) A detailed job application form requesting biographical data found to be predictive of success on the job, pertaining to background, experiences, and preferences. As with a WAB, responses are scored.

blind ad A recruitment ad in which the identity and address of the employer are omitted.

bona fide occupational requirement (BFOR) A justifiable reason for discrimination based on business necessity (that is, required for the safe and efficient operation of the organization) or a requirement that can be clearly defended as intrinsically required by the tasks an employee is expected to perform.

boycott An organized refusal of bargaining unit members and supporters to buy the products or use the services of the organization whose employees are on strike in an effort to exert economic pressure on the employer.

broadbanding Reducing the number of salary grades and ranges into just a few wide levels or "bands," each of which then contains a relatively wide range of jobs and salary levels.

burnout The total depletion of physical and mental resources caused by excessive striving to reach an unrealistic work-related goal.

business unionism The activities of labour unions focusing on economic and welfare issues, including pay and benefits, job security, and working conditions.

C

Canada/Quebec Pension Plan (C/QPP) Programs that provide three types of benefits: retirement income; survivor or death benefits payable to the employee's dependants regardless of age at time of death; and disability benefits payable to employees with disabilities and their dependants. Benefits are payable only to those individuals who make contributions to the plans and/or available to their family members.

capital accumulation programs Long-term incentives most often reserved for senior executives.

career anchor A concern or value that you will not give up if a choice has to be made.

career cycle The stages through which a person's career evolves.

career planning and development The deliberate process through which a person becomes aware of personal career-related attributes and the lifelong series of activities that contribute to his or her career fulfillment.

career-planning workshop A planned learning event in which participants are expected to be actively involved in career-planning exercises and career-skills practice sessions.

case study method A development method in which a trainee is presented with a written description of an organizational problem to diagnose and solve.

caucus session A session in which only the members of one's own bargaining team are present.

central tendency A tendency to rate all employees in the middle of the scale.

certification Recognition for having met certain professional standards.

certification The procedure whereby a labour union obtains a certificate from the relevant LRB declaring that the union is the exclusive bargaining agent for a defined group of employees in a bargaining unit that the LRB considers appropriate for collective bargaining purposes.

Charter of Rights and Freedoms Federal law enacted in 1982 that guarantees fundamental freedoms to all Canadians.

classes Groups of jobs based on a set of rules for each class, such as amount of independent judgment, skill, physical effort, and so forth. Classes usually contain similar jobs—such as all secretaries.

classification/grading method A method for categorizing jobs into groups.

coinsurance The percentage of expenses (in excess of the deductible) that are paid for by the insurance plan.

collective agreement (union contract) A formal agreement between an employer and the union representing a group of its employees regarding terms and conditions of employment.

collective bargaining Negotiations between a union and an employer to arrive at a mutually acceptable collective agreement.

compensable factor A fundamental, compensable element of a job, such as skill, effort, responsibility, and working conditions.

competencies Demonstrable characteristics of a person that enable performance of the job.

competency-based job analysis Describing a job in terms of the measurable, observable behavioural competencies an employee must exhibit to do a job well.

compressed workweek An arrangement that most commonly allows employees to work four ten-hour days instead of the more usual five eight-hour days.

conciliation The use of a neutral third party to help an organization and the union representing a group of its employees to come to a mutually satisfactory collective agreement.

construct validity The extent to which a selection tool measures a theoretical construct or trait deemed necessary to perform the job successfully.

constructive dismissal The employer makes unilateral changes in the employment contract that are unacceptable to the employee, even though the employee has not been formally terminated.

content validity The extent to which a selection instrument, such as a test, adequately samples the knowledge and skills needed to perform the job.

contingent/nonstandard workers Workers who do not have regular full-time employment status.

contract workers Employees who develop work relationships directly with the employer for a specific type of work or period of time.

contrast or candidate-order error An error of judgment on the part of the interviewer because of interviewing one or more very good or very bad candidates just before the interview in question.

controlled experimentation Formal methods for testing the effectiveness of a training program, preferably with a control group and with tests before and after training.

craft union Traditionally, a labour organization representing workers practising the same craft or trade, such as carpentry or plumbing.

criterion-related validity The extent to which a selection tool predicts or significantly correlates with important elements of work behaviour.

critical incident method Keeping a record of uncommonly good or undesirable examples of an employee's work-related behaviour and reviewing the list with the employee at predetermined times.

D

data warehouse A specialized type of database that is optimized for reporting and analysis and is the raw material for managers' decision support.

decertification The process whereby a union is legally deprived of its official recognition as the exclusive bargaining agent for a group of employees.

decline stage The period during which many people are faced with the prospect of having to accept reduced levels of power and responsibility.

deductible The annual amount of health/dental expenses that an employee must pay before insurance benefits will be paid.

deferred profit-sharing plan A plan in which a certain amount of company profits is credited to each employee's account, payable at retirement, termination, or death.

defined benefit pension plan A plan that contains a formula for determining retirement benefits.

defined contribution pension plan A plan in which the employer's contribution to the employees' retirement fund is specified.

Delphi technique A judgmental forecasting method used to arrive at a group decision, typically involving outside experts as well as organizational employees. Ideas are exchanged without face-to-face interaction and feedback is provided and used to fine-tune independent judgments until a consensus is reached.

developmental job rotation A management-training technique that involves moving a trainee from department to department to broaden his or her experience and identify strong and weak points.

diary/log Daily listings made by employees of every activity in which they engage, along with the time each activity takes.

differential validity Confirmation that the selection tool accurately predicts the performance of all possible employee subgroups, including white males, women, visible minorities, persons with disabilities, and Aboriginal people.

disability management A proactive, employer-centred process that coordinates the activities of the employer, the insurance company, and health-care providers in an effort to minimize the impact of injury, disability, or disease in a worker's capacity to successfully perform his or her job.

discipline A procedure intended to correct an employee's behaviour because a rule or procedure has been violated.

discrimination As used in the context of human rights in employment, a distinction, exclusion, or preference, based on one of the prohibited grounds, that has the effect of nullifying or impairing the right of a person to full and equal recognition and exercise of his or her human rights and freedoms.

dismissal Involuntary termination of an employee's employment.

distributive bargaining A win–lose negotiating strategy, such that one party gains at the expense of the other.

distributive justice Fairness of a decision outcome.

diversity management Activities designed to integrate all members of an organization's multicultural workforce and use their diversity to enhance the firm's effectiveness.

downsizing Refers to the process of reducing, usually dramatically, the number of people employed by the firm.

E

early retirement buyout programs Strategies used to accelerate attrition that involve offering attractive buyout packages or the opportunity to retire on full pension with an attractive benefits package.

e-learning Delivery and administration of learning opportunities and support via computer, networked, and web-based technology, to enhance employee performance and development.

electronic HR (e-HR) A form of technology that enables HR professionals to integrate an organization's HR strategies, processes, and human capital to improve overall HR service delivery.

electronic performance monitoring (EPM) Having supervisors electronically monitor the amount of computerized data an employee is processing per day and thereby his or her performance.

electronic performance support systems (EPSS) Computer-based job aids, or sets of computerized tools and displays that automate training, documentation, and phone support.

emotional intelligence (EI) tests Tests that measure ability to monitor one's own emotions and the emotions of others and to use that knowledge to guide thoughts and actions.

employee assistance plan (EAP) A company-sponsored program to help employees cope with personal problems that are interfering with or have the potential to interfere with their job performance, as well as issues affecting their well-being and/or that of their families.

employee benefits Indirect financial payments given to employees. They may include supplementary health and life insurance, vacation, pension, education plans, and discounts on company products.

employee engagement A positive, fulfilling, work-related state of mind characterized by vigour, dedication, and absorption.

employment insurance A federal program that provides income benefits if a person is unable to work through no fault of his or her own.

employee opinion surveys Communication devices that use questionnaires to ask for employees' opinions about the company, management, and work life.

employee orientation (onboarding) A procedure for providing new employees with basic background information about the firm and the job.

employee self-service (ESS) Enables employees to access and manage their personal information directly.

employee share purchase/stock ownership plans (ESOPs) A trust is established to hold shares of company stock purchased for or issued to employees. The trust distributes the stock to employees on retirement, separation from service, or as otherwise prescribed by the plan.

employee wellness program A program that takes a proactive approach to employee health and well-being.

employer branding The image or impression of an organization as an employer based on the benefits of being employed by the organization.

employment (labour) standards legislation Laws present in every Canadian jurisdiction that establish minimum employee entitlements and set a limit on the maximum number of hours of work permitted per day or week.

employment equity program A detailed plan designed to identify and correct existing discrimination, redress past discrimination, and achieve a balanced representation of designated group members in the organization.

employment insurance A federal program that provides income benefits if a person is unable to work through no fault of his or her own.

employment systems review A thorough examination of corporate policies and procedures, collective agreements, and informal practices to determine their impact on designated group members so that existing intentional or systemic barriers can be eliminated.

empowerment Providing workers with the skills and authority to make decisions that would traditionally be made by managers.

enterprise-wide or enterprise resource planning (ERP) system A system that supports enterprise-wide or cross-functional requirements rather than a single department within the organization.

environmental scanning Identifying and analyzing external opportunities and threats that may be crucial to the organization's success.

equality rights Section 15 of the Charter of Rights and Freedoms, which guarantees the right to equal protection and equal benefit of the law without discrimination.

ergonomics An interdisciplinary approach that seeks to integrate and accommodate the physical needs of workers into the design of jobs. It aims to adapt the entire job system—the work, environment, machines, equipment, and processes—to match human characteristics.

ergonomics The art of fitting the workstation and work tools to the individual.

establishment stage The period, roughly from age 24 to 44, that is the heart of most people's work lives.

expatriate assignment failure Early return of an expatriate from a global assignment.

expatriate Employees who are citizens of the country where the parent company is based, who are sent to work in another country.

exploration stage The period from around age 15 to 24 during which a person seriously explores various occupational alternatives, attempting to match these alternatives with his or her interests and abilities.

F

flexible benefits program Individualized benefit plans to accommodate employee needs and preferences.

flextime A plan whereby employees build their workday around a core of midday hours.

flexyear A work arrangement under which employees can choose (at six-month intervals) the number of hours that they want to work each month over the next year.

forced distribution method Predetermined percentages of ratees are placed in various performance categories.

Functional Job Analysis (FJA) A quantitative method for classifying jobs based on types and amounts of responsibility for data, people, and things. Performance standards and training requirements are also identified.

G

gainsharing plan An incentive plan that engages employees in a common effort to achieve productivity objectives and share the gains.

Generation X Individuals born between 1965 and 1980.

Generation Y Individuals born since 1980.

glass ceiling An invisible barrier, caused by attitudinal or organizational bias, which limits the advancement opportunities of qualified designated group members.

global HR system A standardized HR system in all company locations around the world.

globalization The emergence of a single global market for most products and services.

grade/group description A written description of the level of compensable factors required by jobs in each grade. Used to combine similar jobs into grades or classes.

grades Groups of jobs based on a set of rules for each grade, where jobs are similar in difficulty but otherwise different. Grades often contain dissimilar jobs, such as secretaries, mechanics, and firefighters.

graphic rating scale A scale that lists a number of traits and a range of performance for each. The employee is then rated by identifying the score that best describes his or her level of performance for each trait.

grievance A written allegation of a contract violation, filed by an individual bargaining unit member, the union, or management.

group life insurance Insurance provided at lower rates for all employees, including new employees, regardless of health or physical condition.

group termination laws Laws that require an employer to notify employees in the event that an employer decides to terminate a group of employees.

growth stage The period from birth to around age 14 during which the person develops a self-concept by identifying with and interacting with other people, such as family, friends, and teachers.

guaranteed piecework plan The minimum hourly wage plus an incentive for each piece produced above a set number of pieces per hour.

H

halo effect A positive initial impression that distorts an interviewer's rating of a candidate because subsequent information is judged with a positive bias.

halo effect In performance appraisal, the problem that occurs when a supervisor's rating of an employee on one trait biases the rating of that person on other traits.

harassment Unwelcome behaviour that demeans, humiliates, or embarrasses a person and that a reasonable person should have known would be unwelcome.

hiring freeze A common initial response to an employee surplus. Openings are filled by reassigning current employees, and no outsiders are hired.

HR portal A single Internet access point for customized and personalized HR services.

HR technology Any technology that is used to attract, hire, retain and maintain talent, support workforce administration, and optimize workforce management.

HR technology strategy A plan that is aimed at increasing the effectiveness of HR programs, processes, and service delivery by shortening cycle times, increasing customer service levels, reducing costs, and adding new service capabilities.

human capital The knowledge, education, training, skills, and expertise of an organization's workforce.

human relations movement A management philosophy based on the belief that the attitudes and feelings of workers are important and deserve more attention.

human resources information system (HRIS) Integrated system used to gather, store, and analyze information regarding an organization's human resources.

human resources management (HRM) The management of people in organizations to drive successful organizational performance and achievement of the organization's strategic goals.

human resources movement A management philosophy focusing on concern for people and productivity.

human resources planning (HRP) The process of forecasting future human resources requirements to ensure that the organization will have the required number of employees with the necessary skills to meet its strategic objectives.

I

industrial engineering A field of study concerned with analyzing work methods; making work cycles more efficient by modifying, combining, rearranging, or eliminating tasks; and establishing time standards.

industrial union A labour organization representing all workers eligible for union membership in a particular company or industry, including skilled tradespersons.

in-house development centre A company-based method for exposing prospective managers to realistic exercises to develop improved management skills.

insubordination Wilful disregard or disobedience of the boss's authority or legitimate orders; criticizing the boss in public.

integrative bargaining A negotiating strategy in which the possibility of win–win, lose–win, win–lose, and lose–lose outcomes is recognized, and there is acknowledgement that achieving a win–win outcome will depend on mutual trust and problem solving.

intelligence (IQ) tests Tests that measure general intellectual abilities, such as verbal comprehension, inductive reasoning, memory, numerical ability, speed of perception, spatial visualization, and word fluency.

interactional justice Fairness in interpersonal interactions by treating others with dignity and respect.

interactive voice response (IVR) A telephone technology in which a touch-tone telephone is used to interact with a database to acquire information from or enter data into the database.

interest arbitration The imposition of the final terms of a collective agreement.

interest dispute A dispute between an organization and the union representing its employees over the terms of a collective agreement.

interest inventories Tests that compare a candidate's interests with those of people in various occupations.

intranet A network that is inter-connected within one organization, using web technologies for the sharing of information internally.

J

job A group of related activities and duties, held by a single employee or a number of incumbents.

job analysis The procedure for determining the tasks, duties, and responsibilities of each job, and the human attributes (in terms of knowledge, skills, and abilities) required to perform it.

job description A list of the duties, responsibilities, reporting relationships, and working conditions of a job—one product of a job analysis.

job design The process of systematically organizing work into tasks that are required to perform a specific job.

job enlargement (horizontal loading) A technique to relieve monotony and boredom that involves assigning workers additional tasks at the same level of responsibility to increase the number of tasks they have to perform.

job enrichment (vertical loading) Any effort that makes an employee's job more rewarding or satisfying by adding more meaningful tasks and duties.

job evaluation A systematic comparison to determine the relative worth of jobs within a firm.

job instruction training (JIT) The listing of each job's basic tasks, along with key points, in order to provide step-by-step training for employees.**videoconferencing** Connecting two or more distant groups by using audiovisual equipment.

job posting The process of notifying current employees about vacant positions.

job rotation Another technique to relieve monotony and employee boredom that involves systematically moving employees from one job to another.

job sharing A strategy that involves dividing the duties of a single position between two or more employees.

job specification A list of the "human requirements," that is, the requisite knowledge, skills, and abilities, needed to perform the job—another product of a job analysis.

K

KSAs Knowledge, skills, and abilities.

L

labour union (union) An officially recognized association of employees practising a similar trade or employed in the same company or industry who have joined together to present a united front and collective voice in dealing with management.

labour–management relations The ongoing interactions between labour unions and management in organizations.

layoff The temporary withdrawal of employment to workers for economic or business reasons.

learning organization An organization skilled at creating, acquiring, and transferring knowledge and at modifying its behaviour to reflect new knowledge and insights.

local A group of unionized employees in a particular location.

lockout Temporary refusal of a company to continue providing work for bargaining unit employees involved in a labour dispute, which may result in closure of the establishment for a time.

M

maintenance stage The period from about age 45 to 65 during which the person secures his or her place in the world of work.

management assessment centre A strategy used to assess candidates' management potential that uses a combination of realistic exercises, management games, objective testing, presentations, and interviews.

management by objectives (MBO) Involves setting specific measurable goals with each employee and then periodically reviewing the progress made.

management development Any attempt to improve current or future management performance by imparting knowledge, changing attitudes, or increasing skills.

management game A computerized development technique in which teams of managers compete with one another by making decisions regarding realistic but simulated companies.

management inventories Records summarizing the qualifications, interests, and skills of management employees, along with the number and types of employees supervised, duties of such employees, total budget managed, previous managerial duties and responsibilities, and managerial training received.

management self-service (MSS) Enables managers to access a range of information about themselves and about employees who report to them and to process HR-related paperwork that pertains to their staff.

Markov analysis A method of forecasting internal labour supply that involves tracking the pattern of employee movements through various jobs and developing a transitional probability matrix.

mediation The use (usually voluntary) of a neutral third party to help an organization and the union representing its employees to reach a mutually satisfactory collective agreement.

memorandum of settlement A summary of the terms and conditions agreed to by the parties that is submitted to the constituent groups for final approval.

mentoring An experienced individual (the mentor) teaching and training another person (the protégé) who has less knowledge in an area.

merit pay (merit raise) Any salary increase awarded to an employee based on his or her individual performance.

metrics Statistics used to measure activities and results.

metrics (workforce analytics) Statistical measures of the impact of HRM practices on the performance of an organization's human capital.

micro-assessment A series of verbal, paper-based, or computer-based questions and exercises that a candidate is required to complete, covering the range of activities required on the job for which he or she is applying.

mixed (semi-structured) interview An interview format that combines the structured and unstructured techniques.

multiple-hurdle strategy An approach to selection involving a series of successive steps or hurdles. Only candidates clearing the hurdle are permitted to move on to the next step.

must criteria Requirements that are absolutely essential for the job, include a measurable standard of acceptability, or are absolute, and can be screened initially on paper.

mutual gains (interest-based) bargaining A win–win approach based on training in the fundamentals of effective problem solving and conflict resolution, in which the interests of all stakeholders are taken into account.

N

National Occupational Classification (NOC) A reference tool for writing job descriptions and job specifications. Compiled by the federal government, it contains comprehensive, standardized descriptions of about 30 000 occupations and the requirements for each.

nepotism A preference for hiring relatives of current employees.

nominal group technique A decision-making technique that involves a group of experts meeting face to face. Steps include independent idea generation, clarification and open discussion, and private assessment.

O

occupation A collection of jobs that share some or all of a set of main duties.

occupational health and safety legislation Laws intended to protect the health and safety of workers by minimizing work-related accidents and illnesses.

occupational orientation The theory, developed by John Holland, that there are six basic personal orientations that determine the sorts of careers to which people are drawn.

occupational segregation The existence of certain occupations that have traditionally been male dominated and others that have been female dominated.

organization chart A "snapshot" of the firm, depicting the organization's structure in chart form at a particular point in time.

organizational climate The prevailing atmosphere that exists in an organization and its impact on employees.

organizational culture The core values, beliefs, and assumptions that are widely shared by members of an organization.

organizational structure The formal relationships among jobs in an organization.

outplacement counselling A systematic process by which a terminated person is trained and counselled in the techniques of self-appraisal and securing a new position.

outsourcing Subcontracting of work that is not considered part of a company's core business.

outsourcing The practice of contracting with outside vendors to handle specified functions on a permanent basis.

P

paired comparison method Ranking employees by making a chart of all possible pairs of employees for each trait and indicating the better employee of the pair.

panel interview An interview in which a group of interviewers questions the applicant.

pay equity Providing equal pay to male-dominated job classes and female-dominated job classes of equal value to the employer.

pay grade Comprises jobs of approximately equal value.

pay ranges A series of steps or levels within a pay grade, usually based on years of service.

pension plans Plans that provide income when employees reach a predetermined retirement age.

performance analysis Verifying that there is a performance deficiency and determining whether that deficiency should be rectified through training or through some other means (such as transferring the employee).

performance management The process encompassing all activities related to improving employee performance, productivity, and effectiveness.

personality tests Instruments used to measure basic aspects of personality, such as introversion, stability, motivation, neurotic tendency, self-confidence, self-sufficiency, and sociability.

phased retirement An arrangement whereby employees gradually ease into retirement by using reduced workdays and/or shortened workweeks.

physical demands analysis Identification of the senses used and the type, frequency, and amount of physical effort involved in a job.

picket Stationing groups of striking employees, usually carrying signs, at the entrances and exits of the struck operation to publicize the issues in dispute and discourage people from entering or leaving the premises.

piecework A system of pay based on the number of items processed by each individual worker in a unit of time, such as items per hour or items per day.

point method The job evaluation method in which a number of compensable factors are identified, the degree to which each of these factors is present in the job is determined, and an overall point value is calculated.

portability A provision that employees who change jobs can transfer the lump-sum value of the pension they have earned to a locked-in RRSP or their new employer's pension plan.

Position Analysis Questionnaire (PAQ) A questionnaire used to collect quantifiable data concerning the duties and responsibilities of various jobs.

position The collection of tasks and responsibilities performed by one person.

positive measures Initiatives designed to accelerate the entry, development, and promotion of designated group members, aimed at overcoming the residual effects of past discrimination.

pre-hearing vote An alternative mechanism for certification, used in situations in which there is evidence of violations of fair labour practices early in the organizing campaign.

pre-retirement counselling Counselling provided to employees some months (or even years) before retirement, which covers such matters as benefits advice, second careers, and so on.

primary sector Agriculture, fishing and trapping, forestry, and mining.

procedural justice Fairness of the process used to make a decision.

process chart A diagram showing the flow of inputs to and outputs from the job under study.

productivity The ratio of an organization's outputs (goods and services) to its inputs (people, capital, energy, and materials).

profit-sharing plan A plan whereby most or all employees share in the company's profits.

programmed learning A systematic method for teaching job skills that involves presenting questions or facts, allowing the person to respond, and giving the learner immediate feedback on the accuracy of his or her answers.

promotion Movement of an employee from one job to another that is higher in pay, responsibility, and/or organizational level, usually based on merit, seniority, or a combination of both.

R

ratification Formal approval by secret-ballot vote of the bargaining unit members of the agreement negotiated between union and management.

ratio analysis A forecasting technique for determining future staff needs by using ratios between some causal factor (such as sales volume) and the number of employees needed.

realistic job preview (RJP) A strategy used to provide applicants with realistic information—both positive and negative—about the job demands, the organization's expectations, and the work environment.

reality shock The state that results from the discrepancy between what the new employee expects from his or her new job and the realities of it.

reasonable accommodation The adjustment of employment policies and practices that an employer may be expected to make so that no individual is denied benefits, disadvantaged in employment, or prevented from carrying out the essential components of a job because of grounds prohibited in human rights legislation.

recency effect The rating error that occurs when ratings are based on the employee's most recent performance rather than on performance throughout the appraisal period.

recruiter A specialist in recruitment, whose job it is to find and attract capable candidates.

recruitment The process of searching out and attracting qualified job applicants, which begins with the identification of a position that requires staffing and is completed when résumés and/or completed application forms are received from an adequate number of applicants.

red circle pay rate A rate of pay that is above the pay range maximum.

reduced workweek Employees work fewer hours and receive less pay.

regression analysis A statistical technique involving the use of a mathematical formula to project future demands based on an established relationship between an organization's employment level (dependent variable) and some measurable factor of output (independent variable).

regulations Legally binding rules established by the special regulatory bodies created to enforce compliance with the law and aid in its interpretation.

relational database One piece of data stored in several different data files so that information from the separate files can be linked and used together.

reliability The degree to which interviews, tests, and other selection procedures yield comparable data over time; in other words, the degree of dependability, consistency, or stability of the measures used.

repatriation Process of moving the expatriate and his or her family back home from the foreign assignment.

repetitive strain injuries (RSIs) Activity-related soft-tissue injuries of the neck, shoulders, arms, wrist, hands, back, and legs.

replacement charts Visual representations of who will replace whom in the event of a job opening. Likely internal candidates are listed, along with their age, present performance rating, and promotability status.

replacement summaries Lists of likely replacements for each position and their relative strengths and weaknesses, as well as information about current position, performance, promotability, age, and experience.

representation vote A vote conducted by the LRB in which employees in the bargaining unit indicate, by secret ballot, whether or not they want to be represented, or continue to be represented, by a labour union.

request for proposal (RFP) Document requesting that vendors provide a proposal detailing how the implementation of their particular HRIS will meet the organization's needs.

reverse discrimination Giving preference to designated group members to the extent that nonmembers believe they are being discriminated against.

rights arbitration The process involved in the settlement of a rights dispute.

rights dispute A disagreement between an organization and the union representing its employees regarding the interpretation or application of one or more clauses in the current collective agreement.

role-playing A training technique in which trainees act the parts of people in a realistic management situation.

S

Sandwich Generation Individuals with responsibility for rearing young dependants as well as for assisting elderly relatives who are no longer capable of functioning totally independently.

Scanlon plan An incentive plan developed in 1937 by Joseph Scanlon and designed to encourage cooperation, involvement, and sharing of benefits.

scatter plot A graphical method used to help identify the relationship between two variables.

scientific management The process of "scientifically" analyzing manufacturing processes, reducing production costs, and compensating employees based on their performance levels.

secondary sector Manufacturing and construction.

selection interview A procedure designed to predict future job performance on the basis of applicants' oral responses to oral inquiries.

selection ratio The ratio of the number of applicants hired to the total number of applicants.

selection The process of choosing among individuals who have been recruited to fill existing or projected job openings.

seniority Length of service in the bargaining unit.

severance package A lump-sum payment, continuation of benefits for a specified period of time, and other benefits that are provided to employees who are being terminated.

sexual annoyance Sexually related conduct that is hostile, intimidating, or offensive to the employee but has no direct link to tangible job benefits or loss thereof.

sexual coercion Harassment of a sexual nature that results in some direct consequence to the worker's employment status or some gain in or loss of tangible job benefits.

sexual harassment Offensive or humiliating behaviour that is related to a person's sex, as well as behaviour of a sexual nature that creates an intimidating, unwelcome, hostile, or offensive work environment or that could reasonably be thought to put sexual conditions on a person's job or employment opportunities.

short-term disability and sick leave Plans that provide pay to an employee when he or she is unable to work because of a non-work-related illness or injury.

similar-to-me bias The tendency to give higher performance ratings to employees who are perceived to be similar to the rater in some way.

situational interview A series of job-related questions that focus on how the candidate would behave in a given situation.

situational tests Tests in which candidates are presented with hypothetical situations representative of the job for which they are applying and are evaluated on their responses.

skills inventories Manual or computerized records summarizing employees' education, experience, interests, skills, and so on, which are used to identify internal candidates eligible for transfer and/or promotion.

social (reform) unionism Activities of unions directed at furthering the interests of their members by influencing the social and economic policies of governments at all levels, such as speaking out on proposed legislative reforms.

social responsibility The implied, enforced, or felt obligation of managers, acting in their official capacities, to serve or protect the interests of groups other than themselves.

socialization The ongoing process of instilling in all employees the prevailing attitudes, standards, values, and patterns of behaviour that are expected by the organization.

staffing table A pictorial representation of all jobs within the organization, along with the number of current incumbents and future employment requirements (monthly or yearly) for each.

stand-alone system A self-contained system that does not rely on other systems to operate.

standard hour plan A plan by which a worker is paid a basic hourly rate plus an extra percentage of his or her base rate for production exceeding the standard per hour or per day. It is similar to piecework payment but is based on a percentage premium.

statistical strategy A more objective technique used to determine to whom the job should be offered; involves identifying the most valid predictors and weighting them through statistical methods, such as multiple regression.

stock option The right to purchase a stated number of shares of a company stock at today's price at some time in the future.

straight piecework plan A set payment for each piece produced or processed in a factory or shop.

strategy The company's plan for how it will balance its internal strengths and weaknesses with external opportunities and threats in order to maintain a competitive advantage.

strictness/leniency The problem that occurs when a supervisor has a tendency to rate all employees either low or high.

strike The temporary refusal by bargaining unit members to continue working for the employer.

strike vote Legally required in some jurisdictions, it is a vote seeking authorization from bargaining unit members to strike if necessary. A favourable vote does not mean that a strike is inevitable.

structured interview An interview following a set sequence of questions.

succession planning The process of ensuring a suitable supply of successors for current and future senior or key jobs so that the careers of individuals can be effectively planned and managed.

supplemental employee retirement plans Plans that provide the additional pension benefit required for employees to receive their full pension benefit in cases where their full pension benefit exceeds the maximum allowable benefit under the Income Tax Act.

supplemental unemployment benefits (SUBs) A top-up of EI benefits to bring income levels closer to what an employee would receive if on the job.

supportive measures Strategies that enable all employees to achieve better balance between work and other responsibilities.

survivor sickness A range of negative emotions experienced by employees remaining after a major restructuring initiative, which can include feelings of betrayal or violation, guilt, and detachment, and can result in stress symptoms, including depression, increased errors, and reduced performance.

T

task analysis A detailed study of a job to identify the skills and competencies it requires so that an appropriate training program can be instituted.

team A small group of people, with complementary skills, who work toward common goals for which they hold joint responsibility and accountability.

team or group incentive plan A plan in which a production standard is set for a specific work group and its members are paid incentives if the group exceeds the production standard.

team-based job designs Job designs that focus on giving a team, rather than an individual, a whole and meaningful piece of work to do and empowering team members to decide among themselves how to accomplish the work.

termination interview The interview in which an employee is informed of the fact that he or she has been dismissed.

termination Permanent separation from the organization for any reason.

tertiary or service sector Public administration, personal and business services, finance, trade, public utilities, and transportation/communications.

total rewards An integrated package of all rewards (monetary and nonmonetary, extrinsic and intrinsic) gained by employees arising from their employment.

Traditionalists/Silent Generation Individuals born before 1946.

training The process of teaching employees the basic skills/competencies that they need to perform their jobs.

transfer Movement of an employee from one job to another that is relatively equal in pay, responsibility, and/or organizational level.

transfer of training Application of the skills acquired during the training program into the work environment, and the maintenance of these skills over time.

trend analysis The study of a firm's past employment levels over a period of years to predict future needs.

U

unclear performance standards An appraisal scale that is too open to interpretation of traits and standards.

underemployment Being employed in a job that does not fully utilize one's knowledge, skills, and abilities (KSAs).

undue hardship The point to which employers are expected to accommodate under human rights legislative requirements.

unintentional/constructive/systemic discrimination Discrimination that is embedded in policies and practices that appear neutral on the surface and are implemented impartially but have an adverse impact on specific groups of people for reasons that are not job related or required for the safe and efficient operation of the business.

union security clause The contract provisions protecting the interests of the labour union, dealing with the issue of membership requirements and, often, the payment of union dues.

union steward A union member elected by workers in a particular department or area of a firm to act as their union representative.

unstructured interview An unstructured, conversational-style interview. The interviewer pursues points of interest as they come up in response to questions.

utilization analysis The comparison of the internal workforce representation with external workforce availability.

V

validity The accuracy with which a predictor measures what it is intended to measure.

variable pay Any plan that ties pay to productivity or profitability.

vestibule or simulated training Training employees on special off-the-job equipment, as in airplane pilot training, whereby training costs and hazards can be reduced.

vesting Provision that employer money placed in a pension fund cannot be forfeited for any reason.

videoconferencing Connecting two or more distant groups by using audiovisual equipment.

W

wage curve A graphic description of the relationship between the value of the job and the average wage paid for this job.

wage/salary survey A survey aimed at determining prevailing wage rates. A good salary survey provides specific wage rates for comparable jobs. Formal written questionnaire surveys are the most comprehensive.

want ad A recruitment ad describing the job and its specifications, the compensation package, and the hiring employer. The address to which applications and/or résumés should be submitted is also provided.

want criteria Those criteria that represent qualifications that cannot be screened on paper or are not readily measurable, as well as those that are highly desirable but not critical.

web-based application An application that can be accessed from any computer connected to the Internet.

weighted application blank (WAB) A job application form on which applicant responses have been weighted based on their statistical relationship to measures of job success.

wildcat strike A spontaneous walkout, not officially sanctioned by the union leadership, which may be legal or illegal, depending on its timing.

work sharing Employees work three or four days a week and receive EI benefits on their non-workday(s).

work simplification An approach to job design that involves assigning most of the administrative aspects of work (such as planning and organizing) to supervisors and managers, while giving lower-level employees narrowly defined tasks to perform according to methods established and specified by management.

workers' compensation Workers' compensation provides income and medical benefits to victims of work-related accidents or illnesses and/or their dependants, regardless of fault.

Workplace Hazardous Materials Information System (WHMIS) A Canada-wide, legally mandated system designed to protect workers by providing information about hazardous materials in the workplace.

wrongful dismissal An employee dismissal that does not comply with the law or does not comply with a written or implied contractual arrangement.

Y

yield ratio The percentage of applicants that proceed to the next stage of the selection process.

PHOTO CREDITS